C000068855

Collins

Thesaurus

HarperCollins Publishers
Westerhill Road
Bishopbriggs
Glasgow
G64 2QT

Fourth Edition 2010

Reprint 10 9 8 7 6 5 4 3 2 1 0

© HarperCollins Publishers 2009

ISBN 978-0-00-732491-0

Collins® is a registered trademark of
HarperCollins Publishers Limited

www.collinslanguage.com

A catalogue record for this book is
available from the British Library.

Designed by Mark Thomson and
Wolfgang Homola

Computing support by
Thomas Callan

Typeset by Interactive Sciences
Limited, Gloucester

Printed and bound in China by South
China Printing Co. Ltd

Acknowledgements
We would like to thank those
authors and publishers who kindly
gave permission for copyright
material to be used in the Collins
Word Web. We would also like to
thank Times Newspapers Ltd for
providing valuable data.

When you buy a Collins dictionary
or thesaurus and register on
www.collinslanguage.com for the
free online and digital services, you
will not be charged by HarperCollins
for access to Collins free Online
Dictionary content on that website.
However, your operator's charges
for using the internet on your
computer will apply. Costs vary
from operator to operator.
HarperCollins is not responsible for
any charges levied by online service
providers for accessing Collins free
Online Dictionary on
www.collinslanguage.com using
these services.

HarperCollins does not warrant
that the functions contained in
www.collinslanguage.com content
will be uninterrupted or error free,
that defects will be corrected,
or that www.collinslanguage.
com or the server that makes it
available are free of viruses or bugs.
HarperCollins is not responsible for
any access difficulties that may be
experienced due to problems with
network, web, online or mobile
phone connections.

Editorial Staff

William Collins' dream of knowledge for all began with the publication of his first book in 1819. A self-educated mill worker, he not only enriched millions of lives, but also founded a flourishing publishing house. Today, staying true to this spirit, Collins books are packed with inspiration, innovation, and practical expertise. They place you at the centre of a world of possibility and give you exactly what you need to explore it.

Language is the key to this exploration, and at the heart of Collins Dictionaries is language as it is really used. New words, phrases, and meanings spring up every day, and all of them are captured and analysed by the **Collins Corpus**. Constantly updated, and with over 2.5 billion entries, this living language resource is unique to our dictionaries.

Words are tools for life. And a Collins Dictionary makes them work for you.

Collins. Do more.

Contents

Introduction

The **Collins Mini Thesaurus** has proved to be an immensely popular language resource. It has been designed with a clear and attractive layout which highlights its many features, and gives you the tools to express yourself in many different ways.

The headword list has been selected on the basis of frequency, so they are those most likely to be looked up by the user. The key synonym for each sense is shown first, in bold, which not only offers you the most helpful alternative but also lets you identify the sense in question at a glance. Other synonyms are arranged in order of their frequency of occurrence. In addition, all main entry words are printed in colour so that they are quick and easy to find.

The thesaurus offers extensive coverage of English as a world language, with words and phrases from all over the English-speaking world making this a truly international language resource.

As well as generous synonym lists, key antonyms are included for many entry words. But this new edition gives you much more than just synonyms and antonyms.

- The **Related Words** feature enables you to find information such as adjectives and collective nouns associated with several key entries.

- Informative word list panels provide a wealth of material connected with many entry words.

- The **Word Studies** supplement offers advice on how to avoid the most overused words, and contains detailed groups of alternatives for every context and shade of meaning.

- Helpful **Usage Notes** are also included at key entries. These give advice on good English and help you to avoid some of the more common language mistakes.

All these features mean that this new thesaurus is a treasury of useful and practical words and information, arranged in the most helpful way possible.

Features of the Thesaurus

Entry words
in colour

speed NOUN 1 = **rate**, pace
2 = **swiftness**, rush, hurry,
haste, rapidity, quickness
OPPOSITE: slowness
▷ VERB 3 = **race**, rush, hurry,
zoom, career, tear, barrel
(along) (*informal, chiefly U.S. &
Canad.*), gallop **OPPOSITE:** crawl
4 = **help**, advance, aid, boost,
assist, facilitate, expedite
OPPOSITE: hinder

Synonyms offer
a wide range of
alternatives

**Regional
labels**

Usage notes
give advice on
good English

● **USAGE NOTE**
● The past tense of *speed up* is
● *speeded up* (not *sped up*), for
● example *I speeded up to*
● *overtake the lorry.* The past
● participle is also *speeded up*,
● for example *I had already*
● *speeded up when I spotted the*
● *police car.*

**Related
words**
expand your
vocabulary

spider
● **RELATED WORD**
● *fear:* arachnophobia
▷ *See panel* SPIDERS AND OTHER
ARACHNIDS

**Cross
references**

SPIDERS AND OTHER ARACHNIDS	
black widow	red-back (spider) (*Austral.*)
chigger, chigoe, or (*U.S. &*	spider
Canad.) redbug	spider mite
chigoe, chigger, jigger, or *sand*	tarantula
flea	tick
harvestman or (*U.S. & Canad.*)	trap-door spider
daddy-longlegs	whip scorpion
katipo (*N.Z.*)	wolf spider or hunting
mite	spider

Word list panels add an
extra dimension to your
vocabulary

Features of the Thesaurus

Sense numbers

spin VERB 1 = **revolve**, turn, rotate, reel, whirl, twirl, gyrate, pirouette 2 = **reel**, swim, whirl
▷ **PHRASES: spin something out** = **prolong**, extend, lengthen, draw out, drag out, delay, amplify

Idioms and phrases add colour to your language

International English from all regions of the world where English is spoken

spirit NOUN 1 = **soul**, life 2 = **life force**, vital spark, mauri (N.Z.) 3 = **ghost**, phantom, spectre, apparition, atua (N.Z.), kehua (N.Z.) 4 = **courage**, guts (informal), grit, backbone, spunk (informal), gameness 5 = **liveliness**, energy, vigour, life, force, fire, enthusiasm, animation 6 = **attitude**, character, temper, outlook, temperament, disposition
▷ **PLURAL NOUN** 10 = **mood**, feelings, morale, temper, disposition, state of mind, frame of mind

Labels identify areas of usage

Key synonyms given first

Part of speech labels

Fixed phrases

spite NOUN 1 = **malice**, malevolence, ill will, hatred, animosity, venom, spleen, spitefulness **OPPOSITE:** kindness
▷ **VERB** 2 = **annoy**, hurt, injure, harm, vex **OPPOSITE:** benefit
▷ **PHRASES: in spite of** = **despite**, regardless of, notwithstanding, (even) though

Opposites given for many key words

Lists in the Thesaurus

Lists in the Thesaurus

Aa

abandon VERB 1 = **leave**, strand, ditch, forsake, run out on, desert, dump 2 = **stop**, give up, halt, pack in (*Brit. informal*), discontinue, leave off
OPPOSITE: continue 3 = **give up**, yield, surrender, relinquish OPPOSITE: keep
▷ NOUN 4 = **recklessness**, wildness OPPOSITE: restraint
abandonment = **desertion**, leaving, forsaking
abbey = **monastery**, convent, priory, nunnery, friary
abduct = **kidnap**, seize, carry off, snatch (*slang*)
abide = **tolerate**, suffer, accept, bear, endure, put up with, take, stand
▷ PHRASES: abide by something = **obey**, follow, agree to, carry out, observe, fulfil, act on, comply with
abiding = **enduring**, lasting, continuing, permanent, persistent, everlasting OPPOSITE: brief
ability 1 = **capability**, potential, competence, proficiency OPPOSITE: inability 2 = **skill**, talent, expertise, competence,

aptitude, proficiency, cleverness
able = **capable**, qualified, efficient, accomplished, competent, skilful, proficient OPPOSITE: incapable
abnormal = **unusual**, different, odd, strange, extraordinary, remarkable, exceptional, peculiar OPPOSITE: normal
abnormality 1 = **strangeness**, peculiarity, irregularity, singularity 2 = **anomaly**, oddity, exception, peculiarity, deformity, irregularity
abolish = **do away with**, end, destroy, eliminate, cancel, get rid of, ditch (*slang*), throw out OPPOSITE: establish
abolition = **eradication**, ending, end, destruction, wiping out, elimination, cancellation, termination
abort 1 = **terminate** (*a pregnancy*), miscarry 2 = **stop**, end, finish, check, arrest, halt, cease, axe (*informal*)
abortion = **termination**, miscarriage, deliberate miscarriage
abound = **be plentiful**, thrive, flourish, be numerous, proliferate, be abundant, be thick on the ground
about PREPOSITION
1 = **regarding**, on, concerning, dealing with, referring to, relating to, as regards 2 = **near**, around, close to, nearby, beside, adjacent to, in the neighbourhood of

a

▷ ADVERB **3** = **approximately**, around, almost, nearly, approaching, close to, roughly, just about

above 1 = **over**, upon, beyond, on top of, exceeding, higher than **OPPOSITE:** under **2** = **senior to**, over, ahead of, in charge of, higher than, superior to, more powerful than

abroad = **overseas**, out of the country, in foreign lands

abrupt 1 = **sudden**, unexpected, rapid, surprising, quick, rash, precipitate **OPPOSITE:** slow **2** = **curt**, brief, short, rude, impatient, terse, gruff, succinct **OPPOSITE:** polite

absence 1 = **time off**, leave, break, vacation, recess, truancy, absenteeism, nonattendance **2** = **lack**, deficiency, omission, scarcity, want, need, shortage, dearth

absent 1 = **away**, missing, gone, elsewhere, unavailable, nonexistent **OPPOSITE:** present **2** = **absent-minded**, blank, vague, distracted, vacant, preoccupied, oblivious, inattentive **OPPOSITE:** alert ▷ PHRASES: **absent yourself** = **stay away**, withdraw, keep away, play truant

absolute 1 = **complete**, total, perfect, pure, sheer, utter, outright, thorough **2** = **supreme**, sovereign, unlimited, ultimate, full, unconditional, unrestricted,

pre-eminent **3** = **autocratic**, supreme, all-powerful, imperious, domineering, tyrannical

absolutely = **completely**, totally, perfectly, fully, entirely, altogether, wholly, utterly **OPPOSITE:** somewhat

absorb 1 = **soak up**, suck up, receive, digest, imbibe **2** = **engross**, involve, engage, fascinate, rivet, captivate

absorbed = **engrossed**, lost, involved, gripped, fascinated, caught up, wrapped up, preoccupied

absorbing = **fascinating**, interesting, engaging, gripping, compelling, intriguing, enticing, riveting **OPPOSITE:** boring

absorption 1 = **soaking up**, consumption, digestion, sucking up **2** = **immersion**, involvement, concentration, fascination, preoccupation, intentness

abstract ADJECTIVE **1** = **theoretical**, general, academic, speculative, indefinite, hypothetical, notional, abstruse **OPPOSITE:** actual ▷ NOUN **2** = **summary**, résumé, outline, digest, epitome, rundown, synopsis, précis **OPPOSITE:** expansion ▷ VERB **3** = **extract**, draw, pull, remove, separate, withdraw, isolate, pull out **OPPOSITE:** add

absurd = **ridiculous**, crazy

(*informal*), silly, foolish, ludicrous, unreasonable, irrational, senseless **OPPOSITE:** sensible

abundance = plenty, bounty, exuberance, profusion, plethora, affluence, fullness, fruitfulness **OPPOSITE:** shortage

abundant = plentiful, full, rich, liberal, generous, ample, exuberant, teeming **OPPOSITE:** scarce

abuse NOUN
1 = maltreatment, damage, injury, hurt, harm, exploitation, manhandling, ill-treatment
2 = insults, blame, slights, put-downs, censure, reproach, scolding, defamation
3 = misuse, misapplication
▷ VERB 4 = ill-treat, damage, hurt, injure, harm, molest, maltreat, knock about *or* around **OPPOSITE:** care for
5 = insult, offend, curse, put down, malign, scold, disparage, castigate **OPPOSITE:** praise

abusive 1 = violent, rough, cruel, savage, brutal, vicious, destructive, harmful **OPPOSITE:** kind 2 = insulting, offensive, rude, degrading, scathing, contemptuous, disparaging, scurrilous **OPPOSITE:** complimentary

academic ADJECTIVE
1 = scholastic, educational
2 = scholarly, learned, intellectual, literary, erudite, highbrow, studious

3 = theoretical, abstract, speculative, hypothetical, impractical, notional, conjectural
▷ NOUN 4 = scholar, intellectual, don, master, professor, fellow, lecturer, tutor, acca (*Austral. slang*)

accelerate 1 = increase, grow, advance, extend, expand, raise, swell, enlarge **OPPOSITE:** fall
2 = expedite, further, speed up, hasten **OPPOSITE:** delay
3 = speed up, advance, quicken, gather momentum **OPPOSITE:** slow down

acceleration = hastening, hurrying, stepping up (*informal*), speeding up, quickening

accent NOUN
1 = pronunciation, tone, articulation, inflection, brogue, intonation, diction, modulation
▷ VERB 2 = emphasize, stress, highlight, underline, underscore, accentuate

accept 1 = receive, take, gain, pick up, secure, collect, get, obtain 2 = acknowledge, believe, allow, admit, approve, recognize, yield, concede

acceptable = satisfactory, fair, all right, suitable, sufficient, good enough, adequate, tolerable **OPPOSITE:** unsatisfactory

acceptance 1 = accepting, taking, receiving, obtaining, acquiring, reception, receipt
2 = acknowledgement,

agreement, approval, recognition, admission, consent, adoption, assent

accepted = **agreed**, common, established, traditional, approved, acknowledged, recognized, customary **OPPOSITE:** unconventional

access 1 = **admission**, entry, passage 2 = **entrance**, road, approach, entry, path, gate, opening, passage

accessible = **handy**, near, nearby, at hand, within reach, at your fingertips, reachable, achievable **OPPOSITE:** inaccessible

accessory 1 = **extra**, addition, supplement, attachment, adjunct, appendage 2 = **accomplice**, partner, ally, associate (*in crime*), assistant, helper, colleague, collaborator

accident 1 = **crash**, smash, wreck, collision 2 = **misfortune**, disaster, tragedy, setback, calamity, mishap, misadventure 3 = **chance**, fortune, luck, fate, hazard, coincidence, fluke, fortuity

accidental 1 = **unintentional**, unexpected, incidental, unforeseen, unplanned **OPPOSITE:** deliberate 2 = **chance**, random, casual, unplanned, fortuitous, inadvertent

accidentally = **unintentionally**, incidentally, by accident, by chance, inadvertently, unwittingly, randomly, haphazardly **OPPOSITE:** deliberately

acclaim VERB 1 = **praise**, celebrate, honour, cheer, admire, hail, applaud, compliment ▷ NOUN 2 = **praise**, honour, celebration, approval, tribute, applause, kudos, commendation **OPPOSITE:** criticism

accommodate 1 = **house**, put up, take in, lodge, shelter, entertain, cater for 2 = **help**, support, aid, assist, cooperate with, abet, lend a hand to 3 = **adapt**, fit, settle, alter, adjust, modify, comply, reconcile

accommodating = **obliging**, willing, kind, friendly, helpful, polite, cooperative, agreeable **OPPOSITE:** unhelpful

accommodation = **housing**, homes, houses, board, quarters, digs (*Brit. informal*), shelter, lodging(s)

accompaniment 1 = **backing music**, backing, support, obbligato 2 = **supplement**, extra, addition, companion, accessory, complement, decoration, adjunct

accompany 1 = **go with**, lead, partner, guide, attend, conduct, escort, shepherd 2 = **occur with**, belong to, come with, supplement, go together with

accompanying = additional, extra, related, associated, attached, attendant, complementary, supplementary, appended

accomplish = realize, produce, effect, finish, complete, manage, achieve, perform **OPPOSITE:** fail

accomplished = skilled, able, professional, expert, masterly, talented, gifted, polished **OPPOSITE:** unskilled

accomplishment
1 = achievement, feat, act, stroke, triumph, coup, exploit, deed 2 = accomplishing, finishing, carrying out, conclusion, bringing about, execution, completion, fulfilment

accord 1 = treaty, contract, agreement, arrangement, settlement, pact, deal (*informal*) 2 = sympathy, agreement, harmony, unison, rapport, conformity **OPPOSITE:** conflict
▷ **PHRASES:** accord with something = agree with, match, coincide with, fit with, correspond with, conform with, tally with, harmonize with

accordingly 1 = consequently, so, thus, therefore, hence, subsequently, in consequence, ergo 2 = appropriately, correspondingly, properly, suitably, fitly

account NOUN
1 = description, report, story, statement, version, tale, explanation, narrative
2 = importance, standing, concern, value, note, worth, weight, honour
▷ **PLURAL NOUN** 3 (*Commerce*) = ledgers, books, charges, bills, statements, balances, tallies, invoices
▷ **VERB** 4 = consider, rate, value, judge, estimate, think, count, reckon

accountability = responsibility, liability, culpability, answerability, chargeability

accountable = answerable, subject, responsible, obliged, liable, amenable, obligated, chargeable

accountant = auditor, book-keeper, bean counter (*informal*)

accumulate = build up, increase, be stored, collect, gather, pile up, amass, hoard **OPPOSITE:** disperse

accumulation 1 = collection, increase, stock, store, mass, build-up, pile, stack
2 = growth, collection, gathering, build-up

accuracy = exactness, precision, fidelity, authenticity, correctness, closeness, veracity, truthfulness **OPPOSITE:** inaccuracy

accurate 1 = precise, close, correct, careful, strict, exact, faithful, explicit **OPPOSITE:** inaccurate 2 = correct, true, exact, spot-on (Brit. informal)

accurately 1 = **precisely**, correctly, closely, truly, strictly, exactly, faithfully, to the letter 2 = **exactly**, closely, correctly, precisely, strictly, faithfully, explicitly, scrupulously

accusation = **charge**, complaint, allegation, indictment, recrimination, denunciation, incrimination

accuse 1 = **point a** or **the finger at**, blame for, denounce, hold responsible for, impute blame to **OPPOSITE:** exonerate 2 = **charge with**, indict for, impeach for, censure with, incriminate for **OPPOSITE:** absolve

accustom = **familiarize**, train, discipline, adapt, instruct, school, acquaint, acclimatize

accustomed 1 = **used**, trained, familiar, given to, adapted, acquainted, in the habit of, familiarized **OPPOSITE:** unaccustomed 2 = **usual**, established, expected, common, standard, traditional, normal, regular **OPPOSITE:** unusual

ace NOUN 1 (Cards, dice) = **one**, single point 2 (Informal) = **expert**, star, champion, authority, professional, master, specialist, guru ▷ ADJECTIVE 3 (Informal) = **great**, brilliant, fine, wonderful, excellent, outstanding, superb, fantastic

(informal), booshit (Austral. slang), exo (Austral. slang), sik (Austral. slang), ka pai (N.Z.)

ache VERB 1 = **hurt**, suffer, burn, pain, smart, sting, pound, throb ▷ NOUN 2 = **pain**, discomfort, suffering, hurt, throbbing, irritation, tenderness, pounding

achieve = **accomplish**, fulfil, complete, gain, perform, do, get, carry out

achievement = **accomplishment**, effort, feat, deed, stroke, triumph, coup, exploit

acid 1 = **sour**, tart, pungent, acerbic, acrid, vinegary **OPPOSITE:** sweet 2 = **sharp**, cutting, biting, bitter, harsh, barbed, caustic, vitriolic **OPPOSITE:** kindly

acknowledge 1 = **admit**, own up, allow, accept, reveal, grant, declare, recognize **OPPOSITE:** deny 2 = **greet**, address, notice, recognize, salute, accost **OPPOSITE:** snub 3 = **reply to**, answer, notice, recognize, respond to, react to, retort to **OPPOSITE:** ignore

acquaintance 1 = **associate**, contact, ally, colleague, comrade **OPPOSITE:** intimate 2 = **relationship**, connection, fellowship, familiarity **OPPOSITE:** unfamiliarity

acquire = **get**, win, buy, receive, gain, earn, secure, collect **OPPOSITE:** lose

acquisition 1 = acquiring, gaining, procurement, attainment 2 = **purchase**, buy, investment, property, gain, prize, asset, possession

acquit = clear, free, release, excuse, discharge, liberate, vindicate **OPPOSITE:** find guilty
▷ **PHRASES: acquit yourself** = **behave**, bear yourself, conduct yourself, comport yourself

act VERB 1 = **do something**, perform, function 2 = **perform**, mimic
▷ NOUN 3 = **deed**, action, performance, achievement, undertaking, exploit, feat, accomplishment 4 = **pretence**, show, front, performance, display, attitude, pose, posture 5 = **law**, bill, measure, resolution, decree, statute, ordinance, enactment 6 = **performance**, show, turn, production, routine, presentation, gig (*informal*), sketch

acting NOUN 1 = **performance**, playing, performing, theatre, portrayal, impersonation, characterization, stagecraft
▷ ADJECTIVE 2 = **temporary**, substitute, interim, provisional, surrogate, stopgap, pro tem

action NOUN 1 = **deed**, act, performance, achievement, exploit, feat, accomplishment 2 = **measure**, act, manoeuvre 3 = **lawsuit**, case, trial, suit, proceeding, dispute, prosecution, litigation 4 = **energy**, activity, spirit, force, vitality, vigour, liveliness, vim 5 = **effect**, working, process, operation, activity, movement, functioning, motion 6 = **battle**, fight, conflict, clash, contest, encounter, combat, engagement

activate = **start**, move, initiate, rouse, mobilize, set in motion, galvanize **OPPOSITE:** stop

active 1 = **busy**, involved, occupied, lively, energetic, bustling, on the move, strenuous **OPPOSITE:** sluggish 2 = **energetic**, quick, alert, dynamic, lively, vigorous, animated, forceful **OPPOSITE:** inactive 3 = **in operation**, working, acting, at work, in action, operative, in force, effectual

activist = **militant**, partisan

activity 1 = **action**, labour, movement, energy, exercise, spirit, motion, bustle **OPPOSITE:** inaction 2 = **pursuit**, project, scheme, pleasure, interest, hobby, pastime

actor *or* **actress** = **performer**, player, Thespian, luvvie (*informal*)
● **USAGE NOTE**
● The use of *actress* is now very
● much on the decline, and
● women who work in the
● profession invariably prefer to
● be referred to as *actors*.

a

actual = **real**, substantial, concrete, definite, tangible

● USAGE NOTE
● The words *actual* and *actually*
● are often used when
● speaking, but should only be
● used in writing where they
● add something to the
● meaning of a sentence. For
● example, in the sentence *he*
● *actually rather enjoyed the film*,
● the word *actually* is only
● needed if there was originally
● some doubt as to whether he
● would enjoy it.

actually = **really**, in fact, indeed, truly, literally, genuinely, in reality, in truth

acute 1 = **serious**, important, dangerous, critical, crucial, severe, grave, urgent
2 = **sharp**, shooting, powerful, violent, severe, intense, fierce, piercing 3 = **perceptive**, sharp, keen, smart, sensitive, clever, astute, insightful **OPPOSITE:** slow

adamant = **determined**, firm, fixed, stubborn, uncompromising, resolute, unbending, obdurate **OPPOSITE:** flexible

adapt 1 = **adjust**, change, alter, modify, accommodate, conform, acclimatize
2 = **convert**, change, transform, alter, modify, tailor, remodel

adaptation
1 = **acclimatization**, naturalization, familiarization
2 = **conversion**, change, variation, adjustment, transformation, modification, alteration

add 1 = **count up**, total, reckon, compute, add up, tot up **OPPOSITE:** take away
2 = **include**, attach, supplement, adjoin, augment, affix, append

addict 1 = **junkie** (*informal*), freak (*informal*), fiend (*informal*)
2 = **fan**, lover, nut (*slang*), follower, enthusiast, admirer, buff (*informal*), junkie (*informal*)

addicted PHRASES: addicted to = **hooked on**, dependent on, accustomed to (*slang*), habituated to

addiction 1 = **dependence**, habit, obsession, craving, enslavement 2 **with** to = **love of**, passion for, attachment to

addition 1 = **extra**, supplement, increase, gain, bonus, extension, accessory, additive 2 = **inclusion**, adding, increasing, extension, attachment, insertion, incorporation, augmentation **OPPOSITE:** removal
3 = **counting up**, totalling, adding up, computation, totting up **OPPOSITE:** subtraction
▷ **PHRASES:** in addition to = **as well as**, along with, on top of, besides, to boot, additionally, over and above, to say nothing

of, into the bargain

additional = extra, new, other, added, further, fresh, spare, supplementary

address NOUN 1 = location, home, place, house, point, position, situation, site 2 = speech, talk, lecture, discourse, sermon, dissertation, homily, oration
▷ VERB 3 = speak to, talk to, greet, hail, approach, converse with, korero (N.Z.)

adept ADJECTIVE 1 = skilful, able, skilled, expert, practised, accomplished, versed, proficient **OPPOSITE:** unskilled
▷ NOUN 2 = expert, master, genius, hotshot (informal), dab hand (Brit. informal)

adequate 1 = passable, acceptable, average, fair, satisfactory, competent, mediocre, so-so (informal) **OPPOSITE:** inadequate
2 = sufficient, enough **OPPOSITE:** insufficient

adhere to = stick to, attach to, cling to, glue to, fix to, fasten to, hold fast to, paste to

adjacent ADJECTIVE
1 = adjoining, neighbouring, nearby **OPPOSITE:** far away
▷ PREPOSITION 2 with to = next to, touching, close to, neighbouring, beside, near to, adjoining, bordering on

adjoin = connect with or to, join, link with, touch on, border on

adjoining = connecting, touching, bordering, neighbouring, next door, adjacent, abutting

adjourn = postpone, delay, suspend, interrupt, put off, defer, discontinue **OPPOSITE:** continue

adjust 1 = adapt, change, alter, accustom, conform 2 = change, reform, alter, adapt, revise, modify, amend, make conform 3 = modify, alter, adapt

adjustable = alterable, flexible, adaptable, malleable, movable, modifiable

adjustment 1 = alteration, change, tuning, repair, conversion, modifying, adaptation, modification
2 = acclimatization, orientation, change, regulation, amendment, adaptation, revision, modification

administer 1 = manage, run, control, direct, handle, conduct, command, govern 2 = dispense, give, share, provide, apply, assign, allocate, allot 3 = execute, give, provide, apply, perform, carry out, impose, implement

administration
1 = management, government, running, control, handling, direction, conduct, application
2 = directors, board, executive(s), employers
3 = government, leadership,

regime, governing body
administrative = **managerial**, executive, directing, regulatory, governmental, organizational, supervisory, directorial

administrator = **manager**, head, official, director, executive, boss (*informal*), governor, supervisor, baas (*S. African*)

admirable = **praiseworthy**, good, great, fine, wonderful, excellent, brilliant, outstanding, booshit (*Austral. slang*), exo (*Austral. slang*), sik (*Austral. slang*), ka pai (*N.Z.*) **OPPOSITE:** deplorable

admiration = **regard**, wonder, respect, praise, approval, recognition, esteem, appreciation

admire 1 = **respect**, value, prize, honour, praise, appreciate, esteem, approve of **OPPOSITE:** despise 2 = **adore**, like, love, take to, fancy (*Brit. informal*), treasure, cherish, glorify 3 = **marvel at**, look at, appreciate, delight in, wonder at, be amazed by, take pleasure in, gape at

admirer 1 = **fan**, supporter, follower, enthusiast, partisan, disciple, devotee 2 = **suitor**, lover, boyfriend, sweetheart, beau, wooer

admission 1 = **admittance**, access, entry, introduction, entrance, acceptance, initiation, entrée

2 = **confession**, declaration, revelation, allowance, disclosure, acknowledgement, unburdening, divulgence

admit 1 = **confess**, confide, own up, come clean (*informal*) 2 = **allow**, agree, accept, reveal, grant, declare, acknowledge, recognize **OPPOSITE:** deny 3 = **let in**, allow, receive, accept, introduce, take in, initiate, give access to **OPPOSITE:** keep out

adolescence = **teens**, youth, minority, boyhood, girlhood

adolescent ADJECTIVE
1 = **young**, junior, teenage, juvenile, youthful, childish, immature, boyish 2 = **teenage**, young, teen (*informal*)
▷ NOUN 3 = **teenager**, girl, boy, kid (*informal*), youth, lad, minor, young man

adopt 1 = **take on**, follow, choose, maintain, assume, take up, engage in, become involved in 2 = **take in**, raise, nurse, mother, rear, foster, bring up, take care of **OPPOSITE:** abandon

adoption 1 = **fostering**, adopting, taking in
2 = **embracing**, choice, taking up, selection, assumption, endorsement, appropriation, espousal

adore = **love**, honour, admire, worship, esteem, cherish, revere, dote on **OPPOSITE:** hate

adoring = **admiring**, loving, devoted, fond, affectionate, doting **OPPOSITE:** hating

adorn = **decorate**, array, embellish, festoon

adrift ADJECTIVE 1 = **drifting**, afloat, unmoored, unanchored 2 = **aimless**, goalless, directionless, purposeless ▷ ADVERB 3 = **wrong**, astray, off course, amiss, off target, wide of the mark

adult NOUN 1 = **grown-up**, mature person, person of mature age, grown or grown-up person, man *or* woman ▷ ADJECTIVE 2 = **fully grown**, mature, grown-up, of age, ripe, fully fledged, fully developed, full grown 3 = **pornographic**, blue, dirty, obscene, filthy, indecent, lewd, salacious

advance VERB 1 = **progress**, proceed, come forward, make inroads, make headway OPPOSITE: retreat 2 = **accelerate**, speed, promote, hasten, bring forward 3 = **improve**, rise, develop, pick up, progress, upgrade, prosper, make strides 4 = **suggest**, offer, present, propose, advocate, submit, prescribe, put forward OPPOSITE: withhold 5 = **lend**, loan, supply on credit OPPOSITE: withhold payment ▷ NOUN 6 = **down payment**, credit, loan, fee, deposit, retainer, prepayment 7 = **attack**, charge, strike, assault, raid, invasion, offensive, onslaught 8 = **improvement**,

development, gain, growth, breakthrough, step, headway, inroads ▷ ADJECTIVE 9 = **prior**, early, beforehand ▷ PHRASES: **in advance** = **beforehand**, earlier, ahead, previously

advanced = **sophisticated**, foremost, modern, revolutionary, up-to-date, higher, leading, recent OPPOSITE: backward

advancement = **promotion**, rise, gain, progress, improvement, betterment, preferment

advantage 1 = **benefit**, help, profit, favour OPPOSITE: disadvantage 2 = **lead**, sway, dominance, precedence 3 = **superiority**, good

adventure 1 = **venture**, experience, incident, enterprise, undertaking, exploit, occurrence, caper 2 = **excitement**, action, passion, thrill, animation, commotion

adventurous = **daring**, enterprising, bold, reckless, intrepid, daredevil OPPOSITE: cautious

adversary = **opponent**, rival, enemy, competitor, foe, contestant, antagonist OPPOSITE: ally

adverse 1 = **harmful**, damaging, negative, destructive, detrimental,

hurtful, injurious, inopportune **OPPOSITE:** beneficial
2 = **unfavourable**, hostile, unlucky **3** = **negative**, opposing, hostile, contrary, dissenting, unsympathetic, ill-disposed

advert (*Brit. informal*) = **advertisement**, notice, commercial, ad (*informal*), announcement, poster, plug (*informal*), blurb

advertise = **publicize**, promote, plug (*informal*), announce, inform, hype, notify, tout

advertisement = **advert** (*Brit. informal*), notice, commercial, ad (*informal*), announcement, poster, plug (*informal*), blurb

advice = **guidance**, help, opinion, direction, suggestion, instruction, counsel, counselling

advise 1 = **recommend**, suggest, urge, counsel, advocate, caution, prescribe, commend **2** = **notify**, tell, report, announce, warn, declare, inform, acquaint

adviser = **counsellor**, guide, consultant, aide, guru, mentor, helper, confidant

advisory = **advising**, helping, recommending, counselling, consultative

advocate VERB
1 = **recommend**, support, champion, encourage, propose, promote, advise, endorse

OPPOSITE: oppose
▷ NOUN **2** = **supporter**, spokesman, champion, defender, campaigner, promoter, counsellor, proponent **3** (*Law*) = **lawyer**, attorney, solicitor, counsel, barrister

affair 1 = **matter**, business, happening, event, activity, incident, episode, topic
2 = **relationship**, romance, intrigue, fling, liaison, flirtation, amour, dalliance

affect¹ 1 = **influence**, concern, alter, change, manipulate, act on, bear upon, impinge upon
2 = **emotionally move**, touch, upset, overcome, stir, disturb, perturb

affect² = put on, assume, adopt, pretend, imitate, simulate, contrive, aspire to

affected = **pretended**, artificial, contrived, put-on, mannered, unnatural, feigned, insincere **OPPOSITE:** genuine

affection = **fondness**, liking, feeling, love, care, warmth, attachment, goodwill, aroha (*N.Z.*)

affectionate = **fond**, loving, kind, caring, friendly, attached, devoted, tender **OPPOSITE:** cool

affiliate = **associate**, unite, join, link, ally, combine, incorporate, amalgamate

affinity 1 = **attraction**, liking, leaning, sympathy, inclination, rapport, fondness, partiality,

aroha (N.Z.) **OPPOSITE:** hostility
2 = **similarity**, relationship, connection, correspondence, analogy, resemblance, closeness, likeness **OPPOSITE:** difference

affirm 1 = **declare**, state, maintain, swear, assert, testify, pronounce, certify **OPPOSITE:** deny 2 = **confirm**, prove, endorse, ratify, verify, validate, bear out, substantiate **OPPOSITE:** refute

affirmative = **agreeing**, confirming, positive, approving, consenting, favourable, concurring, assenting **OPPOSITE:** negative

afflict = **torment**, trouble, pain, hurt, distress, plague, grieve, harass

affluent = **wealthy**, rich, prosperous, loaded (*slang*), well-off, opulent, well-heeled (*informal*), well-to-do **OPPOSITE:** poor

afford 1 = **have the money for**, manage, bear, pay for, spare, stand, stretch to 2 = **bear**, stand, sustain, allow yourself 3 = **give**, offer, provide, produce, supply, yield, render

affordable = **inexpensive**, cheap, reasonable, moderate, modest, low-cost, economical **OPPOSITE:** expensive

afraid 1 = **scared**, frightened, nervous, terrified, shaken, startled, fearful, cowardly **OPPOSITE:** unafraid

2 = **reluctant**, frightened, scared, unwilling, hesitant, loath, disinclined, unenthusiastic 3 = **sorry**, apologetic, regretful, sad, distressed, unhappy **OPPOSITE:** pleased

after PREPOSITION 1 = **at the end of**, following, subsequent to **OPPOSITE:** before
▷ **ADVERB** 2 = **following**, later, next, succeeding, afterwards, subsequently, thereafter
● RELATED WORD
● *prefix:* post-

aftermath = **effects**, results, wake, consequences, outcome, sequel, end result, upshot

again 1 = **once more**, another time, anew, afresh 2 = **also**, in addition, moreover, besides, furthermore

against 1 = **beside**, on, up against, in contact with, abutting 2 = **opposed to**, anti (*informal*), hostile to, in opposition to, averse to, opposite to 3 = **in opposition to**, resisting, versus, counter to, in the opposite direction of 4 = **in preparation for**, in case of, in anticipation of, in expectation of, in provision for
● RELATED WORDS
● *prefixes:* anti-, contra-,
● counter-

age NOUN 1 = **years**, days, generation, lifetime, length of existence 2 = **old age**, experience, maturity, seniority,

majority, senility, decline (of life), advancing years **OPPOSITE:** youth 3 = **time**, day(s), period, generation, era, epoch
▷ VERB 4 = **grow old**, decline, weather, fade, deteriorate, wither 5 = **mature**, season, condition, soften, mellow, ripen

aged = **old**, getting on, grey, ancient, antique, elderly, antiquated **OPPOSITE:** young

agency 1 = **business**, company, office, firm, department, organization, enterprise, establishment 2 (Old-fashioned) = **medium**, means, activity, vehicle, instrument, mechanism

agenda = **programme**, list, plan, schedule, diary, calendar, timetable

agent 1 = **representative**, rep (informal), negotiator, envoy, surrogate, go-between 2 = **author**, worker, vehicle, instrument, operator, performer, catalyst, doer 3 = **force**, means, power, cause, instrument

aggravate 1 = **make worse**, exaggerate, intensify, worsen, exacerbate, magnify, inflame, increase **OPPOSITE:** improve 2 (Informal) = **annoy**, bother, provoke, irritate, nettle, get on your nerves (informal) **OPPOSITE:** please

aggregate NOUN 1 = **total**, body, whole, amount, collection, mass, sum, combination

▷ ADJECTIVE 2 = **collective**, mixed, combined, collected, accumulated, composite, cumulative
▷ VERB 3 = **combine**, mix, collect, assemble, heap, accumulate, pile, amass

aggression 1 = **hostility**, malice, antagonism, antipathy, ill will, belligerence, destructiveness, pugnacity 2 = **attack**, campaign, injury, assault, raid, invasion, offensive, onslaught

aggressive 1 = **hostile**, offensive, destructive, belligerent, unfriendly, contrary, antagonistic, pugnacious, aggers (Austral. slang), biffo (Austral. slang) **OPPOSITE:** friendly 2 = **forceful**, powerful, convincing, effective, enterprising, dynamic, bold, militant **OPPOSITE:** submissive

agitate 1 = **stir**, beat, shake, disturb, toss, rouse 2 = **upset**, worry, trouble, excite, distract, unnerve, disconcert, fluster **OPPOSITE:** calm

agony = **suffering**, pain, distress, misery, torture, discomfort, torment, hardship

agree 1 = **concur**, be as one, sympathize, assent, see eye to eye, be of the same opinion **OPPOSITE:** disagree 2 = **correspond**, match, coincide, tally, conform 3 = **suit**, get on, befit

agreement 1 = **treaty**,

contract, arrangement, alliance, deal (*informal*), understanding, settlement, bargain **2 = concurrence**, harmony, compliance, union, agreeing, consent, unison, assent **OPPOSITE:** disagreement **3 = correspondence**, similarity, consistency, correlation, conformity, compatibility, congruity **OPPOSITE:** difference

agricultural = farming, country, rural, rustic, agrarian

agriculture = farming, culture, cultivation, husbandry, tillage

ahead 1 = in front, in advance, towards the front, frontwards **2 = at an advantage**, in advance, in the lead **3 = in the lead**, winning, leading, at the head, to the fore, at an advantage **4 = in front**, before, in advance, in the lead

aid NOUN 1 = help, backing, support, benefit, favour, relief, promotion, assistance **OPPOSITE:** hindrance
▷ VERB **2 = help**, support, serve, sustain, assist, avail, subsidize, be of service to **OPPOSITE:** hinder **3 = promote**, help, further, forward, encourage, favour, facilitate, pave the way for

aide = assistant, supporter, attendant, helper, right-hand man, second

ailing 1 = weak, failing, poor, flawed, unstable, unsatisfactory, deficient **2 = ill**, poorly, sick, weak, crook (*Austral. & N.Z. informal*), unwell, infirm, under the weather (*informal*), indisposed

ailment = illness, disease, complaint, disorder, sickness, affliction, malady, infirmity

aim VERB 1 = try for, seek, work for, plan for, strive, set your sights on **2 = point**
▷ NOUN **3 = intention**, point, plan, goal, design, target, purpose, desire

air NOUN 1 = wind, breeze, draught, gust, zephyr **2 = atmosphere**, sky, heavens, aerosphere **3 = tune**, song, theme, melody, strain, lay, aria **4 = manner**, appearance, look, aspect, atmosphere, mood, impression, aura
▷ PLURAL NOUN
5 = affectation, arrogance, pretensions, pomposity, swank (*informal*), hauteur, haughtiness, superciliousness
▷ VERB **6 = publicize**, reveal, exhibit, voice, express, display, circulate, make public **7 = ventilate**, expose, freshen, aerate
● RELATED WORD
● *adjective*: aerial

airborne = flying, floating, in the air, hovering, gliding, in flight, on the wing

airing 1 = ventilation, drying, freshening, aeration **2 = exposure**, display, expression, publicity, vent,

utterance, dissemination
airplane (*U.S. & Canad.*) = **plane**,
aircraft, jet, aeroplane, airliner
aisle = **passageway**, path, lane,
passage, corridor, alley,
gangway
alarm NOUN 1 = **fear**, panic,
anxiety, fright, apprehension,
nervousness, consternation,
trepidation **OPPOSITE:** calmness
2 = **danger signal**, warning,
bell, alert, siren, alarm bell,
hooter, distress signal
▷ VERB 3 = **frighten**, scare,
panic, distress, startle, dismay,
daunt, unnerve **OPPOSITE:** calm
alarming = **frightening**,
shocking, scaring, disturbing,
distressing, startling, horrifying,
menacing
alcoholic NOUN 1 = **drunkard**,
drinker, drunk, toper, lush
(*slang*), tippler, wino (*informal*),
inebriate, alko or alco (*Austral.
slang*)
▷ ADJECTIVE 2 = **intoxicating**,
hard, strong, stiff, brewed,
fermented, distilled
alert ADJECTIVE 1 = **attentive**,
awake, vigilant, watchful, on
the lookout, circumspect,
observant, on guard **OPPOSITE:**
careless 2 = **quick-witted**,
bright, sharp
▷ NOUN 3 = **warning**, signal,
alarm, siren **OPPOSITE:** all clear
▷ VERB 4 = **warn**, signal,
inform, notify, tip off,
forewarn **OPPOSITE:** lull
alien ADJECTIVE 1 = **foreign**,

strange, imported, unknown,
exotic, unfamiliar 2 = **strange**,
new, foreign, novel, unknown,
exotic, unfamiliar, untried
OPPOSITE: similar
▷ NOUN 3 = **foreigner**, incomer,
immigrant, stranger, outsider,
newcomer, asylum seeker
OPPOSITE: citizen
alienate = **antagonize**, anger,
annoy, offend, irritate, hassle
(*informal*), estrange
alienation = **estrangement**,
setting against, separation,
turning away, disaffection,
remoteness
alight¹ 1 = **get off**, descend, get
down, disembark, dismount
2 = **land**, light, settle, come
down, descend, perch, touch
down, come to rest **OPPOSITE:**
take off
alight² = **lit up**, bright, brilliant,
shining, illuminated, fiery
align 1 = **ally**, side, join,
associate, affiliate, cooperate,
sympathize 2 = **line up**, order,
range, regulate, straighten,
even up
alike ADJECTIVE 1 = **similar**,
close, the same, parallel,
resembling, identical,
corresponding, akin **OPPOSITE:**
different
▷ ADVERB 2 = **similarly**,
identically, equally, uniformly,
correspondingly, analogously
OPPOSITE: differently
alive 1 = **living**, breathing,
animate, subsisting, existing,

functioning, in the land of the living (*informal*) **OPPOSITE:** dead **2** = **in existence**, existing, functioning, active, operative, in force, on-going, prevalent **OPPOSITE:** inoperative **3** = **lively**, active, vital, alert, energetic, animated, agile, perky **OPPOSITE:** dull

all PRONOUN 1 = **the whole amount**, everything, the total, the aggregate, the totality, the sum total, the entirety, the entire amount **2** = **every**, each, every single, every one of, each and every

▷ **ADJECTIVE 3** = **complete**, greatest, full, total, perfect, entire, utter

▷ **ADVERB 4** = **completely**, totally, fully, entirely, absolutely, altogether, wholly, utterly

allegation = **claim**, charge, statement, declaration, accusation, assertion, affirmation

allege = **claim**, charge, challenge, state, maintain, declare, assert, uphold **OPPOSITE:** deny

alleged = **claimed**, supposed, declared, assumed, so-called, apparent, stated, described

allegiance = **loyalty**, devotion, fidelity, obedience, constancy, faithfulness **OPPOSITE:** disloyalty

allergic = **sensitive**, affected by, susceptible, hypersensitive

allergy = **sensitivity**, reaction,

susceptibility, antipathy, hypersensitivity, sensitiveness

alleviate = **ease**, reduce, relieve, moderate, soothe, lessen, lighten, allay

alley = **passage**, walk, lane, pathway, alleyway, passageway, backstreet

alliance = **union**, league, association, agreement, marriage, connection, combination, coalition **OPPOSITE:** division

allied 1 = **united**, linked, related, combined, integrated, affiliated, cooperating, in league 2 = **connected**, linked, associated

allocate = **assign**, grant, distribute, designate, set aside, earmark, give out, consign

allocation 1 = **allowance**, share, portion, quota, lot, ration **2** = **assignment**, allowance, allotment

allow VERB 1 = **permit**, approve, enable, sanction, endure, license, tolerate, authorize **OPPOSITE:** prohibit **2** = **let**, permit, sanction, authorize, license, tolerate, consent to, assent to **OPPOSITE:** forbid **3** = **give**, provide, grant, spare, devote, assign, allocate, set aside **4** = **acknowledge**, accept, admit, grant, recognize, yield, concede, confess

▷ **PHRASES: allow for something** = **take something into account**, consider, plan for, accommodate, provide for, make provision for, make allowances for, make concessions for

allowance 1 = **portion**, lot, share, amount, grant, quota, allocation, stint 2 = **pocket money**, grant, fee, payment, ration, handout, remittance 3 = **concession**, discount, reduction, repayment, deduction, rebate

all right 1 = **satisfactory**, O.K. or okay (*informal*), average, fair, sufficient, standard, acceptable, good enough **OPPOSITE:** unsatisfactory 2 = **well**, O.K. or okay (*informal*), whole, sound, fit, safe, healthy, unharmed **OPPOSITE:** ill

ally = **partner**, friend, colleague, associate, mate, comrade, helper, collaborator, cobber (*Austral. & N.Z. old-fashioned informal*), E hoa (*N.Z.*) **OPPOSITE:** opponent
▷ **PHRASES: ally yourself with something** *or* **someone** = **unite with**, associate with, unify, collaborate with, join forces with, band together with

almost = **nearly**, about, close to, virtually, practically, roughly, just about, not quite

alone ADJECTIVE 1 = **solitary**, isolated, separate, apart, by yourself, unaccompanied, on your tod (*slang*) **OPPOSITE:** accompanied 2 = **lonely**, abandoned, isolated, solitary,

desolate, forsaken, forlorn, destitute
▷ ADVERB 3 = **solely**, only, individually, singly, exclusively, uniquely 4 = **by yourself**, independently, unaccompanied, without help, on your own, without assistance **OPPOSITE:** with help

aloud = **out loud**, clearly, plainly, distinctly, audibly, intelligibly

already = **before now**, before, previously, at present, by now, by then, even now, just now

also = **and**, too, further, in addition, as well, moreover, besides, furthermore

alter 1 = **modify**, change, reform, vary, transform, adjust, adapt, revise 2 = **change**, turn, vary, transform, adjust, adapt

alternate VERB
1 = **interchange**, change, fluctuate, take turns, oscillate, chop and change
2 = **intersperse**, interchange, exchange, swap, stagger, rotate
▷ ADJECTIVE 3 = **alternating**, interchanging, every other, rotating, every second, sequential

alternative NOUN
1 = **substitute**, choice, other (*of two*), option, preference, recourse
▷ ADJECTIVE 2 = **different**, other, substitute, alternate

alternatively = **or**, instead,

otherwise, on the other hand, if not, then again, as an alternative, as another option

although = though, while, even if, even though, whilst, albeit, despite the fact that, notwithstanding

altogether 1 = absolutely, quite, completely, totally, perfectly, fully, thoroughly, wholly 2 = completely, fully, entirely, thoroughly, wholly, in every respect **OPPOSITE:** partially 3 = on the whole, generally, mostly, in general, collectively, all things considered, on average, for the most part 4 = in total, in all, all told, taken together, in sum, everything included

- **USAGE NOTE**
- The single-word form
- *altogether* should not be used
- as an alternative to *all*
- *together* because the
- meanings are very distinct.
- *Altogether* is an adverb
- meaning 'absolutely' or, in a
- different sense, ' in total'. *All*
- *together*, however, means 'all
- at the same time' or 'all in the
- same place'. The distinction
- can be seen in the following
- examples: *altogether there were*
- *six or seven families sharing the*
- *flat's facilities means ' in total',*
- while *there were six or seven*
- *families all together in one flat,*
- means 'all crowded in
- together'.

always 1 = habitually, regularly, every time, consistently, invariably, perpetually, without exception, customarily **OPPOSITE:** seldom 2 = forever, for keeps, eternally, for all time, evermore, till the cows come home (*informal*), till Doomsday 3 = continually, constantly, all the time, forever, repeatedly, persistently, perpetually, incessantly

amass = collect, gather, assemble, compile, accumulate, pile up, hoard

amateur = nonprofessional, outsider, layman, dilettante, layperson, non-specialist, dabbler

amaze = astonish, surprise, shock, stun, alarm, stagger, startle, bewilder

amazement = astonishment, surprise, wonder, shock, confusion, admiration, awe, bewilderment

amazing = astonishing, surprising, brilliant, stunning, overwhelming, staggering, sensational (*informal*), bewildering

ambassador = representative, minister, agent, deputy, diplomat, envoy, consul, attaché

ambiguity = vagueness, doubt, uncertainty, obscurity, equivocation, dubiousness

ambiguous = unclear, obscure, vague, dubious, enigmatic, indefinite, inconclusive, indeterminate **OPPOSITE:** clear

ambition 1 = goal, hope, dream, target, aim, wish, purpose, desire 2 = enterprise, longing, drive, spirit, desire, passion, enthusiasm, striving

ambitious = enterprising, spirited, daring, eager, intent, enthusiastic, hopeful, striving **OPPOSITE:** unambitious

ambush VERB 1 = trap, attack, surprise, deceive, dupe, ensnare, waylay, bushwhack (U.S.)
▷ NOUN 2 = trap, snare, lure, waylaying

amend VERB = change, improve, reform, fix, correct, repair, edit, alter
▷ PLURAL NOUN (usually in make amends) = compensation, redress, reparation, restitution, atonement, recompense

amendment 1 = addition, change, adjustment, attachment, adaptation, revision, modification, alteration 2 = change, improvement, repair, edit, remedy, correction, revision, modification

amenity = facility, service, advantage, comfort, convenience

amid or **amidst** 1 = during, among, at a time of, in an atmosphere of 2 = in the middle of, among, surrounded by, amongst, in the midst of

ammunition = munitions, rounds, shot, shells, powder, explosives, armaments

amnesty = general pardon, mercy, pardoning, immunity, forgiveness, reprieve, remission (of penalty), clemency

among or **amongst** 1 = in the midst of, with, together with, in the middle of, amid, surrounded by, amidst, in the thick of 2 = in the group of, one of, part of, included in, in the company of, in the class of, in the number of 3 = between, to

amount 1 = quantity, measure, size, supply, mass, volume, capacity, extent, magnitude
▷ PHRASES: amount to something 1 = add up to, mean, total, equal, constitute, comprise, be equivalent to 2 = come to, become, develop into, advance to, progress to, mature into

● USAGE NOTE
● Although it is common to use
● a plural noun after amount of,
● for example in the amount of
● people and the amount of
● goods, this should be avoided.
● Preferred alternatives would
● be to use quantity, as in the
● quantity of people, or number,
● as in the number of goods.

amphibian
▷ See panel AMPHIBIANS

ample 1 = plenty of, generous,

a

AMPHIBIANS

axolotl
brown-striped frog (*Austral.*)
bullfrog
caecilian
cane toad (*Austral.*)
congo eel or snake
frog or (*Caribbean*) crapaud
Goliath frog
hairy frog
hyla

midwife toad
natterjack
newt or (*dialect or archaic*) eft
olm
Queensland cane toad
salamander
siren
toad or (*Caribbean*) crapaud
tree frog

lavish, abundant, plentiful, expansive, copious, profuse **OPPOSITE:** insufficient 2 = **large**, full, extensive, generous, abundant, bountiful

amply = **fully**, completely, richly, generously, abundantly, profusely, copiously **OPPOSITE:** insufficiently

amuse 1 = **entertain**, please, delight, charm, cheer, tickle **OPPOSITE:** bore 2 = **occupy**, interest, involve, engage, entertain, absorb, engross

amusement 1 = **enjoyment**, entertainment, cheer, mirth, merriment **OPPOSITE:** boredom 2 = **diversion**, fun, pleasure, entertainment 3 = **pastime**, game, sport, joke, entertainment, hobby, recreation, diversion

amusing = **funny**, humorous, comical, droll, interesting, entertaining, comic, enjoyable **OPPOSITE:** boring

anaesthetic NOUN
1 = **painkiller**, narcotic,

sedative, opiate, anodyne, analgesic, soporific
▷ ADJECTIVE 2 = **pain-killing**, dulling, numbing, sedative, deadening, anodyne, analgesic, soporific

analogy = **similarity**, relation, comparison, parallel, correspondence, resemblance, correlation, likeness

analyse 1 = **examine**, test, study, research, survey, investigate, evaluate, inspect 2 = **break down**, separate, divide, resolve, dissect, think through

analysis = **examination**, test, inquiry, investigation, interpretation, breakdown, scanning, evaluation

analytical or **analytic** = **rational**, organized, exact, precise, logical, systematic, inquiring, investigative

anarchy = **lawlessness**, revolution, riot, disorder, confusion, chaos, disorganization

a

OPPOSITE: law and order

anatomy 1 = structure, build, make-up, frame, framework, composition **2 = examination**, study, division, inquiry, investigation, analysis, dissection

ancestor = forefather, predecessor, precursor, forerunner, forebear, antecedent, tupuna or tipuna (N.Z.) **OPPOSITE:** descendant

ancient 1 = classical, old, former, past, bygone, primordial, primeval, olden **2 = very old**, aged, antique, archaic, timeworn **3 = old-fashioned**, dated, outdated, obsolete, out of date, unfashionable, outmoded, passé **OPPOSITE:** up-to-date

and 1 = also, including, along with, together with, in addition to, as well as **2 = moreover**, plus, furthermore

● USAGE NOTE
● The forms *try and do something*
● and *wait and do something*
● should only be used in
● informal or spoken English. In
● more formal writing, use *try*
● *to* and *wait to*, for example:
● *we must try to prevent this*
● *happening* (not *try and*
● *prevent*).

anecdote = story, tale, sketch, short story, yarn, reminiscence, urban myth, urban legend

angel 1 = divine messenger, cherub, archangel, seraph

2 (*Informal*) **= dear**, beauty, saint, treasure, darling, jewel, gem, paragon

anger NOUN 1 = rage, outrage, temper, fury, resentment, wrath, annoyance, ire **OPPOSITE:** calmness

▷ **VERB 2 = enrage**, outrage, annoy, infuriate, incense, gall, madden, exasperate **OPPOSITE:** soothe

angle 1 = gradient, bank, slope, incline, inclination **2 = intersection**, point, edge, corner, bend, elbow, crook, nook **3 = point of view**, position, approach, direction, aspect, perspective, outlook, viewpoint

angry = furious, cross, mad (*informal*), outraged, annoyed, infuriated, incensed, enraged, tooshie (*Austral. slang*), off the air (*Austral. slang*) **OPPOSITE:** calm

● USAGE NOTE
● Some people feel it is more
● correct to talk about being
● *angry with* someone than
● being *angry at* them. In British
● English, *angry with* is still
● more common than *angry at*,
● but *angry at* is used more
● commonly in American
● English.

angst = anxiety, worry, unease, apprehension **OPPOSITE:** peace of mind

anguish = suffering, pain, distress, grief, misery, agony, torment, sorrow, woe

animal NOUN 1 = **creature**, beast, brute 2 = **brute**, devil, monster, savage, beast, bastard (*informal, offensive*), villain, barbarian

▷ ADJECTIVE 3 = **physical**, gross, bodily, sensual, carnal, brutish, bestial

▷ *See panels* AMPHIBIANS, ANIMALS, BIRDS, DINOSAURS, FISH, INSECTS, INVERTEBRATES, MAMMALS, REPTILES

animate ADJECTIVE 1 = **living**, live, moving, alive, breathing, alive and kicking

▷ VERB 2 = **enliven**, excite, inspire, move, fire, stimulate, energize, kindle **OPPOSITE:** inhibit

animated = **lively**, spirited, excited, enthusiastic, passionate, energetic, ebullient, vivacious **OPPOSITE:** listless

animation = **liveliness**, energy, spirit, passion, enthusiasm, excitement, verve, zest

announce = **make known**, tell, report, reveal, declare, advertise, broadcast, disclose **OPPOSITE:** keep secret

announcement
1 = **statement**, communication, broadcast, declaration, advertisement, bulletin, communiqué, proclamation 2 = **declaration**, report, reporting, revelation, proclamation

annoy = **irritate**, trouble, anger,

bother, disturb, plague, hassle (*informal*), madden **OPPOSITE:** soothe

annoying = **irritating**, disturbing, troublesome, maddening, exasperating **OPPOSITE:** delightful

annual 1 = **once a year**, yearly 2 = **yearlong**, yearly

annually 1 = **once a year**, yearly, every year, per year, by the year, every twelve months, per annum 2 = **per year**, yearly, every year, by the year, per annum

anomaly = **irregularity**, exception, abnormality, inconsistency, eccentricity, oddity, peculiarity, incongruity

anonymous 1 = **unnamed**, unknown, unidentified, nameless, unacknowledged, incognito **OPPOSITE:** identified 2 = **unsigned**, uncredited, unattributed **OPPOSITE:** signed

answer VERB 1 = **reply**, explain, respond, resolve, react, return, retort **OPPOSITE:** ask

▷ NOUN 2 = **reply**, response, reaction, explanation, comeback, retort, return, defence **OPPOSITE:** question 3 = **solution**, resolution, explanation 4 = **remedy**, solution

ant NOUN ▷ *See panel* ANTS, BEES, AND WASPS

anthem = **song of praise**, carol, chant, hymn, psalm, paean, chorale, canticle

a

ANIMALS

Collective animals

antelopes	herd	giraffes	herd
apes	shrewdness	gnats	swarm or cloud
asses	pace or herd	goats	herd or tribe
badgers	cete	goldfinches	charm
bears	sloth	grouse	brood, covey, or pack
bees	swarm or grist		
birds	flock, congregation, flight, or volery	gulls	colony
		hares	down or husk
		hawks	cast
bitterns	sedge or siege	hens	brood
boars	sounder	herons	sedge or siege
bucks	brace or lease	herrings	shoal or glean
buffaloes	herd	hounds	pack, mute, or cry
capercailzies	tok		
cats	clowder	insects	swarm
cattle	drove or herd	kangaroos	troop
choughs	chattering	kittens	kindle
colts	rag	lapwings	desert
coots	covert	larks	exaltation
cranes	herd, sedge, or siege	leopards	leap
		lions	pride or troop
crows	murder	mallards	sord or sute
cubs	litter	mares	stud
curlews	herd	martens	richesse
curs	cowardice	moles	labour
deer	herd	monkeys	troop
dolphins	school	mules	barren
doves	flight or dule	nightingales	watch
ducks	paddling or team	owls	parliament
dunlins	flight	oxen	yoke, drove, team, or herd
elk	gang		
fish	shoal, draught, haul, run, or catch	partridges	covey
		peacocks	muster
		pheasants	nye or nide
flies	swarm or grist	pigeons	flock or flight
foxes	skulk	pigs	litter
geese	gaggle or skein	plovers	stand or wing

ANIMALS *continued*			
pochards	flight, rush, bunch, or knob	starlings	murmuration
ponies	herd	swallows	flight
porpoises	school *or* gam	swans	herd *or* bevy
poultry	run	swifts	flock
pups	litter	swine	herd, sounder, *or* dryft
quails	bevy		
rabbits	nest	teal	bunch, knob, *or* spring
racehorses	field *or* string		
ravens	unkindness	whales	school, gam, *or* run
roes	bevy		
rooks	building *or* clamour	whelps	litter
ruffs	hill	whiting	pod
seals	herd *or* pod	wigeon	bunch, company, knob, *or* flight
sheep	flock		
sheldrakes	dopping	wildfowl	plump, sord, *or* sute
snipe	walk *or* wisp		
sparrows	host	wolves	pack, rout, *or* herd
		woodcocks	fall

anthology = collection, selection, treasury, compilation, compendium, miscellany

anticipate 1 = **expect**, predict, prepare for, hope for, envisage, foresee, bank on, foretell 2 = **await**, look forward to, count the hours until

anticipation = expectancy, expectation, foresight, premonition, prescience, forethought

antics = **clowning**, tricks, mischief, pranks, escapades, playfulness, horseplay, tomfoolery

antique NOUN 1 = **period piece**, relic, bygone, heirloom, collector's item, museum piece ▷ ADJECTIVE 2 = **vintage**, classic, antiquarian, olden

anxiety = **uneasiness**, concern, worry, doubt, tension, angst, apprehension, misgiving **OPPOSITE:** confidence

anxious 1 = **eager**, keen, intent, yearning, impatient, itching, desirous **OPPOSITE:** reluctant 2 = **uneasy**, concerned, worried, troubled, nervous, uncomfortable, tense, fearful **OPPOSITE:** confident

apart 1 = **to pieces**, to bits, asunder 2 = **away from each other**, distant from each other 3 = **aside**, away, alone, isolated, to one side, by yourself 4 *with* **from** = **except for**, excepting, other than, excluding, besides, not including, aside from, but

a

ANTS, BEES, AND WASPS

Amazon ant	killer bee
ant or (archaic or dialect) emmet	kootchar (Austral.)
	leafcutter ant
army ant or legionary ant	leafcutter bee
	mason bee
bee	mason wasp
blue ant (Austral.)	minga (Austral.)
bulldog ant, bull ant, or (Austral.) bull Joe	mining bee
	mud dauber
bumblebee or humblebee	native bee or sugarbag fly (Austral.)
carpenter bee	
cicada hunter (Austral.)	Pharaoh ant
cuckoo bee	policeman fly (Austral.)
digger wasp	ruby-tail wasp
driver ant	sand wasp
flower wasp (Austral.)	Sirex wasp (Austral.)
gall wasp	slave ant
honeypot ant or honey ant (Austral.)	spider-hunting wasp
	termite or white ant
honeybee or hive bee	velvet ant
horntail or wood wasp	wasp
ichneumon fly or ichneumon wasp	wood ant
	yellow jacket (U.S. & Canad.)

apartment 1 (U.S.) = **flat**, room, suite, penthouse, crib
2 = **rooms**, quarters, accommodation, living quarters

apathy = **lack of interest**, indifference, inertia, coolness, passivity, nonchalance, torpor, unconcern **OPPOSITE:** interest

apiece = **each**, individually, separately, for each, to each, respectively, from each **OPPOSITE:** all together

apologize = **say sorry**, express regret, ask forgiveness, make an apology, beg pardon

apology = **regret**, explanation, excuse, confession
▷ **PHRASES:** apology for something or someone = **mockery of**, excuse for, imitation of, caricature of, travesty of, poor substitute for

appal = **horrify**, shock, alarm, frighten, outrage, disgust, dishearten, revolt

appalling 1 = **horrifying**, shocking, alarming, awful, terrifying, horrible, dreadful, fearful **OPPOSITE:** reassuring
2 = **awful**, dreadful, horrendous

apparatus 1 = **organization**, system, network, structure, bureaucracy, hierarchy, setup (*informal*), chain of command 2 = **equipment**, tackle, gear, device, tools, mechanism, machinery, appliance

apparent 1 = **seeming**, outward, superficial, ostensible **OPPOSITE:** actual 2 = **obvious**, marked, visible, evident, distinct, manifest, noticeable, unmistakable **OPPOSITE:** unclear

apparently = **seemingly**, outwardly, ostensibly

appeal VERB 1 = **plead**, ask, request, pray, beg, entreat **OPPOSITE:** refuse ▷ NOUN 2 = **plea**, call, application, request, prayer, petition, overture, entreaty **OPPOSITE:** refusal 3 = **attraction**, charm, fascination, beauty, allure **OPPOSITE:** repulsiveness ▷ PHRASES: appeal to someone = **attract**, interest, draw, please, charm, fascinate, tempt, lure

appealing = **attractive**, engaging, charming, desirable, alluring, winsome **OPPOSITE:** repellent

appear 1 = **look** (like *or* as if), seem, occur, look to be, come across as, strike you as 2 = **come into view**, emerge, occur, surface, come out, turn up, be present, show up (*informal*) **OPPOSITE:** disappear

appearance 1 = **look**, form, figure, looks, manner, expression, demeanour, mien (*literary*) 2 = **arrival**, presence, introduction, emergence 3 = **impression**, air, front, image, illusion, guise, façade, pretence

appease 1 = **pacify**, satisfy, calm, soothe, quiet, placate, mollify, conciliate **OPPOSITE:** anger 2 = **ease**, calm, relieve, soothe, alleviate, allay

appendix = **supplement**, postscript, adjunct, appendage, addendum, addition

appetite 1 = **hunger** 2 = **desire**, liking, longing, demand, taste, passion, stomach, hunger **OPPOSITE:** distaste

applaud 1 = **clap**, encourage, praise, cheer, acclaim **OPPOSITE:** boo 2 = **praise**, celebrate, approve, acclaim, compliment, salute, commend, extol **OPPOSITE:** criticize

applause = **ovation**, praise, cheers, approval, clapping, accolade, big hand

appliance = **device**, machine, tool, instrument, implement, mechanism, apparatus, gadget

applicable = **appropriate**, fitting, useful, suitable, relevant, apt, pertinent **OPPOSITE:** inappropriate

applicant = **candidate**, claimant, inquirer

application 1 = **request**,

a

claim, appeal, inquiry, petition, requisition **2 = effort**, work, industry, trouble, struggle, pains, commitment, hard work

apply VERB 1 = request, appeal, put in, petition, inquire, claim, requisition **2 = be relevant**, relate, refer, be fitting, be appropriate, fit, pertain, be applicable **3 = use**, exercise, carry out, employ, implement, practise, exert, enact **4 = put on**, work in, cover with, lay on, paint on, spread on, rub in, smear on
▷ **PHRASES: apply yourself to something = work hard at**, concentrate on, try at, commit yourself to, buckle down to (*informal*), devote yourself to, be diligent in, dedicate yourself to

appoint 1 = assign, name, choose, commission, select, elect, delegate, nominate **OPPOSITE:** fire **2 = decide**, set, choose, establish, fix, arrange, assign, designate **OPPOSITE:** cancel

appointed 1 = decided, set, chosen, established, fixed, arranged, assigned, designated **2 = assigned**, named, chosen, selected, elected, delegated, nominated **3 = equipped**, provided, supplied, furnished, fitted out

appointment 1 = selection, naming, election, choice, nomination, assignment **2 = job**, office, position, post,

situation, place, employment, assignment **3 = meeting**, interview, date, arrangement, engagement, fixture, rendezvous, assignation

appraisal = assessment, opinion, estimate, judgment, evaluation, estimation

appreciate 1 = enjoy, like, value, respect, prize, admire, treasure, rate highly **OPPOSITE:** scorn **2 = be aware of**, understand, realize, recognize, perceive, take account of, be sensitive to, sympathize with **OPPOSITE:** be unaware of **3 = be grateful**, be obliged, be thankful, give thanks, be indebted, be in debt, be appreciative **OPPOSITE:** be ungrateful for **4 = increase**, rise, grow, gain, improve, enhance, soar **OPPOSITE:** fall

appreciation 1 = admiration, enjoyment **2 = gratitude**, thanks, recognition, obligation, acknowledgment, indebtedness, thankfulness, gratefulness **OPPOSITE:** ingratitude **3 = awareness**, understanding, recognition, perception, sympathy, consciousness, sensitivity, realization **OPPOSITE:** ignorance **4 = increase**, rise, gain, growth, improvement, escalation, enhancement **OPPOSITE:** fall

apprehension 1 = anxiety, concern, fear, worry, alarm, suspicion, dread, trepidation

OPPOSITE: confidence
2 = **arrest**, catching, capture,
taking, seizure **OPPOSITE:**
release 3 = **awareness**,
understanding, perception,
grasp, comprehension
OPPOSITE: incomprehension
apprentice = **trainee**, student,
pupil, novice, beginner, learner,
probationer **OPPOSITE:** master
approach VERB 1 = **move
towards**, reach, near, come
close, come near, draw near
2 = **make a proposal to**, speak
to, apply to, appeal to,
proposition, solicit, sound out,
make overtures to 3 = **set
about**, tackle, undertake,
embark on, get down to, launch
into, begin work on, commence
on
▷ NOUN 4 = **advance**, coming,
nearing, appearance, arrival,
drawing near 5 = **access**, way,
drive, road, passage, entrance,
avenue, passageway 6 *often
plural* = **proposal**, offer, appeal,
advance, application, invitation,
proposition, overture 7 = **way**,
means, style, method,
technique, manner
appropriate ADJECTIVE
1 = **suitable**, fitting, relevant, to
the point, apt, pertinent,
befitting, well-suited **OPPOSITE:**
unsuitable
▷ VERB 2 = **seize**, claim,
acquire, confiscate, usurp,
impound, commandeer, take
possession of **OPPOSITE:**

relinquish 3 = **allocate**, allow,
budget, devote, assign,
designate, set aside, earmark
OPPOSITE: withhold 4 = **steal**,
take, nick (*slang, chiefly Brit.*),
pocket, pinch (*informal*), lift
(*informal*), embezzle, pilfer
approval 1 = **consent**,
agreement, sanction, blessing,
permission, recommendation,
endorsement, assent
2 = **favour**, respect, praise,
esteem, acclaim, appreciation,
admiration, applause
OPPOSITE: disapproval
approve = **agree to**, allow,
pass, recommend, permit,
sanction, endorse, authorize
OPPOSITE: veto
▷ PHRASES: **approve of
something** *or* **someone**
= **favour**, like, respect, praise,
admire, commend, have a good
opinion of, regard highly
apt 1 = **appropriate**, fitting,
suitable, relevant, to the point,
pertinent **OPPOSITE:**
inappropriate 2 = **inclined**,
likely, ready, disposed, prone,
liable, given, predisposed
3 = **gifted**, skilled, quick,
talented, sharp, capable, smart,
clever **OPPOSITE:** slow
arbitrary = **random**, chance,
subjective, inconsistent, erratic,
personal, whimsical, capricious
OPPOSITE: logical
arbitration = **decision**,
settlement, judgment,
determination, adjudication

a

arc = curve, bend, bow, arch, crescent, half-moon

arcade = gallery, cloister, portico, colonnade

arch¹ NOUN 1 = **archway**, curve, dome, span, vault 2 = **curve**, bend, bow, crook, arc, hunch, sweep, hump ▷ VERB 3 = **curve**, bridge, bend, bow, span, arc

arch² = **playful**, sly, mischievous, saucy, pert, roguish, frolicsome, waggish

archetypal = **typical**, standard, model, original, classic, ideal, prototypic or prototypical

architect = **designer**, planner, draughtsman, master builder

architecture 1 = **design**, planning, building, construction 2 = **construction**, design, style 3 = **structure**, design, shape, make-up, construction, framework, layout, anatomy

archive NOUN = **record office**, museum, registry, repository ▷ PLURAL NOUN = **records**, papers, accounts, rolls, documents, files, deeds, chronicles

arctic (Informal) = **freezing**, cold, frozen, icy, chilly, glacial, frigid

Arctic = **polar**, far-northern, hyperborean

ardent 1 = **enthusiastic**, keen, eager, avid, zealous OPPOSITE: indifferent 2 = **passionate**, intense, impassioned, lusty, amorous, hot-blooded OPPOSITE: cold

area 1 = **region**, quarter, district, zone, neighbourhood, locality 2 = **part**, section, sector, portion 3 = **realm**, part, department, field, province, sphere, domain

arena 1 = **ring**, ground, field, theatre, bowl, pitch, stadium, enclosure 2 = **scene**, world, area, stage, field, sector, territory, province

argue 1 = **quarrel**, fight, row, clash, dispute, disagree, squabble, bicker 2 = **discuss**, debate, dispute 3 = **claim**, reason, challenge, insist, maintain, allege, assert, uphold

argument 1 = **reason**, case, reasoning, ground(s), defence, logic, polemic, dialectic 2 = **debate**, questioning, claim, discussion, dispute, controversy, plea, assertion 3 = **quarrel**, fight, row, clash, dispute, controversy, disagreement, feud OPPOSITE: agreement

arise 1 = **happen**, start, begin, follow, result, develop, emerge, occur 2 (Old-fashioned) = **get to your feet**, get up, rise, stand up, spring up, leap up 3 = **get up**, wake up, awaken, get out of bed

aristocrat = **noble**, lord, lady, peer, patrician, grandee, aristo (informal), peeress

aristocratic = **upper-class**, lordly, titled, elite, gentlemanly, noble, patrician, blue-blooded

OPPOSITE: common

arm[1] = **upper limb**, limb, appendage

arm[2] VERB 1 = **equip**, provide, supply, array, furnish, issue with, deck out, accoutre

▷ PLURAL NOUN 2 = **weapons**, guns, firearms, weaponry, armaments, ordnance, munitions, instruments of war

armed = **carrying weapons**, protected, equipped, primed, fitted out

armour = **protection**, covering, shield, sheathing, armour plate, chain mail, protective covering

armoured = **protected**, mailed, reinforced, toughened, bulletproof, armour-plated, steel-plated, ironclad

army 1 = **soldiers**, military, troops, armed force, legions, infantry, military force, land force 2 = **vast number**, host, gang, mob, flock, array, legion, swarm

aroma = **scent**, smell, perfume, fragrance, bouquet, savour, odour, redolence

around PREPOSITION
1 = **surrounding**, about, enclosing, encompassing, framing, encircling, on all sides of, on every side of
2 = **approximately**, about, nearly, close to, roughly, just about, in the region of, circa (used with dates)

▷ ADVERB 3 = **everywhere**, about, throughout, all over, here and there, on all sides, in all directions, to and fro
4 = **near**, close, nearby, at hand, close at hand

arouse 1 = **stimulate**, encourage, inspire, prompt, spur, provoke, rouse, stir up **OPPOSITE:** quell 2 = **inflame**, move, excite, spur, provoke, stir up, agitate 3 = **awaken**, wake up, rouse, waken

arrange 1 = **plan**, agree, prepare, determine, organize, construct, devise, contrive, jack up (N.Z. informal) 2 = **put in order**, group, order, sort, position, line up, organize, classify, jack up (N.Z. informal) **OPPOSITE:** disorganize
3 = **adapt**, score, orchestrate, harmonize, instrument

arrangement 1 often plural = **plan**, planning, provision, preparation 2 = **agreement**, contract, settlement, appointment, compromise, deal (informal), pact, compact
3 = **display**, system, structure, organization, exhibition, presentation, classification, alignment 4 = **adaptation**, score, version, interpretation, instrumentation, orchestration, harmonization

array NOUN 1 = **arrangement**, show, supply, display, collection, exhibition, line-up, mixture
2 (Poetic) = **clothing**, dress, clothes, garments, apparel, attire, finery, regalia

▷ **VERB 3** = **arrange**, show, group, present, range, display, parade, exhibit **4** = **dress**, clothe, deck, decorate, adorn, festoon, attire

arrest VERB 1 = **capture**, catch, nick (*slang, chiefly Brit.*), seize, detain, apprehend, take prisoner **OPPOSITE:** release
2 = **stop**, end, limit, block, slow, delay, interrupt, suppress **OPPOSITE:** speed up
3 = **fascinate**, hold, occupy, engage, grip, absorb, entrance, intrigue
▷ **NOUN 4** = **capture**, bust (*informal*), detention, seizure **OPPOSITE:** release
5 = **stoppage**, suppression, obstruction, blockage, hindrance **OPPOSITE:** acceleration

arresting = **striking**, surprising, engaging, stunning, impressive, outstanding, remarkable, noticeable **OPPOSITE:** unremarkable

arrival 1 = **appearance**, coming, arriving, entrance, advent, materialization
2 = **coming**, happening, taking place, emergence, occurrence, materialization **3** = **newcomer**, incomer, visitor, caller, entrant

arrive 1 = **come**, appear, turn up, show up (*informal*), draw near **OPPOSITE:** depart
2 = **occur**, happen, take place
3 (*Informal*) = **succeed**, make it (*informal*), triumph, do well, thrive, flourish, be successful, make good

arrogance = **conceit**, pride, swagger, insolence, high-handedness, haughtiness, superciliousness, disdainfulness **OPPOSITE:** modesty

arrogant = **conceited**, proud, cocky, overbearing, haughty, scornful, egotistical, disdainful **OPPOSITE:** modest

arrow 1 = **dart**, flight, bolt, shaft (*archaic*), quarrel
2 = **pointer**, indicator, marker

arsenal = **armoury**, supply, store, stockpile, storehouse, ammunition dump, arms depot, ordnance depot

art 1 = **artwork**, style of art, fine art, creativity **2** = **skill**, craft, expertise, competence, mastery, ingenuity, virtuosity, cleverness

article 1 = **feature**, story, paper, piece, item, creation, essay, composition **2** = **thing**, piece, unit, item, object, device, tool, implement **3** = **clause**, point, part, section, item, passage, portion, paragraph

articulate ADJECTIVE
1 = **expressive**, clear, coherent, fluent, eloquent, lucid **OPPOSITE:** incoherent
▷ **VERB 2** = **express**, say, state, word, declare, phrase, communicate, utter
3 = **pronounce**, say, talk, speak, voice, utter, enunciate

artificial 1 = **synthetic**,

manufactured, plastic, man-made, non-natural
2 = **insincere**, forced, affected, phoney or phony (*informal*), false, contrived, unnatural, feigned **OPPOSITE:** genuine
3 = **fake**, mock, imitation, bogus, simulated, sham, counterfeit **OPPOSITE:** authentic

artillery = **big guns**, battery, cannon, ordnance, gunnery

artistic 1 = **creative**, cultured, original, sophisticated, refined, aesthetic, discerning, eloquent **OPPOSITE:** untalented
2 = **beautiful**, creative, elegant, stylish, aesthetic, tasteful **OPPOSITE:** unattractive

as CONJUNCTION **1** = **when**, while, just as, at the time that
▷ PREPOSITION **2** = **in the role of**, being, under the name of, in the character of
▷ CONJUNCTION **3** = **in the way that**, like, in the manner that
4 = **since**, because, seeing that, considering that, on account of the fact that

ashamed 1 = **embarrassed**, sorry, guilty, distressed, humiliated, self-conscious, red-faced, mortified **OPPOSITE:** proud **2** = **reluctant**, embarrassed

ashore = **on land**, on the beach, on the shore, aground, to the shore, on dry land, shorewards, landwards

aside ADVERB **1** = **to one side**, separately, apart, beside, out of the way, on one side, to the side
▷ NOUN **2** = **interpolation**, parenthesis

ask 1 = **inquire**, question, quiz, query, interrogate **OPPOSITE:** answer **2** = **request**, appeal to, plead with, demand, beg
3 = **invite**, bid, summon

asleep = **sleeping**, napping, dormant, dozing, slumbering, snoozing (*informal*), fast asleep, sound asleep

aspect 1 = **feature**, side, factor, angle, characteristic, facet
2 = **position**, view, situation, scene, prospect, point of view, outlook **3** = **appearance**, look, air, condition, quality, bearing, attitude, cast

aspiration = **aim**, plan, hope, goal, dream, wish, desire, objective

aspire to = **aim for**, desire, hope for, long for, seek out, wish for, dream about, set your heart on

ass 1 = **donkey**, moke (*slang*)
2 = **fool**, idiot, twit (*informal*, *chiefly Brit.*), oaf, jackass, blockhead, halfwit, numbskull or numskull, dorba or dorb (*Austral. slang*), bogan (*Austral. slang*)

assassin = **murderer**, killer, slayer, liquidator, executioner, hit man (*slang*), hatchet man (*slang*)

assassinate = **murder**, kill, eliminate (*slang*), take out

a

(slang), terminate, hit (slang),
slay, liquidate

assault NOUN 1 = **attack**, raid,
invasion, charge, offensive,
onslaught, foray OPPOSITE:
defence
▷ VERB 2 = **strike**, attack, beat,
knock, bang, slap, smack,
thump

assemble 1 = **gather**, meet,
collect, rally, come together,
muster, congregate OPPOSITE:
scatter 2 = **bring together**,
collect, gather, rally, come
together, muster, amass,
congregate 3 = **put together**,
join, set up, build up, connect,
construct, piece together,
fabricate OPPOSITE: take apart

assembly 1 = **gathering**,
group, meeting, council,
conference, crowd, congress,
collection, hui (N.Z.), runanga
(N.Z.) 2 = **putting together**,
setting up, construction,
building up, connecting, piecing
together

assert 1 = **state**, argue,
maintain, declare, swear,
pronounce, affirm, profess
OPPOSITE: deny 2 = **insist
upon**, stress, defend, uphold,
put forward, press, stand up for
OPPOSITE: retract
▷ PHRASES: assert yourself = **be
forceful**, put your foot down
(informal), put yourself forward,
make your presence felt, exert
your influence

assertion 1 = **statement**,

claim, pronouncement
2 = **insistence**, stressing,
maintenance

assertive = **confident**, positive,
aggressive, forceful, emphatic,
insistent, feisty (informal, chiefly
U.S. & Canad.), pushy (informal)
OPPOSITE: meek

assess 1 = **judge**, estimate,
analyse, evaluate, rate, value,
check out, weigh up
2 = **evaluate**, rate, tax, value,
estimate, fix, impose, levy

assessment 1 = **judgment**,
analysis, evaluation, valuation,
appraisal, rating, opinion,
estimate 2 = **evaluation**,
rating, charge, fee, toll, levy,
valuation

asset NOUN 1 = **benefit**, help,
service, aid, advantage,
strength, resource, attraction,
blessing OPPOSITE:
disadvantage
▷ PLURAL NOUN 2 = **property**,
goods, money, funds, effects,
capital, riches, finance

assign 1 = **give**, set, grant,
allocate, give out, consign,
allot, apportion 2 = **select for**,
post, commission, elect,
appoint, delegate, nominate,
name 3 = **attribute**, credit, put
down, set down, ascribe,
accredit

assignment = **task**, job,
position, post, commission,
exercise, responsibility, duty

assist 1 = **help**, support, aid,
cooperate with, abet, lend a

helping hand to 2 = **facilitate**, help, further, serve, aid, forward, promote, speed up **OPPOSITE:** hinder

assistance = **help**, backing, support, aid, cooperation, helping hand **OPPOSITE:** hindrance

assistant = **helper**, ally, colleague, supporter, aide, second, attendant, accomplice

associate VERB 1 = **connect**, link, ally, identify, join, combine, attach, fasten **OPPOSITE:** separate 2 = **socialize**, mix, accompany, mingle, consort, hobnob **OPPOSITE:** avoid
▷ NOUN 3 = **partner**, friend, ally, colleague, mate (*informal*), companion, comrade, affiliate, cobber (*Austral. & N.Z. old-fashioned informal*), E hoa (*N.Z.*)

association 1 = **group**, club, society, league, band, set, pack, collection 2 = **connection**, union, joining, pairing, combination, mixture, blend, juxtaposition

assorted = **various**, different, mixed, varied, diverse, miscellaneous, sundry, motley **OPPOSITE:** similar

assume 1 = **presume**, think, believe, expect, suppose, imagine, fancy, take for granted **OPPOSITE:** know 2 = **take on**, accept, shoulder, take over, put on, enter upon 3 = **simulate**, affect, adopt, put on, imitate, mimic, feign, impersonate

4 = **take over**, take, appropriate, seize, commandeer **OPPOSITE:** give up

assumed = **false**, made-up, fake, bogus, counterfeit, fictitious, make-believe **OPPOSITE:** real

assumption 1 = **presumption**, belief, guess, hypothesis, inference, conjecture, surmise, supposition 2 = **taking on**, managing, handling, shouldering, putting on, taking up, takeover, acquisition 3 = **seizure**, taking, takeover, acquisition, appropriation, wresting, confiscation, commandeering

assurance 1 = **promise**, statement, guarantee, commitment, pledge, vow, declaration, assertion **OPPOSITE:** lie 2 = **confidence**, conviction, certainty, self-confidence, poise, faith, nerve, aplomb **OPPOSITE:** self-doubt

assure 1 = **convince**, encourage, persuade, satisfy, comfort, reassure, hearten, embolden 2 = **make certain**, ensure, confirm, guarantee, secure, make sure, complete, seal 3 = **promise to**, pledge to, vow to, guarantee to, swear to, confirm to, certify to, give your word to

assured 1 = **confident**, certain, positive, poised, fearless, self-confident, self-assured, dauntless **OPPOSITE:** self-conscious 2 = **certain**, sure, ensured, confirmed, settled, guaranteed, fixed, secure **OPPOSITE:** doubtful

astonish = **amaze**, surprise, stun, stagger, bewilder, astound, daze, confound

astounding = **amazing**, surprising, brilliant, impressive, astonishing, staggering, sensational (*informal*), bewildering

astute = **intelligent**, sharp, clever, subtle, shrewd, cunning, canny, perceptive **OPPOSITE:** stupid

asylum 1 (*Old-fashioned*) = **mental hospital**, hospital, institution, psychiatric hospital, madhouse (*informal*)
2 = **refuge**, haven, safety, protection, preserve, shelter, retreat, harbour

athlete = **sportsperson**, player, runner, competitor, sportsman, contestant, gymnast, sportswoman

athletic ADJECTIVE 1 = **fit**, strong, powerful, healthy, active, trim, strapping, energetic **OPPOSITE:** feeble
▷ PLURAL NOUN 2 = **sports**, games, races, exercises, contests, sporting events, gymnastics, track and field events

atmosphere 1 = **air**, sky, heavens, aerosphere
2 = **feeling**, character, environment, spirit, surroundings, tone, mood, climate

atom = **particle**, bit, spot, trace, molecule, dot, speck

atrocity 1 = **act of cruelty**, crime, horror, evil, outrage, abomination 2 = **cruelty**, horror, brutality, savagery, wickedness, barbarity, viciousness, fiendishness

attach 1 = **affix**, stick, secure, add, join, couple, link, tie **OPPOSITE:** detach 2 = **ascribe**, connect, attribute, assign, associate

attached = **spoken for**, married, partnered, engaged, accompanied
▷ PHRASES: attached to = **fond of**, devoted to, affectionate towards, full of regard for

attachment 1 = **fondness**, liking, feeling, relationship, regard, attraction, affection, affinity, aroha (*N.Z.*) **OPPOSITE:** aversion 2 = **accessory**, fitting, extra, component, extension, supplement, fixture, accoutrement

attack VERB 1 = **assault**, strike (at), mug, ambush, tear into, set upon, lay into (*informal*) **OPPOSITE:** defend 2 = **invade**, occupy, raid, infringe, storm, encroach 3 = **criticize**, blame, abuse, condemn, knock (*informal*), put down, slate (*informal*), have a go (at) (*informal*)
▷ NOUN 4 = **assault**, charge,

campaign, strike, raid, invasion, offensive, blitz **OPPOSITE:** defence **5** = **criticism**, censure, disapproval, abuse, bad press, vilification, denigration, disparagement **6** = **bout**, fit, stroke, seizure, spasm, convulsion, paroxysm

attacker = **assailant**, assaulter, raider, intruder, invader, aggressor, mugger

attain 1 = **obtain**, get, reach, complete, gain, achieve, acquire, fulfil **2** = **reach**, achieve, acquire, accomplish

attempt VERB **1** = **try**, seek, aim, struggle, venture, undertake, strive, endeavour ▷ NOUN **2** = **try**, go (informal), shot (informal), effort, trial, bid, crack (informal), stab (informal) **3** = **attack**

attend 1 = **be present**, go to, visit, frequent, haunt, appear at, turn up at, patronize **OPPOSITE:** be absent **2** = **pay attention**, listen, hear, mark, note, observe, heed, pay heed **OPPOSITE:** ignore ▷ PHRASES: attend to something = apply yourself to, concentrate on, look after, take care of, see to, get to work on, devote yourself to, occupy yourself with

attendance 1 = **presence**, being there, attending, appearance **2** = **turnout**, audience, gate, congregation, house, crowd, throng

attendant NOUN **1** = **assistant**, guard, servant, companion, aide, escort, follower, helper ▷ ADJECTIVE **2** = **accompanying**, related, associated, accessory, consequent, resultant, concomitant

attention 1 = **thinking**, thought, mind, consideration, scrutiny, heed, deliberation, intentness **2** = **care**, support, concern, treatment, looking after, succour, ministration **3** = **awareness**, regard, notice, recognition, consideration, observation, consciousness **OPPOSITE:** inattention

attic = **loft**, garret, roof space **OPPOSITE:** basement

attitude 1 = **opinion**, view, position, approach, mood, perspective, point of view, stance **2** = **position**, bearing, pose, stance, carriage, posture

attract 1 = **allure**, draw, persuade, charm, appeal to, win over, tempt, lure (informal) **OPPOSITE:** repel **2** = **pull**, draw, magnetize

attraction 1 = **appeal**, pull (informal), charm, lure, temptation, fascination, allure, magnetism **2** = **pull**, magnetism

attractive 1 = **seductive**, charming, tempting, pretty, fair, inviting, lovely, pleasant **OPPOSITE:** unattractive

2 = **appealing**, pleasing, inviting, tempting, irresistible **OPPOSITE:** unappealing

attribute VERB 1 = **ascribe**, credit, refer, trace, assign, charge, allocate, put down ▷ NOUN 2 = **quality**, feature, property, character, element, aspect, characteristic, distinction

audience 1 = **spectators**, company, crowd, gathering, gallery, assembly, viewers, listeners 2 = **interview**, meeting, hearing, exchange, reception, consultation

aura = **air**, feeling, quality, atmosphere, tone, mood, ambience

austerity 1 = **plainness**, simplicity, starkness 2 = **asceticism**, self-discipline, sobriety, puritanism, self-denial

authentic 1 = **real**, pure, genuine, valid, undisputed, lawful, bona fide, dinkum (*Austral. & N.Z. informal*), true-to-life **OPPOSITE:** fake 2 = **accurate**, legitimate, authoritative

authenticity 1 = **genuineness**, purity 2 = **accuracy**, certainty, validity, legitimacy, faithfulness, truthfulness

author 1 = **writer**, composer, novelist, hack, creator, scribbler, scribe, wordsmith 2 = **creator**, father, producer, designer, founder, architect, inventor, originator, initiator

authoritarian ADJECTIVE 1 = **strict**, severe, autocratic, dictatorial, dogmatic, tyrannical, doctrinaire **OPPOSITE:** lenient ▷ NOUN 2 = **disciplinarian**, dictator, tyrant, despot, autocrat, absolutist

authoritative 1 = **commanding**, masterly, imposing, assertive, imperious, self-assured **OPPOSITE:** timid 2 = **reliable**, accurate, valid, authentic, definitive, dependable, trustworthy **OPPOSITE:** unreliable

authority 1 *usually plural* = **powers that be**, government, police, officials, the state, management, administration, the system 2 = **prerogative**, influence, power, control, weight, direction, command, licence, mana (*N.Z.*) 3 = **expert**, specialist, professional, master, guru, virtuoso, connoisseur, fundi (*S. African*) 4 = **command**, power, control, rule, management, direction, mastery

authorize 1 = **empower**, commission, enable, entitle, mandate, accredit, give authority to 2 = **permit**, allow, grant, approve, sanction, license, warrant, consent to **OPPOSITE:** forbid

automatic 1 = **mechanical**, automated, mechanized, push-

button, self-propelling **OPPOSITE:** done by hand
2 = **involuntary**, natural, unconscious, mechanical, spontaneous, reflex, instinctive, unwilled **OPPOSITE:** conscious

autonomous = **self-ruling**, free, independent, sovereign, self-sufficient, self-governing, self-determining

autonomy = **independence**, freedom, sovereignty, self-determination, self-government, self-rule, self-sufficiency, home rule, rangatiratanga (N.Z.) **OPPOSITE:** dependency

availability = **accessibility**, readiness, handiness, attainability

available = **accessible**, ready, to hand, handy, at hand, free, to be had, achievable **OPPOSITE:** in use

avalanche 1 = **snow-slide**, landslide, landslip 2 = **large amount**, barrage, torrent, deluge, inundation

avant-garde = **progressive**, pioneering, experimental, innovative, unconventional, ground-breaking **OPPOSITE:** conservative

avenue = **street**, way, course, drive, road, approach, route, path

average NOUN 1 = **standard**, normal, usual, par, mode, mean, medium, norm
▷ ADJECTIVE 2 = **usual**, standard, general, normal, regular, ordinary, typical, commonplace **OPPOSITE:** unusual 3 = **mean**, middle, medium, intermediate, median **OPPOSITE:** minimum
▷ VERB 4 = **make on average**, be on average, even out to, do on average, balance out to
▷ PHRASES: on average = **usually**, generally, normally, typically, for the most part, as a rule

avert 1 = **ward off**, avoid, prevent, frustrate, fend off, preclude, stave off, forestall 2 = **turn away**, turn aside

avoid 1 = **prevent**, stop, frustrate, hamper, foil, inhibit, avert, thwart 2 = **refrain from**, bypass, dodge, eschew, escape, duck (out of) (informal), fight shy of, shirk from 3 = **keep away from**, dodge, shun, evade, steer clear of, bypass

await 1 = **wait for**, expect, look for, look forward to, anticipate, stay for 2 = **be in store for**, wait for, be ready for, lie in wait for, be in readiness for

awake ADJECTIVE 1 = **not sleeping**, sleepless, wide-awake, aware, conscious, aroused, awakened, restless **OPPOSITE:** asleep
▷ VERB 2 = **wake up**, come to, wake, stir, awaken, rouse 3 = **alert**, stimulate, provoke, revive, arouse, stir up, kindle

awaken 1 = **stimulate**,

a

provoke, alert, stir up, kindle
2 = **awake**, wake, revive, arouse, rouse
award NOUN **1** = **prize**, gift, trophy, decoration, grant, bonsela (S. African), koha (N.Z.)
▷ VERB **2** = **present with**, give, grant, hand out, confer, endow, bestow **3** = **grant**, give, confer
aware = **informed**, enlightened, knowledgeable, learned, expert, versed, up to date, in the picture OPPOSITE: ignorant
awareness PHRASES:
awareness of = **knowledge of**, understanding of, recognition of, perception of, consciousness of, realization of, familiarity with
away ADJECTIVE **1** = **absent**, out, gone, elsewhere, abroad, not here, not present, on vacation
▷ ADVERB **2** = **off**, elsewhere, abroad, hence, from here **3** = **aside**, out of the way, to one side **4** = **at a distance**, far, apart, remote, isolated
5 = **continuously**, repeatedly, relentlessly, incessantly, interminably, unremittingly, uninterruptedly
awe NOUN **1** = **wonder**, fear, respect, reverence, horror, terror, dread, admiration OPPOSITE: contempt
▷ VERB **2** = **impress**, amaze, stun, frighten, terrify, astonish, horrify, intimidate
awesome = **awe-inspiring**,

amazing, stunning, impressive, astonishing, formidable, intimidating, breathtaking
awful 1 = **disgusting**, offensive, gross, foul, dreadful, revolting, sickening, frightful, festy (Austral. slang), yucko (Austral. slang) **2** = **bad**, poor, terrible, appalling, foul, rubbish (slang), dreadful, horrendous OPPOSITE: wonderful **3** = **shocking**, dreadful **4** = **unwell**, poorly (informal), ill, terrible, sick, crook (Austral. & N.Z. informal), unhealthy, off-colour, under the weather (informal)
awfully 1 (Informal) = **very**, extremely, terribly, exceptionally, greatly, immensely, exceedingly, dreadfully **2** = **badly**, woefully, dreadfully, disgracefully, wretchedly, unforgivably, reprehensibly
awkward 1 = **embarrassing**, difficult, sensitive, delicate, uncomfortable, humiliating, disconcerting, inconvenient, barro (Austral. slang) OPPOSITE: comfortable **2** = **inconvenient**, difficult, troublesome, cumbersome, unwieldy, unmanageable, clunky (informal) OPPOSITE: convenient
3 = **clumsy**, lumbering, bumbling, unwieldy, ponderous, ungainly, gauche, gawky, unco (Austral. slang) OPPOSITE: graceful
axe NOUN **1** = **hatchet**,

chopper, tomahawk, cleaver, adze
▷ VERB 2 (*Informal*) = **abandon**, end, eliminate, cancel, scrap, cut back, terminate, dispense with 3 (*Informal*) = **dismiss**, fire (*informal*), sack (*informal*), remove, get rid of
▷ PHRASES: the axe (*Informal*) = **the sack** (*informal*), dismissal, the boot (*slang*), termination, the chop (*slang*)
axis = **pivot**, shaft, axle, spindle, centre line

Bb

baas (*S. African*) = **master**, bo (*informal*), chief, ruler, commander, head, overlord, overseer
baby NOUN 1 = **child**, infant, babe, bairn (*Scot.*), newborn child, babe in arms, ankle-biter (*Austral. slang*), tacker (*Austral. slang*)
▷ ADJECTIVE 2 = **small**, little, minute, tiny, mini, wee, miniature, petite
back NOUN 1 = **spine**, backbone, vertebrae, spinal column, vertebral column
2 = **rear**, back end OPPOSITE: front 3 = **reverse**, rear, other side, wrong side, underside, flip side
▷ ADJECTIVE 4 = **rear** OPPOSITE: front 5 = **rearmost**, hind, hindmost 6 = **previous**, earlier, former, past, elapsed OPPOSITE: future 7 = **tail**, end, rear, posterior
▷ VERB 8 = **support**, help, aid, champion, defend, promote, assist, advocate OPPOSITE: oppose 9 = **subsidize**, help, support, sponsor, assist
backbone 1 = **spinal column**,

spine, vertebrae, vertebral column 2 = **strength of character**, character, resolution, nerve, daring, courage, determination, pluck

backer 1 = **supporter**, second, angel (*informal*), patron, promoter, subscriber, helper, benefactor 2 = **advocate**, supporter, patron, sponsor, promoter

backfire = **fail**, founder, flop (*informal*), rebound, boomerang, miscarry, misfire

background 1 = **upbringing**, history, culture, environment, tradition, circumstances 2 = **experience**, grounding, education 3 = **circumstances**, history, conditions, situation, atmosphere, environment, framework, ambience

backing 1 = **support**, encouragement, endorsement, moral support 2 = **assistance**, support, help, aid, sponsorship, patronage

backlash = **reaction**, response, resistance, retaliation, repercussion, counterblast, counteraction

backward
1 = **underdeveloped**, undeveloped 2 = **slow**, behind, retarded, underdeveloped, subnormal, half-witted, slow-witted

backwards *or* **backward**
= **towards the rear**, behind you, in reverse, rearwards

bacteria = **microorganisms**, viruses, bugs (*slang*), germs, microbes, pathogens, bacilli
● **USAGE NOTE**
● *Bacteria* is a plural noun. It is
● therefore incorrect to talk
● about *a bacteria*, even though
● this is quite commonly heard,
● especially in the media. The
● correct singular is *a bacterium*.

bad ADJECTIVE 1 = **harmful**, damaging, dangerous, destructive, unhealthy, detrimental, hurtful, ruinous **OPPOSITE:** beneficial 2 = **poor** 3 = **unfavourable**, distressing, unfortunate, grim, unpleasant, gloomy, adverse 4 = **inferior**, poor, inadequate, faulty, unsatisfactory, defective, imperfect, substandard, bush-league (*Austral. & N.Z. informal*), half-pie (*N.Z. informal*), bodger or bodgie (*Austral. slang*) **OPPOSITE:** satisfactory
5 = **incompetent**, poor, useless, incapable, unfit, inexpert 6 = **grim**, severe, hard, tough 7 = **wicked**, criminal, evil, corrupt, immoral, sinful, depraved **OPPOSITE:** virtuous 8 = **naughty**, defiant, wayward, mischievous, wicked, unruly, impish, undisciplined **OPPOSITE:** well-behaved 9 = **rotten**, off, rank, sour, rancid, mouldy, putrid, festy (*Austral. slang*)

badge 1 = **image**, brand, stamp, identification, crest, emblem, insignia 2 = **mark**, sign, token, hallmark

badger = pester, harry, bother, bug (*informal*), bully, plague, hound, harass

badly 1 = poorly, incorrectly, carelessly, inadequately, imperfectly, ineptly **OPPOSITE:** well 2 = severely, greatly, deeply, seriously, desperately, intensely, exceedingly
3 = unfavourably, unsuccessfully

baffle = puzzle, confuse, stump, bewilder, confound, perplex, mystify, flummox **OPPOSITE:** explain

bag NOUN 1 = sack, container, sac, receptacle
▷ VERB 2 = get, land, score (*slang*), capture, acquire, procure 3 = catch, kill, shoot, capture, acquire, trap

baggage = luggage, things, cases, bags, equipment, gear, suitcases, belongings

baggy = loose, slack, bulging, sagging, sloppy, floppy, roomy, ill-fitting **OPPOSITE:** tight

bail (*Law*) = security, bond, guarantee, pledge, warranty, surety
▷ PHRASES: bail out = escape, withdraw, get away, retreat, make your getaway, break free or out ▶ bail something or someone out (*Informal*) = save, help, release, aid, deliver, recover, rescue, get out

bait NOUN 1 = lure, attraction, incentive, carrot (*informal*), temptation, snare, inducement, decoy
▷ VERB 2 = tease, annoy, irritate, bother, mock, wind up (*Brit. slang*), hound, torment

baked = dry, desert, seared, scorched, barren, sterile, arid, torrid

bakkie (*S. African*) = truck, pick-up, van, lorry, pick-up truck

balance VERB 1 = stabilize, level, steady **OPPOSITE:** overbalance 2 = weigh, consider, compare, estimate, contrast, assess, evaluate, set against 3 (*Accounting*) = calculate, total, determine, estimate, settle, count, square, reckon
▷ NOUN 4 = equilibrium, stability, steadiness, evenness **OPPOSITE:** instability
5 = stability, equanimity, steadiness 6 = parity, equity, fairness, impartiality, equality, correspondence, equivalence
7 = remainder, rest, difference, surplus, residue
8 = composure, stability, restraint, self-control, poise, self-discipline, equanimity, self-restraint

balcony 1 = terrace, veranda 2 = upper circle, gods, gallery

bald 1 = hairless, depilated, baldheaded 2 = plain, direct, frank, straightforward, blunt, rude, forthright, unadorned

ball = sphere, drop, globe, pellet, orb, globule, spheroid

b

balloon = expand, rise, increase, swell, blow up, inflate, bulge, billow

ballot = vote, election, voting, poll, polling, referendum, show of hands

ban VERB 1 = prohibit, bar, block, veto, forbid, boycott, outlaw, banish OPPOSITE: permit 2 = bar, prohibit, exclude, forbid, disqualify, preclude, debar, declare ineligible
▷ NOUN 3 = prohibition, restriction, veto, boycott, embargo, injunction, taboo, disqualification, rahui (N.Z.) OPPOSITE: permission

band[1] 1 = ensemble, group, orchestra, combo 2 = gang, company, group, party, team, body, crowd, pack

band[2] = headband, strip, ribbon

bandage NOUN 1 = dressing, plaster, compress, gauze
▷ VERB 2 = dress, cover, bind, swathe

bandit = robber, outlaw, raider, plunderer, mugger (informal), looter, highwayman, desperado

bang NOUN 1 = explosion, pop, clash, crack, blast, slam, discharge, thunder, thump 2 = blow, knock, stroke, punch, bump, sock (slang), smack, thump
▷ VERB 3 = resound, boom, explode, thunder, thump, clang 4 = bump, knock, elbow, jostle 5 often with on = hit, strike, knock, belt (informal), slam, thump, clatter, pummel
▷ ADVERB 6 = exactly, straight, square, squarely, precisely, slap, smack, plumb (informal)

banish 1 = exclude, ban, dismiss, expel, throw out, eject, evict 2 = expel, exile, outlaw, deport OPPOSITE: admit 3 = get rid of, remove

bank[1] NOUN 1 = financial institution, repository, depository 2 = store, fund, stock, source, supply, reserve, pool, reservoir
▷ VERB 3 = deposit, keep, save

bank[2] NOUN 1 = side, edge, margin, shore, brink 2 = mound, banking, rise, hill, mass, pile, heap, ridge, kopje or koppie (S. African) 3 = mass
▷ VERB 4 = tilt, tip, pitch, heel, slope, incline, slant, cant

bank[3] = row, group, line, range, series, file, rank, sequence

bankrupt = insolvent, broke (informal), ruined, wiped out (informal), impoverished, in the red, destitute, gone bust (informal) OPPOSITE: solvent

bankruptcy = insolvency, failure, disaster, ruin, liquidation

banner = flag, standard, colours, placard, pennant, ensign, streamer

banquet = feast, spread (informal), dinner, meal, revel, repast, hakari (N.Z.)

bar NOUN 1 = public house, pub (informal, chiefly Brit.), counter, inn, saloon, tavern, canteen, watering hole (*facetious slang*) **2 = rod**, staff, stick, stake, rail, pole, paling, shaft **3 = obstacle**, block, barrier, hurdle, hitch, barricade, snag, deterrent **OPPOSITE:** aid ▷ **VERB 4 = lock**, block, secure, attach, bolt, blockade, barricade, fortify **5 = block**, restrict, restrain, hamper, thwart, hinder, obstruct, impede **6 = exclude**, ban, forbid, prohibit, keep out of, disallow, shut out of, blackball **OPPOSITE:** admit

barbarian 1 = savage, monster, beast, brute, yahoo, swine, sadist **2 = lout**, yahoo, bigot, philistine, hoon (*Austral. & N.Z.*), cougan (*Austral. slang*), scozza (*Austral. slang*), bogan (*Austral. slang*), boor, vulgarian

bare 1 = naked, nude, stripped, uncovered, undressed, unclothed, unclad, without a stitch on (*informal*) **OPPOSITE:** dressed **2 = simple**, spare, stark, austere, spartan, unadorned, unembellished, unornamented **OPPOSITE:** adorned **3 = plain**, simple, basic, obvious, sheer, patent, evident, stark

barely = only just, just, hardly, scarcely, at a push **OPPOSITE:** completely

bargain NOUN 1 = good buy, discount purchase, good deal, steal (*informal*), snip (*informal*),

giveaway, cheap purchase **2 = agreement**, deal (*informal*), promise, contract, arrangement, settlement, pledge, pact ▷ **VERB 3 = negotiate**, deal, contract, mediate, covenant, stipulate, transact, cut a deal

barge = canal boat, lighter, narrow boat, flatboat

bark¹ VERB 1 = yap, bay, howl, snarl, growl, yelp, woof ▷ **NOUN 2 = yap**, bay, howl, snarl, growl, yelp, woof

bark² = covering, casing, cover, skin, layer, crust, cortex (*Anatomy, botany*), rind

barracks = camp, quarters, garrison, encampment, billet

barrage 1 = bombardment, attack, bombing, assault, shelling, battery, volley, blitz **2 = torrent**, mass, burst, stream, hail, spate, onslaught, deluge

barren 1 = desolate, empty, desert, waste **OPPOSITE:** fertile **2** (*Old-fashioned*) **= infertile**, sterile, childless, unproductive

barricade NOUN 1 = barrier, wall, fence, blockade, obstruction, rampart, bulwark, palisade ▷ **VERB 2 = bar**, block, defend, secure, lock, bolt, blockade, fortify

barrier = barricade, wall, bar, fence, boundary, obstacle, blockade, obstruction

base¹ NOUN 1 = bottom, floor,

b

lowest part **OPPOSITE:** top
2 = **support**, stand, foot, rest,
bed, bottom, foundation,
pedestal 3 = **foundation**,
institution, organization,
establishment 4 = **centre**,
post, station, camp, settlement,
headquarters, starting point
5 = **home**, house, pad (slang),
residence 6 = **essence**, source,
basis, root, core
▷ VERB 7 = **ground**, found,
build, establish, depend,
construct, derive, hinge
8 = **place**, set, post, station,
establish, locate, install
base² = **dishonourable**, evil,
disgraceful, shameful, immoral,
wicked, sordid, despicable,
scungy (Austral. & N.Z.)
OPPOSITE: honourable
bash NOUN (Informal)
1 = **attempt**, go (informal), try,
shot (informal), bid, crack
(informal), stab (informal)
▷ VERB (Informal) 2 = **hit**, beat,
strike, knock, smash, belt
(informal), slap, sock (slang)
basic ADJECTIVE
1 = **fundamental**, main,
essential, primary, vital,
principal, cardinal, elementary
2 = **vital**, needed, important,
key, necessary, essential,
primary, crucial 3 = **essential**,
key, vital, fundamental
OPPOSITE: secondary 4 = **main**,
key, essential, primary
5 = **plain**, simple, classic,
unfussy, unembellished

▷ PLURAL NOUN 6 = **essentials**,
principles, fundamentals, nuts
and bolts (informal), nitty-gritty
(informal), rudiments, brass
tacks (informal)
basically = **essentially**, mainly,
mostly, principally,
fundamentally, primarily, at
heart, inherently
basis 1 = **arrangement**, way,
system, footing, agreement
2 = **foundation**, support, base,
ground, footing, bottom,
groundwork
bask = **lie**, relax, lounge, sprawl,
loaf, lie about, swim in,
sunbathe, outspan (S. African)
bass = **deep**, low, resonant,
sonorous, low-pitched, deep-
toned
bat NOUN ▷ See panel BATS
batch = **group**, set, lot, crowd,
pack, collection, quantity,
bunch
bath NOUN 1 = **wash**, cleaning,
shower, soak, cleansing, scrub,
scrubbing, douche
▷ VERB 2 = **clean**, wash,
shower, soak, cleanse, scrub,
bathe, rinse
bathe 1 = **swim** 2 = **wash**,
clean, bath, shower, soak,
cleanse, scrub, rinse
3 = **cleanse**, clean, wash, soak,
rinse 4 = **cover**, flood, steep,
engulf, immerse, overrun,
suffuse, wash over
baton = **stick**, club, staff, pole,
rod, crook, cane, mace, mere
(N.Z.), patu (N.Z.)

BATS

flying fox	horseshoe bat	pipistrelle
fruit bat	kalong	serotine
hammerhead	noctule	vampire bat

batter = beat, hit, strike, knock, bang, thrash, pound, buffet

battery = artillery, ordnance, gunnery, gun emplacement, cannonry

battle NOUN 1 = fight, attack, action, struggle, conflict, clash, encounter, combat, biffo (Austral. slang) **OPPOSITE:** peace 2 = conflict, campaign, struggle, dispute, contest, crusade 3 = campaign, drive, movement, push, struggle ▷ VERB 4 = wrestle, war, fight, argue, dispute, grapple, clamour, lock horns 5 = struggle, work, labour, strain, strive, toil, go all out (informal), give it your best shot (informal) ▷ See panel FAMOUS BATTLES

battlefield = battleground, front, field, combat zone, field of battle

batty = crazy, odd, mad, eccentric, peculiar, daft (informal), touched, potty (Brit. informal), porangi (N.Z.)

bay¹ = inlet, sound, gulf, creek, cove, fjord, bight, natural harbour

bay² = recess, opening, corner, niche, compartment, nook, alcove

bay³ VERB = howl, cry, roar (used of hounds), bark, wail, growl, bellow, clamour ▷ NOUN = cry, roar (used of hounds), bark, howl, wail, growl, bellow, clamour

bazaar 1 = market, exchange, fair, marketplace 2 = fair, fête, gala, bring-and-buy

be = be alive, live, exist, survive, breathe, be present, endure

beach = shore, coast, sands, seaside, water's edge, seashore

beached = stranded, grounded, abandoned, deserted, wrecked, ashore, marooned, aground

beacon = signal, sign, beam, flare, lighthouse, bonfire, watchtower

bead = drop, tear, bubble, pearl, dot, drip, blob, droplet

beam VERB 1 = smile, grin 2 = transmit, show, air, broadcast, cable, send out, relay, televise 3 = radiate, flash, shine, glow, glitter, glare, gleam ▷ NOUN 4 = ray, flash, stream, glow, streak, shaft, gleam, glint 5 = rafter, support, timber, spar, plank, girder, joist 6 = smile, grin

bear VERB 1 = carry, take, move, bring, transfer, conduct, transport, haul **OPPOSITE:** put

FAMOUS BATTLES

Aboukir Bay	1798	Manassas	1861; 1862
Actium	31 B.C.	Marathon	490 B.C.
Agincourt	1415	Marengo	1800
Alamo	1836	Marston Moor	1644
Arnhem	1944	Missionary Ridge	1863
Austerlitz	1805	Naseby	1645
Balaklava	1854	Omdurman	1898
Bannockburn	1314	Passchendaele	1917
Barnet	1471	Philippi	42 B.C.
Bautzen	1813	Plains of Abraham	1759
Belleau Wood	1918	Plassey	1757
Blenheim	1704	Plataea	479 B.C.
Borodino	1812	Poltava	1709
Bosworth Field	1485	Prestonpans	1745
Boyne	1690	Pydna	168 B.C.
Cannae	216 B.C.	Quatre Bras	1815
Crécy	1346	Ramillies	1706
Culloden	1746	Roncesvalles	778
Dien Bien Phu	1954	Sadowa or Sadová	1866
Edgehill	1642	Saint-Mihiel	1918
El Alamein	1942	Salamis	480 B.C.
Falkirk	1298; 1746	Sedgemoor	1685
Flodden	1513	Sempach	1386
Gettysburg	1863	Shipka Pass	1877-78
Guadalcanal	1942-3	Somme	1916; 1918
Hastings	1066	Stamford Bridge	1066
Imphal	1944	Tannenberg	1410; 1914
Inkerman	1854	Tewkesbury	1471
Jemappes	1792	Thermopylae	480 B.C.
Jena	1806	Tobruk	1941; 1942
Killiecrankie	1689	Trafalgar	1805
Kursk	1943	Trenton	1776
Ladysmith	1899-1900	Verdun	1916
Leipzig	1813	Vitoria	1813
Lepanto	1571	Wagram	1809
Leyte Gulf	1944	Waterloo	1815
Little Bighorn	1876	Ypres	1914; 1915; 1917; 1918
Lützen	1632	Zama	202 B.C.

down **2** = **support**, shoulder, sustain, endure, uphold, withstand **OPPOSITE:** give up **3** = **display**, have, show, hold, carry, possess **4** = **suffer**, experience, go through, sustain, stomach, endure, brook, abide **5** = **bring yourself to**, allow, accept, permit, endure, tolerate **6** = **produce**, generate, yield, bring forth **7** = **give birth to**, produce, deliver, breed, bring forth, beget **8** = **exhibit**, hold, maintain **9** = **conduct**, carry, move, deport

▷ **PHRASES: bear something out** = **support**, prove, confirm, justify, endorse, uphold, substantiate, corroborate

bearer 1 = **agent**, carrier, courier, herald, envoy, messenger, conveyor, emissary **2** = **carrier**, runner, servant, porter

bearing NOUN 1 usually with on or upon = **relevance**, relation, application, connection, import, reference, significance, pertinence **OPPOSITE:** irrelevance **2** = **manner**, attitude, conduct, aspect, behaviour, posture, demeanour, deportment

▷ **PLURAL NOUN 3** = **way**, course, position, situation, track, aim, direction, location

beast 1 = **animal**, creature, brute **2** = **brute**, monster, savage, barbarian, fiend, swine, ogre, sadist

beastly = **unpleasant**, mean, awful, nasty, rotten, horrid, disagreeable **OPPOSITE:** pleasant

beat VERB 1 = **batter**, hit, strike, knock, pound, smack, thrash, thump **2** = **pound**, strike, hammer, batter, thrash **3** = **throb**, thump, pound, quake, vibrate, pulsate, palpitate **4** = **hit**, strike, bang **5** = **flap**, thrash, flutter, wag **6** = **defeat**, outdo, trounce, overcome, crush, overwhelm, conquer, surpass

▷ **NOUN 7** = **throb**, pounding, pulse, thumping, vibration, pulsating, palpitation, pulsation **8** = **route**, way, course, rounds, path, circuit

▷ **PHRASES: beat someone up** (Informal) = **assault**, attack, batter, thrash, set about, set upon, lay into (informal), beat the living daylights out of (informal)

beaten 1 = **stirred**, mixed, whipped, blended, whisked, frothy, foamy **2** = **defeated**, overcome, overwhelmed, cowed, thwarted, vanquished

beautiful = **attractive**, pretty, lovely, charming, tempting, pleasant, handsome, fetching **OPPOSITE:** ugly

beauty 1 = **attractiveness**, charm, grace, glamour, elegance, loveliness, handsomeness, comeliness **OPPOSITE:** ugliness **2** = **good-**

looker, lovely (*slang*), belle, stunner (*informal*)

because = **since**, as, in that ▷ **PHRASES: because of** = **as a result of**, on account of, by reason of, thanks to, owing to

● **USAGE NOTE**
● The phrase *on account of* can
● provide a useful alternative to
● *because of* in writing. It occurs
● relatively infrequently in
● spoken language, where it is
● sometimes followed by a
● clause, as in *on account of I*
● *don't do drugs*. However, this
● use is considered
● nonstandard.

beckon = **gesture**, sign, wave, indicate, signal, nod, motion, summon

become 1 = **come to be**, develop into, be transformed into, grow into, change into, alter to, mature into, ripen into 2 = **suit**, fit, enhance, flatter, embellish, set off

becoming 1 = **flattering**, pretty, attractive, enhancing, neat, graceful, tasteful, well-chosen **OPPOSITE:** unflattering 2 = **appropriate**, seemly, fitting, suitable, proper, worthy, in keeping, compatible **OPPOSITE:** inappropriate

bed 1 = **bedstead**, couch, berth, cot, bunk, divan 2 = **plot**, area, row, strip, patch, ground, land, garden 3 = **bottom**, ground, floor 4 = **base**, footing, basis, bottom, foundation, underpinning, groundwork, bedrock

bee ▷ *See panel* **ANTS, BEES AND WASPS**

beetle ▷ *See panel* **BEETLES**

before **PREPOSITION** 1 = **earlier than**, ahead of, prior to, in advance of **OPPOSITE:** after 2 = **in front of**, ahead of, in advance of 3 = **in the presence of**, in front of 4 = **ahead of**, in front of, in advance of ▷ **ADVERB** 5 = **previously**, earlier, sooner, in advance, formerly **OPPOSITE:** after 6 = **in the past**, earlier, once, previously, formerly, hitherto, beforehand

● **RELATED WORDS**
● *prefixes:* ante-, fore-, pre-

beforehand = **in advance**, before, earlier, already, sooner, ahead, previously, in anticipation

beg 1 = **implore**, plead with, beseech, request, petition, solicit, entreat 2 = **scrounge**, bum (*informal*), touch (someone) for (*slang*), cadge, sponge on (someone) for, freeload (*slang*), seek charity, solicit charity **OPPOSITE:** give

beggar = **tramp**, bum (*informal*), derelict, drifter, down-and-out, pauper, vagrant, bag lady (*chiefly U.S.*), derro (*Austral. slang*)

begin 1 = **start**, commence, proceed **OPPOSITE:** stop 2 = **commence**, start, initiate,

BEETLES

ambrosia beetle	deathwatch beetle
Asiatic beetle	diving beetle
bacon beetle	dung beetle or chafer
bark beetle	firefly
bee beetle	flea beetle
black beetle or (N.Z.)	furniture beetle
kekerengu or Māori	glow-worm
bug	gold beetle or goldbug
blister beetle	goldsmith beetle
bloody-nosed beetle	ground beetle
boll weevil	Japanese beetle
bombardier beetle	June bug, June beetle, May
burying beetle or sexton	bug, or May beetle
cabinet beetle	ladybird or (U.S. & Canad.)
cardinal beetle	ladybug
carpet beetle or (U.S.) carpet	leaf beetle
bug	leather beetle
chafer	May beetle, cockchafer, or
Christmas beetle or king	June bug
beetle	scarab
click beetle, snapping beetle,	scavenger beetle
or skipjack	snapping beetle
cockchafer, May beetle, or	water beetle
May bug	weevil or snout beetle
Colorado beetle or potato	weevil, pea weevil, or bean
beetle	weevil

embark on, set about, instigate, institute, make a beginning **3** = **start talking**, start, initiate, commence **4** = **come into existence**, start, appear, emerge, arise, originate, come into being **5** = **emerge**, start, spring, stem, derive, originate **OPPOSITE:** end

beginner = **novice**, pupil, amateur, newcomer, starter, trainee, apprentice, learner

OPPOSITE: expert

beginning 1 = **start**, opening, birth, origin, outset, onset, initiation, inauguration **OPPOSITE:** end **2** = **outset**, start, opening, birth, onset, commencement **3** = **origins**

behave 1 = **act 2** *often reflexive* = **be well-behaved**, mind your manners, keep your nose clean, act correctly, conduct yourself properly **OPPOSITE:** misbehave

b

behaviour 1 = **conduct**, ways, actions, bearing, attitude, manner, manners, demeanour 2 = **action**, performance, operation, functioning

behind PREPOSITION 1 = **at the rear of**, at the back of, at the heels of 2 = **after**, following 3 = **supporting**, for, backing, on the side of, in agreement with 4 = **causing**, responsible for, initiating, at the bottom of, instigating 5 = **later than**, after

▷ ADVERB 6 = **after**, next, following, afterwards, subsequently, in the wake (of) OPPOSITE: in advance of 7 = **behind schedule**, delayed, running late, behind time OPPOSITE: ahead 8 = **overdue**, in debt, in arrears, behindhand ▷ NOUN 9 (*Informal*) = **bottom**, butt (*U.S. & Canad. informal*), buttocks, posterior

being 1 = **individual**, creature, human being, living thing 2 = **life**, reality OPPOSITE: nonexistence 3 = **soul**, spirit, substance, creature, essence, organism, entity

beleaguered 1 = **harassed**, troubled, plagued, hassled (*informal*), badgered, persecuted, pestered, vexed 2 = **besieged**, surrounded, blockaded, beset, encircled, assailed, hemmed in

belief 1 = **trust**, confidence, conviction OPPOSITE: disbelief

2 = **faith**, principles, doctrine, ideology, creed, dogma, tenet, credo 3 = **opinion**, feeling, idea, impression, assessment, notion, judgment, point of view

believe 1 = **think**, judge, suppose, estimate, imagine, assume, gather, reckon 2 = **accept**, trust, credit, depend on, rely on, have faith in, swear by, be certain of OPPOSITE: disbelieve

believer = **follower**, supporter, convert, disciple, devotee, apostle, adherent, zealot OPPOSITE: sceptic

bellow VERB 1 = **shout**, cry (out), scream, roar, yell, howl, shriek, bawl ▷ NOUN 2 = **shout**, cry, scream, roar, yell, howl, shriek, bawl

belly = **stomach**, insides (*informal*), gut, abdomen, tummy, paunch, potbelly, corporation (*informal*), puku (*N.Z.*)

belong = **go with**, fit into, be part of, relate to, be connected with, pertain to

belonging = **fellowship**, relationship, association, loyalty, acceptance, attachment, inclusion, affinity

belongings = **possessions**, goods, things, effects, property, stuff, gear, paraphernalia

beloved = **dear**, loved, valued, prized, admired, treasured, precious, darling

below PREPOSITION 1 = **under**,

underneath, lower than
2 = **less than**, lower than
3 = **subordinate to**, subject to, inferior to, lesser than
▷ ADVERB 4 = **lower**, down, under, beneath, underneath
5 = **beneath**, following, at the end, underneath, at the bottom, further on

belt 1 = **waistband**, band, sash, girdle, girth, cummerbund
2 = **conveyor belt**, band, loop, fan belt, drive belt
3 (*Geography*) = **zone**, area, region, section, district, stretch, strip, layer

bemused = **puzzled**, confused, baffled, at sea, bewildered, muddled, perplexed, mystified

bench 1 = **seat**, stall, pew
2 = **worktable**, stand, table, counter, trestle table, workbench
▷ PHRASES: **the bench** = **court**, judges, magistrates, tribunal, judiciary, courtroom

benchmark = **reference point**, gauge, yardstick, measure, level, standard, model, par

bend VERB 1 = **twist**, turn, wind, lean, hook, bow, curve, arch
▷ NOUN 2 = **curve**, turn, corner, twist, angle, bow, loop, arc

beneath PREPOSITION
1 = **under**, below, underneath, lower than **OPPOSITE:** over
2 = **inferior to**, below
3 = **unworthy of**, unfitting for, unsuitable for, inappropriate

for, unbefitting
▷ ADVERB 4 = **underneath**, below, in a lower place
● RELATED WORD
● *prefix:* sub-

beneficial = **favourable**, useful, valuable, helpful, profitable, benign, wholesome, advantageous **OPPOSITE:** harmful

beneficiary 1 = **recipient**, receiver, payee 2 = **heir**, inheritor

benefit NOUN 1 = **good**, help, profit, favour **OPPOSITE:** harm
2 = **advantage**, aid, favour, assistance
▷ VERB 3 = **profit from**, make the most of, gain from, do well out of, reap benefits from, turn to your advantage 4 = **help**, aid, profit, improve, enhance, assist, avail **OPPOSITE:** harm

benign 1 = **benevolent**, kind, kindly, warm, friendly, obliging, sympathetic, compassionate **OPPOSITE:** unkind 2 (*Medical*) = **harmless**, innocent, innocuous, curable, inoffensive, remediable **OPPOSITE:** malignant

bent ADJECTIVE 1 = **misshapen**, twisted, angled, bowed, curved, arched, crooked, distorted **OPPOSITE:** straight
2 = **stooped**, bowed, arched, hunched
▷ NOUN 3 = **inclination**, ability, leaning, tendency, preference, penchant, propensity, aptitude

> **PHRASES: bent on = intent on**, set on, fixed on, predisposed to, resolved on, insistent on

bequeath 1 = **leave**, will, give, grant, hand down, endow, bestow, entrust 2 = **give**, accord, grant, afford, yield, lend, pass on, confer

berth NOUN 1 = **bunk**, bed, hammock, billet 2 (*Nautical*) = **anchorage**, haven, port, harbour, dock, pier, wharf, quay
> **VERB** 3 (*Nautical*) = **anchor**, land, dock, moor, tie up, drop anchor

beside = **next to**, near, close to, neighbouring, alongside, adjacent to, at the side of, abreast of
> **PHRASES: beside yourself = distraught**, desperate, distressed, frantic, frenzied, demented, unhinged, overwrought

● **USAGE NOTE**
● People occasionally confuse
● *beside* and *besides*. *Besides* is
● used for mentioning
● something that adds to what
● you have already said, for
● example: *I didn't feel like going*
● *and besides, I had nothing to*
● *wear. Beside usually means*
● *next to or at the side of*
● *something or someone*, for
● example: *he was standing*
● *beside me* (not *besides me*).

besides PREPOSITION 1 = **apart from**, barring, excepting, other than, excluding, as well (as), in addition to, over and above
> **ADVERB** 2 = **also**, too, further, otherwise, in addition, as well, moreover, furthermore

besiege 1 = **harass**, harry, plague, hound, hassle (*informal*), badger, pester 2 = **surround**, enclose, blockade, encircle, hem in, shut in, lay siege to

best ADJECTIVE 1 = **finest**, leading, supreme, principal, foremost, pre-eminent, unsurpassed, most accomplished
> **NOUN** 2 = **finest**, top, prime, pick, flower, cream, elite, crème de la crème (*French*)
> **ADVERB** 3 = **most highly**, most fully, most deeply

bestow = **present**, give, award, grant, commit, hand out, lavish, impart **OPPOSITE:** obtain

bet VERB 1 = **gamble**, chance, stake, venture, hazard, speculate, wager, risk money
> **NOUN** 2 = **gamble**, risk, stake, venture, speculation, flutter (*informal*), punt, wager

betray 1 = **be disloyal to**, dob in (*Austral. slang*), double-cross (*informal*), stab in the back, be unfaithful to, inform on or against 2 = **give away**, reveal, expose, disclose, uncover, divulge, unmask, let slip

betrayal 1 = **disloyalty**, sell-out (*informal*), deception, treason, treachery, trickery, double-cross (*informal*), breach of trust

OPPOSITE: loyalty

better ADVERB 1 = **to a greater degree**, more completely, more thoroughly 2 = **in a more excellent manner**, more effectively, more attractively, more advantageously, more competently, in a superior way **OPPOSITE:** worse

▷ ADJECTIVE 3 = **well**, stronger, recovering, cured, fully recovered, on the mend (*informal*) **OPPOSITE:** worse 4 = **superior**, finer, higher-quality, surpassing, preferable, more desirable **OPPOSITE:** inferior

between = amidst, among, mid, in the middle of, betwixt
● RELATED WORD
● *prefix:* inter-
● USAGE NOTE
● After *distribute* and words
● with a similar meaning,
● *among* should be used rather
● than *between*: *share out the*
● *sweets among the children* (not
● *between the children*, unless
● there are only two children).

beverage = drink, liquid, liquor, refreshment

beware 1 = **be careful**, look out, watch out, be wary, be cautious, take heed, guard against something 2 = **avoid**, mind

bewilder = confound, confuse, puzzle, baffle, perplex, mystify, flummox, bemuse

bewildered = confused,

puzzled, baffled, at sea, muddled, perplexed, at a loss, mystified

beyond 1 = **on the other side of** 2 = **after**, over, past, above 3 = **past** 4 = **except for**, but, save, apart from, other than, excluding, besides, aside from 5 = **exceeding**, surpassing, superior to, out of reach of 6 = **outside**, over, above

bias NOUN 1 = **prejudice**, leaning, tendency, inclination, favouritism, partiality **OPPOSITE:** impartiality
▷ VERB 2 = **influence**, colour, weight, prejudice, distort, sway, warp, slant

biased = prejudiced, weighted, one-sided, partial, distorted, slanted

bid NOUN 1 = **attempt**, try, effort, go (*informal*), shot (*informal*), stab (*informal*), crack (*informal*) 2 = **offer**, price, amount, advance, proposal, sum, tender
▷ VERB 3 = **make an offer**, offer, propose, submit, tender, proffer 4 = **wish**, say, call, tell, greet 5 = **tell**, ask, order, require, direct, command, instruct

bidding = order, request, command, instruction, summons, beck and call

big 1 = **large**, great, huge, massive, vast, enormous, substantial, extensive **OPPOSITE:** small

2 = **important**, significant, urgent, far-reaching **OPPOSITE:** unimportant 3 = **powerful**, important, prominent, dominant, influential, eminent 4 = **grown-up**, adult, grown, mature, elder, full-grown **OPPOSITE:** young 5 = **generous**, good, noble, gracious, benevolent, altruistic, unselfish, magnanimous

bill¹ NOUN 1 = **charges**, rate, costs, score, account, statement, reckoning, expense 2 = **act of parliament**, measure, proposal, piece of legislation, projected law 3 = **list**, listing, programme, card, schedule, agenda, catalogue, inventory 4 = **advertisement**, notice, poster, leaflet, bulletin, circular, handout, placard ▷ VERB 5 = **charge**, debit, invoice, send a statement to, send an invoice to 6 = **advertise**, post, announce, promote, plug (*informal*), tout, publicize, give advance notice of

bill² = **beak**, nib, neb (*archaic, dialect*), mandible

bind VERB 1 = **oblige**, make, force, require, engage, compel, constrain, necessitate 2 = **tie**, join, stick, secure, wrap, knot, strap, lash **OPPOSITE:** untie ▷ NOUN 3 (*Informal*) = **nuisance**, inconvenience, hassle (*informal*), drag (*informal*), spot (*informal*), difficulty, bore,

dilemma, uphill (*S. African*)

binding = **compulsory**, necessary, mandatory, obligatory, irrevocable, unalterable, indissoluble **OPPOSITE:** optional

binge (*Informal*) = **bout**, spell, fling, feast, stint, spree, orgy, bender (*informal*)

biography = **life story**, life, record, account, profile, memoir, CV, curriculum vitae

bird = **feathered friend**, fowl, songbird
● RELATED WORDS
● *adjective*: avian
● *male*: cock
● *female*: hen
● *young*: chick, fledg(e)ling, nestling
● *collective nouns*: flock, flight
● *habitation*: nest
▷ *See panels* BIRDS, BIRDS OF PREY, SEABIRDS, TYPES OF FOWL

bird of prey ▷ *See panel* BIRDS OF PREY

birth 1 = **childbirth**, delivery, nativity, parturition **OPPOSITE:** death 2 = **ancestry**, stock, blood, background, breeding, pedigree, lineage, parentage
● RELATED WORD
● *adjective*: natal

bit¹ 1 = **slice**, fragment, crumb, morsel 2 = **piece**, scrap 3 = **jot**, iota 4 = **part**

bit² = **curb**, check, brake, restraint, snaffle

bite VERB 1 = **nip**, cut, tear, wound, snap, pierce, pinch,

BIRDS

accentor
amokura (N.Z.)
apostle bird or happy family bird (Austral.)
avocet
axebird (Austral.)
banded dotterel (N.Z.)
banded rail (N.Z.)
bee-eater
bellbird or (N.Z.) koromako or makomako
bittern
blackbird
blackcap
black-fronted tern or tara (N.Z.)
black robin (N.Z.)
blue duck, mountain duck, whio or whistling duck (N.Z.)
boobook (Austral.)
brain-fever bird or (Austral.) pallid cuckoo
brambling
brolga, Australian crane, or (Austral.) native companion
brown creeper or pipipi (N.Z.)
brown duck (N.Z.)
brown kiwi (N.Z.)
budgerigar or (Austral.) zebra parrot
bunting
bush wren (N.Z.)
bustard or (Austral.) plain turkey, plains turkey, or wild turkey
button quail or (Austral.) bustard quail
Californian quail (N.Z.)
canary

capercaillie or capercailzie
chaffinch
chicken or (Austral. informal) chook
chiffchaff
chough
chukar
crane
crossbill
crow or (Scot.) corbie
cuckoo
curlew
dipper or water ouzel
diver
dove or (archaic or poetic) culver
dunlin or red-backed sandpiper
egret
fernbird (N.Z.)
fieldfare
finch
firecrest
flamingo
flycatcher
galah or (Austral.) galar or gillar
godwit
goldcrest
grebe
greenshank
grey-crowned babbler, happy family bird, Happy Jack, or parson bird (Austral.)
grey warbler or riroriro (N.Z.)
grouse
hen harrier or (U.S. & Canad.) marsh harrier
heron
hoopoe

BIRDS continued

jabiru or (Austral.) policeman bird
jackdaw
jaeger (U.S. & Canad.)
jay
kaka (N.Z.)
kakapo (N.Z.)
kakariki (N.Z.)
karoro or blackbacked gull (N.Z.)
kea (N.Z.)
kingfisher or (N.Z.) kotare
kiwi or apteryx
knot
koel or (Austral.) black cuckoo or cooee bird
kokako or blue-wattled crow (N.Z.)
kookaburra, laughing jackass, or (Austral.) bushman's clock, settler's clock, goburra, or great brown kingfisher
kotuku or white heron (N.Z.)
lapwing or green plover
lark
linnet
lorikeet
lyrebird or (Austral.) buln-buln
magpie or (Austral.) piping shrike or piping crow-shrike
magpie lark or (Austral.) mudlark, Murray magpie, mulga, or peewit
Major Mitchell or Leadbeater's cockatoo
makomako (Austral.)
martin

metallic starling or shining starling (Austral.)
miromiro (N.Z.)
mistletoe bird (Austral.)
mohua or bush canary (N.Z.)
New Zealand pigeon or kereru (N.Z.)
nightingale
nightjar, (U.S. & Canad.) goatsucker, or (Austral.) nighthawk
noisy miner or (Austral.) micky or soldier bird
nutcracker
nuthatch
ouzel or ousel
paradise duck or putangitangi (N.Z.)
pardalote (Austral.)
partridge
pheasant
pigeon
pipit or (N.Z.) pihoihoi
pipiwharauroa or bronze-winged cuckoo (N.Z.)
pitta (Austral.)
plover
ptarmigan
puffin
quail
rainbow lorikeet
raven
redpoll
redshank
redstart
redwing
ringneck parrot, Port Lincoln parrot, or buln-buln (Austral.)

b

BIRDS *continued*	
robin or robin redbreast	swallow
roller	swift
rook	thrush or (*poetic*) throstle
ruff	tit
saddlebill or jabiru	topknot pigeon (*Austral.*)
sanderling	tree creeper
sandpiper	tui or parson bird (*N.Z.*)
serin	twite
shrike or butcherbird	wagtail
silver-eye (*Austral.*)	warbler
siskin or (*formerly*)	waxwing
aberdevine	weka, weka rail, Māori hen, or
skylark	wood hen (*N.Z.*)
snipe	whinchat
sparrow	white-eye or (*N.Z.*) blighty,
spoonbill	silvereye, tauhou or waxeye
spotted crake or (*Austral.*)	white-fronted tern or kahawai
water crake	bird (*N.Z.*)
starling	whitethroat
stint	woodcock
stonechat	woodlark
stork	woodpecker
sulphur-crested cockatoo or	wren
white cockatoo	yellowhammer
superb blue wren (*Austral.*)	yellowtail or yellowtail
superb lyrebird (*Austral.*)	kingfisher (*Austral.*)

chew, nibble
▷ **NOUN 2** = **snack**, food, piece,
taste, refreshment, mouthful,
morsel, titbit **3** = **wound**, sting,
pinch, nip, prick
biting 1 = **piercing**, cutting,
sharp, frozen, harsh,
penetrating, arctic, icy
2 = **sarcastic**, cutting, stinging,
scathing, acrimonious, incisive,
virulent, caustic
bitter 1 = **resentful**, angry,

offended, sour, sore,
acrimonious, sullen, miffed
(*informal*) **OPPOSITE:** happy
2 = **freezing**, biting, severe,
intense, raw, fierce, chill,
stinging **OPPOSITE:** mild
3 = **sour**, sharp, acid, harsh,
tart, astringent, acrid,
unsweetened **OPPOSITE:** sweet
bitterness 1 = **resentment**,
hostility, indignation, animosity,
acrimony, rancour, ill feeling,

bad blood **2** = **sourness**, acidity, sharpness, tartness, acerbity

bizarre = **strange**, unusual, extraordinary, fantastic, weird, peculiar, eccentric, ludicrous **OPPOSITE:** normal

black ADJECTIVE **1** = **dark**, raven, ebony, sable, jet, dusky, pitch-black, swarthy **OPPOSITE:** light **2** = **gloomy**, sad, depressing, grim, bleak, hopeless, dismal, ominous **OPPOSITE:** happy **3** = **terrible**, bad, devastating, tragic, fatal, catastrophic, ruinous, calamitous **4** = **wicked**, bad, evil, corrupt, vicious, immoral, depraved, villainous **OPPOSITE:** good **5** = **angry**, cross, furious, hostile, sour, menacing, moody, resentful **OPPOSITE:** happy

- USAGE NOTE
- When referring to people
- with dark skin, the adjective
- *black* or *Black* is used. For
- people of the US whose
- origins lie in Africa, the
- preferred term is *African*
- *American*.

▷ *See panel* SHADES FROM BLACK TO WHITE

blackmail NOUN **1** = **threat**, intimidation, ransom, extortion, hush money (*slang*)

▷ VERB **2** = **threaten**, squeeze, compel, intimidate, coerce, dragoon, extort, hold to ransom

blame VERB **1** = **hold responsible**, accuse, denounce, indict, impeach, incriminate, impute **OPPOSITE:** absolve **2** = **attribute to**, credit to, assign to, put down to, impute to **3** (*used in negative constructions*) = **criticize**, condemn, censure, reproach, chide, find fault with **OPPOSITE:** praise

▷ NOUN **4** = **responsibility**, liability, accountability, onus, culpability, answerability **OPPOSITE:** praise

bland **1** = **dull**, boring, plain, flat, dreary, run-of-the-mill, uninspiring, humdrum **OPPOSITE:** exciting **2** = **tasteless**, insipid, flavourless, thin

blank ADJECTIVE

1 = **unmarked**, white, clear, clean, empty, plain, bare, void **OPPOSITE:** marked **2** = **expressionless**, empty, vague, vacant, deadpan, impassive, poker-faced (*informal*) **OPPOSITE:** expressive

▷ NOUN **3** = **empty space**, space, gap **4** = **void**, vacuum, vacancy, emptiness, nothingness

blanket NOUN **1** = **cover**, rug, coverlet **2** = **covering**, sheet, coat, layer, carpet, cloak, mantle, thickness

▷ VERB **3** = **coat**, cover, hide, mask, conceal, obscure, cloak

blast NOUN **1** = **explosion**, crash, burst, discharge, eruption, detonation **2** = **gust**,

SHADES FROM BLACK TO WHITE			
ash	gunmetal	pearl	sable
black	iron	pitch-black	silver
charcoal	ivory	platinum	slate
cream	jet	putty	steel grey
ebony	off-white	raven	white
grey			

rush, storm, breeze, puff, gale, tempest, squall **3 = blare**, blow, scream, trumpet, wail, resound, clamour, toot

▷ **VERB 4 = blow up**, bomb, destroy, burst, ruin, break up, explode, shatter

blatant = obvious, clear, plain, evident, glaring, manifest, noticeable, conspicuous **OPPOSITE:** subtle

blaze VERB 1 = burn, glow, flare, be on fire, go up in flames, be ablaze, fire, flame **2 = shine**, flash, beam, glow, flare, glare, gleam, radiate

▷ **NOUN 3 = inferno**, fire, flames, bonfire, combustion, conflagration **4 = flash**, glow, glitter, flare, glare, gleam, brilliance, radiance

bleach = lighten, wash out, blanch, whiten

bleak 1 = dismal, dark, depressing, grim, discouraging, gloomy, hopeless, dreary **OPPOSITE:** cheerful

2 = exposed, empty, bare, barren, desolate, windswept, weather-beaten, unsheltered **OPPOSITE:** sheltered

3 = stormy, severe, rough, harsh, tempestuous, intemperate

bleed 1 = lose blood, flow, gush, spurt, shed blood **2 = blend**, run, meet, unite, mix, combine, flow, fuse **3** (*Informal*) **= extort**, milk, squeeze, drain, exhaust, fleece

blend VERB 1 = mix, join, combine, compound, merge, unite, mingle, amalgamate **2 = go well**, match, fit, suit, go with, correspond, complement, coordinate **3 = combine**, mix, link, integrate, merge, unite, amalgamate

▷ **NOUN 4 = mixture**, mix, combination, compound, brew, union, synthesis, alloy

bless 1 = sanctify, dedicate, ordain, exalt, anoint, consecrate, hallow **OPPOSITE:** curse **2 = endow**, give to, provide for, grant for, favour, grace, bestow to **OPPOSITE:** afflict

blessed = holy, sacred, divine, adored, revered, hallowed, sanctified, beatified

blessing 1 = benefit, help, service, favour, gift, windfall, kindness, good fortune

OPPOSITE: disadvantage
2 = approval, backing, support, agreement, favour, sanction, permission, leave **OPPOSITE:** disapproval **3 = benediction**, grace, dedication, thanksgiving, invocation, commendation, consecration, benison **OPPOSITE:** curse

blight NOUN **1 = curse**, suffering, evil, corruption, pollution, plague, hardship, woe **OPPOSITE:** blessing **2 = disease**, pest, fungus, mildew, infestation, pestilence, canker
▷ **VERB 3 = frustrate**, destroy, ruin, crush, mar, dash, wreck, spoil, crool or cruel (*Austral. slang*)

blind 1 = sightless, unsighted, unseeing, eyeless, visionless **OPPOSITE:** sighted **2** *often with* **to = unaware of**, unconscious of, ignorant of, indifferent to, insensitive to, oblivious of, unconcerned about, inconsiderate of **OPPOSITE:** aware **3 = unquestioning**, prejudiced, wholesale, indiscriminate, uncritical, unreasoning, undiscriminating

blindly 1 = thoughtlessly, carelessly, recklessly, indiscriminately, senselessly, heedlessly **2 = wildly**, aimlessly

blink 1 = flutter, wink, bat **2 = flash**, flicker, wink, shimmer, twinkle, glimmer
▷ **PHRASES: on the blink** (*Slang*)

= not working (properly), faulty, defective, playing up, out of action, malfunctioning, out of order

bliss 1 = joy, ecstasy, euphoria, rapture, nirvana, felicity, gladness, blissfulness **OPPOSITE:** misery **2 = beatitude**, blessedness

blister = sore, boil, swelling, cyst, pimple, carbuncle, pustule

blitz = attack, strike, assault, raid, offensive, onslaught, bombardment, bombing campaign

bloc = group, union, league, alliance, coalition, axis

block NOUN **1 = piece**, bar, mass, brick, lump, chunk, hunk, ingot **2 = obstruction**, bar, barrier, obstacle, impediment, hindrance
▷ **VERB 3 = obstruct**, close, stop, plug, choke, clog, stop up, bung up (*informal*) **OPPOSITE:** clear **4 = obscure**, bar, obstruct **5 = shut off**, stop, bar, hamper, obstruct

blockade = stoppage, block, barrier, restriction, obstacle, barricade, obstruction, impediment

bloke (*Informal*) **= man**, person, individual, character (*informal*), guy (*informal*), fellow, chap

blonde *or* **blond 1 = fair**, light, flaxen **2 = fair-haired**, golden-haired, tow-headed

blood 1 = lifeblood, gore, vital fluid **2 = family**, relations,

birth, descent, extraction,
ancestry, lineage, kinship

bloodshed = killing, murder,
massacre, slaughter, slaying,
carnage, butchery, blood-letting

bloody 1 = cruel, fierce, savage,
brutal, vicious, ferocious, cut-
throat, warlike

2 = bloodstained, raw,
bleeding, blood-soaked, blood-
spattered

bloom NOUN 1 = flower, bud,
blossom 2 = prime, flower,
beauty, height, peak,
flourishing, heyday, zenith
3 = glow, freshness, lustre,
radiance **OPPOSITE:** pallor
▷ VERB 4 = flower, blossom,
open, bud **OPPOSITE:** wither
5 = grow, develop, wax
6 = succeed, flourish, thrive,
prosper, fare well **OPPOSITE:** fail

blossom NOUN 1 = flower,
bloom, bud, efflorescence,
floret
▷ VERB 2 = bloom, grow,
develop, mature 3 = succeed,
progress, thrive, flourish,
prosper 4 = flower, bloom, bud

blow¹ VERB 1 = move, carry,
drive, sweep, fling, buffet, waft
2 = be carried, flutter
3 = exhale, breathe, pant, puff
4 = play, sound, pipe, trumpet,
blare, toot
▷ PHRASES: blow something
up 1 = explode, bomb, blast,
detonate, blow sky-high
2 = inflate, pump up, fill,
expand, swell, enlarge, puff up,

distend 3 = magnify, increase,
extend, expand, widen,
broaden, amplify ▶ blow up
1 = explode, burst, shatter,
erupt, detonate 2 (Informal)
= lose your temper, rage, erupt,
see red (informal), become
angry, hit the roof (informal), fly
off the handle (informal), go
crook (Austral. & N.Z. slang),
blow your top

blow² 1 = knock, stroke, punch,
bang, sock (slang), smack,
thump, clout (informal)
2 = setback, shock, disaster,
reverse, disappointment,
catastrophe, misfortune,
bombshell

bludge (Austral. & N.Z. informal)
= slack, skive (Brit. informal),
idle, shirk

blue ADJECTIVE 1 = depressed,
low, sad, unhappy, melancholy,
dejected, despondent,
downcast **OPPOSITE:** happy
2 = smutty, obscene, indecent,
lewd, risqué, X-rated (informal)
OPPOSITE: respectable
▷ PLURAL NOUN
3 = depression, gloom,
melancholy, unhappiness, low
spirits, the dumps (informal),
doldrums
▷ See panel SHADES OF BLUE

blueprint 1 = scheme, plan,
design, system, programme,
proposal, strategy, pattern
2 = plan, scheme, pattern,
draft, outline, sketch

bluff¹ NOUN 1 = deception,

SHADES OF BLUE

aqua	navy blue	saxe blue
aquamarine	Oxford blue	sky blue
azure	peacock blue	steel blue
Cambridge blue	perse	teal
clear blue	royal blue	turquoise
cobalt blue	sapphire	ultramarine
indigo		

fraud, sham, pretence, deceit, bravado, bluster, humbug
▷ VERB 2 = **deceive**, trick, fool, pretend, cheat, con, fake, mislead

bluff² NOUN 1 = **precipice**, bank, peak, cliff, ridge, crag, escarpment, promontory
▷ ADJECTIVE 2 = **hearty**, open, blunt, outspoken, genial, ebullient, jovial, plain-spoken **OPPOSITE:** tactful

blunder NOUN 1 = **mistake**, slip, fault, error, oversight, gaffe, slip-up (informal), indiscretion **OPPOSITE:** correctness
▷ VERB 2 = **make a mistake**, blow it (slang), err, slip up (informal), foul up, put your foot in it (informal) **OPPOSITE:** be correct 3 = **stumble**, fall, reel, stagger, lurch

blunt ADJECTIVE 1 = **frank**, forthright, straightforward, rude, outspoken, bluff, brusque, plain-spoken **OPPOSITE:** tactful 2 = **dull**, rounded, dulled, edgeless, unsharpened **OPPOSITE:** sharp
▷ VERB 3 = **dull**, weaken,

soften, numb, dampen, water down, deaden, take the edge off **OPPOSITE:** stimulate

blur NOUN 1 = **haze**, confusion, fog, obscurity, indistinctness
▷ VERB 2 = **become indistinct**, become vague, become hazy, become fuzzy 3 = **obscure**, make indistinct, mask, obfuscate, make vague, make hazy

blush VERB 1 = **turn red**, colour, glow, flush, redden, go red (as a beetroot), turn scarlet **OPPOSITE:** turn pale
▷ NOUN 2 = **reddening**, colour, glow, flush, pink tinge, rosiness, ruddiness, rosy tint

board NOUN 1 = **plank**, panel, timber, slat, piece of timber 2 = **council**, directors, committee, congress, advisers, panel, assembly, trustees 3 = **meals**, provisions, victuals, daily meals
▷ VERB 4 = **get on**, enter, mount, embark **OPPOSITE:** get off

boast VERB 1 = **brag**, crow, vaunt, talk big (slang), blow your own trumpet, show off, be

proud of, congratulate yourself
on, skite (*Austral. & N.Z. informal*)
OPPOSITE: cover up
2 = **possess**, exhibit
▷ NOUN 3 = **bragging**, big talk
(*slang*) **OPPOSITE:** disclaimer
bob = **bounce**, duck, hop,
oscillate
bodily = **physical**, material,
actual, substantial, tangible,
corporal, carnal, corporeal
body 1 = **physique**, build, form,
figure, shape, frame,
constitution 2 = **torso**, trunk
3 = **corpse**, dead body, remains,
stiff (*slang*), carcass, cadaver
4 = **organization**, company,
group, society, association,
band, congress, institution
5 = **main part**, matter,
material, mass, substance, bulk,
essence 6 = **expanse**, mass
● RELATED WORDS
● *adjectives:* corporal, physical
bog = **marsh**, swamp, slough,
wetlands, fen, mire, quagmire,
morass, pakihi (*N.Z.*)
bogey = **bugbear**, bête noire,
horror, nightmare, bugaboo
bogus = **fake**, false, artificial,
forged, imitation, sham,
fraudulent, counterfeit
OPPOSITE: genuine
Bohemian ADJECTIVE 1 *often
not cap.* = **unconventional**,
alternative, artistic,
unorthodox, arty (*informal*),
offbeat, left bank,
nonconformist **OPPOSITE:**
conventional

▷ NOUN 2 *often not cap.*
= **nonconformist**, rebel, radical,
eccentric, maverick, hippy,
dropout, individualist
boil¹ = **simmer**, bubble, foam,
seethe, fizz, froth, effervesce
boil² = **pustule**, gathering,
swelling, blister, carbuncle
bold 1 = **fearless**, enterprising,
brave, daring, heroic,
adventurous, courageous,
audacious **OPPOSITE:** timid
2 = **impudent**, forward,
confident, rude, cheeky, brazen,
shameless, insolent
OPPOSITE: shy
bolster = **support**, help, boost,
strengthen, reinforce, shore up,
augment
bolt NOUN 1 = **pin**, rod, peg,
rivet 2 = **bar**, catch, lock, latch,
fastener, sliding bar
▷ VERB 3 = **lock**, close, bar,
secure, fasten, latch 4 = **dash**,
fly 5 = **gobble**, stuff, wolf,
cram, gorge, devour, gulp,
guzzle
bomb NOUN 1 = **explosive**,
mine, shell, missile, device,
rocket, grenade, torpedo
▷ VERB 2 = **blow up**, attack,
destroy, assault, shell, blitz,
bombard, torpedo
bombard 1 = **attack**, assault,
besiege, beset, assail
2 = **bomb**, shell, blitz, open fire,
strafe, fire upon
bombardment = **bombing**,
attack, assault, shelling, blitz,
barrage, fusillade

bond NOUN 1 = **tie**, union, coupling, link, association, relation, connection, alliance 2 = **fastening**, tie, chain, cord, shackle, fetter, manacle 3 = **agreement**, word, promise, contract, guarantee, pledge, obligation, covenant
▷ VERB 4 = **form friendships**, connect 5 = **fix**, hold, bind, connect, glue, stick, paste, fasten

bonus 1 = **extra**, prize, gift, reward, premium, dividend 2 = **advantage**, benefit, gain, extra, plus, asset, icing on the cake

book NOUN 1 = **work**, title, volume, publication, tract, tome 2 = **notebook**, album, journal, diary, pad, notepad, exercise book, jotter
▷ VERB 3 = **reserve**, schedule, engage, organize, charter, arrange for, make reservations
▷ PHRASES: **book in** = **register**, enter

booklet = **brochure**, leaflet, hand-out, pamphlet, folder, mailshot, handbill

boom NOUN 1 = **expansion**, increase, development, growth, jump, boost, improvement, upsurge OPPOSITE: decline 2 = **bang**, crash, clash, blast, burst, explosion, roar, thunder
▷ VERB 3 = **increase**, flourish, grow, develop, expand, strengthen, swell, thrive OPPOSITE: fall 4 = **bang**, roll, crash, blast, explode, roar, thunder, rumble

boon 1 = **benefit**, blessing, godsend, gift 2 = **gift**, favour

boost VERB 1 = **increase**, develop, raise, expand, add to, heighten, enlarge, amplify OPPOSITE: decrease
▷ NOUN 2 = **rise**, increase, jump, addition, improvement, expansion, upsurge, upturn OPPOSITE: fall 3 = **encouragement**, help

boot = **kick**, punt, put the boot in(to) (slang), drop-kick

border NOUN 1 = **frontier**, line, limit, bounds, boundary, perimeter, borderline 2 = **edge**, margin, verge, rim
▷ VERB 3 = **edge**, bound, decorate, trim, fringe, rim, hem

bore¹ = **drill**, mine, sink, tunnel, pierce, penetrate, burrow, puncture

bore² VERB 1 = **tire**, fatigue, weary, wear out, jade, be tedious, pall on, send to sleep OPPOSITE: excite
▷ NOUN 2 = **nuisance**, pain (informal), yawn (informal), anorak (informal)

bored = **fed up**, tired, wearied, uninterested, sick and tired (informal), listless, brassed off (Brit. slang), hoha (N.Z.)

boredom = **tedium**, apathy, weariness, monotony, sameness, ennui, flatness, world-weariness OPPOSITE: excitement

boring = uninteresting, dull, tedious, tiresome, monotonous, flat, humdrum, mind-numbing

borrow 1 = take on loan, touch (someone) for (slang), scrounge (informal), cadge, use temporarily **OPPOSITE:** lend 2 = steal, take, copy, adopt, pinch (informal)

boss = manager, head, leader, director, chief, master, employer, supervisor, baas (S. African)
▷ **PHRASES:** boss someone around (Informal) = order around, dominate, bully, oppress, push around (slang)

bother VERB 1 = trouble, concern, worry, alarm, disturb, disconcert, perturb 2 = pester, plague, harass, hassle (informal), inconvenience **OPPOSITE:** help
▷ **NOUN** 3 = trouble, problem, worry, difficulty, fuss, irritation, hassle (informal), nuisance, uphill (S. African) **OPPOSITE:** help

bottle shop (Austral. & N.Z.) = off-licence (Brit.), liquor store (U.S. & Canad.), bottle store (S. African), package store (U.S. & Canad.), offie or offy (Brit. informal)

bottle store (S. African) = off-licence (Brit.), liquor store (U.S. & Canad.), bottle shop (Austral. & N.Z.), package store (U.S. & Canad.), offie or offy (Brit. informal)

bottom NOUN 1 = lowest part, base, foot, bed, floor, foundation, depths **OPPOSITE:** top 2 = underside, sole, underneath, lower side 3 = buttocks, behind (informal), rear, backside, rump, seat, posterior
▷ **ADJECTIVE** 4 = lowest, last **OPPOSITE:** higher

bounce VERB 1 = rebound, recoil, ricochet 2 = bound, spring, jump, leap, skip, gambol
▷ **NOUN** 3 = springiness, give, spring, resilience, elasticity, recoil 4 (Informal) = life, go (informal), energy, zip (informal), vigour, exuberance, dynamism, vivacity

bound¹ 1 = compelled, obliged, forced, committed, pledged, constrained, beholden, duty-bound 2 = tied, fixed, secured, attached, tied up, fastened, pinioned 3 = certain, sure, fated, doomed, destined

bound² 1 = surround, confine, enclose, encircle, hem in, demarcate 2 = limit, restrict, confine, restrain, circumscribe

bound³ VERB 1 = leap, bob, spring, jump, bounce, skip, vault
▷ **NOUN** 2 = leap, bob, spring, jump, bounce, hurdle, skip, vault

boundary 1 = frontier, edge, border, barrier, margin, brink 2 = edges, limits, fringes, extremities 3 = dividing line, borderline

b

bounds = boundary, limit, edge, border, confine, verge, rim, perimeter

bouquet 1 = bunch of flowers, spray, garland, wreath, posy, buttonhole, corsage, nosegay 2 = aroma, smell, scent, perfume, fragrance, savour, odour, redolence

bourgeois = middle-class, traditional, conventional, materialistic, hidebound

bout 1 = period, term, fit, spell, turn, interval 2 = round, series, session, cycle, sequence, stint 3 = fight, match, competition, struggle, contest, set-to, encounter, engagement

bow¹ VERB 1 = bend, bob, nod, stoop, droop, genuflect ▷ NOUN 2 = bending, bob, nod, obeisance, kowtow, genuflection

bow² (*Nautical*) = prow, head, stem, fore, beak

bowels 1 = guts, insides (*informal*), intestines, innards (*informal*), entrails, viscera, vitals 2 = depths, hold, inside, deep, interior, core, belly

bowl¹ = basin, plate, dish, vessel

bowl² = throw, hurl, launch, cast, pitch, toss, fling, chuck (*informal*)

box¹ NOUN 1 = container, case, chest, trunk, pack, package, carton, casket ▷ VERB 2 = pack, package, wrap, encase, bundle up

box² = fight, spar, exchange

blows, prizefight

boxer = fighter, pugilist, prizefighter

boy = lad, kid (*informal*), youth, fellow, youngster, schoolboy, junior, stripling

boycott = embargo, reject, snub, black **OPPOSITE:** support

boyfriend = sweetheart, man, lover, beloved, admirer, suitor, beau, date

brace VERB 1 = steady, support, secure, stabilize 2 = support, strengthen, steady, reinforce, bolster, fortify, buttress ▷ NOUN 3 = support, stay, prop, bolster, bracket, reinforcement, strut, truss

bracing = refreshing, fresh, stimulating, crisp, brisk, exhilarating, invigorating **OPPOSITE:** tiring

brain = intelligence, understanding, sense, intellect

brake NOUN 1 = control, check, curb, restraint, constraint, rein ▷ VERB 2 = slow, decelerate, reduce speed

branch 1 = bough, shoot, arm, spray, limb, sprig, offshoot 2 = office, department, unit, wing, chapter, bureau 3 = division, part, section, subdivision, subsection 4 = discipline, section, subdivision

brand NOUN 1 = trademark 2 = label, mark, sign, stamp,

symbol, logo, trademark, marker

▷ VERB 3 = **stigmatize**, mark, expose, denounce, disgrace, discredit, censure 4 = **mark**, burn, label, stamp, scar

brash = **bold**, rude, cocky, pushy (*informal*), brazen, impertinent, insolent, impudent **OPPOSITE:** timid

brave ADJECTIVE

1 = **courageous**, daring, bold, heroic, adventurous, fearless, resolute, audacious **OPPOSITE:** timid

▷ VERB 2 = **confront**, face, suffer, tackle, endure, defy, withstand, stand up to **OPPOSITE:** give in to

bravery = **courage**, nerve, daring, pluck, spirit, fortitude, heroism, mettle **OPPOSITE:** cowardice

brawl NOUN 1 = **fight**, clash, fray, skirmish, scuffle, punch-up (*Brit. informal*), fracas, altercation, biffo (*Austral. slang*)

▷ VERB 2 = **fight**, scrap (*informal*), wrestle, tussle, scuffle

breach 1 = **nonobservance**, abuse, violation, infringement, trespass, transgression, contravention, infraction **OPPOSITE:** compliance

2 = **opening**, crack, split, gap, rift, rupture, cleft, fissure

bread 1 = **food**, fare, kai (*N.Z. informal*), nourishment, sustenance 2 (*Slang*) = **money**,

cash, dough (*slang*)

breadth 1 = **width**, spread, span, latitude, broadness, wideness 2 = **extent**, range, scale, scope, compass, expanse

break VERB 1 = **shatter**, separate, destroy, crack, snap, smash, crush, fragment **OPPOSITE:** repair 2 = **fracture**, crack, smash 3 = **burst**, tear, split 4 = **disobey**, breach, defy, violate, disregard, flout, infringe, contravene **OPPOSITE:** obey 5 = **stop**, cut, suspend, interrupt, cut short, discontinue 6 = **disturb**, interrupt 7 = **end**, stop, cut, drop, give up, abandon, suspend, interrupt 8 = **weaken**, undermine, tame, subdue, demoralize, dispirit 9 = **be revealed**, be published, be announced, be made public, be proclaimed, be let out 10 = **reveal**, tell, announce, declare, disclose, proclaim, make known 11 = **beat**, top, better, exceed, go beyond, excel, surpass, outstrip

▷ NOUN 12 = **fracture**, opening, tear, hole, split, crack, gap, fissure 13 = **interval**, pause, interlude, intermission 14 = **holiday**, leave, vacation, time off, recess, awayday 15 (*Informal*) = **stroke of luck**, chance, opportunity, advantage, fortune, opening

▷ PHRASES: break off = **stop talking**, pause ▶ break out = **begin**, start, happen, occur,

b

arise, set in, commence, spring up ▶ **break something off** = **detach**, separate, divide, cut off, pull off, sever, part, remove ▶ **break something up** ▶ **stop**, end, suspend, dismantle, terminate, disband, diffuse ▶ **break up 1** = **finish**, be suspended, adjourn **2** = **split up**, separate, part, divorce
breakdown = **collapse**
break-in = **burglary**, robbery, breaking and entering
breakthrough
= **development**, advance, progress, discovery, find, invention, step forward, leap forwards
breast = **bosom(s)**, front, chest, bust
breath = **inhalation**, breathing, pant, gasp, gulp, wheeze, exhalation, respiration
breathe 1 = **inhale and exhale**, pant, gasp, puff, gulp, wheeze, respire, draw in breath **2** = **whisper**, sigh, murmur
breathless 1 = **out of breath**, panting, gasping, gulping, wheezing, short-winded **2** = **excited**, curious, eager, enthusiastic, impatient, on tenterhooks, in suspense
breathtaking = **amazing**, exciting, stunning (informal), impressive, thrilling, magnificent, astonishing, sensational
breed NOUN **1** = **variety**, race, stock, type, species, strain,

pedigree **2** = **kind**, sort, type, variety, brand, stamp ▷ VERB **3** = **rear**, tend, keep, raise, maintain, farm, look after, care for **4** = **reproduce**, multiply, propagate, procreate, produce offspring, bear young, bring forth young **5** = **produce**, cause, create, generate, bring about, arouse, give rise to, stir up
breeding = **refinement**, culture, taste, manners, polish, courtesy, sophistication, cultivation
breeze NOUN **1** = **light wind**, air, draught, gust, waft, zephyr, breath of wind, current of air ▷ VERB **2** = **sweep**, move briskly, pass, sail, hurry, glide, flit
brew VERB **1** = **boil**, make, soak, steep, stew, infuse (tea) **2** = **make**, ferment **3** = **start**, develop, gather, foment **4** = **develop**, form, gather, foment ▷ NOUN **5** = **drink**, preparation, mixture, blend, liquor, beverage, infusion, concoction
bribe NOUN **1** = **inducement**, pay-off (informal), sweetener (slang), kickback (U.S.), backhander (slang), enticement, allurement ▷ VERB **2** = **buy off**, reward, pay off (informal), corrupt, suborn, grease the palm or hand of (slang)
bribery = **corruption**,

inducement, buying off, payola (*informal*), palm-greasing (*slang*)
bridge NOUN 1 = **arch**, span, viaduct, flyover, overpass
▷ VERB 2 = **span**, cross
3 = **reconcile**, resolve
brief ADJECTIVE 1 = **short**, quick, fleeting, swift, short-lived, momentary, ephemeral, transitory OPPOSITE: long
▷ VERB 2 = **inform**, prime, prepare, advise, fill in (*informal*), instruct, put in the picture (*informal*), keep (someone) posted
▷ NOUN 3 = **summary**, résumé, outline, sketch, abstract, digest, epitome, rundown
briefing 1 = **conference**, priming 2 = **instructions**, information, priming, directions, preparation, guidance, rundown
briefly 1 = **quickly**, shortly, hastily, momentarily, hurriedly 2 = **in outline**, in brief, in a nutshell, concisely
brigade 1 = **corps**, company, force, unit, division, troop, squad, team 2 = **group**, band, squad, organization
bright 1 = **vivid**, rich, brilliant, glowing, colourful 2 = **shining**, glowing, dazzling, gleaming, shimmering, radiant, luminous, lustrous 3 = **intelligent**, smart, clever, aware, sharp, enlightened, astute, wide-awake OPPOSITE: stupid
4 = **clever**, smart, ingenious

5 = **sunny**, clear, fair, pleasant, lucid, cloudless, unclouded OPPOSITE: cloudy
brighten 1 = **light up**, shine, glow, gleam, lighten OPPOSITE: dim 2 = **enliven**, animate, make brighter, vitalize
3 = **become brighter**, light up, glow, gleam
brilliance *or* **brilliancy**
1 = **cleverness**, talent, wisdom, distinction, genius, excellence, greatness, inventiveness OPPOSITE: stupidity
2 = **brightness**, intensity, sparkle, dazzle, lustre, radiance, luminosity, vividness OPPOSITE: darkness 3 = **splendour**, glamour, grandeur, magnificence, éclat, illustriousness
brilliant 1 = **intelligent**, sharp, intellectual, clever, profound, penetrating, inventive, perspicacious OPPOSITE: stupid
2 = **expert**, masterly, talented, gifted, accomplished OPPOSITE: untalented 3 = **splendid**, famous, celebrated, outstanding, superb, magnificent, glorious, notable
4 = **bright**, shining, intense, sparkling, glittering, dazzling, vivid, radiant OPPOSITE: dark
brim NOUN 1 = **rim**, edge, border, lip, margin, verge, brink
▷ VERB 2 = **be full**, spill, well over, run over 3 = **fill**, well over, fill up, overflow
bring VERB 1 = **fetch**, take,

carry, bear, transfer, deliver, transport, convey **2 = take**, guide, conduct, escort **3 = cause**, produce, create, effect, occasion, result in, contribute to, inflict

▷ **PHRASES: bring someone up = rear**, raise, support, train, develop, teach, breed, foster ▶ **bring something about = cause**, produce, create, effect, achieve, generate, accomplish, give rise to ▶ **bring something off = accomplish**, achieve, perform, succeed, execute, pull off, carry off ▶ **bring something up = mention**, raise, introduce, point out, refer to, allude to, broach

brink = edge, limit, border, lip, margin, boundary, skirt, frontier

brisk 1 = quick, lively, energetic, active, vigorous, bustling, sprightly, spry **OPPOSITE:** slow **2 = short**, brief, blunt, abrupt, terse, gruff, brusque, monosyllabic

briskly = quickly, smartly, promptly, rapidly, readily, actively, efficiently, energetically

bristle NOUN 1 = hair, spine, thorn, whisker, barb, stubble, prickle

▷ **VERB 2 = stand up**, rise, stand on end **3 = be angry**, rage, seethe, flare up, bridle, see red

brittle = fragile, delicate, crisp, crumbling, frail, crumbly, breakable, friable **OPPOSITE:**

shatterproof

broad 1 = wide, large, ample, generous, expansive **2 = large**, huge, vast, extensive, ample, spacious, expansive, roomy **OPPOSITE:** narrow **3 = full**, general, comprehensive, complete, wide, sweeping, wide-ranging, thorough **4 = universal**, general, common, wide, sweeping, worldwide, widespread, wide-ranging **5 = general**, loose, vague, approximate, indefinite, ill-defined, inexact, unspecific

broadcast NOUN 1 = transmission, show, programme, telecast

▷ **VERB 2 = transmit**, show, air, radio, cable, beam, send out, relay **3 = make public**, report, announce, publish, spread, advertise, proclaim, circulate

broaden = expand, increase, develop, spread, extend, stretch, swell, supplement **OPPOSITE:** restrict

brochure = booklet, advertisement, leaflet, handout, circular, pamphlet, folder, mailshot

broekies (*S. African informal*) **= underpants**, pants, briefs, drawers, knickers, panties, boxer shorts, Y-fronts ®, underdaks (*Austral. slang*)

broke (*Informal*) **= penniless**, short, ruined, bust (*informal*), bankrupt, impoverished, in the red, insolvent **OPPOSITE:** rich

broken 1 = **interrupted**, incomplete, erratic, intermittent, fragmentary, spasmodic, discontinuous 2 = **imperfect**, halting, hesitating, stammering, disjointed 3 = **smashed**, burst, shattered, fragmented, fractured, severed, ruptured, separated 4 = **defective**, not working, imperfect, out of order, on the blink (*slang*), kaput (*informal*)

broker = **dealer**, agent, trader, supplier, merchant, negotiator, mediator, intermediary

bronze = **reddish-brown**, copper, tan, rust, chestnut, brownish

▷ *See panel* SHADES OF BROWN

brood NOUN 1 = **offspring**, issue, clutch, litter, progeny 2 = **children**, family, nearest and dearest, flesh and blood, ainga (*N.Z.*)

▷ VERB 3 = **think**, obsess, muse, ponder, agonize, mull over, mope, ruminate

brook = **stream**, burn (*Scot. & Northern English*), rivulet, beck, watercourse, rill

brother 1 = **male sibling** 2 = **monk**, cleric, friar, religious

● RELATED WORD
● *adjective:* fraternal

brotherly = **fraternal**, friendly, neighbourly, sympathetic, affectionate, kind, amicable

brown ADJECTIVE 1 = **brunette**, bay, coffee, chocolate, chestnut, hazel, dun, auburn 2 = **tanned**, bronze, tan, sunburnt

▷ VERB 3 = **fry**, cook, grill, sear, sauté

▷ *See panel* SHADES OF BROWN

browse 1 = **skim**, scan, glance at, survey, look through, look round, dip into, leaf through 2 = **graze**, eat, feed, nibble

bruise NOUN 1 = **discoloration**, mark, injury, blemish, contusion

▷ VERB 2 = **hurt**, injure, mark 3 = **damage**, mark, mar, discolour

brush¹ NOUN 1 = **broom**, sweeper, besom 2 = **conflict**, clash, confrontation, skirmish, tussle 3 = **encounter**, meeting, confrontation, rendezvous

▷ VERB 4 = **clean**, wash, polish, buff 5 = **touch**, sweep, kiss, stroke, glance, flick, scrape, graze

▷ PHRASES: brush someone off (*Slang*) = **ignore**, reject, dismiss, snub, disregard, scorn, disdain, spurn ▸ brush something up *or* brush up on something = **revise**, study, go over, cram, polish up, read up on, relearn, bone up on (*informal*)

brush² = **shrubs**, bushes, scrub, undergrowth, thicket, copse, brushwood

brutal 1 = **cruel**, savage, vicious, ruthless, callous, sadistic, heartless, inhuman

OPPOSITE: kind 2 = **harsh**,

b

SHADES OF BROWN

amber	café au lait	ginger	rust
auburn	camel	hazel	sable
bay	chestnut	henna	sepia
beige	chocolate	khaki	sienna
biscuit	cinnamon	liver	tan
bisque	cocoa	mahogany	taupe
bronze	coffee	mocha	tawny
buff	copper	nutbrown	terracotta
burnt sienna	dun	oxblood	tortoiseshell
burnt umber	fawn	russet	walnut

tough, severe, rough, rude, indifferent, insensitive, callous
OPPOSITE: sensitive

brutality = cruelty, atrocity, ferocity, savagery, ruthlessness, barbarism, inhumanity, viciousness

bubble NOUN 1 = air ball, drop, bead, blister, blob, droplet, globule
▷ VERB 2 = boil, seethe
3 = foam, fizz, froth, percolate, effervesce 4 = gurgle, splash, murmur, trickle, ripple, babble, burble, lap

bubbly 1 = lively, happy, excited, animated, merry, bouncy, elated, sparky
2 = frothy, sparkling, fizzy, effervescent, carbonated, foamy

buckle NOUN 1 = fastener, catch, clip, clasp, hasp
▷ VERB 2 = fasten, close, secure, hook, clasp 3 = distort, bend, warp, crumple, contort
4 = collapse, bend, twist, fold, give way, subside, cave in, crumple

bud NOUN 1 = shoot, branch, sprout, sprig, offshoot
▷ VERB 2 = develop, grow, shoot, sprout, burgeon, burst forth

budding = developing, beginning, growing, promising, potential, burgeoning, fledgling, embryonic

budge 1 = move, stir
2 = dislodge, move, push, transfer, shift, stir

budget NOUN 1 = allowance, means, funds, income, finances, resources, allocation
▷ VERB 2 = plan, estimate, allocate, cost, ration, apportion

buff[1] ADJECTIVE 1 = fawn, tan, beige, yellowish, straw-coloured, sand-coloured, yellowish-brown
▷ VERB 2 = polish, smooth, brush, shine, rub, wax, brighten, burnish
▷ See panels SHADES OF BROWN, SHADES OF YELLOW

buff[2] (Informal) = expert, fan, addict, enthusiast, admirer, devotee, connoisseur, aficionado, fundi (*S. African*)

buffer = **safeguard**, screen, shield, cushion, intermediary, bulwark

buffet 1 = **smorgasbord** 2 = **snack bar**, café, cafeteria, brasserie, refreshment counter

bug NOUN 1 (*Informal*) = **illness**, disease, virus, infection, disorder, sickness, ailment, affliction 2 = **fault**, error, defect, flaw, glitch, gremlin ▷ VERB 3 = **tap**, eavesdrop, listen in on 4 (*Informal*) = **annoy**, bother, disturb, irritate, hassle (*informal*), pester, vex, get on your nerves (*informal*)

build VERB 1 = **construct**, make, raise, put up, assemble, erect, fabricate, form OPPOSITE: demolish ▷ NOUN 2 = **physique**, form, body, figure, shape, structure, frame

building = **structure**, house, construction, dwelling, erection, edifice, domicile

build-up = **increase**, development, growth, expansion, accumulation, enlargement, escalation

bulge VERB 1 = **swell out**, project, expand, stick out, protrude, puff out, distend 2 = **stick out**, stand out, protrude ▷ NOUN 3 = **lump**, swelling, bump, projection, hump,

protuberance, protrusion OPPOSITE: hollow 4 = **increase**, rise, boost, surge, intensification

bulk 1 = **size**, volume, dimensions, magnitude, substance, immensity, largeness 2 = **weight**, size, mass, heaviness, poundage 3 = **majority**, mass, most, body, best part, lion's share, better part, preponderance

● USAGE NOTE
● The use of a plural noun after
● *bulk*, as in sense 3, although
● common, is considered by
● some to be incorrect and
● should be avoided. This usage
● is most commonly
● encountered, according to
● computer-aided studies of
● language, when referring to
● *funds* and *profits*: *the bulk of
● our profits stem from the sale of
● beer*. The synonyms *majority*
● and *most* would work better
● in this context.

bullet = **projectile**, ball, shot, missile, slug, pellet

bulletin = **report**, account, statement, message, communication, announcement, dispatch, communiqué

bully NOUN 1 = **persecutor**, tough, oppressor, tormentor, bully boy, browbeater, coercer, ruffian ▷ VERB 2 = **persecute**, intimidate, torment, oppress,

b

pick on, victimize, terrorize, push around (*slang*) **3** = **force**, coerce, browbeat, hector, domineer

bump VERB **1** = **knock**, hit, strike, crash, smash, slam, bang **2** = **jerk**, shake, bounce, rattle, jog, lurch, jolt
▷ NOUN **3** = **knock**, blow, impact, collision, thump **4** = **thud**, crash, knock, bang, smack, thump **5** = **lump**, swelling, bulge, hump, nodule, protuberance, contusion

bumper = **exceptional**, excellent, exo (*Austral. slang*), massive, jumbo (*informal*), abundant, whopping (*informal*), bountiful

bunch 1 = **group**, band, crowd, party, team, gathering, gang, flock **2** = **bouquet**, sheaf **3** = **cluster**, clump
▷ PHRASES: bunch together or up = group, mass, collect, assemble, cluster, huddle

bundle NOUN **1** = **bunch**, group, collection, mass, pile, stack, heap, batch
▷ VERB **2** = **push**, thrust, shove, throw, rush, hurry, jostle, hustle
▷ PHRASES: bundle someone up = wrap up, swathe

bungle = **mess up**, blow (*slang*), ruin, spoil, blunder, botch, make a mess of, muff, crool or cruel (*Austral. slang*) OPPOSITE: accomplish

bungling = **incompetent**, blundering, clumsy, inept, cack-

handed (*informal*), maladroit, ham-fisted (*informal*), unco (*Austral. slang*)

bunk or **bunkum** (*Informal*) = **nonsense**, rubbish, garbage (*informal*), hot air (*informal*), twaddle, moonshine, baloney (*informal*), hogwash, bizzo (*Austral. slang*), bull's wool (*Austral. & N.Z. slang*), kak (*S. African taboo slang*)

buoy = **float**, guide, signal, marker, beacon

buoyant 1 = **cheerful**, happy, upbeat (*informal*), carefree, jaunty, chirpy (*informal*), light-hearted OPPOSITE: gloomy **2** = **floating**, light

burden NOUN **1** = **trouble**, worry, weight, responsibility, strain, affliction, onus, millstone **2** = **load**, weight, cargo, freight, consignment, encumbrance
▷ VERB **3** = **weigh down**, worry, load, tax, bother, handicap, oppress, inconvenience

bureau 1 = **agency 2** = **office**, department, section, branch, station, unit, division, subdivision **3** = **desk**, writing desk

bureaucracy 1 = **government**, officials, authorities, administration, the system, civil service, corridors of power **2** = **red tape**, regulations, officialdom

bureaucrat = **official**, officer,

administrator, civil servant, public servant, functionary, mandarin

burglar = housebreaker, thief, robber, pilferer, filcher, cat burglar, sneak thief

burglary = breaking and entering, housebreaking, break-in

burial = funeral, interment, obsequies, entombment, exequies

burn 1 = be on fire, blaze, be ablaze, smoke, flame, glow, flare, go up in flames 2 = set on fire, light, ignite, kindle, incinerate 3 = scorch, toast, sear, char, singe 4 = be passionate, be aroused, be inflamed 5 = seethe, fume, be angry, simmer, smoulder

burning 1 = intense, passionate, eager, ardent, fervent, impassioned, vehement **OPPOSITE:** mild 2 = blazing, fiery, smouldering, glowing 3 = flashing, blazing, flaming, gleaming, fiery 4 = crucial, important, pressing, significant, essential, vital, critical, acute

burrow NOUN 1 = hole, shelter, tunnel, den, lair, retreat ▷ VERB 2 = dig, tunnel, excavate 3 = delve, search, probe, ferret, rummage, forage, fossick (Austral. & N.Z.)

burst VERB 1 = explode, blow up, break, split, crack, shatter, puncture, rupture 2 = rush, run, break, break out, erupt, spout, gush forth 3 = barge, charge, rush, shove ▷ NOUN 4 = rush, surge, outbreak, outburst, spate, gush, torrent, spurt 5 = explosion, crack, blast, bang, discharge ▷ ADJECTIVE 6 = ruptured, flat, punctured, split, rent

bury 1 = inter, lay to rest, entomb, consign to the grave, inhume **OPPOSITE:** dig up 2 = hide, cover, conceal, stash (informal), secrete, stow away **OPPOSITE:** uncover 3 = sink, embed, immerse, enfold 4 = forget

bush = shrub, plant, hedge, thicket, shrubbery ▷ PHRASES: the bush = the wilds, brush, scrub, woodland, backwoods, scrubland

business 1 = trade, selling, industry, manufacturing, commerce, dealings 2 = establishment, company, firm, concern, organization, corporation, venture, enterprise 3 = profession, work, job, line, trade, career, function, employment 4 = matter, issue, subject, point, problem, responsibility, task, duty 5 = concern, affair

businessman = executive, director, manager, merchant, capitalist, administrator, entrepreneur, tycoon

bust¹ = bosom, breasts, chest, front

b

bust² (*Informal*) 1 = **break**, smash, split, burst, shatter, fracture, rupture 2 = **arrest**, catch, raid
▷ **PHRASES: go bust** = **go bankrupt**, fail, be ruined, become insolvent

bustle VERB 1 = **hurry**, rush, fuss, hasten, scuttle, scurry, scamper **OPPOSITE:** idle
▷ NOUN 2 = **activity**, to-do, stir, excitement, fuss, flurry, commotion, ado **OPPOSITE:** inactivity

bustling = **busy**, full, crowded, active, lively, buzzing, humming, swarming

busy 1 = **active**, industrious, rushed off your feet **OPPOSITE:** idle 2 = **occupied with**, working, engaged in, on duty, employed in, hard at work **OPPOSITE:** unoccupied 3 = **hectic**, full, exacting, energetic
▷ **PHRASES: busy yourself** = **occupy yourself**, be engrossed, immerse yourself, involve yourself, absorb yourself, employ yourself, engage yourself

but CONJUNCTION 1 = **however**, still, yet, nevertheless
▷ **PREPOSITION** 2 = **except (for)**, save, bar, barring, excepting, excluding, with the exception of
▷ **ADVERB** 3 = **only**, just, simply, merely

butcher NOUN 1 = **murderer**, killer, slaughterer, slayer, destroyer, executioner, cut-throat, exterminator
▷ **VERB** 2 = **slaughter**, prepare, carve, cut up, dress, cut, clean, joint 3 = **kill**, slaughter, massacre, destroy, cut down, assassinate, slay, liquidate

butt¹ 1 = **end**, handle, shaft, stock, shank, hilt, haft 2 = **stub**, tip, leftover, fag end (*informal*)

butt² = **target**, victim, dupe, laughing stock, Aunt Sally

butt³ = **knock**, push, bump, thrust, ram, shove, poke, prod
▷ **PHRASES: butt in** 1 = **interfere**, meddle, intrude, heckle, barge in (*informal*), stick your nose in, put your oar in 2 = **interrupt**, cut in, break in, chip in (*informal*)

butt⁴ = **cask**, barrel

butterfly
● **RELATED WORDS**
● *young*: caterpillar, chrysalis, or chrysalid
● *enthusiast*: lepidopterist
▷ *See panel* BUTTERFLIES AND MOTHS

buy VERB 1 = **purchase**, get, pay for, obtain, acquire, invest in, shop for, procure **OPPOSITE:** sell
▷ NOUN 2 = **purchase**, deal, bargain, acquisition, steal (*informal*), snip (*informal*), giveaway

by PREPOSITION 1 = **through**, through the agency of 2 = **via**,

b

BUTTERFLIES AND MOTHS

argus
bag moth (N.Z.)
brown-tail moth
cabbage white
cactoblastis
cardinal
carpet moth
clearwing or clearwing moth
death's-head moth
ermine moth or ermine
ghost moth
gipsy moth
grayling
hairstreak
herald moth
hawk moth, sphinx moth, or hummingbird moth
house moth
lackey moth
large white or cabbage white
leopard moth
magpie moth
marbled white
monarch
orange-tip

painted lady
peacock butterfly
peppered moth
privet hawk
processionary moth
purple emperor
puss moth
red admiral
red underwing
ringlet
silver-Y
skipper
small white
snout
speckled wood
swallowtail
swift
tapestry moth
tiger (moth)
umber (moth)
wax moth, honeycomb moth, or bee moth
white
white admiral
winter moth
yellow underwing

over, by way of **3** = **near**, past, along, close to, closest to, neighbouring, next to, beside ▷ ADVERB **4** = **nearby**, close, handy, at hand, within reach
bypass 1 = **get round**, avoid
2 = **go round**, circumvent, depart from, deviate from, pass round, detour round **OPPOSITE:** cross

bystander = **onlooker**, passer-by, spectator, witness, observer, viewer, looker-on
byword = **saying**, slogan, motto, maxim, adage, proverb, epithet, dictum, precept, aphorism, saw, apophthegm

Cc

cab = taxi, minicab, taxicab, hackney carriage

cabin 1 = **room**, berth, quarters, compartment **2** = **hut**, shed, cottage, lodge, shack, chalet, shanty, whare (N.Z.)

cabinet 1 = **cupboard**, case, locker, dresser, closet, press, chiffonier **2** *often cap.* = **council**, committee, administration, ministry, assembly, board

cad (*Old-fashioned, informal*) = **scoundrel** (*slang*), rat (*informal*), bounder (*Brit. old-fashioned slang*), rotter (*slang, chiefly Brit.*), heel

café = **snack bar**, restaurant, cafeteria, coffee shop, brasserie, coffee bar, tearoom, lunchroom

cage = **enclosure**, pen, coop, hutch, pound

cake = **block**, bar, slab, lump, cube, loaf, mass

calculated = **deliberate**, planned, considered, intended, intentional, designed, aimed, purposeful **OPPOSITE:** unplanned

calculating = **scheming**, sharp, shrewd, cunning, sly, devious, manipulative, crafty **OPPOSITE:** direct

calculation 1 = **computation**, working out, reckoning, estimate, forecast, judgment, result, answer **2** = **planning**, intention, deliberation, foresight, contrivance, forethought, premeditation

calibre or (U.S.) **caliber 1** = **worth**, quality, ability, talent, capacity, merit, distinction, stature **2** = **standard**, level, quality, grade **3** = **diameter**, bore, gauge, measure

call VERB **1** = **name**, entitle, dub, designate, term, style, label, describe as **2** = **cry**, shout, scream, yell, whoop **OPPOSITE:** whisper **3** = **phone**, telephone, ring (up) (*informal, chiefly Brit.*) **4** = **hail**, summon **5** = **summon**, gather, rally, assemble, muster, convene **OPPOSITE:** dismiss **6** = **waken**, arouse, rouse ▷ NOUN **7** = **visit 8** = **request**, order, demand, appeal, notice, command, invitation, plea **9** (usually used in a negative construction) = **need**, cause, reason, grounds, occasion, excuse, justification **10** = **attraction**, pull (*informal*), appeal, lure, allure, magnetism **11** = **cry**, shout, scream, yell, whoop **OPPOSITE:** whisper ▷ PHRASES: **call for someone** = **fetch**, pick up, collect ▶ **call**

for something 1 = **demand**, order, request, insist on, cry out for 2 = **require**, need, involve, demand, occasion, entail, necessitate

calling = **profession**, trade, career, mission, vocation, life's work

calm ADJECTIVE 1 = **cool**, relaxed, composed, sedate, collected, dispassionate, unemotional, self-possessed **OPPOSITE:** excited 2 = **still**, quiet, smooth, mild, serene, tranquil, balmy, windless **OPPOSITE:** rough
▷ NOUN 3 = **peacefulness**, peace, serenity 4 = **stillness**, peace, quiet, hush, serenity, tranquillity, repose, peacefulness 5 = **peace**, calmness **OPPOSITE:** disturbance
▷ VERB 6 = **soothe**, quiet, relax, appease, still, allay, assuage, quieten **OPPOSITE:** excite 7 = **placate**, hush, pacify, mollify **OPPOSITE:** aggravate

camouflage NOUN
1 = **protective colouring**
2 = **disguise**, cover, screen, blind, mask, cloak, masquerade, subterfuge
▷ VERB 3 = **disguise**, cover, screen, hide, mask, conceal, obscure, veil **OPPOSITE:** reveal

camp¹ = **camp site**, tents, encampment, bivouac, camping ground

camp² (*Informal*) = **affected**, mannered, artificial, posturing, ostentatious, effeminate

campaign 1 = **drive**, appeal, movement, push (*informal*), offensive, crusade
2 = **operation**, drive, attack, movement, push, offensive, expedition, crusade

canal = **waterway**, channel, passage, conduit, duct, watercourse

cancel 1 = **call off**, drop, forget about 2 = **annul**, abolish, repeal, abort, do away with, revoke, eliminate
▷ PHRASES: cancel something out = **counterbalance**, offset, make up for, compensate for, neutralize, nullify, balance out

cancellation
1 = **abandonment**
2 = **annulment**, abolition, repeal, elimination, revocation

cancer 1 = **growth**, tumour, malignancy 2 = **evil**, corruption, sickness, pestilence

candidate = **contender**, competitor, applicant, nominee, entrant, claimant, contestant, runner

cannabis = **marijuana**, pot (*slang*), dope (*slang*), grass (*slang*), hemp, dagga (*S. African*)

cannon = **gun**, big gun, field gun, mortar

canon 1 = **rule**, standard, principle, regulation, formula, criterion, dictate, statute
2 = **list**, index, catalogue, roll

canopy = **awning**, covering,

shade, sunshade

cap 1 (*Informal*) = **beat**, top, better, exceed, eclipse, surpass, transcend, outstrip 2 = **top**, crown 3 = **complete**, crown

capability = **ability**, means, power, potential, capacity, qualification(s), competence, proficiency **OPPOSITE:** inability

capable 1 = **able**, suited **OPPOSITE:** incapable 2 = **accomplished**, qualified, talented, gifted, efficient, competent, proficient **OPPOSITE:** incompetent

capacity 1 = **ability**, facility, gift, genius, capability, aptitude, aptness, competence or competency 2 = **size**, room, range, space, volume, extent, dimensions, scope 3 = **function**, position, role, post, sphere

cape = **headland**, point, head, peninsula, promontory

capital NOUN 1 = **money**, funds, investment(s), cash, finances, resources, assets, wealth ▷ ADJECTIVE 2 (*Old-fashioned*) = **first-rate**, fine, excellent, superb

capitalism = **private enterprise**, free enterprise, private ownership, laissez faire or laisser faire

capsule 1 = **pill**, tablet, lozenge 2 (*Botany*) = **pod**, case, shell, vessel, sheath, receptacle, seed case

captain 1 = **leader**, boss, master, skipper, head, chief 2 = **commander**, skipper

captivate = **charm**, attract, fascinate, entrance, enchant, enthral, beguile, allure **OPPOSITE:** repel

captive ADJECTIVE 1 = **confined**, caged, imprisoned, locked up, enslaved, incarcerated, ensnared, subjugated ▷ NOUN 2 = **prisoner**, hostage, convict, prisoner of war, detainee, internee

captivity = **confinement**, custody, detention, imprisonment, incarceration, internment

capture VERB 1 = **catch**, arrest, take, bag, secure, seize, collar (*informal*), apprehend **OPPOSITE:** release ▷ NOUN 2 = **arrest**, catching, trapping, imprisonment, seizure, apprehension, taking, taking captive

car 1 = **vehicle**, motor, wheels (*informal*), auto (*U.S.*), automobile, jalopy (*informal*), motorcar, machine 2 (*U.S. & Canad.*) = (railway) **carriage**, coach, cable car, dining car, sleeping car, buffet car, van

cardinal = **principal**, first, leading, chief, main, central, key, essential **OPPOSITE:** secondary

care VERB 1 = **be concerned**, mind, bother, be interested, be

bothered, give a damn, concern yourself
▷ NOUN 2 = **custody**, keeping, control, charge, management, protection, supervision, guardianship 3 = **caution**, attention, pains, consideration, heed, prudence, vigilance, forethought OPPOSITE: carelessness 4 = **worry**, concern, pressure, trouble, responsibility, stress, anxiety, disquiet OPPOSITE: pleasure
▷ PHRASES: care for someone 1 = **look after**, mind, tend, attend, nurse, minister to, watch over 2 = **love**, desire, be fond of, want, prize ▶ care for something or someone = **like**, enjoy, take to, relish, be fond of, be keen on, be partial to ▶ take care of 1 = **look after**, mind, watch, protect, tend, nurse, care for, provide for 2 = **deal with**, manage, cope with, see to, handle

career NOUN 1 = **occupation**, calling, employment, pursuit, vocation, livelihood, life's work
▷ VERB 2 = **rush**, race, speed, tear, dash, barrel (along) (*informal, chiefly U.S. & Canad.*), bolt, hurtle

careful 1 = **cautious**, scrupulous, circumspect, chary, thoughtful, discreet OPPOSITE: careless 2 = **thorough**, full, particular, precise, intensive, in-depth, meticulous, conscientious OPPOSITE: casual

3 = **prudent**, sparing, economical, canny, provident, frugal, thrifty

careless 1 = **slapdash**, irresponsible, sloppy (*informal*), cavalier, offhand, neglectful, slipshod, lackadaisical OPPOSITE: careful
2 = **negligent**, hasty, thoughtless, unthinking, forgetful, absent-minded, remiss OPPOSITE: careful
3 = **nonchalant**, casual, offhand, artless, unstudied OPPOSITE: careful

caretaker = **warden**, keeper, porter, superintendent, curator, custodian, watchman, janitor

cargo = **load**, goods, contents, shipment, freight, merchandise, baggage, consignment

caricature NOUN 1 = **parody**, cartoon, distortion, satire, send-up (*Brit. informal*), travesty, takeoff (*informal*), lampoon
▷ VERB 2 = **parody**, take off (*informal*), mock, distort, ridicule, mimic, send up (*Brit. informal*), lampoon

carnage = **slaughter**, murder, massacre, holocaust, havoc, bloodshed, shambles, mass murder

carnival = **festival**, fair, fête, celebration, gala, jubilee, jamboree, revelry

carnivore ▷ *See panel* CARNIVORES

carol = **song**, hymn, Christmas song

CARNIVORES

aardwolf
arctic fox
badger
bear
binturong
black bear
bobcat
brown bear
caracal or desert lynx
cat
catamount, catamountain, or cat-o'-mountain
cheetah or chetah
cinnamon bear
civet
coyote or prairie wolf
dhole
dingo or (Austral.) native dog or warrigal
dog
ermine
fennec
ferret
fox
genet or genette
giant panda
grey fox (U.S.)
grey wolf or timber wolf
grizzly bear or grizzly
hyena or hyaena
ichneumon
jackal
jaguar
jaguarondi, jaguarundi, or (Austral.) eyra
kinkajou, honey bear, or potto
Kodiak bear
laughing hyena or spotted hyena
leopard or panther
linsang
lion
lynx
margay
marten
meerkat
mink
mongoose
mountain lion
ocelot
otter
otter shrew
palm civet
panda
panther
pine marten or sweet marten
polar bear or (N. Canad.) nanook
polecat
prairie dog
puma or cougar
raccoon, racoon, or coon
raccoon dog
ratel
red fox
sable
sea otter
serval
silver fox
skunk
sloth bear
snow leopard or ounce
stoat
strandwolf
sun bear

CARNIVORES continued	
swift fox *or* kit fox	timber wolf
tayra	weasel
teledu	wolf
tiger	wolverine, glutton, *or*
tiger cat	carcajou

carp VERB 1 = **find fault**, complain, criticize, reproach, quibble, cavil, pick holes **OPPOSITE:** praise

carpenter = **joiner**, cabinet-maker, woodworker

carriage 1 = **vehicle**, coach, trap, gig, cab, wagon, hackney, conveyance 2 = **bearing**, posture, gait, deportment, air

carry VERB 1 = **convey**, take, move, bring, bear, transfer, conduct, transport 2 = **transport**, take, transfer 3 = **transmit**, transfer, spread, pass on 4 = **win**, gain, secure, capture, accomplish ▷ **PHRASES: carry on** 1 = **continue**, last, endure, persist, keep going, persevere 2 (*Informal*) = **make a fuss**, misbehave, create (*slang*), raise Cain ▷ **carry something on** = **engage in**, conduct, carry out, undertake, embark on, enter into ▷ **carry something out** = **perform**, effect, achieve, realize, implement, fulfil, accomplish, execute

carry-on (*Informal, chiefly Brit.*) = **fuss**, disturbance, racket, commotion

carton = **box**, case, pack, package, container

cartoon 1 = **drawing**, parody, satire, caricature, comic strip, takeoff (*informal*), lampoon, sketch 2 = **animation**, animated film, animated cartoon

carve 1 = **sculpt**, cut, chip, whittle, chisel, hew, fashion 2 = **etch**, engrave

cascade NOUN 1 = **waterfall**, falls, torrent, flood, shower, fountain, avalanche, deluge ▷ VERB 2 = **flow**, fall, flood, pour, plunge, surge, spill, tumble

case¹ 1 = **situation**, event, circumstance(s), state, position, condition, context, contingency 2 = **instance**, example, occasion, specimen, occurrence 3 (*Law*) = **lawsuit**, trial, suit, proceedings, dispute, action

case² 1 = **cabinet**, box, chest, holder 2 = **container**, carton, canister, casket, receptacle 3 = **suitcase**, bag, grip, holdall, portmanteau, valise 4 = **crate**, box 5 = **covering**, casing, shell, jacket, envelope, capsule, sheath, wrapper

cash = **money**, funds, notes, currency, silver, brass (*Northern*

English dialect), dough (slang), coinage

cast NOUN 1 = **actors**, company, players, characters, troupe, dramatis personae 2 = **type**, sort, kind, style ▷ VERB 3 = **choose**, name, pick, select, appoint, assign, allot 4 = **bestow**, give, level, direct 5 = **give out**, spread, deposit, shed, distribute, scatter, emit, radiate 6 = **throw**, launch, pitch, toss, thrust, hurl, fling, sling 7 = **mould**, set, found, form, model, shape

caste = **class**, order, rank, status, stratum, social order

castle = **fortress**, keep, palace, tower, chateau, stronghold, citadel

casual 1 = **careless**, relaxed, unconcerned, blasé, offhand, nonchalant, lackadaisical OPPOSITE: serious 2 = **chance**, unexpected, random, accidental, incidental OPPOSITE: planned 3 = **informal**, leisure, sporty, non-dressy OPPOSITE: formal

casualty 1 = **fatality**, death, loss, wounded 2 = **victim**, sufferer

cat = **feline**, pussy (informal), moggy (slang), puss (informal), ballarat (Austral. informal), tabby
- RELATED WORDS
- adjective: feline
- male: tom
- female: tabby
- young: kitten

catalogue or (U.S.) **catalog** NOUN 1 = **list**, record, schedule, index, register, directory, inventory, gazetteer ▷ VERB 2 = **list**, file, index, register, classify, inventory, tabulate, alphabetize

catastrophe = **disaster**, tragedy, calamity, cataclysm, trouble, adversity, fiasco

catch VERB 1 = **capture**, arrest, trap, seize, snare, apprehend, ensnare, entrap OPPOSITE: free 2 = **trap**, capture, snare, ensnare, entrap 3 = **seize**, get, grab, snatch 4 = **grab**, take, grip, seize, grasp, clutch, lay hold of OPPOSITE: release 5 = **discover**, surprise, find out, expose, detect, catch in the act, take unawares 6 = **contract**, get, develop, suffer from, incur, succumb to, go down with OPPOSITE: escape ▷ NOUN 7 = **fastener**, clip, bolt, latch, clasp 8 (Informal) = **drawback**, trick, trap, disadvantage, hitch, snag, stumbling block, fly in the ointment OPPOSITE: advantage ▷ PHRASES: **catch on** 1 (Informal) = **understand**, see, find out, grasp, see through, comprehend, twig (Brit. informal), get the picture 2 = **become popular**, take off, become trendy, come into fashion

catching = **infectious**,

contagious, transferable, communicable, transmittable **OPPOSITE:** non-infectious

category = class, grouping, heading, sort, department, type, division, section

cater PHRASES: cater for something *or* someone
1 = **provide for**, supply, purvey
2 = **take into account**, consider, bear in mind, make allowance for, have regard for

cattle = cows, stock, beasts, livestock, bovines
● RELATED WORDS
● *adjective:* bovine
● *collective nouns:* drove, herd

cause NOUN 1 = **origin**, source, spring, agent, maker, producer, root, beginning **OPPOSITE:** result 2 = **reason**, call, need, grounds, basis, incentive, motive, motivation 3 = **aim**, movement, principle, ideal, enterprise
▷ VERB 4 = **produce**, create, lead to, result in, generate, induce, bring about, give rise to **OPPOSITE:** prevent

caution NOUN 1 = **care**, discretion, heed, prudence, vigilance, alertness, forethought, circumspection **OPPOSITE:** carelessness
2 = **reprimand**, warning, injunction, admonition
▷ VERB 3 = **warn**, urge, advise, alert, tip off, forewarn
4 = **reprimand**, warn, admonish, give an injunction to

cautious = careful, guarded, wary, tentative, prudent, judicious, circumspect, cagey (*informal*) **OPPOSITE:** careless

cavalry = horsemen, horse, mounted troops **OPPOSITE:** infantrymen

cave = hollow, cavern, grotto, den, cavity

cavity = hollow, hole, gap, pit, dent, crater

cease 1 = **stop**, end, finish, come to an end **OPPOSITE:** start 2 = **discontinue**, end, stop, finish, conclude, halt, terminate, break off **OPPOSITE:** begin

celebrate 1 = **rejoice**, party, enjoy yourself, carouse, live it up (*informal*), make merry, put the flags out, kill the fatted calf
2 = **commemorate**, honour, observe, toast, drink to, keep
3 = **perform**, observe, preside over, officiate at, solemnize

celebrated = renowned, popular, famous, distinguished, well-known, prominent, acclaimed, notable **OPPOSITE:** unknown

celebration 1 = **party**, festival, gala, jubilee, festivity, revelry, red-letter day, merrymaking
2 = **commemoration**, honouring, remembrance
3 = **performance**, observance, solemnization

celebrity 1 = **personality**, star, superstar, big name, dignitary, luminary, big shot (*informal*),

V.I.P. **OPPOSITE:** nobody
2 = **fame**, reputation, distinction, prestige, prominence, stardom, renown, repute **OPPOSITE:** obscurity

cell 1 = **room**, chamber, lock-up, compartment, cavity, cubicle, dungeon, stall 2 = **unit**, group, section, core, nucleus, caucus, coterie

cement NOUN 1 = **mortar**, plaster, paste 2 = **sealant**, glue, gum, adhesive
▷ VERB 3 = **stick**, join, bond, attach, seal, glue, plaster, weld

cemetery = **graveyard**, churchyard, burial ground, necropolis, God's acre

censor = **expurgate**, cut, blue-pencil, bowdlerize

censure VERB 1 = **criticize**, blame, condemn, denounce, rebuke, reprimand, reproach, scold **OPPOSITE:** applaud
▷ NOUN 2 = **disapproval**, criticism, blame, condemnation, rebuke, reprimand, reproach, stick (slang) **OPPOSITE:** approval

central 1 = **inner**, middle, mid, interior **OPPOSITE:** outer
2 = **main**, chief, key, essential, primary, principal, fundamental, focal **OPPOSITE:** minor

centre NOUN 1 = **middle**, heart, focus, core, nucleus, hub, pivot, kernel **OPPOSITE:** edge
▷ VERB 2 = **focus**, concentrate, cluster, revolve, converge

ceremonial ADJECTIVE

1 = **formal**, public, official, ritual, stately, solemn, liturgical, courtly **OPPOSITE:** informal
▷ NOUN 2 = **ritual**, ceremony, rite, formality, solemnity

ceremony 1 = **ritual**, service, rite, observance, commemoration, solemnities
2 = **formality**, ceremonial, propriety, decorum

certain 1 = **sure**, convinced, positive, confident, satisfied, assured **OPPOSITE:** unsure
2 = **bound**, sure, fated, destined **OPPOSITE:** unlikely
3 = **inevitable**, unavoidable, inescapable 4 = **known**, true, positive, conclusive, unequivocal, undeniable, irrefutable, unquestionable **OPPOSITE:** doubtful 5 = **fixed**, decided, established, settled, definite **OPPOSITE:** indefinite

certainly = **definitely**, surely, truly, undoubtedly, without doubt, undeniably, indisputably, assuredly

certainty 1 = **confidence**, trust, faith, conviction, assurance, sureness, positiveness **OPPOSITE:** doubt
2 = **inevitability OPPOSITE:** uncertainty 3 = **fact**, truth, reality, sure thing (informal), banker

certificate = **document**, licence, warrant, voucher, diploma, testimonial, authorization, credential(s)

certify = **confirm**, declare,

guarantee, assure, testify, verify, validate, attest

chain NOUN 1 = **tether**, coupling, link, bond, shackle, fetter, manacle 2 = **series**, set, train, string, sequence, succession, progression ▷ VERB 3 = **bind**, confine, restrain, handcuff, shackle, tether, fetter, manacle

chairman *or* **chairwoman** 1 = **director**, president, chief, executive, chairperson 2 = **master of ceremonies**, spokesman, chair, speaker, MC, chairperson

● USAGE NOTE
● The general trend of
● nonsexist language is to find
● a term which can apply to
● both sexes equally, as in the
● use of *actor* to refer to both
● men and women. *Chairman*
● can seem inappropriate when
● applied to a woman, while
● *chairwoman* specifies gender.
● Therefore, the terms *chair* and
● *chairperson* are often preferred
● as alternatives.

challenge NOUN 1 = **dare**, provocation, wero (*N.Z.*) 2 = **test**, trial, opposition, confrontation, ultimatum ▷ VERB 3 = **dispute**, question, tackle, confront, defy, object to, disagree with, take issue with 4 = **dare**, invite, defy, throw down the gauntlet 5 = **test** 6 = **question**, interrogate

chamber 1 = **hall**, room

2 = **council**, assembly, legislature, legislative body 3 = **room**, bedroom, apartment, enclosure, cubicle 4 = **compartment**

champion NOUN 1 = **winner**, hero, victor, conqueror, title holder 2 = **defender**, guardian, patron, backer, protector, upholder ▷ VERB 3 = **support**, back, defend, promote, advocate, fight for, uphold, espouse

chance NOUN 1 = **probability**, odds, possibility, prospect, likelihood OPPOSITE: certainty 2 = **opportunity**, opening, occasion, time 3 = **accident**, fortune, luck, fate, destiny, coincidence, providence OPPOSITE: design 4 = **risk**, speculation, gamble, hazard ▷ VERB 5 = **risk**, try, stake, venture, gamble, hazard, wager

change NOUN 1 = **alteration**, innovation, transformation, modification, mutation, metamorphosis, difference, revolution 2 = **variety**, break (*informal*), departure, variation, novelty, diversion OPPOSITE: monotony 3 = **exchange**, trade, conversion, swap, substitution, interchange ▷ VERB 4 = **alter**, reform, transform, adjust, revise, modify, reorganize, restyle OPPOSITE: keep 5 = **shift**, vary, transform, alter, modify, mutate OPPOSITE: stay 6 = **exchange**, trade, replace, substitute, swap, interchange

channel NOUN 1 = **means**, way, course, approach, medium, route, path, avenue 2 = **strait**, sound, route, passage, canal, waterway 3 = **duct**, artery, groove, gutter, furrow, conduit ▷ VERB 4 = **direct**, guide, conduct, transmit, convey

chant NOUN 1 = **song**, carol, chorus, melody, psalm ▷ VERB 2 = **sing**, chorus, recite, intone, carol

chaos = **disorder**, confusion, mayhem, anarchy, lawlessness, pandemonium, bedlam, tumult **OPPOSITE:** orderliness

chaotic = **disordered**, confused, uncontrolled, anarchic, tumultuous, lawless, riotous, topsy-turvy

chap (*Informal*) = **fellow**, man, person, individual, character, guy (*informal*), bloke (*Brit. informal*)

chapter 1 = **section**, part, stage, division, episode, topic, segment, instalment 2 = **period**, time, stage, phase

character 1 = **personality**, nature, attributes, temperament, complexion, disposition 2 = **nature**, kind, quality, calibre 3 = **reputation**, honour, integrity, good name, rectitude 4 = **role**, part, persona 5 = **eccentric**, card (*informal*), original, oddball

(*informal*) 6 = **symbol**, mark, sign, letter, figure, device, rune, hieroglyph

characteristic NOUN 1 = **feature**, mark, quality, property, attribute, faculty, trait, quirk ▷ ADJECTIVE 2 = **typical**, special, individual, representative, distinguishing, distinctive, peculiar, singular **OPPOSITE:** rare

characterize = **distinguish**, mark, identify, brand, stamp, typify

charge VERB 1 = **accuse**, indict, impeach, incriminate, arraign **OPPOSITE:** acquit 2 = **attack**, assault, assail **OPPOSITE:** retreat 3 = **rush**, storm, stampede 4 = **fill**, load ▷ NOUN 5 = **price**, rate, cost, amount, payment, expense, toll, expenditure 6 = **accusation**, allegation, indictment, imputation **OPPOSITE:** acquittal 7 = **care**, trust, responsibility, custody, safekeeping 8 = **duty**, office, responsibility, remit 9 = **ward**, pupil, protégé, dependant 10 = **attack**, rush, assault, onset, onslaught, stampede, sortie **OPPOSITE:** retreat

charisma = **charm**, appeal, personality, attraction, lure, allure, magnetism, force of personality

charismatic = **charming**, appealing, attractive,

influential, magnetic, enticing, alluring

charitable 1 = **benevolent**, liberal, generous, lavish, philanthropic, bountiful, beneficent **OPPOSITE:** mean 2 = **kind**, understanding, forgiving, sympathetic, favourable, tolerant, indulgent, lenient **OPPOSITE:** unkind

charity 1 = **charitable organization**, fund, movement, trust, endowment 2 = **donations**, help, relief, gift, contributions, assistance, hand-out, philanthropy, koha (N.Z.) **OPPOSITE:** meanness 3 = **kindness**, humanity, goodwill, compassion, generosity, indulgence, altruism, benevolence, aroha (N.Z.) **OPPOSITE:** ill will

charm NOUN 1 = **attraction**, appeal, fascination, allure, magnetism **OPPOSITE:** repulsiveness 2 = **talisman**, trinket, amulet, fetish 3 = **spell**, magic, enchantment, sorcery, makutu (N.Z.)
▷ VERB 4 = **attract**, delight, fascinate, entrance, win over, enchant, captivate, beguile **OPPOSITE:** repel 5 = **persuade**, seduce, coax, beguile, sweet-talk (informal)

charming = **attractive**, pleasing, appealing, fetching, delightful, cute, seductive, captivating **OPPOSITE:** unpleasant

chart NOUN 1 = **table**, diagram, blueprint, graph, plan, map
▷ VERB 2 = **plot**, map out, delineate, sketch, draft, tabulate 3 = **monitor**, follow, record, note, document, register, trace, outline

charter NOUN 1 = **document**, contract, permit, licence, deed, prerogative 2 = **constitution**, laws, rules, code
▷ VERB 3 = **hire**, commission, employ, rent, lease 4 = **authorize**, permit, sanction, entitle, license, empower, give authority

chase VERB 1 = **pursue**, follow, track, hunt, run after, course 2 = **drive away**, drive, expel, hound, send away, send packing, put to flight 3 = **rush**, run, race, shoot, fly, speed, dash, bolt
▷ NOUN 4 = **pursuit**, race, hunt, hunting

chat VERB 1 = **talk**, gossip, jaw (slang), natter, blather, blether (Scot.)
▷ NOUN 2 = **talk**, tête-à-tête, conversation, gossip, heart-to-heart, natter, blather, blether (Scot.), korero (N.Z.)

chatter VERB 1 = **prattle**, chat, rabbit on (Brit. informal), babble, gab (informal), natter, blather, schmooze (slang)
▷ NOUN 2 = **prattle**, chat, gossip, babble, gab (informal), natter, blather, blether (Scot.)

cheap 1 = inexpensive, reduced, keen, reasonable, bargain, low-priced, low-cost, cut-price **OPPOSITE:** expensive **2** = inferior, poor, worthless, second-rate, shoddy, tawdry, tatty, trashy, bodger *or* bodgie (*Austral. slang*) **OPPOSITE:** good **3** (*Informal*) = despicable, mean, contemptible, scungy (*Austral. & N.Z.*) **OPPOSITE:** decent

cheat VERB 1 = deceive, trick, fool, con (*informal*), mislead, rip off (*slang*), fleece, defraud ▷ **NOUN 2** = deceiver, sharper, shark, charlatan, trickster, con man (*informal*), double-crosser (*informal*), swindler, rorter (*Austral. slang*)

check VERB 1 *often with* out = examine, test, study, look at, research, investigate, monitor, vet **OPPOSITE:** overlook **2** = stop, limit, delay, halt, restrain, inhibit, hinder, obstruct **OPPOSITE:** further ▷ **NOUN 3** = examination, test, research, investigation, inspection, scrutiny, once-over (*informal*) **4** = control, limitation, restraint, constraint, obstacle, curb, obstruction, stoppage

cheek (*Informal*) = impudence, nerve, disrespect, audacity, lip (*slang*), temerity, chutzpah (*U.S. & Canad. informal*), insolence

cheeky = impudent, rude, forward, insulting, saucy, audacious, pert, disrespectful

OPPOSITE: respectful

cheer VERB 1 = applaud, hail, acclaim, clap **OPPOSITE:** boo **2** = hearten, encourage, comfort, uplift, brighten, cheer up, buoy up, gladden **OPPOSITE:** dishearten ▷ **NOUN 3** = applause, ovation, plaudits, acclamation ▷ **PHRASES: cheer someone up** = comfort, encourage, hearten, enliven, gladden, gee up, jolly along (*informal*) ▶ **cheer up** = take heart, rally, perk up, buck up (*informal*)

cheerful 1 = happy, optimistic, enthusiastic, jolly, merry, upbeat (*informal*), buoyant, cheery **OPPOSITE:** sad **2** = pleasant, bright **OPPOSITE:** gloomy

chemical = compound, drug, substance, synthetic substance, potion

chemist = pharmacist, apothecary (*obsolete*), dispenser

cherish 1 = cling to, prize, treasure, hold dear, cleave to **OPPOSITE:** despise **2** = care for, love, support, comfort, look after, shelter, nurture, hold dear **OPPOSITE:** neglect **3** = harbour, nurse, sustain, foster, entertain

chest 1 = breast, front **2** = box, case, trunk, crate, coffer, casket, strongbox
● **RELATED WORD**
● *adjective:* pectoral

chew = munch, bite, grind, champ, crunch, gnaw, chomp,

masticate, manducate

chic = stylish, smart, elegant, fashionable, trendy (*Brit. informal*) **OPPOSITE:** unfashionable

chief NOUN 1 = **head**, leader, director, manager, boss (*informal*), captain, master, governor, baas (*S. African*), ariki (*N.Z.*) **OPPOSITE:** subordinate
▷ ADJECTIVE 2 = **primary**, highest, leading, main, prime, key, premier, supreme **OPPOSITE:** minor

chiefly 1 = **especially**, essentially, principally, primarily, above all 2 = **mainly**, largely, usually, mostly, in general, on the whole, predominantly, in the main

child 1 = **youngster**, baby, kid (*informal*), infant, babe, juvenile, toddler, tot, littlie (*Austral. informal*), ankle-biter (*Austral. slang*), tacker (*Austral. slang*)
2 = **offspring**
● **RELATED WORDS**
● *adjective:* filial
● *prefix:* paedo-

childbirth = **child-bearing**, labour, delivery, lying-in, confinement, parturition

childhood = **youth**, minority, infancy, schooldays, immaturity, boyhood *or* girlhood

childish 1 = **youthful**, young, boyish *or* girlish 2 = **immature**, juvenile, foolish, infantile, puerile **OPPOSITE:** mature

chill VERB 1 = **cool**, refrigerate,

freeze 2 = **dishearten**, depress, discourage, dismay, dampen, deject
▷ NOUN 3 = **coldness**, bite, nip, sharpness, coolness, rawness, crispness, frigidity 4 = **shiver**, frisson
▷ ADJECTIVE 5 = **chilly**, biting, sharp, freezing, raw, bleak, chilly, wintry

chilly 1 = **cool**, fresh, sharp, crisp, penetrating, brisk, draughty, nippy **OPPOSITE:** warm 2 = **unfriendly**, hostile, unsympathetic, frigid, unresponsive, unwelcoming **OPPOSITE:** friendly

china[1] = **pottery**, ceramics, ware, porcelain, crockery, tableware, service

china[2] (*Brit. & S. African informal*) = **friend**, pal, mate (*informal*), buddy (*informal*), companion, best friend, intimate, comrade, cobber (*Austral. & N.Z. old-fashioned informal*), E hoa (*N.Z.*)

chip NOUN 1 = **fragment**, shaving, wafer, sliver, shard 2 = **scratch**, nick, notch 3 = **counter**, disc, token
▷ VERB 4 = **nick**, damage, gash 5 = **chisel**, whittle

choice NOUN 1 = **range**, variety, selection, assortment 2 = **selection**, preference, pick 3 = **option**, say, alternative
▷ ADJECTIVE 4 = **best**, prime, select, excellent, exclusive, elite, booshit (*Austral. slang*), exo (*Austral. slang*)

choke 1 = suffocate, stifle, smother, overpower, asphyxiate 2 = strangle, throttle, asphyxiate 3 = block, clog, obstruct, bung, constrict, congest, stop, bar

choose 1 = pick, prefer, select, elect, adopt, opt for, designate, settle upon **OPPOSITE:** reject 2 = wish, want

chop = cut, fell, hack, sever, cleave, hew, lop

chore = task, job, duty, burden, hassle (*informal*), errand

chorus 1 = refrain, response, strain, burden 2 = choir, singers, ensemble, vocalists, choristers

▷ **PHRASES: in chorus** = in unison, as one, all together, in concert, in harmony, in accord, with one voice

christen 1 = baptize, name 2 = name, call, term, style, title, dub, designate

Christmas = festive season, Noël, Xmas (*informal*), Yule (*archaic*), Yuletide (*archaic*)

chronicle VERB 1 = record, tell, report, enter, relate, register, recount, set down ▷ NOUN 2 = record, story, history, account, register, journal, diary, narrative

chuck VERB (*Informal*) 1 = throw, cast, pitch, toss, hurl, fling, sling, heave 2 *often with away* or *out* = throw out, dump (*informal*), scrap, get rid of, ditch (*slang*), dispose of,

dispense with, jettison 3 = give up *or* over, leave, abandon, cease, resign from, pack in 4 (*Austral. & N.Z. informal*) = vomit, throw up (*informal*), spew, heave (*slang*), puke (*slang*), barf (*U.S. slang*), chunder (*slang, chiefly Austral.*)

chuckle = laugh, giggle, snigger, chortle, titter

chum (*Informal*) = friend, mate (*informal*), pal (*informal*), companion, comrade, crony, cobber (*Austral. & N.Z. old-fashioned informal*), E hoa (*N.Z.*)

chunk = piece, block, mass, portion, lump, slab, hunk, nugget

churn 1 = stir up, beat, disturb, swirl, agitate 2 = swirl, toss, seethe

cinema 1 = pictures, movies, picture-house, flicks (*slang*) 2 = films, pictures, movies, big screen (*informal*), motion pictures, silver screen

circle NOUN 1 = ring, disc, hoop, halo 2 = group, company, set, club, society, clique, coterie ▷ VERB 3 = go round, ring, surround, enclose, envelop, encircle, circumscribe, circumnavigate 4 = wheel, spiral

circuit 1 = course, tour, track, route, journey 2 = racetrack, course, track, racecourse 3 = lap, tour, revolution, orbit

circular ADJECTIVE 1 = **round**, ring-shaped 2 = **circuitous**, cyclical, orbital
▷ NOUN 3 = **advertisement**, notice, ad (*informal*), announcement, advert (*Brit. informal*), press release

circulate 1 = **spread**, issue, publish, broadcast, distribute, publicize, disseminate, promulgate 2 = **flow**, revolve, rotate, radiate

circulation 1 = **distribution**, currency, readership 2 = **bloodstream**, blood flow 3 = **flow**, circling, motion, rotation 4 = **spread**, distribution, transmission, dissemination

circumstance 1 *usually plural* = **situation**, condition, contingency, state of affairs, lie of the land 2 *usually plural* = **detail**, event, particular, respect 3 *usually plural* = **situation**, state, means, position, station, status 4 = **chance**, the times, accident, fortune, luck, fate, destiny, providence

cite = **quote**, name, advance, mention, extract, specify, allude to, enumerate

citizen = **inhabitant**, resident, dweller, denizen, subject, townsman
 • RELATED WORD
 • *adjective*: civil

city = **town**, metropolis, municipality, conurbation

 • RELATED WORD
 • *adjective*: civic

civic = **public**, municipal, communal, local

civil 1 = **civic**, political, domestic, municipal **OPPOSITE:** state 2 = **polite**, obliging, courteous, considerate, affable, well-mannered **OPPOSITE:** rude

civilization 1 = **society**, people, community, nation, polity 2 = **culture**, development, education, progress, enlightenment, sophistication, advancement, cultivation

civilize = **cultivate**, educate, refine, tame, enlighten, sophisticate

civilized 1 = **cultured**, educated, sophisticated, enlightened, humane **OPPOSITE:** primitive 2 = **polite**, mannerly, tolerant, gracious, courteous, well-behaved, well-mannered

claim VERB 1 = **assert**, insist, maintain, allege, uphold, profess 2 = **demand**, call for, ask for, insist on
▷ NOUN 3 = **assertion**, statement, allegation, declaration, pretension, affirmation, protestation 4 = **demand**, application, request, petition, call 5 = **right**, title, entitlement

clamour = **noise**, shouting, racket, outcry, din, uproar, commotion, hubbub

clamp NOUN 1 = **vice**, press, grip, bracket, fastener
▷ VERB 2 = **fasten**, fix, secure, brace, make fast

clan 1 = **family**, group, society, tribe, fraternity, brotherhood, ainga (N.Z.), ngai or ngati (N.Z.)
2 = **group**, set, circle, gang, faction, coterie, cabal

clap = **applaud**, cheer, acclaim **OPPOSITE:** boo

clarify = **explain**, interpret, illuminate, clear up, simplify, make plain, elucidate, throw or shed light on

clarity 1 = **clearness**, precision, simplicity, transparency, lucidity, straightforwardness **OPPOSITE:** obscurity
2 = **transparency**, clearness **OPPOSITE:** cloudiness

clash VERB 1 = **conflict**, grapple, wrangle, lock horns, cross swords, war, feud, quarrel
2 = **disagree**, conflict, vary, counter, differ, contradict, diverge, run counter to 3 = **not go**, jar, not match 4 = **crash**, bang, rattle, jar, clatter, jangle, clang, clank
▷ NOUN 5 = **conflict**, fight, brush, confrontation, collision, showdown (informal)
6 = **disagreement**, difference, argument, dispute, dissent, difference of opinion

clasp VERB 1 = **grasp**, hold, press, grip, seize, squeeze, embrace, clutch
▷ NOUN 2 = **grasp**, hold, grip, embrace, hug 3 = **fastening**, catch, grip, hook, pin, clip, buckle, brooch

class NOUN 1 = **group**, set, division, rank 2 = **type**, set, sort, kind, category, genre
▷ VERB 3 = **classify**, group, rate, rank, brand, label, grade, designate

classic ADJECTIVE 1 = **typical**, standard, model, regular, usual, ideal, characteristic, definitive, dinki-di (Austral. informal)
2 = **masterly**, best, finest, world-class, consummate, first-rate **OPPOSITE:** second-rate
3 = **lasting**, enduring, abiding, immortal, undying, ageless, deathless
▷ NOUN 4 = **standard**, masterpiece, prototype, paradigm, exemplar, model

classification = **categorization**, grading, taxonomy, sorting, analysis, arrangement

classify = **categorize**, sort, rank, arrange, grade, catalogue, pigeonhole, tabulate

classy (Informal) = **high-class**, exclusive, superior, elegant, stylish, posh (informal, chiefly Brit.), up-market, top-drawer

clause = **section**, condition, article, chapter, passage, part, paragraph

claw NOUN 1 = **nail**, talon
2 = **pincer**
▷ VERB 3 = **scratch**, tear, dig, rip, scrape, maul, mangulate

(*Austral. slang*), lacerate
clean ADJECTIVE 1 = **hygienic**, fresh, sterile, pure, purified, antiseptic, sterilized, uncontaminated OPPOSITE: contaminated 2 = **spotless**, fresh, immaculate, impeccable, flawless, unblemished, unsullied OPPOSITE: dirty 3 = **moral**, good, pure, decent, innocent, respectable, upright, honourable OPPOSITE: immoral 4 = **complete**, final, whole, total, perfect, entire, decisive, thorough
▷ VERB 5 = **cleanse**, wash, scrub, rinse, launder, scour, purify, disinfect OPPOSITE: dirty
cleanse 1 = **purify**, clear, purge 2 = **absolve**, clear, purge, purify
▷ VERB 3 = **clean**, wash, scrub, rinse, scour
clear ADJECTIVE
1 = **comprehensible**, explicit, understandable OPPOSITE: confused 2 = **distinct**, perceptible OPPOSITE: indistinct 3 = **obvious**, plain, apparent, evident, distinct, pronounced, manifest, blatant OPPOSITE: ambiguous 4 = **certain**, sure, convinced, positive, satisfied, resolved, definite, decided OPPOSITE: confused
5 = **transparent**, see-through, translucent, crystalline, glassy, limpid, pellucid OPPOSITE: opaque 6 = **unobstructed**, open, free, empty, unhindered, unimpeded OPPOSITE: blocked

7 = **bright**, fine, fair, shining, sunny, luminous, cloudless, light OPPOSITE: cloudy
8 = **untroubled**, clean, pure, innocent, immaculate, unblemished, untarnished
▷ VERB 9 = **unblock**, free, loosen, extricate, open, disentangle 10 = **remove**, clean, wipe, cleanse, tidy (up), sweep away 11 = **brighten**, break up, lighten 12 = **pass over**, jump, leap, vault, miss 13 = **absolve**, acquit, vindicate, exonerate OPPOSITE: blame
clear-cut = **straightforward**, specific, plain, precise, black-and-white, explicit, definite, unequivocal
clearly 1 = **obviously**, undoubtedly, evidently, distinctly, markedly, overtly, undeniably, beyond doubt
2 = **legibly**, distinctly
3 = **audibly**, distinctly, intelligibly, comprehensibly
clergy = **priesthood**, ministry, clerics, clergymen, churchmen, the cloth, holy orders
clever 1 = **intelligent**, bright, talented, gifted, smart, knowledgeable, quick-witted OPPOSITE: stupid 2 = **shrewd**, bright, ingenious, resourceful, canny OPPOSITE: unimaginative 3 = **skilful**, talented, gifted OPPOSITE: inept
cliché = **platitude**, stereotype, commonplace, banality, truism, hackneyed phrase

client = customer, consumer, buyer, patron, shopper, patient

cliff = rock face, overhang, crag, precipice, escarpment, scar, bluff

climate = weather, temperature

climax = culmination, top, summit, height, highlight, peak, high point, zenith

climb 1 = ascend, scale, mount, go up, clamber, shin up 2 = clamber, descend, scramble, dismount 3 = rise, go up, soar, ascend, fly up ▷ PHRASES: climb down = back down, withdraw, yield, concede, retreat, surrender, give in, cave in (informal)

clinch 1 = secure, close, confirm, conclude, seal, sew up (informal), set the seal on 2 = settle, decide, determine

cling 1 = clutch, grip, embrace, grasp, hug, hold on to, clasp 2 = stick to, adhere to

clinical = unemotional, cold, scientific, objective, detached, analytic, impersonal, dispassionate

clip¹ VERB 1 = trim, cut, crop, prune, shorten, shear, snip, pare 2 (Informal) = smack, strike, knock, punch, thump, clout (informal), cuff, whack ▷ NOUN 3 (Informal) = smack, strike, knock, punch, thump, clout (informal), cuff, whack

clip² = attach, fix, secure, connect, pin, staple, fasten

cloak NOUN 1 = cape, coat, wrap, mantle 2 = covering, layer, blanket, shroud ▷ VERB 3 = cover, coat, wrap, blanket, shroud, envelop 4 = hide, cover, screen, mask, disguise, conceal, obscure, veil, camouflage

clog = obstruct, block, jam, hinder, impede, congest

close¹ VERB 1 = shut, lock, fasten, secure OPPOSITE: open 2 = shut down, finish, cease 3 = wind up, finish, shut down, terminate 4 = block up, bar, seal OPPOSITE: open 5 = end, finish, complete, conclude, wind up, terminate OPPOSITE: begin 6 = clinch, confirm, secure, conclude, seal, sew up (informal), set the seal on 7 = come together, join, connect OPPOSITE: separate ▷ NOUN 8 = end, ending, finish, conclusion, completion, finale, culmination, denouement

close² ADJECTIVE 1 = near, neighbouring, nearby, handy, adjacent, adjoining, cheek by jowl OPPOSITE: far 2 = intimate, loving, familiar, thick (informal), attached, devoted, confidential, inseparable OPPOSITE: distant 3 = noticeable, marked, strong, distinct, pronounced 4 = careful, detailed, intense, minute, thorough, rigorous, painstaking 5 = even, level, neck and neck, fifty-fifty

(*informal*), evenly matched
6 = **imminent**, near,
impending, at hand, nigh
OPPOSITE: far away **7** = **stifling**,
oppressive, suffocating, stuffy,
humid, sweltering, airless,
muggy **OPPOSITE:** airy
closed 1 = **shut**, locked, sealed,
fastened **OPPOSITE:** open
2 = **shut down**, out of service
3 = **exclusive**, select, restricted
4 = **finished**, over, ended,
decided, settled, concluded,
resolved, terminated
cloth = **fabric**, material, textiles
clothe = **dress**, array, robe,
drape, swathe, attire, fit out,
garb **OPPOSITE:** undress
clothes = **clothing**, wear, dress,
gear (*informal*), outfit, costume,
wardrobe, garments
clothing = **clothes**, wear, dress,
gear (*informal*), outfit, costume,
wardrobe, garments
cloud NOUN 1 = **mist**, haze,
vapour, murk, gloom
▷ **VERB 2** = **confuse**, distort,
impair, muddle, disorient
3 = **darken**, dim, be
overshadowed
clout (*Informal*) **VERB 1** = **hit**,
strike, punch, slap, sock (*slang*),
smack, thump, clobber (*slang*)
▷ **NOUN 2** = **thump**, blow,
punch, slap, sock (*slang*), wallop
(*informal*) **3** = **influence**, power,
authority, pull, weight, prestige,
mana (*N.Z.*)
clown NOUN 1 = **comedian**,
fool, comic, harlequin, joker,

jester, prankster, buffoon
2 = **fool**, idiot, twit (*informal*,
chiefly Brit.), imbecile (*informal*),
ignoramus, dolt, blockhead,
dorba or dorb (*Austral. slang*),
bogan (*Austral. slang*)
▷ **VERB 3** *usually with* **around**
= **play the fool**, mess about,
jest, act the fool
club NOUN 1 = **association**,
company, group, union, society,
lodge, guild, fraternity
2 = **stick**, bat, bludgeon,
truncheon, cosh (*Brit.*), cudgel
▷ **VERB 3** = **beat**, strike,
hammer, batter, bash,
bludgeon, pummel, cosh (*Brit.*)
clue = **indication**, lead, sign,
evidence, suggestion, trace,
hint, suspicion
clump NOUN 1 = **cluster**,
group, bunch, bundle
▷ **VERB 2** = **stomp**, thump,
lumber, tramp, plod, thud
clumsy = **awkward**, lumbering,
bumbling, ponderous, ungainly,
gauche, gawky, uncoordinated,
unco (*Austral. slang*) **OPPOSITE:**
skilful
cluster NOUN 1 = **gathering**,
group, collection, bunch, knot,
clump, assemblage
▷ **VERB 2** = **gather**, group,
collect, bunch, assemble, flock,
huddle
clutch VERB 1 = **hold**, grip,
embrace, grasp, cling to, clasp
2 = **seize**, catch, grab, grasp,
snatch
▷ **PLURAL NOUN 3** = **power**,

hands, control, grip, possession, grasp, custody, sway

clutter NOUN 1 = **untidiness**, mess, disorder, confusion, litter, muddle, disarray, jumble **OPPOSITE:** order
▷ VERB 2 = **litter**, scatter, strew, mess up **OPPOSITE:** tidy

coach NOUN 1 = **instructor**, teacher, trainer, tutor, handler 2 = **bus**, charabanc
▷ VERB 3 = **instruct**, train, prepare, exercise, drill, tutor

coalition = **alliance**, union, association, combination, merger, conjunction, bloc, confederation

coarse 1 = **rough**, crude, unfinished, homespun, impure, unrefined, unprocessed, unpolished **OPPOSITE:** smooth 2 = **vulgar**, rude, indecent, improper, earthy, smutty, ribald, indelicate

coast NOUN 1 = **shore**, border, beach, seaside, coastline, seaboard
▷ VERB 2 = **cruise**, sail, drift, taxi, glide, freewheel

coat NOUN 1 = **fur**, hair, skin, hide, wool, fleece, pelt 2 = **layer**, covering, coating, overlay
▷ VERB 3 = **cover**, spread, plaster, smear

coax = **persuade**, cajole, talk into, wheedle, sweet-talk (informal), prevail upon, entice, allure **OPPOSITE:** bully

cobber (Austral. & N.Z. old-fashioned informal) = **friend**, pal, mate (informal), buddy (informal), china (Brit. & S. African informal), best friend, intimate, comrade, E hoa (N.Z.)

cocktail = **mixture**, combination, compound, blend, mix

cocky or **cockie** (Austral. & N.Z. informal) = **farmer**, smallholder, crofter (Scot.), grazier, agriculturalist, rancher

code 1 = **principles**, rules, manners, custom, convention, ethics, maxim, etiquette, kawa (N.Z.), tikanga (N.Z.) 2 = **cipher**, cryptograph

coherent 1 = **consistent**, reasoned, organized, rational, logical, meaningful, systematic, orderly **OPPOSITE:** inconsistent 2 = **articulate**, lucid, comprehensible, intelligible **OPPOSITE:** unintelligible

coil 1 = **wind**, twist, curl, loop, spiral, twine 2 = **curl**, wind, twist, snake, loop, twine, wreathe

coin NOUN = **money**, change, cash, silver, copper, specie
▷ VERB = **invent**, create, make up, forge, originate, fabricate

coincide 1 = **occur simultaneously**, coexist, synchronize, be concurrent 2 = **agree**, match, accord, square, correspond, tally, concur, harmonize **OPPOSITE:** disagree

coincidence = **chance**,

accident, luck, fluke, stroke of luck, happy accident

cold ADJECTIVE 1 = **chilly**, freezing, bleak, arctic, icy, frosty, wintry, frigid OPPOSITE: hot 2 = **distant**, reserved, indifferent, aloof, frigid, undemonstrative, standoffish OPPOSITE: emotional 3 = **unfriendly**, indifferent, frigid OPPOSITE: friendly ▷ NOUN 4 = **coldness**, chill, frigidity, frostiness, iciness

collaborate 1 = **work together**, team up, join forces, cooperate, play ball (informal), participate 2 = **conspire**, cooperate, collude, fraternize

collaboration 1 = **teamwork**, partnership, cooperation, association, alliance 2 = **conspiring**, cooperation, collusion, fraternization

collaborator 1 = **co-worker**, partner, colleague, associate, team-mate, confederate 2 = **traitor**, turncoat, quisling, fraternizer

collapse VERB 1 = **fall down**, fall, give way, subside, cave in, crumple, fall apart at the seams 2 = **fail**, fold, founder, break down, fall through, come to nothing, go belly-up (informal) ▷ NOUN 3 = **falling down**, ruin, falling apart, cave-in, disintegration, subsidence 4 = **failure**, slump, breakdown, flop, downfall 5 = **faint**, breakdown, blackout

collar (Informal) = **seize**, catch, arrest, grab, capture, nail (informal), nab (informal), apprehend

colleague = **fellow worker**, partner, ally, associate, assistant, team-mate, comrade, helper

collect 1 = **gather**, save, assemble, heap, accumulate, amass, stockpile, hoard OPPOSITE: scatter 2 = **assemble**, meet, rally, cluster, come together, convene, converge, congregate OPPOSITE: disperse

collected = **calm**, cool, composed, heap, serene, unperturbed, unruffled, self-possessed, unperturbable OPPOSITE: nervous

collection 1 = **accumulation**, set, store, mass, pile, heap, stockpile, hoard 2 = **compilation**, accumulation, anthology 3 = **group**, company, crowd, assembly, cluster, assortment 4 = **gathering** 5 = **contribution**, donation, alms 6 = **offering**, offertory

collective 1 = **joint**, united, shared, combined, corporate, unified OPPOSITE: individual 2 = **combined**, aggregate, composite, cumulative OPPOSITE: separate

collide 1 = **crash**, clash, meet head-on, come into collision 2 = **conflict**, clash, be incompatible, be at variance

collision 1 = **crash**, impact, accident, smash, bump, pile-up (informal), prang (informal) 2 = **conflict**, opposition, clash, encounter, disagreement, incompatibility

colony = **settlement**, territory, province, possession, dependency, outpost, dominion, satellite state

colour or (U.S.) **color** NOUN 1 = **hue**, tone, shade, tint, colourway 2 = **paint**, stain, dye, tint, pigment, colorant ▷ VERB 3 = **blush**, flush, redden ▷ See panels SHADES FROM BLACK TO WHITE, SHADES OF BLUE, SHADES OF BROWN, SHADES OF GREEN, SHADES OF ORANGE, SHADES OF PURPLE, SHADES OF RED, SHADES OF YELLOW

colourful 1 = **bright**, brilliant, psychedelic, variegated, multicoloured OPPOSITE: drab 2 = **interesting**, rich, graphic, lively, distinctive, vivid, picturesque OPPOSITE: boring

column 1 = **pillar**, support, post, shaft, upright, obelisk 2 = **line**, row, file, rank, procession, cavalcade

coma = **unconsciousness**, trance, oblivion, stupor

comb 1 = **untangle**, arrange, groom, dress 2 = **search**, hunt through, rake, sift, scour, rummage, ransack, forage, fossick (Austral. & N.Z.)

combat NOUN 1 = **fight**, war, action, battle, conflict, engagement, warfare, skirmish OPPOSITE: peace ▷ VERB 2 = **fight**, oppose, resist, defy, withstand, do battle with OPPOSITE: support

combination 1 = **mixture**, mix, blend, composite, amalgamation, coalescence 2 = **association**, union, alliance, coalition, federation, consortium, syndicate, confederation

combine 1 = **amalgamate**, mix, blend, integrate, merge OPPOSITE: separate 2 = **join together**, link, connect, integrate, merge, amalgamate 3 = **unite**, associate, team up, get together, collaborate, join forces, join together, pool resources OPPOSITE: split up

come VERB 1 = **approach**, near, advance, move towards, draw near 2 = **arrive**, turn up (informal), show up (informal) 3 = **reach**, extend, come up to, come as far as 4 = **happen**, fall, occur, take place, come about, come to pass 5 = **be available**, be made, be offered, be produced, be on offer ▷ PHRASES: come across as something or someone = **seem**, look, seem to be, appear to be, give the impression of being ▶ come across someone = **meet**, encounter, run into, bump into (informal) ▶ come across

something = find, discover, notice, unearth, stumble upon, chance upon 6 = be obtained, be from, issue, emerge, flow, arise, originate, emanate

comeback 1 (*Informal*) = return, revival, rebound, resurgence, rally, recovery, triumph 2 = response, reply, retort, retaliation, riposte, rejoinder

comedian = comic, wit, clown, funny man, humorist, wag, joker, jester, dag (*N.Z. informal*)

comedy 1 = light entertainment, slapstick OPPOSITE: tragedy 2 = humour, fun, joking, farce, jesting, hilarity OPPOSITE: seriousness

comfort NOUN 1 = ease, luxury, wellbeing, opulence 2 = consolation, succour, help, support, relief, compensation OPPOSITE: annoyance
▷ VERB 3 = console, reassure, soothe, hearten, commiserate with OPPOSITE: distress

comfortable 1 = pleasant, homely, relaxing, cosy, agreeable, restful OPPOSITE: unpleasant 2 = at ease, happy, at home, contented, relaxed, serene OPPOSITE: uncomfortable 3 (*Informal*) = well-off, prosperous, affluent, well-to-do, comfortably-off, in clover (*informal*)

comforting = consoling, encouraging, cheering, reassuring, soothing, heart-warming OPPOSITE: upsetting

comic ADJECTIVE 1 = funny, amusing, witty, humorous, farcical, comical, droll, jocular OPPOSITE: sad
▷ NOUN 2 = comedian, funny man, humorist, wit, clown, wag, jester, dag (*N.Z. informal*), buffoon

coming ADJECTIVE
1 = approaching, near, forthcoming, imminent, in store, impending, at hand, nigh
▷ NOUN 2 = arrival, approach, advent

command VERB 1 = order, tell, charge, demand, require, direct, bid, compel OPPOSITE: beg
2 = have authority over, lead, head, control, rule, manage, handle, dominate OPPOSITE: be subordinate to
▷ NOUN 3 = order, demand, instruction, requirement, decree, directive, ultimatum, commandment
4 = domination, control, rule, mastery, power, government
5 = management, power, control, charge, authority, supervision

commander = leader, chief, officer, boss, head, captain, bass (*S. African*), ruler

commanding = dominant, controlling, dominating, superior, decisive, advantageous

commemorate = celebrate, remember, honour, recognize,

salute, pay tribute to,
immortalize **OPPOSITE:** ignore
commence 1 = **embark on**,
start, open, begin, initiate,
originate, instigate, enter upon
OPPOSITE: stop 2 = **start**, open,
begin, go ahead **OPPOSITE:** end
commend 1 = **praise**, acclaim,
applaud, compliment, extol,
approve, speak highly of
OPPOSITE: criticize
2 = **recommend**, suggest,
approve, advocate, endorse
comment VERB 1 = **remark**,
say, note, mention, point out,
observe, utter 2 *usually with* **on**
= **remark on**, explain, talk
about, discuss, speak about, say
something about, allude to,
elucidate
▷ NOUN 3 = **remark**,
statement, observation
4 = **note**, explanation,
illustration, commentary,
exposition, annotation,
elucidation
commentary 1 = **narration**,
report, review, explanation,
description, voice-over
2 = **analysis**, notes, review,
critique, treatise
commentator 1 = **reporter**,
special correspondent,
sportscaster 2 = **critic**,
interpreter, annotator
commercial 1 = **mercantile**,
trading 2 = **materialistic**,
mercenary, profit-making
commission VERB
1 = **appoint**, order, contract,

select, engage, delegate,
nominate, authorize
▷ NOUN 2 = **duty**, task,
mission, mandate, errand
3 = **fee**, cut, percentage,
royalties, rake-off (*slang*)
4 = **committee**, board,
representatives, commissioners,
delegation, deputation
commit 1 = **do**, perform, carry
out, execute, enact, perpetrate
2 = **put in custody**, confine,
imprison **OPPOSITE:** release
commitment 1 = **dedication**,
loyalty, devotion **OPPOSITE:**
indecisiveness
2 = **responsibility**, tie, duty,
obligation, liability,
engagement
common 1 = **usual**, standard,
regular, ordinary, familiar,
conventional, routine, frequent
OPPOSITE: rare 2 = **popular**,
general, accepted, standard,
routine, widespread, universal,
prevailing 3 = **shared**,
collective 4 = **ordinary**,
average, typical, dinki-di
(*Austral. informal*) **OPPOSITE:**
important 5 = **vulgar**, inferior,
coarse, plebeian **OPPOSITE:**
refined 6 = **collective**, public,
community, social, communal
OPPOSITE: personal
commonplace ADJECTIVE
1 = **everyday**, common,
ordinary, widespread, mundane,
banal, run-of-the-mill,
humdrum **OPPOSITE:** rare
▷ NOUN 2 = **cliché**, platitude,

banality, truism, bromide

common sense = good sense, sound judgment, level-headedness, prudence, gumption (*Brit. informal*), horse sense, native intelligence, wit

communal = public, shared, general, joint, collective **OPPOSITE:** private

commune = community, collective, cooperative, kibbutz

communicate 1 = contact, talk, speak, make contact, get in contact 2 = make known, declare, disclose, pass on, proclaim, transmit, convey, impart **OPPOSITE:** keep secret 3 = pass on, transfer, spread, transmit

communication 1 = contact, conversation, correspondence, link, relations 2 = passing on, circulation, transmission, disclosure, imparting, dissemination, conveyance 3 = message, news, report, word, information, statement, announcement, disclosure

communism *usually cap.* = socialism, Marxism, collectivism, Bolshevism, state socialism

communist *often cap.* = socialist, Red (*informal*), Marxist, Bolshevik, collectivist

community = society, people, public, residents, commonwealth, general public, populace, state

commuter = daily traveller, passenger, suburbanite

compact¹ ADJECTIVE 1 = closely packed, solid, thick, dense, compressed, condensed, pressed together **OPPOSITE:** loose 2 = concise, brief, to the point, succinct, terse **OPPOSITE:** lengthy
▷ VERB 3 = pack closely, stuff, cram, compress, condense, tamp **OPPOSITE:** loosen

compact² = agreement, deal, understanding, contract, bond, arrangement, treaty, bargain

companion 1 = friend, partner, ally, colleague, associate, mate (*informal*), comrade, accomplice, cobber (*Austral. & N.Z. old-fashioned informal*) 2 = assistant, aide, escort, attendant

company 1 = business, firm, association, corporation, partnership, establishment, syndicate, house 2 = group, set, community, band, crowd, collection, gathering, assembly 3 = troop, unit, squad, team 4 = companionship, society, presence, fellowship 5 = guests, party, visitors, callers

comparable 1 = equal, equivalent, on a par, tantamount, a match for, proportionate, commensurate, as good as **OPPOSITE:** unequal 2 = similar, related, alike, corresponding, akin, analogous, of a piece, cognate

comparative = **relative**, qualified, by comparison

compare = **contrast**, balance, weigh, set against, juxtapose
▷ **PHRASES: compare to something** = **liken to**, parallel, identify with, equate to, correlate to, mention in the same breath as ▶ **compare with something** = **be as good as**, match, approach, equal, compete with, be on a par with, be the equal of, hold a candle to

comparison 1 = **contrast**, distinction, differentiation, juxtaposition 2 = **similarity**, analogy, resemblance, correlation, likeness, comparability

compartment 1 = **section**, carriage, berth 2 = **bay**, booth, locker, niche, cubicle, alcove, pigeonhole, cubbyhole

compass = **range**, field, area, reach, scope, limit, extent, boundary

compassion = **sympathy**, understanding, pity, humanity, mercy, sorrow, kindness, tenderness, aroha (*N.Z.*)
OPPOSITE: indifference

compassionate
= **sympathetic**, understanding, pitying, humanitarian, charitable, humane, benevolent, merciful **OPPOSITE:** uncaring

compatible 1 = **consistent**, in keeping, congruous **OPPOSITE:** inappropriate 2 = **like-minded**, harmonious, in harmony
OPPOSITE: incompatible

compel = **force**, make, railroad (*informal*), oblige, constrain, coerce, impel, dragoon

compelling 1 = **convincing**, telling, powerful, forceful, conclusive, weighty, cogent, irrefutable 2 = **pressing**, binding, urgent, overriding, imperative, unavoidable, coercive, peremptory 3 = **fascinating**, gripping, irresistible, enchanting, enthralling, hypnotic, spellbinding, mesmeric
OPPOSITE: boring

compensate 1 = **recompense**, repay, refund, reimburse, remunerate, make good 2 = **make amends**, make up for, atone, make it up to someone, pay for, do penance, cancel out, make reparation 3 = **balance**, cancel (out), offset, make up for, redress, counteract, counterbalance

compensation
1 = **reparation**, damages, recompense, remuneration, restitution, reimbursement 2 = **recompense**, amends, reparation, restitution, atonement

compete 1 = **contend**, fight, vie, challenge, struggle, contest, strive 2 = **take part**, participate, be in the running, be a competitor, be a contestant, play

competence 1 = **ability**, skill, talent, capacity, expertise, proficiency, capability **OPPOSITE:** incompetence
2 = **fitness**, suitability, adequacy, appropriateness **OPPOSITE:** inadequacy

competent 1 = **able**, skilled, capable, proficient **OPPOSITE:** incompetent 2 = **fit**, qualified, suitable, adequate **OPPOSITE:** unqualified

competition 1 = **rivalry**, opposition, struggle, strife
2 = **opposition**, field, rivals, challengers 3 = **contest**, event, championship, tournament, head-to-head

competitive 1 = **cut-throat**, aggressive, fierce, ruthless, relentless, antagonistic, dog-eat-dog 2 = **ambitious**, pushing, opposing, aggressive, vying, contentious, combative

competitor 1 = **rival**, adversary, antagonist
2 = **contestant**, participant, contender, challenger, entrant, player, opponent

compilation = **collection**, treasury, accumulation, anthology, assortment, assemblage

compile = **put together**, collect, gather, organize, accumulate, marshal, garner, amass

complacency = **smugness**, satisfaction, contentment, self-congratulation, self-satisfaction

complacent = **smug**, self-satisfied, pleased with yourself, resting on your laurels, contented, satisfied, serene, unconcerned **OPPOSITE:** insecure

complain = **find fault**, moan, grumble, whinge (*informal*), carp, groan, lament, whine

complaint 1 = **protest**, objection, grievance, charge
2 = **grumble**, criticism, moan, lament, grievance, grouse, gripe (*informal*) 3 = **disorder**, problem, disease, upset, illness, sickness, ailment, affliction

complement VERB
1 = **enhance**, complete, improve, boost, crown, add to, set off, heighten
▷ NOUN 2 = **accompaniment**, companion, accessory, completion, finishing touch, rounding-off, adjunct, supplement 3 = **total**, capacity, quota, aggregate, contingent, entirety

● **USAGE NOTE**
● This is sometimes confused
● with *compliment* but the two
● words have very different
● meanings. As the synonyms
● show, the verb form of
● *complement* means 'to
● enhance' and 'to complete'
● something. In contrast,
● common synonyms of
● *compliment* as a verb are
● *praise, commend,* and *flatter.*

complementary = **matching**, companion, corresponding,

compatible, reciprocal, interrelating, interdependent, harmonizing **OPPOSITE:** incompatible

complete ADJECTIVE 1 = **total**, perfect, absolute, utter, outright, thorough, consummate, out-and-out 2 = **whole**, full, entire **OPPOSITE:** partial 3 = **entire**, full, whole, intact, unbroken, faultless **OPPOSITE:** incomplete 4 = **unabridged**, full, entire 5 = **finished**, done, ended, achieved, concluded, fulfilled, accomplished **OPPOSITE:** unfinished

▷ VERB 6 = **perfect**, finish off, round off, crown **OPPOSITE:** spoil 7 = **finish**, conclude, end, close, settle, wrap up (*informal*), finalize **OPPOSITE:** start 8 = **fill in**, fill out

completely = **totally**, entirely, wholly, utterly, perfectly, fully, absolutely, altogether

completion = **finishing**, end, close, conclusion, fulfilment, culmination, fruition

complex ADJECTIVE 1 = **compound**, multiple, composite, manifold, heterogeneous, multifarious 2 = **complicated**, difficult, involved, elaborate, tangled, intricate, tortuous, convoluted **OPPOSITE:** simple

▷ NOUN 3 = **structure**, system, scheme, network, organization, aggregate, composite

4 (*Informal*) = **obsession**, preoccupation, phobia, fixation, fixed idea, idée fixe (*French*)

● USAGE NOTE
● Although *complex* and
● *complicated* are close in
● meaning, care should be
● taken when using one as a
● synonym of the other.
● *Complex* should be used to say
● that something consists of
● several parts rather than that
● it is difficult to understand,
● analyse, or deal with, which
● is what *complicated* inherently
● means. In the following real
● example a clear distinction is
● made between the two
● words: *the British benefits*
● *system is phenomenally complex*
● *and is administered by a*
● *complicated range of agencies.*

complexion 1 = **skin**, colour, colouring, hue, skin tone, pigmentation 2 = **nature**, character, make-up 3 = **perspective**, look, light, appearance, aspect, angle, slant

complexity = **complication**, involvement, intricacy, entanglement

complicate = **make difficult**, confuse, muddle, entangle, involve **OPPOSITE:** simplify

complicated 1 = **involved**, difficult, puzzling, troublesome, problematic, perplexing **OPPOSITE:** simple 2 = **complex**, involved, elaborate, intricate, convoluted, labyrinthine

OPPOSITE: understandable

complication 1 = **problem**, difficulty, obstacle, drawback, snag, uphill (S. African) 2 = **complexity**, web, confusion, intricacy, entanglement

compliment NOUN 1 = **praise**, honour, tribute, bouquet, flattery, eulogy **OPPOSITE:** criticism

▷ PLURAL NOUN 2 = **greetings**, regards, respects, good wishes, salutation **OPPOSITE:** insult 3 = **congratulations**, praise, commendation

▷ VERB 4 = **praise**, flatter, salute, congratulate, pay tribute to, commend, extol, wax lyrical about **OPPOSITE:** criticize

● USAGE NOTE
● Compliment is sometimes
● confused with complement.

complimentary 1 = **flattering**, approving, appreciative, congratulatory, commendatory **OPPOSITE:** critical 2 = **free**, donated, courtesy, honorary, on the house, gratuitous, gratis

comply = **obey**, follow, observe, submit to, conform to, adhere to, abide by, acquiesce with **OPPOSITE:** defy

component NOUN 1 = **part**, piece, unit, item, element, ingredient, constituent

▷ ADJECTIVE 2 = **constituent**, inherent, intrinsic

compose 1 = **put together**, make up, constitute, comprise, make, build, form, fashion **OPPOSITE:** destroy 2 = **create**, write, produce, invent, devise, contrive 3 = **arrange**, make up, construct, put together, order, organize

▷ PHRASES: compose yourself = **calm**, control, collect, quiet, soothe, pull yourself together

composed = **calm**, cool, collected, relaxed, poised, at ease, serene, sedate **OPPOSITE:** agitated

composition 1 = **design**, structure, make-up, organization, arrangement, formation, layout, configuration 2 = **creation**, work, piece, production, opus, masterpiece 3 = **essay**, exercise, treatise, literary work 4 = **production**, creation, making, fashioning, formation, putting together, compilation, formulation

compound NOUN 1 = **combination**, mixture, blend, composite, fusion, synthesis, alloy, medley **OPPOSITE:** element

▷ ADJECTIVE 2 = **complex**, multiple, composite, intricate **OPPOSITE:** simple

▷ VERB 3 = **intensify**, add to, complicate, worsen, heighten, exacerbate, aggravate, magnify **OPPOSITE:** lessen 4 = **combine**, unite, mix, blend, synthesize, amalgamate, intermingle

OPPOSITE: segregate
comprehend = **understand**, see, take in, perceive, grasp, conceive, make out, fathom **OPPOSITE:** misunderstand

comprehension = **understanding**, grasp, conception, realization, intelligence, perception, discernment **OPPOSITE:** incomprehension

comprehensive = **broad**, full, complete, blanket, thorough, inclusive, exhaustive, all-inclusive **OPPOSITE:** limited

compress 1 = **squeeze**, crush, squash, press 2 = **condense**, contract, concentrate, shorten, abbreviate

comprise 1 = **be composed of**, include, contain, consist of, take in, embrace, encompass 2 = **make up**, form, constitute, compose

● **USAGE NOTE**
● The use of of after comprise
● should be avoided: the library
● comprises (not comprises of)
● 6,500,000 books and
● manuscripts. Consist,
● however, should be followed
● by of when used in this way:
● Her crew consisted of children
● from Devon and Cornwall.

compromise NOUN 1 = **give-and-take**, agreement, settlement, accommodation, concession, adjustment, trade-off **OPPOSITE:** disagreement
▷ VERB 2 = **meet halfway**, concede, make concessions, give and take, strike a balance, strike a happy medium, go fifty-fifty (informal) **OPPOSITE:** disagree 3 = **undermine**, expose, embarrass, weaken, prejudice, discredit, jeopardize, dishonour **OPPOSITE:** support

compulsive 1 = **obsessive**, confirmed, chronic, persistent, addictive, uncontrollable, incurable, inveterate
2 = **fascinating**, gripping, absorbing, compelling, captivating, enthralling, hypnotic, engrossing
3 = **irresistible**, overwhelming, compelling, urgent, neurotic, uncontrollable, driving

compulsory = **obligatory**, forced, required, binding, mandatory, imperative, requisite, de rigueur (French) **OPPOSITE:** voluntary

compute = **calculate**, total, count, reckon, figure out, add up, tally, enumerate

comrade = **companion**, friend, partner, ally, colleague, associate, fellow, co-worker, cobber (Austral. & N.Z. old-fashioned informal)

con (Informal) VERB
1 = **swindle**, trick, cheat, rip off (slang), deceive, defraud, dupe, hoodwink
▷ NOUN 2 = **swindle**, trick, fraud, deception, scam (slang), sting (informal)

conceal 1 = **hide**, bury, cover,

screen, disguise, obscure, camouflage **OPPOSITE:** reveal
2 = **keep secret**, hide, disguise, mask, suppress, veil **OPPOSITE:** show

concede 1 = **admit**, allow, accept, acknowledge, own, grant, confess **OPPOSITE:** deny
2 = **give up**, yield, hand over, surrender, relinquish, cede **OPPOSITE:** conquer

conceive 1 = **imagine**, envisage, comprehend, visualize, think, believe, suppose, fancy 2 = **think up**, create, design, devise, formulate, contrive
3 = **become pregnant**, get pregnant, become impregnated

concentrate 1 = **focus your attention on**, focus on, pay attention to, be engrossed in, put your mind to, keep your mind on, apply yourself to, give your mind to **OPPOSITE:** pay no attention to 2 = **focus**, centre, converge, bring to bear
3 = **gather**, collect, cluster, accumulate, congregate **OPPOSITE:** scatter

concentrated 1 = **condensed**, rich, undiluted, reduced, evaporated, thickened, boiled down 2 = **intense**, hard, deep, intensive, all-out (*informal*)

concentration 1 = **attention**, application, absorption, single-mindedness, intentness **OPPOSITE:** inattention
2 = **focusing**, centring,

consolidation, convergence, bringing to bear, intensification, centralization
3 = **convergence**, collection, mass, cluster, accumulation, aggregation **OPPOSITE:** scattering

concept = **idea**, view, image, theory, notion, conception, hypothesis, abstraction

conception 1 = **idea**, plan, design, image, concept, notion
2 = **impregnation**, insemination, fertilization, germination

concern NOUN 1 = **anxiety**, fear, worry, distress, unease, apprehension, misgiving, disquiet 2 = **worry**, care, anxiety 3 = **affair**, issue, matter, consideration 4 = **care**, interest, attentiveness
5 = **business**, job, affair, responsibility, task
6 = **company**, business, firm, organization, corporation, enterprise, establishment
7 = **importance**, interest, bearing, relevance
▷ VERB 8 = **worry**, trouble, bother, disturb, distress, disquiet, perturb, make anxious
9 = **be about**, cover, deal with, go into, relate to, have to do with 10 = **be relevant to**, involve, affect, regard, apply to, bear on, have something to do with, pertain to

concerned 1 = **worried**, troubled, upset, bothered,

disturbed, anxious, distressed, uneasy **OPPOSITE:** indifferent
2 = **involved**, interested, active, mixed up, implicated, privy to
concerning = regarding, about, re, touching, respecting, relating to, on the subject of, with reference to
concession 1 = **compromise**, agreement, settlement, accommodation, adjustment, trade-off, give-and-take
2 = **privilege**, right, permit, licence, entitlement, indulgence, prerogative
3 = **reduction**, saving, grant, discount, allowance
4 = **surrender**, yielding, conceding, renunciation, relinquishment
conclude 1 = **decide**, judge, assume, gather, work out, infer, deduce, surmise 2 = **come to an end**, end, close, finish, wind up **OPPOSITE:** begin 3 = **bring to an end**, end, close, finish, complete, wind up, terminate, round off **OPPOSITE:** begin
4 = **accomplish**, effect, bring about, carry out, pull off
conclusion 1 = **decision**, opinion, conviction, verdict, judgment, deduction, inference
2 = **end**, ending, close, finish, completion, finale, termination, bitter end 3 = **outcome**, result, upshot, consequence, culmination, end result
concrete 1 = **specific**, precise, explicit, definite, clear-cut,

unequivocal **OPPOSITE:** vague
2 = **real**, material, actual, substantial, sensible, tangible, factual **OPPOSITE:** abstract
condemn 1 = **denounce**, damn, criticize, disapprove, censure, reprove, upbraid, blame **OPPOSITE:** approve
2 = **sentence**, convict, damn, doom, pass sentence on **OPPOSITE:** acquit
condemnation
= **denunciation**, blame, censure, disapproval, reproach, stricture, reproof
condition NOUN 1 = **state**, order, shape, nick (*Brit. informal*), trim 2 = **situation**, state, position, status, circumstances
3 = **requirement**, terms, rider, restriction, qualification, limitation, prerequisite, proviso
4 = **health**, shape, fitness, trim, form, kilter, state of health, fettle 5 = **ailment**, problem, complaint, weakness, malady, infirmity
▷ PLURAL NOUN
6 = **circumstances**, situation, environment, surroundings, way of life, milieu
▷ VERB 7 = **train**, teach, adapt, accustom
conditional = **dependent**, limited, qualified, subject to, contingent, provisional, with reservations **OPPOSITE:** unconditional
condone = **overlook**, excuse,

forgive, pardon, turn a blind eye to, look the other way, make allowance for, let pass **OPPOSITE:** condemn

conduct VERB 1 = **carry out**, run, control, manage, direct, handle, organize, administer 2 = **accompany**, lead, escort, guide, steer, convey, usher ▷ NOUN 3 = **management**, running, control, handling, administration, direction, organization, guidance 4 = **behaviour**, ways, bearing, attitude, manners, demeanour, deportment ▷ PHRASES: **conduct yourself** = **behave yourself**, act, carry yourself, acquit yourself, deport yourself, comport yourself

confer 1 = **discuss**, talk, consult, deliberate, discourse, converse 2 = **grant**, give, present, accord, award, hand out, bestow

conference = **meeting**, congress, discussion, convention, forum, consultation, seminar, symposium, hui (*N.Z.*)

confess 1 = **admit**, acknowledge, disclose, confide, own up, come clean (*informal*), divulge **OPPOSITE:** cover up 2 = **declare**, allow, reveal, confirm, concede, assert, affirm, profess

confession = **admission**, revelation, disclosure, acknowledgment, exposure,

unbosoming, avowa

confidant *or* **confidante** = **close friend**, familiar, intimate, crony, alter ego, bosom friend

confide = **tell**, admit, reveal, confess, whisper, disclose, impart, divulge

confidence 1 = **trust**, belief, faith, dependence, reliance, credence **OPPOSITE:** distrust 2 = **self-assurance**, courage, assurance, aplomb, boldness, self-possession, nerve **OPPOSITE:** shyness 3 = **secret** ▷ PHRASES: **in confidence** = **in secrecy**, privately, confidentially, between you and me (and the gatepost), (just) between ourselves

confident 1 = **certain**, sure, convinced, positive, secure, satisfied, counting on **OPPOSITE:** unsure 2 = **self-assured**, positive, assured, bold, self-confident, self-reliant, sure of yourself **OPPOSITE:** insecure

confidential 1 = **secret**, private, intimate, classified, privy, off the record, hush-hush (*informal*) 2 = **secretive**, low, soft, hushed

confine VERB 1 = **imprison**, enclose, shut up, intern, incarcerate, hem in, keep, cage 2 = **restrict**, limit ▷ PLURAL NOUN 3 = **limits**, bounds, boundaries, compass, precincts, circumference, edge

confirm 1 = **prove**, support,

establish, back up, verify, validate, bear out, substantiate **2 = ratify**, establish, sanction, endorse, authorize **3 = strengthen**, establish, fix, secure, reinforce, fortify

confirmation 1 = proof, evidence, testimony, verification, ratification, validation, corroboration, authentication **OPPOSITE:** repudiation **2 = affirmation**, approval, acceptance, endorsement, ratification, assent, agreement **OPPOSITE:** disapproval

confirmed = long-established, seasoned, chronic, hardened, habitual, ingrained, inveterate, dyed-in-the-wool

confiscate = seize, appropriate, impound, commandeer, sequester **OPPOSITE:** give back

conflict NOUN 1 = dispute, difference, opposition, hostility, disagreement, friction, strife, fighting **OPPOSITE:** agreement **2 = struggle**, battle, clash, strife **3 = battle**, war, fight, clash, contest, encounter, combat, strife **OPPOSITE:** peace ▷ **VERB 4 = be incompatible**, clash, differ, disagree, collide, be at variance **OPPOSITE:** agree

conflicting = incompatible, opposing, clashing, contrary, contradictory, inconsistent, paradoxical, discordant **OPPOSITE:** agreeing

conform 1 = fit in, follow, adjust, adapt, comply, obey, fall in with, toe the line **2 = fulfil**, meet, match, suit, satisfy, agree with, obey, abide by

confound = bewilder, baffle, confuse, astound, perplex, mystify, flummox, dumbfound

confront 1 = tackle, deal with, cope with, meet head-on **2 = trouble**, face, perturb, bedevil **3 = challenge**, face, oppose, tackle, encounter, defy, stand up to, accost **OPPOSITE:** evade

confrontation = conflict, fight, contest, set-to (*informal*), encounter, showdown (*informal*), head-to-head

confuse 1 = mix up with, take for, muddle with **2 = bewilder**, puzzle, baffle, perplex, mystify, fluster, faze, flummox **3 = obscure**, cloud, make more difficult

confused 1 = bewildered, puzzled, baffled, at sea, muddled, perplexed, taken aback, disorientated **OPPOSITE:** enlightened **2 = disorderly**, disordered, chaotic, mixed up, jumbled, untidy, in disarray, topsy-turvy **OPPOSITE:** tidy

confusing = bewildering, puzzling, misleading, unclear, baffling, contradictory, perplexing **OPPOSITE:** clear

confusion 1 = bewilderment, doubt, uncertainty **OPPOSITE:** enlightenment **2 = disorder**, chaos, turmoil, upheaval, muddle, shambles, commotion **OPPOSITE:** order

congestion = overcrowding, crowding, jam, clogging, bottleneck

congratulate = compliment, pat on the back, wish joy to

congratulations PLURAL NOUN 1 = good wishes, greetings, compliments, best wishes, felicitations
▷ INTERJECTION 2 = good wishes, greetings, compliments, best wishes, felicitations

congregation = parishioners, brethren, crowd, assembly, flock, fellowship, multitude, throng

congress 1 = meeting, council, conference, assembly, convention, conclave, hui (N.Z.), runanga (N.Z.) 2 = legislature, council, parliament, House of Representatives (N.Z.)

conjure = produce, generate, bring about, give rise to, make, create, effect, produce as if by magic
▷ PHRASES: conjure something up = bring to mind, recall, evoke, recreate, recollect, produce as if by magic

connect 1 = link, join, couple, attach, fasten, affix, unite **OPPOSITE:** separate
2 = associate, join, link, identify, lump together

connected = linked, united,

joined, coupled, related, allied, associated, combined

connection 1 = association, relationship, link, bond, relevance, tie-in
2 = communication, alliance, attachment, liaison, affinity, union 3 = link, coupling, junction, fastening, tie
4 = contact, friend, ally, associate, acquaintance

conquer 1 = seize, obtain, acquire, occupy, overrun, annex, win 2 = defeat, overcome, overthrow, beat, master, crush, overpower, quell **OPPOSITE:** lose to 3 = overcome, beat, defeat, master, overpower

conquest 1 = takeover, coup, invasion, occupation, annexation, subjugation
2 = defeat, victory, triumph, overthrow, rout, mastery

conscience 1 = principles, scruples, moral sense, sense of right and wrong, still small voice 2 = guilt, shame, regret, remorse, contrition, self-reproach

conscious 1 often with of = aware of, alert to, responsive to, sensible of **OPPOSITE:** unaware 2 = deliberate, knowing, studied, calculated, self-conscious, intentional, wilful, premeditated **OPPOSITE:** unintentional 3 = awake, wide-awake, sentient, alive **OPPOSITE:** asleep

consciousness = awareness,

understanding, knowledge, recognition, sensibility, realization, apprehension

consecutive = successive, running, succeeding, in turn, uninterrupted, sequential, in sequence

consensus = agreement, general agreement, unanimity, common consent, unity, harmony, assent, concord, kotahitanga (N.Z.)

● USAGE NOTE
● The original meaning of the
● word *consensus* is a *collective*
● *opinion*. Because the concept
● of 'opinion' is contained
● within this word, a few
● people argue that the phrase
● *a consensus of opinion* is
● incorrect and should be
● avoided. However, this
● common use of the word is
● unlikely to jar with the
● majority of speakers.

consent NOUN 1 = agreement, sanction, approval, go-ahead (informal), permission, compliance, assent, acquiescence **OPPOSITE:** refusal
▷ VERB 2 = agree, approve, permit, concur, assent, acquiesce **OPPOSITE:** refuse

consequence 1 = result, effect, outcome, repercussion, issue, sequel, end result, upshot 2 = importance, concern, moment, value, account, weight, import, significance

consequently = as a result,

thus, therefore, hence, subsequently, accordingly, for that reason, thence

conservation
1 = preservation, saving, protection, maintenance, safeguarding, upkeep, guardianship, safekeeping
2 = economy, saving, thrift, husbandry

conservative ADJECTIVE
1 = traditional, conventional, cautious, sober, reactionary, die-hard, hidebound **OPPOSITE:** radical
▷ NOUN 2 = traditionalist, reactionary, die-hard, stick-in-the-mud (informal) **OPPOSITE:** radical

Conservative ADJECTIVE
1 = Tory, Republican (U.S.), right-wing
▷ NOUN 2 = Tory, Republican (U.S.), right-winger

conserve 1 = save, husband, take care of, hoard, store up, use sparingly **OPPOSITE:** waste
2 = protect, keep, save, preserve

consider 1 = think, see, believe, rate, judge, suppose, deem, view as 2 = think about, reflect on, weigh, contemplate, deliberate, ponder, meditate, ruminate 3 = bear in mind, remember, respect, think about, take into account, reckon with, take into consideration, make allowance for

considerable = large, goodly,

great, marked, substantial, noticeable, plentiful, appreciable **OPPOSITE:** small

considerably = greatly, very much, significantly, remarkably, substantially, markedly, noticeably, appreciably

consideration 1 = thought, review, analysis, examination, reflection, scrutiny, deliberation 2 = thoughtfulness, concern, respect, kindness, tact, considerateness 3 = factor, point, issue, concern, element, aspect 4 = payment, fee, reward, remuneration, recompense, tip

considering = taking into account, in the light of, bearing in mind, in view of, keeping in mind, taking into consideration

consist **PHRASES: consist in something** = lie in, involve, reside in, be expressed by, subsist in, be found or contained in ▶ **consist of something** = **be made up of**, include, contain, incorporate, amount to, comprise, be composed of

consistency 1 = agreement, regularity, uniformity, constancy, steadiness, steadfastness, evenness 2 = texture, density, thickness, firmness, viscosity, compactness

consistent 1 = steady, even, regular, stable, constant, persistent, dependable, unchanging **OPPOSITE:** erratic

2 = compatible, agreeing, in keeping, harmonious, in harmony, consonant, in accord, congruous **OPPOSITE:** incompatible 3 = coherent, logical, compatible, harmonious, consonant **OPPOSITE:** contradictory

consolation = comfort, help, support, relief, cheer, encouragement, solace, succour

console = comfort, cheer, soothe, support, encourage, calm, succour, express sympathy for **OPPOSITE:** distress

consolidate 1 = strengthen, secure, reinforce, fortify, stabilize 2 = combine, unite, join, merge, unify, amalgamate, federate

conspicuous = obvious, clear, patent, evident, noticeable, blatant, salient **OPPOSITE:** inconspicuous

conspiracy = plot, scheme, intrigue, collusion, machination

conspire 1 = plot, scheme, intrigue, manoeuvre, contrive, machinate, plan 2 = **work together**, combine, contribute, cooperate, concur, tend

constant 1 = continuous, sustained, perpetual, interminable, unrelenting, incessant, ceaseless, nonstop **OPPOSITE:** occasional 2 = unchanging, even, fixed, permanent, stable, steady, uniform, invariable **OPPOSITE:** changing 3 = **faithful**, true, devoted, loyal, stalwart, staunch, trustworthy, trusty **OPPOSITE:** undependable

constantly = **continuously**, always, all the time, invariably, continually, endlessly, perpetually, incessantly **OPPOSITE:** occasionally

constituent NOUN 1 = **voter**, elector, member of the electorate 2 = **component**, element, ingredient, part, unit, factor
▷ ADJECTIVE 3 = **component**, basic, essential, integral, elemental

constitute 1 = **represent**, be, consist of, embody, exemplify, be equivalent to 2 = **make up**, form, compose, comprise

constitution 1 = **state of health**, build, body, frame, physique, physical condition 2 = **structure**, form, nature, make-up, composition, character, disposition

constitutional = **legitimate**, official, legal, chartered, statutory, vested

constrain 1 = **restrict**, confine, curb, restrain, constrict, straiten, check 2 = **force**, bind, compel, oblige, necessitate, coerce, impel, pressurize

constraint 1 = **restriction**, limitation, curb, rein, deterrent, hindrance, check 2 = **force**, pressure, necessity, restraint,

compulsion, coercion

construct 1 = **build**, make, form, create, fashion, shape, manufacture, assemble **OPPOSITE:** demolish 2 = **create**, make, form, compose, put together

construction 1 = **building**, creation, composition 2 (*Formal*) = **interpretation**, reading, explanation, rendering, inference

constructive = **helpful**, positive, useful, practical, valuable, productive **OPPOSITE:** unproductive

consult 1 = **ask**, refer to, turn to, take counsel, pick (someone's) brains, question 2 = **confer**, talk, compare notes 3 = **refer to**, check in, look in

consultant = **specialist**, adviser, counsellor, authority

consultation 1 = **discussion**, talk, council, conference, dialogue 2 = **meeting**, interview, session, appointment, examination, deliberation, hearing

consume 1 = **eat**, swallow, devour, put away, gobble (up), eat up 2 = **use up**, spend, waste, absorb, exhaust, squander, dissipate, expend 3 = **destroy**, devastate, demolish, ravage, annihilate, lay waste 4 *often passive* = **obsess**, dominate, absorb, preoccupy, eat up, monopolize, engross

consumer = **buyer**, customer,

user, shopper, purchaser

consumption 1 = using up, use, loss, waste, expenditure, exhaustion, depletion, dissipation 2 (Old-fashioned) = tuberculosis, T.B.

contact NOUN
1 = communication, link, association, connection, correspondence 2 = touch, contiguity 3 = connection, colleague, associate, liaison, acquaintance, confederate
▷ VERB 4 = get or be in touch with, call, reach, approach, write to, speak to, communicate with

contain 1 = hold, incorporate, accommodate, enclose, have capacity for 2 = include, consist of, embrace, comprise, embody, comprehend
3 = restrain, control, hold in, curb, suppress, hold back, stifle, repress

container = holder, vessel, repository, receptacle

contaminate = pollute, infect, stain, corrupt, taint, defile, adulterate, befoul OPPOSITE: purify

contamination = pollution, infection, corruption, poisoning, taint, impurity, contagion, defilement

contemplate 1 = consider, plan, think of, intend, envisage, foresee 2 = think about, consider, ponder, reflect upon, ruminate (upon), muse over,

deliberate over 3 = look at, examine, inspect, gaze at, eye up, view, study, regard

contemporary ADJECTIVE
1 = modern, recent, current, up-to-date, present-day, à la mode, newfangled, present
OPPOSITE: old-fashioned
2 = coexisting, concurrent, contemporaneous
▷ NOUN 3 = peer, fellow, equal

● USAGE NOTE
● Since *contemporary* can mean
● either 'of the present period'
● or 'of the same period', it is
● best to avoid it where
● ambiguity might arise, as in *a*
● *production of Othello in*
● *contemporary dress*. A synonym
● such as *modern* or *present-day*
● would clarify if the first sense
● were being used, while a specific
● term, such as *Elizabethan*,
● would be appropriate for the
● second sense.

contempt = scorn, disdain, mockery, derision, disrespect, disregard OPPOSITE: respect

contend 1 = argue, hold, maintain, allege, assert, affirm
2 = compete, fight, struggle, clash, contest, strive, vie, jostle

content[1] NOUN 1 = subject matter, material, theme, substance, essence, gist
2 = amount, measure, size, load, volume, capacity
▷ PLURAL NOUN
3 = constituents, elements, load, ingredients

content² ADJECTIVE

1 = **satisfied**, happy, pleased, contented, comfortable, fulfilled, at ease, gratified

▷ NOUN 2 = **satisfaction**, ease, pleasure, comfort, peace of mind, gratification, contentment

▷ PHRASES: **content yourself with something** = **satisfy yourself with**, be happy with, be satisfied with, be content with

contented = **satisfied**, happy, pleased, content, comfortable, glad, thankful, gratified **OPPOSITE:** discontented

contentious = **argumentative**, wrangling, bickering, quarrelsome, querulous, cavilling, disputatious, captious

contest NOUN

1 = **competition**, game, match, trial, tournament 2 = **struggle**, fight, battle, conflict, dispute, controversy, combat

▷ VERB 3 = **compete in**, take part in, fight in, go in for, contend for, vie in 4 = **oppose**, question, challenge, argue, debate, dispute, object to, call in or into question

contestant = **competitor**, candidate, participant, contender, entrant, player

context 1 = **circumstances**, conditions, situation, ambience 2 = **frame of reference**, background, framework, relation, connection

contingency = **possibility**, happening, chance, event, incident, accident, emergency, eventuality

continual 1 = **constant**, interminable, incessant, unremitting **OPPOSITE:** erratic 2 = **frequent**, regular, repeated, recurrent **OPPOSITE:** occasional

continually 1 = **constantly**, always, all the time, forever, incessantly, nonstop, interminably 2 = **repeatedly**, often, frequently, many times, over and over, persistently

continuation 1 = **continuing**, lasting, carrying on, keeping up, endurance, perpetuation, prolongation 2 = **addition**, extension, supplement, sequel, resumption, postscript

continue 1 = **keep on**, go on, maintain, sustain, carry on, persist in, persevere, stick at **OPPOSITE:** stop 2 = **go on**, progress, proceed, carry on, keep going 3 = **resume**, return to, take up again, proceed, carry on, recommence, pick up where you left off **OPPOSITE:** stop 4 = **remain**, last, stay, survive, carry on, live on, endure, persist **OPPOSITE:** quit

continuing = **lasting**, sustained, enduring, ongoing, in progress

continuity = **cohesion**, flow, connection, sequence, succession, progression

continuous = **constant**,

extended, prolonged, unbroken, uninterrupted, unceasing **OPPOSITE:** occasional

contract NOUN
1 = **agreement**, commitment, arrangement, settlement, bargain, pact, covenant
▷ VERB 2 = **agree**, negotiate, pledge, bargain, undertake, come to terms, covenant, make a deal **OPPOSITE:** refuse
3 = **constrict**, confine, tighten, shorten, compress, condense, shrivel 4 = **tighten**, narrow, shorten **OPPOSITE:** stretch
5 = **lessen**, reduce, shrink, diminish, decrease, dwindle **OPPOSITE:** increase 6 = **catch**, get, develop, acquire, incur, be infected with, go down with, be afflicted with **OPPOSITE:** avoid

contraction 1 = **tightening**, narrowing, shortening, constricting, shrinkage
2 = **abbreviation**, reduction, shortening, compression

contradict 1 = **dispute**, deny, challenge, belie, fly in the face of, be at variance with
2 = **negate**, deny, rebut, controvert **OPPOSITE:** confirm

contradiction 1 = **conflict**, inconsistency, contravention, incongruity 2 = **negation**, opposite, denial

contradictory = **inconsistent**, conflicting, opposed, opposite, contrary, incompatible, paradoxical

contrary ADJECTIVE

1 = **opposite**, different, opposed, clashing, counter, reverse, adverse, contradictory **OPPOSITE:** in agreement
2 = **perverse**, difficult, awkward, intractable, obstinate, stroppy (*Brit. slang*), cantankerous, disobliging **OPPOSITE:** cooperative
▷ NOUN 3 = **opposite**, reverse, converse, antithesis

contrast NOUN 1 = **difference**, opposition, comparison, distinction, foil, disparity, divergence, dissimilarity
▷ VERB 2 = **differentiate**, compare, oppose, distinguish, set in opposition 3 = **differ**, be contrary, be at variance, be dissimilar

contribute = **give**, provide, supply, donate, subscribe, chip in (*informal*), bestow
▷ PHRASES: contribute to something = **be partly responsible for**, lead to, be instrumental in, be conducive to, help

contribution = **gift**, offering, grant, donation, input, subscription, koha (*N.Z.*)

contributor = **donor**, supporter, patron, subscriber, giver

contrive 1 = **devise**, plan, fabricate, create, design, scheme, manufacture, plot
2 = **manage**, succeed, arrange, manoeuvre

contrived = **forced**, planned,

laboured, strained, artificial,
elaborate, unnatural, overdone
OPPOSITE: natural

control NOUN 1 = **power**,
authority, management,
command, guidance,
supervision, supremacy, charge
2 = **restraint**, check, regulation,
brake, limitation, curb 3 = **self-
discipline**, self-restraint,
restraint, self-command
4 = **switch**, instrument, button,
dial, lever, knob
▷ PLURAL NOUN
5 = **instruments**, dash, dials,
console, dashboard, control
panel
▷ VERB 6 = **have power over**,
manage, direct, handle,
command, govern, administer,
supervise 7 = **limit**, restrict,
curb 8 = **restrain**, limit, check,
contain, curb, hold back,
subdue, repress

controversial = **disputed**,
contentious, at issue,
debatable, under discussion,
open to question, disputable

controversy = **argument**,
debate, row, dispute, quarrel,
squabble, wrangling,
altercation

convene 1 = **call**, gather,
assemble, summon, bring
together, convoke 2 = **meet**,
gather, assemble, come
together, congregate

convenience 1 = **benefit**,
good, advantage
2 = **suitability**, fitness,

appropriateness
3 = **usefulness**, utility
OPPOSITE: uselessness
4 = **accessibility**, availability,
nearness 5 = **appliance**,
facility, comfort, amenity,
labour-saving device, help

convenient 1 = **suitable**, fit,
handy, satisfactory 2 = **useful**,
practical, handy, serviceable,
labour-saving **OPPOSITE:**
useless 3 = **nearby**, available,
accessible, handy, at hand,
within reach, close at hand, just
round the corner **OPPOSITE:**
inaccessible 4 = **appropriate**,
timely, suitable, helpful

convention 1 = **custom**,
practice, tradition, code, usage,
protocol, etiquette, propriety,
kawa (N.Z.), tikanga (N.Z.)
2 = **agreement**, contract,
treaty, bargain, pact, protocol
3 = **assembly**, meeting, council,
conference, congress,
convocation, hui (N.Z.), runanga
(N.Z.)

conventional 1 = **proper**,
conservative, respectable,
genteel, conformist
2 = **ordinary**, standard, normal,
regular, usual 3 = **traditional**,
accepted, orthodox, customary
4 = **unoriginal**, routine,
stereotyped, banal, prosaic,
run-of-the-mill, hackneyed
OPPOSITE: unconventional

converge 1 = **come together**,
meet, join, combine, gather,
merge, coincide, intersect

▷ **PHRASES: converge on something = close in on**, arrive at, move towards, home in on, come together at

conversation = talk, discussion, dialogue, tête-à-tête, conference, chat, gossip, discourse, korero (N.Z.)
● **RELATED WORD**
● *adjective*: colloquial

conversion 1 = change, transformation, metamorphosis **2 = adaptation**, reconstruction, modification, alteration, remodelling, reorganization

convert VERB 1 = change, turn, transform, alter, transpose **2 = adapt**, modify, remodel, reorganize, customize, restyle **3 = reform**, convince, proselytize
▷ **NOUN 4 = neophyte**, disciple, proselyte

convey 1 = communicate, impart, reveal, relate, disclose, make known, tell **2 = carry**, transport, move, bring, bear, conduct, fetch

convict VERB 1 = find guilty, sentence, condemn, imprison, pronounce guilty
▷ **NOUN 2 = prisoner**, criminal, lag (*slang*), felon, jailbird

conviction 1 = belief, view, opinion, principle, faith, persuasion, creed, tenet, kaupapa (N.Z.) **2 = certainty**, confidence, assurance, firmness, certitude

convince 1 = assure, persuade, satisfy, reassure **2 = persuade**, induce, coax, talk into, prevail upon, bring round to the idea of
● **USAGE NOTE**
● The use of *convince* to talk
● about persuading someone
● to do something is
● considered by many British
● speakers to be wrong or
● unacceptable. It would be
● preferable to use an
● alternative such as *persuade*
● or *talk into*.

convincing = persuasive, credible, conclusive, telling, powerful, impressive, plausible, cogent **OPPOSITE:** unconvincing

cool ADJECTIVE 1 = cold, chilled, refreshing, chilly, nippy **OPPOSITE:** warm **2 = calm**, collected, relaxed, composed, sedate, self-controlled, unruffled, unemotional **OPPOSITE:** agitated **3 = unfriendly**, distant, indifferent, aloof, lukewarm, offhand, unenthusiastic, unwelcoming **OPPOSITE:** friendly **4 = unenthusiastic**, indifferent, lukewarm, unwelcoming
▷ **VERB 5 = lose heat**, cool off **OPPOSITE:** warm (up) **6 = make cool**, freeze, chill, refrigerate, cool off **OPPOSITE:** warm (up)
▷ **NOUN 7 = coldness**, chill, coolness **8** (*Slang*) **= calmness**, control, temper, composure, self-control, poise, self-discipline, self-possession

cooperate = work together, collaborate, coordinate, join forces, conspire, pull together, pool resources, combine your efforts **OPPOSITE:** conflict

cooperation = teamwork, unity, collaboration, give-and-take, combined effort, esprit de corps, kotahitanga (N.Z.) **OPPOSITE:** opposition

cooperative 1 = shared, joint, combined, collective, collaborative 2 = helpful, obliging, accommodating, supportive, responsive, onside (informal)

cope = manage, get by (informal), struggle through, survive, carry on, make the grade, hold your own
▷ **PHRASES: cope with something** = deal with, handle, struggle with, grapple with, wrestle with, contend with, weather

copy NOUN 1 = reproduction, duplicate, replica, imitation, forgery, counterfeit, likeness, facsimile **OPPOSITE:** original
▷ **VERB** 2 = reproduce, replicate, duplicate, transcribe, counterfeit **OPPOSITE:** create 3 = imitate, act like, emulate, behave like, follow, repeat, mirror, ape

cord = rope, line, string, twine

cordon = chain, line, ring, barrier, picket line
▷ **PHRASES: cordon something off** = surround, isolate, close

off, fence off, separate, enclose, picket, encircle

core 1 = centre 2 = heart, essence, nucleus, kernel, crux, gist, nub, pith

corner NOUN 1 = angle, joint, crook 2 = bend, curve 3 = space, hideaway, nook, hide-out
▷ **VERB** 4 = trap, catch, run to earth 5 (usually with market as object) = monopolize, take over, dominate, control, hog (slang), engross

corporation 1 = business, company, concern, firm, society, association, organization, enterprise 2 = town council, council, municipal authorities, civic authorities

corps = team, unit, regiment, detachment, company, band, division, troop

corpse = body, remains, carcass, cadaver, stiff (slang)

correct ADJECTIVE
1 = accurate, right, true, exact, precise, flawless, faultless, O.K. or okay (informal) **OPPOSITE:** inaccurate 2 = right, standard, appropriate, acceptable, proper, precise 3 = proper, seemly, standard, fitting, kosher (informal) **OPPOSITE:** inappropriate
▷ **VERB** 4 = rectify, remedy, redress, right, reform, cure, adjust, amend **OPPOSITE:** spoil 5 = rebuke, discipline, reprimand, chide, admonish,

chastise, chasten, reprove
OPPOSITE: praise

correction 1 = **rectification**, improvement, amendment, adjustment, modification, alteration, emendation
2 = **punishment**, discipline, reformation, admonition, chastisement, reproof, castigation

correctly = **rightly**, right, perfectly, properly, precisely, accurately

correctness 1 = **truth**, accuracy, precision, exactitude, exactness, faultlessness
2 = **decorum**, propriety, good manners, civility, good breeding

correspond 1 = **be consistent**, match, agree, accord, fit, square, tally, conform
OPPOSITE: differ
2 = **communicate**, write, keep in touch, exchange letters

correspondence
1 = **communication**, writing, contact 2 = **letters**, post, mail
3 = **relation**, match, agreement, comparison, harmony, coincidence, similarity, correlation

correspondent 1 = **reporter**, journalist, contributor, hack
2 = **letter writer**, pen friend or pen pal

corresponding = **equivalent**, matching, similar, related, complementary, reciprocal, analogous

corridor = **passage**, alley, aisle,

hallway, passageway

corrupt ADJECTIVE
1 = **dishonest**, bent (*slang*), crooked (*informal*), fraudulent, unscrupulous, venal, unprincipled **OPPOSITE:** honest
2 = **depraved**, vicious, degenerate, debased, profligate, dissolute
3 = **distorted**, doctored, altered, falsified
▷ VERB 4 = **bribe**, fix (*informal*), buy off, suborn, grease (someone's) palm (*slang*)
5 = **deprave**, pervert, subvert, debauch **OPPOSITE:** reform
6 = **distort**, doctor, tamper with

corruption 1 = **dishonesty**, fraud, bribery, extortion, venality, shady dealings (*informal*) 2 = **depravity**, vice, evil, perversion, decadence, wickedness, immorality
3 = **distortion**, doctoring, falsification

cosmetic = **superficial**, surface, nonessential

cosmic 1 = **extraterrestrial**, stellar 2 = **universal**, general, overarching

cosmopolitan
= **sophisticated**, cultured, refined, cultivated, urbane, well-travelled, worldly-wise
OPPOSITE: unsophisticated

cost NOUN 1 = **price**, worth, expense, charge, damage (*informal*), amount, payment, outlay 2 = **loss**, suffering, damage, injury, penalty, hurt, expense, harm

▷ **PLURAL NOUN 3** = **expenses**, spending, expenditure, overheads, outgoings, outlay, budget

▷ **VERB 4** = **sell at**, come to, set (someone) back (*informal*), be priced at, command a price of **5** = **lose**, deprive of, cheat of

costly 1 = **expensive**, dear, stiff, steep (*informal*), highly-priced, exorbitant, extortionate **OPPOSITE:** inexpensive
2 = **damaging**, disastrous, harmful, catastrophic, loss-making, ruinous, deleterious

costume = **outfit**, dress, clothing, uniform, ensemble, livery, apparel, attire

cosy 1 = **comfortable**, homely, warm, intimate, snug, comfy (*informal*), sheltered **2** = **snug**, warm, comfortable, sheltered, comfy (*informal*), tucked up **3** = **intimate**, friendly, informal

cottage = **cabin**, lodge, hut, shack, chalet, whare (*N.Z.*)

cough VERB 1 = **clear your throat**, bark, hack
▷ **NOUN 2** = **frog or tickle in your throat**, bark, hack

council 1 = **committee**, governing body, board
2 = **governing body**, parliament, congress, cabinet, panel, assembly, convention, conference, runanga (*N.Z.*)

counsel NOUN 1 = **advice**, information, warning, direction,

suggestion, recommendation, guidance **2** = **legal adviser**, lawyer, attorney, solicitor, advocate, barrister
▷ **VERB 3** = **advise**, recommend, advocate, warn, urge, instruct, exhort

count VERB 1 *often with* **up** = **add (up)**, total, reckon (up), tot up, calculate, compute, tally, number **2** = **matter**, be important, carry weight, tell, rate, weigh, signify
3 = **consider**, judge, regard, deem, think of, rate, look upon **4** = **include**, number among, take into account *or* consideration
▷ **NOUN 5** = **calculation**, poll, reckoning, sum, tally, numbering, computation, enumeration
▷ **PHRASES: count on *or* upon something *or* someone** = **depend on**, trust, rely on, bank on, take for granted, lean on, reckon on, take on trust

counter VERB 1 = **oppose**, meet, block, resist, parry, deflect, repel, rebuff
2 = **retaliate**, answer, reply, respond, retort, hit back, rejoin, strike back **OPPOSITE:** yield
▷ **ADVERB 3** = **opposite to**, against, versus, conversely, in defiance of, at variance with, contrariwise **OPPOSITE:** in accordance with

counterpart = **opposite number**, equal, twin,

equivalent, match, fellow, mate
countless = innumerable, legion, infinite, myriad, untold, limitless, incalculable, immeasurable **OPPOSITE:** limited

country 1 = nation, state, land, commonwealth, kingdom, realm, people 2 = people, community, nation, society, citizens, inhabitants, populace, public 3 = countryside, provinces, sticks (*informal*), farmland, outback (*Austral. & N.Z.*), green belt, backwoods, bush (*N.Z. & S. African*) **OPPOSITE:** town 4 = territory, land, region, terrain

countryside = country, rural areas, outback (*Austral. & N.Z.*), green belt, sticks (*informal*)

county = province, district, shire

coup = masterstroke, feat, stunt, action, exploit, manoeuvre, deed, accomplishment

couple = pair, two, brace, duo, twosome
▷ **PHRASES: couple something to something** = link to, connect to, pair with, unite with, join to, hitch to, yoke to

coupon = slip, ticket, certificate, token, voucher, card

courage = bravery, nerve, resolution, daring, pluck, heroism, mettle, gallantry **OPPOSITE:** cowardice

courageous = brave, daring,

bold, gritty, fearless, gallant, intrepid, valiant **OPPOSITE:** cowardly

courier 1 = messenger, runner, carrier, bearer, envoy 2 = guide, representative, escort, conductor

course NOUN 1 = route, way, line, road, track, direction, path, passage 2 = procedure, plan, policy, programme, method, conduct, behaviour, manner 3 = progression, order, unfolding, development, movement, progress, flow, sequence 4 = classes, programme, schedule, lectures, curriculum 5 = racecourse, circuit 6 = period, time, duration, term, passing
▷ **VERB** 7 = run, flow, stream, gush, race, speed, surge 8 = hunt, follow, chase, pursue
▷ **PHRASES: of course** = naturally, certainly, obviously, definitely, undoubtedly, needless to say, without a doubt, indubitably

court NOUN 1 = law court, bar, bench, tribunal 2 = palace, hall, castle, manor 3 = royal household, train, suite, attendants, entourage, retinue, cortege
▷ **VERB** 4 = cultivate, seek, flatter, solicit, pander to, curry favour with, fawn upon 5 = invite, seek, attract, prompt, provoke, bring about, incite 6 = woo, go (out) with,

date, take out, run after, walk out with, set your cap at

courtesy 1 = **politeness**, good manners, civility, gallantry, graciousness, affability, urbanity 2 = **favour**, kindness, indulgence

courtyard = **yard**, square, piazza, quadrangle, plaza, enclosure, cloister, quad (informal)

cove = **bay**, sound, inlet, anchorage

covenant = **promise**, contract, agreement, commitment, arrangement, pledge, pact

cover VERB 1 = **conceal**, hide, mask, disguise, obscure, veil, cloak, shroud OPPOSITE: reveal 2 = **clothe**, dress, wrap, envelop OPPOSITE: uncover 3 = **overlay**, blanket 4 = **coat**, cake, plaster, smear, envelop, spread, encase, daub 5 = **submerge**, flood, engulf, overrun, wash over 6 = **travel over**, cross, traverse, pass through or over 7 = **protect**, guard, defend, shield 8 = **consider**, deal with, investigate, describe, tell of 9 = **report on**, write about, commentate on, relate, tell of, narrate, write up 10 = **pay for**, fund, provide for, offset, be enough for

▷ NOUN 11 = **protection**, shelter, shield, defence, guard, camouflage, concealment 12 = **insurance**, protection, compensation, indemnity, reimbursement 13 = **covering**, case, top, coating, envelope, lid, canopy, wrapper 14 = **bedclothes**, bedding, sheets, blankets, quilt, duvet, eiderdown 15 = **jacket**, case, wrapper 16 = **disguise**, front, screen, mask, veil, façade, pretext, smoke screen

covering NOUN 1 = **cover**, coating, casing, wrapping, layer, blanket

▷ ADJECTIVE 2 = **explanatory**, accompanying, introductory, descriptive

covet = **long for**, desire, envy, crave, aspire to, yearn for, lust after, set your heart on

coward = **wimp**, chicken (slang), scaredy-cat (informal), yellow-belly (slang)

cowardly = **faint-hearted**, scared, spineless, soft, yellow (informal), weak, chicken (slang), fearful, sookie (N.Z.) OPPOSITE: brave

cowboy = **cowhand**, drover, rancher, stockman, cattleman, herdsman, gaucho (S. American)

crack VERB 1 = **break**, split, burst, snap, fracture, splinter 2 = **snap**, ring, crash, burst, explode, pop, detonate 3 (Informal) = **hit**, clip (informal), slap, smack, clout (informal), cuff, whack 4 = **break**, cleave 5 = **solve**, work out, resolve, clear up, fathom, decipher, suss (out) (slang), get to the bottom of 6 = **break down**, collapse, yield, give in, give way, succumb, lose control, be overcome

▷ NOUN 7 = **break**, chink, gap, fracture, rift, cleft, crevice, fissure 8 = **split**, break, fracture 9 = **snap**, pop, crash, burst, explosion, clap, report 10 (*Informal*) = **blow**, slap, smack, clout (*informal*), cuff, whack, clip (*informal*) 11 (*Informal*) = **joke**, dig, gag (*informal*), quip, jibe, wisecrack, witticism, funny remark

▷ ADJECTIVE 12 (*Slang*) = **first-class**, excellent, ace, elite, superior, world-class, first-rate

crackdown = **clampdown**, crushing, repression, suppression

cracked = **broken**, damaged, split, chipped, flawed, faulty, defective, imperfect

cradle NOUN 1 = **crib**, cot, Moses basket, bassinet 2 = **birthplace**, beginning, source, spring, origin, fount, fountainhead, wellspring

▷ VERB 3 = **hold**, support, rock, nurse, nestle

craft 1 = **vessel**, boat, ship, plane, aircraft, spacecraft 2 = **occupation**, work, business, trade, employment, pursuit, vocation, handicraft 3 = **skill**, art, ability, technique, know-how (*informal*), expertise, aptitude, artistry

craftsman = **skilled worker**, artisan, master, maker, wright, technician, smith

cram 1 = **stuff**, force, jam, shove, compress 2 = **pack**, fill, stuff 3 = **squeeze**, press, pack in 4 = **study**, revise, swot, bone up (*informal*), mug up (*slang*)

cramp[1] = **spasm**, pain, ache, contraction, pang, stitch, convulsion, twinge

cramp[2] = **restrict**, hamper, inhibit, hinder, handicap, constrain, obstruct, impede

cramped = **restricted**, confined, overcrowded, crowded, packed, uncomfortable, closed in, congested **OPPOSITE:** spacious

crash NOUN 1 = **collision**, accident, smash, wreck, prang (*informal*), bump, pile-up (*informal*) 2 = **smash**, clash, boom, bang, thunder, racket, din, clatter 3 = **collapse**, failure, depression, ruin, downfall

▷ VERB 4 = **fall**, plunge, topple, lurch, hurtle, overbalance, fall headlong 5 = **plunge**, hurtle 6 = **collapse**, fail, go under, be ruined, go bust (*informal*), fold up, go to the wall, go belly up (*informal*)

▷ PHRASES: **crash into** = **collide with**, hit, bump into, drive into, plough into

crate = **container**, case, box, packing case, tea chest

crater = **hollow**, hole, depression, dip, cavity

crave 1 = **long for**, yearn for, hanker after, want, desire, hope for, lust after 2 (*Informal*) = **beg**, ask for, seek, petition, pray for, plead for, solicit, implore

craving = **longing**, hope, desire, yen (*informal*), hunger, appetite, yearning, thirst

crawl = **creep**, slither, inch, wriggle, writhe, worm your way, advance slowly **OPPOSITE:** run

▷ **PHRASES: crawl to someone** = **grovel**, creep, fawn, toady, humble yourself

craze = **fad**, fashion, trend, rage, enthusiasm, vogue, mania, infatuation

crazed = **mad**, crazy, raving, insane, lunatic, berko (*Austral. slang*), off the air (*Austral. slang*), porangi (*N.Z.*)

crazy 1 (*Informal*) = **ridiculous**, absurd, foolish, ludicrous, senseless, preposterous, idiotic, nonsensical, porangi (*N.Z.*) **OPPOSITE:** sensible 2 = **insane**, mad, unbalanced, deranged, nuts (*slang*), crazed, demented, off the air (*Austral. slang*), out of your mind, porangi (*N.Z.*) **OPPOSITE:** sane 3 = **fanatical**, wild (*informal*), mad, devoted, enthusiastic, passionate, infatuated **OPPOSITE:** uninterested

cream NOUN 1 = **lotion**, ointment, oil, essence, cosmetic, paste, emulsion, salve 2 = **best**, elite, prime, pick,

flower, crème de la crème (*French*)

▷ **ADJECTIVE** 3 = **off-white**, ivory, yellowish-white

▷ **See panel SHADES FROM BLACK TO WHITE**

creamy 1 = **milky**, buttery 2 = **smooth**, soft, velvety, rich

crease NOUN 1 = **fold**, line, ridge, groove, corrugation 2 = **wrinkle**, line, crow's-foot

▷ **VERB** 3 = **crumple**, rumple, fold, double up, corrugate 4 = **wrinkle**, crumple, screw up

create 1 = **cause**, lead to, occasion, bring about 2 = **make**, produce, invent, compose, devise, originate, formulate, spawn **OPPOSITE:** destroy 3 = **appoint**, make, establish, set up, invest, install, constitute

creation 1 = **universe**, world, nature, cosmos 2 = **invention**, production, achievement, brainchild (*informal*), concoction, handiwork, pièce de résistance (*French*), magnum opus (*Latin*) 3 = **making**, generation, formation, conception, genesis 4 = **setting up**, development, production, institution, foundation, establishment, formation, inception

creative = **imaginative**, gifted, artistic, inventive, original, inspired, clever, ingenious

creativity = **imagination**, inspiration, ingenuity,

originality, inventiveness, cleverness

creator 1 = **maker**, father, author, designer, architect, inventor, originator 2 *usually with cap.* = **God**, Maker

creature 1 = **living thing**, being, animal, beast, brute 2 = **person**, man, woman, individual, soul, human being, mortal

credentials 1 = **qualifications**, ability, skill, fitness, attribute, capability, eligibility, aptitude 2 = **certification**, document, reference(s), papers, licence, passport, testimonial, authorization

credibility = **believability**, reliability, plausibility, trustworthiness

credible 1 = **believable**, possible, likely, reasonable, probable, plausible, conceivable, imaginable **OPPOSITE:** unbelievable 2 = **reliable**, honest, dependable, trustworthy, sincere, trusty **OPPOSITE:** unreliable

credit NOUN 1 = **praise**, honour, recognition, approval, tribute, acclaim, acknowledgment, kudos 2 = **source of satisfaction** *or* **pride**, asset, honour, feather in your cap 3 = **prestige**, reputation, standing, position, influence, regard, status, esteem 4 = **belief**, trust,

confidence, faith, reliance, credence ▷ VERB 5 = **believe**, rely on, have faith in, trust, accept ▷ PHRASES: **credit someone with something** = attribute to, assign to, ascribe to, impute to

creed = **belief**, principles, doctrine, dogma, credo, catechism, articles of faith

creek 1 = **inlet**, bay, cove, bight, firth *or* frith (*Scot.*) 2 (*U.S., Canad., Austral. & N.Z.*) = **stream**, brook, tributary, bayou, rivulet, watercourse, runnel

creep VERB 1 = **sneak**, steal, tiptoe, slink, skulk, approach unnoticed ▷ NOUN 2 (*Slang*) = **bootlicker** (*informal*), sneak, sycophant, crawler (*slang*), toady ▷ PHRASES: **give someone the creeps** (*informal*) = **disgust**, frighten, scare, repel, repulse, make your hair stand on end, make you squirm

crescent = **meniscus**, sickle, new moon

crest 1 = **top**, summit, peak, ridge, highest point, pinnacle, apex, crown 2 = **tuft**, crown, comb, plume, mane 3 = **emblem**, badge, symbol, insignia, bearings, device

crew 1 = **(ship's) company**, hands, (ship's) complement 2 = **team**, squad, gang, corps, posse 3 (*Informal*) = **crowd**, set, bunch (*informal*), band, pack, gang, mob, horde

crime 1 = **offence**, violation, trespass, felony, misdemeanour, misdeed, transgression, unlawful act 2 = **lawbreaking**, corruption, illegality, vice, misconduct, wrongdoing

criminal NOUN

1 = **lawbreaker**, convict, offender, crook (*informal*), villain, culprit, sinner, felon, rorter (*Austral. slang*), skelm (*S. African*)

▷ ADJECTIVE 2 = **unlawful**, illicit, lawless, wrong, illegal, corrupt, crooked (*informal*), immoral OPPOSITE: lawful

3 (*Informal*) = **disgraceful**, ridiculous, foolish, senseless, scandalous, preposterous, deplorable

cripple 1 = **disable**, paralyse, lame, maim, incapacitate, weaken, hamstring

2 = **damage**, destroy, ruin, spoil, impair, put paid to, put out of action OPPOSITE: help

crippled = **disabled**, handicapped, paralysed, lame, incapacitated

crisis 1 = **emergency**, plight, predicament, trouble, deep water, meltdown (*informal*), dire straits 2 = **critical point**, climax, height, crunch (*informal*), turning point, culmination, crux, moment of truth

crisp 1 = **firm**, crunchy, crispy, crumbly, fresh, brittle, unwilted OPPOSITE: soft 2 = **bracing**, fresh, refreshing, brisk, invigorating OPPOSITE: warm

3 = **clean**, smart, trim, neat, tidy, spruce, well-groomed, well-pressed

criterion = **standard**, test, rule, measure, principle, gauge, yardstick, touchstone

● USAGE NOTE
● The word *criteria* is the plural
● of *criterion* and it is incorrect
● to use it as an alternative
● singular form; *these criteria are*
● *not valid* is correct, and so is
● *this criterion is not valid*, but
● not *this criteria is not valid*.

critic 1 = **judge**, authority, expert, analyst, commentator, pundit, reviewer, connoisseur 2 = **fault-finder**, attacker, detractor, knocker (*informal*)

critical 1 = **crucial**, decisive, pressing, serious, vital, urgent, all-important, pivotal OPPOSITE: unimportant

2 = **grave**, serious, acute, precarious OPPOSITE: safe

3 = **disparaging**, disapproving, scathing, derogatory, nit-picking (*informal*), censorious, fault-finding, captious OPPOSITE: complimentary

4 = **analytical**, penetrating, discriminating, discerning, perceptive, judicious OPPOSITE: undiscriminating

criticism 1 = **fault-finding**, censure, disapproval, disparagement, stick (*slang*), flak (*informal*), bad press,

character assassination
2 = **analysis**, assessment, judgment, commentary, evaluation, appreciation, appraisal, critique

criticize = **find fault with**, censure, disapprove of, knock (informal), condemn, carp, put down, slate (informal)
OPPOSITE: praise

crook NOUN 1 (Informal) = **criminal**, rogue, cheat, thief, shark, villain, robber, racketeer, skelm (S. African)
▷ ADJECTIVE 2 (Austral. & N.Z. informal) = **ill**, sick, poorly (informal), unhealthy, seedy (informal), unwell, queasy, out of sorts (informal)
▷ PHRASES: **go (off) crook** (Austral. & N.Z. informal) = **lose your temper**, be furious, rage, go mad, lose it (informal), crack up (informal), see red (informal), blow your top

crooked 1 = **bent**, twisted, curved, irregular, warped, out of shape, misshapen **OPPOSITE:** straight 2 = **deformed**, distorted 3 = **zigzag**, winding, twisting 4 = **at an angle**, uneven, slanting, squint, awry, lopsided, askew, off-centre 5 (Informal) = **dishonest**, criminal, illegal, corrupt, unlawful, shady (informal), fraudulent, bent (slang)
OPPOSITE: honest

crop NOUN 1 = **yield**, produce, gathering, fruits, harvest,

vintage, season's growth
▷ VERB 2 = **graze**, eat, browse, feed on, nibble 3 = **cut**, trim, clip, prune, shear, snip, pare, lop
▷ PHRASES: **crop up** (Informal) = **happen**, appear, emerge, occur, arise, turn up, spring up

cross VERB 1 = **go across**, pass over, traverse, cut across, move across, travel across 2 = **span**, bridge, go across, extend over 3 = **intersect**, intertwine, crisscross 4 = **oppose**, interfere with, obstruct, block, resist, impede 5 = **interbreed**, mix, blend, cross-pollinate, crossbreed, hybridize, cross-fertilize, intercross
▷ NOUN 6 = **crucifix** 7 = **trouble**, worry, trial, load, burden, grief, woe, misfortune 8 = **mixture**, combination, blend, amalgam, amalgamation 9 = **crossroads**, crossing, junction, intersection
▷ ADJECTIVE 10 = **angry**, annoyed, put out, grumpy, short, ill-tempered, irascible, tooshie (Austral. slang), in a bad mood, hoha (N.Z.) **OPPOSITE:** good-humoured
▷ PHRASES: **cross something out or off** = **strike off or out**, eliminate, cancel, delete, bluepencil, score off or out

crouch = **bend down**, kneel, squat, stoop, bow, duck, hunch

crow = **gloat**, triumph, boast, swagger, brag, exult, blow your own trumpet

crowd NOUN 1 = **multitude**, mass, throng, army, host, pack, mob, swarm 2 = **group**, set, lot, circle, gang, bunch (*informal*), clique 3 = **audience**, spectators, house, gate, attendance
▷ VERB 4 = **flock**, mass, collect, gather, stream, surge, swarm, throng 5 = **squeeze**, pack, pile, bundle, cram 6 = **congest**, pack, cram

crowded = **packed**, full, busy, cramped, swarming, teeming, congested, jam-packed

crown NOUN 1 = **coronet**, tiara, diadem, circlet 2 = **laurel wreath**, trophy, prize, honour, garland, laurels, wreath 3 = **high point**, top, tip, summit, crest, pinnacle, apex
▷ VERB 4 = **install**, honour, dignify, ordain, inaugurate 5 = **top**, cap, be on top of, surmount 6 = **cap**, finish, complete, perfect, round off, put the finishing touch to, be the climax *or* culmination of 7 (*Slang*) = **strike**, belt (*informal*), bash, hit over the head, box, punch, cuff, biff (*slang*)
▷ PHRASES: **the Crown** 1 = **monarch**, ruler, sovereign, emperor *or* empress, king *or* queen 2 = **monarchy**, sovereignty, royalty

crucial 1 (*Informal*) = **vital**, important, pressing, essential, urgent, momentous, high-priority 2 = **critical**, central, key, psychological, decisive, pivotal

crude 1 = **rough**, basic, makeshift 2 = **simple**, rudimentary, basic, primitive, coarse, clumsy, rough-and-ready 3 = **vulgar**, dirty, rude, obscene, coarse, indecent, tasteless, smutty **OPPOSITE:** tasteful 4 = **unrefined**, natural, raw, unprocessed **OPPOSITE:** processed

crudely 1 = **roughly**, basically 2 = **simply**, roughly, basically, coarsely 3 = **vulgarly**, rudely, coarsely, crassly, obscenely, lewdly, impolitely, tastelessly

cruel 1 = **brutal**, ruthless, callous, sadistic, inhumane, vicious, monstrous, unkind **OPPOSITE:** kind 2 = **bitter**, ruthless, traumatic, grievous, unrelenting, merciless, pitiless

cruelly 1 = **brutally**, severely, mercilessly, in cold blood, callously, monstrously, sadistically, pitilessly 2 = **bitterly**, deeply, severely, ruthlessly, mercilessly, grievously, pitilessly, traumatically

cruelty = **brutality**, ruthlessness, depravity, inhumanity, barbarity, callousness, spitefulness, mercilessness

cruise NOUN 1 = **sail**, voyage, boat trip, sea trip
▷ VERB 2 = **sail**, coast, voyage 3 = **travel along**, coast, drift,

keep a steady pace

crumb 1 = **bit**, grain, fragment, shred, morsel 2 = **morsel**, scrap, shred, snippet, soupçon (*French*)

crumble 1 = **disintegrate**, collapse, deteriorate, decay, fall apart, degenerate, tumble down, go to pieces 2 = **crush**, fragment, pulverize, pound, grind, powder, granulate 3 = **collapse**, deteriorate, decay, fall apart, degenerate, go to pieces

crumple 1 = **crush**, squash, screw up, scrumple 2 = **crease**, wrinkle, rumple, ruffle, pucker 3 = **collapse**, sink, go down, fall 4 = **break down**, fall, collapse, give way, cave in, go to pieces 5 = **screw up**

crunch VERB 1 = **chomp**, champ, munch, chew noisily, grind
▷ NOUN 2 (*Informal*) = **critical point**, test, crisis, emergency, crux, moment of truth

crusade NOUN 1 = **campaign**, drive, movement, cause, push 2 = **holy war**
▷ VERB 3 = **campaign**, fight, push, struggle, lobby, agitate, work

crush VERB 1 = **squash**, break, squeeze, compress, press, pulverize 2 = **crease**, wrinkle, crumple 3 = **overcome**, overwhelm, put down, subdue, overpower, quash, quell, stamp out 4 = **demoralize**, depress,

devastate, discourage, humble, put down (*slang*), humiliate, squash
▷ NOUN 5 = **crowd**, mob, horde, throng, pack, mass, jam, huddle

crust = **layer**, covering, coating, skin, surface, shell

crustacean ▷ *See panel*
CRUSTACEANS

cry VERB 1 = **weep**, sob, shed tears, blubber, snivel OPPOSITE: laugh 2 = **shout**, scream, roar, yell, howl, call out, exclaim, shriek OPPOSITE: whisper
▷ NOUN 3 = **weep**, sob, bawl, blubber 4 = **shout**, call, scream, roar, yell, howl, shriek, bellow 5 = **appeal**, plea
▷ PLURAL NOUN 6 = **weeping**, sobbing, blubbering, snivelling
▷ PHRASES: cry off (*Informal*) = **back out**, withdraw, quit, excuse yourself

cuddle 1 = **hug**, embrace, fondle, cosset 2 = **pet**, hug, bill and coo
▷ PHRASES: cuddle up = **snuggle**

cue = **signal**, sign, hint, prompt, reminder, suggestion

culminate = **end up**, close, finish, conclude, wind up, climax, come to a head, come to a climax

culprit = **offender**, criminal, felon, guilty party, wrongdoer, miscreant, evildoer, transgressor

cult 1 = **sect**, faction, school,

CRUSTACEANS

barnacle
crab
crayfish, crawfish (U.S.), or (Austral. & N.Z. informal) craw
freshwater shrimp
hermit crab
horseshoe crab or king crab
king prawn
koura (N.Z.)
krill
land crab
langoustine
lobster
oyster crab
prawn
robber crab
sand shrimp
scorpion
sea spider
shrimp
soft-shell crab
spider crab
spiny lobster, rock lobster, crawfish, or langouste

religion, clique, hauhau (N.Z.)
2 = **craze**, fashion, trend, fad
3 = **obsession**, worship, devotion, idolization
cultivate 1 = **farm**, work, plant, tend, till, plough
2 = **develop**, establish, foster
3 = **court**, seek out, run after, dance attendance upon
4 = **improve**, refine
cultural 1 = **ethnic**, national, native, folk, racial 2 = **artistic**, educational, aesthetic, enriching, enlightening, civilizing, edifying
culture 1 = **the arts**
2 = **civilization**, society, customs, way of life
3 = **lifestyle**, habit, way of life, mores 4 = **refinement**, education, enlightenment, sophistication, good taste, urbanity
cultured = **refined**, intellectual, educated, sophisticated, enlightened, well-informed, urbane, highbrow **OPPOSITE:** uneducated

cunning ADJECTIVE 1 = **crafty**, sly, devious, artful, sharp, wily, Machiavellian, shifty **OPPOSITE:** frank 2 = **ingenious**, imaginative, sly, devious, artful, Machiavellian 3 = **skilful**, clever **OPPOSITE:** clumsy
▷ NOUN 4 = **craftiness**, guile, trickery, deviousness, artfulness, slyness **OPPOSITE:** candour 5 = **skill**, subtlety, ingenuity, artifice, cleverness
OPPOSITE: clumsiness
cup 1 = **mug**, goblet, chalice, teacup, beaker, bowl
2 = **trophy**
cupboard = **cabinet**, press
curb VERB 1 = **restrain**, control, check, restrict, suppress, inhibit, hinder, retard
▷ NOUN 2 = **restraint**, control, check, brake, limitation, rein, deterrent, bridle
cure VERB 1 = **make better**,

correct, heal, relieve, remedy, mend, ease 2 = **restore to health**, restore, heal
3 = **preserve**, smoke, dry, salt, pickle
▷ NOUN 4 = **remedy**, treatment, antidote, panacea, nostrum

curiosity 1 = **inquisitiveness**, interest, prying, snooping (*informal*), nosiness (*informal*)
2 = **oddity**, wonder, sight, phenomenon, spectacle, freak, novelty, rarity

curious 1 = **inquisitive**, interested, questioning, searching, inquiring, meddling, prying, nosy (*informal*)
OPPOSITE: uninterested
2 = **strange**, unusual, bizarre, odd, novel, rare, extraordinary, unexpected **OPPOSITE:** ordinary

curl NOUN 1 = **ringlet**, lock
2 = **twist**, spiral, coil, kink, whorl 3 = **crimp**, wave, perm
▷ VERB 4 = **twirl**, turn, bend, twist, curve, loop, spiral, coil
5 = **wind**

curly = **wavy**, curled, curling, fuzzy, frizzy

currency 1 = **money**, coinage, legal tender, notes, coins
2 = **acceptance**, popularity, circulation, vogue, prevalence

current NOUN 1 = **flow**, course, undertow, jet, stream, tide, progression, river 2 = **draught**, flow, breeze, puff 3 = **mood**, feeling, spirit, atmosphere, trend, tendency, undercurrent

▷ ADJECTIVE 4 = **present**, fashionable, up-to-date, contemporary, trendy (*Brit. informal*), topical, present-day, in fashion **OPPOSITE:** out-of-date 5 = **prevalent**, common, accepted, popular, widespread, customary, in circulation

curse VERB 1 = **swear**, cuss (*informal*), blaspheme, take the Lord's name in vain 2 = **abuse**, scold, vilify
▷ NOUN 3 = **oath**, obscenity, blasphemy, expletive, profanity, imprecation, swearword
4 = **malediction**, jinx, anathema, hoodoo (*informal*), excommunication
5 = **affliction**, plague, scourge, trouble, torment, hardship, bane

cursed = **under a curse**, damned, doomed, jinxed, bedevilled, accursed, ill-fated

curtail = **reduce**, diminish, decrease, dock, cut back, shorten, lessen, cut short

curtain = **hanging**, drape (*chiefly U.S.*), portière

curve NOUN 1 = **bend**, turn, loop, arc, curvature
▷ VERB 2 = **bend**, turn, wind, twist, arch, snake, arc, coil

curved = **bent**, rounded, twisted, bowed, arched, serpentine, sinuous

cushion NOUN 1 = **pillow**, pad, bolster, headrest, beanbag, hassock

▷ **VERB** 2 = **protect** 3 = **soften**, dampen, muffle, mitigate, deaden, suppress, stifle

custody 1 = **care**, charge, protection, supervision, safekeeping, keeping
2 = **imprisonment**, detention, confinement, incarceration

custom 1 = **tradition**, practice, convention, ritual, policy, rule, usage, kaupapa (*N.Z.*)
2 = **habit**, way, practice, procedure, routine, wont
3 = **customers**, business, trade, patronage

customary 1 = **usual**, common, accepted, established, traditional, normal, ordinary, conventional **OPPOSITE**: unusual
2 = **accustomed**, regular, usual

customer = **client**, consumer, regular (*informal*), buyer, patron, shopper, purchaser

customs = **import charges**, tax, duty, toll, tariff

cut VERB 1 = **slit**, score, slice, slash, pierce, penetrate
2 = **chop**, split, slice, dissect
3 = **carve**, slice 4 = **sever**, cut in two 5 = **shape**, carve, engrave, chisel, form, score, fashion, whittle 6 = **slash**, wound 7 = **clip**, mow, trim, prune, snip, pare, lop 8 = **trim**, shave, snip 9 = **reduce**, lower, slim (down), diminish, slash, decrease, cut back **OPPOSITE**: increase 10 = **abridge**, edit, shorten, curtail, condense,

abbreviate **OPPOSITE**: extend
11 = **delete**, take out, expurgate
12 = **hurt**, wound, upset, sting, hurt someone's feelings
13 (*Informal*) = **ignore**, avoid, slight, blank (*slang*), snub, spurn, cold-shoulder, turn your back on **OPPOSITE**: greet
14 = **cross**, bisect
▷ **NOUN** 15 = **incision**, nick, stroke, slash, slit 16 = **gash**, nick, wound, slash, laceration
17 = **reduction**, fall, lowering, slash, decrease, cutback
18 (*Informal*) = **share**, piece, slice, percentage, portion
19 = **style**, look, fashion, shape

cutback = **reduction**, cut, retrenchment, economy, decrease, lessening

cute = **appealing**, sweet, attractive, engaging, charming, delightful, lovable, winsome

cutting = **hurtful**, wounding, bitter, malicious, scathing, acrimonious, barbed, sarcastic **OPPOSITE**: kind

cycle = **series of events**, circle, revolution, rotation

cyclone = **typhoon**, hurricane, tornado, whirlwind, tempest, twister (*U.S. Informal*)

cynic = **sceptic**, doubter, pessimist, misanthrope, misanthropist, scoffer

cynical 1 = **sceptical**, mocking, pessimistic, scoffing, contemptuous, scornful, distrustful, derisive **OPPOSITE**: trusting 2 = **unbelieving**,

sceptical, disillusioned,
pessimistic, disbelieving,
mistrustful **OPPOSITE:**
optimistic

cynicism 1 = **scepticism**,
pessimism, misanthropy
2 = **disbelief**, doubt, scepticism,
mistrust

cyst = **sac**, growth, blister, wen,
vesicle, bleb

Dd

d

dab VERB 1 = **pat**, touch, tap
2 = **apply**, daub, stipple
▷ NOUN 3 = **spot**, bit, drop, pat,
smudge, speck 4 = **touch**,
stroke, flick

daft (*Informal, chiefly Brit.*)
1 = **stupid**, crazy, silly, absurd,
foolish, idiotic, witless, crackpot
(*informal*), off the air (*Austral.
slang*) 2 = **crazy**, mad, touched,
nuts (*slang*), crackers (*Brit.
slang*), insane, demented,
deranged, off the air (*Austral.
slang*), porangi (*N.Z.*)

dag (*N.Z. informal*) = **joker**,
comic, wag, wit, comedian,
clown, humorist, prankster
▷ PHRASES: rattle your dags
(*N.Z. informal*) = **hurry up**, get a
move on, step on it (*informal*),
get your skates on (*informal*),
make haste

dagga (*S. African*) = **cannabis**,
marijuana, pot (*slang*), dope
(*slang*), hash (*slang*), grass
(*slang*), weed (*slang*), hemp

daily ADVERB 1 = **every day**,
day by day, once a day
▷ ADJECTIVE 2 = **everyday**,
diurnal, quotidian

dam NOUN 1 = **barrier**, wall,

barrage, obstruction, embankment
▷ **VERB** 2 = **block up**, restrict, hold back, barricade, obstruct
damage VERB 1 = **spoil**, hurt, injure, harm, ruin, crush, devastate, wreck **OPPOSITE:** fix
▷ **NOUN** 2 = **destruction**, harm, loss, injury, suffering, hurt, ruin, devastation **OPPOSITE:** improvement 3 (*Informal*) = **cost**, price, charge, bill, amount, payment, expense, outlay
▷ **PLURAL NOUN** 4 (*Law*) = **compensation**, fine, satisfaction, amends, reparation, restitution, reimbursement, atonement
damaging = **harmful**, detrimental, hurtful, ruinous, deleterious, injurious, disadvantageous **OPPOSITE:** helpful
dame = **lady**, baroness, dowager, grande dame (*French*), noblewoman, peeress
damn = **criticize**, condemn, blast, denounce, put down, censure **OPPOSITE:** praise
damned (*Slang*) = **infernal**, detestable, confounded, hateful, loathsome
damp ADJECTIVE 1 = **moist**, wet, soggy, humid, dank, sopping, clammy, dewy **OPPOSITE:** dry
▷ **NOUN** 2 = **moisture**, liquid, drizzle, dampness, wetness, dankness **OPPOSITE:** dryness

▷ **VERB** 3 = **moisten**, wet, soak, dampen, moisturize
▷ **PHRASES:** damp something down = **curb**, reduce, check, diminish, inhibit, stifle, allay, pour cold water on
dampen 1 = **reduce**, check, moderate, dull, restrain, stifle, lessen 2 = **moisten**, wet, spray, make damp
dance VERB 1 = **prance**, trip, hop, skip, sway, whirl, caper, jig 2 = **caper**, trip, spring, jump, bound, skip, frolic, cavort
▷ **NOUN** 3 = **ball**, social, hop (informal), disco, knees-up (*Brit. informal*), discotheque, B and S (*Austral. informal*)
dancer VERB = **ballerina**, Terpsichorean
danger 1 = **jeopardy**, vulnerability 2 = **hazard**, risk, threat, menace, peril, pitfall
dangerous = **perilous**, risky, hazardous, vulnerable, insecure, unsafe, precarious, breakneck **OPPOSITE:** safe
dangerously = **perilously**, alarmingly, precariously, recklessly, riskily, hazardously, unsafely
dangle 1 = **hang**, swing, trail, sway, flap, hang down 2 = **wave** 3 = **offer**, flourish, brandish, flaunt
dare 1 = **risk doing**, venture, presume, make bold (*archaic*), hazard doing 2 = **challenge**, provoke, defy, taunt, goad, throw down the gauntlet

daring ADJECTIVE 1 = **brave**, bold, adventurous, reckless, fearless, audacious, intrepid, daredevil **OPPOSITE:** timid
▷ NOUN 2 = **bravery**, nerve (*informal*), courage, spirit, bottle (*Brit. slang*), pluck, audacity, boldness **OPPOSITE:** timidity

dark ADJECTIVE 1 = **dim**, murky, shady, shadowy, grey, dingy, unlit, poorly lit 2 = **black**, brunette, ebony, dark-skinned, sable, dusky, swarthy **OPPOSITE:** fair 3 = **evil**, foul, sinister, vile, wicked, infernal 4 = **secret**, hidden, mysterious, concealed 5 = **gloomy**, sad, grim, miserable, bleak, dismal, pessimistic, melancholy **OPPOSITE:** cheerful
▷ NOUN 6 = **darkness**, shadows, gloom, dusk, obscurity, murk, dimness, semi-darkness 7 = **night**, twilight, evening, evo (*Austral. slang*), dusk, night-time, nightfall

darken 1 = **cloud**, obscure, dim, overshadow, blacken **OPPOSITE:** brighten 2 = **make dark**, blacken

darkness = **dark**, shadows, shade, gloom, blackness, murk, duskiness

darling NOUN 1 = **beloved**, love, dear, dearest, angel, treasure, precious, sweetheart
▷ ADJECTIVE 2 = **beloved**, dear, treasured, precious, adored, cherished

dart = **dash**, run, race, shoot, fly, speed, spring, tear

dash VERB 1 = **rush**, run, race, shoot, fly, career, speed, tear **OPPOSITE:** dawdle 2 = **throw**, cast, pitch, slam, toss, hurl, fling, chuck (*informal*) 3 = **crash**, break, smash, shatter, splinter
▷ NOUN 4 = **rush**, run, race, sprint, dart, spurt, sortie 5 = **drop**, little, bit, shot (*informal*), touch, spot, trace, hint **OPPOSITE:** lot 6 (*Old-fashioned*) = **style**, spirit, flair, flourish, verve, panache, élan, brio

dashing 1 (*Old-fashioned*) = **stylish**, smart, elegant, flamboyant, sporty, jaunty, showy 2 = **bold**, spirited, gallant, swashbuckling, debonair **OPPOSITE:** dull

data = **information**, facts, figures, details, intelligence, statistics

date NOUN 1 = **time**, stage, period 2 = **appointment**, meeting, arrangement, commitment, engagement, rendezvous, tryst, assignation 3 = **partner**, escort, friend
▷ VERB 4 = **put a date on**, assign a date to, fix the period of 5 = **become dated**, become old-fashioned
▷ PHRASES: **date from** *or* **date back to** (with a *time* or *date* as object) = **come from**, belong to, originate in, exist from, bear a date of

dated = old-fashioned, outdated, out of date, obsolete, unfashionable, outmoded, passé, old hat **OPPOSITE:** modern

daunting = intimidating, alarming, frightening, discouraging, unnerving, disconcerting, demoralizing, off-putting (*Brit. informal*) **OPPOSITE:** reassuring

dawn NOUN 1 = daybreak, morning, sunrise, daylight, aurora (*poetic*), crack of dawn, sunup, cockcrow 2 (*Literary*) = beginning, start, birth, rise, origin, emergence, advent, genesis
▷ VERB 3 = begin, start, rise, develop, emerge, unfold, originate 4 = grow light, break, brighten, lighten
▷ PHRASES: dawn on *or* upon someone = hit, strike, occur to, register (*informal*), become apparent, come to mind, come into your head

day 1 = twenty-four hours 2 = daytime, daylight 3 = date 4 = time, age, era, period, epoch

daylight = sunlight, sunshine, light of day

daze VERB 1 = stun, shock, paralyse, numb, stupefy, benumb
▷ NOUN 2 (usually used in the phrase in a daze) = shock, confusion, distraction, trance, bewilderment, stupor, trancelike state

dazzle VERB 1 = impress, amaze, overwhelm, astonish, overpower, bowl over (*informal*), take your breath away 2 = blind, confuse, daze, bedazzle
▷ NOUN 3 = splendour, sparkle, glitter, brilliance, magnificence, razzmatazz (*slang*)

dazzling = splendid, brilliant, stunning, glorious, sparkling, glittering, sensational (*informal*), virtuoso **OPPOSITE:** ordinary

dead ADJECTIVE 1 = deceased, departed, late, perished, extinct, defunct, passed away **OPPOSITE:** alive 2 = boring, dull, dreary, flat, plain, humdrum, uninteresting 3 = not working, useless, inactive, inoperative **OPPOSITE:** working 4 = numb, frozen, paralysed, insensitive, inert, deadened, immobilized, unfeeling 5 (usually used of centre, silence, or stop) = total, complete, absolute, utter, outright, thorough, unqualified 6 (*Informal*) = exhausted, tired, worn out, spent, done in (*informal*), all in (*slang*), drained, knackered (*slang*)
▷ NOUN 7 = middle, heart, depth, midst
▷ ADVERB 8 (*Informal*) = exactly, completely, totally, directly, fully, entirely, absolutely, thoroughly

deadline = time limit, cutoff

point, target date or time, limit

deadlock 1 = **impasse**, stalemate, standstill, gridlock, standoff 2 = **tie**, draw, stalemate, impasse, standstill, gridlock, standoff, dead heat

deadly 1 = **lethal**, fatal, deathly, dangerous, devastating, mortal, murderous, malignant 2 (*Informal*) = **boring**, dull, tedious, flat, monotonous, uninteresting, mind-numbing, wearisome

deaf 1 = **hard of hearing**, without hearing, stone deaf 2 = **oblivious**, indifferent, unmoved, unconcerned, unsympathetic, impervious, unhearing

deal NOUN 1 (*Informal*) = **agreement**, understanding, contract, arrangement, bargain, transaction, pact 2 = **amount**, quantity, measure, degree, mass, volume, share, portion
▷ PHRASES: **deal in something** = **sell**, trade in, stock, traffic in, buy and sell ▶ **deal something out** = **distribute**, give, share, assign, allocate, dispense, allot, mete out ▶ **deal with something** = **be concerned with**, involve, concern, touch, regard, apply to, bear on, pertain to ▶ **deal with something or someone** = **handle**, manage, treat, cope with, take care of, see to, attend to, get to grips with

dealer = **trader**, merchant, supplier, wholesaler, purveyor, tradesman

dear ADJECTIVE 1 = **beloved**, close, valued, favourite, prized, treasured, precious, intimate **OPPOSITE:** hated 2 (*Brit. informal*) = **expensive**, costly, high-priced, pricey (*informal*), at a premium, overpriced, exorbitant **OPPOSITE:** cheap
▷ NOUN 3 = **darling**, love, dearest, angel, treasure, precious, beloved, loved one

dearly (*Formal*) 1 = **very much**, greatly, extremely, profoundly 2 = **at great cost**, at a high price

death 1 = **dying**, demise, end, passing, departure **OPPOSITE:** birth 2 = **destruction**, finish, ruin, undoing, extinction, downfall **OPPOSITE:** beginning

deathly = **deathlike**, white, pale, ghastly, wan, pallid, ashen

debacle or **débâcle** = **disaster**, catastrophe, fiasco

debate NOUN 1 = **discussion**, talk, argument, dispute, analysis, conversation, controversy, dialogue
▷ VERB 2 = **discuss**, question, talk about, argue about, dispute, examine, deliberate 3 = **consider**, reflect, think about, weigh, contemplate, deliberate, ponder, ruminate

debris = **remains**, bits, waste, ruins, fragments, rubble, wreckage, detritus

debt = debit, commitment, obligation, liability

▷ **PHRASES: in debt** = owing, liable, in the red (*informal*), in arrears

debtor = borrower, mortgagor

debut = entrance, beginning, launch, coming out, introduction, presentation, first appearance, initiation

decay VERB 1 = rot, spoil, crumble, deteriorate, perish, decompose, moulder, go bad 2 = decline, diminish, crumble, deteriorate, fall off, dwindle, lessen, wane **OPPOSITE:** grow

▷ NOUN 3 = rot, corruption, mould, blight, decomposition, gangrene, canker, caries 4 = decline, collapse, deterioration, failing, fading, degeneration **OPPOSITE:** growth

deceased = dead, late, departed, expired, defunct, lifeless

deceive = take in, trick, fool (*informal*), cheat, con (*informal*), mislead, dupe, swindle

decency 1 = propriety, correctness, decorum, respectability, etiquette 2 = courtesy, politeness, civility, graciousness, urbanity, courteousness

decent 1 = satisfactory, fair, all right, reasonable, sufficient, good enough, adequate, ample **OPPOSITE:** unsatisfactory 2 = proper, becoming, seemly,

fitting, appropriate, suitable, respectable, befitting **OPPOSITE:** improper 3 (*Informal*) = good, kind, friendly, neighbourly, generous, helpful, obliging, accommodating 4 = respectable, pure, proper, modest, chaste, decorous

deception 1 = trickery, fraud, deceit, cunning, treachery, guile, legerdemain **OPPOSITE:** honesty 2 = trick, lie, bluff, hoax, decoy, ruse, subterfuge

decide 1 = make a decision, make up your mind, reach or come to a decision, choose, determine, conclude **OPPOSITE:** hesitate 2 = resolve, answer, determine, conclude, clear up, ordain, adjudicate, adjudge 3 = settle, determine, resolve

decidedly = definitely, clearly, positively, distinctly, downright, unequivocally, unmistakably

decision 1 = judgment, finding, ruling, sentence, resolution, conclusion, verdict, decree 2 = decisiveness, purpose, resolution, resolve, determination, firmness, forcefulness, strength of mind or will

decisive 1 = crucial, significant, critical, influential, momentous, conclusive, fateful **OPPOSITE:** uncertain 2 = resolute, decided, firm, determined, forceful, incisive, trenchant, strong-minded **OPPOSITE:** indecisive

deck = **decorate**, dress, clothe, array, adorn, embellish, festoon, beautify

declaration
1 = **announcement**, proclamation, decree, notice, notification, edict, pronouncement
2 = **affirmation**, profession, assertion, revelation, disclosure, acknowledgment, protestation, avowal 3 = **statement**, testimony

declare 1 = **state**, claim, announce, voice, express, maintain, assert, proclaim
2 = **testify**, state, swear, assert, affirm, bear witness, vouch
3 = **make known**, reveal, show, broadcast, confess, communicate, disclose

decline VERB 1 = **fall**, drop, lower, sink, fade, shrink, diminish, decrease OPPOSITE: rise 2 = **deteriorate**, weaken, pine, decay, worsen, languish, degenerate, droop OPPOSITE: improve 3 = **refuse**, reject, turn down, avoid, spurn, abstain, say 'no' OPPOSITE: accept
▷ NOUN 4 = **depression**, recession, slump, falling off, downturn, dwindling, lessening OPPOSITE: rise
5 = **deterioration**, failing, weakening, decay, worsening, degeneration OPPOSITE: improvement

décor or **decor** = **decoration**, colour scheme, ornamentation, furnishing style

decorate 1 = **adorn**, trim, embroider, ornament, embellish, festoon, beautify, grace 2 = **do up**, paper, paint, wallpaper, renovate (*informal*), furbish 3 = **pin a medal on**, cite, confer an honour on or upon

decoration 1 = **adornment**, trimming, enhancement, elaboration, embellishment, ornamentation, beautification
2 = **ornament**, trimmings, garnish, frill, bauble 3 = **medal**, award, star, ribbon, badge

decorative = **ornamental**, fancy, pretty, attractive, for show, embellishing, showy, beautifying

decrease VERB 1 = **drop**, decline, lessen, lower, shrink, diminish, dwindle, subside
2 = **reduce**, cut, lower, moderate, weaken, diminish, cut down, shorten OPPOSITE: increase
▷ NOUN 3 = **lessening**, decline, reduction, loss, falling off, dwindling, contraction, cutback OPPOSITE: growth

decree NOUN 1 = **law**, order, ruling, act, command, statute, proclamation, edict
2 = **judgment**, finding, ruling, decision, verdict, arbitration
▷ VERB 3 = **order**, rule, command, demand, proclaim, prescribe, pronounce, ordain

dedicate 1 = **devote**, give,

apply, commit, pledge, surrender, give over to **2** = **offer**, address, inscribe

dedicated = **committed**, devoted, enthusiastic, single-minded, zealous, purposeful, wholehearted **OPPOSITE:** indifferent

dedication 1 = **commitment**, loyalty, devotion, allegiance, adherence, single-mindedness, faithfulness, wholeheartedness **OPPOSITE:** indifference **2** = **inscription**, message, address

deduct = **subtract**, remove, take off, take away, reduce by, knock off (*informal*), decrease by **OPPOSITE:** add

deduction 1 = **conclusion**, finding, verdict, judgment, assumption, inference **2** = **reasoning**, thinking, thought, analysis, logic **3** = **discount**, reduction, cut, concession, decrease, rebate, diminution **4** = **subtraction**, reduction, concession

deed 1 = **action**, act, performance, achievement, exploit, feat **2** (*Law*) = **document**, title, contract

deep ADJECTIVE **1** = **big**, wide, broad, profound, yawning, bottomless, unfathomable **OPPOSITE:** shallow **2** = **intense**, great, serious (*informal*), acute, extreme, grave, profound, heartfelt **OPPOSITE:** superficial **3** = **sound**, profound, unbroken,

undisturbed, untroubled **4** = **absorbed**, lost, gripped, preoccupied, immersed, engrossed, rapt **5** = **dark**, strong, rich, intense, vivid **OPPOSITE:** light **6** = **low**, booming, bass, resonant, sonorous, low-pitched **OPPOSITE:** high **7** = **secret**, hidden, mysterious, obscure, abstract, esoteric, mystifying, arcane **8** = **far**, a long way, a good way, miles, a great distance

▷ NOUN **9** = **middle**, heart, midst, dead

▷ PHRASES: **the deep** (*Poetic*) = **the ocean**, the sea, the waves, the main, the high seas, the briny (*informal*)

deepen 1 = **intensify**, increase, grow, strengthen, reinforce, escalate, magnify **2** = **dig out**, excavate, scoop out, hollow out

deeply = **thoroughly**, completely, seriously, sadly, severely, gravely, profoundly, intensely

de facto ADJECTIVE **1** = **actual**, real, existing **

▷ ADVERB **2** = **in fact**, really, actually, in effect, in reality

default VERB **1** = **fail to pay**, dodge, evade, neglect **

▷ NOUN **2** (usually in phrase *by default* or *in default of*) = **failure**, neglect, deficiency, lapse, omission, dereliction **3** = **nonpayment**, evasion

defeat VERB **1** = **beat**, crush,

overwhelm, conquer, master, rout, trounce, vanquish **OPPOSITE:** surrender
2 = **frustrate**, foil, thwart, ruin, baffle, confound, balk, get the better of
▷ NOUN 3 = **conquest**, beating, overthrow, rout **OPPOSITE:** victory 4 = **frustration**, failure, reverse, setback, thwarting

defect NOUN 1 = **deficiency**, failing, fault, error, flaw, imperfection
▷ VERB 2 = **desert**, rebel, quit, revolt, change sides

defence or (U.S.) **defense** NOUN 1 = **protection**, cover, security, guard, shelter, safeguard, immunity
2 = **armaments**, weapons
3 = **argument**, explanation, excuse, plea, justification, vindication, rationalization
4 = **plea** (Law), testimony, denial, alibi, rebuttal
▷ PLURAL NOUN 5 = **shield**, barricade, fortification, buttress, rampart, bulwark, fortified pa (N.Z.)

defend 1 = **protect**, cover, guard, screen, preserve, look after, shelter, shield
2 = **support**, champion, justify, endorse, uphold, vindicate, stand up for, speak up for

defendant = **the accused**, respondent, prisoner at the bar

defender 1 = **supporter**, champion, advocate, sponsor, follower 2 = **protector**, guard,

guardian, escort, bodyguard

defensive 1 = **protective**, watchful, on the defensive, on guard 2 = **oversensitive**, uptight (informal)

defer = **postpone**, delay, put off, suspend, shelve, hold over, procrastinate, put on ice (informal)

defiance = **resistance**, opposition, confrontation, contempt, disregard, disobedience, insolence, insubordination **OPPOSITE:** obedience

defiant = **resisting**, rebellious, daring, bold, provocative, audacious, antagonistic, insolent **OPPOSITE:** obedient

deficiency 1 = **lack**, want, deficit, absence, shortage, scarcity, dearth **OPPOSITE:** sufficiency 2 = **failing**, fault, weakness, defect, flaw, drawback, shortcoming, imperfection

deficit = **shortfall**, shortage, deficiency, loss, arrears

define 1 = **mark out**, outline, limit, bound, delineate, circumscribe, demarcate
2 = **describe**, interpret, characterize, explain, spell out, expound 3 = **establish**, specify, designate

definite 1 = **specific**, exact, precise, clear, particular, fixed, black-and-white, cut-and-dried (informal) **OPPOSITE:** vague
2 = **clear**, black-and-white,

unequivocal, unambiguous, guaranteed, cut-and-dried (*informal*) 3 = **noticeable**, marked, clear, decided, striking, particular, distinct, conspicuous 4 = **certain**, decided, sure, settled, convinced, positive, confident, assured **OPPOSITE:** uncertain

definitely = **certainly**, clearly, surely, absolutely, positively, without doubt, unquestionably, undeniably

definition 1 = **description**, interpretation, explanation, clarification, exposition, elucidation, statement of meaning 2 = **sharpness**, focus, clarity, contrast, precision, distinctness

definitive 1 = **final**, convincing, absolute, clinching, decisive, definite, conclusive, irrefutable 2 = **authoritative**, greatest, ultimate, reliable, exhaustive, superlative

deflect = **turn aside**, bend

defy = **resist**, oppose, confront, brave, disregard, stand up to, spurn, flout

degenerate VERB 1 = **decline**, slip, sink, decrease, deteriorate, worsen, decay, lapse ▷ ADJECTIVE 2 = **depraved**, corrupt, low, perverted, immoral, decadent, debauched, dissolute

degrade = **demean**, disgrace, humiliate, shame, humble, discredit, debase, dishonour

OPPOSITE: ennoble

degree = **amount**, stage, grade

delay VERB 1 = **put off**, suspend, postpone, shelve, defer, hold over 2 = **hold up**, detain, hold back, hinder, obstruct, impede, bog down, set back **OPPOSITE:** speed (up) ▷ NOUN 3 = **hold-up**, wait, setback, interruption, stoppage, impediment, hindrance

delegate NOUN 1 = **representative**, agent, deputy, ambassador, commissioner, envoy, proxy, legate ▷ VERB 2 = **entrust**, transfer, hand over, give, pass on, assign, consign, devolve 3 = **appoint**, commission, select, contract, engage, nominate, designate, mandate

delegation 1 = **deputation**, envoys, contingent, commission, embassy, legation 2 = **commissioning**, assignment, devolution, committal

delete = **remove**, cancel, erase, strike out, obliterate, efface, cross out, expunge

deliberate ADJECTIVE 1 = **intentional**, meant, planned, intended, conscious, calculated, wilful, purposeful **OPPOSITE:** accidental 2 = **careful**, measured, slow, cautious, thoughtful, circumspect, methodical, unhurried **OPPOSITE:** hurried

▷ **VERB 3** = **consider**, think, ponder, discuss, debate, reflect, consult, weigh

deliberately = **intentionally**, on purpose, consciously, knowingly, wilfully, by design, in cold blood, wittingly

deliberation
1 = **consideration**, thought, reflection, calculation, meditation, forethought, circumspection **2** = **discussion**, talk, conference, debate, analysis, conversation, dialogue, consultation

delicacy 1 = **fragility**, flimsiness **2** = **daintiness**, charm, grace, elegance, neatness, prettiness, slenderness, exquisiteness **3** = **difficulty 4** = **sensitivity**, understanding, consideration, diplomacy, discretion, tact, thoughtfulness, sensitiveness **5** = **treat**, luxury, savoury, dainty, morsel, titbit **6** = **lightness**, accuracy, precision, elegance, sensibility, purity, subtlety, refinement

delicate 1 = **fine**, elegant, exquisite, graceful **2** = **subtle**, fine, delicious, faint, refined, understated, dainty **OPPOSITE:** bright **3** = **fragile**, weak, frail, brittle, tender, flimsy, dainty, breakable **4** = **skilled**, precise, deft **5** = **diplomatic**, sensitive, thoughtful, discreet, considerate, tactful **OPPOSITE:** insensitive

delicious = **delectable**, tasty, choice, savoury, dainty, mouthwatering, scrumptious (*informal*), appetizing, lekker (*S. African slang*), yummo (*Austral. slang*) **OPPOSITE:** unpleasant

delight NOUN 1 = **pleasure**, joy, satisfaction, happiness, ecstasy, enjoyment, bliss, glee **OPPOSITE:** displeasure
▷ **VERB 2** = **please**, satisfy, thrill, charm, cheer, amuse, enchant, gratify **OPPOSITE:** displease
▷ **PHRASES: delight in** *or* **take (a) delight in something** *or* **someone** = **like**, love, enjoy, appreciate, relish, savour, revel in, take pleasure in

delightful = **pleasant**, charming, thrilling, enjoyable, enchanting, agreeable, pleasurable, rapturous **OPPOSITE:** unpleasant

deliver 1 = **bring**, carry, bear, transport, distribute, convey, cart **2** *sometimes with* **up** = **hand over**, commit, give up, yield, surrender, turn over, relinquish, make over **3** = **give**, read, present, announce, declare, utter **4** = **strike**, give, deal, launch, direct, aim, administer, inflict **5** (*Dated*) = **release**, free, save, rescue, loose, liberate, ransom, emancipate

delivery 1 = **handing over**, transfer, distribution,

transmission, dispatch, consignment, conveyance **2** = **consignment**, goods, shipment, batch **3** = **speech**, utterance, articulation, intonation, elocution, enunciation **4** = **childbirth**, labour, confinement, parturition

delusion = **misconception**, mistaken idea, misapprehension, fancy, illusion, hallucination, fallacy, false impression

demand VERB **1** = **request**, ask (for), order, expect, claim, seek, insist on, exact **2** = **challenge**, ask, question, inquire **3** = **require**, want, need, involve, call for, entail, necessitate, cry out for **OPPOSITE:** provide ▷ NOUN **4** = **request**, order **5** = **need**, want, call, market, claim, requirement

demanding = **difficult**, trying, hard, taxing, wearing, challenging, tough, exacting **OPPOSITE:** easy

demise 1 = **failure**, end, fall, defeat, collapse, ruin, breakdown, overthrow **2** (*Euphemistic*) = **death**, end, dying, passing, departure

democracy = **self-government**, republic, commonwealth

Democrat ADJECTIVE **1** = **left-wing**, Labour, Liberal ▷ NOUN **2** = **left-winger**, Labour, Liberal

democratic = **self-governing**, popular, representative, autonomous, populist, egalitarian

demolish 1 = **knock down**, level, destroy, dismantle, flatten, tear down, bulldoze, raze **OPPOSITE:** build **2** = **destroy**, wreck, overturn, overthrow, undo

demolition = **knocking down**, levelling, destruction, explosion, wrecking, tearing down, bulldozing, razing

demon 1 = **evil spirit**, devil, fiend, goblin, ghoul, malignant spirit, atua (N.Z.), wairua (N.Z.) **2** = **wizard**, master, ace (*informal*), fiend

demonstrate 1 = **prove**, show, indicate, make clear, manifest, testify to **2** = **show**, express, display, indicate, exhibit, manifest **3** = **march**, protest, rally, object, parade, picket, remonstrate, express disapproval, hikoi (N.Z.) **4** = **describe**, show, explain, teach, illustrate

demonstration 1 = **march**, protest, rally, sit-in, parade, picket, mass lobby, hikoi (N.Z.) **2** = **display**, show, performance, explanation, description, presentation, exposition **3** = **indication**, proof, testimony, confirmation, substantiation **4** = **exhibition**, display, expression, illustration

den 1 = **lair**, hole, shelter, cave, haunt, cavern, hide-out 2 (*Chiefly U.S.*) = **study**, retreat, sanctuary, hideaway, sanctum, cubbyhole

denial 1 = **negation**, contradiction, dissent, retraction, repudiation **OPPOSITE:** admission 2 = **refusal**, veto, rejection, prohibition, rebuff, repulse 3 = **renunciation**, giving up, rejection, abdication, repudiation, forswearing, disavowal, relinquishment

denomination 1 = **religious group**, belief, sect, persuasion, creed, school, hauhau (*N.Z.*) 2 = **unit**, value, size, grade

denounce 1 = **condemn**, attack, censure, revile, vilify, stigmatize 2 = **report**, dob in (*Austral. slang*)

dense 1 = **thick**, heavy, solid, compact, condensed, impenetrable, close-knit **OPPOSITE:** thin 2 = **heavy**, thick, opaque, impenetrable 3 = **stupid** (*Informal*), thick, dull, dumb (*informal*), dozy (*Brit. informal*), stolid, dopey (*informal*), moronic **OPPOSITE:** bright

density 1 = **tightness**, thickness, compactness, impenetrability, denseness 2 = **mass**, bulk, consistency, solidity

dent VERB 1 = **make a dent in**, press in, gouge, hollow, push in

▷ NOUN 2 = **hollow**, chip, indentation, depression, impression, pit, dip, crater, ding (*Austral. & N.Z. dated informal*)

deny 1 = **contradict**, disagree with, rebuff, negate, rebut, refute **OPPOSITE:** admit 2 = **renounce**, reject, retract, repudiate, disown, recant, disclaim 3 = **refuse**, forbid, reject, rule out, turn down, prohibit, withhold, preclude **OPPOSITE:** permit

depart 1 = **leave**, go, withdraw, retire, disappear, quit, retreat, exit **OPPOSITE:** arrive 2 = **deviate**, vary, differ, stray, veer, swerve, diverge, digress

department = **section**, office, unit, station, division, branch, bureau, subdivision

departure 1 = **leaving**, going, retirement, withdrawal, exit, going away, removal, exodus **OPPOSITE:** arrival 2 = **retirement**, going, withdrawal, exit, going away, removal 3 = **shift**, change, difference, variation, innovation, novelty, deviation, divergence

depend 1 = **be determined by**, be based on, be subject to, hang on, rest on, revolve around, hinge on, be subordinate to 2 = **count on**, turn to, trust in, bank on, lean on, rely upon, reckon on

dependent or (*U.S. sometimes*) **dependant** = **reliant**,

d

vulnerable, helpless, powerless, weak, defenceless **OPPOSITE:** independent

▷ **PHRASES: dependent on** or **upon 1 = reliant on**, relying on **2 = determined by**, depending on, subject to, influenced by, conditional on, contingent on

depict 1 = illustrate, portray, picture, paint, outline, draw, sketch, delineate **2 = describe**, present, represent, outline, characterize

deplete = use up, reduce, drain, exhaust, consume, empty, lessen, impoverish **OPPOSITE:** increase

deplore = disapprove of, condemn, object to, denounce, censure, abhor, take a dim view of

deploy (used of troops or military resources) **= use**, station, position, arrange, set out, utilize

deployment (used of troops or military resources) **= use**, stationing, spread, organization, arrangement, positioning, utilization

deport = expel, exile, throw out, oust, banish, expatriate, extradite, evict

depose = oust, dismiss, displace, demote, dethrone, remove from office

deposit NOUN **1 = down payment**, security, stake, pledge, instalment, retainer, part payment

2 = accumulation, mass, build-up, layer **3 = sediment**, grounds, residue, lees, precipitate, silt, dregs

▷ VERB **4 = put**, place, lay, drop **5 = store**, keep, put, bank, lodge, entrust, consign

depot 1 = arsenal, warehouse, storehouse, repository, depository **2** (*Chiefly U.S. & Canad.*) **= bus station**, station, garage, terminus

depreciation = devaluation, fall, drop, depression, slump, deflation

depress 1 = sadden, upset, distress, discourage, grieve, oppress, weigh down, make sad **OPPOSITE:** cheer **2 = lower**, cut, reduce, diminish, decrease, lessen **OPPOSITE:** raise **3 = devalue**, depreciate, cheapen **4 = press down**, push, squeeze, lower, flatten, compress, push down

depressed 1 = sad, blue, unhappy, discouraged, fed up, mournful, dejected, despondent **2 = poverty-stricken**, poor, deprived, disadvantaged, run-down, impoverished, needy **3 = lowered**, devalued, weakened, depreciated, cheapened **4 = sunken**, hollow, recessed, indented, concave

depressing = bleak, sad, discouraging, gloomy, dismal, harrowing, saddening, dispiriting

depression 1 = despair,

d

misery, sadness, dumps (*informal*), the blues, melancholy, unhappiness, despondency 2 = **recession**, slump, economic decline, stagnation, inactivity, hard or bad times 3 = **hollow**, pit, dip, bowl, valley, dent, cavity, indentation

deprivation 1 = **lack**, denial, withdrawal, removal, expropriation, dispossession 2 = **want**, need, hardship, suffering, distress, privation, destitution

deprive = **dispossess**, rob, strip, despoil, bereave

deprived = **poor**, disadvantaged, needy, in need, lacking, bereft, destitute, down at heel **OPPOSITE:** prosperous

depth 1 = **deepness**, drop, measure, extent 2 = **insight**, wisdom, penetration, profundity, discernment, sagacity, astuteness, profoundness **OPPOSITE:** superficiality 3 = **breadth**

deputy = **substitute**, representative, delegate, lieutenant, proxy, surrogate, second-in-command, legate

derelict ADJECTIVE 1 = **abandoned**, deserted, ruined, neglected, discarded, forsaken, dilapidated ▷ NOUN 2 = **tramp**, outcast, drifter, down-and-out, vagrant, bag lady, derro (*Austral. slang*)

descend 1 = **fall**, drop, sink, go down, plunge, dive, tumble, plummet **OPPOSITE:** rise 2 = **get off** 3 = **go down**, come down, walk down, move down, climb down 4 = **slope**, dip, incline, slant ▷ PHRASES: be descended from = **originate from**, derive from, spring from, proceed from, issue from

descent 1 = **fall**, drop, plunge, coming down, swoop 2 = **slope**, drop, dip, incline, slant, declivity 3 = **decline**, deterioration, degeneration 4 = **origin**, extraction, ancestry, lineage, family tree, parentage, genealogy, derivation

describe 1 = **relate**, tell, report, explain, express, recount, recite, narrate 2 = **portray**, depict 3 = **trace**, draw, outline, mark out, delineate

description 1 = **account**, report, explanation, representation, sketch, narrative, portrayal, depiction 2 = **calling**, naming, branding, labelling, dubbing, designation 3 = **kind**, sort, type, order, class, variety, brand, category

desert¹ = **wilderness**, waste, wilds, wasteland

desert² 1 = **abandon**, leave, quit (*informal*), forsake 2 = **leave**, abandon, strand, maroon, walk out on (*informal*), forsake, jilt, leave stranded **OPPOSITE:** take care of 3 = **abscond**

deserted 1 = **empty**, abandoned, desolate, neglected, vacant, derelict, unoccupied 2 = **abandoned**, neglected, forsaken

deserve = **merit**, warrant, be entitled to, have a right to, rate, earn, justify, be worthy of

deserved = **well-earned**, fitting, due, earned, justified, merited, proper, warranted

deserving = **worthy**, righteous, commendable, laudable, praiseworthy, meritorious, estimable **OPPOSITE:** undeserving

design VERB 1 = **plan**, draw, draft, trace, outline, devise, sketch, formulate 2 = **create**, plan, fashion, propose, invent, conceive, originate, fabricate 3 = **intend**, mean, plan, aim, purpose
▷ NOUN 4 = **pattern**, form, style, shape, organization, arrangement, construction 5 = **plan**, drawing, model, scheme, draft, outline, sketch, blueprint 6 = **intention**, end, aim, goal, target, purpose, object, objective

designate 1 = **name**, call, term, style, label, entitle, dub 2 = **choose**, reserve, select, label, flag, assign, allocate, set aside 3 = **appoint**, name, choose, commission, select, elect, delegate, nominate

designer 1 = **couturier** 2 = **producer**, architect, deviser, creator, planner, inventor, originator

desirable 1 = **advantageous**, useful, valuable, helpful, profitable, of service, convenient, worthwhile **OPPOSITE:** disadvantageous 2 = **popular**, sought-after **OPPOSITE:** unpopular 3 = **attractive**, appealing, pretty, fair, inviting, lovely, charming, sexy (*informal*) **OPPOSITE:** unattractive

desire NOUN 1 = **wish**, want, longing, hope, urge, aspiration, craving, thirst 2 = **lust**, passion, libido, appetite, lasciviousness
▷ VERB 3 = **want**, long for, crave, hope for, ache for, wish for, yearn for, thirst for

despair NOUN
1 = **despondency**, depression, misery, gloom, desperation, anguish, hopelessness, dejection
▷ VERB 2 = **lose hope**, give up, lose heart

despatch ▷ *See* DISPATCH

desperate 1 = **grave**, pressing, serious, severe, extreme, urgent, drastic 2 = **last-ditch**, daring, furious, risky, frantic, audacious

desperately = **gravely**, badly, seriously, severely, dangerously, perilously

desperation 1 = **misery**, worry, trouble, despair, agony, anguish, unhappiness, hopelessness 2 = **recklessness**, madness, frenzy, impetuosity, rashness, foolhardiness

despise = **look down on**, loathe, scorn, detest, revile, abhor **OPPOSITE:** admire

despite = **in spite of**, in the face of, regardless of, even with, notwithstanding, in the teeth of, undeterred by

destination = **stop**, station, haven, resting-place, terminus, journey's end

destined = **fated**, meant, intended, certain, bound, doomed, predestined

destiny 1 = **fate**, fortune, lot, portion, doom, nemesis 2 *usually cap.* = **fortune**, chance, karma, providence, kismet, predestination, divine will

destroy 1 = **ruin**, crush, devastate, wreck, shatter, wipe out, demolish, eradicate 2 = **slaughter**, kill

destruction 1 = **ruin**, havoc, wreckage, demolition, devastation, annihilation 2 slaughter, extermination, eradication 3 = **slaughter**

destructive = **devastating**, fatal, deadly, lethal, harmful, damaging, catastrophic, ruinous

detach 1 = **separate**, remove, divide, cut off, sever, disconnect, tear off, disengage **OPPOSITE:** attach 2 = **free**, remove, separate, isolate, cut off, disengage

detached 1 = **objective**, neutral, impartial, reserved, impersonal, disinterested, unbiased, dispassionate **OPPOSITE:** subjective 2 = **separate**, disconnected, discrete, unconnected, undivided

detachment 1 = **indifference**, fairness, neutrality, objectivity, impartiality, coolness, remoteness, nonchalance 2 (*Military*) = **unit**, party, force, body, squad, patrol, task force

detail NOUN 1 = **point**, fact, feature, particular, respect, factor, element, aspect 2 = **fine point**, particular, nicety, triviality 3 (*Military*) = **party**, force, body, duty, squad, assignment, fatigue, detachment ▷ VERB 4 = **list**, relate, catalogue, recount, rehearse, recite, enumerate, itemize

detailed = **comprehensive**, full, complete, minute, particular, thorough, exhaustive, all-embracing **OPPOSITE:** brief

detain 1 = **hold**, arrest, confine, restrain, imprison, intern, take prisoner, hold in custody 2 = **delay**, hold up, hamper, hinder, retard, impede, keep back, slow up *or* down

detect 1 = **discover**, find, uncover, track down, unmask 2 = **notice**, see, spot, note, identify, observe, recognize, perceive

d

detective = **investigator**, cop (*slang*), private eye, sleuth (*informal*), private investigator, gumshoe (*U.S. slang*)

detention = **imprisonment**, custody, quarantine, confinement, incarceration **OPPOSITE:** release

deter 1 = **discourage**, inhibit, put off, frighten, intimidate, dissuade, talk out of 2 = **prevent**, stop

deteriorate = **decline**, worsen, degenerate, slump, go downhill **OPPOSITE:** improve

determination = **resolution**, purpose, resolve, dedication, fortitude, persistence, tenacity, perseverance **OPPOSITE:** indecision

determine 1 = **affect**, decide, regulate, ordain 2 = **settle**, learn, establish, discover, find out, work out, detect, verify 3 = **decide on**, choose, elect, resolve 4 = **decide**, conclude, resolve, make up your mind

determined = **resolute**, firm, dogged, intent, persistent, persevering, single-minded, tenacious

deterrent = **discouragement**, obstacle, curb, restraint, impediment, check, hindrance, disincentive **OPPOSITE:** incentive

devastate = **destroy**, ruin, sack, wreck, demolish, level, ravage, raze

devastation = **destruction**, ruin, havoc, demolition, desolation

develop 1 = **grow**, advance, progress, mature, evolve, flourish, ripen 2 = **establish**, set up, promote, generate, undertake, initiate, embark on, cultivate 3 = **form**, establish, breed, generate, originate 4 = **expand**, extend, work out, elaborate, unfold, enlarge, broaden, amplify

development 1 = **growth**, increase, advance, progress, spread, expansion, evolution, enlargement 2 = **establishment**, forming, generation, institution, invention, initiation, inauguration, instigation 3 = **event**, happening, result, incident, improvement, evolution, unfolding, occurrence

deviant ADJECTIVE 1 = **perverted**, sick (*informal*), twisted, warped, kinky (*slang*) **OPPOSITE:** normal
▷ NOUN 2 = **pervert**, freak, misfit

device 1 = **gadget**, machine, tool, instrument, implement, appliance, apparatus, contraption 2 = **ploy**, scheme, plan, trick, manoeuvre, gambit, stratagem, wile

devil 1 = **evil spirit**, demon, fiend, atua (*N.Z.*), wairua (*N.Z.*) 2 = **brute**, monster, beast, barbarian, fiend, terror, swine,

ogre **3** = **person**, individual, soul, creature, thing, beggar **4** = **scamp**, rogue, rascal, scoundrel, scallywag (*informal*), nointer (*Austral. slang*)
▷ **PHRASES: the Devil** = **Satan**, Lucifer, Prince of Darkness, Mephistopheles, Evil One, Beelzebub, Old Nick (*informal*)

devise = **work out**, design, construct, invent, conceive, formulate, contrive, dream up

devoid *with* **of** = **lacking in**, without, free from, wanting in, bereft of, empty of, deficient in

devote = **dedicate**, give, commit, apply, reserve, pledge, surrender, assign

devoted = **dedicated**, committed, true, constant, loyal, faithful, ardent, staunch **OPPOSITE:** disloyal

devotee = **enthusiast**, fan, supporter, follower, admirer, buff (*informal*), fanatic, adherent

devotion NOUN **1** = **love**, passion, affection, attachment, fondness **2** = **dedication**, commitment, loyalty, allegiance, fidelity, adherence, constancy, faithfulness **OPPOSITE:** indifference
3 = **worship**, reverence, spirituality, holiness, piety, godliness, devoutness **OPPOSITE:** irreverence
▷ **PLURAL NOUN 4** = **prayers**, religious observance, church service, divine office

devour 1 = **eat**, consume, swallow, wolf, gulp, gobble, guzzle, polish off (*informal*) **2** = **enjoy**, take in, read compulsively *or* voraciously

devout = **religious**, godly, pious, pure, holy, orthodox, saintly, reverent **OPPOSITE:** irreverent

diagnose = **identify**, determine, recognize, distinguish, interpret, pronounce, pinpoint

diagnosis = **identification**, discovery, recognition, detection

diagram = **plan**, figure, drawing, chart, representation, sketch, graph

dialogue 1 = **discussion**, conference, exchange, debate **2** = **conversation**, discussion, communication, discourse

diary 1 = **journal**, chronicle **2** = **engagement book**, Filofax ®, appointment book

dictate VERB **1** = **speak**, say, utter, read out
▷ NOUN **2** = **command**, order, decree, demand, direction, injunction, fiat, edict
3 = **principle**, law, rule, standard, code, criterion, maxim
▷ **PHRASES: dictate to someone** = **order (about)**, direct, lay down the law, pronounce to

dictator = **absolute ruler**, tyrant, despot, oppressor, autocrat, absolutist, martinet

dictatorship = **absolute rule**,

tyranny, totalitarianism, authoritarianism, despotism, autocracy, absolutism

dictionary = wordbook, vocabulary, glossary, lexicon

die VERB **1** = **pass away**, expire, perish, croak (*slang*), give up the ghost, snuff it (*slang*), peg out (*informal*), kick the bucket (*slang*), cark it (*Austral. & N.Z. slang*) **OPPOSITE:** live **2** = **stop**, fail, halt, break down, run down, stop working, peter out, fizzle out **3** = **dwindle**, decline, sink, fade, diminish, decrease, decay, wither **OPPOSITE:** increase

▷ **PHRASES: be dying for something** = **long for**, want, desire, crave, yearn for, hunger for, pine for, hanker after

diet¹ NOUN **1** = **food**, provisions, fare, rations, kai (*N.Z. informal*), nourishment, sustenance, victuals **2** = **fast**, regime, abstinence, regimen ▷ VERB **3** = **slim**, fast, lose weight, abstain, eat sparingly **OPPOSITE:** overindulge

diet² *often cap.* = **council**, meeting, parliament, congress, chamber, convention, legislature

differ 1 = **be dissimilar**, contradict, contrast with, vary, belie, depart from, diverge, negate **OPPOSITE:** accord **2** = **disagree**, clash, dispute, dissent **OPPOSITE:** agree

difference 1 = **dissimilarity**, contrast, variation, change, variety, diversity, alteration, discrepancy **OPPOSITE:** similarity **2** = **remainder**, rest, balance, remains, excess **3** = **disagreement**, conflict, argument, clash, dispute, quarrel, contretemps **OPPOSITE:** agreement

different 1 = **dissimilar**, opposed, contrasting, changed, unlike, altered, inconsistent, disparate **2** = **various**, varied, diverse, assorted, miscellaneous, sundry **3** = **unusual**, special, strange, extraordinary, distinctive, peculiar, uncommon, singular

● **USAGE NOTE**
● On the whole, *different from* is
● preferable to *different to* and
● *different than*, both of which
● are considered unacceptable
● by some people. *Different to* is
● often heard in British English,
● but is thought by some
● people to be incorrect; and
● *different than*, though
● acceptable in American
● English, is often regarded as
● unacceptable in British
● English. This makes *different
● from* the safest option: *this
● result is only slightly different
● from that obtained in the US* - or
● you can rephrase the
● sentence: *this result differs only
● slightly from that obtained in
● the US*.

differentiate 1 = **distinguish**,

separate, discriminate,
contrast, mark off, make a
distinction, tell apart, set off or
apart **2** = **make different**,
separate, distinguish,
characterize, single out,
segregate, individualize, mark
off **3** = **become different**,
change, convert, transform,
alter, adapt, modify

difficult 1 = **hard**, tough,
taxing, demanding, challenging,
exacting, formidable, uphill
OPPOSITE: easy
2 = **problematical**, involved,
complex, complicated, obscure,
baffling, intricate, knotty
OPPOSITE: simple
3 = **troublesome**, demanding,
perverse, fussy, fastidious, hard
to please, refractory,
unaccommodating **OPPOSITE:**
cooperative

difficulty 1 = **problem**, trouble,
obstacle, hurdle, dilemma,
complication, snag, uphill
(S. African) **2** = **hardship**, strain,
awkwardness, strenuousness,
arduousness, laboriousness

dig VERB **1** = **hollow out**, mine,
quarry, excavate, scoop out
2 = **delve**, tunnel, burrow
3 = **turn over 4** = **search**, hunt,
root, delve, forage, dig down,
fossick (Austral. & N.Z.)
5 = **poke**, drive, push, stick,
punch, stab, thrust, shove
▷ NOUN **6** = **cutting remark**,
crack (slang), insult, taunt,
sneer, jeer, barb, wisecrack

(informal) **7** = **poke**, thrust,
nudge, prod, jab, punch

digest VERB **1** = **ingest**, absorb,
incorporate, dissolve, assimilate
2 = **take in**, absorb, grasp, soak
up
▷ NOUN **3** = **summary**, résumé,
abstract, epitome, synopsis,
précis, abridgment

dignity 1 = **decorum**, gravity,
majesty, grandeur,
respectability, nobility,
solemnity, courtliness **2** = **self-
importance**, pride, self-esteem,
self-respect

dilemma = **predicament**,
problem, difficulty, spot
(informal), mess, puzzle, plight,
quandary
● USAGE NOTE
● The use of dilemma to refer to
● a problem that seems
● incapable of solution is
● considered by some people to
● be incorrect. To avoid this
● misuse of the word, an
● appropriate alternative such
● as predicament could be used.

dilute 1 = **water down**, thin
(out), weaken, adulterate, make
thinner, cut (informal)
OPPOSITE: condense
2 = **reduce**, weaken, diminish,
temper, decrease, lessen,
diffuse, mitigate **OPPOSITE:**
intensify

dim ADJECTIVE **1** = **poorly lit**,
dark, gloomy, murky, shady,
shadowy, dusky, tenebrous
2 = **cloudy**, grey, gloomy,

dismal, overcast, leaden **OPPOSITE:** bright **3** = **unclear**, obscured, faint, blurred, fuzzy, shadowy, hazy, bleary **OPPOSITE:** distinct **4** = **stupid** (*Informal*), thick, dull, dense, dumb (*informal*), daft (*informal*), dozy (*Brit. informal*), obtuse **OPPOSITE:** bright ▷ **VERB 5** = **turn down**, fade, dull **6** = **grow** *or* **become faint**, fade, dull, grow *or* become dim **7** = **darken**, dull, cloud over

dimension 1 = **aspect**, side, feature, angle, facet **2** = **extent**, size

diminish 1 = **decrease**, decline, lessen, shrink, dwindle, wane, recede, subside **OPPOSITE:** grow **2** = **reduce**, cut, decrease, lessen, lower, curtail **OPPOSITE:** increase

din = **noise**, row, racket, crash, clamour, clatter, uproar, commotion **OPPOSITE:** silence

dine = **eat**, lunch, feast, sup

dinkum (*Austral. & N.Z. informal*) = **genuine**, honest, natural, frank, sincere, candid, upfront (*informal*), artless

dinner 1 = **meal**, main meal, spread (*informal*), repast **2** = **banquet**, feast, repast, hakari (*N.Z.*)

dinosaur ▷ *See panel* DINOSAURS

dip **VERB 1** = **plunge**, immerse, bathe, douse, douse, dunk **2** = **drop (down)**, fall, lower, sink, descend, subside **3** = **slope**, drop (down),

descend, fall, decline, sink, incline, drop away ▷ **NOUN 4** = **plunge**, ducking, soaking, drenching, immersion, douche **5** = **nod**, drop, lowering, slump, sag **6** = **hollow**, hole, depression, pit, basin, trough, concavity ▷ **PHRASES: dip into something** = **sample**, skim, glance at, browse, peruse

diplomacy 1 = **statesmanship**, statecraft, international negotiation **2** = **tact**, skill, sensitivity, craft, discretion, subtlety, delicacy, finesse **OPPOSITE:** tactlessness

diplomat = **official**, ambassador, envoy, statesman, consul, attaché, emissary, chargé d'affaires

diplomatic 1 = **consular**, official, foreign-office, ambassadorial, foreign-politic **2** = **tactful**, politic, sensitive, subtle, delicate, polite, discreet, prudent **OPPOSITE:** tactless

dire = **desperate**, pressing, critical, terrible, crucial, extreme, awful, urgent

direct **ADJECTIVE 1** = **quickest**, shortest **2** = **straight**, through **OPPOSITE:** circuitous **3** = **first-hand**, personal, immediate **OPPOSITE:** indirect **4** = **clear**, specific, plain, absolute, definite, explicit, downright, point-blank **OPPOSITE:** ambiguous **5** = **straightforward**, open,

d

DINOSAURS

allosaur(us)
ankylosaur(us)
apatosaur(us)
atlantosaur(us)
brachiosaur(us)
brontosaur(us)
ceratosaur(us)
compsognathus
dimetrodon
diplodocus
dolichosaur(us)
dromiosaur(us)
elasmosaur(us)
hadrosaur(us)
ichthyosaur(us)
iguanodon or iguanodont

megalosaur(us)
mosasaur(us)
oviraptor
plesiosaur(us)
pteranodon
pterodactyl or pterosaur
protoceratops
stegodon or stegodont
stegosaur(us)
theropod
titanosaur(us)
trachodon
triceratops
tyrannosaur(us)
velociraptor

straight, frank, blunt, honest,
candid, forthright **OPPOSITE:**
indirect 6 = **verbatim**, exact,
word-for-word, strict, accurate,
faithful, letter-for-letter
▷ **ADVERB** 7 = **non-stop**,
straight
▷ **VERB** 8 = **aim**, point, level,
train, focus 9 = **guide**, show,
lead, point the way, point in the
direction of 10 = **control**, run,
manage, lead, guide, handle,
conduct, oversee 11 = **order**,
command, instruct, charge,
demand, require, bid
12 = **address**, send, mail, route,
label
direction NOUN 1 = **way**,
course, line, road, track,
bearing, route, path
2 = **management**, control,
charge, administration,

leadership, command,
guidance, supervision
▷ **PLURAL NOUN**
3 = **instructions**, rules,
information, plan, briefing,
regulations, recommendations,
guidelines
directive = **order**, ruling,
regulation, command,
instruction, decree, mandate,
injunction
directly 1 = **straight**,
unswervingly, without
deviation, by the shortest route,
in a beeline 2 = **immediately**,
promptly, right away,
straightaway 3 (*Old-fashioned*)
= **at once**, as soon as possible,
straightaway, forthwith
4 = **honestly**, openly, frankly,
plainly, point-blank,
unequivocally, truthfully,

d

straightforwardly

director = **controller**, head, leader, manager, chief, executive, governor, administrator, baas (S. African)

dirt 1 = **filth**, muck, grime, dust, mud, impurity, kak (S. African taboo slang) 2 = **soil**, ground, earth, clay, turf, loam

dirty ADJECTIVE 1 = **filthy**, soiled, grubby, foul, muddy, polluted, messy, grimy, festy (Austral. slang) OPPOSITE: clean 2 = **dishonest**, illegal, unfair, cheating, crooked, fraudulent, treacherous, unscrupulous OPPOSITE: honest 3 = **obscene**, indecent, blue, offensive, filthy, pornographic, sleazy, lewd OPPOSITE: decent
▷ VERB 4 = **soil**, foul, stain, spoil, muddy, pollute, blacken, defile OPPOSITE: clean

disability = **handicap**, affliction, disorder, defect, impairment, infirmity

disable = **handicap**, cripple, damage, paralyse, impair, incapacitate, immobilize, enfeeble

disabled = **differently abled**, physically challenged, handicapped, weakened, crippled, paralysed, lame, incapacitated OPPOSITE: able-bodied

● USAGE NOTE
● Referring to people with
● disabilities as the disabled can
● cause offence and should be

● avoided. Instead, refer to
● them as people with
● disabilities or who are physically
● challenged, or, possibly,
● disabled people or differently
● abled people. In general, the
● terms used for disabilities or
● medical conditions should be
● avoided as collective nouns
● for people who have them -
● so, for example, instead of the
● blind, it is preferable to refer
● to sightless people, vision-
● impaired people, or partially-
● sighted people, depending on
● the degree of their condition.

disadvantage 1 = **drawback**, trouble, handicap, nuisance, snag, inconvenience, downside OPPOSITE: advantage 2 = **harm**, loss, damage, injury, hurt, prejudice, detriment, disservice OPPOSITE: benefit

disagree 1 = **differ (in opinion)**, argue, clash, dispute, dissent, quarrel, take issue with, cross swords OPPOSITE: agree 2 = **make ill**, upset, sicken, trouble, hurt, bother, distress, discomfort

disagreement = **argument**, row, conflict, clash, dispute, dissent, quarrel, squabble OPPOSITE: agreement

disappear 1 = **vanish**, recede, evanesce OPPOSITE: appear 2 = **pass**, fade away 3 = **cease**, dissolve, evaporate, perish, die out, pass away, melt away, leave no trace

disappearance 1 = vanishing, going, passing, melting, eclipse, evaporation, evanescence 2 = **flight**, departure 3 = **loss**, losing, mislaying

disappoint = **let down**, dismay, fail, disillusion, dishearten, disenchant, dissatisfy, disgruntle

disappointment 1 = regret, discontent, dissatisfaction, disillusionment, chagrin, disenchantment, dejection, despondency 2 = **letdown**, blow, setback, misfortune, calamity, choker (*informal*) 3 = **frustration**

disapproval = **displeasure**, criticism, objection, condemnation, dissatisfaction, censure, reproach, denunciation

disapprove = **condemn**, object to, dislike, deplore, frown on, take exception to, take a dim view of, find unacceptable **OPPOSITE:** approve

disarm 1 = **demilitarize**, disband, demobilize, deactivate 2 = **win over**, persuade

disarmament = **arms reduction**, demobilization, arms limitation, demilitarization, de-escalation

disarming = **charming**, winning, irresistible, persuasive, likable *or* likeable

disarray 1 = **confusion**, disorder, indiscipline, disunity, disorganization, unruliness **OPPOSITE:** order

2 = **untidiness**, mess, chaos, muddle, clutter, shambles, jumble, hotchpotch **OPPOSITE:** tidiness

disaster 1 = **catastrophe**, trouble, tragedy, ruin, misfortune, adversity, calamity, cataclysm 2 = **failure**, mess, flop (*informal*), catastrophe, debacle, cock-up (*Brit. slang*), washout (*informal*)

disastrous 1 = **terrible**, devastating, tragic, fatal, catastrophic, ruinous, calamitous, cataclysmic 2 = **unsuccessful**

disbelief = **scepticism**, doubt, distrust, mistrust, incredulity, unbelief, dubiety **OPPOSITE:** belief

discard = **get rid of**, drop, throw away or out, reject, abandon, dump (*informal*), dispose of, dispense with **OPPOSITE:** keep

discharge VERB 1 = **release**, free, clear, liberate, pardon, allow to go, set free 2 = **dismiss**, sack (*informal*), fire (*informal*), remove, expel, discard, oust, cashier 3 = **carry out**, perform, fulfil, accomplish, do, effect, realize, observe 4 = **pay**, meet, clear, settle, square (up), honour, satisfy, relieve 5 = **pour forth**, release, leak, emit, dispense, ooze, exude, give off 6 = **fire**, shoot, set off, explode, let off, detonate, let loose (*informal*) ▷ NOUN 7 = **release**, liberation,

clearance, pardon, acquittal
8 = dismissal, notice, removal,
the boot (*slang*), expulsion, the
push (*slang*), marching orders
(*informal*), ejection
9 = emission, ooze, secretion,
excretion, pus, seepage,
suppuration **10 = firing**, report,
shot, blast, burst, explosion,
volley, salvo
disciple 1 = apostle
2 = follower, student,
supporter, pupil, devotee,
apostle, adherent **OPPOSITE:**
teacher
discipline NOUN 1 = control,
authority, regulation,
supervision, orderliness,
strictness **2 = punishment**,
penalty, correction, chastening,
chastisement, castigation
3 = self-control, control,
restraint, self-discipline,
willpower, self-restraint,
orderliness **4 = training**,
practice, exercise, method,
regulation, drill, regimen
5 = field of study, area, subject,
theme, topic, course,
curriculum, speciality
▷ VERB **6 = punish**, correct,
reprimand, castigate, chastise,
chasten, penalize, bring to book
7 = train, educate
disclose 1 = make known,
reveal, publish, relate,
broadcast, confess,
communicate, divulge
OPPOSITE: keep secret
2 = show, reveal, expose,

unveil, uncover, lay bare, bring
to light **OPPOSITE:** hide
disclosure 1 = revelation,
announcement, publication,
leak, admission, declaration,
confession, acknowledgment
2 = uncovering, publication,
revelation, divulgence
discomfort 1 = pain, hurt,
ache, throbbing, irritation,
tenderness, pang, malaise
OPPOSITE: comfort
2 = uneasiness, worry, anxiety,
doubt, distress, misgiving,
qualms, trepidation **OPPOSITE:**
reassurance
3 = inconvenience, trouble,
difficulty, bother, hardship,
irritation, nuisance, uphill
(*S. African*)
discontent = dissatisfaction,
unhappiness, displeasure,
regret, envy, restlessness,
uneasiness
discontented = dissatisfied,
unhappy, fed up, disgruntled,
disaffected, vexed, displeased
OPPOSITE: satisfied
discount NOUN 1 = deduction,
cut, reduction, concession,
rebate
▷ VERB **2 = mark down**,
reduce, lower **3 = disregard**,
reject, ignore, overlook, discard,
set aside, dispel, pass over
discourage 1 = dishearten,
depress, intimidate, overawe,
demoralize, put a damper on,
dispirit, deject **OPPOSITE:**
hearten **2 = put off**, deter,

prevent, dissuade, talk out of
OPPOSITE: encourage
discourse 1 = **conversation**,
talk, discussion, speech,
communication, chat, dialogue
2 = **speech**, essay, lecture,
sermon, treatise, dissertation,
homily, oration, whaikorero
(*N.Z.*)
discover 1 = **find out**, learn,
notice, realize, recognize,
perceive, detect, uncover
2 = **find**, come across, uncover,
unearth, turn up, dig up, come
upon
discovery 1 = **finding out**,
news, revelation, disclosure,
realization 2 = **invention**,
launch, institution, pioneering,
innovation, inauguration
3 = **breakthrough**, find,
development, advance, leap,
invention, step forward,
quantum leap 4 = **finding**,
revelation, uncovering,
disclosure, detection
discredit VERB 1 = **disgrace**,
shame, smear, humiliate, taint,
disparage, vilify, slander
OPPOSITE: honour 2 = **dispute**,
question, challenge, deny,
reject, discount, distrust,
mistrust
▷ NOUN 3 = **disgrace**, scandal,
shame, disrepute, stigma,
ignominy, dishonour, ill-repute
OPPOSITE: honour
discreet = tactful, diplomatic,
guarded, careful, cautious,
wary, prudent, considerate

OPPOSITE: indiscreet
discrepancy = disagreement,
difference, variation, conflict,
contradiction, inconsistency,
disparity, divergence
discretion 1 = tact,
consideration, caution,
diplomacy, prudence, wariness,
carefulness, judiciousness
OPPOSITE: tactlessness
2 = **choice**, will, pleasure,
preference, inclination, volition
discriminate = differentiate,
distinguish, separate, tell the
difference, draw a distinction
▷ PHRASES: discriminate
against someone = treat
differently, single out,
victimize, treat as inferior, show
bias against, show prejudice
against
discriminating = discerning,
particular, refined, cultivated,
selective, tasteful, fastidious
OPPOSITE: undiscriminating
discrimination 1 = prejudice,
bias, injustice, intolerance,
bigotry, favouritism, unfairness
2 = **discernment**, taste,
judgment, perception, subtlety,
refinement
discuss = talk about, consider,
debate, examine, argue about,
deliberate about, converse
about, confer about
discussion 1 = talk, debate,
argument, conference,
conversation, dialogue,
consultation, discourse, korero
(*N.Z.*) 2 = **examination**,

investigation, analysis, scrutiny, dissection

disdain NOUN 1 = **contempt**, scorn, arrogance, derision, haughtiness, superciliousness
▷ VERB 2 = **scorn**, reject, slight, disregard, spurn, deride, look down on, sneer at

disease = **illness**, condition, complaint, infection, disorder, sickness, ailment, affliction

diseased = **unhealthy**, sick, infected, rotten, ailing, sickly, unwell, crook (*Austral. & N.Z. informal*), unsound

disgrace NOUN 1 = **shame**, degradation, disrepute, ignominy, dishonour, infamy, opprobrium, odium OPPOSITE: honour 2 = **scandal**, stain, stigma, blot, blemish
▷ VERB 3 = **shame**, humiliate, discredit, degrade, taint, sully, dishonour, bring shame upon OPPOSITE: honour

disgraceful = **shameful**, shocking, scandalous, unworthy, ignominious, disreputable, contemptible, dishonourable

disgruntled = **discontented**, dissatisfied, annoyed, irritated, put out, grumpy, vexed, displeased, hoha (*N.Z.*)

disguise NOUN 1 = **costume**, mask, camouflage
▷ VERB 2 = **hide**, cover, conceal, screen, mask, suppress, withhold, veil

disguised 1 = **in disguise**,

masked, camouflaged, undercover, incognito 2 = **false**, artificial, forged, fake, mock, imitation, sham, counterfeit

disgust NOUN 1 = **loathing**, revulsion, hatred, dislike, nausea, distaste, aversion, repulsion OPPOSITE: liking 2 = **outrage**, shock, anger, hurt, fury, resentment, wrath, indignation
▷ VERB 3 = **sicken**, offend, revolt, put off, repel, nauseate OPPOSITE: delight

disgusting 1 = **sickening**, foul, revolting, gross, repellent, nauseating, repugnant, loathsome, festy (*Austral. slang*), yucko (*Austral. slang*) 2 = **appalling**, shocking, awful, offensive, dreadful, horrifying

dish 1 = **bowl**, plate, platter, salver 2 = **food**, fare, recipe

dishonest = **deceitful**, corrupt, crooked (*informal*), lying, bent (*slang*), false, cheating, treacherous OPPOSITE: honest

disintegrate = **break up**, crumble, fall apart, separate, shatter, splinter, break apart, go to pieces

dislike VERB 1 = **hate**, object to, loathe, despise, disapprove of, detest, recoil from, take a dim view of OPPOSITE: like
▷ NOUN 2 = **hatred**, hostility, disapproval, distaste, animosity, aversion, displeasure, antipathy OPPOSITE: liking

dismal 1 = **bad**, awful, dreadful, rotten (*informal*), terrible, poor, dire, abysmal 2 = **sad**, gloomy, dark, depressing, discouraging, bleak, dreary, sombre **OPPOSITE:** happy 3 = **gloomy**, depressing, dull, dreary **OPPOSITE:** cheerful

dismantle = **take apart**, strip, demolish, disassemble, take to pieces *or* bits

dismay NOUN 1 = **alarm**, fear, horror, anxiety, dread, apprehension, nervousness, consternation
2 = **disappointment**, frustration, dissatisfaction, disillusionment, chagrin, disenchantment, discouragement
▷ VERB 3 = **alarm**, frighten, scare, panic, distress, terrify, appal, startle 4 = **disappoint**, upset, discourage, daunt, disillusion, let down, dishearten, dispirit

dismiss 1 = **reject**, disregard 2 = **banish**, dispel, discard, set aside, cast out, lay aside, put out of your mind 3 = **sack**, fire (*informal*), remove (*informal*), axe (*informal*), discharge, lay off, cashier, give notice to 4 = **let go**, free, release, discharge, dissolve, liberate, disperse, send away

dismissal = **the sack**, removal, notice, the boot (*slang*), expulsion (*informal*), the push (*slang*), marching orders

(*informal*), the bum's rush

disobey 1 = **defy**, ignore, rebel, disregard, refuse to obey
2 = **infringe**, defy, refuse to obey, flout, violate, contravene, overstep, transgress

disorder 1 = **illness**, disease, complaint, condition, sickness, ailment, affliction, malady
2 = **untidiness**, mess, confusion, chaos, muddle, clutter, shambles, disarray
3 = **disturbance**, riot, turmoil, unrest, uproar, commotion, unruliness, biffo (*Austral. slang*)

disorderly 1 = **untidy**, confused, chaotic, messy, jumbled, shambolic (*informal*), disorganized, higgledy-piggledy (*informal*) **OPPOSITE:** tidy
2 = **unruly**, disruptive, rowdy, turbulent, tumultuous, lawless, riotous, ungovernable

dispatch or **despatch** VERB 1 = **send**, consign 2 = **kill**, murder, destroy, execute, slaughter, assassinate, slay, liquidate 3 = **carry out**, perform, fulfil, effect, finish, achieve, settle, dismiss
▷ NOUN 4 = **message**, news, report, story, account, communication, bulletin, communiqué

dispel = **drive away**, dismiss, eliminate, expel, disperse, banish, chase away

dispense 1 = **distribute**, assign, allocate, allot, dole out, share out, apportion, deal out

2 = **prepare**, measure, supply, mix 3 = **administer**, operate, carry out, implement, enforce, execute, apply, discharge

▷ PHRASES: **dispense with something** or **someone** 1 = **do away with**, give up, cancel, abolish, brush aside, forgo 2 = **do without**, get rid of, dispose of, relinquish

disperse 1 = **scatter**, spread, distribute, strew, diffuse, disseminate, throw about 2 = **break up**, separate, scatter, dissolve, disband OPPOSITE: gather 3 = **dissolve**, break up

displace 1 = **replace**, succeed, supersede, oust, usurp, supplant, take the place of 2 = **move**, shift, disturb, budge, misplace

display VERB 1 = **show**, present, exhibit, put on view OPPOSITE: conceal 2 = **expose**, show, reveal, exhibit, uncover 3 = **demonstrate**, show, reveal, register, expose, disclose, manifest 4 = **show off**, parade, exhibit, sport (*informal*), flash (*informal*), flourish, brandish, flaunt

▷ NOUN 5 = **proof**, exhibition, demonstration, evidence, expression, illustration, revelation, testimony 6 = **exhibition**, show, demonstration, presentation, array 7 = **ostentation**, show, flourish, fanfare, pomp 8 = **show**, exhibition, parade, spectacle, pageant

disposable 1 = **throwaway**, nonreturnable 2 = **available**, expendable, consumable

disposal = **throwing away**, dumping (*informal*), scrapping, removal, discarding, jettisoning, ejection, riddance

▷ PHRASES: **at your disposal** = **available**, ready, to hand, accessible, handy, at hand, on tap, expendable

dispose = **arrange**, put, place, group, order, distribute, array

▷ PHRASES: **dispose of someone** = **kill**, murder, destroy, execute, slaughter, assassinate, slay, liquidate

▶ **dispose of something** 1 = **get rid of**, destroy, dump (*informal*), scrap, discard, unload, jettison, throw out or away 2 = **deal with**, manage, treat, handle, settle, cope with, take care of, see to

disposition 1 = **character**, nature, spirit, make-up, constitution, temper, temperament 2 = **tendency**, inclination, propensity, habit, leaning, bent, bias, proclivity 3 = **arrangement**, grouping, ordering, organization, distribution, placement

dispute NOUN 1 = **disagreement**, conflict, argument, dissent, altercation 2 = **argument**, row, clash, controversy, contention, feud, quarrel, squabble

▷ VERB 3 = **contest**, question, challenge, deny, doubt, oppose, object to, contradict 4 = **argue**, fight, clash, disagree, fall out (*informal*), quarrel, squabble, bicker

disqualify = **ban**, rule out, prohibit, preclude, debar, declare ineligible

disregard VERB 1 = **ignore**, discount, overlook, neglect, pass over, turn a blind eye to, make light of, pay no heed to **OPPOSITE:** pay attention to
▷ NOUN 2 = **ignoring**, neglect, contempt, indifference, negligence, disdain, disrespect

disrupt 1 = **interrupt**, stop, upset, hold up, interfere with, unsettle, obstruct, cut short 2 = **disturb**, upset, confuse, disorder, spoil, disorganize, disarrange

disruption = **disturbance**, interference, interruption, stoppage

disruptive = **disturbing**, upsetting, disorderly, unsettling, troublesome, unruly **OPPOSITE:** well-behaved

dissatisfaction = **discontent**, frustration, resentment, disappointment, irritation, unhappiness, annoyance, displeasure

dissatisfied = **discontented**, frustrated, unhappy, disappointed, fed up, disgruntled, displeased, unsatisfied **OPPOSITE:** satisfied

dissent = **disagreement**, opposition, protest, resistance, refusal, objection, discord, demur **OPPOSITE:** assent

dissident NOUN 1 = **protester**, rebel, dissenter, demonstrator, agitator
▷ ADJECTIVE 2 = **dissenting**, disagreeing, nonconformist, heterodox

dissolve 1 = **melt**, soften, thaw, liquefy, deliquesce 2 = **end**, suspend, break up, wind up, terminate, discontinue, dismantle, disband

distance 1 = **space**, length, extent, range, stretch, gap, interval, span 2 = **aloofness**, reserve, detachment, restraint, stiffness, coolness, coldness, standoffishness

distant 1 = **far-off**, far, remote, abroad, out-of-the-way, far-flung, faraway, outlying **OPPOSITE:** close 2 = **remote** 3 = **reserved**, withdrawn, cool, remote, detached, aloof, unfriendly, reticent **OPPOSITE:** friendly 4 = **faraway**, blank, vague, distracted, vacant, preoccupied, oblivious, absent-minded

distinct 1 = **different**, individual, separate, discrete, unconnected **OPPOSITE:** similar 2 = **striking**, dramatic, outstanding, noticeable, well-defined 3 = **definite**, marked, clear, decided, obvious, evident, noticeable, conspicuous

d

OPPOSITE: vague

distinction 1 = **difference**, contrast, variation, differential, discrepancy, disparity, dissimilarity 2 = **excellence**, importance, fame, merit, prominence, greatness, eminence, repute 3 = **feature**, quality, characteristic, mark, individuality, peculiarity, distinctiveness, particularity 4 = **merit**, honour, integrity, excellence, rectitude

distinctive = **characteristic**, special, individual, unique, typical, peculiar, singular, idiosyncratic OPPOSITE: ordinary

distinctly 1 = **definitely**, clearly, obviously, plainly, patently, decidedly, markedly, noticeably 2 = **clearly**, plainly

distinguish 1 = **differentiate**, determine, separate, discriminate, decide, judge, ascertain, tell the difference 2 = **characterize**, mark, separate, single out, set apart 3 = **make out**, recognize, perceive, know, see, tell, pick out, discern

distinguished = **eminent**, noted, famous, celebrated, well-known, prominent, esteemed, acclaimed OPPOSITE: unknown

distort 1 = **misrepresent**, twist, bias, disguise, pervert, slant, colour, misinterpret 2 = **deform**, bend, twist, warp, buckle, mangle, mangulate (Austral. slang), disfigure, contort

distortion 1 = **misrepresentation**, bias, slant, perversion, falsification 2 = **deformity**, bend, twist, warp, buckle, contortion, malformation, crookedness

distract 1 = **divert**, sidetrack, draw away, turn aside, lead astray, draw or lead away from 2 = **amuse**, occupy, entertain, beguile, engross

distracted = **agitated**, troubled, puzzled, at sea, perplexed, flustered, in a flap (informal)

distraction 1 = **disturbance**, interference, diversion, interruption 2 = **entertainment**, recreation, amusement, diversion, pastime

distraught = **frantic**, desperate, distressed, distracted, worked-up, agitated, overwrought, out of your mind

distress NOUN 1 = **suffering**, pain, worry, grief, misery, torment, sorrow, heartache 2 = **need**, trouble, difficulties, poverty, hard times, hardship, misfortune, adversity ▷ VERB 3 = **upset**, worry, trouble, disturb, grieve, torment, harass, agitate

distressed 1 = **upset**, worried, troubled, distracted, tormented, distraught,

agitated, wretched
2 = **poverty-stricken**, poor, impoverished, needy, destitute, indigent, down at heel, straitened

distressing = **upsetting**, worrying, disturbing, painful, sad, harrowing, heart-breaking

distribute 1 = **hand out**, pass round 2 = **circulate**, deliver, convey 3 = **share**, deal, allocate, dispense, allot, dole out, apportion

distribution 1 = **delivery**, mailing, transportation, handling 2 = **sharing**, division, assignment, rationing, allocation, allotment, apportionment 3 = **spread**, organization, arrangement, placement

district = **area**, region, sector, quarter, parish, neighbourhood, vicinity, locality

distrust VERB 1 = **suspect**, doubt, be wary of, mistrust, disbelieve, be suspicious of OPPOSITE: trust
▷ NOUN 2 = **suspicion**, question, doubt, disbelief, scepticism, mistrust, misgiving, wariness OPPOSITE: trust

disturb 1 = **interrupt**, trouble, bother, plague, disrupt, interfere with, hassle, inconvenience 2 = **upset**, concern, worry, trouble, alarm, distress, unsettle, unnerve OPPOSITE: calm 3 = **muddle**, disorder, mix up, mess up,

jumble up, disarrange

disturbance 1 = **disorder**, fray, brawl, fracas, commotion, rumpus 2 = **upset**, bother, distraction, intrusion, interruption, annoyance

disturbed 1 (*Psychiatry*) = **unbalanced**, troubled, disordered, unstable, neurotic, upset, deranged, maladjusted OPPOSITE: balanced
2 = **worried**, concerned, troubled, upset, bothered, nervous, anxious, uneasy OPPOSITE: calm

disturbing = **worrying**, upsetting, alarming, frightening, distressing, startling, unsettling, harrowing

ditch NOUN 1 = **channel**, drain, trench, dyke, furrow, gully, moat, watercourse
▷ VERB 2 (*Slang*) = **get rid of**, dump (*informal*), scrap, discard, dispose of, dispense with, jettison, throw out *or* overboard 3 (*Slang*) = **leave**, drop, abandon, dump (*informal*), get rid of, forsake

dive VERB 1 = **plunge**, drop, duck, dip, descend, plummet
2 = **go underwater** 3 = **nose-dive**, plunge, crash, swoop, plummet
▷ NOUN 4 = **plunge**, spring, jump, leap, lunge, nose dive

diverse 1 = **various**, mixed, varied, assorted, miscellaneous, several, sundry, motley
2 = **different**, unlike, varying,

d

separate, distinct, disparate, discrete, dissimilar

diversify = **vary**, change, expand, spread out, branch out

diversion 1 = **distraction**, deviation, digression 2 = **pastime**, game, sport, entertainment, hobby, relaxation, recreation, distraction 3 (*Chiefly Brit.*) = **detour**, roundabout way, indirect course 4 (*Chiefly Brit.*) = **deviation**, departure, straying, divergence, digression

diversity 1 = **difference**, multiplicity, heterogeneity, diverseness 2 = **range**, variety, scope, sphere

divert 1 = **redirect**, switch, avert, deflect, deviate, turn aside 2 = **distract**, sidetrack, lead astray, draw or lead away from 3 = **entertain**, delight, amuse, please, charm, gratify, beguile, regale

divide 1 = **separate**, split, segregate, bisect **OPPOSITE:** join 2 *sometimes with* **up** = **share**, distribute, allocate, dispense, allot, mete, deal out 3 = **split**, break up, come between, estrange, cause to disagree

dividend = **bonus**, share, cut (*informal*), gain, extra, plus, portion, divvy (*informal*)

divine ADJECTIVE 1 = **heavenly**, spiritual, holy, immortal, supernatural, celestial, angelic, superhuman 2 = **sacred**,

religious, holy, spiritual, blessed, revered, hallowed, consecrated 3 (*Informal*) = **wonderful**, perfect, beautiful, excellent, lovely, glorious, marvellous, splendid ▷ VERB 4 = **guess**, suppose, perceive, discern, infer, deduce, apprehend, surmise

division 1 = **separation**, dividing, splitting up, partition, cutting up 2 = **sharing**, distribution, assignment, rationing, allocation, allotment, apportionment 3 = **disagreement**, split, rift, rupture, abyss, chasm, variance, discord **OPPOSITE:** unity 4 = **department**, group, branch 5 = **part**, bit, piece, section, class, category, fraction

divorce NOUN 1 = **separation**, split, break-up, parting, split-up, rift, dissolution, annulment ▷ VERB 2 = **separate**, split up, part company, dissolve your marriage

dizzy 1 = **giddy**, faint, light-headed, swimming, reeling, shaky, wobbly, off balance 2 = **confused**, dazzled, at sea, bewildered, muddled, bemused, dazed, disorientated

do VERB 1 = **perform**, achieve, carry out, complete, accomplish, execute, pull off 2 = **make**, prepare, fix, arrange, look after, see to, get ready 3 = **solve**, work out, resolve, figure out, decode, decipher,

puzzle out **4** = **be adequate**, be sufficient, satisfy, suffice, pass muster, cut the mustard, meet requirements **5** = **produce**, make, create, develop, manufacture, construct, invent, fabricate
▷ NOUN **6** (*Informal, chiefly Brit. & N.Z.*) = **party**, gathering, function, event, affair, occasion, celebration, reception
▷ PHRASES: do away with something = **get rid of**, remove, eliminate, abolish, discard, put an end to, dispense with, discontinue ▸ **do without something** *or* **someone** = **manage without**, give up, dispense with, forgo, kick (*informal*), abstain from, get along without

dock¹ NOUN **1** = **port**, haven, harbour, pier, wharf, quay, waterfront, anchorage
▷ VERB **2** = **moor**, land, anchor, put in, tie up, berth, drop anchor **3** (*of spacecraft*) = **link up**, unite, join, couple, rendezvous, hook up

dock² **1** = **cut**, reduce, decrease, diminish, lessen OPPOSITE: increase **2** = **deduct**, subtract **3** = **cut off**, crop, clip, shorten, curtail, cut short

doctor NOUN **1** = **physician**, medic (*informal*), general practitioner, medical practitioner, G.P.
▷ VERB **2** = **change**, alter, interfere with, disguise, pervert,

tamper with, tinker with, misrepresent **3** = **add to**, spike, cut, mix something with something, dilute, water down, adulterate

doctrine = **teaching**, principle, belief, opinion, conviction, creed, dogma, tenet, kaupapa (*N.Z.*)

document NOUN **1** = **paper**, form, certificate, report, record, testimonial, authorization
▷ VERB **2** = **support**, certify, verify, detail, validate, substantiate, corroborate, authenticate

dodge VERB **1** = **duck**, dart, swerve, sidestep, shoot, turn aside **2** = **evade**, avoid, escape, get away from, elude **3** = **avoid**, evade, shirk
▷ NOUN **4** = **trick**, scheme, ploy, trap, device, fraud, manoeuvre, deception

dodgy ADJECTIVE **1** (*Brit., Austral. & N.Z.*) = **nasty**, offensive, unpleasant, revolting, distasteful, repellent, obnoxious, repulsive **2** (*Brit., Austral. & N.Z.*) = **risky**, difficult, tricky, dangerous, delicate, uncertain, dicey (*informal, chiefly Brit.*), chancy (*informal*) **3** = **second rate**, poor, inferior, mediocre, shoddy, bush-league (*Austral. & N.Z. informal*), half-pie (*N.Z. informal*), bodger *or* bodgie (*Austral. slang*)

dog NOUN **1** = **hound**, canine, pooch (*slang*), cur, man's best

friend, kuri or goorie (N.Z.), brak (S. African)
▷ VERB 2 = **plague**, follow, trouble, haunt, hound, torment
3 = **pursue**, follow, track, chase, trail, hound, stalk
▷ PHRASES: go to the dogs (Informal) = **deteriorate**, degenerate, be in decline, go downhill (informal), go down the drain, go to pot, go to ruin
● RELATED WORDS
● adjective: canine
● female: bitch
● young: pup, puppy

dogged = **determined**, persistent, stubborn, resolute, tenacious, steadfast, obstinate, indefatigable OPPOSITE: irresolute

dole = **share**, grant, gift, allowance, handout, koha (N.Z.)
▷ PHRASES: dole something out = **give out**, distribute, assign, allocate, hand out, dispense, allot, apportion

dolphin
● RELATED WORD
● collective noun: school
▷ See panel WHALES AND DOLPHINS

domestic ADJECTIVE 1 = **home**, internal, native, indigenous
2 = **household**, home, family, private 3 = **home-loving**, homely, housewifely, stay-at-home, domesticated
4 = **domesticated**, trained, tame, pet, house-trained
▷ NOUN 5 = **servant**, help,

maid, daily, char (informal), charwoman

dominant 1 = **main**, chief, primary, principal, prominent, predominant, pre-eminent OPPOSITE: minor
2 = **controlling**, ruling, commanding, supreme, governing, superior, authoritative

dominate 1 = **control**, rule, direct, govern, monopolize, tyrannize, have the whip hand over 2 = **tower above**, overlook, survey, stand over, loom over, stand head and shoulders above

domination = **control**, power, rule, authority, influence, command, supremacy, ascendancy

don = **put on**, get into, dress in, pull on, change into, get dressed in, clothe yourself in, slip on or into

donate = **give**, present, contribute, grant, subscribe, endow, entrust, impart

donation = **contribution**, gift, subscription, offering, present, grant, hand-out, koha (N.Z.)

donor = **giver**, contributor, benefactor, philanthropist, donator OPPOSITE: recipient

doom NOUN 1 = **destruction**, ruin, catastrophe, downfall
2 = **fate**, fortune
▷ VERB 3 = **condemn**, sentence, consign, destine

doomed = **hopeless**,

condemned, ill-fated, fated, unhappy, unfortunate, cursed, unlucky

door = **opening**, entry, entrance, exit, doorway

dope NOUN 1 (*Slang*) = **drugs**, narcotics, opiates, dadah (*Austral. slang*) 2 (*Informal*) = **idiot**, fool, twit (*informal, chiefly Brit.*), dunce, simpleton, dimwit (*informal*), nitwit (*informal*), dumb-ass (*slang*), dorba or dorb (*Austral. slang*), bogan (*Austral. slang*)
▷ VERB 3 = **drug**, knock out, sedate, stupefy, anaesthetize, narcotize

dorp (*S. African*) = **town**, village, settlement, municipality, kainga or kaika (*N.Z.*)

dose 1 = **measure**, amount, allowance, portion, prescription, ration, draught, dosage 2 = **quantity**, measure, supply, portion

dot NOUN 1 = **spot**, point, mark, fleck, jot, speck, speckle
▷ VERB 2 = **spot**, stud, fleck, speckle
▷ PHRASES: **on the dot** = **on time**, promptly, precisely, exactly (*informal*), to the minute, on the button (*informal*), punctually

double ADJECTIVE
1 = **matching**, coupled, paired, twin, duplicate, in pairs
2 = **dual**, enigmatic, twofold
▷ VERB 3 = **multiply by two**, duplicate, increase twofold,

enlarge, magnify 4 = **fold up** *or* **over**
▷ NOUN 5 = **twin**, lookalike, spitting image, clone, replica, dead ringer (*slang*), Doppelgänger, duplicate
▷ PHRASES: **at** *or* **on the double** = **at once**, now, immediately, directly, quickly, promptly, straight away, right away
▶ **double as something** *or* **someone** = **function as**, serve as

doubt NOUN 1 = **uncertainty**, confusion, hesitation, suspense, indecision, hesitancy, lack of conviction, irresolution
OPPOSITE: certainty
2 = **suspicion**, scepticism, distrust, apprehension, mistrust, misgivings, qualms
OPPOSITE: belief
▷ VERB 3 = **be uncertain**, be sceptical, be dubious
4 = **waver**, hesitate, vacillate, fluctuate 5 = **disbelieve**, question, suspect, query, distrust, mistrust, lack confidence in OPPOSITE: believe

doubtful 1 = **unlikely**, unclear, dubious, questionable, improbable, debatable, equivocal OPPOSITE: certain
2 = **unsure**, uncertain, hesitant, suspicious, hesitating, sceptical, tentative, wavering OPPOSITE: certain

doubtless = **probably**, presumably, most likely

down ADJECTIVE

1 = **depressed**, low, sad, unhappy, discouraged, miserable, fed up, dejected
▷ VERB 2 (*Informal*) = **swallow**, drink (down), drain, gulp (down), put away (*informal*), toss off

downfall = **ruin**, fall, destruction, collapse, disgrace, overthrow, undoing, comeuppance (*slang*)

downgrade = **demote**, degrade, take down a peg (*informal*), lower or reduce in rank **OPPOSITE:** promote

downright = **complete**, absolute, utter, total, plain, outright, unqualified, out-and-out

down-to-earth = **sensible**, practical, realistic, matter-of-fact, sane, no-nonsense, unsentimental, plain-spoken

downward = **descending**, declining, heading down, earthward

draft NOUN 1 = **outline**, plan, sketch, version, rough, abstract 2 = **money order**, bill (of exchange), cheque, postal order
▷ VERB 3 = **outline**, write, plan, produce, create, design, draw, compose

drag VERB 1 = **pull**, draw, haul, trail, tow, tug, jerk, lug
▷ NOUN 2 (*Slang*) = **nuisance**, bore, bother, pest, hassle (*informal*), inconvenience, annoyance

drain VERB 1 = **remove**, draw, empty, withdraw, tap, pump, bleed 2 = **empty** 3 = **flow out**, leak, trickle, ooze, seep, exude, well out, effuse 4 = **drink up**, swallow, finish, put away (*informal*), quaff, gulp down 5 = **exhaust**, wear out, strain, weaken, fatigue, debilitate, tire out, enfeeble 6 = **consume**, exhaust, empty, use up, sap, dissipate
▷ NOUN 7 = **sewer**, channel, pipe, sink, ditch, trench, conduit, duct 8 = **reduction**, strain, drag, exhaustion, sapping, depletion

drama 1 = **play**, show, stage show, dramatization 2 = **theatre**, acting, stagecraft, dramaturgy 3 = **excitement**, crisis, spectacle, turmoil, histrionics

dramatic 1 = **exciting**, thrilling, tense, sensational, breathtaking, electrifying, melodramatic, climactic 2 = **theatrical**, Thespian, dramaturgical 3 = **expressive** 4 = **powerful**, striking, impressive, vivid, jaw-dropping **OPPOSITE:** ordinary

drape = **cover**, wrap, fold, swathe

drastic = **extreme**, strong, radical, desperate, severe, harsh

draught 1 = **breeze**, current, movement, flow, puff, gust, current of air 2 = **drink**

draw VERB 1 = **sketch**, design,

outline, trace, portray, paint, depict, mark out **2 = pull**, drag, haul, tow, tug **3 = extract**, take, remove **4 = deduce**, make, take, derive, infer **5 = attract 6 = entice** ▷ **NOUN 7 = tie**, deadlock, stalemate, impasse, dead heat **8** (*Informal*) **= appeal**, pull (*informal*), charm, attraction, lure, temptation, fascination, allure ▷ **PHRASES: draw on** *or* **upon something = make use of**, use, employ, rely on, exploit, extract, take from, fall back on

drawback = disadvantage, difficulty, handicap, deficiency, flaw, hitch, snag, downside **OPPOSITE:** advantage

drawing = picture, illustration, representation, cartoon, sketch, portrayal, depiction, study

drawn = tense, worn, stressed, tired, pinched, haggard

dread VERB 1 = fear, shrink from, cringe at the thought of, quail from, shudder to think about, have cold feet about (*informal*), tremble to think about ▷ **NOUN 2 = fear**, alarm, horror, terror, dismay, fright, apprehension, trepidation

dreadful 1 = terrible, shocking, awful, appalling, horrible, fearful, hideous, atrocious **2 = serious**, terrible, awful, horrendous, monstrous, abysmal **3 = awful**, terrible, horrendous, frightful

dream NOUN 1 = vision, illusion, delusion, hallucination **2 = ambition**, wish, fantasy, desire, pipe dream **3 = daydream 4 = delight**, pleasure, joy, beauty, treasure, gem, marvel, pearler (*Austral. slang*) ▷ **VERB 5 = have dreams**, hallucinate **6 = daydream**, stargaze, build castles in the air or in Spain ▷ **PHRASES: dream of something** *or* **someone = daydream about**, fantasize about

dreamer = idealist, visionary, daydreamer, utopian, escapist, Walter Mitty, fantasist

dreary = dull, boring, tedious, drab, tiresome, monotonous, humdrum, uneventful **OPPOSITE:** exciting

drench = soak, flood, wet, drown, steep, swamp, saturate, inundate

dress NOUN 1 = frock, gown, robe **2 = clothing**, clothes, costume, garments, apparel, attire, garb, togs ▷ **VERB 3 = put on clothes**, don clothes, slip on or into something **OPPOSITE:** undress **4 = clothe 5 = bandage**, treat, plaster, bind up **6 = arrange**, prepare, get ready

dribble 1 = run, drip, trickle, drop, leak, ooze, seep, fall in drops **2 = drool**, drivel, slaver, slobber, drip saliva

drift VERB 1 = **float**, go (aimlessly), bob, coast, slip, sail, slide, glide 2 = **wander**, stroll, stray, roam, meander, rove, range 3 = **stray**, wander, digress, get off the point 4 = **pile up**, gather, accumulate, amass, bank up
▷ NOUN 5 = **pile**, bank, mass, heap, mound, accumulation 6 = **meaning**, point, gist, direction, import, intention, tendency, significance

drill NOUN 1 = **bit**, borer, gimlet, boring tool 2 = **training**, exercise, discipline, instruction, preparation, repetition 3 = **practice**
▷ VERB 4 = **bore**, pierce, penetrate, sink in, puncture, perforate 5 = **train**, coach, teach, exercise, discipline, practise, instruct, rehearse

drink VERB 1 = **swallow**, sip, suck, gulp, sup, guzzle, imbibe, quaff 2 = **booze** (*informal*), tipple, tope, hit the bottle (*informal*)
▷ NOUN 3 = **glass**, cup, draught 4 = **beverage**, refreshment, potion, liquid 5 = **alcohol**, booze (*informal*), liquor, spirits, the bottle (*informal*), hooch or hootch (*informal, chiefly U.S. & Canad.*)

drip VERB 1 = **drop**, splash, sprinkle, trickle, dribble, exude, plop

▷ NOUN 2 = **drop**, bead, trickle, dribble, droplet, globule, pearl 3 (*Informal*) = **weakling**, wet (*Brit. informal*), weed (*informal*), softie (*informal*), mummy's boy (*informal*), namby-pamby

drive VERB 1 = **go (by car)**, ride (by car), motor, travel by car 2 = **operate**, manage, direct, guide, handle, steer 3 = **push**, propel 4 = **thrust**, push, hammer, ram 5 = **herd**, urge, impel 6 = **force**, press, prompt, spur, prod, constrain, coerce, goad
▷ NOUN 7 = **run**, ride, trip, journey, spin (*informal*), outing, excursion, jaunt 8 = **initiative**, energy, enterprise, ambition, motivation, zip (*informal*), vigour, get-up-and-go (*informal*) 9 = **campaign**, push (*informal*), crusade, action, effort, appeal

drop VERB 1 = **fall**, decline, diminish 2 often with **away** = **decline**, fall, sink 3 = **plunge**, fall, tumble, descend, plummet 4 = **drip**, trickle, dribble, fall in drops 5 = **sink**, fall, descend 6 = **quit**, give up, axe (*informal*), kick (*informal*), relinquish, discontinue
▷ NOUN 7 = **decrease**, fall, cut, lowering, decline, reduction, slump, fall-off 8 = **droplet**, bead, globule, bubble, pearl, drip 9 = **dash**, shot (*informal*), spot, trace, sip, tot, trickle, mouthful 10 = **fall**, plunge, descent

▷ **PHRASES: drop off 1 = fall asleep**, nod (off), doze (off), snooze (*informal*), have forty winks (*informal*) **2 = decrease**, lower, decline, shrink, diminish, dwindle, lessen, subside ▷ **drop out = leave**, stop, give up, withdraw, quit, pull out, fall by the wayside ▷ **drop out of something = discontinue**, give up, quit

drought = water shortage, dryness, dry spell, aridity **OPPOSITE:** flood

drove *often plural* **= herd**, company, crowds, collection, mob, flocks, swarm, horde

drown 1 = go down, go under **2 = drench**, flood, soak, steep, swamp, saturate, engulf, submerge **3 = overwhelm**, overcome, wipe out, overpower, obliterate, swallow up

drug NOUN 1 = medication, medicine, remedy, physic, medicament **2 = dope** (*slang*), narcotic (*slang*), stimulant, opiate, dadah (*Austral. slang*) ▷ **VERB 3 = knock out**, dope (*slang*), numb, deaden, stupefy, anaesthetize

drum = pound, beat, tap, rap, thrash, tattoo, throb, pulsate ▷ **PHRASES: drum something into someone = drive into**, hammer into, instil into, din into, harp on about to

drunk ADJECTIVE 1 = intoxicated, plastered (*slang*), drunken, merry (*Brit.*

informal), under the influence (*informal*), tipsy, legless (*informal*), inebriated, out to it (*Austral. & N.Z. slang*), babalas (*S. African*) ▷ **NOUN 2 = drunkard**, alcoholic, lush (*slang*), boozer (*informal*), wino (*informal*), inebriate, alko or alco (*Austral. slang*)

dry ADJECTIVE 1 = dehydrated, dried-up, arid, parched, desiccated **OPPOSITE:** wet **2 = thirsty**, parched **3 = sarcastic**, cynical, low-key, sly, sardonic, deadpan, droll, ironical **4 = dull**, boring, tedious, dreary, tiresome, monotonous, run-of-the-mill, humdrum **OPPOSITE:** interesting **5 = plain**, simple, bare, basic, stark, unembellished ▷ **VERB 6 = drain**, make dry **7** *often with* **out = dehydrate**, make dry, desiccate, sear, parch, dehumidify **OPPOSITE:** wet ▷ **PHRASES: dry up** or **out = become dry**, harden, wither, shrivel up, wizen

dual = twofold, double, twin, matched, paired, duplicate, binary, duplex

dubious 1 = suspect, suspicious, crooked, dodgy (*Brit., Austral. & N.Z. informal*), questionable, unreliable, fishy (*informal*), disreputable **OPPOSITE:** trustworthy

2 = **unsure**, uncertain, suspicious, hesitating, doubtful, sceptical, tentative, wavering **OPPOSITE:** sure

duck 1 = **bob**, drop, lower, bend, bow, dodge, crouch, stoop 2 (*Informal*) = **dodge**, avoid, escape, evade, elude, sidestep, shirk 3 = **dunk**, wet, plunge, dip, submerge, immerse, douse, souse

due ADJECTIVE 1 = **expected**, scheduled 2 = **fitting**, deserved, appropriate, justified, suitable, merited, proper, rightful 3 = **payable**, outstanding, owed, owing, unpaid, in arrears
▷ ADVERB 4 = **directly**, dead, straight, exactly, undeviatingly
▷ NOUN 5 = **right(s)**, privilege, deserts, merits, comeuppance (*informal*)
▷ PLURAL NOUN
6 = **membership fee**, charges, fee, contribution, levy

duel NOUN 1 = **single combat**, affair of honour 2 = **contest**, fight, competition, clash, encounter, engagement, rivalry
▷ VERB 3 = **fight**, struggle, clash, compete, contest, contend, vie with, lock horns

duff (*Brit., Austral. & N.Z. informal*) = **bad**, poor, useless, inferior, unsatisfactory, defective, imperfect, substandard, bodger *or* bodgie (*Austral. slang*)

dull ADJECTIVE 1 = **boring**, tedious, dreary, flat, plain, monotonous, run-of-the-mill, humdrum **OPPOSITE:** exciting 2 = **lifeless**, indifferent, apathetic, listless, unresponsive, passionless **OPPOSITE:** lively 3 = **cloudy**, dim, gloomy, dismal, overcast, leaden **OPPOSITE:** bright 4 = **blunt**, blunted, unsharpened **OPPOSITE:** sharp
▷ VERB 5 = **relieve**, blunt, lessen, moderate, soften, alleviate, allay, take the edge off

duly 1 = **properly**, fittingly, correctly, appropriately, accordingly, suitably, deservedly, rightfully 2 = **on time**, promptly, punctually, at the proper time

dumb 1 = **unable to speak**, mute **OPPOSITE:** articulate 2 = **silent**, mute, speechless, tongue-tied, wordless, voiceless, soundless, mum 3 (*Informal*) = **stupid**, thick, dull, foolish, dense, unintelligent, asinine, dim-witted (*informal*) **OPPOSITE:** clever

dummy NOUN 1 = **model**, figure, mannequin, form, manikin 2 = **imitation**, copy, duplicate, sham, counterfeit, replica 3 (*Slang*) = **fool**, idiot, dunce, oaf, simpleton, nitwit (*informal*), blockhead, dumb-ass (*slang*), dorba *or* dorb (*Austral. slang*), bogan (*Austral. slang*)
▷ ADJECTIVE 4 = **imitation**, false, fake, artificial, mock,

bogus, simulated, sham

dump VERB 1 = **drop**, deposit, throw down, let fall, fling down 2 = **get rid of**, tip, dispose of, unload, jettison, empty out, throw away *or* out 3 = **scrap**, get rid of, abolish, put an end to, discontinue, jettison, put paid to
▷ NOUN 4 = **rubbish tip**, tip, junkyard, rubbish heap, refuse heap 5 (*Informal*) = **pigsty**, hole (*informal*), slum, hovel

dunny (*Austral. & N.Z. old-fashioned informal*) = **toilet**, lavatory, bathroom, loo (*Brit. informal*), W.C., bog (*slang*), Gents *or* Ladies, can (*U.S. & Canad. slang*), bogger (*Austral. slang*), brasco (*Austral. slang*)

duplicate VERB 1 = **repeat**, reproduce, copy, clone, replicate 2 = **copy**
▷ ADJECTIVE 3 = **identical**, matched, matching, twin, corresponding, twofold
▷ NOUN 4 = **copy**, facsimile 5 = **photocopy**, copy, reproduction, replica, carbon copy

durable 1 = **hard-wearing**, strong, tough, reliable, resistant, sturdy, long-lasting OPPOSITE: fragile 2 = **enduring**, continuing, dependable, unwavering, unfaltering

duration = **length**, time, period, term, stretch, extent, spell, span

dusk = **twilight**, evening, evo (*Austral. slang*), nightfall, sunset, dark, sundown, eventide, gloaming (*Scot. poetic*) OPPOSITE: dawn

dust NOUN 1 = **grime**, grit, powder 2 = **particles**
▷ VERB 3 = **sprinkle**, cover, powder, spread, spray, scatter, sift, dredge

dusty = **dirty**, grubby, unclean, unswept

duty 1 = **responsibility**, job, task, work, role, function, obligation, assignment 2 = **tax**, toll, levy, tariff, excise
▷ PHRASES: on duty = **at work**, busy, engaged, on active service

dwarf VERB 1 = **tower above** *or* **over**, dominate, overlook, stand over, loom over, stand head and shoulders above 2 = **eclipse**, tower above *or* over, put in the shade, diminish
▷ ADJECTIVE 3 = **miniature**, small, baby, tiny, diminutive, bonsai, undersized
▷ NOUN 4 = **gnome**, midget, Lilliputian, Tom Thumb, pygmy *or* pigmy

dwell (*Formal or literary*) = **live**, reside, lodge, abide

dwelling (*Formal or literary*) = **home**, house, residence, abode, quarters, lodging, habitation, domicile, whare (*N.Z.*)

dwindle = **lessen**, decline, fade, shrink, diminish, decrease, wane, subside OPPOSITE: increase

dye VERB 1 = **colour**, stain, tint, tinge, pigment
▷ NOUN 2 = **colouring**, colour, pigment, stain, tint, tinge, colorant

dying 1 = **near death**, moribund, in extremis (*Latin*), at death's door, not long for this world 2 = **final**, last, parting, departing 3 = **failing**, declining, foundering, diminishing, decreasing, dwindling, subsiding

dynamic = **energetic**, powerful, vital, go-ahead, lively, animated, high-powered, forceful OPPOSITE: apathetic

dynasty = **empire**, house, rule, regime, sovereignty

Ee

each DETERMINER 1 = **every**, every single
▷ PRONOUN 2 = **every one**, all, each one, each and every one, one and all
▷ ADVERB 3 = **apiece**, individually, for each, to each, respectively, per person, per head, per capita

● USAGE NOTE
● *Each* is a singular pronoun
● and should be used with a
● singular verb - for example,
● *each of the candidates was*
● *interviewed separately* (not *were*
● *interviewed separately*).

eager 1 = **anxious**, keen, hungry, impatient, itching, thirsty OPPOSITE: unenthusiastic 2 = **keen**, interested, intense, enthusiastic, passionate, avid (*informal*), fervent OPPOSITE: uninterested

ear = **sensitivity**, taste, discrimination, appreciation

early ADVERB 1 = **in good time**, beforehand, ahead of schedule, in advance, with time to spare OPPOSITE: late 2 = **too soon**, before the usual time,

prematurely, ahead of time
OPPOSITE: late
▷ ADJECTIVE 3 = **first**, opening,
initial, introductory
4 = **premature**, forward,
advanced, untimely,
unseasonable **OPPOSITE:**
belated 5 = **primitive**, first,
earliest, young, original,
undeveloped, primordial,
primeval **OPPOSITE:** developed

earmark 1 = **set aside**, reserve,
label, flag, allocate, designate,
mark out 2 = **mark out**,
identify, designate

earn 1 = **be paid**, make, get,
receive, gain, net, collect, bring
in 2 = **deserve**, win, gain,
attain, justify, merit, warrant,
be entitled to

earnest 1 = **serious**, grave,
intense, dedicated, sincere,
thoughtful, solemn, ardent
OPPOSITE: frivolous
2 = **determined**, dogged,
intent, persistent, persevering,
resolute, wholehearted
OPPOSITE: half-hearted

earnings = **income**, pay, wages,
revenue, proceeds, salary,
receipts, remuneration

earth 1 = **world**, planet, globe,
sphere, orb, earthly sphere
2 = **ground**, land, dry land,
terra firma 3 = **soil**, ground,
land, dust, clay, dirt, turf, silt

earthly 1 = **worldly**, material,
secular, mortal, temporal,
human **OPPOSITE:** spiritual
2 = **sensual**, worldly, physical,

fleshly, bodily, carnal
3 (*Informal*) = **possible**, likely,
practical, feasible, conceivable,
imaginable

ease NOUN
1 = **straightforwardness**,
simplicity, readiness
2 = **comfort**, luxury, leisure,
relaxation, prosperity, affluence,
rest, repose **OPPOSITE:** hardship
3 = **peace of mind**, peace,
content, quiet, comfort,
happiness, serenity, tranquillity
OPPOSITE: agitation
▷ VERB 4 = **relieve**, calm,
soothe, lessen, alleviate,
lighten, lower, relax **OPPOSITE:**
aggravate 5 = **reduce**,
diminish, lessen, slacken
6 = **move carefully**, edge, slip,
inch, slide, creep, manoeuvre

easily = **without difficulty**,
smoothly, readily, comfortably,
effortlessly, with ease,
straightforwardly

easy 1 = **simple**,
straightforward, no trouble, not
difficult, effortless, painless,
uncomplicated, child's play
(*informal*) **OPPOSITE:** hard
2 = **untroubled**, relaxed,
peaceful, serene, tranquil, quiet
3 = **carefree**, comfortable,
leisurely, trouble-free,
untroubled, cushy (*informal*)
OPPOSITE: difficult
4 = **tolerant**, soft, mild, laid-
back (*informal*), indulgent, easy-
going, lenient, permissive
OPPOSITE: strict

eat 1 = **consume**, swallow, chew, scoff (*slang*), devour, munch, tuck into (*informal*), put away 2 = **have a meal**, lunch, breakfast, dine, snack, feed, graze (*informal*), have lunch

ebb VERB 1 = **flow back**, go out, withdraw, retreat, wane, recede 2 = **decline**, flag, diminish, decrease, dwindle, lessen, subside, fall away
▷ NOUN 3 = **flowing back**, going out, withdrawal, retreat, wane, low water, low tide, outgoing tide

eccentric ADJECTIVE 1 = **odd**, strange, peculiar, irregular, quirky, unconventional, idiosyncratic, outlandish
OPPOSITE: normal
▷ NOUN 2 = **crank** (*informal*), character (*informal*), oddball (*informal*), nonconformist, weirdo or weirdie (*informal*)

echo NOUN 1 = **reverberation**, ringing, repetition, answer, resonance, resounding 2 = **copy**, reflection, clone, reproduction, imitation, duplicate, double, reiteration
▷ VERB 3 = **reverberate**, repeat, resound, ring, resonate 4 = **recall**, reflect, copy, mirror, resemble, imitate, ape

eclipse NOUN 1 = **obscuring**, covering, blocking, shading, dimming, extinction, darkening, blotting out
▷ VERB 2 = **surpass**, exceed, overshadow, excel, transcend, outdo, outclass, outshine

economic 1 = **financial**, industrial, commercial 2 = **profitable**, successful, commercial, rewarding, productive, lucrative, worthwhile, viable 3 (*Informal*) = **economical**, cheap, reasonable, modest, low-priced, inexpensive

economical 1 = **thrifty**, sparing, careful, prudent, provident, frugal, parsimonious, scrimping OPPOSITE: extravagant 2 = **efficient**, sparing, cost-effective, money-saving, time-saving OPPOSITE: wasteful

economy 1 = **financial system**, financial state 2 = **thrift**, restraint, prudence, husbandry, frugality, parsimony

ecstasy = **rapture**, delight, joy, bliss, euphoria, fervour, elation OPPOSITE: agony

ecstatic = **rapturous**, entranced, joyous, elated, overjoyed, blissful, euphoric, enraptured

edge NOUN 1 = **border**, side, limit, outline, boundary, fringe, verge, brink 2 = **verge**, point, brink, threshold 3 = **advantage**, lead, dominance, superiority, upper hand, head start, ascendancy, whip hand 4 = **power**, force, bite, effectiveness, incisiveness, powerful quality 5 = **sharpness**, point, bitterness, keenness

▷ VERB 6 = **inch**, ease, creep, slink, steal, sidle, move slowly

7 = **border**, fringe, hem, pipe

▷ PHRASES: on edge = **tense**, nervous, impatient, irritable, apprehensive, edgy, ill at ease, on tenterhooks

edit = **revise**, improve, correct, polish, adapt, rewrite, condense, redraft

edition = **version**, copy, issue, programme (TV, Radio), printing, volume, impression, publication

educate = **teach**, school, train, develop, improve, inform, discipline, tutor

educated 1 = **cultured**, intellectual, learned, sophisticated, refined, cultivated, enlightened, knowledgeable OPPOSITE: uncultured 2 = **taught**, schooled, coached, informed, tutored, instructed, nurtured, well-informed OPPOSITE: uneducated

education 1 = **teaching**, schooling, training, development, discipline, instruction, nurture, tuition

2 = **learning**, schooling, cultivation, refinement

educational 1 = **academic**, school, learning, teaching, scholastic, pedagogical, pedagogic 2 = **instructive**, useful, cultural, illuminating, enlightening, informative, instructional, edifying

eerie = **uncanny**, strange, frightening, ghostly, weird, mysterious, scary (informal), sinister

effect NOUN 1 = **result**, consequence, conclusion, outcome, event, end result, upshot 2 = **impression**, feeling, impact, influence 3 = **purpose**, impression, sense, intent, essence, thread, tenor

▷ PLURAL NOUN

4 = **belongings**, goods, things, property, stuff, gear, possessions, paraphernalia

▷ VERB 5 = **bring about**, produce, complete, achieve, perform, fulfil, accomplish, execute

● USAGE NOTE

● It is quite common for the
● verb effect to be mistakenly
● used where affect is intended.
● Effect is relatively uncommon
● and rather formal, and is a
● synonym of 'bring about'.
● Conversely, the noun effect is
● quite often mistakenly
● written with an initial a. The
● following are correct: the
● group is still recovering from the
● effects of the recession; they
● really are powerless to effect any
● change. The next two
● examples are incorrect: the
● full affects of the shutdown
● won't be felt for several more
● days; men whose lack of hair
● doesn't effect their self-esteem.

effective 1 = **efficient**,

successful, useful, active, capable, valuable, helpful, adequate **OPPOSITE:** ineffective **2 = powerful**, strong, convincing, persuasive, telling, impressive, compelling, forceful **OPPOSITE:** weak **3 = virtual**, essential, practical, implied, implicit, tacit, unacknowledged **4 = in operation**, official, current, legal, active, in effect, valid, operative **OPPOSITE:** inoperative

efficiency 1 = effectiveness, power, economy, productivity, organization, cost-effectiveness, orderliness **2 = competence**, expertise, capability, professionalism, proficiency, adeptness

efficient 1 = effective, successful, structured, productive, systematic, streamlined, cost-effective, methodical **OPPOSITE:** inefficient **2 = competent**, professional, capable, organized, productive, proficient, businesslike, well-organized **OPPOSITE:** incompetent

effort 1 = attempt, try, endeavour, shot (*informal*), bid, essay, go (*informal*), stab (*informal*) **2 = exertion**, work, trouble, energy, struggle, application, graft, toil

egg = ovum, gamete, germ cell ▷ **PHRASES: egg someone on = incite**, push, encourage, urge,

prompt, spur, provoke, prod

eject 1 = throw out, remove, turn out, expel (*slang*), oust, banish, drive out, evict **2 = bail out**, escape, get out

elaborate ADJECTIVE 1 = complicated, detailed, studied, complex, precise, thorough, intricate, painstaking **2 = ornate**, involved, complex, fancy, complicated, intricate, baroque, ornamented **OPPOSITE:** plain ▷ **VERB 3 = develop**, flesh out **4 = expand (upon)**, extend, enlarge (on), amplify, embellish, flesh out, add detail (to) **OPPOSITE:** simplify

elastic 1 = flexible, supple, rubbery, pliable, plastic, springy, pliant, tensile **OPPOSITE:** rigid **2 = adaptable**, yielding, variable, flexible, accommodating, tolerant, adjustable, supple **OPPOSITE:** inflexible

elbow = joint, angle, curve

elder ADJECTIVE 1 = older, first, senior, first-born ▷ **NOUN 2 = older person**, senior

elect 1 = vote for, choose, pick, determine, select, appoint, opt for, settle on **2 = choose**, decide, prefer, select, opt

election 1 = vote, poll, ballot, referendum, franchise, plebiscite, show of hands **2 = appointment**, picking, choice, selection

electric 1 = electric-powered, powered, cordless, battery-operated, electrically-charged, mains-operated 2 = **charged**, exciting, stirring, thrilling, stimulating, dynamic, tense, rousing

elegance = **style**, taste, grace, dignity, sophistication, grandeur, refinement, gracefulness

elegant = **stylish**, fine, sophisticated, delicate, handsome, refined, chic, exquisite **OPPOSITE:** inelegant

element NOUN
1 = **component**, part, unit, section, factor, principle, aspect, foundation 2 = **group**, faction, clique, set, party, circle 3 = **trace**, suggestion, hint, dash, suspicion, tinge, smattering, soupçon
▷ PLURAL NOUN 4 = **weather conditions**, climate, the weather, wind and rain, atmospheric conditions, powers of nature
▷ PHRASES: be in your element = **be in a situation you enjoy**, be in your natural environment, be in familiar surroundings

elementary = **simple**, clear, easy, plain, straightforward, rudimentary, uncomplicated, undemanding **OPPOSITE:** complicated

elevate 1 = **promote**, raise, advance, upgrade, exalt, kick upstairs (*informal*), aggrandize, give advancement to
2 = **increase**, lift, raise, step up, intensify, move up, hoist, raise high 3 = **raise**, lift, heighten, uplift, hoist, lift up, raise up, hike up

elevated 1 = **exalted**, important, august, grand, superior, noble, dignified, high-ranking 2 = **high-minded**, fine, grand, noble, inflated, dignified, sublime, lofty **OPPOSITE:** humble 3 = **raised**, high, lifted up, upraised

elicit 1 = **bring about**, cause, derive, bring out, evoke, give rise to, draw out, bring forth 2 = **obtain**, extract, exact, evoke, wrest, draw out, extort

eligible 1 = **entitled**, fit, qualified, suitable **OPPOSITE:** ineligible 2 = **available**, free, single, unmarried, unattached

eliminate = **remove**, end, stop, withdraw, get rid of, abolish, cut out, dispose of

elite = **aristocracy**, best, pick, cream, upper class, nobility, crème de la crème (*French*), flower **OPPOSITE:** rabble

eloquent 1 = **silver-tongued**, moving, powerful, effective, stirring, articulate, persuasive, forceful **OPPOSITE:** inarticulate 2 = **expressive**, telling, pointed, significant, vivid, meaningful, indicative, suggestive

elsewhere = **in or to another place**, away, abroad, hence (*archaic*), somewhere else, not

here, in other places, in or to a
different place

elude 1 = **evade**, escape, lose,
avoid, flee, duck (*informal*),
dodge, get away from
2 = **escape**, baffle, frustrate,
puzzle, stump, foil, be beyond
(someone), thwart

● USAGE NOTE
● *Elude* is sometimes wrongly
● used where *allude* is meant:
● *he was alluding* (not *eluding*) to
● *his previous visit to the city*.

elusive 1 = **difficult to catch**,
tricky, slippery, difficult to find,
evasive, shifty 2 = **indefinable**,
fleeting, subtle, indefinite,
transient, intangible,
indescribable, transitory

● USAGE NOTE
● The spelling of *elusive*, as in a
● shy, *elusive character*, should be
● noted. This adjective derives
● from the verb *elude*, and
● should not be confused with
● the rare word *illusive* meaning
● 'not real' or 'based on illusion'.

emanate = **flow**, emerge,
spring, proceed, arise, stem,
derive, originate

embargo NOUN 1 = **ban**, bar,
restriction, boycott, restraint,
prohibition, moratorium,
stoppage, rahui (*N.Z.*)
▷ VERB 2 = **block**, stop, bar,
ban, restrict, boycott, prohibit,
blacklist

embark = **go aboard**, climb
aboard, board ship, step aboard,
go on board, take ship

OPPOSITE: get off
▷ PHRASES: embark on
something = **begin**, start,
launch, enter, take up, set out,
set about, plunge into

embarrass = **shame**, distress,
show up (*informal*), humiliate,
disconcert, fluster, mortify,
discomfit

embarrassed = **ashamed**,
shamed, uncomfortable,
awkward, abashed, humiliated,
uneasy, unsettled

embarrassing = **humiliating**,
upsetting, compromising,
delicate, uncomfortable,
awkward, sensitive,
troublesome, barro (*Austral.
slang*)

embarrassment 1 = **shame**,
distress, showing up (*informal*),
humiliation, discomfort,
unease, self-consciousness,
awkwardness 2 = **problem**,
difficulty, nuisance, source of
trouble, thorn in your flesh
3 = **predicament**, problem,
difficulty (*informal*), mess, jam
(*informal*), plight, scrape
(*informal*), pickle (*informal*)

embody 1 = **personify**,
represent, stand for, manifest,
exemplify, symbolize, typify,
actualize 2 = **incorporate**,
include, contain, combine,
collect, take in, encompass

embrace VERB 1 = **hug**, hold,
cuddle, seize, squeeze, clasp,
envelop, canoodle (*slang*)
2 = **accept**, support, welcome,

adopt, take up, seize, espouse, take on board **3 = include**, involve, cover, contain, take in, incorporate, comprise, encompass
▷ NOUN **4 = hug**, hold, cuddle, squeeze, clinch (*slang*), clasp

embroil = involve, mix up, implicate, entangle, mire, ensnare, enmesh

embryo 1 = foetus, unborn child, fertilized egg **2 = germ**, beginning, source, root, seed, nucleus, rudiment

emerge 1 = come out, appear, surface, rise, arise, turn up, spring up, emanate OPPOSITE: withdraw **2 = become apparent**, come out, become known, come to light, crop up, transpire, become evident, come out in the wash

emergence 1 = coming, development, arrival, surfacing, rise, appearance, arising, turning up **2 = disclosure**, publishing, broadcasting, broadcast, publication, declaration, revelation, becoming known

emergency NOUN **1 = crisis**, danger, difficulty, accident, disaster, necessity, plight, scrape (*informal*)
▷ ADJECTIVE **2 = urgent**, crisis, immediate **3 = alternative**, extra, additional, substitute, replacement, temporary, makeshift, stopgap

emigrate = move abroad, move, relocate, migrate, resettle, leave your country

eminent = prominent, noted, respected, famous, celebrated, distinguished, well-known, esteemed OPPOSITE: unknown

emission = giving off *or* **out**, release, shedding, leak, radiation, discharge, transmission, ejaculation

emit 1 = give off, release, leak, transmit, discharge, send out, radiate, eject OPPOSITE: absorb **2 = utter**, produce, voice, give out, let out

emotion 1 = feeling, spirit, soul, passion, excitement, sensation, sentiment, fervour **2 = instinct**, sentiment, sensibility, intuition, tenderness, gut feeling, soft-heartedness

emotional 1 = psychological, private, personal, hidden, spiritual, inner **2 = moving**, touching, affecting, stirring, sentimental, poignant, emotive, heart-rending **3 = passionate**, sentimental, temperamental, excitable, demonstrative, hot-blooded **4 = emotive**, sensitive, controversial, delicate, contentious, heated, inflammatory, touchy

emphasis 1 = importance, attention, weight, significance, stress, priority, prominence **2 = stress**, accent, force, weight

emphasize 1 = highlight, stress, underline, draw

attention to, dwell on, play up, make a point of, give priority to **OPPOSITE:** minimize **2 = stress**, accentuate, lay stress on

emphatic 1 = forceful, positive, definite, vigorous, unmistakable, insistent, unequivocal, vehement **OPPOSITE:** hesitant **2 = significant**, pronounced, decisive, resounding, conclusive

empire 1 = kingdom, territory, province, federation, commonwealth, realm, domain **2 = organization**, company, business, firm, concern, corporation, consortium, syndicate

empirical or **empiric = first-hand**, direct, observed, practical, actual, experimental, pragmatic, factual **OPPOSITE:** hypothetical

employ 1 = hire, commission, appoint, take on, retain, engage, recruit, sign up **2 = use**, apply, exercise, exert, make use of, utilize, ply, bring to bear **3 = spend**, fill, occupy, involve, engage, take up, make use of, use up

employed 1 = working, in work, having a job, in employment, in a job, earning your living **OPPOSITE:** out of work **2 = busy**, active, occupied, engaged, hard at work, in harness, rushed off your feet **OPPOSITE:** idle

employee = worker, labourer,

workman, staff member, member of staff, hand, wage-earner, white-collar worker

employer 1 = boss (*informal*), manager, head, leader, director, chief, owner, master, baas (*S. African*) **2 = company**, business, firm, organization, establishment, outfit (*informal*)

employment 1 = job, work, position, trade, post, situation, profession, occupation **2 = taking on**, commissioning, appointing, hire, hiring, retaining, engaging, appointment **3 = use**, application, exertion, exercise, utilization

empower 1 = authorize, allow, commission, qualify, permit, sanction, entitle, delegate **2 = enable**, equip, emancipate, give means to, enfranchise

empty ADJECTIVE 1 = bare, clear, abandoned, deserted, vacant, free, void, desolate **OPPOSITE:** full **2 = meaningless**, cheap, hollow, vain, idle, futile, insincere **3 = worthless**, meaningless, hollow, pointless, futile, senseless, fruitless, inane **OPPOSITE:** meaningful ▷ **VERB 4 = clear**, drain, void, unload, pour out, unpack, remove the contents of **OPPOSITE:** fill **5 = exhaust**, consume the contents of, void, deplete, use up **OPPOSITE:** replenish **6 = evacuate**, clear, vacate, MT (S.M.S.)

emulate = imitate, follow, copy, mirror, echo, mimic, model yourself on

enable 1 = **allow**, permit, empower, give someone the opportunity, give someone the means **OPPOSITE:** prevent 2 = **authorize**, allow, permit, qualify, sanction, entitle, license, warrant **OPPOSITE:** stop

enact 1 = **establish**, order, command, approve, sanction, proclaim, decree, authorize 2 = **perform**, play, present, stage, represent, put on, portray, depict

enchant = fascinate, delight, charm, entrance, dazzle, captivate, enthral, beguile

enclose or **inclose** 1 = **surround**, circle, bound, fence, confine, close in, wall in, encircle 2 = **send with**, include, put in, insert

encompass 1 = **include**, hold, cover, admit, deal with, contain, take in, embrace 2 = **surround**, circle, enclose, close in, envelop, encircle, fence in, ring

encounter VERB 1 = **experience**, meet, face, suffer, have, go through, sustain, endure 2 = **meet**, confront, come across, bump into (informal), run across, come upon, chance upon, meet by chance
▷ NOUN 3 = **meeting**, brush,

confrontation, rendezvous, chance meeting 4 = **battle**, conflict, clash, contest, run-in (informal), confrontation, head-to-head

encourage 1 = **inspire**, comfort, cheer, reassure, console, hearten, cheer up, embolden **OPPOSITE:** discourage 2 = **urge**, persuade, prompt, spur, coax, egg on **OPPOSITE:** dissuade 3 = **promote**, back, support, increase, foster, advocate, stimulate, endorse **OPPOSITE:** prevent

encouragement 1 = **inspiration**, support, comfort, comforting, cheer, cheering, reassurance, morale boosting 2 = **urging**, prompting, stimulus, persuasion, coaxing, egging on, incitement 3 = **promotion**, backing, support, endorsement, stimulation, furtherance

end NOUN 1 = **close**, ending, finish, expiry, expiration **OPPOSITE:** beginning 2 = **conclusion**, ending, climax, completion, finale, culmination, denouement, consummation **OPPOSITE:** start 3 = **finish**, close, stop, resolution, conclusion, closure, completion, termination 4 = **extremity**, limit, edge, border, extent, extreme, margin, boundary 5 = **tip**, point, head, peak, extremity 6 = **purpose**, point,

reason, goal, target, aim, object, mission **7 = outcome**, resolution, conclusion
8 = death, dying, ruin, destruction, passing on, doom, demise, extinction
9 = remnant, butt, stub, scrap, fragment, stump, remainder, leftover
▷ VERB **10 = stop**, finish, halt, cease, wind up, terminate, call off, discontinue **OPPOSITE:** start
11 = finish, close, conclude, wind up, culminate, terminate, come to an end, draw to a close **OPPOSITE:** begin

endanger = put at risk, risk, threaten, compromise, jeopardize, imperil, put in danger, expose to danger **OPPOSITE:** save

endearing = attractive, winning, pleasing, appealing, sweet, engaging, charming, pleasant

endeavour (Formal) VERB
1 = try, labour, attempt, aim, struggle, venture, strive, aspire
▷ NOUN **2 = attempt**, try, effort, trial, bid, venture, enterprise, undertaking

ending = finish, end, close, conclusion, summing up, completion, finale, culmination **OPPOSITE:** start

endless = eternal, infinite, continual, unlimited, interminable, incessant, boundless, everlasting **OPPOSITE:** temporary

endorse 1 = approve, back, support, champion, promote, recommend, advocate, uphold
2 = sign, initial, countersign, sign on the back of

endorsement = approval, backing, support, favour, recommendation, acceptance, agreement, upholding

endow 1 = provide, favour, grace, bless, supply, furnish, endue **2 = finance**, fund, pay for, award, confer, bestow, bequeath, donate money to
3 = imbue

endowment = provision, funding, award, grant, gift, contribution, subsidy, donation, koha (N.Z.)

endurance 1 = staying power, strength, resolution, determination, patience, stamina, fortitude, persistence
2 = permanence, stability, continuity, duration, longevity, durability, continuance

endure 1 = experience, suffer, bear, meet, encounter, cope with, sustain, undergo **2 = last**, continue, remain, stay, stand, go on, survive, live on

enemy = foe, rival, opponent, the opposition, competitor, the other side, adversary, antagonist **OPPOSITE:** friend

energetic 1 = forceful, determined, active, aggressive, dynamic, vigorous, hard-hitting, strenuous **2 = lively**, active, dynamic, vigorous, animated,

tireless, bouncy, indefatigable
OPPOSITE: lethargic
3 = **strenuous**, hard, taxing,
demanding, tough, exhausting,
vigorous, arduous
energy 1 = **strength**, might,
stamina, forcefulness
2 = **liveliness**, drive,
determination, pep, vitality,
vigour, verve, resilience
3 = **power**
enforce 1 = **carry out**, apply,
implement, fulfil, execute,
administer, put into effect, put
into action 2 = **impose**, force,
insist on
engage 1 *with* **in** = **participate
in**, join in, take part in,
undertake, embark on, enter
into, become involved in, set
about 2 = **captivate**, catch,
arrest, fix, capture 3 = **occupy**,
involve, draw, grip, absorb,
preoccupy, immerse, engross
4 = **employ**, appoint, take on,
hire, retain, recruit, enlist, enrol
OPPOSITE: dismiss 5 = **set
going**, apply, trigger, activate,
switch on, energize, bring into
operation 6 (*Military*) = **begin
battle with**, attack, take on,
encounter, fall on, battle with,
meet, assail
engaged 1 = **occupied**,
working, employed, busy, tied
up 2 = **betrothed**, promised,
pledged, affianced, promised in
marriage **OPPOSITE:**
unattached 3 = **in use**, busy,
tied up, unavailable **OPPOSITE:**

available
engagement
1 = **appointment**, meeting,
interview, date, commitment,
arrangement, rendezvous
2 = **betrothal**, marriage
contract, troth (*archaic*),
agreement to marry 3 = **battle**,
fight, conflict, action, struggle,
clash, encounter, combat
4 = **participation**, joining,
taking part, involvement
engaging = **charming**,
interesting, pleasing, attractive,
lovely, entertaining, winning,
fetching (*informal*) **OPPOSITE:**
unpleasant
engine = **machine**, motor,
mechanism, generator, dynamo
engineer NOUN 1 = **designer**,
producer, architect, developer,
deviser, creator, planner,
inventor 2 = **worker**, specialist,
operator, practitioner,
operative, driver, conductor,
technician
▷ VERB 3 = **design**, plan,
create, construct, devise
4 = **bring about**, plan, effect,
set up (*informal*), scheme,
arrange, plot, mastermind
engraving = **print**, carving,
etching, inscription, plate,
woodcut, dry point
engulf 1 = **immerse**, swamp,
submerge, overrun, inundate,
envelop, swallow up
2 = **overwhelm**, overcome,
crush, swamp
enhance = **improve**, better,

increase, lift, boost, add to, strengthen, reinforce **OPPOSITE:** reduce

enjoy 1 = **take pleasure in** or **from**, like, love, appreciate, relish, delight in, be pleased with, be fond of **OPPOSITE:** hate 2 = **have**, use, own, experience, possess, have the benefit of, reap the benefits of, be blessed or favoured with

enjoyable = **pleasurable**, good, great, fine, nice, satisfying, lovely, entertaining **OPPOSITE:** unpleasant

enjoyment 1 = **pleasure**, liking, fun, delight, entertainment, joy, happiness, relish 2 = **benefit**, use, advantage, favour, possession, blessing

enlarge 1 = **expand**, increase, extend, add to, build up, widen, intensify, broaden **OPPOSITE:** reduce 2 = **grow**, increase, extend, expand, swell, become bigger, puff up, grow larger ▷ **PHRASES: enlarge on something** = **expand on**, develop, add to, fill out, elaborate on, flesh out, expatiate on, give further details about

enlighten = **inform**, tell, teach, advise, counsel, educate, instruct, illuminate

enlightened = **informed**, aware, reasonable, educated, sophisticated, cultivated, open-minded, knowledgeable

OPPOSITE: ignorant

enlightenment = **understanding**, learning, education, knowledge, instruction, awareness, wisdom, insight

enlist 1 = **join up**, join, enter (into), register, volunteer, sign up, enrol 2 = **recruit**, take on, hire, sign up, call up, muster, mobilize, conscript 3 = **obtain**, get, gain, secure, engage, procure

enormous = **huge**, massive, vast, extensive, tremendous, gross, immense, gigantic **OPPOSITE:** tiny

enough DETERMINER 1 = **sufficient**, adequate, ample, abundant, as much as you need, as much as is necessary ▷ PRONOUN 2 = **sufficiency**, plenty, sufficient, abundance, adequacy, right amount, ample supply ▷ ADVERB 3 = **sufficiently**, amply, reasonably, adequately, satisfactorily, abundantly, tolerably

enquire ▷ See INQUIRE

enquiry ▷ See INQUIRY

enrage = **anger**, infuriate, incense, madden, inflame, exasperate, antagonize, make angry **OPPOSITE:** calm

enrich 1 = **enhance**, develop, improve, boost, supplement, refine, heighten, augment 2 = **make rich**, make wealthy, make affluent, make prosperous, make well-off

enrol 1 = **enlist**, register, be accepted, be admitted, join up, put your name down for, sign up or on 2 = **recruit**, take on, enlist

en route = on or along the way, travelling, on the road, in transit, on the journey

ensemble 1 = **group**, company, band, troupe, cast, orchestra, chorus 2 = **collection**, set, body, whole, total, sum, combination, entity 3 = **outfit**, suit, get-up (informal), costume

ensue = follow, result, develop, proceed, arise, stem, derive, issue **OPPOSITE:** come first

ensure 1 = **make certain**, guarantee, secure, make sure, confirm, warrant, certify 2 = **protect**, defend, secure, safeguard, guard, make safe

entail = involve, require, produce, demand, call for, occasion, need, bring about

enter VERB 1 = **come** or **go in** or **into**, arrive, set foot in somewhere, cross the threshold of somewhere, make an entrance **OPPOSITE:** exit 2 = **penetrate**, get in, pierce, pass into, perforate 3 = **join**, start work at, begin work at, enrol in, enlist in **OPPOSITE:** leave 4 = **participate in**, join (in), be involved in, get involved in, play a part in, partake in, associate yourself with, start to be in 5 = **begin**, start, take up,

move into, commence, set out on, embark upon 6 = **compete in**, contest, join in, fight, sign up for, go in for 7 = **record**, note, register, log, list, write down, take down, inscribe

enterprise 1 = **firm**, company, business, concern, operation, organization, establishment, commercial undertaking 2 = **venture**, operation, project, adventure, undertaking, programme, pursuit, endeavour 3 = **initiative**, energy, daring, enthusiasm, imagination, drive, ingenuity, originality

enterprising = resourceful, original, spirited, daring, bold, enthusiastic, imaginative, energetic

entertain 1 = **amuse**, interest, please, delight, charm, enthral, cheer, regale 2 = **show hospitality to**, receive, accommodate, treat, put up, lodge, be host to, have company of 3 = **consider**, imagine, think about, contemplate, conceive of, bear in mind, keep in mind, give thought to

entertainment 1 = **enjoyment**, fun, pleasure, leisure, relaxation, recreation, amusement 2 = **pastime**, show, sport, performance, treat, presentation, leisure activity

enthusiasm = keenness, interest, passion, motivation,

relish, zeal, zest, fervour
enthusiast = fan, supporter, lover, follower, addict, buff (*informal*), fanatic, devotee
enthusiastic = keen, committed, eager, passionate, vigorous, avid, fervent, zealous **OPPOSITE:** apathetic
entice = lure, attract, invite, persuade, tempt, induce, seduce, lead on
entire = whole, full, complete, total, gross
entirely = completely, totally, absolutely, fully, altogether, thoroughly, wholly, utterly **OPPOSITE:** partly
entitle 1 = give the right to, allow, enable, permit, sanction, license, authorize, empower 2 = call, name, title, term, label, dub, christen, give the title of
entity = thing, being, individual, object, substance, creature, organism
entrance¹ 1 = way in, opening, door, approach, access, entry, gate, passage **OPPOSITE:** exit 2 = appearance, coming in, entry, arrival, introduction **OPPOSITE:** exit 3 = admission, access, entry, entrée, admittance, permission to enter, right of entry
entrance² 1 = enchant, delight, charm, fascinate, dazzle, captivate, enthral, beguile **OPPOSITE:** bore 2 = mesmerize, bewitch, hypnotize, put a spell on, cast a

spell on, put in a trance
entrant = competitor, player, candidate, entry, participant, applicant, contender, contestant
entrenched or **intrenched** = fixed, set, rooted, well-established, ingrained, deep-seated, deep-rooted, unshakeable or unshakable
entrepreneur = businessman or businesswoman, tycoon, executive, industrialist, speculator, magnate, impresario, business executive
entrust or **intrust** 1 = give custody of, deliver, commit, delegate, hand over, turn over, confide 2 = assign
entry 1 = admission, access, entrance, admittance, entrée, permission to enter, right of entry 2 = coming in, entering, appearance, arrival, entrance **OPPOSITE:** exit 3 = introduction, presentation, initiation, inauguration, induction, debut, investiture 4 = record, listing, account, note, statement, item 5 = way in, opening, door, approach, access, gate, passage, entrance
envelope = wrapping, casing, case, covering, cover, jacket, sleeve, wrapper
environment 1 = surroundings, setting, conditions, situation, medium, circumstances, background, atmosphere 2 = habitat,

home, surroundings, territory, terrain, locality, natural home

environmental = ecological, green

environmentalist
= conservationist, ecologist, green

envisage 1 = imagine, contemplate, conceive (of), visualize, picture, fancy, think up, conceptualize 2 = foresee, see, expect, predict, anticipate, envision

envoy 1 = ambassador, diplomat, emissary
2 = messenger, agent, representative, delegate, courier, intermediary, emissary

envy NOUN 1 = covetousness, resentment, jealousy, bitterness, resentfulness, enviousness (informal)
▷ VERB 2 = be jealous (of), resent, begrudge, be envious (of) 3 = covet, desire, crave, aspire to, yearn for, hanker after

epidemic 1 = outbreak, plague, growth, spread, scourge, contagion 2 = spate, plague, outbreak, wave, rash, eruption, upsurge

episode 1 = event, experience, happening, matter, affair, incident, adventure, occurrence
2 = instalment, part, act, scene, section, chapter, passage
3 = period, attack, spell, phase, bout

equal ADJECTIVE 1 = identical, the same, matching,

equivalent, uniform, alike, corresponding OPPOSITE: unequal 2 = fair, just, impartial, egalitarian, unbiased, even-handed OPPOSITE: unfair
3 = even, balanced, fifty-fifty (informal), evenly matched OPPOSITE: uneven
▷ NOUN 4 = match, equivalent, twin, counterpart
▷ VERB 5 = amount to, make, come to, total, level, parallel, tie with, equate OPPOSITE: be unequal to 6 = be equal to, match, reach 7 = be as good as, match, compare with, equate with, measure up to, be as great as

equality 1 = fairness, equal opportunity, equal treatment, egalitarianism, fair treatment, justness OPPOSITE: inequality
2 = sameness, balance, identity, similarity, correspondence, parity, likeness, uniformity OPPOSITE: disparity

equate 1 = identify, associate, connect, compare, relate, mention in the same breath, think of in connection with
2 = make equal, match, even up 3 = be equal to, parallel, compare with, liken, be commensurate with, correspond with or to

equation = equating, comparison, parallel, correspondence

equilibrium = stability,

balance, symmetry, steadiness, evenness, equipoise

equip 1 = **supply**, provide for, stock, arm, array, furnish, fit out, kit out 2 = **prepare**, qualify, educate, get ready

equipment = **apparatus**, stock, supplies, stuff, tackle, gear, tools, provisions

equitable = **even-handed**, just, fair, reasonable, proper, honest, impartial, unbiased

equivalent NOUN 1 = **equal**, counterpart, twin, parallel, match, opposite number
▷ ADJECTIVE 2 = **equal**, same, comparable, parallel, identical, alike, corresponding, tantamount OPPOSITE: different

era = **age**, time, period, date, generation, epoch, day or days

eradicate = **wipe out**, eliminate, remove, destroy, get rid of, erase, extinguish, obliterate

erase 1 = **delete**, cancel out, wipe out, remove, eradicate, obliterate, blot out, expunge 2 = **rub out**, remove, wipe out, delete

erect VERB 1 = **build**, raise, set up, construct, put up, assemble, put together OPPOSITE: demolish 2 = **found**, establish, form, create, set up, institute, organize, put up
▷ ADJECTIVE 3 = **upright**, straight, stiff, vertical, elevated, perpendicular, pricked-up

OPPOSITE: bent

erode 1 = **disintegrate**, crumble, deteriorate, corrode, break up, grind down, waste away, wear down or away 2 = **destroy**, consume, crumble, eat away, corrode, break up, grind down, abrade 3 = **weaken**, destroy, undermine, diminish, impair, lessen, wear away

erosion 1 = **disintegration**, deterioration, wearing down or away, grinding down 2 = **deterioration**, undermining, destruction, weakening, attrition, eating away, abrasion, grinding down

erotic = **sexual**, sexy (informal), crude, explicit, sensual, seductive, vulgar, voluptuous

erratic = **unpredictable**, variable, unstable, irregular, inconsistent, uneven, unreliable, wayward OPPOSITE: regular

error = **mistake**, slip, blunder, oversight, howler (informal), bloomer (Brit. informal), miscalculation, solecism

erupt 1 = **explode**, blow up, emit lava 2 = **discharge**, expel, emit, eject, spout, throw off, pour forth, spew forth or out 3 = **gush**, burst out, pour forth, belch forth, spew forth or out 4 = **start**, break out, begin, explode, flare up, burst out, boil over 5 (Medical) = **break out**, appear, flare up

escalate 1 = **grow**, increase, extend, intensify, expand, surge, mount, heighten **OPPOSITE:** decrease 2 = **increase**, develop, extend, intensify, expand, build up, heighten **OPPOSITE:** lessen

escape VERB 1 = **get away**, flee, take off, fly, bolt, slip away, abscond, make a break for it 2 = **avoid**, miss, evade, dodge, shun, elude, duck, steer clear of 3 = **leak out**, flow out, gush out, emanate, seep out, exude, spill out, pour forth
▷ NOUN 4 = **getaway**, break, flight, break-out 5 = **avoidance**, evasion, circumvention 6 = **relaxation**, recreation, distraction, diversion, pastime 7 = **leak**, emission, outpouring, seepage, issue, emanation

escort NOUN 1 = **guard**, bodyguard, train, convoy, entourage, retinue, cortege 2 = **companion**, partner, attendant, guide, beau, chaperon
▷ VERB 3 = **accompany**, lead, partner, conduct, guide, shepherd, usher, chaperon

especially 1 = **notably**, mostly, strikingly, conspicuously, outstandingly 2 = **very**, specially, extremely, remarkably, unusually, exceptionally, markedly, uncommonly

espionage = **spying**, intelligence, surveillance, counter-intelligence, undercover work

essay NOUN 1 = **composition**, study, paper, article, piece, assignment, discourse, tract
▷ VERB 2 (Formal) = **attempt**, try, undertake, endeavour

essence 1 = **fundamental nature**, nature, being, heart, spirit, soul, core, substance 2 = **concentrate**, spirits, extract, tincture, distillate

essential ADJECTIVE 1 = **vital**, important, needed, necessary, critical, crucial, key, indispensable **OPPOSITE:** unimportant 2 = **fundamental**, main, basic, principal, cardinal, elementary, innate, intrinsic **OPPOSITE:** secondary
▷ NOUN 3 = **prerequisite**, fundamental, necessity, must, basic, sine qua non (Latin), rudiment

establish 1 = **set up**, found, create, institute, constitute, inaugurate 2 = **prove**, confirm, demonstrate, certify, verify, substantiate, corroborate, authenticate 3 = **secure**, form, ground, settle

establishment 1 = **creation**, founding, setting up, foundation, institution, organization, formation, installation 2 = **organization**, company, business, firm, concern, operation, institution, corporation
▷ PHRASES: the Establishment = the authorities, the system,

the powers that be, the ruling class

estate 1 = **lands**, property, area, grounds, domain, manor, holdings 2 = **area**, centre, park, development, site, zone, plot 3 (*Law*) = **property**, capital, assets, fortune, goods, effects, wealth, possessions

esteem NOUN 1 = **respect**, regard, honour, admiration, reverence, estimation, veneration
▷ VERB 2 = **respect**, admire, think highly of, love, value, prize, treasure, revere

estimate VERB 1 = **calculate roughly**, value, guess, judge, reckon, assess, evaluate, gauge 2 = **think**, believe, consider, rate, judge, hold, rank, reckon
▷ NOUN 3 = **approximate calculation**, guess, assessment, judgment, valuation, guesstimate (*informal*), rough calculation, ballpark figure (*informal*) 4 = **assessment**, opinion, belief, appraisal, evaluation, judgment, estimation

estuary = **inlet**, mouth, creek, firth, fjord

etch 1 = **engrave**, cut, impress, stamp, carve, imprint, inscribe 2 = **corrode**, eat into, burn into

etching = **print**, carving, engraving, imprint, inscription

eternal 1 = **everlasting**, lasting, permanent, enduring, endless, perpetual, timeless,

unending OPPOSITE: transitory 2 = **interminable**, endless, infinite, continual, immortal, never-ending, everlasting OPPOSITE: occasional

eternity 1 (*Theology*) = **the afterlife**, heaven, paradise, the next world, the hereafter 2 = **perpetuity**, immortality, infinity, timelessness, endlessness 3 = **ages**

ethical 1 = **moral**, behavioural 2 = **right**, morally acceptable, good, just, fair, responsible, principled OPPOSITE: unethical

ethics = **moral code**, standards, principles, morals, conscience, morality, moral values, moral principles, tikanga (*N.Z.*)

ethnic *or* **ethnical** = **cultural**, national, traditional, native, folk, racial, genetic, indigenous

euphoria = **elation**, joy, ecstasy, rapture, exhilaration, jubilation OPPOSITE: despondency

evacuate 1 = **remove**, clear, withdraw, expel, move out, send to a safe place 2 = **abandon**, leave, clear, desert, quit, withdraw from, pull out of, move out of

evade 1 = **avoid**, escape, dodge, get away from, elude, steer clear of, sidestep, duck OPPOSITE: face 2 = **avoid answering**, parry, fend off, fudge, hedge, equivocate

evaluate = **assess**, rate, judge, estimate, reckon, weigh, calculate, gauge

evaporate 1 = **disappear**, vaporize, dematerialize, vanish, dissolve, dry up, fade away, melt away 2 = **dry up**, dry, dehydrate, vaporize, desiccate 3 = **fade away**, disappear, vanish, dissolve, melt away

eve 1 = **night before**, day before, vigil 2 = **brink**, point, edge, verge, threshold

even ADJECTIVE 1 = **regular**, stable, constant, steady, smooth, uniform, unbroken, uninterrupted **OPPOSITE:** variable 2 = **level**, straight, flat, smooth, true, steady, uniform, parallel **OPPOSITE:** uneven 3 = **equal**, like, matching, similar, identical, comparable **OPPOSITE:** unequal 4 = **equally matched**, level, tied, on a par, neck and neck, fifty-fifty (*informal*), all square **OPPOSITE:** ill-matched 5 = **square**, quits, on the same level, on an equal footing 6 = **calm**, composed, cool, well-balanced, placid, unruffled, imperturbable, even-tempered **OPPOSITE:** excitable

evening = **dusk** (*archaic*), night, sunset, twilight, sundown, gloaming (*Scot. poetic*), close of day, evo (*Austral. slang*)

event 1 = **incident**, happening, experience, affair, occasion, proceeding, business, circumstance 2 = **competition**, game, tournament, contest, bout

eventual = **final**, overall, concluding, ultimate

eventually = **in the end**, finally, one day, after all, some time, ultimately, at the end of the day, when all is said and done

ever 1 = **at any time**, at all, in any case, at any point, by any chance, on any occasion, at any period 2 = **always**, for ever, at all times, evermore 3 = **constantly**, continually, perpetually

every = **each**, each and every, every single

everybody = **everyone**, each one, the whole world, each person, every person, all and sundry, one and all
▷ EVERYONE

everyday = **ordinary**, common, usual, routine, stock, customary, mundane, run-of-the-mill **OPPOSITE:** unusual

everyone = **everybody**, each one, the whole world, each person, every person, all and sundry, one and all

● **USAGE NOTE**
● *Everyone* and *everybody* are
● interchangeable, and can be
● used as synonyms of each
● other in any context. Care
● should be taken, however, to
● distinguish between *everyone*
● as a single word and *every one*
● as two words, the latter form
● correctly being used to refer
● to each individual person or
● thing in a particular group:
● *every one of them is wrong.*

everything = all, the lot, the whole lot, each thing

everywhere 1 = all over, all around, the world over, high and low, in every nook and cranny, far and wide or near, to or in every place 2 = all around, all over, in every nook and cranny, ubiquitously, far and wide or near, to or in every place

evidence NOUN 1 = proof, grounds, demonstration, confirmation, verification, corroboration, authentication, substantiation 2 = sign(s), suggestion, trace, indication 3 = testimony, statement, submission, avowal
▷ VERB 4 = show, prove, reveal, display, indicate, witness, demonstrate, exhibit

evident = obvious, clear, plain, apparent, visible, manifest, noticeable, unmistakable
OPPOSITE: hidden

evidently 1 = obviously, clearly, plainly, undoubtedly, manifestly, without question, unmistakably 2 = apparently, seemingly, outwardly, ostensibly, so it seems, to all appearances

evil NOUN 1 = wickedness, bad, vice, sin, wrongdoing, depravity, badness, villainy 2 = harm, suffering, hurt, woe 3 = act of cruelty, crime, ill, horror, outrage, misfortune, mischief, affliction
▷ ADJECTIVE 4 = wicked, bad,

malicious, immoral, sinful, malevolent, depraved, villainous 5 = harmful, disastrous, destructive, dire, catastrophic, pernicious, ruinous 6 = demonic, satanic, diabolical, hellish, devilish, infernal, fiendish 7 = offensive, nasty, foul, unpleasant, vile, noxious, disagreeable, pestilential 8 = unfortunate, unfavourable, ruinous, calamitous

evoke = arouse, cause, induce, awaken, give rise to, stir up, rekindle, summon up
OPPOSITE: suppress

evolution 1 = rise, development, adaptation, natural selection, Darwinism, survival of the fittest 2 = development, growth, advance, progress, working out, expansion, extension, unfolding

evolve 1 = develop, metamorphose, adapt yourself 2 = grow, develop, advance, progress, mature 3 = work out, develop, progress, expand, unfold

exact ADJECTIVE 1 = accurate, correct, true, right, specific, precise, definite, faultless
OPPOSITE: approximate
▷ VERB 2 = demand, claim, force, command, extract, compel, extort 3 = inflict, apply, administer, mete out, deal out

exacting 1 = demanding,

hard, taxing, difficult, tough **OPPOSITE:** easy **2 = strict**, severe, harsh, rigorous, stringent

exactly 1 = accurately, correctly, precisely, faithfully, explicitly, scrupulously, truthfully, unerringly **2 = precisely**, specifically, bang on (*informal*), to the letter

exaggerate = overstate, enlarge, embroider, amplify, embellish, overestimate, overemphasize, pile it on about (*informal*)

examination 1 = checkup, analysis, going-over (*informal*), exploration, health check, check **2 = exam**, test, research, paper, investigation, practical, assessment, quiz

examine 1 = inspect, study, survey, investigate, explore, analyse, scrutinize, peruse **2 = check**, analyse, check over **3 = test**, question, assess, quiz, evaluate, appraise **4 = question**, quiz, interrogate, cross-examine, grill (*informal*), give the third degree to (*informal*)

example 1 = instance, specimen, case, sample, illustration, particular case, particular instance, typical case **2 = illustration**, model, ideal, standard, prototype, paradigm, archetype, paragon **3 = warning**, lesson, caution, deterrent

exceed 1 = surpass, better, pass, eclipse, beat, cap (*informal*), top, be over **2 = go over the limit of**, go beyond, overstep

excel = be superior, eclipse, beat, surpass, transcend, outdo, outshine ▷ **PHRASES: excel in** *or* **at something = be good at**, shine at, be proficient in, show talent in, be skilful at, be talented at

excellence = high quality, merit, distinction, goodness, superiority, greatness, supremacy, eminence

excellent = outstanding, good, great, fine, cool (*informal*), brilliant, very good, superb, booshit (*Austral. slang*), exo (*Austral. slang*), sik (*Austral. slang*) **OPPOSITE:** terrible

except *or* **except for** PREPOSITION **1 = apart from**, but for, saving, barring, excepting, other than, excluding, omitting ▷ VERB **2 = exclude**, leave out, omit, disregard, pass over

exception = special case, freak, anomaly, inconsistency, deviation, oddity, peculiarity, irregularity

exceptional 1 = remarkable, special, excellent, extraordinary, outstanding, superior, first-class, marvellous **OPPOSITE:** average **2 = unusual**, special, odd, strange, extraordinary, unprecedented, peculiar, abnormal **OPPOSITE:** ordinary

excerpt = **extract**, part, piece, section, selection, passage, fragment, quotation

excess 1 = **surfeit**, surplus, overload, glut, superabundance, superfluity **OPPOSITE:** shortage
2 = **overindulgence**, extravagance, profligacy, debauchery, dissipation, intemperance, indulgence, prodigality **OPPOSITE:** moderation

excessive 1 = **immoderate**, too much, extreme, exaggerated, unreasonable, disproportionate, undue, uncontrolled **2** = **inordinate**, unfair, unreasonable, disproportionate, undue, unwarranted, exorbitant, extortionate

exchange VERB
1 = **interchange**, change, trade, switch, swap, barter, give to each other, give to one another
▷ **NOUN 2** = **conversation**, talk, word, discussion, chat, dialogue, natter, powwow
3 = **interchange**, trade, switch, swap, trafficking, swapping, substitution, barter

excite 1 = **thrill**, inspire, stir, provoke, animate, rouse, exhilarate, inflame **2** = **arouse**, provoke, rouse, stir up
3 = **titillate**, thrill, stimulate, turn on (*slang*), arouse, get going (*informal*), electrify

excitement = **exhilaration**, action, activity, passion, thrill, animation, furore, agitation

exciting 1 = **stimulating**, dramatic, gripping, stirring, thrilling, sensational, rousing, exhilarating **OPPOSITE:** boring
2 = **titillating**, stimulating, arousing, erotic

exclaim = **cry out**, declare, shout, proclaim, yell, utter, call out

exclude 1 = **keep out**, bar, ban, refuse, forbid, boycott, prohibit, disallow **OPPOSITE:** let in
2 = **omit**, reject, eliminate, rule out, miss out, leave out **OPPOSITE:** include
3 = **eliminate**, reject, ignore, rule out, leave out, set aside, omit, pass over

exclusion 1 = **ban**, bar, veto, boycott, embargo, prohibition, disqualification
2 = **elimination**, missing out, rejection, leaving out, omission

exclusive 1 = **select**, fashionable, stylish, restricted, posh (*informal, chiefly Brit.*), chic, high-class, up-market **OPPOSITE:** unrestricted
2 = **sole**, full, whole, complete, total, entire, absolute, undivided **OPPOSITE:** shared
3 = **entire**, full, whole, complete, total, absolute, undivided **4** = **limited**, unique, restricted, confined, peculiar

excursion = **trip**, tour, journey, outing, expedition, ramble, day trip, jaunt, awayday

excuse NOUN 1 = **justification**, reason, explanation, defence, grounds, plea, apology, vindication **OPPOSITE:** accusation

▷ VERB 2 = **justify**, explain, defend, vindicate, mitigate, apologize for, make excuses for **OPPOSITE:** blame 3 = **forgive**, pardon, overlook, tolerate, acquit, turn a blind eye to, exonerate, make allowances for 4 = **free**, relieve, exempt, release, spare, discharge, let off, absolve **OPPOSITE:** convict

execute 1 = **put to death**, kill, shoot, hang, behead, decapitate, guillotine, electrocute 2 = **carry out**, effect, implement, accomplish, discharge, administer, prosecute, enact 3 = **perform**, carry out, accomplish

execution 1 = **killing**, hanging, the death penalty, the rope, capital punishment, beheading, the electric chair, the guillotine 2 = **carrying out**, performance, operation, administration, prosecution, enforcement, implementation, accomplishment

executive NOUN 1 = **administrator**, official, director, manager, chairman, managing director, controller, chief executive officer 2 = **administration**, government, directors, management, leadership, hierarchy, directorate

▷ ADJECTIVE 3 = **administrative**, controlling, directing, governing, regulating, decision-making, managerial

exemplify = **show**, represent, display, demonstrate, illustrate, exhibit, embody, serve as an example of

exempt ADJECTIVE 1 = **immune**, free, excepted, excused, released, spared, not liable to **OPPOSITE:** liable

▷ VERB 2 = **grant immunity**, free, excuse, release, spare, relieve, discharge, let off

exemption = **immunity**, freedom, relief, exception, discharge, release, dispensation, absolution

exercise VERB 1 = **put to use**, use, apply, employ, exert, utilize, bring to bear, avail yourself of 2 = **train**, work out, practise, keep fit, do exercises

▷ NOUN 3 = **use**, practice, application, operation, discharge, implementation, fulfilment, utilization 4 = **exertion**, training, activity, work, labour, effort, movement, toil 5 = **manoeuvre**, campaign, operation, movement, deployment 6 = **task**, problem, lesson, assignment, practice

exert = **apply**, use, exercise, employ, wield, make use of, utilize, bring to bear

▷ PHRASES: **exert yourself**

= **make an effort**, work, labour, struggle, strain, strive, endeavour, toil

exhaust 1 = **tire out**, fatigue, drain, weaken, weary, sap, wear out, debilitate **2** = **use up**, spend, consume, waste, go through, run through, deplete, squander

exhausted 1 = **worn out**, tired out, drained, spent, bushed (*informal*), done in (*informal*), all in (*slang*), fatigued **OPPOSITE:** invigorated **2** = **used up**, consumed, spent, finished, depleted, dissipated, expended **OPPOSITE:** replenished

exhaustion 1 = **tiredness**, fatigue, weariness, debilitation **2** = **depletion**, emptying, consumption, using up

exhibit 1 = **show**, reveal, display, demonstrate, express, indicate, manifest **2** = **display**, show, set out, parade, unveil, put on view

exhibition 1 = **show**, display, representation, presentation, spectacle, showcase, exposition **2** = **display**, show, performance, demonstration, revelation

exile NOUN **1** = **banishment**, expulsion, deportation, eviction, expatriation **2** = **expatriate**, refugee, outcast, émigré, deportee ▷ VERB **3** = **banish**, expel, throw out, deport, drive out, eject, expatriate, cast out

exist 1 = **live**, be present, survive, endure, be in existence, be, have breath **2** = **occur**, be present **3** = **survive**, stay alive, make ends meet, subsist, eke out a living, scrape by, scrimp and save, support yourself

existence 1 = **reality**, being, life, subsistence, actuality **2** = **life**, situation, way of life, life style

existent = **in existence**, living, existing, surviving, standing, present, alive, extant

exit NOUN **1** = **way out**, door, gate, outlet, doorway, gateway, escape route **OPPOSITE:** entry **2** = **departure**, withdrawal, retreat, farewell, going, goodbye, exodus, decamping ▷ VERB **3** = **depart**, leave, go out, withdraw, retire, quit, retreat, go away **OPPOSITE:** enter

exodus = **departure**, withdrawal, retreat, leaving, flight, exit, migration, evacuation

exotic 1 = **unusual**, striking, strange, fascinating, mysterious, colourful, glamorous, unfamiliar **OPPOSITE:** ordinary **2** = **foreign**, alien, tropical, external, naturalized

expand 1 = **get bigger**, increase, grow, extend, swell, widen, enlarge, become bigger **OPPOSITE:** contract **2** = **make bigger**, increase, develop, extend, widen, enlarge,

broaden, magnify **OPPOSITE:** reduce **3** = **spread (out)**, stretch (out), unfold, unravel, diffuse, unfurl, unroll
▷ **PHRASES: expand on something** = **go into detail about**, embellish, elaborate on, develop, flesh out, expound on, enlarge on, expatiate on

expansion 1 = **increase**, development, growth, spread, magnification, amplification **2** = **enlargement**, increase, growth, opening out

expatriate NOUN **1** = **exile**, refugee, emigrant, émigré
▷ **ADJECTIVE 2** = **exiled**, refugee, banished, emigrant, émigré, expat

expect 1 = **think**, believe, suppose, assume, trust, imagine, reckon, presume **2** = **anticipate**, look forward to, predict, envisage, await, hope for, contemplate **3** = **require**, demand, want, call for, ask for, hope for, insist on

expectation 1 = **projection**, supposition, assumption, belief, forecast, likelihood, probability, presumption **2** = **anticipation**, hope, promise, excitement, expectancy, apprehension, suspense

expedition = **journey**, mission, voyage, tour, quest, trek

expel 1 = **throw out**, exclude, ban, dismiss, kick out (*informal*), ask to leave, turf out (*informal*), debar **OPPOSITE:** let in

2 = **banish**, exile, deport, evict, force to leave **OPPOSITE:** take in **3** = **drive out**, discharge, force out, let out, eject, issue, spew, belch

expenditure 1 = **spending**, payment, expense, outgoings, cost, outlay **2** = **consumption**, using, output

expense = **cost**, charge, expenditure, payment, spending, outlay

expensive = **costly**, high-priced, lavish, extravagant, dear, stiff, steep (*informal*), pricey **OPPOSITE:** cheap

experience NOUN **1** = **knowledge**, practice, skill, contact, expertise, involvement, exposure, participation **2** = **event**, affair, incident, happening, encounter, episode, adventure, occurrence
▷ **VERB 3** = **undergo**, feel, face, taste, go through, sample, encounter, endure

experienced = **knowledgeable**, skilled, tried, tested, seasoned, expert, veteran, practised **OPPOSITE:** inexperienced

experiment NOUN **1** = **test**, trial, investigation, examination, procedure, demonstration, observation, try-out **2** = **research**, investigation, analysis, observation, research and development, experimentation
▷ **VERB 3** = **test**, investigate,

trial, research, try, examine, pilot, sample

experimental 1 = test, trial, pilot, preliminary, provisional, tentative, speculative, exploratory **2 = innovative**, new, original, radical, creative, ingenious, avant-garde, inventive

expert NOUN 1 = specialist, authority, professional, master, genius, guru, pundit, maestro, fundi (*S. African*) **OPPOSITE:** amateur
▷ **ADJECTIVE 2 = skilful**, experienced, professional, masterly, qualified, talented, outstanding, practised **OPPOSITE:** unskilled

expertise = skill, knowledge, know-how (*informal*), facility, judgment, mastery, proficiency, adroitness

expire 1 = become invalid, end, finish, conclude, close, stop, run out, cease **2 = die**, depart, perish, kick the bucket (*informal*), depart this life, meet your maker, cark it (*Austral. & N.Z. slang*), pass away *or* on

explain 1 = make clear *or* **plain**, describe, teach, define, resolve, clarify, clear up, simplify **2 = account for**, excuse, justify, give a reason for

explanation 1 = reason, answer, account, excuse, motive, justification, vindication **2 = description**, report, definition, teaching, interpretation, illustration, clarification, simplification

explicit 1 = clear, obvious, specific, direct, precise, straightforward, definite, overt **OPPOSITE:** vague **2 = frank**, specific, graphic, unambiguous, unrestricted, unrestrained, uncensored **OPPOSITE:** indirect

explode 1 = blow up, erupt, burst, go off, shatter **2 = detonate**, set off, discharge, let off **3 = lose your temper**, rage, erupt, become angry, hit the roof (*informal*), go crook (*Austral. & N.Z. slang*) **4 = increase**, grow, develop, extend, advance, shoot up, soar, boost **5 = disprove**, discredit, refute, demolish, repudiate, put paid to, invalidate, debunk

exploit VERB 1 = take advantage of, abuse, use, manipulate, milk, misuse, ill-treat, play on *or* upon **2 = make the best use of**, use, make use of, utilize, cash in on (*informal*), capitalize on, use to good advantage, profit by *or* from
▷ **NOUN 3 = feat**, act, achievement, enterprise, adventure, stunt, deed, accomplishment

exploitation = misuse, abuse, manipulation, using, ill-treatment

exploration 1 = expedition, tour, trip, survey, travel, journey, reconnaissance

2 = **investigation**, research, survey, search, inquiry, analysis, examination, inspection

explore 1 = **travel around**, tour, survey, scout, reconnoitre 2 = **investigate**, consider, research, survey, search, examine, probe, look into

explosion 1 = **blast**, crack, burst, bang, discharge, report, blowing up, clap 2 = **increase**, rise, development, growth, boost, expansion, enlargement, escalation 3 = **outburst**, fit, storm, attack, surge, flare-up, eruption 4 = **outbreak**, flare-up, eruption, upsurge

explosive NOUN 1 = **bomb**, mine, shell, missile, rocket, grenade, charge, torpedo ▷ ADJECTIVE 2 = **unstable**, dangerous, volatile, hazardous, unsafe, perilous, combustible, inflammable 3 = **sudden**, rapid, marked, unexpected, startling, swift, abrupt 4 = **fiery**, violent, volatile, stormy, touchy, vehement

expose 1 = **uncover**, show, reveal, display, exhibit, present, unveil, lay bare **OPPOSITE:** hide 2 = **make vulnerable**, subject, endanger, leave open, jeopardize, put at risk, imperil, lay open

exposure 1 = **hypothermia**, frostbite, extreme cold, intense cold 2 = **uncovering**, showing, display, exhibition, revelation, presentation, unveiling

express VERB 1 = **state**, communicate, convey, articulate, say, word, voice, declare 2 = **show**, indicate, exhibit, demonstrate, reveal, intimate, convey, signify ▷ ADJECTIVE 3 = **explicit**, clear, plain, distinct, definite, unambiguous, categorical 4 = **specific**, exclusive, particular, sole, special, singular, clear-cut, especial 5 = **fast**, direct, rapid, priority, prompt, swift, high-speed, speedy

expression 1 = **statement**, declaration, announcement, communication, utterance, articulation 2 = **indication**, demonstration, exhibition, display, showing, show, sign, symbol 3 = **look**, countenance, face, air, appearance, aspect 4 = **phrase**, saying, word, term, remark, maxim, idiom, adage

expressive = **vivid**, striking, telling, moving, poignant, eloquent **OPPOSITE:** impassive

expulsion 1 = **ejection**, exclusion, dismissal, removal, eviction, banishment 2 = **discharge**, emission, spewing, secretion, excretion, ejection, seepage, suppuration

exquisite 1 = **beautiful**, elegant, graceful, pleasing, attractive, lovely, charming, comely **OPPOSITE:** unattractive 2 = **fine**, beautiful, lovely, elegant, precious, delicate, dainty 3 = **intense**, acute, severe, sharp, keen, extreme

extend VERB 1 = **spread out**, reach, stretch 2 = **stretch**, stretch out, spread out, straighten out 3 = **last**, continue, go on, stretch, carry on 4 = **protrude**, project, stand out, bulge, stick out, hang, overhang, jut out 5 = **widen**, increase, expand, add to, enhance, supplement, enlarge, broaden **OPPOSITE:** reduce 6 = **make longer**, prolong, lengthen, draw out, spin out, drag out **OPPOSITE:** shorten 7 = **offer**, present, confer, stick out, impart, proffer **OPPOSITE:** withdraw

extension 1 = **annexe**, addition, supplement, appendix, appendage 2 = **lengthening**, extra time, continuation, additional period of time 3 = **development**, expansion, widening, increase, broadening, enlargement, diversification

extensive 1 = **large**, considerable, substantial, spacious, wide, broad, expansive **OPPOSITE:** confined 2 = **comprehensive**, complete, wide, pervasive **OPPOSITE:** restricted 3 = **great**, vast, widespread, large-scale, far-reaching, far-flung, voluminous **OPPOSITE:** limited

extent 1 = **magnitude**, amount, scale, level, stretch,

expanse 2 = **size**, area, length, width, breadth

exterior NOUN 1 = **outside**, face, surface, covering, skin, shell, coating, façade
▷ ADJECTIVE 2 = **outer**, outside, external, surface, outward, outermost **OPPOSITE:** inner

external 1 = **outer**, outside, surface, outward, exterior, outermost **OPPOSITE:** internal 2 = **foreign**, international, alien, extrinsic **OPPOSITE:** domestic 3 = **outside**, visiting **OPPOSITE:** inside

extinct = **dead**, lost, gone, vanished, defunct **OPPOSITE:** living

extinction = **dying out**, destruction, abolition, oblivion, extermination, annihilation, eradication, obliteration

extra ADJECTIVE 1 = **additional**, more, added, further, supplementary, auxiliary, ancillary **OPPOSITE:** vital 2 = **surplus**, excess, spare, redundant, unused, leftover, superfluous
▷ NOUN 3 = **addition**, bonus, supplement, accessory **OPPOSITE:** necessity
▷ ADVERB 4 = **in addition**, additionally, over and above 5 = **exceptionally**, very, specially, especially, particularly, extremely, remarkably, unusually

extract VERB 1 = **take out**, draw, pull, remove, withdraw, pull out, bring out 2 = **pull out**, remove, take out, draw, uproot, pluck out 3 = **elicit**, obtain, force, draw, derive, glean, coerce

▷ NOUN 4 = **passage**, selection, excerpt, cutting, clipping, quotation, citation 5 = **essence**, solution, concentrate, juice, distillation

● USAGE NOTE
● People sometimes use *extract*
● where *extricate* would be
● better. Although both words
● can refer to a physical act of
● removal from a place, *extract*
● has a more general sense
● than *extricate*. *Extricate* has
● additional overtones of
● 'difficulty', and is most
● commonly used with
● reference to getting a person
● - particularly *yourself* - out of
● a situation. So, for example,
● you might say *he will find it*
● *difficult to extricate himself* (not
● *extract himself*) *from this*
● *situation*.

extraordinary
1 = **remarkable**, outstanding, amazing, fantastic, astonishing, exceptional, phenomenal, extremely good **OPPOSITE:** unremarkable 2 = **unusual**, strange, remarkable, uncommon **OPPOSITE:** ordinary
extravagant 1 = **wasteful**, lavish, prodigal, profligate, spendthrift **OPPOSITE:** economical 2 = **excessive**,

outrageous, over the top (*slang*), unreasonable, preposterous **OPPOSITE:** moderate
extreme ADJECTIVE 1 = **great**, highest, supreme, acute, severe, maximum, intense, ultimate **OPPOSITE:** mild 2 = **severe**, radical, strict, harsh, rigid, drastic, uncompromising 3 = **radical**, excessive, fanatical, immoderate **OPPOSITE:** moderate 4 = **farthest**, furthest, far, remotest, far-off, outermost, most distant **OPPOSITE:** nearest

▷ NOUN 5 = **limit**, end, edge, opposite, pole, boundary, antithesis, extremity
extremely = **very**, particularly, severely, terribly, unusually, exceptionally, extraordinarily, tremendously
extremist NOUN 1 = **radical**, activist, militant, fanatic, die-hard, bigot, zealot

▷ ADJECTIVE 2 = **extreme**, wild, passionate, frenzied, obsessive, fanatical, fervent, zealous
eye NOUN 1 = **eyeball**, optic (*informal*), organ of vision, organ of sight 2 *often plural* = **eyesight**, sight, vision, perception, ability to see, power of seeing 3 = **appreciation**, taste, recognition, judgment, discrimination, perception, discernment 4 = **observance**, observation, surveillance, vigil, watch, lookout 5 = **centre**,

heart, middle, mid, core,
nucleus
▷ VERB 6 = **look at**, view, study,
watch, survey, observe,
contemplate, check out
(*informal*)
eyesight = **vision**, sight,
observation, perception, ability
to see, range of vision, power of
seeing, power of sight
eyesore = **mess**, blight, blot,
blemish, sight (*informal*),horror,
disgrace, atrocity, ugliness,
monstrosity, disfigurement

fable 1 = **legend**, myth, parable,
allegory, story, tale 2 = **fiction**,
fantasy, myth, invention, yarn
(*informal*), fabrication, urban
myth, tall story (*informal*)
OPPOSITE: fact
fabric 1 = **cloth**, material, stuff,
textile, web 2 = **framework**,
structure, make-up,
organization, frame,
foundations, construction,
constitution 3 = **structure**,
foundations, construction,
framework
fabulous 1 (*Informal*)
= **wonderful**, excellent, brilliant,
superb, spectacular, fantastic
(*informal*), marvellous,
sensational (*informal*) **OPPOSITE:**
ordinary 2 = **astounding**,
amazing, extraordinary,
remarkable, incredible,
astonishing, unbelievable,
breathtaking 3 = **legendary**,
imaginary, mythical, fictitious,
made-up, fantastic, invented,
unreal
façade 1 = **front**, face, exterior
2 = **show**, front, appearance,
mask, exterior, guise, pretence,
semblance

face NOUN 1 = **countenance**, features, profile, mug (*slang*), visage 2 = **expression**, look, air, appearance, aspect, countenance 3 = **side**, front, outside, surface, exterior, elevation, vertical surface
▷ VERB 4 = **look onto**, overlook, be opposite, look out on, front onto 5 = **confront**, meet, encounter, deal with, oppose, tackle, experience, brave 6 *often with* **up to** = **accept**, deal with, tackle, acknowledge, cope with, confront, come to terms with, meet head-on

facilitate = **further**, help, forward, promote, speed up, pave the way for, make easy, expedite OPPOSITE: hinder

facility 1 *often plural* = **amenity**, means, aid, opportunity, advantage, resource, equipment, provision 2 = **opportunity**, possibility, convenience 3 = **ability**, skill, efficiency, fluency, proficiency, dexterity, adroitness 4 = **ease**, fluency, effortlessness OPPOSITE: difficulty

fact 1 = **truth**, reality, certainty, verity OPPOSITE: fiction 2 = **event**, happening, act, performance, incident, deed, occurrence, fait accompli (*French*)

faction 1 = **group**, set, party, gang, bloc, contingent, clique, coterie 2 = **dissension**, division, conflict, rebellion, disagreement, variance, discord, infighting OPPOSITE: agreement

factor = **element**, part, cause, influence, item, aspect, characteristic, consideration
● USAGE NOTE
● In strict usage, *factor* should only be used to refer to something which contributes to a result. It should not be used to refer to a part of something, such as a plan or arrangement; more appropriate alternatives to *factor* in this sense are words such as *component* or *element*.

factory = **works**, plant, mill, workshop, assembly line, shop floor

factual = **true**, authentic, real, correct, genuine, exact, precise, dinkum (*Austral. & N.Z. informal*), true-to-life OPPOSITE: fictitious

faculty NOUN 1 = **ability**, power, skill, facility, capacity, propensity, aptitude OPPOSITE: failing 2 = **department**, school 3 = **teaching staff**, staff, teachers, professors, lecturers (*chiefly U.S.*)
▷ PLURAL NOUN 4 = **powers**, reason, senses, intelligence, wits, capabilities, mental abilities, physical abilities

fad = **craze**, fashion, trend, rage, vogue, whim, mania

fade 1 = **become pale**, bleach, wash out, discolour, lose colour, decolour **2 = make pale**, dim, bleach, wash out, blanch, discolour, decolour **3 = grow dim**, fade away, become less loud **4 = dwindle**, disappear, vanish, melt away, decline, dissolve, wane, die away

fail VERB **1 = be unsuccessful**, founder, fall, break down, flop (*informal*), fizzle out (*informal*), come unstuck, miscarry OPPOSITE: succeed **2 = disappoint**, abandon, desert, neglect, omit, let down, forsake, be disloyal to **3 = stop working**, stop, die, break down, stall, cut out, malfunction, conk out (*informal*) **4 = wither**, perish, sag, waste away, shrivel up **5 = go bankrupt**, collapse, fold (*informal*), close down, go under, go bust (*informal*), go out of business, be wound up **6 = decline**, deteriorate, degenerate **7 = give out**, dim, peter out, die away, grow dim
▷ PHRASES: **without fail**
= without exception, regularly, constantly, invariably, religiously, unfailingly, conscientiously, like clockwork

failing NOUN **1 = shortcoming**, fault, weakness, defect, deficiency, flaw, drawback, blemish OPPOSITE: strength
▷ PREPOSITION **2 = in the absence of**, lacking, in default of

failure 1 = lack of success, defeat, collapse, breakdown,

overthrow, miscarriage, fiasco, downfall OPPOSITE: success **2 = loser**, disappointment, flop (*informal*), write-off, no-hoper (*chiefly Austral.*), dud (*informal*), black sheep, washout (*informal*), dead duck (*slang*) **3 = bankruptcy**, crash, collapse, ruin, closure, winding up, downfall, going under OPPOSITE: prosperity

faint ADJECTIVE **1 = dim**, low, soft, faded, distant, vague, unclear, muted OPPOSITE: clear **2 = slight**, weak, feeble, unenthusiastic, remote, slim, vague, slender **3 = dizzy**, giddy, light-headed, weak, exhausted, wobbly, muzzy, woozy (*informal*) OPPOSITE: energetic
▷ VERB **4 = pass out**, black out, lose consciousness, keel over (*informal*), go out, collapse, swoon (*literary*), flake out (*informal*)
▷ NOUN **5 = blackout**, collapse, coma, swoon (*literary*), unconsciousness

faintly 1 = slightly, rather, a little, somewhat, dimly **2 = softly**, weakly, feebly, in a whisper, indistinctly, unclearly

fair¹ ADJECTIVE **1 = unbiased**, impartial, even-handed, unprejudiced, just, reasonable, proper, legitimate OPPOSITE: unfair **2 = respectable**, average, reasonable, decent, acceptable, moderate, adequate, satisfactory

3 = **light**, golden, blonde, blond, yellowish, fair-haired, light-coloured, flaxen-haired
4 = **fine**, clear, dry, bright, pleasant, sunny, cloudless, unclouded 5 = **beautiful**, pretty, attractive, lovely, handsome, good-looking, bonny, comely **OPPOSITE:** ugly

fair² = **carnival**, show, fête, festival, exhibition, mart, bazaar, gala

fairly 1 = **equitably**, objectively, legitimately, honestly, justly, lawfully, without prejudice, dispassionately
2 = **moderately**, rather, quite, somewhat, reasonably, adequately, pretty well, tolerably 3 = **positively**, really, simply, absolutely
4 = **deservedly**, objectively, honestly, justifiably, justly, impartially, equitably, without fear or favour

fairness = **impartiality**, justice, equity, legitimacy, decency, disinterestedness, rightfulness, equitableness

fairy = **sprite**, elf, brownie, pixie, puck, imp, leprechaun, peri

fairy tale *or* **fairy story**
1 = **folk tale**, romance, traditional story 2 = **lie**, fiction, invention, fabrication, untruth, urban myth, tall story, urban legend

faith 1 = **confidence**, trust, credit, conviction, assurance, dependence, reliance, credence
OPPOSITE: distrust 2 = **religion**, church, belief, persuasion, creed, communion, denomination, dogma
OPPOSITE: agnosticism

faithful 1 = **loyal**, true, committed, constant, devoted, dedicated, reliable, staunch
OPPOSITE: disloyal
2 = **accurate**, close, true, strict, exact, precise

fake ADJECTIVE 1 = **artificial**, false, forged, counterfeit, put-on, pretend (*informal*), mock, imitation **OPPOSITE:** genuine
▷ NOUN 2 = **forgery**, copy, fraud, reproduction, dummy, imitation, hoax, counterfeit
3 = **charlatan**, deceiver, sham, quack
▷ VERB 4 = **forge**, copy, reproduce, fabricate, counterfeit, falsify 5 = **sham**, put on, pretend, simulate, feign, go through the motions of

fall VERB 1 = **drop**, plunge, tumble, plummet, collapse, sink, go down, come down
OPPOSITE: rise 2 = **decrease**, drop, decline, go down, slump, diminish, dwindle, lessen
OPPOSITE: increase 3 = **be overthrown**, surrender, succumb, submit, capitulate, be conquered, pass into enemy hands **OPPOSITE:** triumph
4 = **be killed**, die, perish, meet your end **OPPOSITE:** survive
5 = **occur**, happen, come about, chance, take place, befall

▷ NOUN 6 = **drop**, slip, plunge, dive, tumble, descent, plummet, nose dive
7 = **decrease**, drop, lowering, decline, reduction, slump, dip, lessening 8 = **collapse**, defeat, downfall, ruin, destruction, overthrow, submission, capitulation

false 1 = **incorrect**, wrong, mistaken, misleading, faulty, inaccurate, invalid, erroneous **OPPOSITE:** correct 2 = **untrue**, fraudulent, trumped up, fallacious, untruthful **OPPOSITE:** true 3 = **artificial**, forged, fake, reproduction, replica, imitation, bogus, simulated **OPPOSITE:** real

falter 1 = **hesitate**, delay, waver, vacillate **OPPOSITE:** persevere 2 = **tumble**, totter 3 = **stutter**, pause, stumble, hesitate, stammer

fame = **prominence**, glory, celebrity, stardom, reputation, honour, prestige, stature, illustriousness, **OPPOSITE:** obscurity

familiar 1 = **well-known**, recognized, common, ordinary, routine, frequent, accustomed, customary **OPPOSITE:** unfamiliar 2 = **friendly**, close, dear, intimate, amicable **OPPOSITE:** formal 3 = **relaxed**, easy, friendly, comfortable, intimate, casual, amicable 4 = **disrespectful**, forward, bold, intrusive, presumptuous,

impudent, overfamiliar

familiarity 1 = **acquaintance**, experience, understanding, knowledge, awareness, grasp **OPPOSITE:** unfamiliarity 2 = **friendliness**, intimacy, ease, openness, informality, sociability **OPPOSITE:** formality 3 = **disrespect**, forwardness, overfamiliarity, cheek, presumption, boldness **OPPOSITE:** respect

family 1 = **relations**, relatives, household, folk (*informal*), kin, nuclear family, next of kin, kith and kin, ainga (*N.Z.*) 2 = **children**, kids (*informal*), offspring, little ones, littlies (*Austral. informal*) 3 = **ancestors**, house, race, tribe, clan, dynasty, line of descent 4 = **species**, group, class, system, order, network, genre, subdivision

● USAGE NOTE
● Some careful writers insist
● that a singular verb should
● always be used with
● collective nouns such as
● *government*, *team*, *family*,
● *committee*, and *class*, for
● example: *the class is doing a*
● *project on Vikings; the company*
● *is mounting a big sales*
● *campaign*. In British usage,
● however, a plural verb is
● often used with a collective
● noun, especially where the
● emphasis is on a collection of
● individual objects or people

rather than a group regarded as a unit: *the family are all on holiday*. The most important thing to remember is never to treat the same collective noun as both singular and plural in the same sentence: *the family is well and sends its best wishes* or *the family are well and send their best wishes*, but not *the family is well and send their best wishes*.

famine = hunger, want, starvation, deprivation, scarcity, dearth

famous = well-known, celebrated, acclaimed, noted, distinguished, prominent, legendary, renowned **OPPOSITE:** unknown

fan[1] NOUN 1 = blower, ventilator, air conditioner
▷ VERB 2 = blow, cool, refresh, air-condition, ventilate

fan[2] = supporter, lover, follower, enthusiast, admirer, buff (*informal*), devotee, aficionado

fanatic = extremist, activist, militant, bigot, zealot

fancy ADJECTIVE 1 = elaborate, decorative, extravagant, intricate, baroque, ornamental, ornate, embellished **OPPOSITE:** plain
▷ NOUN 2 = whim, thought, idea, desire, urge, notion, humour, impulse 3 = delusion, dream, vision, fantasy, daydream, chimera
▷ VERB 4 = wish for, want,

desire, hope for, long for, crave, yearn for, thirst for 5 (*Informal*) = be attracted to, find attractive, lust after, like, take to, be captivated by, have a thing about (*informal*), have eyes for 6 = suppose, think, believe, imagine, reckon, conjecture, think likely

fantastic 1 (*Informal*) = wonderful, great, excellent, very good, smashing (*informal*), superb, tremendous (*informal*), magnificent, booshit (*Austral. slang*), exo (*Austral. slang*), sik (*Austral. slang*) **OPPOSITE:** ordinary 2 = strange, bizarre, grotesque, fanciful, outlandish 3 = implausible, unlikely, incredible, absurd, preposterous, cock-and-bull (*informal*)

fantasy or (*Archaic*) **phantasy** 1 = daydream, dream, wish, reverie, flight of fancy, pipe dream 2 = imagination, fancy, invention, creativity, originality

far ADVERB 1 = a long way, miles, deep, a good way, afar, a great distance 2 = much, greatly, very much, extremely, significantly, considerably, decidedly, markedly
▷ ADJECTIVE 3 *often with* off = remote, distant, far-flung, faraway, out-of-the-way, far-off, outlying, off the beaten track **OPPOSITE:** near

farce 1 = comedy, satire, slapstick, burlesque, buffoonery

2 = **mockery**, joke, nonsense, parody, shambles, sham, travesty

fare NOUN 1 = **charge**, price, ticket price, ticket money 2 = **food**, provisions, board, rations, kai (*N.Z. informal*), nourishment, sustenance, victuals, nutriment
▷ VERB 3 = **get on**, do, manage, make out, prosper, get along

farewell INTERJECTION 1 = **goodbye**, bye (*informal*), so long, see you, take care, good morning, bye-bye (*informal*), good day, haere ra (*N.Z.*)
▷ NOUN 2 = **goodbye**, parting, departure, leave-taking, adieu, valediction, sendoff (*informal*)

farm NOUN 1 = **smallholding**, ranch (*chiefly U.S. & Canad.*), farmstead, station (*Austral. & N.Z.*), vineyard, plantation, croft (*Scot.*), grange, homestead
▷ VERB 2 = **cultivate**, work, plant, grow crops on, keep animals on

fascinate = **entrance**, absorb, intrigue, rivet, captivate, enthral, beguile, transfix **OPPOSITE:** bore

fascinating = **captivating**, engaging, gripping, compelling, intriguing, very interesting, irresistible, enticing **OPPOSITE:** boring

fascination = **attraction**, pull, magic, charm, lure, allure, magnetism, enchantment

fashion NOUN 1 = **style**, look, trend, rage, custom, mode, vogue, craze 2 = **method**, way, style, manner, mode
▷ VERB 3 = **make**, shape, cast, construct, form, create, manufacture, forge

fashionable = **popular**, in fashion, trendy (*Brit. informal*), in (*informal*), modern, with it (*informal*), stylish, chic **OPPOSITE:** unfashionable

fast¹ ADJECTIVE 1 = **quick**, flying, rapid, fleet, swift, speedy, brisk, hasty **OPPOSITE:** slow 2 = **fixed**, firm, sound, stuck, secure, tight, jammed, fastened **OPPOSITE:** unstable 3 = **dissipated**, wild, exciting, loose, extravagant, reckless, self-indulgent, wanton 4 = **close**, firm, devoted, faithful, steadfast
▷ ADVERB 5 = **quickly**, rapidly, swiftly, hastily, hurriedly, speedily, in haste, at full speed **OPPOSITE:** slowly 6 = **securely**, firmly, tightly, fixedly 7 = **fixedly**, firmly, soundly, deeply, securely, tightly

fast² VERB 1 = **go hungry**, abstain, go without food, deny yourself
▷ NOUN 2 = **fasting**, diet, abstinence

fasten 1 = **secure**, close, do up 2 = **tie**, bind, tie up 3 = **fix**, join, link, connect, attach, affix

fat ADJECTIVE 1 = **overweight**, large, heavy, plump, stout, obese, tubby, portly **OPPOSITE:** thin **2** = fatty, greasy, adipose, oleaginous, oily **OPPOSITE:** lean

▷ NOUN **3** = **fatness**, flesh, bulk, obesity, flab, blubber, paunch, fatty tissue

fatal 1 = **disastrous**, devastating, crippling, catastrophic, ruinous, calamitous, baleful, baneful **OPPOSITE:** minor **2** = **lethal**, deadly, mortal, causing death, final, killing, terminal, malignant **OPPOSITE:** harmless

fate 1 = **destiny**, chance, fortune, luck, the stars, providence, nemesis, kismet **2** = **fortune**, destiny, lot, portion, cup, horoscope

fated = **destined**, doomed, predestined, preordained, foreordained

father NOUN **1** = **daddy** (*informal*), dad (*informal*), male parent, pop (*U.S. informal*), old man (*Brit. informal*), pa (*informal*), papa (*old-fashioned informal*), pater **2** = **founder**, author, maker, architect, creator, inventor, originator, prime mover **3** *usually cap.* = **priest**, minister, vicar, parson, pastor, cleric, churchman, padre (*informal*) **4** *usually plural* = **forefather**, predecessor, ancestor, forebear, progenitor, tupuna *or* tipuna (*N.Z.*)

▷ VERB **5** = **sire**, parent, conceive, bring to life, beget, procreate, bring into being,
give life to, get

fatherly = **paternal**, kindly, protective, supportive, benign, affectionate, patriarchal, benevolent

fatigue NOUN **1** = **tiredness**, lethargy, weariness, heaviness, languor, listlessness **OPPOSITE:** freshness

▷ VERB **2** = **tire**, exhaust, weaken, weary, drain, wear out, take it out of (*informal*), tire out **OPPOSITE:** refresh

fatty = **greasy**, fat, creamy, oily, adipose, oleaginous, suety, rich

fault NOUN **1** = **responsibility**, liability, guilt, accountability, culpability **2** = **mistake**, slip, error, blunder, lapse, oversight, indiscretion, howler (*informal*) **3** = **failing**, weakness, defect, deficiency, flaw, shortcoming, blemish, imperfection **OPPOSITE:** strength

▷ VERB **4** = **criticize**, blame, complain, condemn, moan about, censure, hold (someone) responsible, find fault with

▷ PHRASES: **find fault with something** *or* **someone** = **criticize**, complain about, whinge about (*informal*), whine about (*informal*), quibble, carp at, take to task, pick holes in

▶ **to a fault** = **excessively**, unduly, in the extreme, overmuch, immoderately

faulty 1 = **defective**, damaged, malfunctioning, broken, flawed, impaired, imperfect, out of order 2 = **incorrect**, flawed, unsound

favour NOUN 1 = **approval**, goodwill, commendation, approbation OPPOSITE: disapproval 2 = **favouritism**, preferential treatment 3 = **support**, backing, aid, assistance, patronage, good opinion 4 = **good turn**, service, benefit, courtesy, kindness, indulgence, boon, good deed OPPOSITE: wrong
▷ VERB 5 = **prefer**, opt for, like better, incline towards, choose, pick, desire, go for OPPOSITE: object to 6 = **indulge**, reward, side with, smile upon 7 = **support**, champion, encourage, approve, advocate, subscribe to, commend, stand up for OPPOSITE: oppose 8 = **help**, benefit

favourable 1 = **positive**, encouraging, approving, praising, reassuring, enthusiastic, sympathetic, commending OPPOSITE: disapproving 2 = **affirmative**, agreeing, confirming, positive, assenting, corroborative 3 = **advantageous**, promising, encouraging, suitable, helpful, beneficial, auspicious, opportune OPPOSITE: disadvantageous

favourite ADJECTIVE
1 = **preferred**, favoured, best-loved, most-liked, special, choice, dearest, pet

▷ NOUN 2 = **darling**, pet, blue-eyed boy (*informal*), beloved, idol, fave (*informal*), teacher's pet, the apple of your eye

fear NOUN 1 = **dread**, horror, panic, terror, fright, alarm, trepidation, fearfulness 2 = **bugbear**, bête noire, horror, nightmare, anxiety, terror, dread, spectre
▷ VERB 3 = **be afraid of**, dread, shudder at, be fearful of, tremble at, be terrified by, take fright at, shake in your shoes about 4 = **regret**, feel, suspect, have a feeling, have a hunch, have a sneaking suspicion, have a funny feeling
▷ PHRASES: **fear for something** or **someone** = **worry about**, be anxious about, feel concern for

fearful 1 = **scared**, afraid, alarmed, frightened, nervous, terrified, petrified OPPOSITE: unafraid 2 = **timid**, afraid, frightened, scared, alarmed, nervous, uneasy, jumpy OPPOSITE: brave 3 = **frightful**, terrible, awful, dreadful, horrific, dire, horrendous, gruesome

feasible = **practicable**, possible, reasonable, viable, workable, achievable, attainable, likely OPPOSITE: impracticable

feast NOUN 1 = **banquet**, repast, spread (*informal*), dinner, treat, hakari (*N.Z.*) 2 = **festival**, holiday, fête, celebration, holy day, red-letter day, religious

festival, saint's day
▷ **VERB 3** = **eat your fill**, wine and dine, overindulge, consume, indulge, gorge, devour, pig out (*slang*)

feat = **accomplishment**, act, performance, achievement, enterprise, undertaking, exploit, deed

feather NOUN **1** = **plume**
▷ **PLURAL NOUN 2** = **plumage**, plumes, down

feature NOUN **1** = **aspect**, quality, characteristic, property, factor, trait, hallmark, facet **2** = **article**, report, story, piece, item, column **3** = **highlight**, attraction, speciality, main item
▷ **PLURAL NOUN 4** = **face**, countenance, physiognomy, lineaments
▷ **VERB 5** = **spotlight**, present, emphasize, play up, foreground, give prominence to **6** = **star**, appear, participate, play a part

federation = **union**, league, association, alliance, combination, coalition, partnership, consortium

fed up = **cheesed off**, depressed, bored, tired, discontented, dissatisfied, glum, sick and tired (*informal*), hoha (*N.Z.*)

fee = **charge**, price, cost, bill, payment, wage, salary, toll

feeble 1 = **weak**, frail, debilitated, sickly, puny, weedy (*informal*), infirm, effete
OPPOSITE: strong

2 = **inadequate**, pathetic, insufficient, lame
3 = **unconvincing**, poor, thin, tame, pathetic, lame, flimsy, paltry **OPPOSITE:** effective

feed VERB **1** = **cater for**, provide for, nourish, provide with food, supply, sustain, cook for, wine and dine **2** = **graze**, eat, browse, pasture **3** = **eat**, drink milk
▷ **NOUN 4** = **food**, fodder, provender, pasturage **5** (*Informal*) = **meal**, spread (*informal*), dinner, lunch, tea, breakfast, feast, supper

feel VERB **1** = **experience**, bear **2** = **touch**, handle, manipulate, finger, stroke, paw, caress, fondle **3** = **be aware of 4** = **perceive**, detect, discern, experience, notice, observe **5** = **sense**, be aware, be convinced, have a feeling, intuit **6** = **believe**, consider, judge, deem, think, hold
▷ **NOUN 7** = **texture**, finish, touch, surface, surface quality **8** = **impression**, feeling, air, sense, quality, atmosphere, mood, aura

feeling NOUN **1** = **emotion**, sentiment **2** = **opinion**, view, attitude, belief, point of view, instinct, inclination
3 = **passion**, emotion, intensity, warmth **4** = **ardour**, love, care, warmth, tenderness, fervour **5** = **sympathy**, understanding, concern, pity, sensitivity,

compassion, sorrow, sensibility
6 = **sensation**, sense, impression, awareness
7 = **sense of touch**, perception, sensation **8** = **impression**, idea, sense, notion, suspicion, hunch, inkling, presentiment
9 = **atmosphere**, mood, aura, ambience, feel, air, quality

fell 1 = **cut down**, cut, level, demolish, knock down, hew
2 = **knock down**, floor

fellow 1 (*Old-fashioned*) = **man**, person, individual, character, guy (*informal*), bloke (*Brit. informal*), chap (*informal*)
2 = **associate**, colleague, peer, partner, companion, comrade, crony

fellowship 1 = **society**, club, league, association, organization, guild, fraternity, brotherhood **2** = **camaraderie**, brotherhood, companionship, sociability

feminine = **womanly**, pretty, soft, gentle, tender, delicate, ladylike **OPPOSITE:** masculine

fence NOUN **1** = **barrier**, wall, defence, railings, hedge, barricade, hedgerow, rampart
▷ VERB **2** *often with* **in** *or* **off** = **enclose**, surround, bound, protect, pen, confine, encircle

ferocious 1 = **fierce**, violent, savage, ravening, predatory, rapacious, wild **OPPOSITE:** gentle **2** = **cruel**, bitter, brutal, vicious, ruthless, bloodthirsty

ferry NOUN **1** = **ferry boat**,

boat, ship, passenger boat, packet boat, packet
▷ VERB **2** = **transport**, bring, carry, ship, take, run, shuttle, convey

fertile = **productive**, rich, lush, prolific, abundant, plentiful, fruitful, teeming **OPPOSITE:** barren

fertility = **fruitfulness**, abundance, richness, fecundity, luxuriance, productiveness

fertilizer = **compost**, muck, manure, dung, bone meal, dressing

festival 1 = **celebration**, fair, carnival, gala, fête, entertainment, jubilee, fiesta
2 = **holy day**, holiday, feast, commemoration, feast day, red-letter day, saint's day, fiesta

festive = **celebratory**, happy, merry, jubilant, cheery, joyous, joyful, jovial **OPPOSITE:** mournful

fetch 1 = **bring**, pick up, collect, go and get, get, carry, deliver, transport **2** = **sell for**, make, raise, earn, realize, go for, yield, bring in

fetching = **attractive**, charming, cute, enticing, captivating, alluring, winsome

feud NOUN **1** = **hostility**, row, conflict, argument, disagreement, rivalry, quarrel, vendetta
▷ VERB **2** = **quarrel**, row, clash, dispute, fall out, contend, war, squabble

fever = **excitement**, frenzy, ferment, agitation, fervour, restlessness, delirium

few = **not many**, one or two, scarcely any, rare, meagre, negligible, sporadic, sparse

fiasco = **flop**, failure, disaster, mess (*informal*), catastrophe, debacle, cock-up (*Brit. slang*), washout (*informal*)

fibre = **thread**, strand, filament, tendril, pile, texture, wisp

fiction 1 = **tale**, story, novel, legend, myth, romance, narration, creative writing
2 = **lie**, invention, fabrication, falsehood, untruth, urban myth, tall story, urban legend

fictional = **imaginary**, made-up, invented, legendary, unreal, nonexistent

fiddle VERB 1 *usually with* **with** = **fidget**, play, finger, tamper, mess about *or* around 2 *usually with* **with** = **tinker**, adjust, interfere, mess about *or* around
3 (*Informal*) = **cheat**, cook (*informal*), fix, diddle (*informal*), wangle (*informal*)
▷ NOUN 4 (*Brit. informal*) = **fraud**, racket, scam (*slang*), fix, swindle 5 = **violin**

fiddling = **trivial**, small, petty, trifling, insignificant, unimportant, pettifogging, futile

fidelity 1 = **loyalty**, devotion, allegiance, constancy, faithfulness, dependability, trustworthiness, staunchness

OPPOSITE: disloyalty
2 = **accuracy**, precision, correspondence, closeness, faithfulness, exactness, scrupulousness OPPOSITE: inaccuracy

field NOUN 1 = **meadow**, land, green, lea (*poetic*), pasture
2 = **speciality**, line, area, department, territory, discipline, province, sphere
3 = **line**, reach, sweep
4 = **competitors**, competition, candidates, runners, applicants, entrants, contestants
▷ VERB 5 (*Informal*) = **deal with**, answer, handle, respond to, reply to, deflect, turn aside
6 (*Sport*) = **retrieve**, return, stop, catch, pick up

fierce 1 = **ferocious**, wild, dangerous, cruel, savage, brutal, aggressive, menacing, aggers (*Austral. slang*), biffo (*Austral. slang*) OPPOSITE: gentle
2 = **intense**, strong, keen, relentless, cut-throat
3 = **stormy**, strong, powerful, violent, intense, raging, furious, howling OPPOSITE: tranquil

fiercely = **ferociously**, savagely, passionately, furiously, viciously, tooth and nail, tigerishly, with no holds barred

fiery 1 = **burning**, flaming, blazing, on fire, ablaze, aflame, afire 2 = **excitable**, fierce, passionate, irritable, impetuous, irascible, hot-headed

fight VERB 1 = **oppose**, campaign against, dispute, contest, resist, defy, contend, withstand 2 = **battle**, combat, do battle 3 = **engage in**, conduct, wage, pursue, carry on
▷ NOUN 4 = **battle**, campaign, movement, struggle
5 = **conflict**, clash, contest, encounter 6 = **brawl**, scrap (*informal*), confrontation, rumble (*U.S. & N.Z. slang*), duel, skirmish, tussle, biffo (*Austral. slang*) 7 = **row**, argument, dispute, quarrel, squabble 8 = **resistance**, spirit, pluck, militancy, belligerence, pluckiness

fighter 1 = **boxer**, wrestler, pugilist, prize fighter
2 = **soldier**, warrior, fighting man, man-at-arms

figure NOUN 1 = **digit**, character, symbol, number, numeral 2 = **shape**, build, body, frame, proportions, physique
3 = **personage**, person, individual, character, personality, celebrity, big name, dignitary 4 = **diagram**, drawing, picture, illustration, representation, sketch
5 = **design**, shape, pattern
6 = **price**, cost, value, amount, total, sum
▷ VERB 7 *usually with* **in** = **feature**, act, appear, contribute to, play a part, be featured 8 = **calculate**, work

out, compute, tot up, total, count, reckon, tally
▷ PHRASES: **figure something or someone out** = **understand**, make out, fathom, see, solve, comprehend, make sense of, decipher

figurehead = **nominal head**, titular head, front man, puppet, mouthpiece

file¹ NOUN 1 = **folder**, case, portfolio, binder 2 = **dossier**, record, information, data, documents, case history, report, case 3 = **line**, row, chain, column, queue, procession
▷ VERB 4 = **arrange**, order, classify, put in place, categorize, pigeonhole, put in order
5 = **register**, record, enter, log, put on record 6 = **march**, troop, parade, walk in line, walk behind one another

file² = **smooth**, shape, polish, rub, scrape, rasp, abrade

fill VERB 1 = **top up**, fill up, make full, become full, brim over 2 = **swell**, expand, become bloated, extend, balloon, fatten 3 = **pack**, crowd, squeeze, cram, throng 4 = **stock**, supply, pack, load 5 = **plug**, close, stop, seal, cork, bung, block up, stop up 6 = **saturate**, charge, pervade, permeate, imbue, impregnate, suffuse 7 = **fulfil**, hold, perform, carry out, occupy, execute, discharge
8 *often with* **up** = **satisfy**, stuff,

glut, satiate

filling NOUN 1 = **stuffing**, padding, filler, wadding, inside, insides, contents
▷ ADJECTIVE 2 = **satisfying**, heavy, square, substantial, ample

film NOUN 1 = **movie**, picture, flick (*slang*), motion picture
2 = **cinema**, the movies
3 = **layer**, covering, cover, skin, coating, dusting, tissue, membrane
▷ VERB 4 = **photograph**, record, shoot, video, videotape, take 5 = **adapt for the screen**, make into a film

filter VERB 1 = **purify**, treat, strain, refine, riddle, sift, sieve, winnow 2 = **trickle**, seep, percolate, escape, leak, penetrate, ooze, dribble
▷ NOUN 3 = **sieve**, mesh, gauze, strainer, membrane, riddle, sifter

filthy 1 = **dirty**, foul, polluted, squalid, slimy, unclean, putrid, festy (*Austral. slang*) 2 = **grimy**, muddy, blackened, grubby, begrimed, festy (*Austral. slang*)
3 = **obscene**, corrupt, indecent, pornographic, lewd, depraved, impure, smutty

final 1 = **last**, latest, closing, finishing, concluding, ultimate, terminal OPPOSITE: first
2 = **irrevocable**, absolute, definitive, decided, settled, definite, conclusive, irrefutable

finale = **climax**, ending, close,

conclusion, culmination, denouement, last part, epilogue OPPOSITE: opening

finally 1 = **eventually**, at last, in the end, ultimately, at length, at long last, after a long time
2 = **lastly**, in the end, ultimately
3 = **in conclusion**, lastly, in closing, to conclude, to sum up, in summary

finance VERB 1 = **fund**, back, support, pay for, guarantee, invest in, underwrite, endow
▷ NOUN 2 = **economics**, business, money, banking, accounts, investment, commerce
▷ PLURAL NOUN = **resources**, money, funds, capital, cash, affairs, budgeting, assets

financial = **economic**, business, commercial, monetary, fiscal, pecuniary

find VERB 1 = **discover**, uncover, spot, locate, detect, come across, hit upon, put your finger on OPPOSITE: lose
2 = **encounter**, meet, recognize
3 = **observe**, learn, note, discover, notice, realize, come up with, perceive
▷ NOUN 4 = **discovery**, catch, asset, bargain, acquisition, good buy
▷ PHRASES: find something out = **learn**, discover, realize, observe, perceive, detect, become aware, come to know

fine¹ ADJECTIVE 1 = **excellent**, good, striking, masterly, very good, impressive, outstanding, magnificent **OPPOSITE:** poor **2** = **satisfactory**, good, all right, suitable, acceptable, convenient, fair, O.K. *or* okay (*informal*) **3** = **thin**, light, narrow, wispy **4** = **delicate**, light, thin, sheer, flimsy, wispy, gossamer, diaphanous **OPPOSITE:** coarse **5** = **stylish**, expensive, elegant, refined, tasteful, quality **6** = **exquisite**, delicate, fragile, dainty **7** = **minute**, exact, precise, nice **8** = **keen**, minute, nice, sharp, acute, subtle, precise, hairsplitting **9** = **brilliant**, quick, keen, alert, clever, penetrating, astute **10** = **sunny**, clear, fair, dry, bright, pleasant, clement, balmy **OPPOSITE:** cloudy

fine² NOUN **1** = **penalty**, damages, punishment, forfeit, financial penalty

▷ VERB **2** = **penalize**, charge, punish

finger = **touch**, feel, handle, play with, manipulate, paw (*informal*), maul, toy with

finish VERB **1** = **stop**, close, complete, conclude, cease, wrap up (*informal*), terminate, round off **OPPOSITE:** start **2** = **get done**, complete, conclude **3** = **end**, stop, conclude, wind up, terminate **4** = **consume**, dispose of, devour, polish off, eat, get through **5** = **use up**, empty,

exhaust **6** = **coat**, polish, stain, texture, wax, varnish, gild, veneer **7** *usually with* **off** = **destroy**, defeat, overcome, bring down, ruin, dispose of, rout, put an end to **8** *usually with* **off** = **kill**, murder, destroy, massacre, butcher, slaughter, slay, exterminate

▷ NOUN **9** = **end**, close, conclusion, run-in, completion, finale, culmination, cessation **OPPOSITE:** beginning **10** = **surface**, polish, shine, texture, glaze, veneer, lacquer, lustre

finished 1 = **over**, done, through, ended, closed, complete, executed, finalized **OPPOSITE:** begun **2** = **ruined**, done for (*informal*), doomed, through, lost, defeated, wiped out, undone

fire NOUN **1** = **flames**, blaze, combustion, inferno, conflagration, holocaust **2** = **passion**, energy, spirit, enthusiasm, excitement, intensity, sparkle, vitality **3** = **bombardment**, shooting, firing, shelling, hail, volley, barrage, gunfire

▷ VERB **4** = **let off**, shoot, shell, set off, discharge, detonate **5** = **shoot**, explode, discharge, detonate, pull the trigger **6** (*Informal*) = **dismiss**, sack (*informal*), get rid of, discharge, lay off, make redundant, cashier, give notice **7** *sometimes* with **up** = **inspire**, excite, stir, stimulate, motivate, awaken, animate, rouse

fireworks 1 = **pyrotechnics**, illuminations, feux d'artifice 2 (*Informal*) = **trouble**, row, storm, rage, uproar, hysterics

firm¹ ADJECTIVE 1 = **hard**, solid, dense, set, stiff, compacted, rigid, inflexible **OPPOSITE:** soft 2 = **secure**, fixed, rooted, stable, steady, fast, embedded, immovable **OPPOSITE:** unstable 3 = **strong**, close, tight, steady 4 = **strict**, unshakeable, resolute, inflexible, unyielding, unbending 5 = **determined**, resolved, definite, set on, adamant, resolute, inflexible, unyielding **OPPOSITE:** wavering 6 = **definite**, hard, clear, confirmed, settled, fixed, hard-and-fast, cut-and-dried (*informal*)

firm² = **company**, business, concern, association, organization, corporation, venture, enterprise

firmly 1 = **securely**, safely, tightly 2 = **immovably**, securely, steadily, like a rock, unflinchingly, unshakeably 3 = **steadily**, securely, tightly, unflinchingly 4 = **resolutely**, staunchly, steadfastly, definitely, unwaveringly, unchangeably

first ADJECTIVE 1 = **earliest**, original, primordial 2 = **initial**, opening, earliest, maiden,

introductory 3 = **top**, best, winning, premier 4 = **elementary**, key, basic, primary, fundamental, cardinal, rudimentary, elemental 5 = **foremost**, highest, greatest, leading, head, ruling, chief, prime ▷ ADVERB 6 = **to begin with**, firstly, initially, at the beginning, in the first place, beforehand, to start with, at the outset ▷ NOUN 7 = **novelty**, innovation, originality, new experience ▷ PHRASES: **from the first** = **from the start**, from the beginning, from the outset, from the very beginning, from the introduction, from the starting point, from the inception, from the commencement

fish = **angle**, net, cast, trawl ▷ *See panels* FISH, SHARKS

fit¹ VERB 1 = **adapt**, shape, arrange, alter, adjust, modify, tweak (*informal*), customize 2 = **place**, insert 3 = **suit**, meet, match, belong to, conform to, correspond to, accord with, be appropriate to 4 = **equip**, provide, arm, prepare, fit out, kit out ▷ ADJECTIVE 5 = **appropriate**, suitable, right, becoming, seemly, fitting, skilled, correct **OPPOSITE:** inappropriate 6 = **healthy**, strong, robust, sturdy, well, trim, strapping,

FISH

Types of fish

ahuru (N.Z.)
alewife
albacore
alfonsino
amberjack
anabas
anchovy
angelfish
archerfish
argentine
aua (N.Z.)
Australian salmon, native salmon, salmon trout, bay trout or kahawai (N.Z. & Austral.)
barbel
barracouta or (Austral.) hake
barracuda
barramundi or (Austral.) barra or giant perch
bass
beluga
bib, pout, or whiting pout
black cod or Māori chief (N.Z.)
blackfish or (Austral.) nigger
bleak
blenny
blowfish or (Austral.) toado
blue cod, rock cod, or (N.Z.) rawaru, pakirikiri, or patutuki
bluefin tuna
bluefish or snapper
blue nose (N.Z.)
bonito or (Austral.) horse mackerel
bony bream (Austral.)

bowfin or dogfish
bream or (Austral.) brim
brill
brook trout or speckled trout
brown trout
bullhead
bully or (N.Z.) pakoko, titarakura, or toitoi
burbot, eelpout, or ling
butterfish, greenbone, or (N.Z.) koaea or marari
capelin or caplin
carp
catfish
Chinook salmon, quinnat salmon, or king salmon
chub
cisco or lake herring
clingfish
coalfish or (Brit.) saithe or coley
cockabully
cod or codfish
coelacanth
coho or silver salmon
coley
conger
coral trout
dab
dace
dart (Austral.)
darter
dory
dragonet
eel or (N.Z.) tuna
eelpout
electric eel
fighting fish or betta

FISH *continued*

filefish

flatfish *or (N.Z.)* flattie

flathead

flounder *or (N.Z.)* patiki

flying fish

flying gurnard

garpike, garfish, gar, *or (Austral.)* ballahoo

geelbek

gemfish *or (Austral.)* hake

goby

golden perch, freshwater bream, Murray perch, *or* yellow-belly *(Austral.)*

goldfish

gourami

grayling *or (Austral.)* yarra

herring

grenadier *or* rat-tail

groper *or* grouper

grunion

grunt

gudgeon

gunnel

guppy

gurnard *or* gurnet

haddock

hagfish, hag *or* blind eel

hake

halfbeak

halibut

hapuku *(Austral. & N.Z.)*

herring

hogfish

hoki *(N.Z.)*

horse mackerel

jewelfish

jewfish *or (Austral. informal)* jewie

John Dory

kelpfish *or (Austral. informal)* kelpie

killifish

kingfish

kingklip *(S. Afr.)*

kokanee

kokopu *(N.Z.)*

lamprey *or* lamper eel

leatherjacket

lemon sole

ling *or (Austral.)* beardie

loach

luderick *or (N.Z.)* parore

lumpfish *or* lumpsucker

lungfish

mackerel *or (colloquial)* shiner

mangrove Jack *(Austral.)*

manta, manta ray, devilfish, *or* devil ray

maomao *(N.Z.)*

marlin *or* spearfish

menhaden

miller's thumb

minnow *or (Scot.)* baggie

minnow

mirror carp

moki *or* blue moki *(N.Z.)*

molly

monkfish *or (U.S.)* goosefish

moray

morwong, black perch, *or (N.Z.)* porae

mudfish

mudskipper

opah, moonfish, *or* kingfish

FISH continued

orange roughy (*Austral.*)
orfe
ouananiche
ox-eye herring (*Austral.*)
parore, blackfish, black rockfish or mangrove fish (*N.Z.*)
parrotfish
pearl perch (*Austral.*)
perch or (*Austral.*) redfin
pickerel
pike, luce, or jackfish
pikeperch
pilchard or (*Austral. informal*) pillie
pilot fish
pipefish or needlefish
piranha or piraña
plaice
pollack or pollock
pollan
pompano
porae (*N.Z.*)
porcupine fish or globefish
porgy or pogy
pout
powan or lake herring
puffer or globefish
rainbow trout
ray
redfin
redfish
red mullet or (*U.S.*) goatfish
red salmon
red snapper
remora
ribbonfish
roach
rock bass

rockfish or (*formerly*) rock salmon
rockling
rudd
ruffe, ruff, or pope
salmon
sand eel, sand lance, or launce
sardine
sauger
saury or skipper
sawfish
scad
scaldfish
scorpion fish
scup or northern porgy
sea bass
sea bream
sea horse
sea scorpion
sea snail or snailfish
sea trout
Sergeant Baker
shad
shanny
shiner
Siamese fighting fish
sild
silver belly (*N.Z.*)
silverfish
silverside or silversides
skate
skipjack or skipjack tuna
smelt
smooth hound
snapper, red bream, or (*Austral.*) wollomai or wollamai
snipefish or bellows fish

FISH *continued*

snoek
snook
sockeye *or* red salmon
sole
Spanish mackerel *or*
   Queensland kingfish
sprat
steelhead
stickleback
stingray
stonefish
sturgeon
sucker
sunfish
surgeonfish
swordfish
swordtail
tailor
tarakihi *or* terakihi (*N.Z.*)
tarpon
tarwhine
tautog *or* blackfish
tench
toadfish
tommy rough *or* tommy ruff
   (*Austral.*)

trevalla (*Austral.*)
trevally, araara *or* samson fish
   (*Austral. & N.Z.*)
triggerfish
trout
trunkfish, boxfish, *or* cowfish
tuna *or* tunny
turbot
vendace
wahoo
walleye, walleyed pike, *or*
   dory
warehou (*N.Z.*)
weever
whitebait
whitefish
whiting
witch
wobbegong, wobbygong, *or*
   wobegong
wolffish *or* catfish
wrasse
yellowfin (*N.Z.*)
yellow jack

hale **OPPOSITE:** unfit
fit² 1 = **seizure**, attack, bout,
spasm, convulsion, paroxysm
2 = **bout**, burst, outbreak,
outburst, spell
fitness 1 = **appropriateness**,
competence, readiness,
eligibility, suitability, propriety,
aptness 2 = **health**, strength,
good health, vigour, good
condition, wellness, robustness
fitting NOUN 1 = **accessory**,

part, piece, unit, component,
attachment
▷ ADJECTIVE 2 = **appropriate**,
suitable, proper, apt, right,
becoming, seemly, correct
OPPOSITE: unsuitable
fix VERB 1 = **place**, join, stick,
attach, set, position, plant, link
2 = **decide**, set, choose,
establish, determine, settle,
arrange, arrive at 3 = **arrange**,
organize, sort out, see to, fix

up, make arrangements for
4 = **repair**, mend, service,
correct, restore, see to,
overhaul, patch up **5** = **focus**,
direct at, fasten on **6** (*Informal*)
= **rig**, set up (*informal*),
influence, manipulate, fiddle
(*informal*)
▷ NOUN **7** (*Informal*) = **mess**,
corner, difficulty, dilemma,
embarrassment, plight, pickle
(*informal*), uphill (*S. African*)
▷ PHRASES: **fix someone up**
= **provide**, supply, bring about,
lay on, arrange for ▸ **fix
something up** = **arrange**, plan,
settle, fix, organize, sort out,
agree on, make
arrangements for
fixed 1 = **inflexible**, set, steady,
resolute, unwavering
OPPOSITE: wavering
2 = **immovable**, set,
established, secure, rooted,
permanent, rigid **OPPOSITE:**
mobile **3** = **agreed**, set,
planned, decided, established,
settled, arranged, resolved
fizz 1 = **bubble**, froth, fizzle,
effervesce, produce bubbles
2 = **sputter**, buzz, sparkle, hiss,
crackle
flag¹ NOUN **1** = **banner**,
standard, colours, pennant,
ensign, streamer, pennon
▷ VERB **2** = **mark**, identify,
indicate, label, pick out, note
▷ PHRASES: **flag something or
someone down** = **hail**, stop,
signal, wave down

flag² = **weaken**, fade, weary,
falter, wilt, wane, sag, languish
flagging = **weakening**,
declining, waning, fading,
deteriorating, wearying,
faltering, wilting
flair 1 = **ability**, feel, talent, gift,
genius, faculty, mastery, knack
2 = **style**, taste, dash, chic,
elegance, panache,
discernment, stylishness
flake NOUN **1** = **chip**, scale,
layer, peeling, shaving, wafer,
sliver
▷ VERB **2** = **chip**, peel (off),
blister
flamboyant 1 = **camp**
(*informal*), dashing, theatrical,
swashbuckling **2** = **showy**,
elaborate, extravagant, ornate,
ostentatious **3** = **colourful**,
striking, brilliant, glamorous,
stylish, dazzling, glitzy (*slang*),
showy
flame NOUN **1** = **fire**, light,
spark, glow, blaze, brightness,
inferno **2** (*Informal*)
= **sweetheart**, partner, lover,
girlfriend, boyfriend, heart-
throb (*Brit.*), beau
▷ VERB **3** = **burn**, flash, shine,
glow, blaze, flare, glare
flank NOUN **1** = **side**, hip, thigh, loin
2 = **wing**, side, sector, aspect
flap VERB **1** = **flutter**, wave, flail
2 = **beat**, wave, thrash, flutter,
wag, vibrate, shake
▷ NOUN **3** = **flutter**, beating,
waving, shaking, swinging,
swish **4** (*Informal*) = **panic**,

state (*informal*), agitation, commotion, sweat (*informal*), dither (*chiefly Brit.*), fluster, tizzy (*informal*)

flare NOUN 1 = **flame**, burst, flash, blaze, glare, flicker
▷ VERB 2 = **blaze**, flame, glare, flicker, burn up 3 = **widen**, spread, broaden, spread out, dilate, splay

flash NOUN 1 = **blaze**, burst, spark, beam, streak, flare, dazzle, glare
▷ VERB 2 = **blaze**, shine, beam, sparkle, flare, glare, gleam, light up 3 = **speed**, race, shoot, fly, tear, dash, whistle, streak
4 (*Informal*) = **show quickly**, display, expose, exhibit, flourish, show off, flaunt
▷ ADJECTIVE 5 (*Informal*) = **ostentatious**, smart, trendy, showy

flat¹ ADJECTIVE 1 = **even**, level, levelled, smooth, horizontal **OPPOSITE:** uneven
2 = **punctured**, collapsed, burst, blown out, deflated, empty 3 = **used up**, finished, empty, drained, expired
4 = **absolute**, firm, positive, explicit, definite, outright, downright, unequivocal
5 = **dull**, dead, empty, boring, depressing, tedious, lacklustre, tiresome **OPPOSITE:** exciting
6 = **without energy**, empty, weak, tired, depressed, drained, weary, worn out
7 = **monotonous**, boring, dull,

tedious, tiresome, unchanging
▷ ADVERB 8 = **completely**, directly, absolutely, categorically, precisely, exactly, utterly, outright
▷ PHRASES: flat out (*Informal*) = **at full speed**, all out, to the full, hell for leather (*informal*), as hard as possible, at full tilt, for all you are worth

flat² = **apartment**, rooms, quarters, digs, suite, penthouse, living quarters

flatly = **absolutely**, completely, positively, categorically, unequivocally, unhesitatingly

flatten 1 = **level**, squash, compress, trample, iron out, even out, smooth off
2 = **destroy**, level, ruin, demolish, knock down, pull down, raze

flatter 1 = **praise**, compliment, pander to, sweet-talk (*informal*), wheedle, soft-soap (*informal*), butter up 2 = **suit**, become, enhance, set off, embellish, do something for, show to advantage

flattering 1 = **becoming**, kind, effective, enhancing, well-chosen **OPPOSITE:** unflattering
2 = **ingratiating**, complimentary, fawning, fulsome, laudatory, adulatory **OPPOSITE:** uncomplimentary

flavour NOUN 1 = **taste**, seasoning, flavouring, savour, relish, smack, aroma, zest **OPPOSITE:** blandness

2 = **quality**, feeling, feel, style, character, tone, essence, tinge
▷ VERB 3 = **season**, spice, add flavour to, enrich, infuse, imbue, pep up, leaven

flaw = **weakness**, failing, defect, weak spot, fault, blemish, imperfection, chink in your armour

flawed 1 = **damaged**, defective, imperfect, blemished, faulty
2 = **erroneous**, incorrect, invalid, wrong, mistaken, false, faulty, unsound

flee = **run away**, escape, bolt, fly, take off (*informal*), depart, run off, take flight

fleet = **navy**, task force, flotilla, armada

fleeting = **momentary**, passing, brief, temporary, short-lived, transient, ephemeral, transitory **OPPOSITE:** lasting

flesh 1 = **fat**, muscle, tissue, brawn 2 = **fatness**, fat, adipose tissue, corpulence, weight
3 = **meat** 4 = **physical nature**, carnality, human nature, flesh and blood, sinful nature
▷ PHRASES: **your own flesh and blood** = **family**, blood, relations, relatives, kin, kith and kin, blood relations, kinsfolk, ainga (N.Z.)

flexibility 1 = **elasticity**, pliability, springiness, pliancy, give (*informal*) 2 = **adaptability**, openness, versatility, adjustability
3 = **complaisance**,

accommodation, give and take, amenability

flexible 1 = **pliable**, plastic, elastic, supple, lithe, springy, pliant, stretchy **OPPOSITE:** rigid
2 = **adaptable**, open, variable, adjustable, discretionary **OPPOSITE:** inflexible

flick 1 = **jerk**, pull, tug, lurch, jolt 2 = **strike**, tap, remove quickly, hit, touch, stroke, flip, whisk
▷ PHRASES: **flick through something** = **browse**, glance at, skim, leaf through, flip through, thumb through, skip through

flicker VERB 1 = **twinkle**, flash, sparkle, flare, shimmer, gutter, glimmer 2 = **flutter**, waver, quiver, vibrate
▷ NOUN 3 = **glimmer**, flash, spark, flare, gleam 4 = **trace**, breath, spark, glimmer, iota

flight¹ 1 = **journey**, trip, voyage
2 = **aviation**, flying, aeronautics
3 = **flock**, group, unit, cloud, formation, squadron, swarm, flying group

flight² = **escape**, fleeing, departure, retreat, exit, running away, exodus, getaway

fling VERB 1 = **throw**, toss, hurl, launch, cast, propel, sling, catapult
▷ NOUN 2 = **binge**, good time, bash, party, spree, night on the town, rave-up (*Brit. slang*)

flip VERB 1 = **flick**, switch, snap, slick 2 = **spin**, turn, overturn,

turn over, roll over **3** = **toss**, throw, flick, fling, sling
▷ **NOUN 4** = **toss**, throw, spin, snap, flick

flirt VERB **1** = **chat up**, lead on (*informal*), make advances at, make eyes at, philander, make sheep's eyes at **2** *usually with* **with** = **toy with**, consider, entertain, play with, dabble in, trifle with, give a thought to, expose yourself to
▷ **NOUN 3** = **tease**, philanderer, coquette, heart-breaker

float 1 = **glide**, sail, drift, move gently, bob, coast, slide, be carried **2** = **be buoyant**, hang, hover **OPPOSITE:** sink **3** = **launch**, offer, sell, set up, promote, get going **OPPOSITE:** dissolve

floating 1 = **uncommitted**, wavering, undecided, indecisive, vacillating, sitting on the fence (*informal*), unaffiliated, independent **2** = **free**, wandering, variable, fluctuating, unattached, movable

flock NOUN **1** = **herd**, group, flight, drove, colony, gaggle, skein **2** = **crowd**, company, group, host, collection, mass, gathering, herd
▷ **VERB 3** = **stream**, crowd, mass, swarm, throng **4** = **gather**, crowd, mass, collect, assemble, herd, huddle, converge

flog = **beat**, whip, lash, thrash,

whack, scourge, hit hard, trounce

flood NOUN **1** = **deluge**, downpour, inundation, tide, overflow, torrent, spate **2** = **torrent**, flow, rush, stream, tide, abundance, glut, profusion **3** = **series**, stream, avalanche, barrage, spate, torrent **4** = **outpouring**, rush, stream, surge, torrent
▷ **VERB 5** = **immerse**, swamp, submerge, inundate, drown, cover with water **6** = **pour over**, swamp, run over, overflow, inundate, surge **7** = **engulf**, sweep into, overwhelm, surge into, swarm into, pour into **8** = **saturate**, fill, choke, swamp, glut, oversupply, overfill **9** = **stream**, flow, rush, pour, surge

floor NOUN **1** = **ground 2** = **storey**, level, stage, tier
▷ **VERB 3** (*Informal*) = **disconcert**, stump, baffle, confound, throw (*informal*), defeat, puzzle, bewilder **4** = **knock down**, fell, knock over, prostrate, deck (*slang*)

flop VERB **1** = **slump**, fall, drop, collapse, sink **2** = **hang down**, hang, dangle, sag, droop **3** (*Informal*) = **fail**, fold (*informal*), founder, fall flat, come unstuck, misfire, go belly-up (*slang*) **OPPOSITE:** succeed
▷ **NOUN 4** (*Informal*) = **failure**, disaster, fiasco, debacle, washout (*informal*), nonstarter

OPPOSITE: success

floppy = droopy, soft, loose, limp, sagging, baggy, flaccid, pendulous

floral = flowery, flower-patterned

flounder 1 = falter, struggle, stall, slow down, run into trouble, come unstuck (*informal*), be in difficulties, hit a bad patch 2 = dither, struggle, blunder, be confused, falter, be in the dark, be out of your depth 3 = struggle, struggle, toss, thrash, stumble, fumble, grope

● USAGE NOTE
● *Flounder* is sometimes
● wrongly used where *founder* is
● meant: *the project foundered*
● (not *floundered*) *because of lack*
● *of funds.*

flourish VERB 1 = thrive, increase, advance, progress, boom, bloom, blossom, prosper OPPOSITE: fail 2 = succeed, move ahead, go places (*informal*) 3 = grow, thrive, flower, succeed, bloom, blossom, prosper, bloom 4 = wave, brandish, display, shake, wield, flaunt
▷ NOUN 5 = wave, sweep, brandish, swish, swing, twirl 6 = show, display, parade, fanfare 7 = curlicue, sweep, decoration, swirl, plume, embellishment, ornamentation

flourishing = thriving, successful, blooming, prospering, rampant, going

places, in the pink

flow VERB 1 = run, course, rush, sweep, move, pass, roll, flood 2 = pour, move, sweep, flood, stream 3 = issue, follow, result, emerge, spring, proceed, arise, derive
▷ NOUN 4 = stream, current, movement, motion, course, flood, drift, tide

flower NOUN 1 = bloom, blossom, efflorescence 2 = elite, best, prime, finest, pick, choice, cream, crème de la crème (*French*) 3 = height, prime, peak
▷ VERB 4 = bloom, open, mature, flourish, unfold, blossom 5 = blossom, grow, develop, progress, mature, thrive, flourish, bloom

● RELATED WORD
● *adjective:* floral

fluctuate 1 = change, swing, vary, alternate, waver, veer, seesaw 2 = shift, oscillate

fluent = effortless, natural, articulate, well-versed, voluble

fluid NOUN 1 = liquid, solution, juice, liquor, sap
▷ ADJECTIVE 2 = liquid, flowing, watery, molten, melted, runny, liquefied OPPOSITE: solid

flurry 1 = commotion, stir, bustle, flutter, excitement, fuss, disturbance, ado 2 = gust, shower, gale, swirl, squall, storm

flush[1] VERB 1 = blush, colour, glow, redden, turn red, go red

2 *often with* **out** = **cleanse**, wash out, rinse out, flood, swill, hose down **3** = **expel**, drive, dislodge
▷ NOUN **4** = **blush**, colour, glow, reddening, redness, rosiness

flush² **1** = **level**, even, true, flat, square **2** (*Informal*) = **wealthy**, rich, well-off, in the money (*informal*), well-heeled (*informal*), replete, moneyed

flutter VERB **1** = **beat**, flap, tremble, ripple, waver, quiver, vibrate, palpitate **2** = **flit**
▷ NOUN **3** = **tremor**, tremble, shiver, shudder, palpitation **4** = **vibration**, twitching, quiver **5** = **agitation**, state (*informal*), confusion, excitement, flap (*informal*), dither (*chiefly Brit.*), commotion, fluster

fly¹ VERB **1** = **take wing**, soar, glide, wing, sail, hover, flutter, flit **2** = **pilot**, control, operate, steer, manoeuvre, navigate **3** = **airlift**, send by plane, take by plane, take in an aircraft **4** = **flutter**, wave, float, flap **5** = **display**, show, flourish, brandish **6** = **rush**, race, shoot, career, speed, tear, dash, hurry **7** = **pass swiftly**, pass, glide, slip away, roll on, flit, elapse, run its course **8** = **leave**, get away, escape, flee, run for it, skedaddle (*informal*), take to your heels

fly² ▷ *See panel* FLIES

flying = **hurried**, brief, rushed, fleeting, short-lived, hasty, transitory

foam NOUN **1** = **froth**, spray, bubbles, lather, suds, spume, head
▷ VERB **2** = **bubble**, boil, fizz, froth, lather, effervesce

focus VERB **1** = **concentrate**, centre, spotlight, direct, aim, pinpoint, zoom in **2** = **fix**, train, direct, aim
▷ NOUN **3** = **centre**, focal point, central point **4** = **focal point**, heart, target, hub

foe = **enemy**, rival, opponent, adversary, antagonist
OPPOSITE: friend

fog = **mist**, gloom, haze, smog, murk, miasma, peasouper (*informal*)

foil¹ = **thwart**, stop, defeat, disappoint, counter, frustrate, hamper, balk

foil² = **complement**, relief, contrast, antithesis

fold VERB **1** = **bend**, crease, double over **2** (*Informal*) = **go bankrupt**, fail, crash, collapse, founder, shut down, go under, go bust (*informal*)
▷ NOUN **3** = **crease**, gather, bend, overlap, wrinkle, pleat, ruffle, furrow

folk **1** = **people**, persons, individuals, men and women, humanity, inhabitants, mankind, mortals **2** *usually plural* = **family**, parents, relations, relatives, tribe, clan, kin, kindred, ainga (*N.Z.*)

FLIES

aphid *or* plant louse	gadfly
aphis	gallfly
blackfly *or* bean aphid	gnat
blowfly, bluebottle, *or* (*Austral.* *informal*) blowie	green blowfly *or* (*Austral.* *informal*) blue-arsed fly
botfly	greenfly
bushfly	horsefly *or* cleg
crane fly *or* (*Brit.*) daddy-longlegs	housefly
	hover fly
damselfly	lacewing
dragonfly *or* (*colloquial*) devil's darning-needle	mayfly *or* dayfly
	sandfly
drosophila, fruit fly, *or* vinegar fly	stonefly
	tsetse fly *or* tzetze fly
fly	warble fly
fruit fly	whitefly

follow VERB 1 = **accompany**, attend, escort, go behind, tag along behind, come behind 2 = **pursue**, track, dog, hunt, chase, shadow, trail, hound **OPPOSITE: avoid** 3 = **come after**, go after, come next **OPPOSITE: precede** 4 = **result**, issue, develop, spring, flow, proceed, arise, ensue 5 = **obey**, observe, adhere to, stick to, heed, conform to, keep to, pay attention to **OPPOSITE: ignore** 6 = **succeed**, replace, come after, take over from, come next, supersede, supplant, take the place of 7 = **understand**, realize, appreciate, take in, grasp, catch on (*informal*), comprehend, fathom 8 = **keep up with**, support, be interested in, cultivate, be a fan of, keep abreast of

follower = **supporter**, fan, disciple, devotee, apostle, pupil, adherent, groupie (*slang*) **OPPOSITE: leader**

following ADJECTIVE 1 = **next**, subsequent, successive, ensuing, later, succeeding, consequent 2 = **coming**, about to be mentioned ▷ NOUN 3 = **supporters**, backing, train, fans, suite, clientele, entourage, coterie

folly = **foolishness**, nonsense, madness, stupidity, indiscretion, lunacy, imprudence, rashness **OPPOSITE: wisdom**

fond 1 = **loving**, caring, warm, devoted, tender, adoring, affectionate, indulgent **OPPOSITE: indifferent**

2 = unrealistic, empty, naive, vain, foolish, deluded, overoptimistic, delusive **OPPOSITE:** sensible

▷ **PHRASES: fond of**
1 = attached to, in love with, keen on, attracted to, having a soft spot for, enamoured of
2 = keen on, into (*informal*), hooked on, partial to, having a soft spot for, addicted to

fondly 1 = lovingly, tenderly, affectionately, amorously, dearly, possessively, with affection, indulgently
2 = unrealistically, stupidly, vainly, foolishly, naively, credulously

food = nourishment, fare, diet, tucker (*Austral. & N.Z. informal*), rations, nutrition, cuisine, refreshment, nibbles, kai (*N.Z. informal*)

fool NOUN 1 = simpleton, idiot, mug (*Brit. slang*), dummy (*slang*), git (*Brit. slang*), twit (*informal, chiefly Brit.*), dunce, imbecile (*informal*), dorba or dorb (*Austral. slang*), bogan (*Austral. slang*) **OPPOSITE:** genius **2 = dupe**, mug (*Brit. slang*), sucker (*slang*), stooge (*slang*), laughing stock, pushover (*informal*), fall guy (*informal*) **3 = jester**, clown, harlequin, buffoon, court jester
▷ **VERB 4 = deceive**, mislead, delude, trick, take in, con (*informal*), dupe, beguile

foolish = unwise, silly, absurd, rash, senseless, foolhardy, ill-judged, imprudent **OPPOSITE:** sensible

footing 1 = basis, foundation, base position, groundwork
2 = relationship, position, basis, standing, rank, status, grade

footpath (*Austral. & N.Z.*) **= pavement**, sidewalk (*U.S. & Canad.*)

footstep = step, tread, footfall

foray = raid, sally, incursion, inroad, attack, assault, invasion, swoop

forbid = prohibit, ban, disallow, exclude, rule out, veto, outlaw, preclude **OPPOSITE:** permit

● **USAGE NOTE**
● Traditionally, it has been
● considered more correct to
● talk about *forbidding someone*
● *to do something*, rather than
● *forbidding someone from doing*
● *something*. Recently, however,
● the *from* option has become
● generally more acceptable, so
● that *he was forbidden to come*
● *in* and *he was forbidden from*
● *coming in* may both now be
● considered correct.

forbidden = prohibited, banned, vetoed, outlawed, taboo, out of bounds, proscribed

forbidding = threatening, severe, frightening, hostile, menacing, sinister, daunting, ominous **OPPOSITE:** inviting

force VERB 1 = compel, make,

drive, press, oblige, constrain, coerce, impel **2 = push**, thrust, propel **3 = break open**, blast, wrench, prise, wrest
▷ NOUN **4 = compulsion**, pressure, violence, constraint, oppression, coercion, duress, arm-twisting (*informal*)
5 = power, might, pressure, energy, strength, momentum, impulse, vigour **OPPOSITE:** weakness **6 = intensity**, vigour, vehemence, fierceness, emphasis **7 = army**, unit, company, host, troop, squad, patrol, regiment
▷ PHRASES: **in force 1 = valid**, working, current, effective, binding, operative, operational, in operation **2 = in great numbers**, all together, in full strength

forced 1 = compulsory, enforced, mandatory, obligatory, involuntary, conscripted **OPPOSITE:** voluntary **2 = false**, affected, strained, wooden, stiff, artificial, contrived, unnatural **OPPOSITE:** natural

forceful 1 = dynamic, powerful, assertive **OPPOSITE:** weak **2 = powerful**, strong, convincing, effective, compelling, persuasive, cogent

forecast NOUN **1 = prediction**, prognosis, guess, prophecy, conjecture, forewarning
▷ VERB **2 = predict**, anticipate, foresee, foretell, divine,

prophesy, augur, forewarn

forefront = lead, centre, front, fore, spearhead, prominence, vanguard, foreground

foreign = alien, exotic, unknown, strange, imported, remote, external, unfamiliar **OPPOSITE:** native

foreigner = alien, incomer, immigrant, non-native, stranger, settler

foremost = leading, best, highest, chief, prime, primary, supreme, most important

foresee = predict, forecast, anticipate, envisage, prophesy, foretell

forever 1 = evermore, always, ever, for good, for keeps, for all time, in perpetuity, till the cows come home (*informal*)
2 = constantly, always, all the time, continually, endlessly, persistently, eternally, perpetually

- USAGE NOTE
- *Forever* and *for ever* can both
- be used to say that
- something is without end.
- For all other meanings, *forever*
- is the preferred form.

forfeit VERB **1 = relinquish**, lose, give up, surrender, renounce, be deprived of, say goodbye to, be stripped of
▷ NOUN **2 = penalty**, fine, damages, forfeiture, loss, mulct

forge 1 = form, build, create, establish, set up, fashion, shape, frame **2 = fake**, copy, reproduce, imitate, counterfeit, feign, falsify **3** = **create**, make, work, found, form, model, fashion, shape

forget 1 = **neglect**, overlook, omit, not remember, be remiss, fail to remember **2** = **leave behind**, lose, lose sight of, mislay

forgive = **excuse**, pardon, not hold something against, understand, acquit, condone, let off (*informal*), turn a blind eye to **OPPOSITE:** blame

forgiveness = **pardon**, mercy, absolution, exoneration, amnesty, acquittal, remission

forgotten = **unremembered**, lost, past, left behind, omitted, bygone, past recall

fork = **branch**, part, separate, split, divide, diverge, subdivide, bifurcate

forked = **branching**, split, branched, divided, angled, pronged, zigzag, Y-shaped

form NOUN **1** = **type**, sort, kind, variety, class, style **2** = **shape**, formation, configuration, structure, pattern, appearance **3** = **condition**, health, shape, nick (*informal*), fitness, trim, fettle **4** = **document**, paper, sheet, questionnaire, application **5** = **procedure**, etiquette, use, custom, convention, usage, protocol, wont, kawa (*N.Z.*), tikanga (*N.Z.*) **6** = **class**, year, set, rank, grade, stream

▷ VERB **7** = **arrange**, combine, line up, organize, assemble, draw up **8** = **make**, produce, fashion, build, create, shape, construct, forge **9** = **constitute**, make up, compose, comprise **10** = **establish**, start, launch **11** = **take shape**, grow, develop, materialize, rise, appear, come into being, crystallize **12** = **draw up**, devise, formulate, organize **13** = **develop**, pick up, acquire, cultivate, contract

formal 1 = **serious**, stiff, detached, official, correct, conventional, remote, precise **OPPOSITE:** informal **2** = **official**, authorized, endorsed, certified, solemn **3** = **ceremonial**, traditional, solemn, ritualistic, dressy **4** = **conventional**, established, traditional

formality 1 = **correctness**, seriousness, decorum, protocol, etiquette **2** = **convention**, procedure, custom, ritual, rite

format = **arrangement**, form, style, make-up, look, plan, design, type

formation 1 = **establishment**, founding, forming, setting up, starting, production, generation, manufacture **2** = **development**, shaping, constitution, moulding, genesis **3** = **arrangement**, grouping, design, structure, pattern, organization, array, configuration, rank

former = **previous**, one-time, erstwhile, earlier, prior, sometime, foregoing **OPPOSITE:** current

formerly = **previously**, earlier, in the past, at one time, before, lately, once

formidable 1 = **impressive**, great, powerful, tremendous, mighty, terrific, awesome, invincible 2 = **intimidating**, threatening, terrifying, menacing, dismaying, fearful, daunting, frightful **OPPOSITE:** encouraging

formula = **method**, plan, policy, rule, principle, procedure, recipe, blueprint

formulate 1 = **devise**, plan, develop, prepare, work out, invent, forge, draw up 2 = **express**, detail, frame, define, specify, articulate, set down, put into words

fort = **fortress**, keep, camp, tower, castle, garrison, stronghold, citadel, fortified pa (N.Z.)

▷ **PHRASES: hold the fort** (Informal) = **take responsibility**, cover, stand in, carry on, take over the reins, deputize, keep things on an even keel

forte = **speciality**, strength, talent, strong point, métier, long suit (informal), gift **OPPOSITE:** weak point

forth 1 (Formal or old-fashioned) = **forward**, out, away, ahead,

onward, outward 2 = **out**

forthcoming 1 = **approaching**, coming, expected, future, imminent, prospective, impending, upcoming 2 = **available**, ready, accessible, at hand, in evidence, obtainable, on tap (informal) 3 = **communicative**, open, free, informative, expansive, sociable, chatty, talkative

fortify 1 = **protect**, defend, strengthen, reinforce, support, shore up, augment, buttress 2 = **strengthen**, add alcohol to **OPPOSITE:** dishearten

fortitude = **courage**, strength, resolution, grit, bravery, backbone, perseverance, valour

fortress = **castle**, fort, stronghold, citadel, redoubt, fastness, fortified pa (N.Z.)

fortunate 1 = **lucky**, favoured, jammy (Brit. slang), in luck **OPPOSITE:** unfortunate 2 = **well-off**, rich, successful, wealthy, prosperous, affluent, opulent, well-heeled (informal) 3 = **providential**, fortuitous, felicitous, timely, helpful, convenient, favourable, advantageous

fortunately = **luckily**, happily, as luck would have it, providentially, by good luck, by a happy chance

fortune NOUN 1 = **wealth**, means, property, riches, resources, assets, possessions, treasure **OPPOSITE:** poverty

2 = **luck**, fluke (*informal*), stroke of luck, serendipity, twist of fate, run of luck **3** = **chance**, fate, destiny, providence, the stars, Lady Luck, kismet
▷ PLURAL NOUN = **destiny**, lot, experiences, history, condition, success, means, adventures

forward ADVERB **1** = **forth**, on, ahead, onwards **OPPOSITE:** backward(s) **2** = **on**, onward, onwards
▷ ADJECTIVE **3** = **leading**, first, head, front, advance, foremost **4** = **future**, advanced, premature, prospective **5** = **presumptuous**, familiar, bold, cheeky, brash, pushy (*informal*), brazen, shameless **OPPOSITE:** shy
▷ VERB **6** = **further**, advance, promote, assist, hurry, hasten, expedite **7** = **send on**, send, post, pass on, dispatch, redirect

fossick (*Austral. & N.Z.*) = **search**, hunt, explore, ferret, check, forage, rummage

foster **1** = **bring up**, mother, raise, nurse, look after, rear, care for, take care of **2** = **develop**, support, further, encourage, feed, promote, stimulate, uphold **OPPOSITE:** suppress

foul ADJECTIVE **1** = **dirty**, unpleasant, stinking, filthy, grubby, repellent, squalid, repulsive, festy (*Austral. slang*), yucko (*Austral. slang*) **OPPOSITE:** clean **2** = **obscene**, crude, indecent, blue, abusive, coarse, vulgar, lewd **3** = **unfair**, illegal, crooked, shady (*informal*), fraudulent, dishonest, unscrupulous, underhand **4** = **offensive**, bad, wrong, evil, corrupt, disgraceful, shameful, immoral **OPPOSITE:** admirable
▷ VERB **5** = **dirty**, stain, contaminate, pollute, taint, sully, defile, besmirch **OPPOSITE:** clean

found = **establish**, start, set up, begin, create, institute, organize, constitute

foundation **1** = **basis** **2** *often plural* = **substructure**, underpinning, groundwork, bedrock, base, footing, bottom **3** = **setting up**, institution, instituting, organization, settlement, establishment, initiating, originating

founder[1] = **initiator**, father, author, architect, creator, beginner, inventor, originator

founder[2] **1** = **fail**, collapse, break down, fall through, be unsuccessful, come unstuck, miscarry, misfire **2** = **sink**, go down, be lost, submerge, capsize, go to the bottom

● USAGE NOTE
● *Founder* is sometimes wrongly
● used where *flounder* is meant:
● *this unexpected turn of events*
● *left him floundering* (not
● *foundering*).

fountain **1** = **font**, spring, reservoir, spout, fount, water feature, well **2** = **jet**, stream, spray, gush **3** = **source**, fount, wellspring, cause, origin, derivation, fountainhead

fowl = **poultry**
▷ *See panel* TYPES OF FOWL

foyer = **entrance hall**, lobby, reception area, vestibule, anteroom, antechamber

fraction = **percentage**, share, section, slice, portion

fracture NOUN **1** = **break**, split, crack **2** = **cleft**, opening, split, crack, rift, rupture, crevice, fissure
▷ VERB **3** = **break**, crack **4** = **split**, separate, divide, rend, fragment, splinter, rupture

fragile 1 = **unstable**, weak, vulnerable, delicate, uncertain, insecure, precarious, flimsy **2** = **fine**, weak, delicate, frail, brittle, flimsy, dainty, easily broken **OPPOSITE:** durable **3** = **delicate**, fine, charming, elegant, neat, exquisite, graceful, petite **4** = **unwell**, poorly, weak, delicate, crook (*Austral. & N.Z. informal*), shaky, frail, feeble, sickly

fragment NOUN **1** = **piece**, bit, scrap, particle, portion, shred, speck, sliver
▷ VERB **2** = **break**, shatter, crumble, disintegrate, splinter, come apart, break into pieces, come to pieces **OPPOSITE:** fuse **3** = **break up**, split up

fragrance 1 = **scent**, smell, perfume, bouquet, aroma,

sweet smell, sweet odour, redolence **OPPOSITE:** stink **2** = **perfume**, scent, cologne, eau de toilette, eau de Cologne, toilet water, Cologne water

fragrant = **aromatic**, perfumed, balmy, redolent, sweet-smelling, sweet-scented, odorous **OPPOSITE:** stinking

frail 1 = **feeble**, weak, puny, infirm **OPPOSITE:** strong **2** = **flimsy**, weak, vulnerable, delicate, fragile, insubstantial

frame NOUN **1** = **casing**, framework, structure, shell, construction, skeleton, chassis **2** = **physique**, build, form, body, figure, anatomy, carcass
▷ VERB **3** = **mount**, case, enclose **4** = **surround**, ring, enclose, encompass, envelop, encircle, hem in **5** = **devise**, draft, compose, sketch, put together, draw up, formulate, map out
▷ PHRASES: **frame of mind** = **mood**, state, attitude, humour, temper, outlook, disposition, mind-set

framework 1 = **system**, plan, order, scheme, arrangement, the bare bones **2** = **structure**, body, frame, foundation, shell, skeleton

frank = **candid**, open, direct, straightforward, blunt, sincere, outspoken, honest **OPPOSITE:** secretive

frankly 1 = **honestly**, sincerely, in truth, candidly, to tell you the

TYPES OF FOWL

barnacle goose	moorhen
brush turkey or scrub turkey	Muscovy duck or musk duck
bufflehead	mute swan
Canada goose	paradise duck
canvasback	pintail
chicken or (Austral. slang)	pochard
chook	redhead
cock or cockerel	Rhode Island Red chicken
duck	scaup or scaup duck
eider or eider duck	screamer
gadwall	shelduck
goldeneye	shoveler
goosander	smew
goose	snow goose
greylag or greylag goose	sultan
hen	swan
mallard	teal
mallee fowl or (Austral.) gnow	trumpeter swan
mandarin duck	turkey
megapode	whooper or whooper swan
merganser or sawbill	wigeon or widgeon

truth, to be frank, to be frank with someone, to be honest
2 = openly, freely, directly, plainly, bluntly, candidly, without reserve

frantic 1 = frenzied, wild, furious, distracted, distraught, berserk, at the end of your tether, beside yourself, berko (*Austral. slang*) **OPPOSITE:** calm
2 = hectic, desperate, frenzied, fraught (*informal*), frenetic

fraternity
1 = companionship, fellowship, brotherhood, kinship, camaraderie **2 = circle**, company, guild

3 = brotherhood, club, union, society, league, association
fraud 1 = deception, deceit, treachery, swindling, trickery, duplicity, double-dealing, chicanery **OPPOSITE:** honesty
2 = scam, deception (*slang*)
3 = hoax, trick, con (*informal*), deception, sham, spoof (*informal*), prank, swindle
4 (*Informal*) **= impostor**, fake, hoaxer, pretender, charlatan, fraudster, swindler, phoney or phony (*informal*)

fraudulent = deceitful, crooked (*informal*), untrue, sham, treacherous, dishonest,

swinding, double-dealing
OPPOSITE: genuine

fray = wear thin, wear, rub, wear out, chafe

freak ADJECTIVE 1 = abnormal, chance, unusual, exceptional, unparalleled
▷ NOUN 2 (*Informal*)
= enthusiast, fan, nut (*slang*), addict, buff (*informal*), fanatic, devotee, fiend (*informal*)
3 = aberration, eccentric, anomaly, oddity, monstrosity, malformation 4 = weirdo *or* weirdie (*informal*), eccentric, character (*informal*), oddball (*informal*), nonconformist

free ADJECTIVE
1 = complimentary, for free (*informal*), for nothing, unpaid, for love, free of charge, on the house, without charge
2 = allowed, permitted, unrestricted, unimpeded, clear, able 3 = at liberty, loose, liberated, at large, on the loose **OPPOSITE:** confined
4 = independent, unfettered, footloose 5 = available, empty, spare, vacant, unused, unoccupied, untaken
6 = generous, liberal, lavish, unstinting, unsparing
OPPOSITE: mean
▷ VERB 7 = clear, disengage, cut loose, release, rescue, extricate 8 = release, liberate, let out, set free, deliver, loose, untie, unchain **OPPOSITE:** confine 9 = disentangle,

extricate, disengage, loose, unravel, disconnect, untangle

freedom 1 = independence, democracy, sovereignty, self-determination, emancipation, autarchy, rangatiratanga (*N.Z.*)
2 = liberty, release, discharge, emancipation, deliverance
OPPOSITE: captivity 3 = licence, latitude, free rein, opportunity, discretion, carte blanche, blank cheque **OPPOSITE:** restriction

freely 1 = abundantly, liberally, lavishly, extravagantly, copiously, unstintingly, amply
2 = openly, frankly, plainly, candidly, unreservedly, straightforwardly, without reserve 3 = willingly, readily, voluntarily, spontaneously, without prompting, of your own free will, of your own accord

freeway (*U.S. & Austral.*)
= motorway (*Brit.*), autobahn (*German*), autoroute (*French*), autostrada (*Italian*)

freeze 1 = ice over *or* up, harden, stiffen, solidify, become solid 2 = chill 3 = fix, hold, limit, hold up 4 = suspend, stop, shelve, curb, cut short, discontinue

freezing 1 = icy, biting, bitter, raw, chill, arctic, frosty, glacial
2 = frozen, very cold

freight 1 = transportation, traffic, delivery, carriage, shipment, haulage, conveyance, transport 2 = cargo, goods, load, delivery, burden, shipment, merchandise, consignment

French = Gallic

frenzied = **uncontrolled**, wild, crazy, furious, frantic, frenetic, feverish, rabid

frenzy = **fury**, passion, rage, seizure, hysteria, paroxysm, derangement **OPPOSITE**: calm

frequent ADJECTIVE

1 = **common**, repeated, usual, familiar, everyday, persistent, customary, recurrent **OPPOSITE**: infrequent

▷ VERB 2 = **visit**, attend, haunt, be found at, patronize, hang out at (*informal*), visit often, go to regularly **OPPOSITE**: keep away

frequently = **often**, commonly, repeatedly, many times, habitually, not infrequently, much **OPPOSITE**: infrequently

fresh ADJECTIVE 1 = **additional**, more, new, other, added, further, extra, supplementary 2 = **natural**, unprocessed, unpreserved **OPPOSITE**: preserved 3 = **new**, original, novel, different, recent, modern, up-to-date, unorthodox **OPPOSITE**: old 4 = **invigorating**, clean, pure, crisp, bracing, refreshing, brisk, unpolluted **OPPOSITE**: stale 5 = **cool**, cold, refreshing, brisk, chilly, nippy 6 = **lively**, keen, alert, refreshed, vigorous, energetic, sprightly, spry

OPPOSITE: weary 7 = **cheeky** (*Informal*), impertinent, forward, familiar, audacious, disrespectful, presumptuous, insolent **OPPOSITE**: well-mannered

fret = **worry**, brood, agonize, obsess, lose sleep, upset yourself, distress yourself

friction 1 = **conflict**, hostility, resentment, disagreement, animosity, discord, bad blood, dissension 2 = **resistance**, rubbing, scraping, grating, rasping, chafing, abrasion 3 = **rubbing**, scraping, grating, rasping, chafing, abrasion

friend 1 = **companion**, pal, mate (*informal*), buddy (*informal*), best friend, close friend, comrade, chum (*informal*), cobber (*Austral. & N.Z.*), E hoa (*N.Z. old-fashioned informal*) **OPPOSITE**: foe 2 = **supporter**, ally, associate, sponsor, patron, well-wisher

friendly 1 ADJECTIVE = **amiable**, welcoming, warm, neighbourly, pally (*informal*), helpful, sympathetic, affectionate

▷ ADJECTIVE 2 = **amicable**, warm, familiar, pleasant, intimate, informal, cordial, congenial **OPPOSITE**: unfriendly

friendship 1 = **attachment**, relationship, bond, link, association, tie

2 = **friendliness**, affection, harmony, goodwill, intimacy,

familiarity, rapport, companionship **OPPOSITE:** unfriendliness

fright 1 = **fear**, shock, alarm, horror, panic, dread, consternation, trepidation **OPPOSITE:** courage 2 = **scare**, start, turn, surprise, shock, jolt, the creeps (*informal*), the willies (*slang*)

frighten = **scare**, shock, alarm, terrify, startle, intimidate, unnerve, petrify **OPPOSITE:** reassure

frightened = **afraid**, alarmed, scared, terrified, shocked, startled, petrified, flustered

frightening = **terrifying**, shocking, alarming, startling, horrifying, menacing, scary (*informal*), fearful

fringe NOUN 1 = **border**, edging, edge, trimming, hem, frill, flounce 2 = **edge**, limits, border, margin, outskirts, perimeter, periphery, borderline
▷ ADJECTIVE 3 = **unofficial**, alternative, radical, innovative, avant-garde, unconventional, unorthodox

frog ▷ *See panel* AMPHIBIANS

front NOUN 1 = **head**, start, lead, forefront 2 = **exterior**, face, façade, frontage 3 = **foreground**, fore, forefront, nearest part 4 = **front line**, trenches, vanguard, firing line 5 (*Informal*) = **disguise**, cover, blind, mask, cover-up, cloak, façade, pretext

▷ ADJECTIVE 6 = **foremost**, at the front **OPPOSITE:** back 7 = **leading**, first, lead, head, foremost, topmost
▷ VERB 8 = **face onto**, overlook, look out on, have a view of, look over *or* onto

frontier = **border**, limit, edge, boundary, verge, perimeter, borderline, dividing line

frost = **hoarfrost**, freeze, rime

frown VERB 1 = **glare**, scowl, glower, make a face, look daggers, knit your brows, lour *or* lower
▷ NOUN 2 = **scowl**, glare, glower, dirty look

frozen 1 = **icy**, hard, solid, frosted, arctic, ice-covered, icebound 2 = **chilled**, cold, iced, refrigerated, ice-cold 3 = **ice-cold**, freezing, numb, very cold, frigid, frozen stiff

fruit 1 = **produce**, crop, yield, harvest 2 *often plural* = **result**, reward, outcome, end result, return, effect, benefit, profit

frustrate = **thwart**, stop, check, block, defeat, disappoint, counter, spoil, crool *or* cruel (*Austral. slang*) **OPPOSITE:** further

frustrated = **disappointed**, discouraged, infuriated, exasperated, resentful, embittered, disheartened

frustration 1 = **annoyance**, disappointment, resentment, irritation, grievance, dissatisfaction, exasperation, vexation 2 = **obstruction**, blocking, foiling, spoiling, thwarting, circumvention

fudge = misrepresent, hedge, stall, flannel (*Brit. informal*), equivocate

fuel = incitement, ammunition, provocation, incentive

fugitive = runaway, refugee, deserter, escapee

fulfil 1 = **carry out**, perform, complete, achieve, accomplish **OPPOSITE:** neglect 2 = **achieve**, realize, satisfy, attain, consummate, bring to fruition 3 = **satisfy**, please, content, cheer, refresh, gratify, make happy 4 = **comply with**, meet, fill, satisfy, observe, obey, conform to, answer

fulfilment = achievement, implementation, completion, accomplishment, realization, attainment, consummation

full ADJECTIVE 1 = **filled**, stocked, brimming, replete, complete, loaded, saturated **OPPOSITE:** empty 2 = **satiated**, having had enough, replete 3 = **extensive**, complete, generous, adequate, ample, abundant, plentiful **OPPOSITE:** incomplete 4 = **comprehensive**, complete, exhaustive, all-embracing 5 = **rounded**, strong, rich, powerful, intense, pungent 6 = **plump**, rounded, voluptuous, shapely, well-rounded, buxom, curvaceous 7 = **voluminous**, large, loose, baggy, billowing, puffy, capacious, loose-fitting **OPPOSITE:** tight 8 = **rich**, strong, deep, loud, distinct, resonant, sonorous, clear **OPPOSITE:** thin

full-scale = major, wide-ranging, all-out, sweeping, comprehensive, thorough, in-depth, exhaustive

fully 1 = **completely**, totally, perfectly, entirely, altogether, thoroughly, wholly, utterly 2 = **in all respects**, completely, totally, entirely, altogether, thoroughly, wholly

fumble = grope, flounder, scrabble, feel around

fume VERB 1 = **rage**, seethe, see red (*informal*), storm, rant, smoulder, get hot under the collar (*informal*) ▷ PLURAL NOUN 2 = **smoke**, gas, exhaust, pollution, vapour, smog

fun NOUN 1 = **amusement**, sport, pleasure, entertainment, recreation, enjoyment, merriment, jollity 2 = **enjoyment**, pleasure, mirth **OPPOSITE:** gloom ▷ ADJECTIVE 3 = **enjoyable**, entertaining, pleasant, amusing, lively, diverting, witty, convivial ▷ PHRASES **make fun of something or someone** = mock, tease, ridicule, poke fun at, laugh at, mimic, parody, send up (*Brit. informal*)

function NOUN 1 = **purpose**, business, job, use, role, responsibility, task, duty 2 = **reception**, party, affair, gathering, bash (*informal*), social occasion, soiree, do (*informal*) ▷ VERB 3 = **work**, run, operate, perform, go 4 = **act**, operate, perform, behave, do duty, have the role of

functional 1 = **practical**, utilitarian, serviceable, hard-wearing, useful 2 = **working**, operative, operational, going, prepared, ready, viable, up and running

fund NOUN 1 = **reserve**, stock, supply, store, collection, pool ▷ PLURAL NOUN 2 = **money**, capital, cash, finance, means, savings, resources, assets ▷ VERB 3 = **finance**, back, support, pay for, subsidize, provide money for, put up the money for

fundamental 1 = **central**, key, basic, essential, primary, principal, cardinal OPPOSITE: incidental 2 = **basic**, essential, underlying, profound, elementary, rudimentary

fundamentally 1 = **basically**, at heart, at bottom 2 = **essentially**, radically, basically, primarily, profoundly, intrinsically

fundi (*S. African*) = **expert**

funeral = **burial**, committal, laying to rest, cremation,

interment, obsequies, entombment

funny 1 = **humorous**, amusing, comical, entertaining, comic, witty, hilarious, riotous OPPOSITE: unfunny 2 = **comic**, comical 3 = **peculiar**, odd, strange, unusual, bizarre, curious, weird, mysterious 4 = **ill**, poorly (*informal*), sick, odd, crook (*Austral. & N.Z. informal*), ailing, unhealthy, unwell, off-colour (*informal*)

furious 1 = **angry**, raging, fuming, infuriated, incensed, enraged, inflamed, very angry, tooshie (*Austral. slang*) OPPOSITE: pleased 2 = **violent**, intense, fierce, savage, turbulent, vehement, unrestrained

furnish 1 = **decorate**, fit out, stock, equip 2 = **supply**, give, offer, provide, present, grant, hand out

furniture = **household goods**, furnishings, fittings, house fittings, goods, things (*informal*), possessions, appliances

furore = **commotion**, to-do, stir, disturbance, outcry, uproar, hullabaloo

further *or* **farther** ADVERB 1 = **in addition**, moreover, besides, furthermore, also, to boot, additionally, into the bargain ▷ ADJECTIVE 2 = **additional**, more, new, other, extra, fresh, supplementary

▷ VERB 3 = **promote**, help, develop, forward, encourage, advance, work for, assist **OPPOSITE:** hinder

furthermore = **moreover**, further, in addition, besides, too, as well, to boot, additionally

furthest *or* **farthest** = **most distant**, extreme, ultimate, remotest, furthermost, outmost

fury 1 = **anger**, passion, rage, madness, frenzy, wrath, impetuosity **OPPOSITE:** calmness 2 = **violence**, force, intensity, severity, ferocity, savagery, vehemence, fierceness **OPPOSITE:** peace

fuss NOUN 1 = **commotion**, to-do, bother, stir, excitement, ado, hue and cry, palaver 2 = **bother**, trouble, struggle, hassle (*informal*), nuisance, inconvenience, hindrance 3 = **complaint**, row, protest, objection, trouble, argument, squabble, furore ▷ VERB 4 = **worry**, flap (*informal*), fret, fidget, take pains, be agitated, get worked up

futile = **useless**, vain, unsuccessful, pointless, worthless, fruitless, ineffectual, unprofitable **OPPOSITE:** useful

future NOUN 1 = **time to come**, hereafter, what lies ahead 2 = **prospect**, expectation, outlook

▷ ADJECTIVE 3 = **forthcoming**, coming, later, approaching, to come, succeeding, fated, subsequent **OPPOSITE:** past

fuzzy 1 = **frizzy**, fluffy, woolly, downy 2 = **indistinct**, blurred, vague, distorted, unclear, bleary, out of focus, ill-defined **OPPOSITE:** distinct

f

Gg

gadget = **device**, thing, appliance, machine, tool, implement, invention, instrument

gag¹ NOUN 1 = **muzzle**, tie, restraint
▷ VERB 2 = **suppress**, silence, muffle, curb, stifle, muzzle, quieten 3 = **retch**, heave

gag² (*Informal*) = **joke**, crack (*slang*), funny (*informal*), quip, pun, jest, wisecrack (*informal*), witticism

gain VERB 1 = **acquire**, get, receive, pick up, secure, collect, gather, obtain 2 = **profit**, get, land, secure, collect, gather, capture, acquire **OPPOSITE:** lose 3 = **put on**, increase in, gather, build up 4 = **attain**, get, reach, get to, secure, obtain, acquire, arrive at
▷ NOUN 5 = **rise**, increase, growth, advance, improvement, upsurge, upturn, upswing 6 = **profit**, return, benefit, advantage, yield, dividend **OPPOSITE:** loss
▷ PLURAL NOUN 7 = **profits**, earnings, revenue, proceeds, winnings, takings

▷ PHRASES: gain on something *or* someone = **get nearer to**, close in on, approach, catch up with, narrow the gap on

gala = **festival**, fête, celebration, carnival, festivity, pageant, jamboree

gale 1 = **storm**, hurricane, tornado, cyclone, blast, typhoon, tempest, squall 2 (*Informal*) = **outburst**, scream, roar, fit, storm, shout, burst, explosion

gall = **annoy**, provoke, irritate, trouble, disturb, madden, exasperate, vex

gallop 1 = **run**, race, career, speed, bolt 2 = **dash**, run, race, career, speed, rush, sprint

gamble NOUN 1 = **risk**, chance, venture, lottery, speculation, uncertainty, leap in the dark **OPPOSITE:** certainty 2 = **bet**, flutter (*informal*), punt (*chiefly Brit.*), wager
▷ VERB 3 = **take a chance**, speculate, stick your neck out (*informal*) 4 = **risk**, chance, hazard, wager 5 = **bet**, play, game, speculate, punt, wager, have a flutter (*informal*)

game NOUN 1 = **pastime**, sport, activity, entertainment, recreation, distraction, amusement, diversion **OPPOSITE:** job 2 = **match**, meeting, event, competition, tournament, clash, contest, head-to-head 3 = **amusement**, joke, entertainment, diversion

4 = **wild animals** or **birds**, prey, quarry **5** = **scheme**, plan, design, trick, plot, tactic, manoeuvre, ploy
▷ ADJECTIVE **6** = **willing**, prepared, ready, keen, eager, interested, desirous **7** = **brave**, courageous, spirited, daring, persistent, gritty, intrepid, plucky OPPOSITE: cowardly

gang = **group**, crowd, pack, company, band, bunch, mob

gangster = **hoodlum** (chiefly U.S.), crook (informal), bandit, hood (U.S. slang), robber, mobster (U.S. slang), racketeer, ruffian, tsotsi (S. African)

gap 1 = **opening**, space, hole, break, crack, slot, aperture, cleft **2** = **interval**, pause, interruption, respite, lull, interlude, breathing space, hiatus **3** = **difference**, gulf, contrast, disagreement, discrepancy, inconsistency, disparity, divergence

gape 1 = **stare**, wonder, goggle, gawp (Brit. slang), gawk **2** = **open**, split, crack, yawn

gaping = **wide**, great, open, broad, vast, yawning, wide open, cavernous

garland NOUN **1** = **wreath**, band, bays, crown, honours, laurels, festoon, chaplet
▷ VERB **2** = **adorn**, crown, deck, festoon, wreathe

garment often plural = **clothes**, dress, clothing, gear (slang), uniform, outfit, costume, apparel, attire

garnish NOUN **1** = **decoration**, embellishment, adornment, ornamentation, trimming
▷ VERB **2** = **decorate**, adorn, ornament, embellish, trim
OPPOSITE: strip

garrison NOUN **1** = **troops**, group, unit, section, command, armed force, detachment **2** = **fort**, fortress, camp, base, post, station, stronghold, fortification, fortified pa (N.Z.)
▷ VERB **3** = **station**, position, post, install, assign, put on duty

gas 1 = **fumes**, vapour **2** (U.S., Canad. & N.Z.) = **petrol**, gasoline

gasp VERB **1** = **pant**, blow, puff, choke, gulp, catch your breath
▷ NOUN **2** = **pant**, puff, gulp, sharp intake of breath

gate = **barrier**, opening, door, entrance, exit, gateway, portal

gather VERB **1** = **congregate**, assemble, collect, meet, mass, come together, muster, converge OPPOSITE: scatter **2** = **assemble**, collect, bring together, muster, call together OPPOSITE: disperse **3** = **collect**, assemble, accumulate, mass, muster, garner, amass, stockpile **4** = **pick**, harvest, pluck, reap, glean **5** = **build up**, rise, increase, grow, expand, swell, intensify, heighten **6** = **understand**, believe, hear, learn, assume, conclude, presume, infer **7** = **fold**, tuck, pleat

gathering 1 = **assembly**, group, crowd, meeting, conference, company, congress, mass, hui (N.Z.), runanga (N.Z.) 2 = **collecting**, obtaining, attainment

gauge VERB 1 = **measure**, calculate, evaluate, value, determine, count, weigh, compute 2 = **judge**, estimate, guess, assess, evaluate, rate, appraise, reckon ▷ NOUN 3 = **meter**, dial, measuring instrument

gay ADJECTIVE 1 = **homosexual**, lesbian, queer (informal or derogatory), moffie (S. African slang) 2 = **cheerful**, lively, sparkling, merry, upbeat (informal), buoyant, cheery, carefree OPPOSITE: sad 3 = **colourful**, rich, bright, brilliant, vivid, flamboyant, flashy, showy OPPOSITE: drab ▷ NOUN 4 = **homosexual**, lesbian, auntie or aunty (Austral. slang), lily (Austral. slang) OPPOSITE: heterosexual

● USAGE NOTE
● By far the most common and
● up-to-date use of the word
● gay is in reference to being
● homosexual. Other senses of
● the word have become
● uncommon and dated.

gaze VERB 1 = **stare**, look, view, watch, regard, gape ▷ NOUN 2 = **stare**, look, fixed look

gazette = **newspaper**, paper, journal, periodical, news-sheet

gear NOUN 1 = **mechanism**, works, machinery, cogs, cogwheels, gearwheels 2 = **equipment**, supplies, tackle, tools, instruments, apparatus, paraphernalia, accoutrements 3 = **clothing**, wear, dress, clothes, outfit, costume, garments, togs ▷ VERB 4 with to or towards = **equip**, fit, adjust, adapt

gem 1 = **precious stone**, jewel, stone 2 = **treasure**, prize, jewel, pearl, masterpiece, humdinger (slang), taonga (N.Z.)

general 1 = **widespread**, accepted, popular, public, common, broad, extensive, universal OPPOSITE: individual 2 = **overall**, complete, total, global, comprehensive, blanket, inclusive, all-embracing OPPOSITE: restricted 3 = **universal**, overall, widespread, collective, across-the-board OPPOSITE: exceptional 4 = **vague**, loose, blanket, sweeping, unclear, approximate, woolly, indefinite OPPOSITE: specific

generally 1 = **usually**, commonly, typically, normally, on the whole, by and large, ordinarily, as a rule OPPOSITE: occasionally 2 = **commonly**, widely, publicly, universally, extensively, popularly, conventionally, customarily OPPOSITE: individually

generate = produce, create, make, cause, give rise to, engender **OPPOSITE:** end

generation 1 = age group, peer group 2 = age, period, era, time, lifetime, span, epoch

generic 1 = collective, general, common, wide, comprehensive, universal, blanket, inclusive **OPPOSITE:** specific

generosity 1 = liberality, charity, bounty, munificence, beneficence, largesse or largess 2 = magnanimity, goodness, kindness, selflessness, charity, unselfishness, high-mindedness, nobleness

generous 1 = liberal, lavish, charitable, hospitable, bountiful, open-handed, unstinting, beneficent **OPPOSITE:** mean 2 = magnanimous, kind, noble, good, high-minded, unselfish, big-hearted 3 = plentiful, lavish, ample, abundant, full, rich, liberal, copious **OPPOSITE:** meagre

genesis 1 = beginning, origin, start, birth, creation, formation, inception **OPPOSITE:** end

genius 1 = brilliance, ability, talent, capacity, gift, bent, excellence, flair 2 = master, expert, mastermind, maestro, virtuoso, whiz (*informal*), hotshot (*informal*), brainbox, fundi (*S. African*) **OPPOSITE:** dunce

genre = type, group, order, sort, kind, class, style, species

gentle 1 = kind, kindly, tender, mild, humane, compassionate, meek, placid **OPPOSITE:** unkind 2 = slow, easy, slight, moderate, gradual, imperceptible 3 = moderate, light, soft, slight, mild, soothing **OPPOSITE:** violent

gentlemanly = chivalrous, refined, polite, civil, courteous, gallant, genteel, well-mannered

genuine 1 = authentic, real, actual, true, valid, legitimate, veritable, bona fide, dinkum (*Austral. & N.Z. informal*) **OPPOSITE:** counterfeit 2 = heartfelt, sincere, honest, earnest, real, true, frank, unaffected **OPPOSITE:** affected 3 = sincere, honest, frank, candid, dinkum (*Austral. & N.Z. informal*), guileless **OPPOSITE:** hypocritical

germ 1 = microbe, virus, bug (*informal*), bacterium, bacillus, microorganism 2 = beginning, root, seed, origin, spark, embryo, rudiment

gesture NOUN 1 = sign, action, signal, motion, indication, gesticulation
▷ VERB 2 = signal, sign, wave, indicate, motion, beckon, gesticulate

get VERB 1 = become, grow, turn, come to be 2 = persuade, convince, induce, influence, entice, incite, impel, prevail

g

upon **3** (*Informal*) = **annoy**, upset, anger, disturb, trouble, bug (*informal*), irritate, gall **4** = **obtain**, receive, gain, acquire, win, land, net, pick up **5** = **fetch**, bring, collect **6** = **understand**, follow, catch, see, realize, take in, perceive, grasp **7** = **catch**, develop, contract, succumb to, fall victim to, go down with, come down with **8** = **arrest**, catch, grab, capture, seize, take, nab (*informal*), apprehend
▷ **PHRASES: get at someone** = **criticize**, attack, blame, put down, knock (*informal*), nag, pick on, disparage ▶ **get at something 1** = **reach**, touch, grasp, get (a) hold of, stretch to **2** = **find out**, learn, reach, reveal, discover, acquire, detect, uncover **3** = **imply**, mean, suggest, hint, intimate, lead up to, insinuate ▶ **get by** = **manage**, survive, cope, fare, exist, get along, make do, muddle through ▶ **get something across** = **communicate**, pass on, transmit, convey, impart, bring home, make known, put over

ghastly = **horrible**, shocking, terrible, awful, dreadful, horrendous, hideous, frightful **OPPOSITE:** lovely

ghost 1 = **spirit**, soul, phantom, spectre, spook (*informal*), apparition, wraith, atua (*N.Z.*), kehua (*N.Z.*), wairua (*N.Z.*)

2 = **trace**, shadow, suggestion, hint, suspicion, glimmer, semblance
● **RELATED WORD**
● *adjective*: spectral

ghostly = **unearthly**, phantom, eerie, supernatural, spooky (*informal*), spectral

giant ADJECTIVE **1** = **huge**, vast, enormous, tremendous, immense, titanic, gigantic, monumental **OPPOSITE:** tiny
▷ NOUN **2** = **ogre**, monster, titan, colossus

gidday or **g'day** (*Austral. & N.Z.*) = **hello**, hi (*informal*), greetings, how do you do?, good morning, good evening, good afternoon, welcome, kia ora (*N.Z.*)

gift 1 = **donation**, offering, present, contribution, grant, legacy, hand-out, endowment, bonsela (*S. African*), koha (*N.Z.*) **2** = **talent**, ability, capacity, genius, power, capability, flair, knack

gifted = **talented**, able, skilled, expert, masterly, brilliant, capable, clever **OPPOSITE:** talentless

gigantic = **huge**, large, giant, massive, enormous, tremendous, immense, titanic **OPPOSITE:** tiny

giggle VERB = **laugh**, chuckle, snigger, chortle, titter, twitter
▷ NOUN = **laugh**, chuckle, snigger, chortle, titter, twitter

girl = **female child**, lass, lassie (*informal*), miss, maiden

give VERB 1 = **perform**, do, carry out, execute 2 = **communicate**, announce, transmit, pronounce, utter, issue 3 = **produce**, make, cause, occasion, engender 4 = **present**, contribute, donate, provide, supply, award, grant, deliver **OPPOSITE:** take 5 = **concede**, allow, grant 6 = **surrender**, yield, devote, hand over, relinquish, part with ▷ **PHRASES: give in = admit defeat**, yield, concede, collapse, quit, submit, surrender, succumb ▶ **give something away = reveal**, expose, leak, disclose, betray, uncover, let out, divulge ▶ **give something off or out = emit**, produce, release, discharge, send out, throw out, exude ▶ **give something up = abandon**, stop, quit, cease, renounce, leave off, desist

glad 1 = **happy**, pleased, delighted, contented, gratified, joyful, overjoyed **OPPOSITE:** unhappy 2 (Archaic) = **pleasing**, happy, cheering, pleasant, cheerful, gratifying

gladly 1 = **happily**, cheerfully, gleefully 2 = **willingly**, freely, happily, readily, cheerfully, with pleasure **OPPOSITE:** reluctantly

glamorous 1 = **attractive**, elegant, dazzling **OPPOSITE:** unglamorous 2 = **exciting**, glittering, prestigious, glossy

OPPOSITE: unglamorous

glamour 1 = **charm**, appeal, beauty, attraction, fascination, allure, enchantment 2 = **excitement**, magic, thrill, romance, prestige, glitz (slang)

glance VERB 1 = **peek**, look, view, glimpse, peep **OPPOSITE:** scrutinize ▷ NOUN 2 = **peek**, look, glimpse, peep, dekko (slang) **OPPOSITE:** good look

● USAGE NOTE
● Care should be taken not to
● confuse glance and glimpse: he
● caught a glimpse (not glance) of
● her making her way through
● the crowd; he gave a quick
● glance (not glimpse) at his
● watch. A glance is a deliberate
● action, while a glimpse seems
● opportunistic.

glare VERB 1 = **scowl**, frown, glower, look daggers, lour or lower 2 = **dazzle**, blaze, flare, flame ▷ NOUN 3 = **scowl**, frown, glower, dirty look, black look, lour or lower 4 = **dazzle**, glow, blaze, flame, brilliance

glaring 1 = **obvious**, gross, outrageous, manifest, blatant, conspicuous, flagrant, unconcealed **OPPOSITE:** inconspicuous 2 = **dazzling**, strong, bright, glowing, blazing **OPPOSITE:** subdued

glaze NOUN 1 = **coat**, finish, polish, shine, gloss, varnish, enamel, lacquer

(archaic), maid (archaic)

▷ VERB 2 = **coat**, polish, gloss, varnish, enamel, lacquer

gleam VERB 1 = **shine**, flash, glow, sparkle, glitter, shimmer, glint, glimmer

▷ NOUN 2 = **glimmer**, flash, beam, glow, sparkle 3 = **trace**, suggestion, hint, flicker, glimmer, inkling

glide = **slip**, sail, slide

glimpse NOUN 1 = **look**, sighting, sight, glance, peep, peek

▷ VERB 2 = **catch sight of**, spot, sight, view, spy, espy

glitter VERB 1 = **shine**, flash, sparkle, glare, gleam, shimmer, twinkle, glint

▷ NOUN 2 = **glamour**, show, display, splendour, tinsel, pageantry, gaudiness, showiness 3 = **sparkle**, flash, shine, glare, gleam, sheen, shimmer, brightness

global 1 = **worldwide**, world, international, universal 2 = **comprehensive**, general, total, unlimited, exhaustive, all-inclusive **OPPOSITE:** limited

globe = **planet**, world, earth, sphere, orb

gloom 1 = **darkness**, dark, shadow, shade, twilight, dusk, obscurity, blackness **OPPOSITE:** light 2 = **depression**, sorrow, woe, melancholy, unhappiness, despondency, dejection, low spirits **OPPOSITE:** happiness

gloomy 1 = **dark**, dull, dim, dismal, black, grey, murky,

dreary **OPPOSITE:** light 2 = **miserable**, sad, pessimistic, melancholy, glum, dejected, dispirited, downcast **OPPOSITE:** happy 3 = **depressing**, bad, dreary, sombre, dispiriting, disheartening, cheerless

glorious 1 = **splendid**, beautiful, brilliant, shining, superb, gorgeous, dazzling **OPPOSITE:** dull 2 = **delightful**, fine, wonderful, excellent, marvellous, gorgeous 3 = **illustrious**, famous, celebrated, distinguished, honoured, magnificent, renowned, eminent **OPPOSITE:** ordinary

glory NOUN 1 = **honour**, praise, fame, distinction, acclaim, prestige, eminence, renown **OPPOSITE:** shame 2 = **splendour**, majesty, greatness, grandeur, nobility, pomp, magnificence, pageantry

▷ VERB 3 = **triumph**, boast, relish, revel, exult, take delight, pride yourself

gloss¹ = **shine**, gleam, sheen, polish, brightness, veneer, lustre, patina

gloss² NOUN 1 = **interpretation**, comment, note, explanation, commentary, translation, footnote, elucidation

▷ VERB 2 = **interpret**, explain, comment, translate, annotate, elucidate

glossy = shiny, polished, shining, glazed, bright, silky, glassy, lustrous **OPPOSITE:** dull

glow NOUN 1 = light, gleam, splendour, glimmer, brilliance, brightness, radiance, luminosity **OPPOSITE:** dullness
▷ VERB 2 = shine, burn, gleam, brighten, glimmer, smoulder 3 = be pink

glowing 1 = complimentary, enthusiastic, rave (*informal*), ecstatic, rhapsodic, laudatory, adulatory **OPPOSITE:** scathing 2 = aglow, bright, radiant **OPPOSITE:** pale

glue NOUN 1 = adhesive, cement, gum, paste
▷ VERB 2 = stick, fix, seal, cement, gum, paste, affix

go VERB 1 = move, travel, advance, journey, proceed, pass, set off **OPPOSITE:** stay 2 = leave, withdraw, depart, move out, slope off, make tracks 3 = elapse, pass, flow, fly by, expire, lapse, slip away 4 = be given, be spent, be awarded, be allotted 5 = function, work, run, move, operate, perform **OPPOSITE:** fail 6 = match, blend, correspond, fit, suit, chime, harmonize 7 = serve, help, tend
▷ NOUN 8 = attempt, try, effort, bid, shot (*informal*), crack (*informal*) 9 = turn, shot (*informal*), stint 10 (*Informal*) = energy, life, drive, spirit, vitality, vigour, verve, force

▷ PHRASES: go off 1 = depart, leave, quit, go away, move out, decamp, slope off 2 = explode, fire, blow up, detonate, come about 3 (*Informal*) = go bad, turn, spoil, rot, go stale ▶ go out 1 = see someone, court, date (*informal, chiefly U.S.*), woo, go steady (*informal*), be romantically involved with 2 = be extinguished, die out, fade out ▶ go through something 1 = suffer, experience, bear, endure, brave, undergo, tolerate, withstand 2 = search, look through, rummage through, rifle through, hunt through, fossick through (*Austral. & N.Z.*), ferret about in 3 = examine, check, search, explore, look through

goal = aim, end, target, purpose, object, intention, objective, ambition

god = deity, immortal, divinity, divine being, supreme being, atua (*N.Z.*)
▷ *See panel* GODS AND GODDESSES

godly = devout, religious, holy, righteous, pious, good, saintly, god-fearing

gogga (*S. African*) = insect, bug, creepy-crawly (*Brit. informal*)

golden 1 = yellow, blonde, blond, flaxen **OPPOSITE:** dark 2 = successful, glorious, prosperous, rich, flourishing, halcyon **OPPOSITE:** worst 3 = promising, excellent,

GODS AND GODDESSES

Greek

Aeolus	winds
Aphrodite	love and beauty
Apollo	light, youth, and music
Ares	war
Artemis	hunting and the moon
Asclepius	healing
Athene *or* Pallas Athene	wisdom
Bacchus	wine
Boreas	north wind
Cronos	fertility of the earth
Demeter	agriculture
Dionysus	wine
Eos	dawn
Eros	love
Fates	destiny
Gaea *or* Gaia	the earth
Graces	charm and beauty
Hades	underworld
Hebe	youth and spring
Hecate	underworld
Helios	sun
Hephaestus	fire and metalworking
Hera	queen of the gods
Hermes	messenger of the gods
Horae *or* the Hours	seasons
Hymen	marriage
Hyperion	sun
Hypnos	sleep
Iris	rainbow
Momus	blame and mockery
Morpheus	sleep and dreams
Nemesis	vengeance
Nike	victory
Pan	woods and shepherds
Poseidon	sea and earthquakes
Rhea	fertility
Selene	moon

GODS AND GODDESSES *continued*

Uranus	sky
Zephyrus	west wind
Zeus	king of the gods
Roman	
Aesculapius	medicine
Apollo	light, youth, and music
Aurora	dawn
Bacchus	wine
Bellona	war
Bona Dea	fertility
Ceres	agriculture
Cupid	love
Cybele	nature
Diana	hunting and the moon
Faunus	forests
Flora	flowers
Janus	doors and beginnings
Juno	queen of the gods
Jupiter *or* Jove	king of the gods
Lares	household
Luna	moon
Mars	war
Mercury	messenger of the gods
Minerva	wisdom
Neptune	sea
Penates	storeroom
Phoebus	sun
Pluto	underworld
Quirinus	war
Saturn	agriculture and vegetation
Sol	sun
Somnus	sleep
Trivia	crossroads
Venus	love
Victoria	victory
Vulcan	fire and metalworking

favourable, opportune
OPPOSITE: unfavourable

▷ *See panels* SHADES OF ORANGE,
SHADES OF YELLOW

gone 1 = **missing**, lost, away, vanished, absent, astray 2 = **past**, over, ended, finished, elapsed

good ADJECTIVE 1 = **excellent**, great, fine, pleasing, acceptable, first-class, splendid, satisfactory, booshit (*Austral. slang*), exo (*Austral. slang*), sik (*Austral. slang*) OPPOSITE: bad 2 = **proficient**, able, skilled, expert, talented, clever, accomplished, first-class OPPOSITE: bad 3 = **beneficial**, useful, helpful, favourable, wholesome, advantageous OPPOSITE: harmful 4 = **honourable**, moral, worthy, ethical, upright, admirable, honest, righteous OPPOSITE: bad 5 = **well-behaved**, polite, orderly, obedient, dutiful, well-mannered OPPOSITE: naughty 6 = **kind**, kindly, friendly, obliging, charitable, humane, benevolent, merciful OPPOSITE: unkind 7 = **true**, real, genuine, proper, dinkum (*Austral. & N.Z. informal*) 8 = **full**, complete, extensive OPPOSITE: scant 9 = **considerable**, large, substantial, sufficient, adequate, ample 10 = **valid**, convincing, compelling, legitimate, authentic, persuasive, bona fide OPPOSITE: invalid 11 = **convenient**, timely, fitting, appropriate, suitable OPPOSITE: inconvenient ▷ NOUN 12 = **benefit**, interest, gain, advantage, use, profit, welfare, usefulness OPPOSITE: disadvantage 13 = **virtue**, goodness, righteousness, worth, merit, excellence, morality, rectitude OPPOSITE: evil ▷ PHRASES: for good = **permanently**, finally, for ever, once and for all, irrevocably

goodbye NOUN 1 = **farewell**, parting, leave-taking ▷ INTERJECTION 2 = **farewell**, see you, see you later, ciao (*Italian*), cheerio, adieu, la la, au revoir (*French*), haere ra (*N.Z.*)

goodness 1 = **virtue**, honour, merit, integrity, morality, honesty, righteousness, probity OPPOSITE: badness 2 = **excellence**, value, quality, worth, merit, superiority 3 = **nutrition**, benefit, advantage, wholesomeness, salubriousness 4 = **kindness**, charity, humanity, goodwill, mercy, compassion, generosity, friendliness

goods 1 = **merchandise**, stock, products, stuff, commodities, wares 2 = **property**, things, effects, gear, possessions, belongings, trappings, paraphernalia

goodwill = **friendliness**, friendship, benevolence, amity, kindliness

gore[1] = **blood**, slaughter, bloodshed, carnage, butchery

gore[2] = **pierce**, wound, transfix

gorge NOUN 1 = **ravine**, canyon, pass, chasm, cleft, fissure, defile, gulch
▷ VERB 2 = **overeat**, devour, gobble, wolf, gulp, guzzle 3 *usually reflexive* = **stuff**, feed, cram, glut

gorgeous 1 = **magnificent**, beautiful, superb, spectacular, splendid, dazzling, sumptuous OPPOSITE: shabby
2 = **delightful**, good, great, wonderful, excellent, lovely, fantastic, pleasant OPPOSITE: awful 3 (*Informal*) = **beautiful**, lovely, stunning (*informal*), elegant, handsome, exquisite, ravishing OPPOSITE: ugly

gospel 1 = **doctrine**, news, teachings, message, revelation, creed, credo, tidings 2 = **truth**, fact, certainty, the last word

gossip NOUN 1 = **idle talk**, scandal, hearsay, tittle-tattle, small talk, chitchat, blether, chinwag (*Brit. informal*)
2 = **busybody**, chatterbox (*informal*), chatterer, scandalmonger, gossipmonger
▷ VERB 3 = **chat**, chatter, jaw (*slang*), blether

gourmet = **connoisseur**, foodie (*informal*), bon vivant (*French*), epicure, gastronome

govern 1 = **rule**, lead, control, command, manage, direct, guide, handle 2 = **restrain**, control, check, master, discipline, regulate, curb, tame

government
1 = **administration**, executive, ministry, regime, powers-that-be 2 = **rule**, authority, administration, sovereignty, governance, statecraft

governor = **leader**, administrator, ruler, head, director, manager, chief, executive, baas (*S. African*)

gown = **dress**, costume, garment, robe, frock, garb, habit

grab = **snatch**, catch, seize, capture, grip, grasp, clutch, snap up

grace NOUN 1 = **elegance**, poise, ease, polish, refinement, fluency, suppleness, gracefulness OPPOSITE: ungainliness 2 = **manners**, decency, etiquette, consideration, propriety, tact, decorum OPPOSITE: bad manners 3 = **indulgence**, mercy, pardon, reprieve 4 = **benevolence**, favour, goodness, goodwill, generosity, kindness, kindliness OPPOSITE: ill will 5 = **prayer**, thanks, blessing, thanksgiving, benediction 6 = **favour**, regard, respect, approval, approbation, good opinion OPPOSITE: disfavour
▷ VERB 7 = **adorn**, enhance, decorate, enrich, set off, ornament, embellish
8 = **honour**, favour, dignify OPPOSITE: insult

g

graceful 1 = **elegant**, easy, pleasing, beautiful **OPPOSITE:** inelegant 2 = **polite**, mannerly, charming, gracious, civil, courteous, well-mannered

gracious = **courteous**, polite, civil, accommodating, kind, friendly, cordial, well-mannered **OPPOSITE:** ungracious

grade VERB 1 = **classify**, rate, order, class, group, sort, range, rank
▷ NOUN 2 = **class** 3 degree 4 = **level**, rank, group, class, stage, category, echelon

gradual = **steady**, slow, regular, gentle, progressive, piecemeal, unhurried **OPPOSITE:** sudden

gradually = **steadily**, slowly, progressively, gently, step by step, little by little, by degrees, unhurriedly

graduate 1 = **mark off**, grade, proportion, regulate, gauge, calibrate, measure out 2 = **classify**, rank, grade, group, order, sort, arrange

graft NOUN 1 = **shoot**, bud, implant, sprout, splice, scion 2 (Informal) = **labour**, work, effort, struggle, sweat, toil, slog, exertion
▷ VERB 3 = **join**, insert, transplant, implant, splice, affix 4 = **work**, labour, struggle, sweat (informal), slave, strive, toil

grain 1 = **seed**, kernel, grist 2 = **cereal**, corn 3 = **bit**, piece, trace, scrap, particle, fragment, speck, morsel 4 = **texture**, pattern, surface, fibre, weave, nap

grand 1 = **impressive**, great, large, magnificent, imposing, splendid, regal, stately **OPPOSITE:** unimposing 2 = **ambitious**, great, grandiose 3 = **superior**, great, dignified, stately 4 = **excellent**, great (informal), fine, wonderful, outstanding, smashing (informal), first-class, splendid **OPPOSITE:** bad

grandeur = **splendour**, glory, majesty, nobility, pomp, magnificence, sumptuousness, sublimity

grant NOUN 1 = **award**, allowance, donation, endowment, gift, subsidy, hand-out
▷ VERB 2 = **give**, allow, present, award, permit, assign, allocate, hand out 3 = **accept**, allow, admit, acknowledge, concede

graphic 1 = **vivid**, clear, detailed, striking, explicit, expressive **OPPOSITE:** vague 2 = **pictorial**, visual, diagrammatic **OPPOSITE:** impressionistic

grapple 1 = **deal**, tackle, struggle, take on, confront, get to grips, address yourself to 2 = **struggle**, fight, combat, wrestle, battle, clash, tussle, scuffle

grasp VERB 1 = **grip**, hold, catch, grab, seize, snatch,

clutch, clinch 2 = **understand**,
realize, take in, get, see, catch
on, comprehend, catch or get
the drift of
▷ NOUN 3 = **grip**, hold,
possession, embrace, clutches,
clasp 4 = **understanding**,
knowledge, grip, awareness,
mastery, comprehension
5 = **reach**, power, control,
scope

grasping = **greedy**, acquisitive,
rapacious, avaricious, covetous,
snoep (S. African informal)
OPPOSITE: generous

grate 1 = **shred**, mince,
pulverize 2 = **scrape**, grind,
rub, scratch, creak, rasp

grateful = **thankful**, obliged, in
(someone's) debt, indebted,
appreciative, beholden

grating¹ = **grille**, grid, grate,
lattice, trellis, gridiron

grating² = **irritating**, harsh,
annoying, jarring, unpleasant,
raucous, strident, discordant
OPPOSITE: pleasing

gratitude = **thankfulness**,
thanks, recognition, obligation,
appreciation, indebtedness,
gratefulness OPPOSITE:
ingratitude

grave¹ = **tomb**, vault, crypt,
mausoleum, sepulchre, pit,
burying place

grave² 1 = **serious**, important,
critical, pressing, threatening,
dangerous, acute, severe
OPPOSITE: trifling 2 = **solemn**,
sober, sombre, dour, unsmiling

OPPOSITE: carefree

graveyard = **cemetery**,
churchyard, burial ground,
charnel house, necropolis

gravity 1 = **seriousness**,
importance, significance,
urgency, severity, acuteness,
weightiness, momentousness
OPPOSITE: triviality
2 = **solemnity**, seriousness,
gravitas OPPOSITE: frivolity

graze¹ = **feed**, crop, browse,
pasture

graze² VERB 1 = **scratch**, skin,
scrape, chafe, abrade
2 = **touch**, brush, rub, scrape,
shave, skim, glance off
▷ NOUN 3 = **scratch**, scrape,
abrasion

greasy = **fatty**, slippery, oily,
slimy, oleaginous

great ADJECTIVE 1 = **large**, big,
huge, vast, enormous,
immense, gigantic, prodigious
OPPOSITE: small
2 = **important**, serious,
significant, critical, crucial,
momentous OPPOSITE:
unimportant 3 = **famous**,
outstanding, remarkable,
prominent, renowned, eminent,
illustrious, noteworthy
4 (Informal) = **excellent**, fine,
wonderful, superb, fantastic
(informal), tremendous
(informal), marvellous (informal),
terrific (informal), booshit
(Austral. slang), exo (Austral.
slang), sik (Austral. slang)
OPPOSITE: poor 5 = **very**, really,

extremely, exceedingly
greatly = **very much**, hugely, vastly, considerably, remarkably, enormously, immensely, tremendously
greatness 1 = **grandeur**, glory, majesty, splendour, pomp, magnificence 2 = **fame**, glory, celebrity, distinction, eminence, note, renown, illustriousness
greed or **greediness**
1 = **gluttony**, voracity
2 = **avarice**, longing, desire, hunger, craving, selfishness, acquisitiveness, covetousness **OPPOSITE:** generosity
greedy 1 = **gluttonous**, insatiable, voracious, ravenous, piggish 2 = **avaricious**, grasping, selfish, insatiable, acquisitive, rapacious, materialistic, desirous **OPPOSITE:** generous
green ADJECTIVE 1 = **verdant**, leafy, grassy 2 = **ecological**, conservationist, environment-friendly, ozone-friendly, non-polluting 3 = **inexperienced**, new, raw, naive, immature, gullible, untrained, wet behind the ears (informal) 4 = **jealous**, grudging, resentful, envious, covetous
▷ NOUN 5 = **lawn**, common, turf, sward
▷ See panel SHADES OF GREEN
greet 1 = **salute**, hail, say hello to, address, accost
2 = **welcome**, meet, receive, karanga (N.Z.), mihi (N.Z.)

3 = **receive**, take, respond to, react to
greeting = **welcome**, reception, salute, address, salutation, hongi (N.Z.), kia ora (N.Z.)
grey 1 = **dull**, dark, dim, gloomy, drab 2 = **boring**, dull, anonymous, faceless, colourless, nondescript, characterless 3 = **pale**, wan, pallid, ashen 4 = **ambiguous**, uncertain, neutral, unclear, debatable
▷ See panel SHADES FROM BLACK TO WHITE
grief = **sadness**, suffering, regret, distress, misery, sorrow, woe, anguish **OPPOSITE:** joy
grievance = **complaint**, gripe (informal), axe to grind
grieve 1 = **mourn**, suffer, weep, lament 2 = **sadden**, hurt, injure, distress, wound, pain, afflict, upset **OPPOSITE:** gladden
grim = **terrible**, severe, harsh, forbidding, formidable, sinister
grind VERB 1 = **crush**, mill, powder, grate, pulverize, pound, abrade, granulate
2 = **press**, push, crush, jam, mash, force down 3 = **grate**, scrape, gnash 4 = **sharpen**, polish, sand, smooth, whet
▷ NOUN 5 (Informal) = **hard work**, labour, sweat (informal), chore, toil, drudgery
grip VERB 1 = **grasp**, hold, catch, seize, clutch, clasp, take hold of 2 = **engross**, fascinate, absorb, entrance, hold, compel,

SHADES OF GREEN		
apple green	lime green	pistachio
aquamarine	Lincoln green	sea green
avocado	Nile green	teal
emerald green	olive	turquoise
jade	pea green	

rivet, enthral

▷ **NOUN 3** = **clasp**, hold, grasp **4** = **control**, rule, influence, command, power, possession, domination, mastery **5** = **hold**, purchase, friction, traction **6** = **understanding**, sense, command, awareness, grasp, appreciation, mastery, comprehension

gripping = **fascinating**, exciting, thrilling, entrancing, compelling, riveting, enthralling, engrossing

grit NOUN 1 = **gravel**, sand, dust, pebbles **2** = **courage**, spirit, resolution, determination, guts (*informal*), backbone, fortitude, tenacity

▷ **VERB 3** = **clench**, grind, grate, gnash

gritty 1 = **rough**, sandy, dusty, rasping, gravelly, granular **2** = **courageous**, dogged, determined, spirited, brave, resolute, tenacious, plucky

groan VERB 1 = **moan**, cry, sigh **2** (*Informal*) = **complain**, object, moan, grumble, gripe (*informal*), carp, lament, whine

▷ **NOUN 3** = **moan**, cry, sigh, whine **4** (*Informal*) = **complaint**, protest, objection, grumble,

grouse, gripe (*informal*)

groom NOUN 1 = **stableman**, stableboy, hostler *or* ostler (*archaic*) **2** = **newly-wed**, husband, bridegroom, marriage partner

▷ **VERB 3** = **brush**, clean, tend, rub down, curry **4** = **smarten up**, clean, tidy, preen, spruce up, primp **5** = **train**, prime, prepare, coach, ready, educate, drill, nurture

groove = **indentation**, cut, hollow, channel, trench, flute, trough, furrow

grope = **feel**, search, fumble, flounder, fish, scrabble, cast about, fossick (*Austral. & N.Z.*)

gross ADJECTIVE 1 = **flagrant**, blatant, rank, sheer, utter, grievous, heinous, unmitigated **OPPOSITE:** qualified **2** = **vulgar**, offensive, crude, obscene, coarse, indelicate **OPPOSITE:** decent **3** = **fat**, obese, overweight, hulking, corpulent **OPPOSITE:** slim **4** = **total**, whole, entire, aggregate, before tax, before deductions **OPPOSITE:** net

▷ **VERB 5** = **earn**, make, take, bring in, rake in (*informal*)

grotesque 1 = **unnatural**,

bizarre, strange, fantastic, distorted, deformed, outlandish, freakish **OPPOSITE:** natural 2 = **absurd**, preposterous **OPPOSITE:** natural

ground NOUN 1 = **earth**, land, dry land, terra firma 2 = **arena**, pitch, stadium, park (*informal*), field, enclosure
▷ PLURAL NOUN 3 = **estate**, land, fields, gardens, territory 4 = **reason**, cause, basis, occasion, foundation, excuse, motive, justification 5 = **dregs**, lees, deposit, sediment
▷ VERB 6 = **base**, found, establish, set, settle, fix 7 = **instruct**, train, teach, initiate, tutor, acquaint with, familiarize with

group NOUN 1 = **crowd**, party, band, pack, gang, bunch
▷ VERB 2 = **arrange**, order, sort, class, classify, marshal, bracket

grove = **wood**, plantation, covert, thicket, copse, coppice, spinney

grow 1 = **develop**, get bigger **OPPOSITE:** shrink 2 = **get bigger**, spread, swell, stretch, expand, enlarge, multiply 3 = **cultivate**, produce, raise, farm, breed, nurture, propagate 4 = **become**, get, turn, come to be 5 = **originate**, spring, arise, stem, issue 6 = **improve**, advance, progress, succeed, thrive, flourish, prosper

grown-up NOUN 1 = **adult**, man, woman
▷ ADJECTIVE 2 = **mature**, adult, of age, fully-grown

growth 1 = **increase**, development, expansion, proliferation, enlargement, multiplication **OPPOSITE:** decline 2 = **progress**, success, improvement, expansion, advance, prosperity **OPPOSITE:** failure 3 (*Medical*) = **tumour**, cancer, swelling, lump, carcinoma (*Pathology*), sarcoma (*Medical*)

grudge NOUN 1 = **resentment**, bitterness, grievance, dislike, animosity, antipathy, enmity, rancour **OPPOSITE:** goodwill
▷ VERB 2 = **resent**, mind, envy, covet, begrudge **OPPOSITE:** welcome

gruelling = **exhausting**, demanding, tiring, taxing, severe, punishing, strenuous, arduous **OPPOSITE:** easy

gruesome = **horrific**, shocking, terrible, horrible, grim, ghastly, grisly, macabre **OPPOSITE:** pleasant

grumble VERB 1 = **complain**, moan, gripe (*informal*), whinge (*informal*), carp, whine, grouse, bleat 2 = **rumble**, growl, gurgle
▷ NOUN 3 = **complaint**, protest, objection, moan, grievance, grouse, gripe (*informal*), grouch (*informal*) 4 = **rumble**, growl, gurgle

guarantee VERB 1 = **ensure**,

secure, assure, warrant, make certain 2 = **promise**, pledge, undertake
▷ NOUN 3 = **promise**, pledge, assurance, certainty, word of honour 4 = **warranty**, contract, bond

guard VERB 1 = **protect**, defend, secure, mind, preserve, shield, safeguard, watch over
▷ NOUN 2 = **sentry**, warder, warden, custodian, watch, lookout, watchman, sentinel
3 = **shield**, security, defence, screen, protection, safeguard, buffer

guarded = **cautious**, reserved, careful, suspicious, wary, prudent, reticent, circumspect

guardian = **keeper**, champion, defender, guard, warden, curator, protector, custodian

guerrilla = **freedom fighter**, partisan, underground fighter

guess VERB 1 = **estimate**, predict, work out, speculate, conjecture, postulate, hypothesize OPPOSITE: know
2 = **suppose**, think, believe, suspect, judge, imagine, reckon, fancy
▷ NOUN 3 = **estimate**, speculation, judgment, hypothesis, conjecture, shot in the dark OPPOSITE: certainty
4 = **supposition**, idea, theory, hypothesis

guest = **visitor**, company, caller, manu(w)hiri (N.Z.)

guidance = **advice**, direction, leadership, instruction, help, management, teaching, counselling

guide NOUN 1 = **handbook**, manual, guidebook, instructions, catalogue
2 = **directory**, street map
3 = **escort**, leader, usher
4 = **pointer**, sign, landmark, marker, beacon, signpost, guiding light, lodestar
5 = **model**, example, standard, ideal, inspiration, paradigm
▷ VERB 6 = **lead**, direct, escort, conduct, accompany, shepherd, usher, show the way 7 = **steer**, control, manage, direct, handle, command, manoeuvre
8 = **supervise**, train, teach, influence, advise, counsel, instruct, oversee

guild = **society**, union, league, association, company, club, order, organization

guilt 1 = **shame**, regret, remorse, contrition, guilty conscience, self-reproach OPPOSITE: pride
2 = **culpability**, blame, responsibility, misconduct, wickedness, sinfulness, guiltiness OPPOSITE: innocence

guilty 1 = **ashamed**, sorry, rueful, sheepish, contrite, remorseful, regretful, shamefaced OPPOSITE: proud
2 = **culpable**, responsible, to blame, offending, erring, at fault, reprehensible, blameworthy, felonious

g

OPPOSITE: innocent

guise 1 = **form**, appearance, shape, aspect, mode, semblance 2 = **pretence**, disguise, aspect, semblance

gulf 1 = **bay**, bight, sea inlet 2 = **chasm**, opening, split, gap, separation, void, rift, abyss

gum NOUN 1 = **glue**, adhesive, resin, cement, paste
▷ VERB 2 = **stick**, glue, affix, cement, paste

gun = **firearm**, shooter (*slang*), piece (*slang*), handgun

gunman = **armed man**, gunslinger (*U.S. slang*)

guru 1 = **authority**, expert, leader, master, pundit, Svengali, fundi (*S. African*) 2 = **teacher**, mentor, sage, master, tutor

gush VERB 1 = **flow**, run, rush, flood, pour, stream, cascade, spurt 2 = **enthuse**, rave, spout, overstate, effuse
▷ NOUN 3 = **stream**, flow, rush, flood, jet, cascade, torrent, spurt

gut NOUN 1 (*Informal*) = **paunch**, belly, spare tyre (*Brit. slang*), potbelly, puku (*N.Z.*)
▷ PLURAL NOUN 2 = **intestines**, insides (*informal*), stomach, belly, bowels, innards (*informal*), entrails 3 (*Informal*) = **courage**, spirit, nerve, daring, pluck, backbone, bottle (*slang*), audacity
▷ VERB 4 = **disembowel**, clean 5 = **ravage**, empty, clean out, despoil

▷ ADJECTIVE 6 = **instinctive**, natural, basic, spontaneous, intuitive, involuntary, heartfelt, unthinking

gutter = **drain**, channel, ditch, trench, trough, conduit, sluice

guy (*Informal*) = **man**, person, fellow, lad, bloke (*Brit. informal*), chap

Gypsy *or* **Gipsy** = **traveller**, roamer, wanderer, Bohemian, rover, rambler, nomad, Romany

Hh

habit 1 = **mannerism**, custom, way, practice, characteristic, tendency, quirk, propensity 2 = **addiction**, dependence, compulsion

hack¹ = **cut**, chop, slash, mutilate, mangle, mangulate (*Austral. slang*), hew, lacerate

hack² = **reporter**, writer, correspondent, journalist, scribbler, contributor, literary hack

hail¹ 1 = **acclaim**, honour, acknowledge, cheer, applaud **OPPOSITE:** condemn 2 = **salute**, greet, address, welcome, say hello to, halloo **OPPOSITE:** snub 3 = **flag down**, summon, signal to, wave down

▷ **PHRASES: hail from somewhere** = **come from**, be born in, originate in, be a native of, have your roots in

hail² NOUN 1 = **hailstones**, sleet, hailstorm, frozen rain 2 = **shower**, rain, storm, battery, volley, barrage, bombardment, downpour

▷ **VERB** 3 = **rain**, shower, pelt 4 = **batter**, rain, bombard, pelt, rain down on, beat down upon

hair = **locks**, mane, tresses, shock, mop, head of hair

hairdresser = **stylist**, barber, coiffeur *or* coiffeuse

hairy 1 = **shaggy**, woolly, furry, stubbly, bushy, unshaven, hirsute 2 (*Slang*) = **dangerous**, risky, unpredictable, hazardous, perilous

hale (*Old-fashioned*) = **healthy**, well, strong, sound, fit, flourishing, robust, vigorous

half NOUN 1 = **fifty per cent**, equal part

▷ **ADJECTIVE** 2 = **partial**, limited, moderate, halved

▷ **ADVERB** 3 = **partially**, partly, in part

halfway ADVERB 1 = **midway**, to *or* in the middle

▷ **ADJECTIVE** 2 = **midway**, middle, mid, central, intermediate, equidistant

hall 1 = **passage**, lobby, corridor, hallway, foyer, entry, passageway, entrance hall 2 = **meeting place**, chamber, auditorium, concert hall, assembly room

hallmark 1 = **trademark**, sure sign, telltale sign 2 (*Brit.*) = **mark**, sign, device, stamp, seal, symbol

halt VERB 1 = **stop**, break off, stand still, wait, rest **OPPOSITE:** continue 2 = **come to an end**, stop, cease 3 = **hold back**, end, check, block, curb, terminate, cut short, bring to an end **OPPOSITE:** aid

▷ NOUN 4 = **stop**, end, close, pause, standstill, stoppage **OPPOSITE:** continuation

halting = **faltering**, stumbling, awkward, hesitant, laboured, stammering, stuttering

halve 1 = **cut in half**, reduce by fifty per cent, decrease by fifty per cent, lessen by fifty per cent 2 = **split in two**, cut in half, bisect, divide in two, share equally, divide equally

hammer 1 = **hit**, drive, knock, beat, strike, tap, bang 2 (*Informal*) = **defeat**, beat, thrash, trounce, run rings around (*informal*), wipe the floor with (*informal*), drub

hamper = **hinder**, handicap, prevent, restrict, frustrate, hamstring, interfere with, obstruct **OPPOSITE:** help

hand NOUN 1 = **palm**, fist, paw (*informal*), mitt (*slang*) 2 = **worker**, employee, labourer, workman, operative, craftsman, artisan, hired man 3 = **round of applause**, clap, ovation, big hand 4 = **writing**, script, handwriting, calligraphy ▷ VERB 5 = **give**, pass, hand over, present to, deliver

handbook = **guidebook**, guide, manual, instruction book

handcuff VERB 1 = **shackle**, secure, restrain, fetter, manacle ▷ PLURAL NOUN 2 = **shackles**, cuffs (*informal*), fetters, manacles

handful = **few**, sprinkling, small

amount, smattering, small number **OPPOSITE:** a lot

handicap NOUN 1 = **disability**, defect, impairment, physical abnormality 2 = **disadvantage**, barrier, restriction, obstacle, limitation, drawback, stumbling block, impediment **OPPOSITE:** advantage 3 = **advantage**, head start ▷ VERB 4 = **hinder**, limit, restrict, burden, hamstring, hamper, hold back, impede **OPPOSITE:** help

handle NOUN 1 = **grip**, hilt, haft, stock ▷ VERB 2 = **manage**, deal with, tackle, cope with 3 = **deal with**, manage, direct, guide, manipulate, manoeuvre 5 = **hold**, feel, touch, pick up, finger, grasp

handsome 1 = **good-looking**, attractive, gorgeous, elegant, personable, dishy (*informal*, *chiefly Brit.*), comely **OPPOSITE:** ugly 2 = **generous**, large, princely, liberal, considerable, lavish, ample, abundant **OPPOSITE:** mean

handy 1 = **useful**, practical, helpful, neat, convenient, easy to use, manageable, user-friendly **OPPOSITE:** useless 2 = **convenient**, close, available, nearby, accessible, on hand, at hand, within reach **OPPOSITE:** inconvenient 3 = **skilful**, skilled, expert, adept, deft, proficient, adroit, dexterous **OPPOSITE:** unskilled

hang 1 = **dangle**, swing, suspend 2 = **lower**, suspend, dangle 3 = **lean** 4 = **execute**, lynch, string up (*informal*) ▷ **PHRASES: get the hang of something** = **grasp**, understand, learn, master, comprehend, catch on to, acquire the technique of ▶ **hang back** = **be reluctant**, hesitate, hold back, recoil, demur

hangover = **aftereffects**, morning after (*informal*)

hang-up (*informal*) = **preoccupation**, thing (*informal*), problem, block, difficulty, obsession, mania, inhibition

hank = **coil**, roll, length, bunch, piece, loop, clump, skein

happen 1 = **occur**, take place, come about, result, develop, transpire (*informal*), come to pass 2 = **chance**, turn out (*informal*)

happening = **event**, incident, experience, affair, proceeding, episode, occurrence

happily 1 = **luckily**, fortunately, providentially, opportunely 2 = **joyfully**, cheerfully, gleefully, blithely, merrily, gaily, joyously 3 = **willingly**, freely, gladly, with pleasure

happiness = **pleasure**, delight, joy, satisfaction, ecstasy, bliss, contentment, elation **OPPOSITE:** unhappiness

happy 1 = **pleased**, delighted, content, thrilled, glad, cheerful, merry, ecstatic 2 = **contented**, joyful, blissful **OPPOSITE:** sad 3 = **fortunate**, lucky, timely, favourable, auspicious, propitious, advantageous **OPPOSITE:** unfortunate

harass = **annoy**, trouble, bother, harry, plague, hound, hassle (*informal*), persecute

harassed = **hassled**, worried, troubled, strained, under pressure, tormented, distraught (*informal*), vexed

harassment = **hassle**, trouble, bother, irritation, persecution (*informal*), nuisance, annoyance, pestering

harbour NOUN 1 = **port**, haven, dock, mooring, marina, pier, wharf, anchorage ▷ VERB 2 = **hold**, bear, maintain, nurse, retain, foster, entertain, nurture 3 = **shelter**, protect, hide, shield, provide refuge, give asylum to

hard ADJECTIVE 1 = **tough**, strong, firm, solid, stiff, rigid, resistant, compressed **OPPOSITE:** soft 2 = **difficult**, involved, complicated, puzzling, intricate, perplexing, impenetrable, thorny **OPPOSITE:** easy 3 = **exhausting**, tough, exacting, rigorous, gruelling, strenuous, arduous, laborious **OPPOSITE:** easy 4 = **harsh**, cold, cruel, stern, callous, unkind,

h

unsympathetic, pitiless
OPPOSITE: kind 5 = grim,
painful, distressing, harsh,
unpleasant, intolerable,
grievous, disagreeable
▷ **ADVERB 6 = strenuously**,
steadily, persistently, doggedly,
diligently, energetically,
industriously, untiringly
7 = intently, closely, carefully,
sharply, keenly **8 = forcefully**,
strongly, heavily, sharply,
severely, fiercely, vigorously,
intensely **OPPOSITE: softly**

harden 1 = solidify, set, freeze,
cake, bake, clot, thicken, stiffen
2 = accustom, season,
toughen, train, inure, habituate

hardened 1 = habitual,
chronic, shameless, inveterate,
incorrigible **OPPOSITE:**
occasional **2 = seasoned**,
experienced, accustomed,
toughened, inured, habituated
OPPOSITE: naive

hardly 1 = barely, only just,
scarcely, just, with difficulty,
with effort **OPPOSITE:**
completely **2 = only just**, just,
barely, scarcely

hardship = suffering, need,
difficulty, misfortune, adversity,
tribulation, privation **OPPOSITE:**
ease

hardy = strong, tough, robust,
sound, rugged, sturdy, stout
OPPOSITE: frail

hare
● **RELATED WORDS**
● *adjective:* leporine

● *male:* buck
● *female:* doe
● *young:* leveret
● *habitation:* down, husk

harm VERB 1 = injure, hurt,
wound, abuse, ill-treat,
maltreat **OPPOSITE: heal**
2 = damage, hurt, ruin, spoil
▷ **NOUN 3 = injury**, suffering,
damage, ill, hurt, distress
4 = damage, loss, ill, hurt,
misfortune, mischief **OPPOSITE:**
good

harmful = damaging,
dangerous, negative,
destructive, hazardous,
unhealthy, detrimental, hurtful
OPPOSITE: harmless

harmless 1 = safe, benign,
wholesome, innocuous,
nontoxic **OPPOSITE: dangerous**
2 = inoffensive, innocent,
innocuous, gentle, tame,
unobjectionable

harmony 1 = accord, peace,
agreement, friendship,
sympathy, cooperation,
rapport, compatibility
OPPOSITE: conflict 2 = tune,
melody, unison, tunefulness,
euphony **OPPOSITE: discord**

harness VERB 1 = exploit,
control, channel, employ,
utilize, mobilize
▷ **NOUN 2 = equipment**, tackle,
gear, tack

harrowing = distressing,
disturbing, painful, terrifying,
traumatic, tormenting,
agonizing, nerve-racking

harry = **pester**, bother, plague, harass, hassle (*informal*), badger, chivvy

harsh 1 = **severe**, hard, tough, stark, austere, inhospitable 2 = **bleak**, freezing, severe, icy 3 = **cruel**, savage, ruthless, barbarous, pitiless 4 = **hard**, severe, cruel, stern, pitiless **OPPOSITE:** kind 5 = **drastic**, punitive, Draconian 6 = **raucous**, rough, grating, strident, rasping, discordant, guttural, dissonant **OPPOSITE:** soft

harshly = **severely**, roughly, cruelly, strictly, sternly, brutally

harvest NOUN 1 = **harvesting**, picking, gathering, collecting, reaping, harvest-time 2 = **crop**, yield, year's growth, produce ▷ VERB 3 = **gather**, pick, collect, bring in, pluck, reap

hassle (*Informal*) NOUN 1 = **trouble**, problem, difficulty, bother, grief (*informal*), uphill (*S. African*), inconvenience ▷ VERB 2 = **bother**, bug (*informal*), annoy, hound, harass, badger, pester

hasten = **rush**, race, fly, speed, dash, hurry (up), scurry, make haste **OPPOSITE:** dawdle

hastily 1 = **quickly**, rapidly, promptly, speedily 2 = **hurriedly**, rashly, precipitately, impetuously

hatch 1 = **incubate**, breed, sit on, brood, bring forth 2 = **devise**, design, invent, put together, conceive, brew, formulate, contrive

hate VERB 1 = **detest**, loathe, despise, dislike, abhor, recoil from, not be able to bear **OPPOSITE:** love 2 = **dislike**, detest, shrink from, recoil from, not be able to bear **OPPOSITE:** like 3 = **be unwilling**, regret, be reluctant, hesitate, be sorry, be loath, feel disinclined ▷ NOUN 4 = **dislike**, hostility, hatred, loathing, animosity, aversion, antipathy, enmity **OPPOSITE:** love

hatred = **hate**, dislike, animosity, aversion, revulsion, antipathy, enmity, repugnance **OPPOSITE:** love

haul VERB 1 = **drag**, draw, pull, heave ▷ NOUN 2 = **yield**, gain, spoils, catch, harvest, loot, takings, booty

haunt VERB 1 = **plague**, trouble, obsess, torment, possess, stay with, recur, prey on ▷ NOUN 2 = **meeting place**, hangout (*informal*), rendezvous, stamping ground

haunted 1 = **possessed**, ghostly, cursed, eerie, spooky (*informal*), jinxed 2 = **preoccupied**, worried, troubled, plagued, obsessed, tormented

haunting = **evocative**, poignant, unforgettable

have VERB 1 = **own**, keep,

possess, hold, retain, boast, be the owner of **2 = get**, obtain, take, receive, accept, gain, secure, acquire **3 = suffer**, experience, undergo, sustain, endure, be suffering from **4 = give birth to**, bear, deliver, bring forth, beget **5 = experience**, go through, undergo, meet with, come across, run into, be faced with

▷ **PHRASES: have someone on = tease**, kid (*informal*), wind up (*Brit. slang*), trick, deceive, take the mickey, pull someone's leg ▶ **have something on = wear**, be wearing, be dressed in, be clothed in, be attired in ▶ **have to 1 = must**, should, be forced, ought, be obliged, be bound, have got to, be compelled **2 = have got to**, must

haven = sanctuary, shelter, retreat, asylum, refuge, oasis, sanctum

havoc 1 = devastation, damage, destruction, ruin **2** (*Informal*) **= disorder**, confusion, chaos, disruption, mayhem, shambles

hazard NOUN 1 = danger, risk, threat, problem, menace, peril, jeopardy, pitfall ▷ **VERB 2 = jeopardize**, risk, endanger, threaten, expose, imperil, put in jeopardy ▷ **PHRASES: hazard a guess = guess**, conjecture, presume, take a guess

hazardous = dangerous, risky,

difficult, insecure, unsafe, precarious, perilous, dicey (*informal, chiefly Brit.*) **OPPOSITE:** safe

haze = mist, cloud, fog, obscurity, vapour

head NOUN 1 = skull, crown, pate, nut (*slang*), loaf (*slang*) **2 = mind**, reasoning, understanding, thought, sense, brain, brains (*informal*), intelligence **3 = top**, crown, summit, peak, crest, pinnacle **4** (*Informal*) **= head teacher**, principal **5 = leader**, president, director, manager, chief, boss (*informal*), captain, master ▷ **ADJECTIVE 6 = chief**, main, leading, first, prime, premier, supreme, principal ▷ **VERB 7 = lead**, precede, be the leader of, be *or* go first, be *or* go at the front of, lead the way **8 = top**, lead, crown, cap **9 = be in charge of**, run, manage, lead, control, direct, guide, command ▷ **PHRASES: go to your head 1 = intoxicate 2 = make someone conceited**, puff someone up, make someone full of themselves ▶ **head over heels = completely**, thoroughly, utterly, intensely, wholeheartedly, uncontrollably

headache 1 = migraine, head (*informal*), neuralgia **2 = problem** (*Informal*), worry, trouble, bother, nuisance, inconvenience, bane, vexation

heading = title, name, caption, headline, rubric

heady 1 = exciting, thrilling, stimulating, exhilarating, intoxicating 2 = intoxicating, strong, potent, inebriating

heal 1 *sometimes with up* = mend, get better, get well, cure, regenerate, show improvement 2 = cure, restore, mend, make better, remedy, make good, make well **OPPOSITE:** injure

health 1 = condition, state, shape, constitution, fettle 2 = wellbeing, strength, fitness, vigour, good condition, soundness, robustness, healthiness **OPPOSITE:** illness 3 = state, condition, shape

healthy 1 = well, fit, strong, active, robust, in good shape (*informal*), in the pink, in fine fettle **OPPOSITE:** ill 2 = wholesome, beneficial, nourishing, nutritious, salutary, hygienic, salubrious **OPPOSITE:** unwholesome 3 = invigorating, beneficial, salutary, salubrious

heap NOUN 1 = pile, lot, collection, mass, stack, mound, accumulation, hoard 2 *often plural* (*Informal*) = a lot, lots (*informal*), plenty, masses, load(s) (*informal*), great deal, tons, stack(s) ▷ VERB 3 *sometimes with up* = pile, collect, gather, stack, accumulate, amass, hoard

▷ PHRASES: heap something on someone = load with, confer on, assign to, bestow on, shower upon

hear 1 = overhear, catch, detect 2 = listen to 3 (*Law*) = try, judge, examine, investigate 4 = learn, discover, find out, pick up, gather, ascertain, get wind of (*informal*)

hearing = inquiry, trial, investigation, industrial tribunal

heart 1 = emotions, feelings, love, affection 2 = nature, character, soul, constitution, essence, temperament, disposition 3 = root, core, centre, nucleus, hub, gist, nitty-gritty (*informal*), nub 4 = courage, will, spirit, purpose, bottle (*Brit. informal*), resolution, resolve, stomach ▷ PHRASES: by heart = from *or* by memory, verbatim, word for word, pat, word-perfect, by rote, off by heart, off pat

heat VERB 1 *sometimes with up* = warm (up), cook, boil, roast, reheat, make hot **OPPOSITE:** chill ▷ NOUN 2 = warmth, hotness, temperature **OPPOSITE:** cold 3 = hot weather, warmth, closeness, high temperature, heatwave, warm weather, hot climate, mugginess 4 = passion, excitement, intensity, fury, fervour, vehemence **OPPOSITE:** calmness

h

heated 1 = **impassioned**, intense, spirited, excited, angry, furious, fierce, lively **OPPOSITE:** calm 2 = **wound up**, worked up, keyed up, het up (*informal*)

heaven 1 = **paradise**, next world, hereafter, nirvana (*Buddhism, Hinduism*), bliss, Zion (*Christianity*), life everlasting, Elysium *or* Elysian fields (*Greek myth*) 2 (*Informal*) = **happiness**, paradise, ecstasy, bliss, utopia, rapture, seventh heaven
▷ **PHRASES: the heavens** (*Old-fashioned*) = **sky**, ether, firmament

heavenly 1 = **celestial**, holy, divine, blessed, immortal, angelic **OPPOSITE:** earthly 2 (*Informal*) = **wonderful**, lovely, delightful, beautiful, divine (*informal*), exquisite, sublime, blissful **OPPOSITE:** awful

heavily 1 = **excessively**, to excess, very much, a great deal, considerably, copiously, without restraint, immoderately 2 = **densely**, closely, thickly, compactly 3 = **hard**, clumsily, awkwardly, weightily

heavy 1 = **weighty**, large, massive, hefty, bulky, ponderous **OPPOSITE:** light 2 = **intensive**, severe, serious, concentrated, fierce, excessive, relentless 3 = **considerable**, large, huge, substantial, abundant, copious, profuse **OPPOSITE:** slight

hectic = **frantic**, chaotic, heated, animated, turbulent, frenetic, feverish **OPPOSITE:** peaceful

hedge = **prevaricate**, evade, sidestep, duck, dodge, flannel (*Brit. informal*), equivocate, temporize
▷ **PHRASES: hedge against something** = **protect against**, insure against, guard against, safeguard against, shield against, cover against

heed (*Formal*) VERB 1 = **pay attention to**, listen to, take notice of, follow, consider, note, observe, obey **OPPOSITE:** ignore
▷ **NOUN** 2 = **thought**, care, mind, attention, regard, respect, notice **OPPOSITE:** disregard

heel (*Slang*) = **swine**, cad (*Brit. informal*), bounder (*Brit. old-fashioned slang*), rotter (*slang, chiefly Brit.*)

hefty (*Informal*) = **big**, strong, massive, strapping, robust, muscular, burly, hulking **OPPOSITE:** small

height 1 = **tallness**, stature, highness, loftiness **OPPOSITE:** shortness 2 = **altitude**, measurement, highness, elevation, tallness **OPPOSITE:** depth 3 = **peak**, top, crown, summit, crest, pinnacle, apex **OPPOSITE:** valley 4 = **culmination**, climax, zenith, limit, maximum, ultimate **OPPOSITE:** low point

heighten = **intensify**, increase, add to, improve, strengthen, enhance, sharpen, magnify

heir = **successor**, beneficiary, inheritor, heiress (*fem.*), next in line

hell 1 = **the underworld**, the abyss, Hades (*Greek myth*), hellfire, the inferno, fire and brimstone, the nether world, the bad fire (*informal*)
2 (*Informal*) = **torment**, suffering, agony, nightmare, misery, ordeal, anguish, wretchedness

hello = **hi** (*informal*), greetings, how do you do?, good morning, good evening, good afternoon, welcome, kia ora (*N.Z.*), gidday or g'day (*Austral. & N.Z.*)

helm (*Nautical*) = **tiller**, wheel, rudder

help VERB 1 *sometimes with out* = **aid**, support, assist, cooperate with, abet, lend a hand, succour **OPPOSITE:** hinder 2 = **improve**, ease, relieve, facilitate, alleviate, mitigate, ameliorate **OPPOSITE:** make worse
3 = **assist**, aid, support
4 = **resist**, refrain from, avoid, prevent, keep from
▷ NOUN 5 = **assistance**, aid, support, advice, guidance, cooperation, helping hand **OPPOSITE:** hindrance

helper = **assistant**, ally, supporter, mate, second, aide, attendant, collaborator

helpful 1 = **cooperative**, accommodating, kind, friendly, neighbourly, sympathetic, supportive, considerate
2 = **useful**, practical, profitable, constructive 3 = **beneficial**, advantageous

helping = **portion**, serving, ration, piece, dollop (*informal*), plateful

helpless = **powerless**, weak, disabled, incapable, paralysed, impotent, infirm **OPPOSITE:** powerful

hem = **edge**, border, margin, trimming, fringe
▷ PHRASES: hem something or someone in 1 = **surround**, confine, enclose, shut in
2 = **restrict**, confine, beset, circumscribe

hence = **therefore**, thus, consequently, for this reason, in consequence, ergo, on that account

herald VERB 1 = **indicate**, promise, usher in, presage, portend, foretoken
▷ NOUN 2 (*Often literary*) = **forerunner**, sign, signal, indication, token, omen, precursor, harbinger
3 = **messenger**, courier, proclaimer, announcer, crier, town crier

herd = **flock**, crowd, collection, mass, drove, mob, swarm, horde

hereditary 1 = **genetic**, inborn, inbred, transmissible, inheritable 2 (*Law*) = **inherited**, passed down, traditional, ancestral

heritage = inheritance, legacy, birthright, tradition, endowment, bequest

hero 1 = protagonist, leading man 2 = star, champion, victor, superstar, conqueror 3 = idol, favourite, pin-up (*slang*), fave (*informal*)

heroic = courageous, brave, daring, fearless, gallant, intrepid, valiant, lion-hearted **OPPOSITE:** cowardly

heroine 1 = protagonist, leading lady, diva, prima donna 2 = idol, favourite, pin-up (*slang*), fave (*informal*)

● USAGE NOTE
● Note that the word *heroine*,
● meaning 'a female hero', has
● an *e* at the end. The drug
● *heroin* is spelled without a
● final *e*.

hesitate 1 = waver, delay, pause, wait, doubt, falter, dither (*chiefly Brit.*), vacillate **OPPOSITE:** be decisive 2 = be reluctant, be unwilling, shrink from, think twice, scruple, demur, hang back, be disinclined **OPPOSITE:** be determined

hesitation = reluctance, reservation(s), misgiving(s), ambivalence, qualm(s), unwillingness, scruple(s), compunction

hidden 1 = secret, veiled, latent 2 = concealed, secret, covert, unseen, clandestine, secreted, under wraps

hide¹ 1 = conceal, stash (*informal*), secrete, put out of sight **OPPOSITE:** display 2 = go into hiding, take cover, keep out of sight, hole up, lie low, go underground, go to ground, go to earth 3 = keep secret, suppress, withhold, keep quiet about, hush up, draw a veil over, keep dark, keep under your hat **OPPOSITE:** disclose 4 = obscure, cover, mask, disguise, conceal, veil, cloak, shroud **OPPOSITE:** reveal

hide² = skin, leather, pelt

hideous = ugly, revolting, ghastly, monstrous, grotesque, gruesome, grisly, unsightly **OPPOSITE:** beautiful

hiding (*Informal*) = beating, whipping, thrashing, licking (*informal*), spanking, walloping (*informal*), drubbing

hierarchy = grading, ranking, social order, pecking order, class system, social stratum

high ADJECTIVE 1 = tall, towering, soaring, steep, elevated, lofty **OPPOSITE:** short 2 = extreme, great, acute, severe, extraordinary, excessive **OPPOSITE:** low 3 = strong, violent, extreme, blustery, squally, sharp 4 = important, chief, powerful, superior, eminent, exalted **OPPOSITE:** lowly 5 = high-pitched, piercing, shrill, penetrating,

strident, sharp, acute, piping
OPPOSITE: deep 6 (*Informal*)
= **intoxicated**, stoned (*slang*),
tripping (*informal*)
▷ **ADVERB** 7 = **way up**, aloft, far
up, to a great height

high-flown = **extravagant**,
elaborate, pretentious,
exaggerated, inflated, lofty,
grandiose, overblown
OPPOSITE: straightforward

highlight VERB
1 = **emphasize**, stress, accent,
show up, underline, spotlight,
accentuate, call attention to
OPPOSITE: play down
▷ **NOUN** 2 = **high point**, peak,
climax, feature, focus, focal
point, high spot **OPPOSITE:** low
point

highly = **extremely**, very,
greatly, vastly, exceptionally,
immensely, tremendously

hijack = **seize**, take over,
commandeer, expropriate

hike NOUN 1 = **walk**, march,
trek, ramble, tramp, traipse
▷ **VERB** 2 = **walk**, march, trek,
ramble, tramp, back-pack

hilarious 1 = **funny**,
entertaining, amusing,
hysterical, humorous, comical,
side-splitting 2 = **merry**,
uproarious, rollicking **OPPOSITE:**
serious

hill = **mount**, fell, height,
mound, hilltop, tor, knoll,
hillock, kopje or koppie (*S.
African*)

hinder = **obstruct**, stop, check,

block, delay, frustrate,
handicap, interrupt **OPPOSITE:**
help

hint NOUN 1 = **clue**,
suggestion, implication,
indication, pointer, allusion,
innuendo, intimation 2 *often
plural* = **advice**, help, tip(s),
suggestion(s), pointer(s)
3 = **trace**, touch, suggestion,
dash, suspicion, tinge,
undertone
▷ **VERB** 4 *sometimes with at*
= **suggest**, indicate, imply,
intimate, insinuate

hire VERB 1 = **employ**,
commission, take on, engage,
appoint, sign up, enlist
2 = **rent**, charter, lease, let,
engage
▷ **NOUN** 3 = **rental**, hiring, rent,
lease 4 = **charge**, rental, price,
cost, fee

hiss VERB 1 = **whistle**, wheeze,
whiz, whirr, sibilate 2 = **jeer**,
mock, deride
▷ **NOUN** 3 = **fizz**, buzz, hissing,
fizzing, sibilation

historic = **significant**, notable,
momentous, famous,
extraordinary, outstanding,
remarkable, ground-breaking
OPPOSITE: unimportant
● **USAGE NOTE**
● Although *historic* and
● *historical* are similarly spelt
● they are very different in
● meaning and should not be
● used interchangeably. A
● distinction is usually made

- between *historic*, which
- means 'important' or
- 'significant', and *historical*,
- which means 'pertaining to
- history': *a historic decision; a*
- *historical perspective.*

historical = factual, real, documented, actual, authentic, attested **OPPOSITE:** contemporary

▷ See **HISTORIC**

history 1 = the past, antiquity, yesterday, yesteryear, olden days 2 = chronicle, record, story, account, narrative, recital, annals

hit VERB 1 = strike, beat, knock, bang, slap, smack, thump, clout (*informal*) 2 = collide with, run into, bump into, clash with, smash into, crash against, bang into 3 = affect, damage, harm, ruin, devastate, overwhelm, touch, impact on 4 = reach, gain, achieve, arrive at, accomplish, attain

▷ NOUN 5 = shot, blow 6 = blow, knock, stroke, belt (*informal*), rap, slap, smack, clout (*informal*) 7 = success, winner, triumph, smash (*informal*), sensation

▷ PHRASES: hit it off (*Informal*) = get on (well) with, click (*slang*), be on good terms, get on like a house on fire (*informal*)

▶ hit on *or* upon something = think up, discover, arrive at, invent, stumble on, light upon,

strike upon, stumble on

hitch NOUN 1 = problem, catch, difficulty, hold-up, obstacle, drawback, snag, uphill (*S. African*), impediment

▷ VERB 2 (*Informal*) = hitchhike, thumb a lift 3 = fasten, join, attach, couple, tie, connect, harness, tether

▷ PHRASES: hitch something up = pull up, tug, jerk, yank

hitherto (*Formal*) = previously, so far, until now, thus far, heretofore

hobby = pastime, relaxation, leisure pursuit, diversion, avocation, (leisure) activity

hoist VERB 1 = raise, lift, erect, elevate, heave

▷ NOUN 2 = lift, crane, elevator, winch

hold VERB 1 = embrace, grasp, clutch, hug, squeeze, cradle, clasp, enfold 2 = restrain, check **OPPOSITE:** release 3 = accommodate, take, contain, seat, have a capacity for 4 = consider, think, believe, judge, regard, assume, reckon, deem **OPPOSITE:** deny 5 = occupy, have, fill, maintain, retain, possess, hold down (*informal*) 6 = conduct, convene, call, run, preside over **OPPOSITE:** cancel 7 = detain, confine, imprison, impound **OPPOSITE:** release

▷ NOUN 8 = grip, grasp, clasp 9 = foothold, footing 10 = control, influence, mastery, mana (N.Z.)

holder 1 = **owner**, bearer, possessor, keeper, proprietor 2 = **case**, cover, container

hold-up 1 = **robbery**, theft, mugging (informal), stick-up (slang, chiefly U.S.) 2 = **delay**, wait, hitch, setback, snag, traffic jam, stoppage, bottleneck

hole 1 = **cavity**, pit, hollow, chamber, cave, cavern 2 = **opening**, crack, tear, gap, breach, vent, puncture, aperture 3 = **burrow**, den, earth, shelter, lair 4 (*Informal*) = **hovel**, dump (informal), dive (slang), slum 5 (*Informal*) = **predicament**, spot (informal), fix (informal), mess, jam (informal), dilemma, scrape (informal), hot water (informal)

holiday 1 = **vacation**, leave, break, time off, recess 2 = **festival**, fête, celebration, feast, gala

hollow ADJECTIVE 1 = **empty**, vacant, void, unfilled **OPPOSITE:** solid 2 = **worthless**, useless, vain, meaningless, pointless, futile, fruitless **OPPOSITE:** meaningful 3 = **dull**, low, deep, muted, toneless, reverberant **OPPOSITE:** vibrant ▷ NOUN 4 = **cavity**, hole, bowl, depression, pit, basin, crater, trough **OPPOSITE:** mound 5 = **valley**, dale, glen, dell, dingle **OPPOSITE:** hill ▷ VERB 6 *often followed by* **out**

= **scoop out**, dig out, excavate, gouge out

holocaust 1 = **devastation**, destruction, genocide, annihilation, conflagration 2 = **genocide**, massacre, annihilation

holy 1 = **sacred**, blessed, hallowed, venerable, consecrated, sacrosanct, sanctified **OPPOSITE:** unsanctified 2 = **devout**, godly, religious, pure, righteous, pious, virtuous, saintly **OPPOSITE:** sinful

homage = **respect**, honour, worship, devotion, reverence, deference, adulation, adoration **OPPOSITE:** contempt

home NOUN 1 = **dwelling**, house, residence, abode, habitation, pad (slang), domicile 2 = **birthplace**, homeland, home town, native land ▷ ADJECTIVE 3 = **domestic**, local, internal, native ▷ PHRASES: at home 1 = **in**, present, available 2 = **at ease**, relaxed, comfortable, content, at peace ▶ bring something home to someone = **make clear**, emphasize, drive home, press home, impress upon

homeland = **native land**, birthplace, motherland, fatherland, country of origin, mother country

homeless = **destitute**, displaced, dispossessed, down-and-out

homely 1 = **comfortable**, welcoming, friendly, cosy, homespun 2 = **plain**, simple, ordinary, modest **OPPOSITE:** elaborate

homicide = **murder**, killing, manslaughter, slaying, bloodshed

hone 1 = **improve**, better, enhance, upgrade, refine, sharpen, help 2 = **sharpen**, point, grind, edge, file, polish, whet

- **USAGE NOTE**
- *Hone* is sometimes wrongly
- used where *home* is meant:
- *this device makes it easier to*
- *home in on* (not *hone in on*) *the*
- *target.*

honest 1 = **trustworthy**, upright, ethical, honourable, reputable, truthful, virtuous, law-abiding **OPPOSITE:** dishonest 2 = **open**, direct, frank, plain, sincere, candid, forthright, upfront (*informal*) **OPPOSITE:** secretive

honestly 1 = **ethically**, legally, lawfully, honourably, by fair means 2 = **frankly**, plainly, candidly, straight (out), truthfully, to your face, in all sincerity

honesty 1 = **integrity**, honour, virtue, morality, probity, rectitude, truthfulness, trustworthiness 2 = **frankness**, openness, sincerity, candour, bluntness, outspokenness, straightforwardness

honorary = **nominal**, unofficial, titular, in name or title only

honour NOUN 1 = **integrity**, morality, honesty, goodness, fairness, decency, probity, rectitude **OPPOSITE:** dishonour 2 = **prestige**, credit, reputation, glory, fame, distinction, dignity, renown **OPPOSITE:** disgrace 3 = **reputation**, standing, prestige, image, status, stature, good name, cachet 4 = **acclaim**, praise, recognition, compliments, homage, accolades, commendation **OPPOSITE:** contempt 5 = **privilege**, credit, pleasure, compliment ▷ VERB 6 = **acclaim**, praise, decorate, commemorate, commend 7 = **respect**, value, esteem, prize, appreciate, adore **OPPOSITE:** scorn 8 = **fulfil**, keep, carry out, observe, discharge, live up to, be true to 9 = **pay**, take, accept, pass, acknowledge **OPPOSITE:** refuse

honourable 1 = **principled**, moral, ethical, fair, upright, honest, virtuous, trustworthy 2 = **proper**, respectable, virtuous, creditable

hook NOUN 1 = **fastener**, catch, link, peg, clasp ▷ VERB 2 = **fasten**, fix, secure, clasp 3 = **catch**, land, trap, entrap

hooked 1 = **bent**, curved, aquiline, hook-shaped 2 (*Informal*) = **obsessed**,

addicted, taken, devoted,
turned on (*slang*), enamoured
3 (*Informal*) = **addicted**,
dependent, using (*informal*),
having a habit

hooligan = **delinquent**, vandal,
hoon (*Austral. & N.Z.*), ruffian,
lager lout, yob or yobbo (*Brit.
slang*), cougan (*Austral. slang*),
scozza (*Austral. slang*), bogan
(*Austral. slang*)

hoop = **ring**, band, loop, wheel,
round, girdle, circlet

hop VERB 1 = **jump**, spring,
bound, leap, skip, vault, caper
▷ NOUN 2 = **jump**, step, spring,
bound, leap, bounce, skip, vault

hope VERB 1 = **believe**, look
forward to, cross your fingers
▷ NOUN 2 = **belief**, confidence,
expectation, longing, dream,
desire, ambition, assumption
OPPOSITE: despair

hopeful 1 = **optimistic**,
confident, looking forward to,
buoyant, sanguine, expectant
OPPOSITE: despairing
2 = **promising**, encouraging,
bright, reassuring, rosy,
heartening, auspicious
OPPOSITE: unpromising

hopefully = **optimistically**,
confidently, expectantly, with
anticipation

● **USAGE NOTE**
● Some people object to the
● use of *hopefully* as a synonym
● for the phrase 'it is hoped
● that' in a sentence such as
● *hopefully I'll be able to attend*

● *the meeting.* This use of the
● adverb first appeared in
● America in the 1960s, but it
● has rapidly established itself
● elsewhere. There are really no
● strong grounds for objecting
● to it, since we accept other
● sentence adverbials that fulfil
● a similar function, for
● example *unfortunately*, which
● means 'it is unfortunate that'
● in a sentence such as
● *unfortunately I won't be able to*
● *attend the meeting.*

hopeless = **impossible**,
pointless, futile, useless, vain,
no-win, unattainable

horde = **crowd**, mob, swarm,
host, band, pack, drove, gang

horizon = **skyline**, view, vista

horizontal = **level**, flat, parallel

horrible 1 (*Informal*) = **dreadful**,
terrible, awful, nasty, cruel,
mean, unpleasant, horrid
OPPOSITE: wonderful
2 = **terrible**, appalling,
terrifying, shocking, grim,
dreadful, revolting, ghastly

horrific = **horrifying**, shocking,
appalling, awful, terrifying,
dreadful, horrendous, ghastly

horrify 1 = **terrify**, alarm,
frighten, scare, intimidate,
petrify, make your hair stand on
end **OPPOSITE:** comfort
2 = **shock**, appal, dismay,
sicken, outrage **OPPOSITE:**
delight

horror 1 = **terror**, fear, alarm,
panic, dread, fright,

consternation, trepidation
2 = **hatred**, disgust, loathing,
aversion, revulsion, repugnance,
odium, detestation **OPPOSITE:**
love

horse = **nag**, mount, mare, colt,
filly, stallion, steed (*archaic or
literary*), moke (*Austral. slang*),
yarraman *or* yarramin (*Austral.*),
gee-gee (*slang*)

hospitality = **welcome**,
warmth, kindness, friendliness,
sociability, conviviality,
neighbourliness, cordiality

host¹ *or* **hostess** NOUN
1 = **master of ceremonies**,
proprietor, innkeeper, landlord
or landlady **2** = **presenter**,
compere (*Brit.*), anchorman *or*
anchorwoman
▷ VERB **3** = **present**, introduce,
compere (*Brit.*), front (*informal*)

host NOUN **1** = **multitude**, lot,
load (*informal*), wealth, array,
myriad, great quantity, large
number
▷ NOUN **2** = **crowd**, army, pack,
drove, mob, herd, legion,
swarm

hostage = **captive**, prisoner,
pawn

hostile **1** = **antagonistic**,
opposed, contrary, ill-disposed
2 = **unfriendly**, belligerent,
antagonistic, rancorous, ill-
disposed **OPPOSITE:** friendly
3 = **inhospitable**, adverse,
uncongenial, unsympathetic,
unwelcoming **OPPOSITE:**
hospitable

hostility NOUN
1 = **unfriendliness**, hatred,
animosity, spite, bitterness,
malice, venom, enmity
OPPOSITE: friendliness
2 = **opposition**, resentment,
antipathy, antagonism,
antagonism, ill feeling, ill-will,
animus **OPPOSITE:** approval
▷ PLURAL NOUN **3** = **warfare**,
war, fighting, conflict, combat,
armed conflict **OPPOSITE:** peace

hot ADJECTIVE **1** = **heated**,
boiling, steaming, roasting,
searing, scorching, scalding
2 = **warm**, close, stifling,
humid, torrid, sultry,
sweltering, balmy **OPPOSITE:**
cold **3** = **spicy**, pungent,
peppery, piquant, biting, sharp
OPPOSITE: mild **4** = **intense**,
passionate, heated, spirited,
fierce, lively, animated, ardent
5 = **new**, latest, fresh, recent,
up to date, just out, up to the
minute, bang up to date
(*informal*) **OPPOSITE:** old
6 = **popular**, hip, fashionable,
cool, in demand, sought-after,
must-see, in vogue **OPPOSITE:**
unpopular **7** = **fierce**, intense,
strong, keen, competitive, cut-
throat **8** = **fiery**, violent,
raging, passionate, stormy
OPPOSITE: calm

hound = **harass**, harry, bother,
provoke, annoy, torment, hassle
(*informal*), badger

house NOUN **1** = **home**,
residence, dwelling, pad (*slang*),

homestead, abode, habitation, domicile, whare (N.Z.) **2** = **household**, family **3** = **firm**, company, business, organization, outfit (*informal*) **4** = **assembly**, parliament, Commons, legislative body **5** = **dynasty**, tribe, clan ▷ VERB **6** = **accommodate**, quarter, take in, put up, lodge, harbour, billet **7** = **contain**, keep, hold, cover, store, protect, shelter **8** = **take**, accommodate, sleep, provide shelter for, give a bed to ▷ PHRASES: **on the house** = **free**, for free (*informal*), for nothing, free of charge, gratis

household = **family**, home, house, family circle, ainga (N.Z.)

housing 1 = **accommodation**, homes, houses, dwellings, domiciles **2** = **case**, casing, covering, cover, shell, jacket, holder, container

hover 1 = **float**, fly, hang, drift, flutter **2** = **linger**, loiter, hang about *or* around (*informal*) **3** = **waver**, fluctuate, dither (*chiefly Brit.*), oscillate, vacillate

however = **but**, nevertheless, still, though, yet, nonetheless, notwithstanding, anyhow

howl VERB **1** = **bay**, cry **2** = **cry**, scream, roar, weep, yell, wail, shriek, bellow ▷ NOUN **3** = **baying**, cry, bay, bark, barking, yelping **4** = **cry**, scream, roar, bay, wail, shriek, clamour, bawl

hub = **centre**, heart, focus, core, middle, focal point, nerve centre

huddle VERB **1** = **curl up**, crouch, hunch up **2** = **crowd**, press, gather, collect, squeeze, cluster, flock, herd ▷ NOUN **3** (*Informal*) = **discussion**, conference, meeting, hui (N.Z.), powwow, confab (*informal*), korero (N.Z.)

hue = **colour**, tone, shade, dye, tint, tinge

hug VERB **1** = **embrace**, cuddle, squeeze, clasp, enfold, hold close, take in your arms ▷ NOUN **2** = **embrace**, squeeze, bear hug, clinch (*slang*), clasp

huge = **enormous**, large, massive, vast, tremendous, immense, gigantic, monumental OPPOSITE: tiny

hui (N.Z.) = **meeting**, gathering, assembly, conference, congress, rally, convention, get-together (*informal*)

hull = **framework**, casing, body, covering, frame

hum 1 = **drone**, buzz, murmur, throb, vibrate, purr, thrum, whir **2** (*Informal*) = **be busy**, buzz, bustle, stir, pulse, pulsate

human ADJECTIVE **1** = **mortal**, manlike OPPOSITE: nonhuman ▷ NOUN **2** = **human being**, person, individual, creature, mortal, man *or* woman OPPOSITE: nonhuman

humane = **kind**, compassionate, understanding, forgiving, tender, sympathetic,

h

benign, merciful **OPPOSITE:** cruel

humanitarian ADJECTIVE
1 = **compassionate**, charitable, humane, benevolent, altruistic
2 = **charitable**, philanthropic, public-spirited
▷ NOUN = **philanthropist**, benefactor, Good Samaritan, altruist

humanity 1 = **the human race**, man, mankind, people, mortals, humankind, Homo sapiens 2 = **human nature**, mortality 3 = **kindness**, charity, compassion, sympathy, mercy, philanthropy, fellow feeling, kind-heartedness

humble ADJECTIVE 1 = **modest**, meek, unassuming, unpretentious, self-effacing, unostentatious **OPPOSITE:** proud 2 = **lowly**, poor, mean, simple, ordinary, modest, obscure, undistinguished **OPPOSITE:** distinguished
▷ VERB 3 = **humiliate**, disgrace, crush, subdue, chasten, put (someone) in their place, take down a peg (*informal*) **OPPOSITE:** exalt

humidity = **damp**, moisture, dampness, wetness, moistness, dankness, clamminess, mugginess

humiliate = **embarrass**, shame, humble, crush, put down, degrade, chasten, mortify **OPPOSITE:** honour

humiliating = **embarrassing**, shaming, humbling, mortifying, crushing, degrading, ignominious, barro (*Austral. slang*)

humiliation = **embarrassment**, shame, disgrace, humbling, put-down, degradation, indignity, ignominy

humorous = **funny**, comic, amusing, entertaining, witty, comical, droll, jocular **OPPOSITE:** serious

humour NOUN 1 = **comedy**, funniness, fun, amusement, funny side, jocularity, facetiousness, ludicrousness **OPPOSITE:** seriousness
2 = **mood**, spirits, temper, disposition, frame of mind
3 = **joking**, comedy, wit, farce, jesting, wisecracks (*informal*), witticisms
▷ VERB 4 = **indulge**, accommodate, go along with, flatter, gratify, pander to, mollify **OPPOSITE:** oppose

hunch NOUN 1 = **feeling**, idea, impression, suspicion, intuition, premonition, inkling, presentiment
▷ VERB 2 = **crouch**, bend, curve, arch, draw in

hunger 1 = **appetite**, emptiness, hungriness, ravenousness 2 = **starvation**, famine, malnutrition, undernourishment 3 = **desire**, appetite, craving, ache, lust, yearning, itch, thirst

▷ PHRASES: hunger for or after something or someone = **want**, desire, crave, long for, wish for, yearn for, hanker after, ache for

hungry 1 = **starving**, ravenous, famished, starved, empty, voracious, peckish (*informal, chiefly Brit.*) 2 = **eager**, keen, craving, yearning, greedy, avid, desirous, covetous

hunk = **lump**, piece, chunk, block, mass, wedge, slab, nugget

hunt VERB 1 = **stalk**, track, chase, pursue, trail, hound ▷ NOUN 2 = **search**, hunting, investigation, chase, pursuit, quest ▷ PHRASES: hunt for something or someone = **search for**, look for, seek for, forage for, scour for, fossick for (*Austral. & N.Z.*), ferret about for

hurdle 1 = **obstacle**, difficulty, barrier, handicap, hazard, uphill (*S. African*), obstruction, stumbling block 2 = **fence**, barrier, barricade

hurl = **throw**, fling, launch, cast, pitch, toss, propel, sling

hurricane = **storm**, gale, tornado, cyclone, typhoon, tempest, twister (*U.S. informal*), willy-willy (*Austral.*)

hurried 1 = **hasty**, quick, brief, rushed, short, swift, speedy 2 = **rushed**, perfunctory, speedy, hasty, cursory

hurry VERB 1 = **rush**, fly, dash,

scurry, scoot **OPPOSITE**: dawdle 2 = **make haste**, rush, get a move on (*informal*), step on it (*informal*) ▷ NOUN 3 = **rush**, haste, speed, urgency, flurry, quickness **OPPOSITE**: slowness

hurt VERB 1 = **injure**, damage, wound, cut, disable, bruise, scrape, impair **OPPOSITE**: heal 2 = **ache**, be sore, be painful, burn, smart, sting, throb, be tender 3 = **harm**, injure, ill-treat, maltreat 4 = **upset**, distress, pain, wound, annoy, grieve, sadden ▷ NOUN 5 = **distress**, suffering, pain, grief, misery, sorrow, heartache, wretchedness **OPPOSITE**: happiness ▷ ADJECTIVE 6 = **injured**, wounded, damaged, harmed, cut, bruised, scarred **OPPOSITE**: healed 7 = **upset**, wounded, crushed, offended, aggrieved, tooshie (*Austral. slang*) **OPPOSITE**: calmed

hurtle = **rush**, charge, race, shoot, fly, speed, tear, crash

husband NOUN 1 = **partner**, spouse, mate, better half (*humorous*) ▷ VERB 2 = **conserve**, budget, save, store, hoard, economize on, use economically **OPPOSITE**: squander

hush VERB 1 = **quieten**, silence, mute, muzzle, shush ▷ NOUN 2 = **quiet**, silence, calm, peace, tranquillity,

stillness, peacefulness

hut 1 = **cabin**, shack, shanty, hovel, w!whare (*N.Z.*) 2 = **shed**, outhouse, lean-to, lockup

hybrid 1 = **crossbreed**, cross, mixture, compound, composite, amalgam, mongrel, half-breed 2 = **mixture**, compound, composite, amalgam

hygiene = **cleanliness**, sanitation, disinfection, sterility

hymn 1 = **religious song**, song of praise, carol, chant, anthem, psalm, paean 2 = **song of praise**, anthem, paean

hype (*Slang*) = **publicity**, promotion, plugging (*informal*), razzmatazz (*slang*), brouhaha, ballyhoo (*informal*)

hypocrisy = **insincerity**, pretence, deception, cant, duplicity, deceitfulness **OPPOSITE:** sincerity

hypothesis = **theory**, premise, proposition, assumption, thesis, postulate, supposition

hysteria = **frenzy**, panic, madness, agitation, delirium, hysterics

hysterical 1 = **frenzied**, frantic, raving, distracted, distraught, crazed, overwrought, berko (*Austral. slang*) **OPPOSITE:** calm 2 (*Informal*) = **hilarious**, uproarious, side-splitting, comical **OPPOSITE:** serious

icy 1 = **cold**, freezing, bitter, biting, raw, chill, chilly, frosty **OPPOSITE:** hot 2 = **slippery**, glassy, slippy (*informal or dialect*), like a sheet of glass 3 = **unfriendly**, cold, distant, aloof, frosty, frigid, unwelcoming **OPPOSITE:** friendly

idea 1 = **notion**, thought, view, teaching, opinion, belief, conclusion, hypothesis 2 = **understanding**, thought, view, opinion, concept, impression, perception 3 = **intention**, aim, purpose, object, plan, objective

● USAGE NOTE
● It is usually considered
● correct to say that someone
● has *the idea of doing something*,
● rather than *the idea to do*
● *something*. For example, you
● would say *he had the idea of*
● *taking a holiday*, not *he had the*
● *idea to take a holiday*.

ideal NOUN 1 = **epitome**, standard, dream, pattern, perfection, last word, paragon 2 = **model**, prototype, paradigm

▷ ADJECTIVE 3 = **perfect**, best, model, classic, simpleton, ultimate, archetypal, exemplary **OPPOSITE:** imperfect

ideally = **in a perfect world**, all things being equal, if you had your way

identical = **alike**, matching, twin, duplicate, indistinguishable, interchangeable **OPPOSITE:** different

identification 1 = **discovery**, recognition, determining, establishment, diagnosis, confirmation, divination 2 = **recognition**, naming, distinguishing, confirmation, pinpointing 3 = **connection**, relationship, association 4 = **understanding**, relationship, involvement, unity, sympathy, empathy, rapport, fellow feeling

identify 1 = **recognize**, place, name, remember, spot, diagnose, make out, pinpoint 2 = **establish**, spot, confirm, demonstrate, pick out, certify, verify, mark out
▷ PHRASES: **identify something or someone with something or someone** = **equate with**, associate with ▶ **identify with someone** = **relate to**, respond to, feel for, empathize with

identity = **individuality**, self, character, personality, existence, originality, separateness

idiot = **fool**, moron, twit (*informal, chiefly Brit.*), chump, imbecile, cretin, simpleton, halfwit, galah (*Austral. & N.Z. informal*), dorba or dorb (*Austral. slang*), bogan (*Austral. slang*)

idle ADJECTIVE 1 = **unoccupied**, unemployed, redundant, inactive **OPPOSITE:** occupied 2 = **unused**, inactive, out of order, out of service 3 = **lazy**, slow, slack, sluggish, lax, negligent, inactive, inert **OPPOSITE:** busy 4 = **useless**, vain, pointless, unsuccessful, ineffective, worthless, futile, fruitless **OPPOSITE:** useful
▷ VERB 5 *often with* **away** = **fritter**, lounge, potter, loaf, dally, loiter, dawdle, laze

idol 1 = **hero**, pin-up, favourite, pet, darling, beloved (*slang*), fave (*informal*) 2 = **graven image**, god, deity

if 1 = **provided**, assuming, given that, providing, supposing, presuming, on condition that, as long as 2 = **when**, whenever, every time, any time

ignite 1 = **catch fire**, burn, burst into flames, inflame, flare up, take fire 2 = **set fire to**, light, set alight, torch, kindle

ignorance 1 = **lack of education**, stupidity, foolishness **OPPOSITE:** knowledge 2 *with of* = **unawareness of**, inexperience of, unfamiliarity with, innocence of, unconsciousness of

ignorant 1 = **uneducated**, illiterate **OPPOSITE:** educated **2** = **insensitive**, rude, crass **3** with of = **uninformed of**, unaware of, oblivious to, innocent of, unconscious of, inexperienced of, uninitiated about, unenlightened about **OPPOSITE:** informed

ignore 1 = **pay no attention to**, neglect, disregard, slight, overlook, scorn, spurn, rebuff **OPPOSITE:** pay attention to **2** = **overlook**, discount, disregard, reject, neglect, shrug off, pass over, brush aside **3** = **snub**, slight, rebuff

ill ADJECTIVE 1 = **unwell**, sick, poorly (*informal*), diseased, weak, crook (*Austral. & N.Z. slang*), ailing, frail **OPPOSITE:** healthy **2** = **harmful**, bad, damaging, evil, foul, unfortunate, destructive, detrimental **OPPOSITE:** favourable

▷ **NOUN 3** = **problem**, trouble, suffering, worry, injury, hurt, strain, harm **OPPOSITE:** good ▷ **ADVERB 4** = **badly**, unfortunately, unfavourably, inauspiciously **5** = **hardly**, barely, scarcely, just, only just, by no means, at a push **OPPOSITE:** well

illegal = **unlawful**, banned, forbidden, prohibited, criminal, outlawed, illicit, unlicensed **OPPOSITE:** legal

illicit 1 = **illegal**, criminal, prohibited, unlawful, illegitimate, unlicensed, unauthorized, felonious **OPPOSITE:** legal **2** = **forbidden**, improper, immoral, guilty, clandestine, furtive

illness = **sickness**, disease, infection, disorder, bug (*informal*), ailment, affliction, malady

illuminate 1 = **light up**, brighten **OPPOSITE:** darken **2** = **explain**, interpret, make clear, clarify, clear up, enlighten, shed light on, elucidate **OPPOSITE:** obscure

illuminating = **informative**, revealing, enlightening, helpful, explanatory, instructive **OPPOSITE:** confusing

illusion 1 = **delusion**, misconception, misapprehension, fancy, fallacy, false impression, false belief **2** = **false impression**, appearance, impression, deception, fallacy **OPPOSITE:** reality **3** = **fantasy**, vision, hallucination, trick, spectre, mirage, daydream, apparition

illustrate 1 = **demonstrate**, emphasize **2** = **explain**, sum up, summarize, bring home, point up, elucidate

illustrated = **pictured**, decorated, pictorial

illustration 1 = **example**, case, instance, sample, specimen, exemplar **2** = **picture**, drawing,

painting, image, print, plate, figure, portrait
image 1 = **thought**, idea, vision, concept, impression, perception, mental picture, conceptualization 2 = **figure of speech** 3 = **reflection**, likeness, mirror image 4 = **figure**, idol, icon, fetish, talisman 5 = **replica**, copy, reproduction, counterpart, clone, facsimile, spitting image (*informal*), Doppelgänger 6 = **picture**, photo, photograph, representation, reproduction, snapshot
imaginary = **fictional**, made-up, invented, imagined, unreal, hypothetical, fictitious, illusory **OPPOSITE:** real
imagination 1 = **creativity**, vision, invention, ingenuity, enterprise, originality, inventiveness, resourcefulness 2 = **mind's eye**, fancy
imaginative = **creative**, original, inspired, enterprising, clever, ingenious, inventive **OPPOSITE:** unimaginative
imagine 1 = **envisage**, see, picture, plan, think of, conjure up, envision, visualize 2 = **believe**, think, suppose, assume, suspect, guess (*informal, chiefly U.S. & Canad.*), take it, reckon
imitate 1 = **copy**, follow, repeat, echo, emulate, ape, simulate, mirror 2 = **do an impression of**, mimic, copy

imitation NOUN 1 = **replica**, fake, reproduction, sham, forgery, counterfeiting, likeness, duplication 2 = **copying**, resemblance, mimicry 3 = **impression**, impersonation ▷ ADJECTIVE 4 = **artificial**, mock, reproduction, dummy, synthetic, man-made, simulated, sham **OPPOSITE:** real
immaculate 1 = **clean**, spotless, neat, spruce, squeaky-clean, spick-and-span **OPPOSITE:** dirty 2 = **pure**, perfect, impeccable, flawless, faultless, above reproach **OPPOSITE:** corrupt 3 = **perfect**, flawless, impeccable, faultless, unblemished, untarnished, unexceptionable **OPPOSITE:** tainted
immediate 1 = **instant**, prompt, instantaneous, quick, on-the-spot, split-second **OPPOSITE:** later 2 = **nearest**, next, direct, close, near **OPPOSITE:** far
immediately = **at once**, now, instantly, straight away, directly, promptly, right away, without delay
immense = **huge**, great, massive, vast, enormous, extensive, tremendous, very big **OPPOSITE:** tiny
immerse 1 = **engross**, involve, absorb, busy, occupy, engage 2 = **plunge**, dip, submerge, sink, duck, bathe, douse, dunk
immigrant = **settler**, incomer,

alien, stranger, outsider, newcomer, migrant, emigrant

imminent = near, coming, close, approaching, gathering, forthcoming, looming, impending **OPPOSITE:** remote

immoral = wicked, bad, wrong, corrupt, indecent, sinful, unethical, depraved **OPPOSITE:** moral

immortal ADJECTIVE
1 = timeless, eternal, everlasting, lasting, traditional, classic, enduring, perennial **OPPOSITE:** ephemeral
2 = undying, eternal, imperishable, deathless **OPPOSITE:** mortal
▷ NOUN 3 = hero, genius, great
4 = god, goddess, deity, divine being, immortal being, atua (N.Z.)

immune PHRASES: immune from = exempt from, free from
▶ immune to 1 = resistant to, free from, protected from, safe from, not open to, spared from, secure against, invulnerable to
2 = unaffected by, invulnerable to

immunity 1 = exemption, amnesty, indemnity, release, freedom, invulnerability 2 with to = resistance to, protection from, resilience to, inoculation against, immunization from **OPPOSITE:** susceptibility to

impact NOUN 1 = effect, influence, consequences, impression, repercussions, ramifications 2 = collision, contact, crash, knock, stroke, smash, bump, thump
▷ VERB 3 = hit, strike, crash, clash, crush, ram, smack, collide

impair = worsen, reduce, damage, injure, harm, undermine, weaken, diminish **OPPOSITE:** improve

impaired = damaged, flawed, faulty, defective, imperfect, unsound

impasse = deadlock, stalemate, standstill, dead end, standoff

impatient 1 = cross, annoyed, irritated, prickly, touchy, bad-tempered, intolerant, ill-tempered **OPPOSITE:** easy-going
2 = eager, longing, keen, anxious, hungry, enthusiastic, restless, avid **OPPOSITE:** calm

impeccable = faultless, perfect, immaculate, flawless, squeaky-clean, unblemished, unimpeachable, irreproachable **OPPOSITE:** flawed

impending = looming, coming, approaching, near, forthcoming, imminent, upcoming, in the pipeline

imperative = urgent, essential, pressing, vital, crucial **OPPOSITE:** unnecessary

imperial = royal, regal, kingly, queenly, princely, sovereign, majestic, monarchial

impetus 1 = incentive, push, spur, motivation, impulse, stimulus, catalyst, goad
2 = force, power, energy,

momentum

implant 1 = **insert**, fix, graft
2 = **instil**, infuse, inculcate

implement VERB 1 = **carry out**, effect, carry through, complete, apply, perform, realize, fulfil **OPPOSITE:** hinder
▷ NOUN 2 = **tool**, machine, device, instrument, appliance, apparatus, gadget, utensil

implicate = **incriminate**, involve, embroil, entangle, inculpate **OPPOSITE:** dissociate
▷ PHRASES: implicate something or someone in something = **involve in**, associate with

implication NOUN
1 = **suggestion**, hint, inference, meaning, significance, presumption, overtone, innuendo
▷ PLURAL NOUN
2 = **consequences**, result, developments, upshot

implicit 1 = **implied**, understood, suggested, hinted at, taken for granted, unspoken, inferred, tacit
OPPOSITE: explicit
2 = **inherent**, underlying, intrinsic, latent, ingrained, inbuilt 3 = **absolute**, full, complete, firm, fixed, constant, utter, outright

implied = **suggested**, indirect, hinted at, implicit, unspoken, tacit, undeclared, unstated

imply 1 = **suggest**, hint, insinuate, indicate, intimate,

signify 2 = **involve**, mean, entail, require, indicate, point to, signify, presuppose

import VERB 1 = **bring in**, buy in, ship in, introduce
▷ NOUN 2 (Formal)
= **significance**, concern, value, weight, consequence, substance, moment, magnitude
3 = **meaning**, implication, significance, sense, intention, substance, drift, thrust

importance 1 = **significance**, interest, concern, moment, value, weight, import, consequence 2 = **prestige**, standing, status, rule, authority, influence, distinction, esteem, mana (N.Z.)

important 1 = **significant**, critical, substantial, urgent, serious, far-reaching, momentous, seminal
OPPOSITE: unimportant
2 = **powerful**, prominent, commanding, dominant, influential, eminent, high-ranking, authoritative

impose PHRASES: impose something on or upon someone 1 = **levy**, introduce, charge, establish, fix, institute, decree, ordain 2 = **inflict**, force, enforce, visit, press, apply, thrust, saddle (someone) with

imposing = **impressive**, striking, grand, powerful, commanding, awesome, majestic, dignified **OPPOSITE:** unimposing

i

imposition 1 = application, introduction, levying 2 = intrusion, liberty, presumption

impossible 1 = not possible, out of the question, impracticable, unfeasible 2 = unachievable, out of the question, vain, unthinkable, inconceivable, far-fetched, unworkable, implausible **OPPOSITE:** possible 3 = absurd, crazy (informal), ridiculous, outrageous, ludicrous, unreasonable, preposterous, farcical

impotence = powerlessness, inability, helplessness, weakness, incompetence, paralysis, frailty, incapacity **OPPOSITE:** powerfulness

impoverish 1 = bankrupt, ruin, beggar, break 2 = deplete, drain, exhaust, diminish, use up, sap, wear out, reduce

impoverished = poor, needy, destitute, bankrupt, poverty-stricken, impecunious, penurious **OPPOSITE:** rich

impress = excite, move, strike, touch, affect, inspire, amaze, overcome
▷ **PHRASES: impress something on or upon someone** = stress, bring home to, instil in, drum into, knock into, emphasize to, fix in, inculcate in

impression 1 = idea, feeling, thought, sense, view, assessment, judgment, reaction 2 = effect, influence, impact 3 = imitation, parody, impersonation, send-up (Brit. informal), takeoff (informal) 4 = mark, imprint, stamp, outline, hollow, dent, indentation

impressive = grand, striking, splendid, good, great (informal), fine, powerful, exciting **OPPOSITE:** unimpressive

imprint NOUN 1 = mark, impression, stamp, indentation ▷ **VERB** 2 = engrave, print, stamp, impress, etch, emboss

imprison = jail, confine, detain, lock up, put away, intern, incarcerate, send down (informal) **OPPOSITE:** free

imprisoned = jailed, confined, locked up, inside (slang), in jail, captive, behind bars, incarcerated

imprisonment = confinement, custody, detention, captivity, incarceration

improbable 1 = doubtful, unlikely, dubious, questionable, fanciful, far-fetched, implausible **OPPOSITE:** probable 2 = unconvincing, weak, unbelievable, preposterous **OPPOSITE:** convincing

improper 1 = inappropriate, unfit, unsuitable, out of place, unwarranted, uncalled-for **OPPOSITE:** appropriate 2 = indecent, vulgar, suggestive, unseemly,

untoward, risqué, smutty,
unbecoming **OPPOSITE:** decent
improve 1 = enhance, better,
add to, upgrade, touch up,
ameliorate **OPPOSITE:** worsen
2 = get better, pick up, develop,
advance
improvement
1 = enhancement,
advancement, betterment
2 = advance, development,
progress, recovery, upswing
improvise 1 = devise, contrive,
concoct, throw together
2 = ad-lib, invent, busk, wing it
(*informal*), play it by ear
(*informal*), extemporize, speak
off the cuff (*informal*)
impulse = urge, longing, wish,
notion, yearning, inclination,
itch, whim
inaccurate = incorrect, wrong,
mistaken, faulty, unreliable,
defective, erroneous, unsound
OPPOSITE: accurate
inadequacy 1 = shortage,
poverty, dearth, paucity,
insufficiency, meagreness,
scantiness 2 = incompetence,
inability, deficiency, incapacity,
ineffectiveness
3 = shortcoming, failing,
weakness, defect, imperfection
inadequate 1 = insufficient,
meagre, poor, lacking, scant,
sparse, sketchy **OPPOSITE:**
adequate 2 = incapable,
incompetent, faulty, deficient,
unqualified, not up to scratch
(*informal*) **OPPOSITE:** capable

inadvertently
= unintentionally, accidentally,
by accident, mistakenly,
unwittingly, by mistake,
involuntarily **OPPOSITE:**
deliberately
inaugural = first, opening,
initial, maiden, introductory
incarnation = embodiment,
manifestation, epitome, type,
personification
incense = anger, infuriate,
enrage, irritate, madden,
inflame, rile (*informal*), make
your blood boil (*informal*)
incensed = angry, furious,
fuming, infuriated, enraged,
maddened, indignant, irate,
tooshie (*Austral. slang*), off the
air (*Austral. slang*)
incentive = inducement,
encouragement, spur, lure, bait,
motivation, carrot (*informal*),
stimulus **OPPOSITE:** disincentive
incident 1 = disturbance,
scene, clash, disorder,
confrontation, brawl, fracas,
commotion 2 = adventure,
drama, excitement, crisis,
spectacle 3 = happening,
event, affair, business, fact,
matter, occasion, episode
incidentally = by the way, in
passing, en passant (*French*),
parenthetically, by the bye
inclination 1 = desire, longing,
aspiration, craving, hankering
2 = tendency, liking,
disposition, penchant,
propensity, predisposition,

predilection, proclivity
OPPOSITE: aversion

incline VERB 1 = **predispose**,
influence, persuade, prejudice,
sway, dispose
▷ NOUN 2 = **slope**, rise, dip,
grade, descent, ascent, gradient

inclined 1 = **disposed**, given,
prone, likely, liable, apt,
predisposed 2 = **willing**,
minded, disposed

include 1 = **contain**, involve,
incorporate, cover, consist of,
take in, embrace, comprise
OPPOSITE: exclude 2 = **count**
3 = **add**, enter, put in, insert

inclusion = **addition**,
incorporation, introduction,
insertion **OPPOSITE:** exclusion

inclusive = **comprehensive**,
general, global, sweeping,
blanket, umbrella, across-the-
board, all-embracing **OPPOSITE:**
limited

income = **revenue**, earnings,
pay, returns, profits, wages,
yield, proceeds

incoming 1 = **arriving**,
landing, approaching, entering,
returning, homeward
OPPOSITE: departing 2 = **new**

incompatible = **inconsistent**,
conflicting, contradictory,
incongruous, unsuited,
mismatched **OPPOSITE:**
compatible

incompetence = **ineptitude**,
inability, inadequacy, incapacity,
ineffectiveness, uselessness,
unfitness, incapability

incompetent = **inept**, useless,
incapable, floundering,
bungling, unfit, ineffectual,
inexpert **OPPOSITE:** competent

incomplete = **unfinished**,
partial, wanting, deficient,
imperfect, fragmentary, half-pie
(*N.Z. informal*) **OPPOSITE:**
complete

inconsistency
1 = **unreliability**, instability,
unpredictability, fickleness,
unsteadiness
2 = **incompatibility**,
discrepancy, disparity,
disagreement, variance,
divergence, incongruity

inconsistent 1 = **changeable**,
variable, unpredictable,
unstable, erratic, fickle,
capricious, unsteady **OPPOSITE:**
consistent 2 = **incompatible**,
conflicting, at odds,
contradictory, incongruous,
discordant, out of step,
irreconcilable **OPPOSITE:**
compatible

inconvenience NOUN
1 = **trouble**, difficulty, bother,
fuss, disadvantage, disturbance,
disruption, nuisance, uphill (*S.
African*)
▷ VERB 2 = **trouble**, bother,
disturb, upset, disrupt, put out,
discommode

incorporate 1 = **include**,
contain, take in, embrace,
integrate, encompass,
assimilate, comprise of
2 = **integrate**, include, absorb,

merge, fuse, assimilate, subsume 3 = **blend**, combine, compound, mingle

incorrect 1 = **false**, wrong, mistaken, flawed, faulty, inaccurate, untrue, erroneous **OPPOSITE:** correct

increase VERB 1 = **raise**, extend, boost, expand, develop, advance, strengthen, widen **OPPOSITE:** decrease 2 = **grow**, develop, spread, expand, swell, enlarge, escalate, multiply **OPPOSITE:** shrink
▷ NOUN 3 = **growth**, rise, development, gain, expansion, extension, proliferation, enlargement

increasingly = **progressively**, more and more

incredible 1 (*Informal*) = **amazing**, wonderful, stunning, extraordinary, overwhelming, astonishing, staggering, sensational (*informal*) 2 = **unbelievable**, unthinkable, improbable, inconceivable, preposterous, unconvincing, unimaginable, far-fetched

incumbent NOUN 1 = **holder**, keeper, bearer
▷ ADJECTIVE (*Formal*) 2 = **obligatory**, required, necessary, essential, binding, compulsory, mandatory, imperative

incur = **sustain**, experience, suffer, gain, earn, collect, meet with, provoke

indecent 1 = **obscene**, lewd, dirty, inappropriate, rude, crude, filthy, improper **OPPOSITE:** decent
2 = **unbecoming**, unsuitable, vulgar, unseemly, undignified, indecorous **OPPOSITE:** proper

indeed 1 = **certainly**, yes, definitely, surely, truly, undoubtedly, without doubt, indisputably 2 = **really**, actually, in fact, certainly, genuinely, in truth, in actuality

indefinitely = **endlessly**, continually, for ever, ad infinitum

independence = **freedom**, liberty, autonomy, sovereignty, self-rule, self-sufficiency, self-reliance, rangatiratanga (*N.Z.*) **OPPOSITE:** subjugation

independent 1 = **separate**, unattached, uncontrolled, unconstrained **OPPOSITE:** controlled 2 = **self-sufficient**, free, liberated, self-contained, self-reliant, self-supporting 3 = **self-governing**, free, autonomous, liberated, sovereign, self-determining, nonaligned **OPPOSITE:** subject

independently = **separately**, alone, solo, on your own, by yourself, unaided, individually, autonomously

indicate 1 = **show**, suggest, reveal, display, demonstrate, point to, imply, manifest
2 = **imply**, suggest, hint, intimate, signify, insinuate

i

3 = **point to**, point out, specify, gesture towards, designate
4 = **register**, show, record, read, express, display, demonstrate
indication = **sign**, mark, evidence, suggestion, symptom, hint, clue, manifestation
indicator = **sign**, mark, measure, guide, signal, symbol, meter, gauge
indict = **charge**, accuse, prosecute, summon, impeach, arraign
indictment = **charge**, allegation, prosecution, accusation, impeachment, summons, arraignment
indifference = **disregard**, apathy, negligence, detachment, coolness, coldness, nonchalance, aloofness **OPPOSITE:** concern
indifferent 1 = **unconcerned**, detached, cold, cool, callous, aloof, unmoved, unsympathetic **OPPOSITE:** concerned
2 = **mediocre**, ordinary, moderate, so-so (*informal*), passable, undistinguished, no great shakes (*informal*), half-pie (*N.Z. informal*) **OPPOSITE:** excellent
indignation = **resentment**, anger, rage, exasperation, pique, umbrage
indirect 1 = **related**, secondary, subsidiary, incidental, unintended 2 = **circuitous**, roundabout, curving,

wandering, rambling, deviant, meandering, tortuous **OPPOSITE:** direct
indispensable = **essential**, necessary, needed, key, vital, crucial, imperative, requisite **OPPOSITE:** dispensable
individual ADJECTIVE
1 = **separate**, independent, isolated, lone, solitary **OPPOSITE:** collective
2 = **unique**, special, fresh, novel, exclusive, singular, idiosyncratic, unorthodox **OPPOSITE:** conventional
▷ NOUN 3 = **person**, being, human, unit, character, soul, creature
individually = **separately**, independently, singly, one by one, one at a time
induce 1 = **cause**, produce, create, effect, lead to, occasion, generate, bring about **OPPOSITE:** prevent
2 = **persuade**, encourage, influence, convince, urge, prompt, sway, entice **OPPOSITE:** dissuade
indulge 1 = **gratify**, satisfy, feed, give way to, yield to, pander to, gladden 2 = **spoil**, pamper, cosset, humour, give in to, coddle, mollycoddle, overindulge
▷ PHRASES: indulge yourself = **treat yourself**, splash out, spoil yourself, luxuriate in something, overindulge yourself
indulgence 1 = **luxury**, treat,

extravagance, favour, privilege
2 = gratification, satisfaction,
fulfilment, appeasement,
satiation
industrialist = capitalist,
tycoon, magnate,
manufacturer, captain of
industry, big businessman
industry 1 = business,
production, manufacturing,
trade, commerce **2 = trade**,
world, business, service, line,
field, profession, occupation
3 = diligence, effort, labour,
hard work, trouble, activity,
application, endeavour
ineffective 1 = unproductive,
useless, futile, vain,
unsuccessful, pointless,
fruitless, ineffectual **OPPOSITE:**
effective **2 = inefficient**,
useless, poor, powerless, unfit,
worthless, inept, impotent
inefficient 1 = wasteful,
uneconomical, profligate
2 = incompetent, inept, weak,
bungling, ineffectual,
disorganized **OPPOSITE:**
efficient
inequality = disparity,
prejudice, difference, bias,
diversity, irregularity,
unevenness, disproportion
inevitable = unavoidable,
inescapable, inexorable, sure,
certain, fixed, assured, fated
OPPOSITE: avoidable
inevitably = unavoidably,
naturally, necessarily, surely,
certainly, as a result,

automatically, consequently
inexpensive = cheap,
reasonable, budget, bargain,
modest, economical **OPPOSITE:**
expensive
inexperienced = new, green,
raw, callow, immature, untried,
unpractised, unversed
OPPOSITE: experienced
infamous = notorious,
ignominious, disreputable, ill-
famed **OPPOSITE:** esteemed
infancy = beginnings, start,
birth, roots, seeds, origins,
dawn, outset **OPPOSITE:** end
infant = baby, child, babe,
toddler, tot, bairn (*Scot.*), littlie
(*Austral. informal*), ankle-biter
(*Austral. slang*), tacker (*Austral.
slang*)
infect 1 = contaminate
2 = pollute, poison, corrupt,
contaminate, taint, defile
3 = affect, move, upset,
overcome, stir, disturb
infection = disease, condition,
complaint, illness, virus,
disorder, corruption, poison
infectious = catching,
spreading, contagious,
communicable, virulent,
transmittable
inferior ADJECTIVE **1 = lower**,
minor, secondary, subsidiary,
lesser, humble, subordinate,
lowly **OPPOSITE:** superior
▷ NOUN **2 = underling**, junior,
subordinate, lesser, menial,
minion
infertility = sterility,

barrenness, unproductiveness, infecundity

infiltrate = **penetrate**, pervade, permeate, percolate, filter through to, make inroads into, sneak into (*informal*), insinuate yourself

infinite 1 = **vast**, enormous, immense, countless, measureless 2 = **limitless**, endless, unlimited, eternal, never-ending, boundless, everlasting, inexhaustible **OPPOSITE:** finite

inflame = **enrage**, stimulate, provoke, excite, anger, arouse, rouse, infuriate **OPPOSITE:** calm

inflamed = **swollen**, sore, red, hot, infected, fevered

inflate 1 = **blow up**, pump up, swell, dilate, distend, bloat, puff up or out **OPPOSITE:** deflate 2 = **increase**, expand, enlarge **OPPOSITE:** diminish 3 = **exaggerate**, embroider, embellish, enlarge, amplify, overstate, overestimate, overemphasize

inflated = **exaggerated**, swollen, overblown

inflation = **increase**, expansion, extension, swelling, escalation, enlargement

inflict = **impose**, administer, visit, apply, deliver, levy, wreak, mete or deal out

influence NOUN 1 = **control**, power, authority, direction, command, domination, supremacy, mastery, mana

(*N.Z.*) 2 = **power**, authority, pull (*informal*), importance, prestige, clout (*informal*), leverage 3 = **spell**, hold, power, weight, magic, sway, allure, magnetism ▷ VERB 4 = **affect**, have an effect on, have an impact on, control, concern, direct, guide, bear upon 5 = **persuade**, prompt, urge, induce, entice, coax, incite, instigate

influential 1 = **important**, powerful, telling, leading, inspiring, potent, authoritative, weighty **OPPOSITE:** unimportant 2 = **instrumental**, important, significant, crucial

influx = **arrival**, rush, invasion, incursion, inundation, inrush

inform = **tell**, advise, notify, instruct, enlighten, communicate to, tip someone off ▷ PHRASES: **inform on someone** = **betray**, denounce, shop (*slang, chiefly Brit.*), give someone away, incriminate, blow the whistle on (*informal*), grass on (*Brit. slang*), double-cross (*informal*), dob someone in (*Austral. & N.Z. slang*)

informal 1 = **natural**, relaxed, casual, familiar, unofficial, laid-back, easy-going, colloquial 2 = **relaxed**, easy, comfortable, simple, natural, casual, cosy, laid-back (*informal*) **OPPOSITE:** formal 3 = **casual**, comfortable, leisure, everyday, simple **4 = unofficial**, irregular **OPPOSITE:** official

information = facts, news, report, message, notice, knowledge, data, intelligence, drum (*Austral. informal*)

informative = instructive, revealing, educational, forthcoming, illuminating, enlightening, chatty, communicative

informed = knowledgeable, up to date, enlightened, learned, expert, familiar, versed, in the picture

infuriate = enrage, anger, provoke, irritate, incense, madden, exasperate, rile **OPPOSITE:** soothe

infuriating = annoying, irritating, provoking, galling, maddening, exasperating, vexatious

ingenious = creative, original, brilliant, clever, bright, shrewd, inventive, crafty **OPPOSITE:** unimaginative

ingredient = component, part, element, feature, piece, unit, item, aspect

inhabit = live in, occupy, populate, reside in, dwell in, abide in

inhabitant = occupant, resident, citizen, local, native, tenant, inmate, dweller

inhabited = populated, peopled, occupied, developed, settled, tenanted, colonized

inhale = breathe in, gasp, draw in, suck in, respire **OPPOSITE:** exhale

inherent = intrinsic, natural, essential, native, fundamental, hereditary, instinctive, innate **OPPOSITE:** extraneous

inherit = be left, come into, be willed, succeed to, fall heir to

inheritance = legacy, heritage, bequest, birthright, patrimony

inhibit 1 = hinder, check, frustrate, curb, restrain, constrain, obstruct, impede **OPPOSITE:** further **2 = prevent**, stop, frustrate **OPPOSITE:** allow

inhibited = shy, reserved, guarded, subdued, repressed, constrained, self-conscious, reticent **OPPOSITE:** uninhibited

initial = opening, first, earliest, beginning, primary, maiden, introductory, embryonic **OPPOSITE:** final

initially = at first, first, firstly, originally, primarily, in the beginning, at or in the beginning

initiate VERB **1 = begin**, start, open, launch, kick off (*informal*), embark on, originate, set about **2 = introduce**, admit, enlist, enrol, launch, establish, invest, recruit
▷ NOUN **3 = novice**, member, pupil, convert, amateur, newcomer, beginner, trainee
▷ PHRASES: **initiate someone into something = instruct in**, train in, coach in, acquaint with, drill in, make aware of,

teach about, tutor in
initiative 1 = **advantage**,
start, lead, upper hand
2 = **enterprise**, drive, energy,
leadership, ambition, daring,
enthusiasm, dynamism
inject 1 = **vaccinate**,
administer, inoculate
2 = **introduce**, bring in, insert,
instil, infuse, breathe
injection 1 = **vaccination**, shot
(*informal*), jab (*informal*), dose,
booster, immunization,
inoculation 2 = **introduction**,
investment, insertion,
advancement, dose, infusion
injunction = **order**, ruling,
command, instruction,
mandate, precept, exhortation
injure 1 = **hurt**, wound, harm,
damage, smash, crush, mar,
shatter, mangulate (*Austral.
slang*) 2 = **damage**, harm, ruin,
wreck, spoil, impair, crool or
cruel (*Austral. slang*)
3 = **undermine**, damage
injured = **hurt**, damaged,
wounded, broken, cut, crushed,
disabled, weakened, crook
(*Austral. & N.Z. slang*)
injury 1 = **wound**, cut, damage,
trauma (*Pathology*), gash, lesion,
laceration 2 = **harm**, suffering,
damage, ill, hurt, disability,
misfortune, affliction
3 = **wrong**, offence, insult,
detriment, disservice
injustice 1 = **unfairness**,
discrimination, prejudice, bias,
inequality, oppression,

intolerance, bigotry **OPPOSITE:**
justice 2 = **wrong**, injury,
crime, error, offence, sin,
misdeed, transgression
inland = **interior**, internal,
upcountry
inner 1 = **inside**, internal,
interior, inward **OPPOSITE:**
outer 2 = **central**, middle,
internal, interior 3 = **hidden**,
deep, secret, underlying,
obscure, repressed, unrevealed
OPPOSITE: obvious
innocence 1 = **naiveté**,
simplicity, inexperience,
credulity, gullibility,
ingenuousness, artlessness,
unworldliness **OPPOSITE:**
worldliness 2 = **blamelessness**,
clean hands, uprightness,
irreproachability, guiltlessness
OPPOSITE: guilt 3 = **chastity**,
virtue, purity, modesty, celibacy,
continence, maidenhood
innocent 1 = **not guilty**, in the
clear, blameless, clean, honest,
uninvolved, irreproachable,
guiltless **OPPOSITE:** guilty
2 = **naive**, open, trusting,
simple, childlike, gullible,
unsophisticated, unworldly
OPPOSITE: worldly
3 = **harmless**, innocuous,
inoffensive, well-meant,
unobjectionable, well-
intentioned
innovation 1 = **change**,
revolution, departure,
introduction, variation,
transformation, upheaval,

alteration 2 = **newness**,
novelty, originality, freshness,
modernization, uniqueness
inquest = **inquiry**,
investigation, probe, inquisition
inquire *or* **enquire** = **ask**,
question, query, quiz
▷ **PHRASES: inquire into
something** = **investigate**,
study, examine, research,
explore, look into, probe into,
make inquiries into
inquiry *or* **enquiry**
1 = **question**, query,
investigation
2 = **investigation**, study,
review, survey, examination,
probe, inspection, exploration
3 = **research**, investigation,
analysis, inspection,
exploration, interrogation
insane 1 = **mad**, crazy, mentally
ill, crazed, demented, deranged,
out of your mind, off the air
(*Austral. slang*), porangi (*N.Z.*)
OPPOSITE: sane 2 = **stupid**,
foolish, daft (*informal*),
irresponsible, irrational,
senseless, preposterous,
impractical **OPPOSITE:**
reasonable
insect = **bug**, creepy-crawly
(*Brit. informal*), gogga (*S. African
informal*)
▷ *See panels* **BEETLES,
BUTTERFLIES AND MOTHS, FLIES,
INSECTS**
insecure 1 = **unconfident**,
worried, anxious, afraid, shy,
uncertain, unsure, timid

OPPOSITE: confident
2 = **unsafe**, exposed,
vulnerable, wide-open,
unprotected, defenceless,
unguarded **OPPOSITE:** safe
insecurity = **anxiety**, fear,
worry, uncertainty **OPPOSITE:**
confidence
insert = **put**, place, position,
slip, slide, slot, thrust, stick in
inside **NOUN** 1 = **interior**,
contents, core, nucleus
▷ **PLURAL NOUN** 2 (*Informal*)
= **stomach**, guts, belly, bowels,
innards (*informal*), entrails,
viscera, vitals
▷ **ADJECTIVE** 3 = **inner**, internal,
interior, inward **OPPOSITE:**
outside 4 = **confidential**,
private, secret, internal,
exclusive, restricted, privileged,
classified
▷ **ADVERB** 5 = **indoors**, in,
within, under cover
insight 1 = **understanding**,
perception, sense, knowledge,
vision, judgment, awareness,
grasp 2 *with* **into**
= **understanding of**, perception
of, awareness of, experience of,
description of, introduction to,
observation of, judgment of
insignificant = **unimportant**,
minor, irrelevant, petty, trivial,
meaningless, trifling, paltry
OPPOSITE: important
insist 1 **lay down the law**, put
your foot down (*informal*)
2 = **demand**, order, require,
command, dictate, entreat

INSECTS

Types of insect

body louse, cootie (*U.S. &*
N.Z.), or (*N.Z. slang*) kutu
bookworm
caddis worm or caseworm
cankerworm
cochineal or cochineal
insect
cockroach
crab (louse)
cricket
earwig, or (*Scot. dialect*)
clipshears, or clipshear
flea
grasshopper
katydid
locust
louse or (*N.Z.*) kutu

mantis or praying mantis
measuring worm, looper, or
inchworm
midge
mosquito
nit
phylloxera
scale insect
silkworm
silverfish
stick insect or (*U.S. &*
Canad.) walking stick
thrips
treehopper
weta (*N.Z.*)
wireworm
woodworm

---

3 = **assert**, state, maintain,
claim, declare, repeat, vow,
swear
insistence 1 = **demand**,
command, dictate, entreaty,
importunity **2** = **assertion**,
claim, statement, declaration,
persistence, pronouncement
inspect 1 = **examine**, check,
look at, view, survey, look over,
scrutinize, go over *or* through
2 = **check**, examine,
investigate, look at, survey, vet,
look over, go over *or* through
inspection 1 = **examination**,
investigation, scrutiny, once-
over (*informal*) **2** = **check**,
search, investigation, review,
survey, examination, scrutiny,
once-over (*informal*)

inspector = **examiner**,
investigator, supervisor,
monitor, superintendent,
auditor, censor, surveyor
inspiration 1 = **imagination**,
creativity, ingenuity, insight,
originality, inventiveness,
cleverness **2** = **motivation**,
example, model, boost, spur,
incentive, revelation, stimulus
OPPOSITE: deterrent
3 = **influence**, spur, stimulus,
muse
inspire 1 = **motivate**,
stimulate, encourage, influence,
spur, animate, enliven,
galvanize **OPPOSITE:** discourage
2 = **give rise to**, produce, result
in, engender
inspired 1 = **brilliant**,

wonderful, impressive, outstanding, thrilling, memorable, dazzling, superlative 2 = **stimulated**, uplifted, exhilarated, enthused, elated

inspiring = **uplifting**, exciting, moving, stirring, stimulating, rousing, exhilarating, heartening **OPPOSITE:** uninspiring

instability 1 = **uncertainty**, insecurity, vulnerability, volatility, unpredictability, fluctuation, impermanence, unsteadiness **OPPOSITE:** stability 2 = **imbalance**, variability, unpredictability, unsteadiness, changeableness

install 1 = **set up**, put in, place, position, station, establish, lay, fix 2 = **institute**, establish, introduce, invest, ordain, inaugurate, induct 3 = **settle**, position, plant, establish, lodge, ensconce

installation 1 = **setting up**, fitting, instalment, placing, positioning, establishment 2 = **appointment**, ordination, inauguration, induction, investiture

instalment 1 = **payment**, repayment, part payment 2 = **part**, section, chapter, episode, portion, division

instance NOUN 1 = **example**, case, occurrence, occasion, sample, illustration
▷ VERB 2 = **name**, mention,

identify, point out, advance, quote, refer to, point to

instant NOUN 1 = **moment**, second, flash, split second, jiffy (*informal*), trice, twinkling of an eye (*informal*) 2 = **time**, point, hour, moment, stage, occasion, phase, juncture
▷ ADJECTIVE 3 = **immediate**, prompt, instantaneous, direct, quick, on-the-spot, split-second 4 = **ready-made**, fast, convenience, ready-mixed, ready-cooked, precooked

instantly = **immediately**, at once, straight away, now, directly, right away, instantaneously, this minute

instead = **rather**, alternatively, preferably, in preference, in lieu, on second thoughts
▷ PHRASES: instead of = **in place of**, rather than, in preference to, in lieu of, in contrast with

instinct 1 = **natural inclination**, talent, tendency, faculty, inclination, knack, predisposition, proclivity 2 = **talent**, skill, gift, capacity, bent, genius, faculty, knack 3 = **intuition**, impulse

instinctive = **natural**, inborn, automatic, unconscious, inherent, spontaneous, reflex, innate **OPPOSITE:** acquired

instinctively = **intuitively**, naturally, automatically, without thinking, involuntarily, by instinct

institute NOUN
1 = **establishment**, body, centre, school, university, society, association, college
▷ VERB 2 = **establish**, start, found, launch, set up, introduce, fix, organize **OPPOSITE:** end

institution 1 = **establishment**, body, centre, school, university, society, association, college
2 = **custom**, practice, tradition, law, rule, procedure, convention, ritual

institutional = **conventional**, accepted, established, formal, routine, orthodox, procedural

instruct 1 = **order**, tell, direct, charge, bid, command, mandate, enjoin 2 = **teach**, school, train, coach, educate, drill, tutor

instruction NOUN 1 = **order**, ruling, command, rule, demand, regulation, dictate, decree
2 = **teaching**, schooling, training, grounding, education, coaching, lesson(s), guidance
▷ PLURAL NOUN
3 = **information**, rules, advice, directions, recommendations, guidance, specifications

instructor = **teacher**, coach, guide, adviser, trainer, demonstrator, tutor, mentor

instrument 1 = **tool**, device, implement, mechanism, appliance, apparatus, gadget, contraption (*informal*)
2 = **agent**, means, medium, agency, vehicle, mechanism, organ

instrumental = **active**, involved, influential, useful, helpful, contributory

insufficient = **inadequate**, scant, meagre, short, sparse, deficient, lacking **OPPOSITE:** ample

insulate = **isolate**, protect, screen, defend, shelter, shield, cut off, cushion

insult VERB = **offend**, abuse, wound, slight, put down, snub, malign, affront **OPPOSITE:** praise
▷ NOUN 1 = **jibe**, slight, put-down, abuse, snub, barb, affront, abusive remark
2 = **offence**, slight, snub, slur, affront, slap in the face (*informal*), kick in the teeth (*informal*), insolence

insulting = **offensive**, rude, abusive, degrading, contemptuous, disparaging, scurrilous, insolent **OPPOSITE:** complimentary

insurance 1 = **assurance**, cover, security, protection, safeguard, indemnity
2 = **protection**, security, guarantee, shelter, safeguard, warranty

insure 1 = **assure**, cover, protect, guarantee, warrant, underwrite, indemnify
2 = **protect**, cover, safeguard

intact = **undamaged**, whole, complete, sound, perfect, entire, unscathed, unbroken **OPPOSITE:** damaged

integral = **essential**, basic, fundamental, necessary, component, constituent, indispensable, intrinsic **OPPOSITE:** inessential

integrate = **join**, unite, combine, blend, incorporate, merge, fuse, assimilate **OPPOSITE:** separate

integrity 1 = **honesty**, principle, honour, virtue, goodness, morality, purity, probity **OPPOSITE:** dishonesty 2 = **unity**, unification, cohesion, coherence, wholeness, soundness, completeness

intellect = **intelligence**, mind, reason, understanding, sense, brains (*informal*), judgment

intellectual ADJECTIVE 1 = **scholarly**, learned, academic, lettered, intelligent, cerebral, erudite, scholastic **OPPOSITE:** stupid ▷ NOUN 2 = **academic**, expert, genius, thinker, master, mastermind, maestro, highbrow, fundi (*S. African*), acca (*Austral. slang*) **OPPOSITE:** idiot

intelligence 1 = **intellect**, understanding, brains (*informal*), sense, knowledge, judgment, wit, perception **OPPOSITE:** stupidity 2 = **information**, news, facts, report, findings, knowledge, data, notification **OPPOSITE:** misinformation

intelligent = **clever**, bright,

smart, sharp, enlightened, knowledgeable, well-informed, brainy (*informal*) **OPPOSITE:** stupid

intend = **plan**, mean, aim, propose, purpose, have in mind or view

intense 1 = **extreme**, great, severe, fierce, deep, powerful, supreme, acute **OPPOSITE:** mild 2 = **fierce**, tough 3 = **passionate**, emotional, fierce, heightened, ardent, fanatical, fervent, heartfelt **OPPOSITE:** indifferent

● USAGE NOTE
● *Intense* is sometimes wrongly
● used where *intensive* is
● meant: *the land is under*
● *intensive* (not *intense*)
● *cultivation. Intensely* is
● sometimes wrongly used
● where *intently* is meant: *he*
● *listened intently* (not *intensely*).

intensify 1 = **increase**, raise, add to, strengthen, reinforce, widen, heighten, sharpen **OPPOSITE:** decrease 2 = **escalate**, increase, widen, deepen

intensity 1 = **force**, strength, fierceness 2 = **passion**, emotion, fervour, force, strength, fanaticism, ardour, vehemence

intensive = **concentrated**, thorough, exhaustive, full, demanding, detailed, complete, serious

intent ADJECTIVE 1 = **absorbed**,

intense, fascinated,
preoccupied, enthralled,
attentive, watchful, engrossed
OPPOSITE: indifferent
▷ NOUN 2 = **intention**, aim,
purpose, meaning, end, plan,
goal, design **OPPOSITE:** chance
intention = **aim**, plan, idea,
goal, end, design, target, wish
inter = **bury**, lay to rest, entomb,
consign to the grave
intercept = **catch**, stop, block,
seize, cut off, interrupt, head
off, obstruct
intercourse 1 = **sexual
intercourse**, sex (informal),
copulation, coitus, carnal
knowledge 2 = **contact**,
communication, commerce,
dealings
interest NOUN 1 often plural
= **hobby**, activity, pursuit,
entertainment, recreation,
amusement, preoccupation,
diversion 2 often plural
= **advantage**, good, benefit,
profit 3 = **stake**, investment
▷ VERB 4 = **arouse your
curiosity**, fascinate, attract,
grip, entertain, intrigue, divert,
captivate **OPPOSITE:** bore
interested 1 = **curious**,
attracted, excited, drawn, keen,
gripped, fascinated, captivated
OPPOSITE: uninterested
2 = **involved**, concerned,
affected, implicated
interesting = **intriguing**,
absorbing, appealing,
attractive, engaging, gripping,

entrancing, stimulating
OPPOSITE: uninteresting
interface = **connection**, link,
boundary, border, frontier
interfere = **meddle**, intervene,
intrude, butt in, tamper, pry,
encroach, stick your oar in
(informal)
▷ PHRASES: **interfere with
something or someone**
= **conflict with**, check, clash,
handicap, hamper, disrupt,
inhibit, thwart
interference = **intrusion**,
intervention, meddling,
opposition, conflict,
obstruction, prying
interim = **temporary**,
provisional, makeshift, acting,
caretaker, improvised, stopgap
interior NOUN 1 = **inside**,
centre, heart, middle, depths,
core, nucleus
▷ ADJECTIVE 2 = **inside**,
internal, inner **OPPOSITE:**
exterior 3 = **mental**, emotional,
psychological, private, personal,
secret, hidden, spiritual
intermediary = **mediator**,
agent, middleman, broker,
go-between
intermediate = **middle**, mid,
halfway, in-between (informal),
midway, intervening,
transitional, median
internal 1 = **domestic**, home,
national, local, civic, in-house,
intramural 2 = **inner**, inside,
interior **OPPOSITE:** external
international = **global**, world,

worldwide, universal, cosmopolitan, intercontinental

Internet PHRASES: **the Internet = the information superhighway**, the net (*informal*), the web (*informal*), the World Wide Web, cyberspace

interpret 1 = **take**, understand, explain, construe 2 = **translate**, transliterate 3 = **explain**, make sense of, decode, decipher, elucidate 4 = **understand**, read, crack, solve, figure out (*informal*), comprehend, decode, deduce 5 = **portray**, present, perform, render, depict, enact, act out

interpretation 1 = **explanation**, analysis, exposition, elucidation 2 = **performance**, portrayal, presentation, reading, rendition 3 = **reading**, study, review, version, analysis, explanation, examination, evaluation

interpreter = **translator**

interrogation = **questioning**, inquiry, examination, grilling (*informal*), cross-examination, inquisition, third degree (*informal*)

interrupt 1 = **intrude**, disturb, intervene, interfere (with), break in, heckle, butt in, barge in (*informal*) 2 = **suspend**, stop, end, delay, cease, postpone, shelve, put off

interruption 1 = **disruption**, break, disturbance, hitch, intrusion 2 = **stoppage**, pause, suspension

interval 1 = **period**, spell, space, stretch, pause, span 2 = **break**, interlude, intermission, rest, gap, pause, respite, lull 3 = **delay**, gap, hold-up, stoppage 4 = **stretch**, space

intervene 1 = **step in** (*informal*), interfere, mediate, intrude, intercede, arbitrate, take a hand (*informal*) 2 = **interrupt**, involve yourself 3 = **happen**, occur, take place, follow, arise, ensue, befall, materialize

intervention = **mediation**, interference, intrusion, arbitration, conciliation, agency

interview NOUN 1 = **meeting** 2 = **audience**, talk, conference, exchange, dialogue, consultation, press conference ▷ VERB 3 = **examine**, talk to 4 = **question**, interrogate, examine, investigate, pump, grill (*informal*), quiz, cross-examine

interviewer = **questioner**, reporter, investigator, examiner, interrogator

intimacy = **familiarity**, closeness, confidentiality OPPOSITE: aloofness

intimate[1] ADJECTIVE 1 = **close**, dear, loving, near, familiar, thick (*informal*), devoted, confidential OPPOSITE: distant 2 = **private**, personal, confidential, special,

individual, secret, exclusive
OPPOSITE: public 3 = detailed,
minute, full, deep, particular,
immediate, comprehensive,
profound **4 = cosy**, relaxed,
friendly, informal, harmonious,
snug, comfy (*informal*), warm
▷ NOUN **5 = friend**, close
friend, crony, cobber (*Austral. &
N.Z. old-fashioned informal*),
confidant or confidante,
(constant) companion, E hoa
(*N.Z.*) **OPPOSITE: stranger**

intimate² **1 = suggest**,
indicate, hint, imply, insinuate
2 = announce, state, declare,
communicate, make known

intimately **1 = closely**,
personally, warmly, familiarly,
tenderly, affectionately,
confidentially, confidingly
2 = fully, very well, thoroughly,
in detail, inside out

intimidate = frighten,
pressure, threaten, scare, bully,
plague, hound, daunt

intimidation = bullying,
pressure, threat(s), menaces,
coercion, arm-twisting
(*informal*), browbeating,
terrorization

intricate = complicated,
involved, complex, fancy,
elaborate, tangled, tortuous,
convoluted **OPPOSITE: simple**

intrigue NOUN **1 = plot**,
scheme, conspiracy,
manoeuvre, collusion,
stratagem, chicanery, wile
2 = affair, romance, intimacy,

liaison, amour
▷ VERB **3 = interest**, fascinate,
attract, rivet, titillate **4 = plot**,
scheme, manoeuvre, conspire,
connive, machinate

intriguing = interesting,
fascinating, absorbing, exciting,
engaging, gripping, stimulating,
compelling

introduce **1 = bring in**,
establish, set up, start, found,
launch, institute, pioneer
2 = present, acquaint, make
known, familiarize
3 = suggest, air, advance,
submit, bring up, put forward,
broach, moot **4 = add**, insert,
inject, throw in (*informal*), infuse

introduction **1 = launch**,
institution, pioneering,
inauguration **OPPOSITE:**
elimination **2 = opening**,
prelude, preface, lead-in,
preamble, foreword, prologue,
intro (*informal*) **OPPOSITE:**
conclusion

introductory **1 = preliminary**,
first, initial, inaugural,
preparatory **OPPOSITE:**
concluding **2 = starting**,
opening, initial

intruder = trespasser, invader,
prowler, interloper, infiltrator,
gate-crasher (*informal*)

intrusion **1 = interruption**,
interference, infringement,
trespass, encroachment
2 = invasion, breach,
infringement, encroachment,
infraction, usurpation

intuition 1 = instinct, perception, insight, sixth sense 2 = feeling, idea, impression, suspicion, premonition, inkling, presentiment

invade 1 = attack, storm, assault, capture, occupy, seize, raid, overwhelm 2 = infest, swarm, overrun, ravage, beset, pervade, permeate

invader = attacker, raider, plunderer, aggressor, trespasser

invalid¹ NOUN 1 = patient, sufferer, convalescent, valetudinarian
▷ ADJECTIVE 2 = disabled, ill, sick, ailing, frail, infirm, bedridden

invalid² 1 = null and void, void, worthless, inoperative
OPPOSITE: valid
2 = unfounded, false, illogical, irrational, unsound, fallacious
OPPOSITE: sound

invaluable = precious, valuable, priceless, inestimable, worth your or its weight in gold
OPPOSITE: worthless

invariably = always, regularly, constantly, repeatedly, consistently, continually, eternally, habitually

invasion 1 = attack, assault, capture, takeover, raid, offensive, occupation, conquering 2 = intrusion, breach, violation, disturbance, disruption, infringement, encroachment, infraction

invent 1 = create, make, produce, design, discover, manufacture, devise, conceive 2 = make up, devise, concoct, forge, fake, fabricate, feign, falsify

invention 1 = creation, machine, device, design, instrument, discovery, innovation, gadget
2 = development, design, production, setting up, foundation, construction, creation, discovery 3 = fiction, fantasy, lie, yarn, fabrication, falsehood, untruth
4 = creativity, imagination, initiative, enterprise, genius, ingenuity, originality, inventiveness

inventive = creative, original, innovative, imaginative, inspired, fertile, ingenious, resourceful OPPOSITE: uninspired

inventor = creator, maker, author, designer, architect, coiner, originator

inventory = list, record, catalogue, listing, account, roll, file, register

invertebrate ▷ See panels CRUSTACEANS, INVERTEBRATES, SNAILS, SLUGS AND OTHER GASTROPODS, SPIDERS AND OTHER ARACHNIDS

invest 1 = spend, expend, advance, venture, put in, devote, lay out, sink in
2 = empower, provide, charge, sanction, license, authorize

INVERTEBRATES

Types of invertebrate

amoeba or (U.S.) ameba
animalcule or animalculum
arthropod
bardy, bardie, or bardi
  (Austral.)
bivalve
blue-ringed octopus (Austral.)
Bluff oyster (N.Z.)
box jellyfish or (Austral.) sea
  wasp
brachiopod or lamp shell
brandling
bryozoan or (colloquial) sea
  mat
centipede
chiton or coat-of-mail shell
clam
cone (shell)
coral
ctenophore or comb jelly
cunjevoi or cunje (Austral.)
cuttlefish or cuttle
daphnia
earthworm
eelworm
gastropodart
horseleech
jellyfish or (Austral. slang)
  blubber
kina (N.Z.)
lancelet or amphioxus
leech
lugworm, lug, or lobworm
millipede, millepede, or
  milleped
mollusc
mussel

octopus or devilfish
oyster
paper nautilus, nautilus, or
  argonaut
pearly nautilus, nautilus, or
  chambered nautilus
piddock
pipi or ugari (Austral.)
Portuguese man-of-war or
  (Austral.) bluebottle
quahog, hard-shell clam,
  hard-shell, or round clam
ragworm or (U.S.) clamworm
razor-shell or (U.S.) razor clam
red coral or precious coral
roundworm
sandworm or (Austral.)
  pumpworm
scallop
sea anemone
sea cucumber
sea lily
sea mouse
sea squirt
sea urchin
seed oyster
sponge
squid
starfish
tapeworm
tardigrade or water bear
teredo or shipworm
trepang or bêche-de-mer
tube worm
tubifex
tusk shell or tooth shell
worm

▷ **PHRASES: invest in something** = buy, get, purchase, pay for, obtain, acquire, procure

investigate = examine, study, research, go into, explore, look into, inspect, probe into, make inquiries about

investigation = examination, study, inquiry, review, search, survey, probe, inspection

investigator = examiner, researcher, monitor, detective, analyser, explorer, scrutinizer, inquirer

investment 1 = investing, backing, funding, financing, contribution, speculation, transaction, expenditure 2 = stake, interest, share, concern, portion, ante (*informal*) 3 = buy, asset, acquisition, venture, risk, gamble

invisible = unseen, imperceptible, indiscernible, unseeable **OPPOSITE:** visible

invitation = request, call, invite (*informal*), summons

invite 1 = ask 2 = request, look for, bid for, appeal for 3 = encourage, attract, cause, court, ask for (*informal*), generate, foster, tempt

inviting = tempting, appealing, attractive, welcoming, enticing, seductive, alluring, mouthwatering **OPPOSITE:** uninviting

invoke 1 = apply, use, implement, initiate, resort to,

put into effect 2 = **call upon**, appeal to, pray to, petition, beseech, entreat, supplicate

involve 1 = entail, mean, require, occasion, imply, give rise to, necessitate 2 = concern, draw in, bear on

involved = complicated, complex, intricate, hard, confused, confusing, elaborate, tangled **OPPOSITE:** straightforward

involvement = connection, interest, association, commitment, attachment

inward 1 = incoming, entering, inbound, ingoing 2 = internal, inner, private, personal, inside, secret, hidden, interior **OPPOSITE:** outward

Ireland = Hibernia (*Latin*)

iron 1 = ferrous, ferric 2 = inflexible, hard, strong, tough, rigid, adamant, unconditional, steely **OPPOSITE:** weak

▷ **PHRASES: iron something out** = settle, resolve, sort out, get rid of, reconcile, clear up, put right, straighten out

● **RELATED WORDS**
● *adjectives:* ferric, ferrous

ironic *or* **ironical** 1 = sarcastic, dry, acid, bitter, mocking, wry, satirical, tongue-in-cheek 2 = paradoxical, contradictory, puzzling, baffling, confounding, enigmatic, incongruous

irony 1 = sarcasm, mockery, ridicule, satire, cynicism,

derision 2 = **paradox**,
incongruity

irrational = **illogical**, crazy,
absurd, unreasonable,
preposterous, nonsensical
OPPOSITE: rational

irregular 1 = **variable**, erratic,
occasional, random, casual,
shaky, sporadic, haphazard
OPPOSITE: steady 2 = **uneven**,
rough, ragged, crooked, jagged,
bumpy, contorted, lopsided
OPPOSITE: even
3 = **inappropriate**,
unconventional, unethical,
unusual, extraordinary,
exceptional, peculiar, unofficial
4 = **unofficial**, underground,
guerrilla, resistance, partisan,
rogue, paramilitary, mercenary

irrelevant = **unconnected**,
unrelated, unimportant,
inappropriate, peripheral,
immaterial, extraneous, beside
the point **OPPOSITE:** relevant

irresistible = **overwhelming**,
compelling, overpowering,
urgent, compulsive

irresponsible = **thoughtless**,
reckless, careless, unreliable,
untrustworthy, shiftless,
scatterbrained **OPPOSITE:**
responsible

irritate 1 = **annoy**, anger,
bother, needle (*informal*),
infuriate, exasperate, nettle, irk
OPPOSITE: placate 2 = **inflame**,
pain, rub, scratch, scrape, chafe

irritated = **annoyed**, cross,
angry, bothered, put out,

exasperated, nettled, vexed,
tooshie (*Austral. slang*), hoha
(*N.Z.*)

irritating = **annoying**, trying,
infuriating, disturbing, nagging,
troublesome, maddening,
irksome **OPPOSITE:** pleasing

irritation 1 = **annoyance**,
anger, fury, resentment, gall,
indignation, displeasure,
exasperation **OPPOSITE:**
pleasure 2 = **nuisance**, irritant,
drag (*informal*), pain in the neck
(*informal*), thorn in your flesh

island = **isle**, atoll, islet, ait or
eyot (*dialect*), cay or key
● RELATED WORD
● *adjective:* insular

isolate 1 = **separate**, break up,
cut off, detach, split up,
insulate, segregate, disconnect
2 = **quarantine**

isolated 1 = **remote**, far, distant,
lonely, out-of-the-way, hidden,
secluded, inaccessible

isolation = **separation**,
segregation, detachment,
solitude, seclusion, remoteness

issue NOUN 1 = **topic**, point,
matter, problem, question,
subject, theme 2 = **point**,
question, bone of contention
3 = **edition**, printing, copy,
publication, number, version
4 = **children**, offspring, babies,
kids (*informal*), heirs,
descendants, progeny
OPPOSITE: parent
▷ VERB 5 = **give out**, release,
publish, announce, deliver,

spread, broadcast, distribute
▷ **PHRASES: take issue with
something** *or* **someone
= disagree with**, question,
challenge, oppose, dispute,
object to, argue with, take
exception to

itch VERB 1 = **prickle**, tickle,
tingle 2 = **long**, ache, crave,
pine, hunger, lust, yearn,
hanker
▷ NOUN 3 = **irritation**, tingling,
prickling, itchiness 4 = **desire**,
longing, craving, passion, yen
(*informal*), hunger, lust, yearning

item 1 = **article**, thing, object,
piece, unit, component
2 = **matter**, point, issue, case,
question, concern, detail,
subject 3 = **report**, story, piece,
account, note, feature, notice,
article

itinerary = **schedule**,
programme, route, timetable

Jj

jab VERB 1 = **poke**, dig, punch,
thrust, tap, stab, nudge, prod
▷ NOUN 2 = **poke**, dig, punch,
thrust, tap, stab, nudge, prod

jacket = **covering**, casing, case,
cover, skin, shell, coat,
wrapping

jackpot = **prize**, winnings,
award, reward, bonanza

jail NOUN 1 = **prison**,
penitentiary (*U.S.*),
confinement, dungeon, nick
(*Brit. slang*), slammer (*slang*),
reformatory, boob (*Austral.
slang*)
▷ VERB 2 = **imprison**, confine,
detain, lock up, put away,
intern, incarcerate, send down

jam NOUN 1 = **predicament**,
tight spot, situation, trouble,
hole (*slang*), fix (*informal*), mess,
pinch
▷ VERB 2 = **pack**, force, press,
stuff, squeeze, ram, wedge,
cram 3 = **crowd**, throng, crush,
mass, surge, flock, swarm,
congregate 4 = **congest**, block,
clog, stick, stall, obstruct

jar[1] = **pot**, container, drum, vase,
jug, pitcher, urn, crock

jar[2] 1 *usually with* **on** = **irritate**,

annoy, offend, nettle, irk, grate on, get on your nerves (*informal*) **2 = jolt**, rock, shake, bump, rattle, vibrate, convulse

jargon = parlance, idiom, usage, argot

jaw PLURAL NOUN **1 = opening**, entrance, mouth
▷ VERB **2** (*Informal*) **= talk**, chat, gossip, chatter, spout, natter

jealous 1 = suspicious, protective, wary, doubtful, sceptical, vigilant, watchful, possessive **OPPOSITE:** trusting **2 = envious**, grudging, resentful, green, green with envy, desirous, covetous **OPPOSITE:** satisfied

jealousy = suspicion, mistrust, possessiveness, doubt, spite, resentment, wariness, dubiety

jeer VERB **1 = mock**, deride, heckle, barrack, ridicule, taunt, scoff, gibe **OPPOSITE:** cheer
▷ NOUN **2 = mockery**, abuse, ridicule, taunt, boo, derision, gibe, catcall **OPPOSITE:** applause

jeopardy = danger, risk, peril, vulnerability, insecurity

jerk VERB **1 = jolt**, bang, bump, lurch
▷ NOUN **2 = lurch**, movement, thrust, twitch, jolt

jet NOUN **1 = stream**, current, spring, flow, rush, flood, burst, spray
▷ VERB **2 = fly**, wing, cruise, soar, zoom

jewel 1 = gemstone, gem,

ornament, sparkler (*informal*), rock (*slang*) **2 = treasure**, wonder, darling, pearl, gem, paragon, pride and joy, taonga (*N.Z.*)

jewellery = jewels, treasure, gems, trinkets, ornaments, finery, regalia

job 1 = position, work, calling, business, field, career, employment, profession **2 = task**, duty, work, venture, enterprise, undertaking, assignment, chore

jobless = unemployed, redundant, out of work, inactive, unoccupied, idle

jog 1 = run, trot, canter, lope **2 = nudge**, push, shake, prod **3 = stimulate**, stir, prod

join 1 = enrol in, enter, sign up for, enlist in **2 = connect**, unite, couple, link, combine, attach, fasten, add **OPPOSITE:** detach

joint ADJECTIVE **1 = shared**, mutual, collective, communal, united, joined, allied, combined
▷ NOUN **2 = junction**, connection, brace, bracket, hinge, intersection, node, nexus

jointly = collectively, together, in conjunction, as one, in common, mutually, in partnership, in league **OPPOSITE:** separately

joke NOUN **1 = jest**, gag (*informal*), wisecrack (*informal*), witticism, crack (*informal*), pun, one-liner (*informal*) **2 = laugh**, jest, jape **3 = prank**,

trick, practical joke, lark
(*informal*), escapade, jape
4 = **laughing stock**, clown,
buffoon
▷ VERB **5** = **jest**, kid (*informal*),
mock, tease, taunt, quip,
banter, play the fool
joker = **comedian**, comic, wit,
clown, wag, jester, prankster,
buffoon
jolly = **happy**, cheerful, merry,
upbeat (*informal*), playful,
cheery, genial, chirpy (*informal*)
OPPOSITE: miserable
jolt VERB **1** = **jerk**, push, shake,
knock, jar, shove, jog, jostle
2 = **surprise**, stun, disturb,
stagger, startle, perturb,
discompose
▷ NOUN **3** = **jerk**, start, jump,
shake, bump, jar, jog, lurch
4 = **surprise**, blow, shock,
setback, bombshell, bolt from
the blue
journal **1** = **magazine**,
publication, gazette, periodical
2 = **newspaper**, paper, daily,
weekly, monthly **3** = **diary**,
record, history, log, notebook,
chronicle, annals, yearbook
journalist = **reporter**, writer,
correspondent, newsman *or*
newswoman, commentator,
broadcaster, hack (*derogatory*),
columnist
journey NOUN **1** = **trip**, drive,
tour, flight, excursion, trek,
expedition, voyage
2 = **progress**, voyage,
pilgrimage, odyssey

▷ VERB **3** = **travel**, go, move,
tour, progress, proceed, wander,
trek, go walkabout (*Austral.*)
joy = **delight**, pleasure,
satisfaction, ecstasy,
enjoyment, bliss, glee, rapture
OPPOSITE: sorrow
jubilee = **celebration**, holiday,
festival, festivity
judge NOUN **1** = **magistrate**,
justice, beak (*Brit. slang*), His,
Her *or* Your Honour **2** = **referee**,
expert, specialist, umpire,
mediator, examiner,
connoisseur, assessor
3 = **critic**, assessor, arbiter
▷ VERB **4** = **adjudicate**, referee,
umpire, mediate, officiate,
arbitrate **5** = **evaluate**, rate,
consider, view, value, esteem
6 = **estimate**, guess, assess,
calculate, evaluate, gauge
judgment **1** = **opinion**, view,
estimate, belief, assessment,
diagnosis, valuation, appraisal
2 = **verdict**, finding, ruling,
decision, sentence, decree,
arbitration, adjudication
3 = **sense**, good sense,
understanding, discrimination,
perception, wisdom, wit,
prudence
judicial = **legal**, official
jug = **container**, pitcher, urn,
carafe, creamer (*U.S. & Canad.*),
vessel, jar, crock
juggle = **manipulate**, change,
alter, modify, manoeuvre
juice **1** = **liquid**, extract, fluid,
liquor, sap, nectar

2 = **secretion**, serum

juicy 1 = **moist**, lush, succulent 2 (*Informal*) = **interesting**, colourful, sensational, vivid, provocative, spicy (*informal*), suggestive, racy

jumble NOUN 1 = **muddle**, mixture, mess, disorder, confusion, clutter, disarray, mishmash

▷ VERB 2 = **mix**, mistake, confuse, disorder, shuffle, muddle, disorganize

jumbo = **giant**, large, huge, immense, gigantic, oversized **OPPOSITE:** tiny

jump VERB 1 = **leap**, spring, bound, bounce, hop, skip 2 = **vault**, hurdle, go over, sail over, hop over 3 = **spring**, bound, bounce 4 = **recoil**, start, jolt, flinch, shake, jerk, quake, shudder 5 = **increase**, rise, climb, escalate, advance, soar, surge, spiral 6 = **miss**, avoid, skip, omit, evade

▷ NOUN 7 = **leap**, spring, skip, bound, hop, vault 8 = **rise**, increase, upswing, advance, upsurge, upturn, increment

jumped-up = **conceited**, arrogant, pompous, overbearing, presumptuous, insolent

jumper = **sweater**, top, jersey, cardigan, woolly, pullover

junior 1 = **minor**, lower, secondary, lesser, subordinate, inferior 2 = **younger OPPOSITE:** senior

junk = **rubbish**, refuse, waste, scrap, litter, debris, garbage (*chiefly U.S.*), trash

jurisdiction 1 = **authority**, power, control, rule, influence, command, mana (*N.Z.*) 2 = **range**, area, field, bounds, province, scope, sphere, compass

just ADVERB 1 = **recently**, lately, only now 2 = **merely**, only, simply, solely 3 = **barely**, hardly, by a whisker, by the skin of your teeth 4 = **exactly**, really, quite, completely, totally, perfectly, entirely, truly

▷ ADJECTIVE 5 = **fair**, good, legitimate, upright, honest, equitable, conscientious, virtuous **OPPOSITE:** unfair 6 = **fitting**, due, correct, deserved, appropriate, justified, decent, merited **OPPOSITE:** inappropriate

- USAGE NOTE
- The expression *just exactly* is
- considered to be poor style
- because, since both words
- mean the same thing, only
- one or the other is needed.
- Use *just - it's just what they
- want -* or *exactly - it's exactly
- what they want*, but not both
- together.

justice 1 = **fairness**, equity, integrity, honesty, decency, rightfulness, right **OPPOSITE:** injustice 2 = **justness**, fairness, legitimacy, right, integrity, honesty, legality, rightfulness

3 = **judge**, magistrate, beak
(*Brit. slang*), His, Her or Your
Honour
justification = **reason**,
grounds, defence, basis, excuse,
warrant, rationale, vindication
justify = **explain**, support,
warrant, defend, excuse,
uphold, vindicate, exonerate
juvenile NOUN 1 = **child**,
youth, minor, girl, boy,
teenager, infant, adolescent
OPPOSITE: adult
▷ ADJECTIVE 2 = **young**, junior,
adolescent, youthful, immature
OPPOSITE: adult 3 = **immature**,
childish, infantile, puerile,
young, youthful, inexperienced,
callow

Kk

kai (*N.Z. informal*) = **food**, grub
(*slang*), provisions, fare, tucker
(*Austral. & N.Z. informal*),
refreshment, foodstuffs
kak (*S. African taboo*) 1 = **faeces**,
excrement, manure, dung,
droppings, waste matter
2 = **rubbish**, nonsense, garbage
(*informal*), rot, drivel, tripe
(*informal*), bizzo (*Austral. slang*),
bull's wool (*Austral. & N.Z. slang*)
keen 1 = **eager**, intense,
enthusiastic, passionate,
ardent, avid, fervent,
impassioned **OPPOSITE:**
unenthusiastic 2 = **earnest**,
fierce, intense, vehement,
passionate, heightened, ardent,
fanatical 3 = **sharp**, incisive,
cutting, edged, razor-like
OPPOSITE: dull 4 = **perceptive**,
quick, sharp, acute, smart,
wise, clever, shrewd **OPPOSITE:**
obtuse 5 = **intense**, strong,
fierce, relentless, cut-throat
keep¹ VERB 1 *usually with* **from**
= **prevent**, restrain, hinder, keep
back 2 = **hold on to**, maintain,
retain, save, preserve, nurture,
cherish, conserve **OPPOSITE:**
lose 3 = **store**, put, place,

house, hold, deposit, stack, stow **4** = **carry**, stock, sell, supply, handle **5** = **support**, maintain, sustain, provide for, mind, fund, finance, feed **6** = **raise**, own, maintain, tend, farm, breed, look after, rear **7** = **manage**, run, administer, be in charge (of), direct, handle, supervise **8** = **delay**, detain, hinder, impede, obstruct, set back **OPPOSITE: release**
▷ NOUN **9** = **board**, food, maintenance, living, kai (*N.Z. informal*)
▷ PHRASES: **keep something up 1** = **continue**, make, maintain, carry on, persist in, persevere with **2** = **maintain**, sustain, perpetuate, retain, preserve, prolong ▶ **keep up** = **keep pace**

keep² = **tower**, castle

keeper = **curator**, guardian, steward, attendant, caretaker, preserver

keeping = **care**, charge, protection, possession, custody, guardianship, safekeeping
▷ PHRASES: **in keeping with** = **in agreement with**, in harmony with, in accord with, in compliance with, in conformity with, in balance with, in correspondence with, in proportion with

key NOUN **1** = **opener**, door key, latchkey **2** = **answer**
▷ ADJECTIVE **3** = **essential**, leading, major, main, important, necessary, vital, crucial **OPPOSITE: minor**

kia ora (*N.Z.*) = **hello**, hi (*informal*), greetings, gidday or g'day (*Austral. & N.Z.*), how do you do?, good morning, good evening, good afternoon

kick VERB **1** = **boot**, knock, punt **2** (*Informal*) = **give up**, break, stop, abandon, quit, cease, eschew, leave off
▷ NOUN **3** (*Informal*) = **thrill**, buzz (*slang*), tingle, high (*slang*)
▷ PHRASES: **kick off** (*Informal*) = **begin**, start, open, commence, initiate, get on the road ▶ **kick someone out** (*Informal*) = **dismiss**, remove, get rid of, expel, eject, evict, sack (*informal*)

kid¹ (*Informal*) = **child**, baby, teenager, youngster, infant, adolescent, juvenile, toddler, littlie (*Austral. informal*), ankle-biter (*Austral. slang*), tacker (*Austral. slang*)

kid² = **tease**, joke, trick, fool, pretend, wind up (*Brit. slang*), hoax, delude

kidnap = **abduct**, capture, seize, snatch (*slang*), hijack, hold to ransom

kill 1 = **slay**, murder, execute, slaughter, destroy, massacre, butcher, cut down **2** (*Informal*) = **destroy**, crush, scotch, stop, halt, wreck, shatter, suppress

killer = **murderer**, slayer, hit man (*slang*), butcher, gunman, assassin, terminator, executioner

k

killing NOUN 1 = **murder**, massacre, slaughter, dispatch, manslaughter, elimination, slaying, homicide

▷ ADJECTIVE 2 (*Informal*) = **tiring**, taxing, exhausting, punishing, fatiguing, gruelling, sapping, debilitating

▷ PHRASES: **make a killing** (*Informal*) = **profit**, gain, clean up (*informal*), be lucky, be successful, make a fortune, strike it rich (*informal*), make a bomb (*slang*)

kind¹ 1 = **class**, sort, type, variety, brand, category, genre 2 = **sort**, set, type, family, species, breed

● USAGE NOTE
● It is common in informal
● speech to combine singular
● and plural in sentences like
● *children enjoy those kind of*
● *stories*. However, this is not
● acceptable in careful writing,
● where the plural must be
● used consistently: *children*
● *enjoy those kinds of stories*.

kind² = **considerate**, kindly, concerned, friendly, generous, obliging, charitable, benign OPPOSITE: unkind

kindly ADJECTIVE
1 = **benevolent**, kind, caring, warm, helpful, pleasant, sympathetic, benign OPPOSITE: cruel

▷ ADVERB 2 = **benevolently**, politely, generously, thoughtfully, tenderly, lovingly, cordially, affectionately OPPOSITE: unkindly

kindness = **goodwill**, understanding, charity, humanity, compassion, generosity, philanthropy, benevolence OPPOSITE: malice

king = **ruler**, monarch, sovereign, leader, lord, Crown, emperor, head of state

kingdom = **country**, state, nation, territory, realm

kiss VERB 1 = **peck** (*informal*), osculate, neck (*informal*) 2 = **brush**, touch, shave, scrape, graze, glance off, stroke

▷ NOUN 3 = **peck** (*informal*), snog (*Brit. slang*), smacker (*slang*), French kiss, osculation

kit 1 = **equipment**, materials, tackle, tools, apparatus, paraphernalia 2 = **gear**, things, stuff, equipment, uniform

▷ PHRASES: **kit something** or **someone out** or **up** = **equip**, fit, supply, provide with, arm, stock, costume, furnish

knack = **skill**, art, ability, facility, talent, gift, capacity, trick OPPOSITE: ineptitude

kneel = **genuflect**, stoop

knickers = **underwear**, smalls, briefs, drawers, panties, bloomers

knife NOUN 1 = **blade**, carver, cutter

▷ VERB 2 = **cut**, wound, stab, slash, thrust, pierce, spear, jab

knit 1 = **join**, unite, link, tie, bond, combine, bind, weave

2 = **heal**, unite, join, link, bind, fasten, intertwine 3 = **furrow**, tighten, knot, wrinkle, crease, screw up, pucker, scrunch up

knob = **ball**, stud, knot, lump, bump, projection, hump, protrusion

knock VERB 1 = **bang**, strike, tap, rap, thump, pummel 2 = **hit**, strike, punch, belt (*informal*), smack, thump, cuff 3 (*Informal*) = **criticize**, condemn, put down, run down, abuse, slate (*informal*), censure, denigrate ▷ NOUN 4 = **knocking**, pounding, beating, tap, bang, banging, rap, thump 5 = **bang**, blow, impact, jar, collision, jolt, smash 6 = **blow**, hit, punch, crack, clip, slap, bash, smack 7 (*Informal*) = **setback**, check, defeat, blow, reverse, disappointment, hold-up, hitch ▷ PHRASES: **knock about or around** = **wander**, travel, roam, rove, range, drift, stray, ramble, go walkabout (*Austral.*) ▶ **knock about or around with someone** = **mix with**, associate with, mingle with, consort with, hobnob with, socialize with, accompany ▶ **knock off** (*Informal*) = **stop work**, get out, call it a day (*informal*), finish work, clock off, clock out ▶ **knock someone about or around** = **hit**, attack, beat, strike, abuse, injure, assault, batter ▶ **knock someone down**

= **run over**, hit, run down, knock over, mow down ▶ **knock something down** = **demolish**, destroy, flatten, tear down, level, fell, dismantle, bulldoze ▶ **knock something off** (*Slang*) = **steal**, take, nick (*slang, chiefly Brit.*), thieve, rob, pinch

knockout 1 = **killer blow**, coup de grâce (*French*), KO or K.O. (*slang*) 2 (*Informal*) = **success**, hit, winner, triumph, smash, sensation, smash hit **OPPOSITE:** failure

knot NOUN 1 = **connection**, tie, bond, joint, loop, ligature ▷ VERB 2 = **tie**, secure, bind, loop, tether

know 1 = **have knowledge of**, see, understand, recognize, perceive, be aware of, be conscious of 2 = **be acquainted with**, recognize, be familiar with, be friends with, be friendly with, have knowledge of, have dealings with, socialize with **OPPOSITE:** be unfamiliar with 3 *sometimes with* **about** *or* **of** = **be familiar with**, understand, comprehend, have knowledge of, be acquainted with, feel certain of, have dealings in, be versed in **OPPOSITE:** be ignorant of

know-how (*Informal*) = **expertise**, ability, skill, knowledge, facility, talent, command, capability

knowing = **meaningful**, significant, expressive,

enigmatic, suggestive

knowledge
1 = **understanding**, sense, judgment, perception, awareness, insight, grasp, appreciation 2 = **learning**, education, intelligence, instruction, wisdom, scholarship, enlightenment, erudition **OPPOSITE:** ignorance 3 = **acquaintance**, intimacy, familiarity **OPPOSITE:** unfamiliarity

knowledgeable 1 = **well-informed**, conversant, au fait (*French*), experienced, aware, familiar, in the know (*informal*), cognizant 2 = **intelligent**, learned, educated, scholarly, erudite

known = **famous**, well-known, celebrated, noted, acknowledged, recognized, avowed **OPPOSITE:** unknown

kopje or **koppie** (*S. African*) = **hill**, down (*archaic*), fell, mount, hilltop, knoll, hillock, brae (*Scot.*)

LI

label NOUN 1 = **tag**, ticket, tab, marker, sticker
▷ VERB 2 = **tag**, mark, stamp, ticket, tab

labour NOUN 1 = **workers**, employees, workforce, labourers, hands 2 = **work**, effort, employment, toil, industry 3 = **childbirth**, birth, delivery, parturition
▷ VERB 4 = **work**, toil, strive, work hard, sweat (*informal*), slave, endeavour, slog away (*informal*) **OPPOSITE:** rest
5 = **struggle**, work, strain, work hard, strive, grapple, toil, make an effort
6 = **overemphasize**, stress, elaborate, exaggerate, strain, dwell on, overdo, go on about
7 *usually with* **under** = **be disadvantaged by**, suffer from, be a victim of, be burdened by

Labour = **left-wing**, Democrat (*U.S.*)

laboured = **difficult**, forced, strained, heavy, awkward

labourer = **worker**, manual worker, hand, blue-collar worker, drudge, navvy (*Brit. informal*)

lace NOUN 1 = **netting**, net, filigree, meshwork, openwork 2 = **cord**, tie, string, lacing, shoelace, bootlace ▷ VERB 3 = **fasten**, tie, tie up, do up, secure, bind, thread 4 = **mix**, drug, doctor, add to, spike, contaminate, fortify, adulterate 5 = **intertwine**, interweave, entwine, twine, interlink

lack NOUN 1 = **shortage**, want, absence, deficiency, need, inadequacy, scarcity, dearth **OPPOSITE:** abundance ▷ VERB 2 = **miss**, want, need, require, not have, be without, be short of, be in need of **OPPOSITE:** have

lad = **boy**, kid (*informal*), guy (*informal*), youth, fellow, youngster, juvenile, nipper (*informal*)

laden = **loaded**, burdened, full, charged, weighed down, encumbered

lady 1 = **gentlewoman**, duchess, noble, dame, baroness, countess, aristocrat, viscountess 2 = **woman**, female, girl, damsel, charlie (*Austral. slang*), chook (*Austral. slang*), wahine (*N.Z.*)

lag = **hang back**, delay, trail, linger, loiter, straggle, dawdle, tarry

laid-back = **relaxed**, calm, casual, easy-going, unflappable (*informal*), unhurried, free and easy **OPPOSITE:** tense

lake = **pond**, pool, reservoir, loch (*Scot.*), lagoon, mere, lough (*Irish*), tarn

lame 1 = **disabled**, handicapped, crippled, limping, hobbling, game 2 = **unconvincing**, poor, pathetic, inadequate, thin, weak, feeble, unsatisfactory

lament VERB 1 = **bemoan**, grieve, mourn, weep over, complain about, regret, wail about, deplore ▷ NOUN 2 = **complaint**, moan, wailing, lamentation 3 = **dirge**, requiem, elegy, threnody

land NOUN 1 = **ground**, earth, dry land, terra firma 2 = **soil**, ground, earth, clay, dirt, sod, loam 3 = **countryside**, farmland 4 (*Law*) = **property**, grounds, estate, real estate, realty, acreage 5 = **country**, nation, region, state, district, territory, province, kingdom ▷ VERB 6 = **arrive**, dock, put down, moor, alight, touch down, disembark, come to rest 7 (*Informal*) = **gain**, get, win, secure, acquire ▷ PHRASES: **land up** = **end up**, turn up, wind up, finish up, fetch up (*informal*)
● RELATED WORD
● *adjective:* terrestrial

landlord 1 = **owner**, landowner, proprietor, freeholder, lessor, landholder 2 = **innkeeper**, host, hotelier

landmark 1 = **feature**,

spectacle, monument
2 = **milestone**, turning point, watershed, critical point

landscape = **scenery**, country, view, land, scene, prospect, countryside, outlook

landslide = **landslip**, avalanche, rockfall

lane = **road**, street, track, path, way, passage, trail, pathway

language 1 = **tongue**, dialect, vernacular, patois **2** = **speech**, communication, expression, speaking, talk, talking, discourse, parlance

languish 1 = **decline**, fade away, wither away, flag, weaken, wilt **OPPOSITE:** flourish **2** (*Literary*) = **waste away**, suffer, rot, be abandoned, be neglected **for OPPOSITE:** thrive **3** *often with* **for** = **pine**, long, desire, hunger, yearn, hanker

lap[1] = **circuit**, tour, leg, stretch, circle, orbit, loop

lap[2] **1** = **ripple**, wash, splash, swish, gurgle, slosh, purl, plash **2** = **drink**, sip, lick, swallow, gulp, sup
▷ **PHRASES: lap something up** = **relish**, like, enjoy, delight in, savour, revel in, wallow in, accept eagerly

lapse NOUN 1 = **decline**, fall, drop, deterioration
2 = **mistake**, failing, fault, failure, error, slip, negligence, omission **3** = **interval**, break, gap, pause, interruption, lull, breathing space, intermission
▷ **VERB 4** = **slip**, fall, decline, sink, drop, slide, deteriorate, degenerate **5** = **end**, stop, run out, expire, terminate

lapsed = **expired**, ended, finished, run out, invalid, out of date, discontinued

large ADJECTIVE 1 = **big**, great, huge, heavy, massive, vast, enormous, tall **OPPOSITE:** small **2** = **massive**, great, big, huge, vast, enormous, considerable, substantial **OPPOSITE:** small
▷ **PHRASES: at large 1** = **in general**, generally, chiefly, mainly, as a whole, in the main **2** = **free**, on the run, fugitive, at liberty, on the loose, unchained, unconfined ▸ **by and large** = **on the whole**, generally, mostly, in general, all things considered, predominantly, in the main, all in all

largely = **mainly**, generally, chiefly, mostly, principally, primarily, predominantly, by and large

large-scale = **wide-ranging**, global, sweeping, broad, wide, extensive, wholesale

lash[1] **VERB 1** = **pound**, beat, strike, hammer, drum, smack (*dialect*) **2** = **censure**, attack, blast, put down, criticize, slate (*informal, chiefly Brit.*), scold, tear into (*informal*) **3** = **whip**, beat, thrash, birch, flog, scourge
▷ **NOUN 4** = **blow**, hit, strike, stroke, stripe, swipe (*informal*)

lash[2] = **fasten**, tie, secure, bind,

strap, make fast, tether

last¹ ADJECTIVE 1 = **most recent**, latest, previous
2 = **hindmost**, final, at the end, remotest, furthest behind, most distant, rearmost **OPPOSITE:** foremost 3 = **final**, closing, concluding, ultimate **OPPOSITE:** first
▷ ADVERB 4 = **in** or **at the end**, after, behind, in the rear, bringing up the rear
▷ PHRASES: **the last word** 1 = **final decision**, final say, final statement, conclusive comment 2 = **leading**, finest, cream, supreme, elite, foremost, pre-eminent, unsurpassed

● USAGE NOTE
● Since *last* can mean either
● *after all others* or *most recent*, it
● is better to avoid using this
● word where ambiguity might
● arise, as in *her last novel*. Final
● or *latest* should be used as
● alternatives in such contexts
● to avoid any possible
● confusion.

last² = **continue**, remain, survive, carry on, endure, persist, keep on, abide **OPPOSITE:** end

lasting = **continuing**, long-term, permanent, enduring, remaining, abiding, long-standing, perennial **OPPOSITE:** passing

latch NOUN 1 = **fastening**, catch, bar, lock, hook, bolt

▷ VERB 2 = **fasten**, bar, secure, bolt, make fast

late ADJECTIVE 1 = **overdue**, delayed, last-minute, belated, tardy, behind time, behindhand **OPPOSITE:** early 2 = **dead**, deceased, departed, passed on, former, defunct **OPPOSITE:** alive 3 = **recent**, new, advanced, fresh **OPPOSITE:** old
▷ ADVERB 4 = **behind time**, belatedly, tardily, behindhand, dilatorily **OPPOSITE:** early

lately = **recently**, of late, just now, in recent times, not long ago, latterly

later ADVERB = **afterwards**, after, eventually, in time, subsequently, later on, thereafter, in a while
▷ ADJECTIVE = **subsequent**, next, following, ensuing **OPPOSITE:** earlier

latest = **up-to-date**, current, fresh, newest, modern, most recent, up-to-the-minute

latitude = **scope**, liberty, freedom, play, space, licence, leeway, laxity

latter PRONOUN = **second**, last, last-mentioned, second-mentioned
▷ ADJECTIVE = **last**, ending, closing, final, concluding **OPPOSITE:** earlier

● USAGE NOTE
● *The latter* should only be used
● to specify the second of two
● items, for example in *if I had*
● *to choose between the hovercraft*

- *and the ferry, I would opt for the*
- *latter.* Where there are three
- or more items, the last can be
- referred to as the *last-named,*
- but not the *latter.*

laugh VERB 1 = **chuckle**, giggle, snigger, cackle, chortle, guffaw, titter, be in stitches ▷ NOUN 2 = **chortle**, giggle, chuckle, snigger, guffaw, titter 3 (*Informal*) = **joke**, scream (*informal*), hoot (*informal*), lark (*informal*), prank 4 (*Informal*) = **clown**, character (*informal*), scream (*informal*), entertainer, card (*informal*), joker, hoot (*informal*) ▷ PHRASES: **laugh something off** = **disregard**, ignore, dismiss, overlook, shrug off, minimize, brush aside, make light of

laughter = **amusement**, entertainment, humour, glee, fun, mirth, hilarity, merriment

launch 1 = **propel**, fire, dispatch, discharge, project, send off, set in motion, send into orbit 2 = **begin**, start, open, initiate, introduce, found, set up, originate ▷ PHRASES: **launch into something** = **start enthusiastically**, begin, initiate, embark on, instigate, inaugurate, embark upon

laurel PHRASES: **rest on your laurels** = **sit back**, relax, take it easy, relax your efforts

lavatory = **toilet**, bathroom, loo (*Brit. informal*), privy, cloakroom (*Brit.*), urinal, latrine,

washroom, dunny (*Austral. & N.Z. old-fashioned informal*), bogger (*Austral. slang*), brasco (*Austral. slang*)

lavish ADJECTIVE 1 = **grand**, magnificent, splendid, abundant, copious, profuse OPPOSITE: stingy 2 = **extravagant**, wild, excessive, exaggerated, wasteful, prodigal, unrestrained, immoderate OPPOSITE: thrifty 3 = **generous**, free, liberal, bountiful, open-handed, unstinting, munificent OPPOSITE: stingy ▷ VERB 4 = **shower**, pour, heap, deluge, dissipate OPPOSITE: stint

law 1 = **constitution**, code, legislation, charter 2 = **statute**, act, bill, rule, order, command, regulation, resolution 3 = **principle**, code, canon, precept, axiom, kaupapa (*N.Z.*) 4 = **the legal profession**, the bar, barristers

lawsuit = **case**, action, trial, suit, proceedings, dispute, prosecution, legal action

lawyer = **legal adviser**, attorney, solicitor, counsel, advocate, barrister, counsellor, legal representative

lay[1] VERB 1 = **place**, put, set, spread, plant, leave, deposit, put down 2 = **devise**, plan, design, prepare, work out, plot, hatch, contrive 3 = **produce**, bear, deposit 4 = **arrange**, prepare, make, organize, position, set out, devise, put together 5 = **attribute**, assign, allocate, allot, ascribe, impute 6 = **put forward**, offer, present, advance, lodge, submit, bring forward 7 = **bet**, stake, venture, gamble, chance, risk, hazard, wager

▷ **PHRASES: lay someone off** = **dismiss**, fire (*informal*), release, sack (*informal*), pay off, discharge, let go, make redundant ▶ **lay someone out** (*Informal*) = **knock out**, fell, floor, knock unconscious, knock for six ▶ **lay something out** 1 = **arrange**, order, design, display, exhibit, put out, spread out 2 (*Informal*) = **spend**, pay, invest, fork out (*slang*), expend, shell out (*informal*), disburse

● **USAGE NOTE**
● In standard English, the verb
● *to lay* (meaning 'to put
● something somewhere')
● always needs an object, for
● example *the Queen laid a*
● *wreath*. By contrast, the verb
● *to lie* is always used without
● an object, for example *he was*
● *just lying there*.

lay² 1 = **nonclerical**, secular, non-ordained

2 = **nonspecialist**, amateur, unqualified, untrained, inexpert, nonprofessional

layer = **tier**, level, seam, stratum

layout = **arrangement**, design, outline, format, plan, formation

lazy 1 = **idle**, inactive, indolent, slack, negligent, inert, workshy, slothful **OPPOSITE:** industrious

2 = **lethargic**, languorous, slow-moving, languid, sleepy, sluggish, drowsy, somnolent **OPPOSITE:** quick

leach = **extract**, strain, drain, filter, seep, percolate

lead VERB 1 = **go in front (of)**, head, be in front, be at the head (of), walk in front (of)

2 = **guide**, conduct, steer, escort, precede, usher, pilot, show the way 3 = **connect to**, link, open onto 4 = **be ahead (of)**, be first, exceed, be winning, excel, surpass, come first, transcend 5 = **command**, rule, govern, preside over, head, control, manage, direct

6 = **live**, have, spend, experience, pass, undergo 7 = **result in**, cause, produce, contribute, generate, bring about, bring on, give rise to 8 = **cause**, prompt, persuade, move, draw, influence, motivate, prevail

▷ NOUN 9 = **first place**, winning position, primary position, vanguard

10 = **advantage**, start, edge, margin, winning margin 11 = **example**, direction, leadership, guidance, model, pattern 12 = **clue**, suggestion, hint, indication, pointer, tip-off

13 = **leading role**, principal, protagonist, title role, principal

part **14** = **leash**, line, cord, rein, tether
▷ ADJECTIVE **15** = **main**, prime, top, leading, first, head, chief, premier
▷ PHRASES: **lead someone on** = **entice**, tempt, lure, mislead, draw on, seduce, deceive, beguile ▶ **lead up to something** = **introduce**, prepare for, pave the way for

leader = **principal**, president, head, chief, boss (*informal*), director, manager, chairman, baas (*S. African*) OPPOSITE: follower

leadership 1 = **authority**, control, influence, command, premiership, captaincy, governance, headship **2** = **guidance**, government, authority, management, direction, supervision, domination, superintendency

leading = **principal**, top, major, main, first, highest, greatest, chief OPPOSITE: minor

leaf 1 = **frond**, blade, cotyledon **2** = **page**, sheet, folio
▷ PHRASES: **leaf through something** (with *book*, *magazine* etc. as object) = **skim**, glance, scan, browse, look through, dip into, flick through, flip through

leaflet = **booklet**, notice, brochure, circular, flyer, tract, pamphlet, handout

leafy = **green**, shaded, shady, verdant

league 1 = **association**, union, alliance, coalition, group, corporation, partnership, federation **2** (*Informal*) = **class**, group, level, category

leak VERB **1** = **escape**, pass, spill, release, drip, trickle, ooze, seep **2** = **disclose**, tell, reveal, pass on, give away, make public, divulge, let slip
▷ NOUN **3** = **leakage**, discharge, drip, seepage, percolation **4** = **hole**, opening, crack, puncture, aperture, chink, crevice, fissure **5** = **disclosure**, exposé, exposure, admission, revelation, uncovering, betrayal, unearthing

lean[1] = **bend**, tip, slope, incline, tilt, heel, slant **2** = **rest**, prop, be supported, recline, repose **3** = **tend**, prefer, favour, incline, be prone to, be disposed to
▷ PHRASES: **lean on someone** = **depend on**, trust, rely on, cling to, count on, have faith in

lean[2] = **thin**, slim, slender, skinny, angular, trim, spare, gaunt OPPOSITE: fat

leaning = **tendency**, bias, inclination, bent, disposition, penchant, propensity, predilection

leap VERB **1** = **jump**, spring, bound, bounce, hop, skip
▷ NOUN **2** = **jump**, spring, bound, vault **3** = **rise**, change, increase, soaring, surge, escalation, upsurge, upswing

▷ PHRASES: **leap at something** = **accept eagerly**, seize on, jump at

learn 1 = **master**, grasp, pick up, take in, familiarize yourself with 2 = **discover**, hear, understand, find out about, become aware, discern, ascertain, come to know 3 = **memorize**, commit to memory, learn by heart, learn by rote, learn parrot-fashion, get off pat

learned = **scholarly**, academic, intellectual, versed, well-informed, erudite, highbrow, well-read OPPOSITE: uneducated

learner = **student**, novice, beginner, apprentice, neophyte, tyro OPPOSITE: expert

learning = **knowledge**, study, education, scholarship, enlightenment

lease = **hire**, rent, let, loan, charter, rent out, hire out

least = **smallest**, meanest, fewest, lowest, tiniest, minimum, slightest, minimal

leave VERB 1 = **depart from**, withdraw from, go from, escape from, quit, flee, exit, pull out of OPPOSITE: arrive 2 = **quit**, give up, get out of, resign from, drop out of 3 = **give up**, abandon, dump (informal), drop, surrender, ditch (informal), chuck (informal), discard OPPOSITE: stay with 4 = **entrust**, commit, delegate, refer, hand over, assign, consign, allot 5 = **bequeath**, will, transfer, endow, confer, hand down 6 = **forget**, leave behind, mislay 7 = **cause**, produce, result in, generate, deposit

▷ NOUN 8 = **holiday**, break, vacation, time off, sabbatical, leave of absence, furlough 9 = **permission**, freedom, sanction, liberty, concession, consent, allowance, warrant OPPOSITE: refusal 10 = **departure**, parting, withdrawal, goodbye, farewell, retirement, leave-taking, adieu OPPOSITE: arrival

▷ PHRASES: **leave something or someone out** = **omit**, exclude, miss out, forget, reject, ignore, overlook, neglect

lecture NOUN 1 = **talk**, address, speech, lesson, instruction, presentation, discourse, sermon 2 = **telling-off** (informal), rebuke, reprimand, talking-to (informal), scolding, dressing-down (informal), reproof

▷ VERB 3 = **talk**, speak, teach, address, discourse, spout, expound, hold forth 4 = **tell off** (informal), berate, scold, reprimand, censure, castigate, admonish, reprove

lees = **sediment**, grounds, deposit, dregs

left 1 = **left-hand**, port, larboard (Nautical) 2 = (of politics)

= **socialist**, radical, left-wing, leftist

left-wing = **socialist**, communist, red (*informal*), radical, revolutionary, militant, Bolshevik, Leninist

leg 1 = **limb**, member, shank, lower limb, pin (*informal*), stump (*informal*) **2** = **support**, prop, brace, upright **3** = **stage**, part, section, stretch, lap, segment, portion
▷ **PHRASES: pull someone's leg** (*Informal*) = **tease**, trick, fool, kid (*informal*), wind up (*Brit. slang*), hoax, make fun of, lead up the garden path

legacy = **bequest**, inheritance, gift, estate, heirloom

legal 1 = **judicial**, judiciary, forensic, juridical, jurisdictive **2** = **lawful**, allowed, sanctioned, constitutional, valid, legitimate, authorized, permissible

legend 1 = **myth**, story, tale, fiction, saga, fable, folk tale, folk story **2** = **celebrity**, star, phenomenon, genius, prodigy, luminary, megastar (*informal*) **3** = **inscription**, title, caption, device, motto, rubric

legendary 1 = **famous**, celebrated, well-known, acclaimed, renowned, famed, immortal, illustrious **OPPOSITE:** unknown **2** = **mythical**, fabled, traditional, romantic, fabulous, fictitious, storybook, apocryphal **OPPOSITE:** factual

legion 1 = **army**, company, force, division, troop, brigade **2** = **multitude**, host, mass, drove, number, horde, myriad, throng

legislation 1 = **law**, act, ruling, rule, bill, measure, regulation, charter **2** = **lawmaking**, regulation, prescription, enactment

legislative = **law-making**, judicial, law-giving

legislator = **lawmaker**, lawgiver

legislature = **parliament**, congress, senate, assembly, chamber

legitimate ADJECTIVE
1 = **lawful**, legal, genuine, authentic, authorized, rightful, kosher (*informal*), dinkum (*Austral. & N.Z. informal*), licit **OPPOSITE:** unlawful
2 = **reasonable**, correct, sensible, valid, warranted, logical, justifiable, well-founded, admissible **OPPOSITE:** unreasonable
▷ VERB **3** = **legitimize**, allow, permit, sanction, authorize, legalize, pronounce lawful

leisure = **spare**, free, rest, ease, relaxation, recreation **OPPOSITE:** work

lekker (*S. African slang*) = **delicious**, tasty, luscious, palatable, delectable, mouthwatering, scrumptious (*informal*), appetizing, yummo (*Austral. slang*)

lemon

● **RELATED WORDS**
● *adjectives*: citric, citrous
▷ *See panel* **SHADES OF YELLOW**

lend 1 = **loan**, advance, sub (*Brit. informal*) 2 = **give**, provide, add, supply, grant, confer, bestow, impart
▷ **PHRASES: lend itself to something = be appropriate for**, suit, be suitable for, be appropriate to, be serviceable for

length 1 = **distance**, reach, measure, extent, longitude 2 = **duration**, term, period, space, stretch, span, expanse 3 = **piece**, measure, section, segment, portion
▷ **PHRASES: at length** 1 = **at last**, finally, eventually, in time, in the end, at long last 2 = **for a long time**, completely, fully, thoroughly, for hours, in detail, for ages, in depth

lengthen 1 = **extend**, continue, increase, stretch, expand, elongate **OPPOSITE:** shorten 2 = **protract**, extend, prolong, draw out, spin out, make longer

lengthy 1 = **protracted**, long, prolonged, tedious, drawn-out, interminable, long-winded, long-drawn-out 2 = **very long**, rambling, interminable, long-winded, wordy, discursive, extended **OPPOSITE:** brief

lesbian = **homosexual**, gay, les (*slang*), sapphic, lesbo (*slang*)

less DETERMINER 1 = **smaller**, shorter, not so much
▷ **PREPOSITION** 2 = **minus**, without, lacking, excepting, subtracting
● **USAGE NOTE**
● *Less* should not be confused
● with *fewer*. *Less* refers strictly
● only to quantity and not to
● number: *there is less water*
● *than before*. *Fewer* means
● smaller in number: *there are*
● *fewer people than before*.

lessen 1 = **reduce**, lower, diminish, decrease, ease, narrow, minimize **OPPOSITE:** increase 2 = **grow less**, diminish, decrease, contract, ease, shrink

lesser = **lower**, secondary, subsidiary, inferior, less important **OPPOSITE:** greater

lesson 1 = **class**, schooling, period, teaching, coaching, session, instruction, lecture 2 = **example**, warning, message, moral, deterrent 3 = **Bible reading**, reading, text, Bible passage, Scripture passage

let VERB 1 = **allow**, permit, authorize, give the go-ahead, give permission 2 = **lease**, hire, rent, rent out, hire out, sublease
▷ **PHRASES: let on** (*Informal*) 3 = **reveal**, disclose, say, tell, admit, give away, divulge, let slip ▶ **let someone down = disappoint**, fail, abandon, desert, disillusion, fall short,

leave stranded, leave in the lurch ▸ **let someone off** = **excuse**, release, discharge, pardon, spare, forgive, exempt, exonerate ▸ **let something down** = **deflate**, empty, exhaust, flatten, puncture ▸ **let something off** 1 = **fire**, explode, set off, discharge, detonate 2 = **emit**, release, leak, exude, give off ▸ **let something** or **someone in** = **admit**, include, receive, welcome, greet, take in, incorporate, give access to ▸ **let something out** 1 = **release**, discharge 2 = **emit**, make, produce, give vent to ▸ **let up** = **stop**, diminish, decrease, subside, relax, ease (up), moderate, lessen

lethal = **deadly**, terminal, fatal, dangerous, devastating, destructive, mortal, murderous **OPPOSITE:** harmless

letter 1 = **message**, line, note, communication, dispatch, missive, epistle 2 = **character**, mark, sign, symbol

level NOUN 1 = **position**, standard, degree, grade, standing, stage, rank, status ▷ ADJECTIVE 2 = **equal**, balanced, at the same height 3 = **horizontal**, even, flat, smooth, uniform **OPPOSITE:** slanted 4 = **even**, tied, equal, drawn, neck and neck, all square, level pegging ▷ VERB 5 = **equalize**, balance,

even up 6 = **destroy**, devastate, demolish, flatten, knock down, pull down, tear down, bulldoze **OPPOSITE:** build 7 = **direct**, point, turn, train, aim, focus 8 = **flatten**, plane, smooth, even off or out ▷ PHRASES: on the level (*Informal*) = **honest**, genuine, straight, fair, square, dinkum (*Austral. & N.Z. informal*), above board

lever NOUN 1 = **handle**, bar ▷ VERB 2 = **prise**, force

leverage 1 = **influence**, authority, pull (*informal*), weight, clout (*informal*) 2 = **force**, hold, pull, strength, grip, grasp

levy NOUN 1 = **tax**, fee, toll, tariff, duty, excise, exaction ▷ VERB 2 = **impose**, charge, collect, demand, exact

liability 1 = **disadvantage**, burden, drawback, inconvenience, handicap, nuisance, hindrance, millstone 2 = **responsibility**, accountability, culpability, answerability

liable 1 = **likely**, tending, inclined, disposed, prone, apt 2 = **vulnerable**, subject, exposed, prone, susceptible, open, at risk of 3 = **responsible**, accountable, answerable, obligated

● USAGE NOTE
● In the past, it was considered
● incorrect to use *liable* to

- mean 'probable' or 'likely', as
- in it's *liable to happen soon*.
- However, this usage is now
- generally considered
- acceptable.

liaison 1 = **contact**,
communication, connection,
interchange 2 = **intermediary**,
contact, hook-up 3 = **affair**,
romance, intrigue, fling, love
affair, amour, entanglement

liar = **falsifier**, perjurer, fibber,
fabricator

libel NOUN 1 = **defamation**,
misrepresentation, denigration,
smear, calumny, aspersion
▷ VERB 2 = **defame**, smear,
slur, blacken, malign, denigrate,
revile, vilify

liberal 1 = **tolerant**, open-
minded, permissive, indulgent,
easy-going, broad-minded
OPPOSITE: intolerant
2 = **progressive**, radical,
reformist, libertarian, forward-
looking, free-thinking
OPPOSITE: conservative
3 = **abundant**, generous,
handsome, lavish, ample, rich,
plentiful, copious **OPPOSITE:**
limited 4 = **generous**, kind,
charitable, extravagant, open-
hearted, bountiful,
magnanimous, open-handed
OPPOSITE: stingy

liberate = **free**, release, rescue,
save, deliver, let out, set free, let
loose **OPPOSITE:** imprison

liberty = **independence**,
sovereignty, liberation,

autonomy, immunity, self-
determination, emancipation,
self-government **OPPOSITE:**
restraint
▷ PHRASES: **at liberty** 1 = **free**,
escaped, unlimited, at large,
not confined, untied, on the
loose, unchained 2 = **able**, free,
allowed, permitted, entitled,
authorized ▶ **take liberties** or a
liberty = **not show enough
respect**, show disrespect, act
presumptuously, behave too
familiarly, behave impertinently

licence NOUN 1 = **certificate**,
document, permit, charter,
warrant 2 = **permission**, the
right, authority, leave, sanction,
liberty, immunity, entitlement
OPPOSITE: denial 3 = **freedom**,
creativity, latitude,
independence, liberty,
deviation, leeway, free rein
OPPOSITE: restraint 4 = **laxity**,
excess, indulgence,
irresponsibility, licentiousness,
immoderation **OPPOSITE:**
moderation
▷ PHRASES: **under licence**
= **with permission**, under a
charter, under warrant, under a
permit, with authorization,
under a patent

license = **permit**, sanction,
allow, warrant, authorize,
empower, certify, accredit
OPPOSITE: forbid

lick VERB 1 = **taste**, lap, tongue
2 (*Informal*) = **beat**, defeat,
overcome, rout, outstrip,

outdo, trounce, vanquish 3 (*of flames*) = **flicker**, touch, flick, dart, ripple, play over
▷ NOUN 4 = **dab**, bit, touch, stroke 5 (*Informal*) = **pace**, rate, speed, clip (*informal*)

lie[1] NOUN 1 = **falsehood**, deceit, fabrication, fib, fiction, invention, deception, untruth
▷ VERB 2 = **fib**, fabricate, falsify, prevaricate, not tell the truth, equivocate, dissimulate, tell untruths
▷ PHRASES: **give the lie to something** = **disprove**, expose, discredit, contradict, refute, negate, invalidate, rebut

lie[2] 1 = **recline**, rest, lounge, sprawl, stretch out, loll, repose 2 = **be placed**, be, rest, exist, be situated 3 = **be situated**, sit, be located, be positioned 4 = **be buried**, remain, rest, be, be entombed

life 1 = **being**, existence, vitality, sentience 2 = **existence**, being, lifetime, time, days, span 3 = **way of life**, situation, conduct, behaviour, life style 4 = **liveliness**, energy, spirit, vitality, animation, vigour, verve, zest 5 = **biography**, story, history, profile, confessions, autobiography, memoirs, life story

lifelong = **long-lasting**, enduring, lasting, persistent, long-standing, perennial

lifetime = **existence**, time, day(s), span

lift VERB 1 = **raise**, pick up, hoist, draw up, elevate, uplift, heave up, upraise OPPOSITE: lower 2 = **revoke**, end, remove, withdraw, stop, cancel, terminate, rescind OPPOSITE: impose 3 = **disappear**, clear, vanish, disperse, dissipate, rise, be dispelled
▷ NOUN 4 = **boost**, encouragement, stimulus, pick-me-up, fillip, shot in the arm (*informal*), gee-up OPPOSITE: blow 5 = **elevator** (*chiefly U.S.*), hoist, paternoster 6 = **ride**, run, drive, hitch (*informal*)
▷ PHRASES: **lift off** = **take off**, be launched, blast off, take to the air

light[1] NOUN 1 = **brightness**, illumination, luminosity, shining, glow, glare, gleam, brilliance OPPOSITE: dark 2 = **lamp**, torch, candle, flare, beacon, lantern, taper 3 = **match**, spark, flame, lighter 4 = **aspect**, context, angle, point of view, interpretation, viewpoint, slant, standpoint
▷ ADJECTIVE 5 = **bright**, brilliant, shining, illuminated, luminous, well-lit, lustrous, well-illuminated OPPOSITE: dark 6 = **pale**, fair, faded, blonde, blond, bleached, pastel, light-coloured OPPOSITE: dark
▷ VERB 7 = **illuminate**, light up, brighten OPPOSITE: darken 8 = **ignite**, inflame, kindle, touch off, set alight OPPOSITE:

extinguish

▷ PHRASES: **light up 1** = **cheer**, shine, blaze, sparkle, animate, brighten, lighten, irradiate **2** = **shine**, flash, beam, blaze, sparkle, flare, glare, gleam

light² ADJECTIVE

1 = **insubstantial**, thin, slight, portable, buoyant, airy, flimsy, underweight **OPPOSITE:** heavy **2** = **weak**, soft, gentle, moderate, slight, mild, faint, indistinct **OPPOSITE:** strong **3** = **digestible**, modest, frugal **OPPOSITE:** substantial **4** = **insignificant**, small, slight, petty, trivial, trifling, inconsequential, inconsiderable **OPPOSITE:** serious **5** = **light-hearted**, funny, entertaining, amusing, witty, humorous, frivolous, unserious **OPPOSITE:** serious **6** = **nimble**, graceful, deft, agile, sprightly, lithe, limber, lissom **OPPOSITE:** clumsy

▷ PHRASES: **light on** or **upon something 1** = **settle**, land, perch, alight **2** = **come across**, find, discover, encounter, stumble on, hit upon, happen upon

lighten¹ = **brighten**, illuminate, light up, irradiate, become light

lighten² **1** = **ease**, relieve, alleviate, allay, reduce, lessen, mitigate, assuage **OPPOSITE:** intensify **2** = **cheer**, lift, revive, brighten, perk up, buoy up **OPPOSITE:** depress

lightly 1 = **moderately**, thinly, slightly, sparsely, sparingly **OPPOSITE:** heavily **2** = **gently**, softly, slightly, faintly, delicately **OPPOSITE:** forcefully **3** = **carelessly**, breezily, thoughtlessly, flippantly, frivolously, heedlessly **OPPOSITE:** seriously **4** = **easily**, simply, readily, effortlessly, unthinkingly, without thought, flippantly, heedlessly **OPPOSITE:** with difficulty

lightweight 1 = **thin**, fine, delicate, sheer, flimsy, gossamer, diaphanous, filmy **2** = **unimportant**, shallow, trivial, insignificant, slight, petty, worthless, trifling **OPPOSITE:** significant

like¹ = **similar to**, same as, equivalent to, parallel to, identical to, alike, corresponding to, comparable to **OPPOSITE:** different

● USAGE NOTE
● The use of *like* to mean 'such
● as' was in the past considered
● undesirable in formal writing,
● but has now become
● acceptable, for example in *I*
● *enjoy team sports like football*
● *and rugby.* However, the
● common use of *look like* and
● *seem like* to mean 'look or
● seem as if' is thought by
● many people to be incorrect
● or nonstandard. You might
● say *it looks as if* (or *as though*)
● *he's coming*, but it is still wise

● to avoid it *looks like he's*
● *coming*, particularly in formal
● or written contexts.

like² 1 = **enjoy**, love, delight in, go for, relish, savour, revel in, be fond of **OPPOSITE:** dislike 2 = **admire**, approve of, appreciate, prize, take to, esteem, cherish, hold dear **OPPOSITE:** dislike 3 = **wish**, want, choose, prefer, desire, fancy, care, feel inclined

likelihood = **probability**, chance, possibility, prospect

likely 1 = **inclined**, disposed, prone, liable, tending, apt 2 = **probable**, expected, anticipated, odds-on, on the cards, to be expected 3 = **plausible**, possible, reasonable, credible, feasible, believable

liken = **compare**, match, relate, parallel, equate, set beside

likewise = **similarly**, the same, in the same way, in similar fashion, in like manner

liking = **fondness**, love, taste, weakness, preference, affection, inclination, penchant **OPPOSITE:** dislike

limb 1 = **part**, member, arm, leg, wing, extremity, appendage 2 = **branch**, spur, projection, offshoot, bough

limelight = **publicity**, recognition, fame, the spotlight, attention, prominence, stardom, public eye

limit NOUN 1 = **end**, ultimate, deadline, breaking point, extremity 2 = **boundary**, edge, border, frontier, perimeter ▷ VERB 3 = **restrict**, control, check, bound, confine, curb, restrain, ration

limitation 1 = **restriction**, control, check, curb, restraint, constraint 2 = **weakness**, failing, qualification, reservation, defect, flaw, shortcoming, imperfection

limited = **restricted**, controlled, checked, bounded, confined, curbed, constrained, finite **OPPOSITE:** unlimited

limp¹ VERB 1 = **hobble**, stagger, stumble, shuffle, hop, falter, shamble, totter ▷ NOUN 2 = **lameness**, hobble

limp² = **floppy**, soft, slack, drooping, flabby, pliable, flaccid **OPPOSITE:** stiff

line NOUN 1 = **stroke**, mark, score, band, scratch, slash, streak, stripe 2 = **wrinkle**, mark, crease, furrow, crow's foot 3 = **row**, queue, rank, file, column, convoy, procession 4 = **string**, cable, wire, rope, thread, cord 5 = **trajectory**, way, course, track, channel, direction, route, path 6 = **boundary**, limit, edge, border, frontier, partition, borderline 7 = **occupation**, work, calling, business, job, area, trade, field ▷ VERB 8 = **border**, edge, bound, fringe **9** = **mark**, crease, furrow, rule, score

▷ **PHRASES: in line for** = **due for**, shortlisted for, in the running for

lined 1 = **wrinkled**, worn, furrowed, wizened **2** = **ruled**, feint

line-up = **arrangement**, team, row, selection, array

linger = **stay**, remain, stop, wait, delay, hang around, idle, dally

link NOUN **1** = **connection**, relationship, association, tie-up, affinity **2** = **relationship**, association, bond, connection, attachment, affinity **3** = **component**, part, piece, element, constituent

▷ VERB **4** = **associate**, relate, identify, connect, bracket **5** = **connect**, join, unite, couple, tie, bind, attach, fasten

OPPOSITE: separate

lip 1 = **edge**, rim, brim, margin, brink **2** (*Slang*) = **impudence**, insolence, impertinence, cheek (*informal*), effrontery, backchat (*informal*), brass neck (*informal*)

liquid NOUN **1** = **fluid**, solution, juice, sap

▷ ADJECTIVE **2** = **fluid**, running, flowing, melted, watery, molten, runny, aqueous **3** (*of assets*) = **convertible**, disposable, negotiable, realizable

liquor 1 = **alcohol**, drink, spirits, booze (*informal*), hard

stuff (*informal*), strong drink **2** = **juice**, stock, liquid, extract, broth

list¹ NOUN **1** = **inventory**, record, series, roll, index, register, catalogue, directory

▷ VERB **2** = **itemize**, record, enter, register, catalogue, enumerate, note down, tabulate

list² VERB **1** = **lean**, tip, incline, tilt, heel over, careen

▷ NOUN **2** = **tilt**, leaning, slant, cant

listen 1 = **hear**, attend, pay attention, lend an ear, prick up your ears **2** = **pay attention**, observe, obey, mind, heed, take notice, take note of, take heed of

literacy = **education**, learning, knowledge

literal 1 = **exact**, close, strict, accurate, faithful, verbatim, word for word **2** = **actual**, real, true, simple, plain, genuine, bona fide, unvarnished

literally = **exactly**, really, closely, actually, truly, precisely, strictly, faithfully

literary = **well-read**, learned, formal, intellectual, scholarly, erudite, bookish

literate = **educated**, informed, knowledgeable

literature = **writings**, letters, compositions, lore, creative writing

▷ *See panel* **SHAKESPEARE**

litigation = **lawsuit**, case,

litter NOUN 1 = **rubbish**, refuse, waste, junk, debris, garbage (*chiefly U.S.*), trash, muck 2 = **brood**, young, offspring, progeny
▷ VERB 3 = **clutter**, mess up, clutter up, be scattered about, disorder, disarrange, derange 4 = **scatter**, spread, shower, strew

little ADJECTIVE 1 = **small**, minute, short, tiny, wee, compact, miniature, diminutive **OPPOSITE:** big 2 = **young**, small, junior, infant, immature, undeveloped, babyish
▷ ADVERB 3 = **hardly**, barely, scarcely **OPPOSITE:** much 4 = **rarely**, seldom, scarcely, not often, infrequently, hardly ever **OPPOSITE:** always
▷ NOUN 5 = **bit**, touch, spot, trace, hint, particle, fragment, speck **OPPOSITE:** lot
▷ PHRASES: **a little** = **to a small extent**, slightly, to some extent, to a certain extent, to a small degree

live[1] 1 = **dwell**, board, settle, lodge, occupy, abide, inhabit, reside 2 = **exist**, last, prevail, be, have being, breathe, persist, be alive 3 = **survive**, get along, make a living, make ends meet, subsist, eke out a living, support yourself, maintain yourself 4 = **thrive**, flourish, prosper, have fun, enjoy yourself, live life to the full

live[2] 1 = **living**, alive, breathing, animate 2 = **active**, unexploded 3 = **topical**, important, pressing, current, hot, burning, controversial, prevalent

livelihood = **occupation**, work, employment, living, job, bread and butter (*informal*)

lively 1 = **animated**, spirited, quick, keen, active, alert, dynamic, vigorous **OPPOSITE:** dull 2 = **vivid**, strong, striking, bright, exciting, stimulating, bold, colourful **OPPOSITE:** dull 3 = **enthusiastic**, strong, keen, stimulating, eager, formidable, vigorous, animated

living NOUN 1 = **lifestyle**, ways, situation, conduct, behaviour, customs, lifestyle, way of life
▷ ADJECTIVE 2 = **alive**, existing, moving, active, breathing, animate **OPPOSITE:** dead 3 = **current**, present, active, contemporary, in use, extant **OPPOSITE:** obsolete

lizard ▷ *See panel* REPTILES

load VERB 1 = **fill**, stuff, pack, pile, stack, heap, cram, freight 2 = **make ready**, charge, prime
▷ NOUN 3 = **cargo**, delivery, haul, shipment, batch, freight, consignment 4 = **oppression**, charge, worry, trouble, weight, responsibility, burden, onus
▷ PHRASES: **load someone down** = **burden**, worry, oppress, weigh down, saddle with,

encumber, snow under

loaded 1 = **tricky**, charged, sensitive, delicate, manipulative, emotive, insidious, artful 2 = **biased**, weighted, rigged, distorted 3 (*Slang*) = **rich**, wealthy, affluent, well off, flush (*informal*), well-heeled (*informal*), well-to-do, moneyed

loaf¹ 1 = **lump**, block, cake, cube, slab 2 (*Slang*) = **head**, mind, sense, common sense, nous (*Brit. slang*), gumption (*Brit. informal*)

loaf² = **idle**, hang around, take it easy, lie around, loiter, laze, lounge around

loan NOUN 1 = **advance**, credit, overdraft
▷ VERB 2 = **lend**, advance, let out

loathe = **hate**, dislike, despise, detest, abhor, abominate

loathing = **hatred**, hate, disgust, aversion, revulsion, antipathy, repulsion, abhorrence

lobby VERB 1 = **campaign**, press, pressure, push, influence, promote, urge, persuade
▷ NOUN 2 = **pressure group**, group, camp, faction, lobbyists, interest group, special-interest group, ginger group
3 = **corridor**, passage, entrance, porch, hallway, foyer, entrance hall, vestibule

lobola (*S. African*) = **dowry**, portion, marriage settlement

local ADJECTIVE 1 = **community**, regional 2 = **confined**, limited, restricted
▷ NOUN 3 = **resident**, native, inhabitant

locate 1 = **find**, discover, detect, come across, track down, pinpoint, unearth, pin down 2 = **place**, put, set, position, seat, site, establish, settle

location = **place**, point, setting, position, situation, spot, venue, locale

lock¹ VERB 1 = **fasten**, close, secure, shut, bar, seal, bolt 2 = **unite**, join, link, engage, clench, entangle, interlock, entwine 3 = **embrace**, press, grasp, clutch, hug, enclose, clasp, encircle
▷ NOUN 4 = **fastening**, catch, bolt, clasp, padlock
▷ PHRASES: lock someone up = **imprison**, jail, confine, cage, detain, shut up, incarcerate, send down (*informal*), put behind bars

lock² = **strand**, curl, tuft, tress, ringlet

lodge NOUN 1 = **cabin**, shelter, cottage, hut, chalet, gatehouse 2 = **society**, group, club, section, wing, chapter, branch
▷ VERB 3 = **register**, enter, file, submit, put on record 4 = **stay**, room, board, reside 5 = **stick**, remain, implant, come to rest, imbed

lodging *often plural*
= **accommodation**, rooms, apartments, quarters, digs (*Brit. informal*), shelter, residence, abode

lofty 1 = **noble**, grand, distinguished, renowned, elevated, dignified, illustrious, exalted **OPPOSITE:** humble
2 = **high**, raised, towering, soaring, elevated **OPPOSITE:** low 3 = **haughty**, proud, arrogant, patronizing, condescending, disdainful, supercilious **OPPOSITE:** modest

log NOUN 1 = **stump**, block, branch, chunk, trunk
2 = **record**, account, register, journal, diary, logbook
▷ VERB 3 = **record**, enter, note, register, chart, put down, set down

logic = **reason**, reasoning, sense, good sense

logical 1 = **rational**, clear, reasoned, sound, consistent, valid, coherent, well-organized **OPPOSITE:** illogical
2 = **reasonable**, sensible, natural, wise, plausible **OPPOSITE:** unlikely

lone = **solitary**, single, one, only, sole, unaccompanied

loneliness = **solitude**, isolation, desolation, seclusion

lonely 1 = **solitary**, alone, isolated, abandoned, lone, withdrawn, single, forsaken **OPPOSITE:** accompanied
2 = **desolate**, deserted, remote, isolated, out-of-the-way, secluded, uninhabited, godforsaken **OPPOSITE:** crowded

lonesome (*Chiefly U.S. & Canad.*)
= **lonely**, gloomy, dreary, desolate, forlorn, friendless, companionless

long[1] 1 = **elongated**, extended, stretched, expanded, extensive, lengthy, far-reaching, spread out **OPPOSITE:** short
2 = **prolonged**, sustained, lengthy, lingering, protracted, interminable, spun out, long-drawn-out **OPPOSITE:** brief

long[2] = **desire**, want, wish, burn, pine, lust, crave, yearn

longing = **desire**, hope, wish, burning, urge, ambition, hunger, yen (*informal*)
OPPOSITE: indifference

long-standing = **established**, fixed, enduring, abiding, long-lasting, long-established, time-honoured

look VERB 1 = **see**, view, consider, watch, eye, study, survey, examine 2 = **search**, seek, hunt, forage, fossick (*Austral. & N.Z.*) 3 = **consider**, contemplate 4 = **face**, overlook 5 = **hope**, expect, await, anticipate, reckon on
6 = **seem**, appear, look like, strike you as
▷ NOUN 7 = **glimpse**, view, glance, observation, sight, examination, gaze, inspection
8 = **appearance**, bearing, air,

style, aspect, manner, expression, impression

▷ **PHRASES: look after something** *or* **someone = take care of**, mind, protect, tend, guard, nurse, care for, supervise ▶ **look down on** *or* **upon someone = disdain**, despise, scorn, sneer at, spurn, contemn (*formal*) ▶ **look forward to something = anticipate**, expect, look for, wait for, await, hope for, long for ▶ **look out for something = be careful of**, beware, watch out for, pay attention to, be wary of, keep an eye out for ▶ **look someone up = visit**, call on, drop in on (*informal*), look in on ▶ **look something up = research**, find, search for, hunt for, track down, seek out ▶ **look up = improve**, develop, advance, pick up, progress, get better, shape up (*informal*), perk up ▶ **look up to someone = respect**, honour, admire, esteem, revere, defer to, think highly of

lookout 1 = **watchman**, guard, sentry, sentinel 2 = **guard**, sentry, sentinel 2 = **guard**, vigil 3 = **watchtower**, post, observatory, observation post 4 (*Informal*) = **concern**, business, worry

loom = **appear**, emerge, hover, take shape, threaten, bulk, menace, come into view

loop NOUN 1 = **curve**, ring, circle, twist, curl, spiral, coil, twirl

▷ VERB 2 = **twist**, turn, roll, knot, curl, spiral, coil, wind round

loophole = **let-out**, escape, excuse

loose ADJECTIVE 1 = **free**, detached, insecure, unfettered, unrestricted, untied, unattached, unfastened 2 = **slack**, easy, relaxed, sloppy, loose-fitting **OPPOSITE:** tight 3 (*Old-fashioned*) = **promiscuous**, fast, abandoned, immoral, dissipated, profligate, debauched, dissolute **OPPOSITE:** chaste 4 = **vague**, random, inaccurate, rambling, imprecise, ill-defined, indistinct, inexact **OPPOSITE:** precise

▷ VERB 5 = **free**, release, liberate, detach, unleash, disconnect, set free, untie **OPPOSITE:** fasten

loosen = **untie**, undo, release, separate, detach, unloose

▷ **PHRASES: loosen up = relax**, chill (*slang*), soften, unwind, go easy (*informal*), hang loose, outspan (*S. African*), ease up *or* off

loot VERB 1 = **plunder**, rob, raid, sack, rifle, ravage, ransack, pillage

▷ NOUN 2 = **plunder**, goods, prize, haul, spoils, booty, swag (*slang*)

lord 1 = **peer**, nobleman, count, duke, gentleman, earl, noble, baron 2 = **ruler**, leader, chief, master, governor, commander, superior, liege

▷ **PHRASES: lord it over someone = boss around** or **about** (informal), order around, threaten, bully, menace, intimidate, hector, bluster ▶ **the Lord** or **Our Lord = Jesus Christ**, God, Christ, Messiah, Jehovah, the Almighty

lose 1 = **be defeated**, be beaten, lose out, come to grief 2 = **mislay**, drop, forget, be deprived of, lose track of, misplace 3 = **forfeit**, miss, yield, be deprived of, pass up (informal)

loser = **failure**, flop (informal), also-ran, no-hoper (Austral. slang), dud (informal), non-achiever

loss 1 = **losing**, waste, squandering, forfeiture **OPPOSITE:** gain 2 sometimes plural = **deficit**, debt, deficiency, debit, depletion **OPPOSITE:** gain 3 = **damage**, cost, injury, hurt, harm **OPPOSITE:** advantage

▷ **PHRASES: at a loss = confused**, puzzled, baffled, bewildered, helpless, stumped, perplexed, mystified

lost = **missing**, disappeared, vanished, wayward, misplaced, mislaid

lot 1 = **bunch** (informal), group, crowd, crew, set, band, quantity, assortment 2 = **destiny**, situation, circumstances, fortune, chance, accident, fate, doom

▷ **PHRASES: a lot** or **lots** 1 = **plenty**, scores, masses (informal), load(s) (informal), wealth, piles (informal), a great deal, stack(s) 2 = **often**, regularly, a great deal, frequently, a good deal

lotion = **cream**, solution, balm, salve, liniment, embrocation

lottery 1 = **raffle**, draw, lotto (Brit., N.Z. & S. African), sweepstake 2 = **gamble**, chance, risk, hazard, toss-up (informal)

loud 1 = **noisy**, booming, roaring, thundering, forte (Music), resounding, deafening, thunderous **OPPOSITE:** quiet 2 = **garish**, bold, glaring, flamboyant, brash, flashy, lurid, gaudy **OPPOSITE:** sombre

loudly = **noisily**, vigorously, vehemently, vociferously, uproariously, lustily, shrilly, fortissimo (Music)

lounge VERB 1 = **relax**, loaf, sprawl, lie about, take it easy, loiter, loll, laze, outspan (S. African)

▷ **NOUN** 2 = **sitting room**, living room, parlour, drawing room, front room, reception room, television room

love VERB 1 = **adore**, care for, treasure, cherish, prize, worship, be devoted to, dote on **OPPOSITE:** hate 2 = **enjoy**, like, appreciate, relish, delight in, savour, take pleasure in, have a

soft spot for **OPPOSITE:** dislike
▷ **NOUN 3** = **passion**, affection, warmth, attachment, intimacy, devotion, tenderness, adoration, aroha (N.Z.)
OPPOSITE: hatred **4** = **liking**, taste, bent for, weakness for, relish for, enjoyment, devotion to, penchant for **5** = **beloved**, dear, dearest, lover, darling, honey, sweetheart, truelove
OPPOSITE: enemy
6 = **sympathy**, understanding, pity, humanity, warmth, mercy, sorrow, kindness, aroha (N.Z.)
▷ **PHRASES:** make love = have sexual intercourse, have sex, go to bed, sleep together, do it (informal), mate, have sexual relations, have it off (slang)
love affair = romance, relationship, affair, intrigue, liaison, amour
lovely 1 = **beautiful**, appealing, attractive, charming, pretty, handsome, good-looking, exquisite **OPPOSITE:** ugly
2 = **wonderful**, pleasing, nice, pleasant, engaging, marvellous, delightful, enjoyable **OPPOSITE:** horrible
lover = **sweetheart**, beloved, loved one, flame (informal), mistress, admirer, suitor, woman friend
loving 1 = **affectionate**, dear, devoted, tender, fond, doting, amorous, warm-hearted
OPPOSITE: cruel **2** = **tender**, kind, caring, warm, gentle,

sympathetic, considerate
low ADJECTIVE 1 = **small**, little, short, stunted, squat
OPPOSITE: tall **2** = **inferior**, bad, poor, inadequate, unsatisfactory, deficient, second-rate, shoddy, half-pie (N.Z. informal), bodger or bodgie (Austral. slang) **3** = **quiet**, soft, gentle, whispered, muted, subdued, hushed, muffled
OPPOSITE: loud **4** = **dejected**, depressed, miserable, fed up, moody, gloomy, glum, despondent **OPPOSITE:** happy
5 = **coarse**, common, rough, crude, rude, vulgar, undignified, disreputable **6** = **ill**, weak, frail, stricken, debilitated **OPPOSITE:** strong
lower ADJECTIVE
1 = **subordinate**, under, smaller, junior, minor, secondary, lesser, inferior **2** = **reduced**, cut, diminished, decreased, lessened, curtailed **OPPOSITE:** increased
▷ **VERB 3** = **drop**, sink, depress, let down, submerge, take down, let fall **OPPOSITE:** raise
4 = **lessen**, cut, reduce, diminish, slash, decrease, prune, minimize **OPPOSITE:** increase
low-key = **subdued**, quiet, restrained, muted, understated, toned down
loyal = **faithful**, true, devoted, dependable, constant, staunch, trustworthy, trusty **OPPOSITE:**

treacherous

loyalty = faithfulness, commitment, devotion, allegiance, fidelity, homage, obedience, constancy

luck 1 = good fortune, success, advantage, prosperity, blessing, windfall, godsend, serendipity 2 = fortune, lot, stars, chance, accident, fate, destiny, twist of fate
▷ PHRASES: **in luck** = fortunate, successful, favoured, well-off, jammy (Brit. slang) ▷ **out of luck** = unfortunate, cursed, unlucky, unsuccessful

luckily = fortunately, happily, opportunely

lucky = fortunate, successful, favoured, charmed, blessed, jammy (Brit. slang), serendipitous OPPOSITE: unlucky

lucrative = profitable, rewarding, productive, fruitful, well-paid, advantageous, remunerative

ludicrous = ridiculous, crazy, absurd, preposterous, silly, laughable, farcical, outlandish OPPOSITE: sensible

luggage = baggage, things, cases, bags, gear, suitcases, paraphernalia, impedimenta

lull NOUN 1 = respite, pause, quiet, silence, calm, hush, let-up (informal)
▷ VERB 2 = calm, soothe, subdue, quell, allay, pacify, tranquillize

lumber¹ VERB 1 (Brit. informal) = burden, land, load, saddle, encumber
▷ NOUN 2 (Brit.) = junk, refuse, rubbish, trash, clutter, jumble

lumber² = plod, shuffle, shamble, trudge, stump, waddle, trundle

lumbering = awkward, heavy, hulking, ponderous, ungainly

lump NOUN 1 = piece, ball, block, mass, chunk, hunk, nugget 2 = swelling, growth, bump, tumour, bulge, hump, protrusion
▷ VERB 3 = group, throw, mass, combine, collect, pool, consolidate, conglomerate

lunatic NOUN 1 = madman, maniac, psychopath, nutcase (slang)
▷ ADJECTIVE 2 = mad, crazy, insane, irrational, daft, deranged, crackpot (informal), crackbrained, off the air (Austral. slang)

lunge VERB 1 = pounce, charge, dive, leap, plunge, thrust
▷ NOUN 2 = thrust, charge, pounce, spring, swing, jab

lurch 1 = tilt, roll, pitch, list, rock, lean, heel 2 = stagger, reel, stumble, weave, sway, totter

lure VERB 1 = tempt, draw, attract, invite, trick, seduce, entice, allure
▷ NOUN 2 = temptation, attraction, incentive, bait,

carrot (*informal*), inducement, enticement, allurement

lurk = hide, sneak, prowl, lie in wait, slink, skulk, conceal yourself

lush 1 = abundant, green, flourishing, dense, rank, verdant 2 = luxurious, grand, elaborate, lavish, extravagant, sumptuous, plush (*informal*), ornate

lust 1 = lechery, sensuality, lewdness, lasciviousness 2 = desire, longing, passion, appetite, craving, greed, thirst
▷ PHRASES: **lust for** or **after someone** = desire, want, crave, yearn for, covet, hunger for or after ▶ **lust for** or **after something** = desire, crave, yearn for, covet

luxurious = sumptuous, expensive, comfortable, magnificent, splendid, lavish, plush (*informal*), opulent
● USAGE NOTE
● *Luxurious* is sometimes
● wrongly used where *luxuriant*
● is meant: *he had a luxuriant*
● (not *luxurious*) *moustache; the*
● *walls were covered with a*
● *luxuriant growth of wisteria.*

luxury 1 = opulence, splendour, richness, extravagance, affluence, hedonism, a bed of roses, the life of Riley OPPOSITE: poverty 2 = extravagance, treat, extra, indulgence, frill OPPOSITE: necessity

lying NOUN 1 = dishonesty, perjury, deceit, misrepresentation, mendacity, untruthfulness
▷ ADJECTIVE 2 = deceitful, false, deceiving, treacherous, dishonest, two-faced, mendacious, perfidious
OPPOSITE: truthful

lyrical = enthusiastic, inspired, poetic, impassioned, effusive, rhapsodic

WORD STUDIES

BAD

BAD is such a commonly-used word that it has come to lose much of its effectiveness. Depending on the sense and context of what you are saying, there are many other much more expressive words that can be used instead.

1   **If you would like to describe something as having a harmful effect, you could try:**
    extremely **damaging** • **destructive** effect • **detrimental** impact • **harmful** effects • **unhealthy** lifestyle • **unpleasant** side-effects

2   **If you would like to describe something that has made someone feel upset or uneasy, you could try:**
    distressing images • **disturbing** news • **grim** time • **painful** memories • **traumatic** period • **unsettling** atmosphere • **upsetting** experience

3   **If you would like to describe something that has, or is causing physical pain, you could try:**
    acute attack • **agonizing** death • **excruciating** pain • **intense** cramps • **painful** back • **serious** knee problems • **severe** stomach pains • **terrible** migraine

4   **If you would like to describe something or someone that lacks skill, you could try:**
    incompetent managers • **inept** performance • **poor** judge • **useless** at …

5   **If you would like to describe poor quality, you could try:**
    defective products • **deficient** diet • **faulty** goods • **imperfect** work • **inadequate** work conditions • **inferior** quality • **pathetic** excuse • **poor** housing • **sorry** state of affairs • **unsatisfactory** service

6 **If you would like to describe something or someone with an evil character, you could try:**
morally corrupt court • **criminal** actions • **depraved** criminals • **evil** man • **immoral** act • **sinful** act • **villainous** characters • **wicked** stepmother • something **wrong**

7 **If you would like to describe children who are behaving badly, you could try:**
disobedient children • **mischievous** little scamp • **naughty** boy • **undisciplined** pupils • **unruly** kids

8 **If you're talking or writing about food, you could try:**
mouldy cheese • This meat's **gone off** • **rancid** butter • **rotten** eggs • **sour** milk

9 **If you're talking about language, you could try:**
obscene lyrics • **offensive** language • **rude** words • **vulgar** expression

BEST

There are a number of alternatives for the word **BEST** which will make your writing more interesting.

1   **If you would like to describe something as being of the highest standard, you could try:**
    the **finest** wines • **first-rate** performance • **foremost** painter • **greatest** film • Britain's **leading** actors • England's **outstanding** tennis players • **pre-eminent** pop act • London's **principal** publishing houses • **superlative** products • **supreme** achievement • **top** athletes

2   **If you would like to describe something as the most desirable thing, you could try:**
    correct thing • **most desirable** outcome • **most fitting** location • **right** person

3   **If you would like to describe something as the best or most preferred of its kind, you could try:**
    the **cream** of Scottish artists • the **elite** of the sporting world • the **finest** wine • the **pick** of the crop

Like best, the word **BETTER** can be replaced with a number of alternatives to add variety and interest to your written and spoken English.

1 **If you want to describe something as being of higher quality or worth, you could try:**
no **finer** place • much **grander** house • **greater** prize • **higher-quality** service • much **nicer** room • **preferable** to • far **superior** to yours • **surpassing** quality • **worthier** cause

2 **If you want to describe someone as having greater skill, you could use:**
the **greater** writer • **more advanced** skiers • **more expert** at some things • **more skilful** player • **more talented** than he is

3 **If you want to describe someone as having improved health, you could say:**
now I'm **cured** • a lot **fitter** • **fully recovered** • much **healthier** • definitely **improving** • **on the mend** now (*informal*) • she's **recovering** • getting **stronger** • feeling **well** again

BIG

A cautionary tale: a teacher was trying to get her class to substitute more interesting words for very commonly-used ones in their writing. She noticed that one boy had described a castle as "big" in his essay, and asked him to write the sentence again in a more creative way. He came back with the following: "I saw a castle which was big, and when I say big, I mean big."

1   If you would like to describe something that is large in size, you could try:
    colossal statue • **enormous** building • **gigantic** creature • **great** commotion • **huge** cake • **immense** task • **large** map • **massive** display • **significant** difference • **vast** stadium

2   If you would like to describe an intense issue or problem, you could try:
    grave crisis • **momentous** decision • **serious** disadvantage • **urgent** need • **weighty** problem

3   If you would like to describe someone or their actions as generous, you could try: **gracious** host • **benevolent** ruler • **kind-hearted** stranger • **noble** gesture • **heroic** deed • **unselfish** act

4   If you would like to emphasize something or someone's importance, you could try:
    eminent politician • **important** influence • **influential** figure • **leading** screenwriters • **major** role • **powerful** businessman • **principal** guest • **prominent** jazz musician • **significant** investor

5   If you would like to describe someone or something that is grown-up, you could try: **elder** sibling • **full-grown** animal • **mature** tree • **grown** man

BREAK

The word **BREAK** is often over-used. There are lots of more descriptive words which you can use to give additional information about how something breaks, so try to choose one of them instead.

1   **If something hard cracks, or you crack it, it becomes slightly damaged, with lines appearing on its surface:**
    A gas main had **cracked** under my garden.
    To get at the coconut flesh, **crack** the shell with a hammer.

2   **If something fractures, or you fracture it, it gets a slight crack in it:**
    One strut had **fractured** and had to be repaired.
    You've **fractured** a rib.

3   **If something snaps, or you snap it, it breaks suddenly, with a sharp cracking noise:**
    A twig **snapped** under his foot.
    She gripped the pipe in both hands, trying to **snap** it in half.

4   **If something splits, or you split it, it breaks into two or more parts:**
    In the severe gale, the ship **split** in two.
    We **split** the boards down the middle.

5   **If something splinters, or you splinter it, it breaks into thin, sharp pieces:**
    The ruler **splintered** into pieces.
    The stone hit the glass, **splintering** it.

6   **If something fragments, or is fragmented, it breaks or separates into small parts:**
    The rock began to **fragment** and crumble.

BREAK

7   **If something crumbles, or you crumble it, it breaks into many small pieces:**
    Under the pressure, the flint **crumbled** into fragments.
    Crumble the cheese into a bowl.

8   **If something shatters, it breaks into many small pieces:**
    safety glass that won't **shatter** if it's hit

9   **If something disintegrates, it breaks into many pieces and is destroyed:**
    The car's windscreen **disintegrated** with the impact of the crash.

10 **If you smash something, or it smashes, it breaks into many small pieces, often because it has been hit or dropped:**
    Someone had **smashed** a bottle.
    Two glasses fell off the table and **smashed** into pieces.

11 **If you wreck or demolish something, you completely destroy it:**
    The bridge was **wrecked** by the storms.
    The hurricane **demolished** houses across the area.

CALL

Depending on which sense of **CALL** you are thinking of, there are a number of words which you can substitute for it to make your language more interesting.

1. **If you are talking about giving someone or something a name, you could try:**
   christen his first-born son Arthur • **designated** an "area of natural beauty" • the man **dubbed** "the world's greatest living explorer" • they **named** their child

2. **If you are describing something as being a particular way, you could try:**
   I **consider** myself • I'm not what you'd **describe** as • do you **judge** this • He **referred to** her as • widely **regarded** as • **termed** as political • people will **think** us

3. **If you are talking about using the telephone, you could try:**
   Contact us immediately • **phone** me • I'll **ring** you • please **telephone**

4. **If you are talking about someone saying something loudly, you could try:**
   he **announced** • she **cried** • she **cried out** • he **shouted** to me • **yelled** over to us

5. **If you are talking about sending for someone, you could try:**
   please **fetch** • **sent** for • I was **summoned**

6. **If you are talking about bringing a group of things or people together, you could try:**
   they **assembled** the group • **convened** a council • **gathered** together **muster** an army • **summoned** to a meeting

7. **If you are talking about paying someone a visit, you could try:**
   drop in (informal) • **pop in** (informal) • **stop by**

9

CLOSE

CLOSE is another over-used word. Depending on whether you are talking about people or things which are close in distance or in time, the closeness of personal relationships, a closeness in resemblance between two things, or you are referring to a description or translation, you can use various other words as substitutes.

1   If you would like to describe something that is CLOSE in distance, you could try:
    at hand • adjacent buildings • adjoining stall
    • keep something handy • quite near • nearby shop
    • neighbouring table

2   If you would like to describe people who have a CLOSE relationship, you could try:
    attached to one another • dear companion • deeply devoted couple • too familiar • very friendly • intimate friends
    • loving relationship

3   If you would like to describe something which is going to happen soon, you could try:
    My birthday is approaching • the time is at hand • is coming • a deal is imminent • impending disaster • the day is near

4   If you would like to describe people or things that have a resemblance, you could try:
    distinct resemblance • marked similarity • pronounced similarities to • strong resemblance

5   If you are talking about a description or translation, you could try:
    accurate description • exact translation • faithful rendition
    • literal interpretation • precise detail • strict account

CUT

There are many useful alternatives for the word **CUT**. Different words can be used instead, depending on what it is that is being cut, what is being used to do the cutting, and how deep or extensive the cutting is.

1   If you **nick** something, you make a small cut on its surface:
    He **nicked** his chin while he was shaving.

2   If you **score** something, you cut a line or lines on its surface:
    Lightly **score** the surface of the steaks with a cook's knife.

3   If you **pierce** something with a sharp object, or a sharp object pierces it, the object goes through it and makes a hole in it:
    Pierce the skin of the potato with a fork.
    One bullet had **pierced** his lung.

4   If something **penetrates** an object, it goes inside it or passes through it:
    a spider with fangs big enough to **penetrate** the skin

5   If you **slit** something, you make a long narrow cut in it: He began to **slit** open each envelope.

6   If you **gash** or **slash** something, you make a long, deep cut in it:
    He **gashed** his leg on the barbed wire.
    She threatened to **slash** her wrists.

7   If you **clip** something, you cut small pieces from it in order to shape it:
    I saw an old man out **clipping** his hedge.

8   If you **trim** something, you cut off small amounts of it to make it look neater:
    I have my hair **trimmed** every eight weeks.

CUT

9 **If you pare something, you cut off its skin or outer layer:**
   She was sitting **paring** her nails with a pair of clippers.

10 **If you prune a tree or bush, you cut off some of its branches:**
   Apple trees can be **pruned** once they've lost their leaves.

11 **If you mow grass, you cut it with a lawnmower:**
   He **mowed** the lawn and did various other chores.

12 **If you snip something, you cut it with scissors or shears:**
   The hairdresser **snipped** off my split ends.

13 **If you split or divide something, you cut it into two or more parts:**
   Split the planks down the middle.
   Divide the pastry into four equal parts.

14 **If you sever something, you cut it off or cut right through it:**
   He **severed** the tendon of his thumb in an industrial accident.

15 **If you saw something, you cut it with a saw:**
   Your father is **sawing** wood in the garden.

16 **If you hack something, you cut it using rough strokes:**
   Matthew desperately **hacked** through the straps.

17 **If you slice something, you cut it into thin pieces:**
   I **sliced** the beef into thin strips.

18 **If you chop something, you cut it into pieces with strong downward movements of a knife or axe:**
   You will need to **chop** the onions very finely.

19 **If you carve an object, you make it by cutting it out of a substance such as wood or stone:**
   He **carves** these figures from pine.

20 **If you carve meat, you cut slices from it:**
Andrew began to **carve** the roast.

21 **If you hew stone or wood, you cut it, perhaps with an axe. This is an old-fashioned word:**
He felled, peeled and **hewed** his own timber.

22 **If you hew something out of stone or wood, you make it by cutting it from stone or wood:**
medieval monasteries **hewn** out of the rockface

23 **If you lop something off, you cut it off with one quick stroke:**
Somebody has **lopped** the heads off our tulips.

24 **If you dock an animal's tail, you cut it off:**
I think it is cruel to **dock** the tail of any animal.

EAT

There are a number of more descriptive words which you can use instead of the basic **EAT**, to say something about the way in which a person eats.

1   If you **consume** something, you eat it. This is a formal word:
    Andrew would **consume** nearly a pound of cheese a day.

2   When an animal **feeds**, or **feeds on** something, it eats:
    After a few days the caterpillars stopped **feeding**.
    Slugs **feed on** decaying plant material.

3   If you **swallow** something, you make it go from your mouth into your stomach:
    Snakes **swallow** their prey whole.

4   If you **snack**, you eat things between meals:
    Instead of **snacking** on crisps and chocolate, eat fruit.

5   If you **chew** something, you break it up with your teeth so that it is easier to swallow:
    I pulled out a filling while I was **chewing** a toffee.

6   If you **nibble** food, you eat it by biting very small pieces of it, perhaps because you are not very hungry:
    She **nibbled** at a piece of dry toast.

7   If you **munch** food, you eat it by chewing it slowly, thoroughly, and rather noisily:
    Luke **munched** his sandwiches appreciatively.

8   If you **stuff yourself**, you eat a lot of food:
    They'd **stuffed** themselves with sweets before dinner.

9   If you gobble, guzzle, wolf (down), or scoff food, you eat it
     quickly and greedily. Guzzle, wolf (down), and scoff are all
     informal words:
     Pete **gobbled** all the stew before anyone else arrived.
     women who **guzzle** chocolate whenever they are unhappy
     I was back in the changing room **wolfing** sandwiches.
     She bought a hot dog from a stand and **wolfed** it down.
     You greedy so-and-so! You've **scoffed** the lot!

10 If you devour something, you eat it quickly and eagerly:
     She **devoured** half an apple pie.

END

END is a commonly over-used word. Depending on your context, you can use the following substitutes to add variety and interest to your writing.

1   **If you would like to describe the END of a period of time, you could try:**
    by the **close** of last year • **ending** of a great era • the **expiry** of his period • nearing its **finish**

2   **If you would like to describe the END of an event, you could try:**
    the dramatic **climax** • the **close** • the **conclusion** of • the remarkable **culmination** • tragic **ending** • grand **finale** • a disappointing **finish**

3   **If you would like to describe the furthest-away part of something, you could try:**
    the **boundaries** of the paths • beyond the **bounds** • the **edge** of the cliff • the western **extremity** • official city **limits** • beyond the forest **margin**

4   **If you would like to describe the point of something long or sharp, you could try:**
    the southernmost **point** • the **tip**

5   **If you would like to describe a leftover piece of something, you could try:**
    a cigarette **butt** • trimmings and **leftovers** • **remnants** of fabric • **scraps** of spare material • a ticket **stub** • The **stump** of his left arm

6   **If you would like to describe the purpose of doing something, you could try:**
    united by a common **aim** • working towards the same **goal** • real **intentions** • the stated **object** • the **objective** of • the true **purpose** • business **reasons**

Some words used to describe a person who is overweight can be more hurtful or insulting than others. There are also words to describe varying degrees of being overweight.

1   Someone who is overweight weighs more than is considered healthy. However, you can be just a little overweight as well as very overweight:
    Since having my baby, I feel slightly **overweight**.

2   If you say someone is podgy, you mean that they are slightly FAT. This is an informal word:
    Eddie's getting a little **podgy** round the middle.

3   If you describe someone as fleshy, you mean that they are slightly too FAT:
    He was well-built, but too **fleshy** to be an imposing figure.

4   A chubby, tubby or stout person is rather FAT:
    I was greeted by a small, **chubby** man.
    He had been a short, **tubby** child who was taunted about his weight.
    a tall, **stout** man with gray hair

5   A portly person is rather FAT. This word is mostly used to describe men:
    a **portly**, middle-aged man

6   You can use the word plump to describe someone who is rather FAT or rounded, usually when you think this is a good quality:
    Maria was a pretty little thing, small and **plump** with a mass of dark curls.

FAT

7   If you describe a woman's figure as rounded or curvy you
    mean that it is attractive because it is well-developed and
    not too thin:
    a beautiful woman with blue eyes and a full, **rounded** figure
    she's very **curvy**

8   A roly-poly person is pleasantly FAT and round. This is an
    informal word:
    a short, **roly-poly** little woman with laughing eyes

9   If you describe a woman as buxom, you mean that she
    looks healthy and attractive and has a rounded body and
    big breasts:
    Melissa was a tall, **buxom** blonde.

10 If you describe someone as obese, you mean that they
    are fatter than overweight, perhaps to the point of being
    unhealthy:
    Obese people tend to have higher blood pressure than lean
    people.

GOOD

Like bad, the word **GOOD** is used in so many ways to describe so many things that it has lost a great deal of its effectiveness. A wide range of alternatives is available to you for every context in which you might be tempted to use **GOOD**; try to vary your language and vocabulary by choosing these instead.

1 **If you would like to describe something that is of GOOD quality, you could try:**
   acceptable standard • **awesome** special effects (slang) • **excellent** meal • **fine** wines • **first-class** game • **first-rate** service • **great** book • **satisfactory** quality • **splendid** hotel • **super** recipe (informal) • **superb** selection

2 **If you would like to describe a GOOD experience, you could try:**
   agreeable evening • **delightful** few hours • **enjoyable** trip • **lovely** time in Paris • **pleasant** stay • **satisfactory** season

3 **If you would like to describe something that has a beneficial effect, you could try:**
   advantageous changes • **beneficial** effects • **favourable** conditions • **positive** results

4 **If you would like to describe someone or something that is morally virtuous, you could try:**
   commendable character • **decent** person • **ethical** stance • **honest** citizens • **honourable** person • morally **righteous** people • morally **upright** • **virtuous** life • **worthy** causes

5 **If you would like to describe a kind and thoughtful person or action, you could try:**
   kindly and **benevolent** • too **charitable** • He's **considerate** to his sisters • **generous** and selfless nature • a **gracious** and genial host • a **humane** and caring woman • it's very **kind** of you • **kind-hearted** colleagues • a **kindly** soul • an **obliging** fellow • **thoughtful** of him to offer

19

GOOD

6   If you would like to describe someone who is skilled at
    something, you could try:
    able student • an **accomplished** pianist • **adept** at
    manipulating the press • very **capable** nanny • very **clever** at
    raising money • careful and **competent** worker • **efficient**
    manager • **expert** cyclists • **first-rate** teacher • **proficient**
    driver • **skilled** carpenter • most **talented** musicians

7   If you would like to describe someone's behaviour, you
    could try:
    disciplined behaviour • meek and **docile** child • a dutiful wife
    and three **obedient** children • **orderly** behaviour • polite and
    well-behaved

8   If you would like to describe any kind of GOOD advice, you
    could try:
    thoughtful and **constructive** input • **helpful** suggestions
    • **sound** advice • **practical** guidelines • **useful** tips

9   If you would like to describe a GOOD idea, you could try:
    judicious approach • **practical** solution • **prudent** strategy
    for economic recovery • a **sensible** way • a **wise** plan

10 If you would like to describe a GOOD price, sum of money,
    amount or quantity, you could try:
    ample supply • a **considerable** income • **fair** bit over
    the asking price • a **large** profit • **reasonable** number
    • **substantial** amount

11 If you would like to describe a person's mood, you could try:
    buoyant spirits • **cheerful** nature • **genial** mood • **happy**
    disposition • **optimistic** frame of mind • **sunny** mood

There are a number of ways in which the word **GREAT** can be used, depending on what you are referring to. But why not make your language more interesting and use one of the following instead?

1   **If you would like to describe something that is GREAT in size, you could try:**
    a **big** house • a **colossal** tomb • a **huge** marquee • **large** pile of logs • an **enormous** hall • **extensive** range of stock • **gigantic** theme park • an **immense** building • **stupendous** sum of money • **tremendous** challenge • a **vast** area

2   **If you would like to describe something that is GREAT in degree, you could try:**
    a **high** degree of risk • **excessive** speeds • **extravagant** claims • **extreme** violence • **tremendous** strength

3   **If you would like to describe something that is GREAT in importance, you could try:**
    one of our **chief** problems • an **important** question • our **main** competitor • **major** issue in the next election • a **momentous** occasion • Our **principal** aim • a **serious** deficiency in the system • a **significant** step towards peace

4   **If you would like to describe someone or something that is famous, you could try:**
    the **celebrated** author • a **distinguished** baritone • **eminent** French scientists • the **famed** Australian actor • a **famous** artist • the world's most **illustrious** ballerinas • a **notable** chess player • Scotland's most **prominent** historian • the **renowned** heart surgeon

5   **If you would like to describe someone's skill, you could try:**
    an **excellent** maths teacher • suitable only for **expert** skiers • a **masterly** display • an **outstanding** cricketer • the most **skilful** snooker player • a **skilled** boxer • a **superb** goalkeeper • a **superlative** thriller writer • a **talented** management team

GREAT

6   **If you would like describe the quality of something or someone, you could try:**
a **beaut** place to live (Australian, New Zealand) • good food and **fine** wines • **excellent** pasta sauce • **superb** works of art • **fantastic** firework display (informal) • their **first-rate** service • **marvellous** rooftop restaurant (informal) • **outstanding** works of art • **superb** staircase made from oak • a **terrific** party • You've done a **tremendous** job • a **wonderful** time

HAPPY is another over-used word. You can vary your language by choosing one of the alternatives shown here.

1 **If you would like to describe someone or something as displaying a cheerful nature or mood, you could try:**
a **cheerful** disposition • a **cheery** face • You're very **chirpy** today (informal) • a **jolly** fat man • a **merry** laugh • her **unfailingly** sunny nature

2 **If you would like to describe a feeling of joy at something, you could try:**
delighted with their new home • I was **ecstatic** to see Marianne again • **elated** that she had won • He is understandably **euphoric** • **glad** to be back • a **joyful** pride in his work • They were **jubilant** over their election victory • **overjoyed** to be reunited • We're very **pleased** • I'm just **thrilled** • The team are **over the moon** with this result (informal)

3 **If you would like to describe something that causes joy, you could try:**
the **agreeable** task • **blissful** marriage • truly **festive** occasion • a **gratifying** relationship • a **joyful** event • the **joyous** news • a **pleasurable** memory

4 **If you would like to describe someone who is willing to do something, you could try:**
She was **content** just to sit • always **glad** to be of service • **pleased** to take you there myself • I'd be **prepared** to talk • He's **ready** to help anyone • I'm **willing** to wait

5 **If you would like to describe something as lucky, you could try:**
an **auspicious** start • a **convenient** outcome • a **favourable** result • a very **fortunate** situation • a **lucky** chance • hardly an **opportune** moment • his **timely** arrival

HIGH

HIGH is another word which has a number of meanings. Depending on just what you are describing as **HIGH**, you have a whole range of substitutes to choose from to give your writing some added variety and expressiveness.

1 **If you are describing a building, ceiling or mountain, you could try:**
   an apartment in an **elevated** position • **lofty** towers and spires • a **soaring** spire • the **steep** hill • **tall** walls • **towering** red sandstone cliffs

2 **If you are describing a HIGH amount or HIGH degree of something, you could try:**
   state of **acute** anxiety • driving at **excessive** speed • drinking **extraordinary** quantities • under **extreme** pressure • a **great** level of interest • **severe** penalties

3 **If you are describing the cost or price of something, you could try:**
   costly premiums • too **dear** • **expensive** prices • charges are very **steep** (informal)

4 **If you are describing the wind, you could try:**
   blustery breezes • **extreme** wind and cold • thunder and **squally** winds • **strong** gusts • **violent** gales

5 **If you are describing someone or something important, you could try:**
   chief position in the company • most **eminent** scientists • an **important** post • in **exalted** circles • an **influential** place • a **leading** figure • the **most** powerful • her **pre-eminent** position • **prominent** political figures • their **superior** status

6 **If you are describing a voice or a sound, you could try:**
high-pitched cry • a **penetrating** whistle • a **piercing** note
• **shrill** scream • **soprano** voice

7 **If you are describing a person's spirits, you could try:**
in **buoyant** spirits • in such **cheerful** spirits • that **elated**
feeling • an **exhilarated** frame of mind • his **exuberant**
moods • I felt **joyful** • in a very **merry** mood

HIT

The word **HIT** is often over-used. There are a number of more descriptive words which you can use to give additional information about the way in which something is **HIT**, or how hard it is **HIT**.

1   If you **strike** someone or something, you HIT them deliberately. This is a formal word:
    She stepped forward and **struck** him across the mouth.

2   If you **tap** something, you HIT it with a quick light blow or series of blows:
    Tap the egg gently with a teaspoon to crack the shell.

3   If you **rap** something, or rap on it, you HIT it with a series of quick blows:
    rapping the glass with the knuckles of his right hand
    He **rapped on** the door with his cane.

4   If you **slap** or **smack** someone, you hit them with the palm of your hand:
    I **slapped** him hard across the face.
    She **smacked** the child on the side of the head.

5   If you **swat** something such as an insect, you HIT it with a quick, swinging movement using your hand or a flat object:
    Every time a fly came near, I **swatted** it with a newspaper.

6   If you **knock** someone or something, you HIT it roughly, especially so that it falls or moves:
    She accidentally **knocked** the tin off the shelf.

7   If you **beat** something, you HIT it hard, usually several times or continuously for a period of time:
    a circle of men **beating** drums

8   If you **hammer** something, you HIT it hard several times to make a noise:
    We had to **hammer** the door and shout to attract their attention.

9   If you **pound** something, you HIT it with great force, usually loudly and repeatedly:
    He **pounded** the table with both fists.

10 If you **batter** someone or something, you HIT them very hard, using your fists or a heavy object:
    He **battered** her round the head with a club.

11 If you **bang** something, you HIT it hard, making a loud noise:
    We **banged** on the door and shouted to be let out.

12 If you **belt** someone, you HIT them very hard. This is an informal word:
    She drew back her fist and **belted** him right in the stomach.

13 If you **bash** someone or something, you HIT them hard. This is an informal word:
    The chef was **bashed** over the head with a bottle.

14 If you **whack** someone or something, you HIT them hard. This is an informal word:
    Someone **whacked** me with a baseball bat.

15 If you **wallop** someone or something, you HIT them very hard, often causing a dull sound. This is an informal word:
    Once, she **walloped** me over the head with a frying pan.

16 If you **thump** someone or something, you HIT them hard, usually with your fist:
    I'm warning you, if you don't shut up, I'll **thump** you.

LITTLE

Depending on what you are describing, you can choose from any of the following alternatives instead of the over-used word LITTLE.

1   **If you are describing an object or the physical size of something, you could try:**
    dainty sandwiches and cakes • **dwarf** tulips • a **mini** laptop • **miniature** toy boats • **minute** particles of soil • **pygmy** goats • a **skimpy** bikini • a **small** table • **tiny** pieces • a **wee** bit of cake

2   **If you are describing someone's height, you could try:**
    dainty Japanese girl • his **diminutive** stature • **petite** women • too **short** • a **short, squat** figure • a **tiny** woman • a **wee** guy

3   **If you are describing the duration of an action or event, you could try:**
    a **brief** pause • a **fleeting** glimpse • a **hasty** peek • a **momentary** lapse • a **quick** smile • a **short** break

4   **If you are describing the quantity of something, you could try:**
    hardly any work • **not much** difference • **meagre** pay increase • **measly** ration of food • a **paltry** salary • He paid **scant** attention

5   **If you are describing someone's age, you could try:**
    my **baby** sister • her **infant** son • two **small** kids • a **young** child

6   If you are describing the importance of something, you could try:
    an **insignificant** detail • a **minor** squabble • Their **influence** is negligible • **petty** complaints • a **trifling** problem • **trivial** matters • an **unimportant** event

7   If you are describing a small amount of something, you could try:
    a **bit** of peace • a **dash** of bravado • a **fragment** of skin tissue • with just a **hint** of coriander • a **small amount** of cash • a **spot** of milk • a **touch** of irritation • a **trace** of blood

LOOK

All of the following words mean to **LOOK**, but each one has an extra shade of meaning which makes it a more expressive substitute for the word look in particular situations or contexts.

1   If you glance, peek, or peep at something, you LOOK at it quickly, and often secretly:
    He **glanced** at his watch as she spoke.
    She **peeked** at him through the curtains.
    He **peeped** at me to see if I was watching him.

2   If you scan something written or printed, you LOOK at it quickly:
    She **scanned** the advertisement pages of the newspapers.

3   If you eye or regard someone or something, you LOOK at them carefully:
    The waiters **eyed** him with suspicion.
    He **regarded** me curiously.

4   If you gaze or stare at someone or something, you LOOK at them steadily for a long time, for example because you find them interesting or because you are thinking about something else. Staring is often thought to be rude, but gazing is not:
    She sat **gazing** into the fire for a long time.
    They **stared** silently into each other's eyes.

5   If you observe or watch someone or something, you LOOK at them for a period of time to see what they are doing or what is happening:
    A man was **observing** him from across the square.
    I hate people **watching** me while I eat.

6   If you **survey** or **view** someone or something, you LOOK at the whole of them carefully:
    He stood up and **surveyed** the crowd.
    The mourners filed past to **view** the body.

7   If you **examine**, **scrutinize**, or **study** something, you LOOK at it very carefully, often to find out information from it:
    He **examined** all the evidence.
    He **scrutinized** her passport and stamped it.
    We **studied** the menu for several minutes.

8   If you **glare**, **glower**, or **scowl** at someone, you stare at them angrily:
    He **glared** resentfully at me.
    She stood **glowering** at me with her arms crossed.
    She **scowled** at the two men as they came into the room.

9   If you **peer** or **squint** at something, you try to see it more clearly by narrowing or screwing up your eyes as you LOOK at it:
    He was **peering** at me through the keyhole.
    She **squinted** at the blackboard, trying to read what was on it.

10 If you **gape** at someone or something, you LOOK at them in surprise, usually with your mouth open:
    She was **gaping** at the wreckage, lost for words.

11 If you **goggle** at someone or something, you LOOK at them with your eyes wide open, usually because you are surprised by them:
    He **goggled** at me in disbelief.

12 If you **ogle** someone, you LOOK at them in a way that makes it very obvious that you find them attractive:
    I hate the way he **ogles** every woman who goes by.

MARK

MARK is rather a vague word. Depending on what you are referring to, there are a number of more interesting synonyms which you can use in its place.

1 **If you would like to describe a stain, you could try:**
   an ink **blot** • a **line** of dirt • a lipstick **smudge** • a grease **spot** • a **stain** • a **streak** of mud

2 **If you would like to describe a damaged area, you could try:**
   slight **blemishes** • purple **blotches** • cuts and **bruises** • a tiny **dent** • little **nicks** on his chin • a jagged **scar** • a long **scratch**

3 **If you would like to describe a written or printed symbol, you could try:**
   with Chinese **characters** • the company's **emblem** • the Papal **insignia** • a multiplication **sign** • date **stamp** on the front • a flag bearing the **symbol**

4 **If you would like to describe a characteristic of something, you could try:**
   the essential **attributes** • a defining **characteristic** • fundamental **features** • the **hallmark** • a **measure** • a **symptom** • a common **trait**

5 **If you would like to describe something that is an indication of something else, you could try:**
   a **gesture** of goodwill • an **indication** of his regard • a **sign** of respect • a **symbol** of mourning • a **token** of our friendship

MOVE

MOVE is not a very expressive word. If you can use a more descriptive substitute to say something about the way in which a person or thing moves, it will give your writing variety and interest.

1   **When a person crawls, they MOVE forwards on their hands and knees:**
    As he tried to **crawl** away, he was kicked in the head.

2   **When an insect crawls somewhere, it MOVES there quite slowly:**
    I watched the moth **crawl** up the outside of the lampshade.

3   **If a person or animal creeps somewhere, they MOVE quietly and slowly:**
    I tried to **creep** upstairs without being heard.

4   **To inch somewhere means to MOVE there very carefully and slowly:**
    He began to **inch** along the ledge.

5   **If you edge somewhere, you MOVE very slowly in that direction:**
    He **edged** closer to the telephone.

6   **If a person or animal slithers somewhere, they MOVE by sliding along the ground in an uneven way:**
    Robert lost his footing and **slithered** down the bank.
    The snake **slithered** into the water.

7   **If you wriggle somewhere, for example through a small gap, you MOVE there by twisting and turning your body:**
    I **wriggled** through a gap in the fence.

MOVE

8   When people or small animals scamper or scuttle
    somewhere, they MOVE there quickly with small, light
    steps:
    The children got off the bus and **scampered** into the
    playground.
    The crabs **scuttled** along the muddy bank.

9   When people or small animals scurry somewhere, they
    MOVE there quickly and hurriedly, often because they are
    frightened:
    The attack began, sending residents **scurrying** for cover.

10 If you hurry, race, or rush somewhere, you go there as
    quickly as you can:
    Claire **hurried** along the road.
    He **raced** across town to the hospital.
    A schoolgirl **rushed** into a burning building to save a baby.

11 If you hasten somewhere, you hurry there. This is a literary
    word:
    He **hastened** along the corridor to Grace's room.

12 If you hare off somewhere, you go there very quickly. This is
    an informal British word:
    She **hared off** to ring the doctor.

13 If you dash, dart, or shoot somewhere, you run or go there
    quickly and suddenly:
    She jumped up and **dashed** out of the room.
    The girl turned and **darted** away through the trees.
    They had almost reached the boat when a figure **shot** past
    them.

14 If you say that someone or something **flies** in a particular direction, you are emphasizing that they MOVE there with a lot of speed and force:
I **flew** downstairs to answer the door.

15 If you **tear** somewhere, you MOVE there very quickly, often in an uncontrolled or dangerous way:
Without looking to the left or right, he **tore** off down the road.

16 When you **run**, you MOVE quickly because you are in a hurry to get somewhere:
I excused myself and **ran** back to the telephone.

17 If you **jog**, you run slowly:
She **jogged** off in the direction he had indicated.

18 If you **sprint**, you run as fast as you can over a short distance:
The sergeant **sprinted** to the car.

19 If you **gallop**, you run somewhere very quickly:
They were **galloping** round the garden playing football.

20 If a person or animal **bolts**, they suddenly start to run very fast, often because something has frightened them:
I made some excuse and **bolted** towards the exit.

21 If a group of animals or people **stampede**, they run in a wild, uncontrolled way:
The crowd **stampeded** out of the hall.

NEW

Depending on the sense of **NEW** which you mean, there are a number of alternatives which you can use to vary your writing and make it more interesting.

1   **If you would like to describe something that has been recently discovered or created, you could try:**
    the company's most **advanced** drugs • the **current** gossip • **fresh** footprints • **ground-breaking** discovery • all the **latest** films • **ultra-modern** shopping mall • most **recent** novel • **up-to-date** computers • **up-to-the-minute** information

2   **If you would like to describe something that has not been used or owned before, you could try:** a **brand new** car • a **fresh** page • **unused** wedding dresses

3   **If you would like to describe something that is unfamiliar, you could try:**
    a completely **different** idea • a **novel** way • an **original** idea • a **strange** country • the **unaccustomed** experience • visiting **unfamiliar** places • completely **unknown**

OLD

Depending on the sense of **OLD** which you mean, there are a number of alternatives which you can use to vary your writing and make it more interesting.

1   **If you are describing someone who has lived for a long time, you could try:**
    an **aged** parent • her **ancient** grandparents • an **elderly** man • a **venerable** father-figure

2   **If you are describing something in the past, you could try:**
    relics of **ancient** cultures • rituals of a **bygone** civilization • an **earlier** marriage • those **early** days • his **ex**-wife • a **former** lover • in **olden** times • one-**time** president • **past** grievances • **previous** tenants • **prior** criminal convictions • those **remote** days

3   **If you are describing something that is out of date, you could try:**
    antiquated teaching methods • **archaic** practices • very much **behind the times** • sounds quite **dated** • These computers are **obsolete** • an **old-fashioned** style • **outdated** attitudes • working with **outmoded** equipment • a make of car that is now **out of date** • That kind of music is **passé**

37

NICE

When you are writing or talking and you are going to use the word **NICE**, try to think of a more descriptive and interesting word instead. Here are some ideas for words and phrases that you might use to describe different aspects of people and things.

1 **If you are describing someone's appearance, you could try:**
   an **attractive** young lady • looking very **beautiful** • a very **cute** girl • he was **dishy** • Her son is **good-looking** • he's really **gorgeous** • a very **handsome** young man • a **lovely** woman • You look very **pretty**

2 **If you are describing an object, place or view, you could try:**
   beautiful little antique shop • **charming** little fishing village • **delightful** place • **lovely** old English garden • a **pretty** room

3 **If you are describing an item of clothing, you could try:**
   chic designer frock • very **elegant** dress • a **fetching** outfit • a **smart** navy-blue suit • such **stylish** clothes

4 **If you are describing an event or occasion, you could try:**
   very **agreeable** • a **delightful** time • much more **enjoyable** • such a **fantastic** party • a **lovely** holiday • a very **pleasant** experience • the **pleasurable** sensation

5 **If you are describing someone's personality, you could try:**
   very **amiable** man • very **considerate** towards his sisters • very **friendly** to strangers • unfailingly **good-natured** • **kind** to everyone • a **kindly** old man • an immensely **likeable** chap • a very **thoughtful** gesture

6 **If you are describing food or drink, you could try:**
   An **appetizing** smell • some **delectable** raspberries • food here is **delicious** • **luscious** peaches • **mouthwatering** dessert • serving **tasty** dishes

7   **If you are describing the weather, you could try:**
a **beautiful** morning • the weather is **fine** • a **glorious** day

8   **If you are describing a room, flat or house, you could try:**
a **comfortable** home • a **cosy** parlour • a **homely** atmosphere
• a very **relaxing** room

SAY

There are a number of more interesting or creative words you can use in place of the basic verbs **SAY**, speak, and talk, if you want to describe the way in which a person says something.

1   If you mention something, you SAY something about it, usually briefly:
    He never mentioned that he was married.

2   If you observe that something is the case, you make a comment about it, especially when it is something you have noticed or thought about a lot:
    "He's a very loyal friend," Daniel observed.

3   If you announce something, you tell people about it publicly or officially:
    "We're engaged!" she announced.

4   If someone asserts a fact or belief, they state it firmly:
    "The facts are clear," the Prime Minister asserted.

5   If you declare that something is true, you SAY that it is true in a firm, deliberate way:
    "I'm absolutely thrilled with the result," he declared.

6   If you put in a remark, you interrupt someone or add to what they have said with the remark:
    "Not that it's any of your business," Helen put in.

7   When people chat, they talk to each other in a friendly and informal way:
    We were just chatting in the corridor.

8   If you converse with someone, you talk to them. This is a formal word:
    They were conversing in German.

9 When people **natter**, they talk casually for a long time about unimportant things:
Susan and her friend were still **nattering** when I left.

10 If you **gossip** with someone, you talk informally, especially about other people or events:
We sat and **gossiped** well into the evening.

11 If you **explain** something, you give details about it so that it can be understood:
"We weren't married at that point," she **explained**.

12 If you **ask** something, you SAY it in the form of a question because you want to know the answer:
"How is Frank?" he **asked**.

13 If you **inquire** about something, you ask for information about it. This is a formal word:
"Is something wrong?" he **inquired**.

14 To **query** or **question** means to ask a question:
"Can I help you?" the assistant **queried**.
"What if something goes wrong?" he **questioned** anxiously.

15 When you **answer** or **reply** to someone who has just spoken, you SAY something back to them:
"When are you leaving?" she asked. "Tomorrow," he **answered**.
"That's a nice outfit," he commented. "Thanks," she **replied**.

16 When you **respond** to something that has been said, you react to it by saying something yourself:
"Are you well enough to carry on?" "Of course," she **responded** scornfully.

SAY

17 To **retort** means to reply angrily to someone. This is a formal word:
    "I don't agree," James said. "Who cares what you think?" she **retorted**.

18 If someone **babbles**, they talk in a confused or excited way:
    "I'm so excited I don't know what I'm doing," she **babbled**.

19 If you **chatter**, you talk quickly and excitedly about things which are not important:
    Everyone was **chattering** away in different languages.

20 If you **gabble**, you SAY things so quickly that it is difficult for people to understand you:
    Marcello sat on his knee and **gabbled** excitedly.

21 If you **prattle**, you talk a great deal about something unimportant:
    She was **prattling** on about this guy she had met the night before.

22 If someone **rambles**, they talk but do not make much sense because they keep going off the subject: an old man who **rambled** about his feud with his neighbours

23 If someone **breathes** something, they SAY it very quietly. This is a literary word:
    "Oh, thank God you're here," he **breathed**.

24 When you **whisper**, you SAY something very quietly, using your breath rather than your throat:
    "Keep your voice down," I **whispered**.

25 If you **hiss** something, you SAY it forcefully in a whisper:
    "Stay here and don't make a sound," he **hissed**.

26 **If you mumble, you speak very quietly and not at all clearly, so that your words are hard to make out:**
"I didn't know I was meant to do it," she **mumbled**.

27 **If you murmur something, you speak very quietly, so that not many people can hear you:**
"How convenient," I **murmured**.

28 **If you mutter, you speak very quietly, often because you are complaining about something:**
"Oh great," he **muttered**, "That's all I need."

29 **If you croak something, you SAY it in a low, rough voice:**
"Water!" he **croaked**.

30 **If you grunt something, you SAY it in a low voice, often because you are annoyed or not interested:**
"Rubbish," I **grunted**, "You just didn't try hard enough."

31 **If you rasp something, you SAY it in a harsh, unpleasant voice:**
"Get into the car," he **rasped**.

32 **If you groan or moan something, you SAY it in a low voice, usually because you are unhappy or in pain:**
"My leg - I think it's broken," Eric **groaned**.
"I can't stand it any longer," she **moaned**.

33 **When someone growls something, they SAY it in a low, rough, and angry voice:**
"I ought to kill you for this," Sharpe **growled**.

34 **If you snap at someone, you speak to them in a sharp, unfriendly way:**
"Of course you can't have it," he **snapped**.

SHORT

Some words used to describe a person who is **SHORT** can be more hurtful or insulting than others.

1 A **little** or **small** person is not large in physical size:
   She was too **little** to reach the books on the top shelf.
   She is **small** for her age.

2 A **diminutive** person is very small:
   a **diminutive** figure standing at the entrance

3 A **tiny** person is extremely small:
   Though she was **tiny**, she had a loud voice.

4 If you describe a woman as **petite**, you are politely saying that she is small and not fat. This is a complimentary word:
   a **petite** blonde woman

5 If you describe someone as **dumpy**, you mean they are **SHORT** and fat. This is an uncomplimentary word:
   a **dumpy** woman in a baggy tracksuit

6 If you describe someone as **squat**, you mean that they are **SHORT** and thick, usually in an unattractive way:
   Eddie was a short, **squat** fellow in his mid-forties.

SMALL

Depending on the sense of **SMALL** which you mean, there are a number of alternatives which you can use to vary your writing and make it more interesting.

1. **If you are describing an object or the physical size of something, you could try:**
   We sat around a **little** table • a **miniature** camera • a pair of **minuscule** shorts • Only a **minute** amount is needed • The living room is **tiny**

2. **If you are describing an area, you could try:**
   only a **little** distance from the station • squeeze through a **narrow** space • a **restricted** habitat

3. **If you are describing a business, you could try:**
   humble corner shop • The company started from **modest** beginnings • a **small-scale** cheese industry • an **unpretentious** restaurant

4. **If you are describing the size of a person, you could try:**
   a **diminutive** figure • a **dumpy** woman • too **little** to reach • **petite** blonde woman • a **short**, squat fellow • she was **tiny**

5. **If you are describing someone's age, you could try:**
   my **baby** sister • an **infant** prodigy • when you were **little** • a **young** child

6. **If you are describing the importance of something, you could try:**
   a seemingly **inconsequential** event • an **insignificant** village in the hills • such a fuss over such a **little** thing • a **minor** detail • The impact of the strike will be **negligible** • over the most **petty** things • It will only make a **slight** difference • These are **trifling** objections • bogged down in **trivial** details • a comparatively **unimportant** event

STRONG

STRONG is an over-used word. Depending on what you are referring to, there are many substitutes which you can use in its place to add variety and interest to your writing.

1   **If you are describing a person who has powerful muscles, you could try:**
    He was tall and **athletic** • a **brawny** young rugby player • a big, **burly** man • a **powerful** bodybuilder • she was lean and **muscular** • a big, **strapping** fellow • a fit, **well-built** runner

2   **If you are describing a person who is in good physical condition, you could try:**
    She is positively **blooming** with health • It won't be long till you're **fit** again • a **healthy** child • He's **in good condition** • a **robust** child • in **sound** physical condition

3   **If you are describing a person who is confident and courageous, you could try:**
    be **brave** for the children's sake • a **courageous** leader • a **plucky** schoolgirl • You've always been **resilient** • feisty, **self-confident** women • You have to be **tough**

4   **If you are describing an object that is able to withstand rough treatment, you could try:**
    made of **durable** plastic • **hard-wearing** cotton overalls • a **heavy-duty** canvas bag • **reinforced** concrete supports • a camera mounted on a **sturdy** tripod • a **substantial** boat with a powerful rigging • a **tough** vehicle designed for all terrains • You need a **well-built** fence all round the garden

5 **If you are describing feelings which are great in degree or intensity, you could try:**
acute feelings of self-consciousness • an **ardent** admirer • a **deep** resentment • my **fervent** hope • He inspires **fierce** loyalty • an **intense** dislike • a **keen** interest in football • a **passionate** believer • his **profound** distrust • His announcement sparked off **vehement** criticism • His plans met with **violent** hostility • his **zealous** religious beliefs

6 **If you are describing an argument which is convincing or supported by a lot of evidence, you could try:**
a **compelling** case • a **convincing** theory • some **effective** arguments against • **persuasive** reasons justifying the move • a **sound** case for using organically-grown produce • the most **telling** condemnation of the system

7 **If you are describing a very noticeable smell, you could try:**
an **overpowering** aftershave • a **powerful** smell of ammonia • the **pungent** aroma of oregano

8 **If you are describing food or drink that has a powerful flavour, you could try:**
a **hot** curry • the **overpowering** taste of chillies • a **piquant** sauce • a liqueur with a **powerful** aniseed flavour • I love the **sharp** taste of pickles • Avoid **spicy** foods and alcohol

9 **If you are describing a person's accent as being very noticeable, you could try:**
a **distinct** American drawl • a **marked** West country accent • his **noticeable** southern accent • **unmistakeable** Latin accent

10 **If you are describing very bright colours, you could try:**
She always dresses in **bold** colours • **bright** reds and blues • **Brilliant** jewel colours • **glaring** red Chanel dress • shirts with **loud** patterns

THIN

Some words which you might use to describe someone who is **THIN** are complimentary, some are neutral, and others are definitely uncomplimentary.

1 A **slender** person is attractively THIN and graceful:
   a tall, **slender** lady in a straw hat

2 A **slim** person has an attractively THIN and well-shaped body:
   a pretty, **slim** girl with blue eyes

3 A **slight** person has a fairly THIN and delicate-looking body:
   He is a **slight**, bespectacled, intellectual figure.

4 A **light** person does not weigh very much:
   You need to be **light** to be a dancer.

5 Someone who is **spare** is tall and not at all fat. This is a literary word:
   She was thin and **spare**, with a sharp, intelligent face.

6 If you describe someone as **lean**, you mean that they are THIN but look strong and healthy:
   Like most athletes, she was **lean** and muscular.

7 If you say someone is **lanky**, you mean that they are tall and THIN and move rather awkwardly:
   He had grown into a **lanky** teenager.

8 A **skinny** person is extremely THIN, in a way that you find unattractive. This is an informal word:
   I don't think these **skinny** supermodels are at all sexy.

9   If you say a person is scraggy or scrawny, you mean that
    they look unattractive because they are so THIN:
      a **scraggy**, shrill, neurotic woman
      a **scrawny** child of fifteen

10 Someone who is bony has very little flesh covering their
    bones:
      a **bony** old woman dressed in black

11 If someone is underweight, they are too THIN and therefore
    not healthy:
      Nearly a third of the girls were severely **underweight**.

12 A person or animal that is emaciated is very THIN and weak
    from illness or lack of food:
      horrific television pictures of **emaciated** prisoners

WALK

There are a number of more interesting or creative words you can use in place of the basic verb **WALK**, if you want to say something about the way in which a person walks.

1. If you **step** in a particular direction, you move your foot in that direction:
   I **stepped** carefully over the piles of rubbish.

2. If you **tread** in a particular way, you WALK in that way. This is rather a literary word:
   She **trod** carefully across the grass.

3. If you **amble** or **stroll**, you WALK in a slow, relaxed way:
   We **ambled** along the beach hand in hand.
   They **strolled** down the High Street, looking in shop windows.

4. If you **saunter**, you WALK in a slow, casual way:
   He was **sauntering** along as if he had all the time in the world.

5. If you **wander**, you WALK around in a casual way, often without intending to go anywhere in particular:
   Khachi was **wandering** aimlessly about in the garden.

6. If you **tiptoe**, you WALK very quietly without putting your heels on the ground, so as not to be heard:
   She slipped out of bed and **tiptoed** to the window.

7. If you **toddle**, you WALK unsteadily, with short quick steps. This word is most often used of babies or small children:
   My daughter **toddles** around after me wherever I go.

8. If you **mince**, you WALK with quick, small steps in a put-on, effeminate way:
   drag artists **mincing** around the stage in tight dresses and high heels

9   If you pace, you WALK up and down a small area, usually because you are anxious or impatient:
    As he waited, he **paced** nervously around the room.

10 If you stride, you WALK with quick, long steps:
    He turned abruptly and **strode** off down the corridor.

11 If you march, you WALK quickly and in a determined way, perhaps because you are angry:
    She **marched** into the office and demanded to see the manager.

12 If you stamp, you put your feet down very hard when you WALK, usually because you are angry:
    "I'm leaving!" he shouted as he **stamped** out of the room.

13 If you flounce, you WALK quickly and with exaggerated movements, in a way that shows you are annoyed or upset about something:
    She **flounced** out of the room in a huff.

14 If you stalk, you WALK in a stiff, proud, or angry way:
    He **stalked** out of the meeting, slamming the door.

15 If you lurch, you WALK with sudden, jerky movements:
    He **lurched** around the room as if he was drunk.

16 If you stagger or totter, you WALK very unsteadily, often because you are ill or drunk:
    He **staggered** home from the pub every night.
    I had to **totter** around on crutches for six weeks.

17 If you reel, you WALK about in an unsteady way as if you are going to fall:
    He lost his balance and **reeled** back.

WALK

18 **If you stumble, you trip while you are walking and almost fall:**
I **stumbled** into the phone box and dialled 999.

19 **If you hike or ramble, you WALK some distance in the countryside for pleasure:**
They **hiked** along a remote trail.
a relaxing holiday spent **rambling** over the fells

20 **If you trek, you make a journey across difficult country by walking:**
This year we're going **trekking** in Nepal.

21 **You can also use trek to describe someone walking rather slowly and unwillingly, usually because they are tired:**
We **trekked** all round the shops looking for white shoes.

22 **If you plod, tramp, or trudge, you WALK slowly, with heavy steps, often because you are tired:**
He **plodded** about after me, looking bored.
They spent all day **tramping** through the snow.
We had to **trudge** all the way back up the hill.

WIDE

There are a number of ways in which the word **WIDE** can be used, depending on what you are referring to. But you can make your language more interesting by using one of the following instead.

1   **If you would like to describe something measuring a large distance from side to side, you could try:**
    a large woman with an **ample** bosom • ridiculously **baggy** trousers • His shoulders were **broad** • an **expansive** play area • The grounds were more **extensive** • a **full** skirt • an **immense** body of water • in **large** rivers and lakes • I like **roomy** jackets • a **spacious** kitchen • long **sweeping** curve • **vast** stretches of land • a **voluminous** trench coat

2   **If you would like to describe something that is extensive in scope, you could try:**
    ample scope here for the imagination • **broad** range of issues • very **catholic** tastes in music • an **encyclopedic** knowledge of the subject • treatment of the topic is **exhaustive** • **comprehensive** guide • **extensive** press coverage • introduce **far-ranging** reforms • **immense** range of holiday activities • an **inclusive** survey • **large** selection of goods • **vast** range of products • **wide-ranging** but simple

3   **If you would like to describe the extent to which something is opened or extended, you could try:**
    He opened the map out **completely** so that we could see • She extended the aerial **fully** • His mouth was **fully open** in astonishment • Spread it **right out** to the edges

Mm

machine 1 = **appliance**, device, apparatus, engine, tool, instrument, mechanism, gadget 2 = **system**, structure, organization, machinery, setup (*informal*)

machinery = **equipment**, gear, instruments, apparatus, technology, tackle, tools, gadgetry

macho = **manly**, masculine, chauvinist, virile

mad ADJECTIVE 1 = **insane**, crazy (*informal*), nuts (*slang*), raving, unstable, psychotic, demented, deranged, off the air (*Austral. slang*) OPPOSITE: sane 2 = **foolish**, absurd, wild, stupid, daft (*informal*), irrational, senseless, preposterous OPPOSITE: sensible 3 (*Informal*) = **angry**, furious, incensed, enraged, livid (*informal*), berserk, berko (*Austral. slang*), tooshie (*Austral. slang*), off the air (*Austral. slang*) OPPOSITE: calm 4 = **enthusiastic**, wild, crazy (*informal*), ardent, fanatical, avid, impassioned, infatuated OPPOSITE: nonchalant 5 = **frenzied**, wild, excited, frenetic, uncontrolled, unrestrained

madden = **infuriate**, irritate, incense, enrage, upset, annoy, inflame, drive you crazy OPPOSITE: calm

madly 1 (*Informal*) = **passionately**, wildly, desperately, intensely, to distraction, devotedly 2 = **foolishly**, wildly, absurdly, ludicrously, irrationally, senselessly 3 = **energetically**, wildly, furiously, excitedly, recklessly, speedily, like mad (*informal*) 4 = **insanely**, frantically, hysterically, crazily, deliriously, distractedly, frenziedly

madness 1 = **insanity**, mental illness, delusion, mania, dementia, distraction, aberration, psychosis 2 = **foolishness**, nonsense, folly, absurdity, idiocy, wildness, daftness (*informal*), foolhardiness

magazine = **journal**, publication, supplement, rag (*informal*), issue, glossy (*informal*), pamphlet, periodical

magic NOUN 1 = **sorcery**, wizardry, witchcraft, enchantment, black art, necromancy 2 = **conjuring**, illusion, trickery, sleight of hand, legerdemain, prestidigitation 3 = **charm**, power, glamour, fascination, magnetism, enchantment

m

▷ ADJECTIVE 4 = **miraculous**, entrancing, charming, fascinating, marvellous, magical, enchanting, bewitching, spellbinding, sorcerous

magician 1 = **conjuror**, illusionist, prestidigitator 2 = **sorcerer**, witch, wizard, illusionist, warlock, necromancer, enchanter *or* enchantress

magistrate = **judge**, justice, justice of the peace, J.P.

magnetic = **attractive**, irresistible, seductive, captivating, charming, fascinating, charismatic, hypnotic **OPPOSITE:** repulsive

magnificent 1 = **splendid**, impressive, imposing, glorious, gorgeous, majestic, regal, sublime **OPPOSITE:** ordinary 2 = **brilliant**, fine, excellent, outstanding, superb, splendid

magnify 1 = **enlarge**, increase, boost, expand, intensify, blow up (*informal*), heighten, amplify **OPPOSITE:** reduce 2 = **make worse**, exaggerate, intensify, worsen, exacerbate, increase, inflame 3 = **exaggerate**, overstate, inflate, overplay, overemphasize **OPPOSITE:** understate

magnitude 1 = **importance**, consequence, significance, moment, note, weight, greatness **OPPOSITE:** unimportance 2 = **immensity**, size, extent, enormity, volume, vastness **OPPOSITE:** smallness 3 = **intensity**, amplitude

maid 1 = **servant**, chambermaid, housemaid, menial, maidservant, female servant, domestic (*archaic*), parlourmaid 2 (*Literary*) = **girl**, maiden, lass, damsel, lassie (*informal*), wench

maiden NOUN 1 (*Literary*) = **girl**, maid, lass, damsel, virgin, lassie (*informal*), wench ▷ ADJECTIVE 2 = **first**, initial, inaugural, introductory 3 = **unmarried**, unwed

mail NOUN 1 = **letters**, post, correspondence ▷ VERB 2 = **post**, send, forward, e-mail, dispatch

main ADJECTIVE 1 = **chief**, leading, head, central, essential, primary, principal, foremost **OPPOSITE:** minor ▷ PLURAL NOUN 2 = **pipeline**, channel, pipe, conduit, duct 3 = **cable**, line, electricity supply, mains supply ▷ PHRASES: in the main = on the whole, generally, mainly, mostly, in general, for the most part

mainly = **chiefly**, mostly, largely, principally, primarily, on the whole, predominantly, in the main

mainstream = **conventional**, general, established, received, accepted, current, prevailing, orthodox **OPPOSITE:**

unconventional

maintain 1 = **continue**, retain, preserve, sustain, carry on, keep up, prolong, perpetuate **OPPOSITE:** end 2 = **assert**, state, claim, insist, declare, contend, profess, avow **OPPOSITE:** disavow 3 = **look after**, care for, take care of, conserve, keep in good condition

maintenance 1 = **upkeep**, keeping, care, repairs, conservation, nurture, preservation 2 = **allowance**, support, keep, alimony 3 = **continuation**, carrying-on, perpetuation, prolongation

majestic = **grand**, magnificent, impressive, superb, splendid, regal, stately, monumental **OPPOSITE:** modest

majesty = **grandeur**, glory, splendour, magnificence, nobility **OPPOSITE:** triviality

major 1 = **important**, critical, significant, great, serious, crucial, outstanding, notable 2 = **main**, higher, greater, bigger, leading, chief, senior, supreme **OPPOSITE:** minor

majority 1 = **most**, mass, bulk, best part, better part, lion's share, preponderance, greater number 2 = **adulthood**, maturity, age of consent, seniority, manhood or womanhood

● **USAGE NOTE**
● *The majority of* should always

● refer to a countable number
● of things or people. If you are
● talking about an amount or
● quantity, rather than a
● countable number, use *most*
● *of*, as in *most of the harvest was*
● *saved* (not *the majority of the*
● *harvest was saved*).

make VERB 1 = **produce**, cause, create, effect, lead to, generate, bring about, give rise to 2 = **perform**, do, effect, carry out, execute 3 = **force**, cause, compel, oblige, require, oblige, induce, constrain 4 = **create**, build, produce, manufacture, form, fashion, construct, assemble 5 = **earn**, get, gain, net, win, clear, obtain, bring in 6 = **amount to**, total, constitute, add up to, count as, tot up to (informal)

▷ NOUN 7 = **brand**, sort, style, model, kind, type, variety, marque

▷ PHRASES: **make for something** = **head for**, aim for, head towards, be bound for ▶ **make it** (Informal) = **succeed**, prosper, arrive (informal), get on, crack it (informal) ▶ **make off** = **flee**, clear out (informal), bolt, take to your heels, run away or off ▶ **make something up** = **invent**, create, construct, compose, frame, coin, devise, originate ▶ **make up** = **settle your differences**, bury the hatchet, call it quits, declare a truce, be friends again ▶ **make**

m

up for something
= **compensate for**, make
amends for, atone for, balance
out, offset, make recompense
for ▶ make up something
1 = **form**, account for,
constitute, compose, comprise
2 = **complete**, supply, fill,
round off

maker = **manufacturer**,
producer, builder, constructor

makeshift = **temporary**,
provisional, substitute,
expedient, stopgap

make-up 1 = **cosmetics**, paint
(*informal*), powder, face
(*informal*), greasepaint (*Theatre*)
2 = **nature**, character,
constitution, temperament,
disposition 3 = **structure**,
organization, arrangement,
construction, assembly,
constitution, format,
composition

making NOUN 1 = **creation**,
production, manufacture,
construction, assembly,
composition, fabrication
▷ PLURAL NOUN
2 = **beginnings**, potential,
capacity, ingredients

male = **masculine**, manly,
macho, virile OPPOSITE: female

malicious = **spiteful**,
malevolent, resentful, vengeful,
rancorous, ill-disposed, ill-
natured OPPOSITE: benevolent

mammal ▷ *See panels* BATS,
CARNIVORES, EXTINCT
MAMMALS, MARSUPIALS,
MONKEYS, APES AND OTHER
PRIMATES, RODENTS, SEA
MAMMALS, WHALES AND
DOLPHINS

mammoth = **colossal**, huge,
giant, massive, enormous,
immense, gigantic,
monumental OPPOSITE: tiny

man NOUN 1 = **male**, guy
(*informal*), fellow (*informal*),
gentleman, bloke (*Brit.
informal*), chap (*Brit. informal*),
dude (*U.S. informal*), geezer
(*informal*) 2 = **human**, human
being, person, individual, soul
3 = **mankind**, humanity,
people, human race,
humankind, Homo sapiens
▷ VERB 4 = **staff**, people, crew,
occupy, garrison

mana (*N.Z.*) = **authority**,
influence, power, might,
standing, status, importance,
eminence

manage 1 = **be in charge of**,
run, handle, direct, conduct,
command, administer,
supervise 2 = **organize**, use,
handle, regulate 3 = **cope**,
survive, succeed, carry on,
make do, get by (*informal*),
muddle through 4 = **perform**,
do, achieve, carry out,
undertake, cope with,
accomplish, contrive
5 = **control**, handle, manipulate

management
1 = **administration**, control,
running, operation, handling,
direction, command, supervision

EXTINCT MAMMALS		
apeman	glyptodont	quagga
aurochs	mammoth	sabre-toothed tiger *or*
australopithecine	mastodon	cat
eohippus	megathere	tarpan

2 = **directors**, board, executive(s), administration, employers

manager = **supervisor**, head, director, executive, boss (*informal*), governor, administrator, organizer, baas (*S. African*)

mandate = **command**, order, commission, instruction, decree, directive, edict

mandatory = **compulsory**, required, binding, obligatory, requisite **OPPOSITE:** optional

manhood = **manliness**, masculinity, virility

manifest ADJECTIVE
1 = **obvious**, apparent, patent, evident, clear, glaring, noticeable, blatant **OPPOSITE:** concealed
▷ VERB **2** = **display**, show, reveal, express, demonstrate, expose, exhibit **OPPOSITE:** conceal

manifestation 1 = **sign**, symptom, indication, mark, example, evidence, proof, testimony **2** = **display**, show, exhibition, expression, demonstration

manipulate 1 = **influence**, control, direct, negotiate, exploit, manoeuvre **2** = **work**,

use, operate, handle

mankind = **people**, man, humanity, human race, humankind, Homo sapiens
● USAGE NOTE
● Some people object to the
● use of *mankind* to refer to all
● human beings on the
● grounds that it is sexist. A
● preferable term is *humankind*,
● which refers to both men and
● women.

manly = **virile**, masculine, strong, brave, bold, strapping, vigorous, courageous **OPPOSITE:** effeminate

man-made = **artificial**, manufactured, mock, synthetic, ersatz

manner NOUN **1** = **style**, way, fashion, method, custom, mode
2 = **behaviour**, air, bearing, conduct, aspect, demeanour **3** = **type**, form, sort, kind, variety, brand, category
▷ PLURAL NOUN **4** = **conduct**, behaviour, demeanour
5 = **politeness**, courtesy, etiquette, refinement, decorum, p's and q's **6** = **protocol**, customs, social graces

mannered = **affected**, artificial, pretentious, stilted, arty-farty (*informal*) **OPPOSITE:** natural

m

manoeuvre VERB 1 = **scheme**, wangle (*informal*), machinate 2 = **manipulate**, arrange, organize, set up, engineer, fix, orchestrate, contrive ▷ NOUN 3 = **stratagem**, scheme, trick, tactic, intrigue, dodge, ploy, ruse 4 *often plural* = **movement**, operation, exercise, war game

mansion = **residence**, manor, hall, villa, seat

mantle 1 = **covering**, screen, curtain, blanket, veil, shroud, canopy, pall 2 = **cloak**, wrap, cape, hood, shawl

manual ADJECTIVE 1 = **physical**, human 2 = **hand-operated**, hand, non-automatic ▷ NOUN 3 = **handbook**, guide, instructions, bible

manufacture VERB 1 = **make**, build, produce, construct, create, turn out, assemble, put together 2 = **concoct**, make up, invent, devise, fabricate, think up, cook up (*informal*), trump up ▷ NOUN 3 = **making**, production, construction, assembly, creation

manufacturer = **maker**, producer, builder, creator, industrialist, constructor

many DETERMINER 1 = **numerous**, various, countless, abundant, myriad, innumerable, manifold, umpteen (*informal*)

▷ PRONOUN 2 = **a lot**, lots (*informal*), plenty, scores, heaps (*informal*)

mar 1 = **harm**, damage, hurt, spoil, stain, taint, tarnish 2 = **ruin**, spoil, scar, flaw, impair, detract from, deform, blemish OPPOSITE: improve

march VERB 1 = **parade**, walk, file, pace, stride, swagger 2 = **walk**, strut, storm, sweep, stride, flounce ▷ NOUN 3 = **walk**, trek, slog, yomp (*Brit. informal*), routemarch 4 = **progress**, development, advance, evolution, progression

margin = **edge**, side, border, boundary, verge, brink, rim, perimeter

marginal 1 = **insignificant**, small, minor, slight, minimal, negligible 2 = **borderline**, bordering, on the edge, peripheral

marijuana = **cannabis**, pot (*slang*), dope (*slang*), grass (*slang*), hemp, dagga (*S. African*)

marine = **nautical**, maritime, naval, seafaring, seagoing

mariner = **sailor**, seaman, sea dog, seafarer, salt

marital = **matrimonial**, nuptial, conjugal, connubial

maritime 1 = **nautical**, marine, naval, oceanic, seafaring 2 = **coastal**, seaside, littoral

mark NOUN 1 = **spot**, stain, streak, smudge, line, scratch, scar, blot 2 = **characteristic**,

feature, standard, quality, measure, stamp, attribute, criterion **3** = **indication**, sign, symbol, token **4** = **brand**, impression, label, device, flag, symbol, token, emblem **5** = **target**, goal, aim, purpose, object, objective
▷ VERB **6** = **scar**, scratch, stain, streak, blot, smudge, blemish **7** = **label**, identify, brand, flag, stamp, characterize **8** = **grade**, correct, assess, evaluate, appraise **9** = **distinguish**, show, illustrate, exemplify, denote **10** = **observe**, mind, note, notice, attend to, pay attention to, pay heed to

marked = **noticeable**, clear, decided, striking, obvious, prominent, patent, distinct **OPPOSITE:** imperceptible

markedly = **noticeably**, clearly, obviously, considerably, distinctly, decidedly, strikingly, conspicuously

market NOUN **1** = **fair**, mart, bazaar, souk (*Arabic*)
▷ VERB **2** = **sell**, promote, retail, peddle, vend

maroon = **abandon**, leave, desert, strand, leave high and dry (*informal*)

marriage = **wedding**, match, nuptials, wedlock, matrimony

marry 1 = **tie the knot** (*informal*), wed, get hitched (*slang*) **2** = **unite**, join, link, bond, ally, merge, knit, unify

marsh = **swamp**, bog, slough,

fen, quagmire, morass

marshal 1 = **conduct**, take, lead, guide, steer, escort, shepherd, usher **2** = **arrange**, group, order, line up, organize, deploy, array, draw up

marsupial ▷ *See panel*
MARSUPIALS

martial = **military**, belligerent, warlike, bellicose

marvel VERB **1** = **be amazed**, wonder, gape, be awed
▷ NOUN **2** = **wonder**, phenomenon, miracle, portent **3** = **genius**, prodigy

marvellous = **excellent**, great (*informal*), wonderful, brilliant, amazing, extraordinary, superb, spectacular, booshit (*Austral. slang*), exo (*Austral. slang*), sik (*Austral. slang*) **OPPOSITE:** terrible

masculine = **male**, manly, mannish, manlike, virile

mask NOUN **1** = **façade**, disguise, front, cover, screen, veil, guise, camouflage
▷ VERB **2** = **disguise**, hide, conceal, obscure, cover (up), screen, blanket, veil

mass NOUN **1** = **lot**, collection, load, pile, quantity, bunch, stack, heap **2** = **piece**, block, lump, chunk, hunk **3** = **size**, matter, weight, extent, bulk, magnitude, greatness
▷ ADJECTIVE **4** = **large-scale**, general, widespread, extensive, universal, wholesale, indiscriminate

MARSUPIALS

bandicoot

Bennett's tree kangaroo or tcharibeena

bettong

bilby, rabbit(-eared) bandicoot, long-eared bandicoot, dalgyte, or dalgite

bobuck or mountain (brushtail) possum

boodie (rat), burrowing rat-kangaroo, Lesueur's rat-kangaroo, tungoo, or tungo

boongary or Lumholtz's tree kangaroo

bridled nail-tail wallaby or merrin

brush-tail(ed) possum

burramys or (mountain) pygmy possum

crest-tailed marsupial mouse, Cannings' little dog, or mulgara

crescent nail-tail wallaby or wurrung

cuscus

dasyurid, dasyure, native cat, marsupial cat, or wild cat

dibbler

diprotodon

dunnart

fluffy glider or yellow-bellied glider

flying phalanger, flying squirrel, glider, or pongo

green ringtail possum or toolah

hare-wallaby

honey mouse, honey possum, noolbenger, or tait

jerboa, jerboa pouched mouse, jerboa kangaroo, or kultarr

kangaroo or (Austral. informal) roo

koala (bear) or (Austral.) native bear

kowari

larapinta or Darling Downs dunnart

marlu

marsupial mole

marsupial mouse

munning

ningaui

northern native cat or satanellus

numbat or banded anteater

opossum or possum

pademelon or paddymelon

phalanger

pitchi-pitchi or wuhl-wuhl

platypus, duck-billed platypus, or duckbill

potoroo

pygmy glider, feather glider, or flying mouse

quokka

quoll

rat kangaroo

squirrel glider

sugar glider

tammar, damar, or dama

Tasmanian devil or ursine dasyure

thylacine, Tasmanian wolf, or Tasmanian tiger

tiger cat or spotted native cat

tree kangaroo

MARSUPIALS continued

tuan, phascogale, or wambenger	warabi
wallaby	wombat or (Austral.) badger
wallaroo, uroo, or biggada	yapok
	yallara

▷ VERB 5 = **gather**, assemble, accumulate, collect, rally, swarm, throng, congregate

massacre NOUN
1 = **slaughter**, murder, holocaust, carnage, extermination, annihilation, butchery, blood bath
▷ VERB 2 = **slaughter**, kill, murder, butcher, wipe out, exterminate, mow down, cut to pieces

massage NOUN 1 = **rub-down**, manipulation
▷ VERB 2 = **rub down**, manipulate, knead
3 = **manipulate**, alter, distort, doctor, cook (informal), fix (informal), rig, fiddle (informal)

massive = **huge**, big, enormous, immense, hefty, gigantic, monumental, mammoth **OPPOSITE:** tiny

master NOUN 1 = **lord**, ruler, commander, chief, director, manager, boss (informal), head, baas (S. African) **OPPOSITE:** servant 2 = **expert**, maestro, ace (informal), genius, wizard, virtuoso, doyen, past master, fundi (S. African) **OPPOSITE:** amateur 3 = **teacher**, tutor, instructor **OPPOSITE:** student

▷ ADJECTIVE 4 = **main**, principal, chief, prime, foremost, predominant **OPPOSITE:** lesser
▷ VERB 5 = **learn**, understand, pick up, grasp, get the hang of (informal), know inside out, know backwards
6 = **overcome**, defeat, conquer, tame, triumph over, vanquish **OPPOSITE:** give in to

masterly = **skilful**, expert, crack (informal), supreme, world-class, consummate, first-rate, masterful

mastermind VERB 1 = **plan**, manage, direct, organize, devise, conceive
▷ NOUN 2 = **organizer**, director, manager, engineer, brain(s) (informal), architect, planner

masterpiece = **classic**, tour de force (French), pièce de résistance (French), magnum opus (Latin), jewel

mastery 1 = **understanding**, skill, know-how, expertise, prowess, finesse, proficiency, virtuosity 2 = **control**, command, domination, superiority, supremacy, upper hand, ascendancy, mana (N.Z.), whip hand

match NOUN 1 = **game**, test,

competition, trial, tie, contest, fixture, bout **2 = marriage**, pairing, alliance, partnership **3 = equal**, rival, peer, counterpart
▷ VERB **4 = correspond with**, go with, fit with, harmonize with **5 = correspond**, agree, accord, square, coincide, tally, conform, match up **6 = rival**, equal, compete with, compare with, emulate, measure up to

matching = identical, like, twin, equivalent, corresponding, coordinating
OPPOSITE: different

mate NOUN **1** (*Informal*) = **friend**, pal (*informal*), companion, buddy (*informal*), comrade, chum (*informal*), mucker (*Brit. informal*), crony, cobber (*Austral. & N.Z. old-fashioned informal*), E hoa (*N.Z.*) **2 = partner**, lover, companion, spouse, consort, helpmeet, husband *or* wife **3 = assistant**, subordinate, apprentice, helper, accomplice, sidekick (*informal*) **4 = colleague**, associate, companion
▷ VERB **5 = pair**, couple, breed

material NOUN **1 = substance**, matter, stuff **2 = cloth**, fabric, textile **3 = information**, details, facts, notes, evidence, particulars, data, info (*informal*)
▷ ADJECTIVE **4 = physical**, solid, substantial, concrete, bodily, tangible, palpable, corporeal **5 = relevant**, important,

significant, essential, vital, serious, meaningful, applicable

materially = significantly, much, greatly, essentially, seriously, gravely, substantially
OPPOSITE: insignificantly

maternal = motherly, protective, nurturing, maternalistic

maternity = motherhood, parenthood, motherliness

matted = tangled, knotted, unkempt, knotty, tousled, ratty, uncombed

matter NOUN **1 = situation**, concern, business, question, event, subject, affair, incident **2 = substance**, material, body, stuff
▷ VERB **3 = be important**, make a difference, count, be relevant, make any difference, carry weight, cut any ice (*informal*), be of account

matter-of-fact = unsentimental, plain, sober, down-to-earth, mundane, prosaic, deadpan, unimaginative

mature VERB **1 = develop**, grow up, bloom, blossom, come of age, age
▷ ADJECTIVE **2 = matured**, seasoned, ripe, mellow **3 = grown-up**, adult, of age, fully fledged, full-grown
OPPOSITE: immature

maturity 1 = adulthood, puberty, coming of age, pubescence, manhood *or* womanhood **OPPOSITE:** immaturity **2** = ripeness

maul 1 = mangle, claw, lacerate, tear, mangulate (*Austral. slang*) **2** = ill-treat, abuse, batter, molest, manhandle

maverick NOUN 1 = rebel, radical, dissenter, individualist, protester, eccentric, heretic, nonconformist **OPPOSITE:** traditionalist
▷ **ADJECTIVE 2** = rebel, radical, dissenting, individualistic, eccentric, heretical, iconoclastic, nonconformist

maximum ADJECTIVE
1 = greatest, highest, supreme, paramount, utmost, most, topmost **OPPOSITE:** minimal
▷ **NOUN 2** = top, peak, ceiling, utmost, upper limit **OPPOSITE:** minimum

maybe = perhaps, possibly, perchance (*archaic*)

mayhem = chaos, trouble, violence, disorder, destruction, confusion, havoc, fracas

maze = web, confusion, tangle, labyrinth, imbroglio, complex network

meadow = field, pasture, grassland, lea (*poetic*)

mean¹ 1 = signify, indicate, represent, express, stand for, convey, spell out, symbolize **2** = imply, suggest, intend, hint at, insinuate **3** = intend, want, plan, expect, design, aim, wish,

think, have in mind
● **USAGE NOTE**
● In standard British English,
● *mean* should not be followed
● by *for* when expressing
● intention. *I didn't mean this to*
● *happen* is acceptable, but not *I*
● *didn't mean for this to happen.*

mean² 1 = miserly, stingy, parsimonious, niggardly, mercenary, penny-pinching, ungenerous, tight-fisted, snoep (*S. African informal*) **OPPOSITE:** generous **2** = dishonourable, petty, shameful, shabby, vile, callous, sordid, despicable, scungy (*Austral. & N.Z.*) **OPPOSITE:** honourable

mean³ NOUN 1 = average, middle, balance, norm, midpoint
▷ **ADJECTIVE 2** = average, middle, standard

meaning 1 = significance, message, substance, drift, connotation, gist **2** = definition, sense

meaningful = significant, important, material, useful, relevant, valid, worthwhile, purposeful **OPPOSITE:** trivial

meaningless = nonsensical, senseless, inconsequential, inane **OPPOSITE:** worthwhile

means 1 = method, way, process, medium, agency, instrument, mode **2** = money, funds, capital, income, resources, fortune, wealth, affluence

m

▷ **PHRASES: by all means**
= **certainly**, surely, of course,
definitely, doubtlessly ▶ **by no
means = in no way**, definitely
not, not in the least, on no
account

meantime or **meanwhile** = **at
the same time**, simultaneously,
concurrently

meanwhile or **meantime**
= **for now**, in the interim

measure VERB 1 = **quantify**,
determine, assess, weigh,
calculate, evaluate, compute,
gauge
▷ NOUN 2 = **quantity**, share,
amount, allowance, portion,
quota, ration, allotment
3 = **action**, act, step, procedure,
means, control, initiative,
manoeuvre 4 = **gauge**, rule,
scale, metre, ruler, yardstick
5 = **law**, act, bill, legislation,
resolution, statute

measured 1 = **steady**, even,
slow, regular, dignified, stately,
solemn, leisurely
2 = **considered**, reasoned,
studied, calculated, deliberate,
sober, well-thought-out

measurement = **calculation**,
assessment, evaluation,
valuation, computation,
calibration, mensuration

meat = **food**, flesh, kai (N.Z.
informal)

mechanical 1 = **automatic**,
automated, mechanized,
power-driven, motor-driven
OPPOSITE: manual

2 = **unthinking**, routine,
automatic, instinctive,
involuntary, impersonal,
cursory, perfunctory **OPPOSITE:**
conscious

mechanism 1 = **process**, way,
means, system, operation,
agency, method, technique
2 = **machine**, device, tool,
instrument, appliance,
apparatus, contrivance

mediate = **intervene**, step in
(informal), intercede, referee,
umpire, reconcile, arbitrate,
conciliate

mediation = **arbitration**,
intervention, reconciliation,
conciliation, intercession

mediator = **negotiator**,
arbitrator, referee, umpire,
intermediary, middleman,
arbiter, peacemaker

medicine = **remedy**, drug, cure,
prescription, medication,
nostrum, medicament

mediocre = **second-rate**,
average, ordinary, indifferent,
middling, pedestrian, inferior,
so-so (informal), half-pie (N.Z.
informal) **OPPOSITE:** excellent

meditation = **reflection**,
thought, study, musing,
pondering, contemplation,
rumination, cogitation

medium ADJECTIVE
1 = **average**, mean, middle,
middling, fair, intermediate,
midway, mediocre **OPPOSITE:**
extraordinary
▷ NOUN 2 = **spiritualist**, seer,

clairvoyant, fortune teller, channeller 3 = **middle**, mean, centre, average, compromise, midpoint

meet VERB 1 = **encounter**, come across, run into, happen on, find, contact, confront, bump into (*informal*) OPPOSITE: avoid 2 = **gather**, collect, assemble, get together, come together, muster, convene, congregate OPPOSITE: disperse 3 = **fulfil**, match (up to), answer, satisfy, discharge, comply with, come up to, conform to OPPOSITE: fall short of 4 = **experience**, face, suffer, bear, go through, encounter, endure, undergo 5 = **converge**, join, cross, touch, connect, come together, link up, intersect OPPOSITE: diverge

meeting 1 = **conference**, gathering, assembly, congress, session, convention, get-together (*informal*), reunion, hui (N.Z.) 2 = **encounter**, introduction, confrontation, engagement, rendezvous, tryst, assignation

melancholy ADJECTIVE 1 = **sad**, depressed, miserable, gloomy, glum, mournful, despondent, dispirited OPPOSITE: happy ▷ NOUN 2 = **sadness**, depression, misery, gloom, sorrow, unhappiness, despondency, dejection OPPOSITE: happiness

mellow ADJECTIVE 1 = **full-flavoured**, rich, sweet, delicate 2 = **ripe**, mature, ripened OPPOSITE: unripe ▷ VERB 3 = **relax**, improve, settle, calm, mature, soften, sweeten 4 = **season**, develop, improve, ripen

melody 1 = **tune**, song, theme, air, music, strain 2 = **tunefulness**, harmony, musicality, euphony, melodiousness

melt 1 = **dissolve**, run, soften, fuse, thaw, defrost, liquefy, unfreeze 2 *often with* **away** = **disappear**, fade, vanish, dissolve, disperse, evaporate, evanesce 3 = **soften**, relax, disarm, mollify

member = **representative**, associate, supporter, fellow, subscriber, comrade, disciple

membership 1 = **participation**, belonging, fellowship, enrolment 2 = **members**, body, associates, fellows

memoir = **account**, life, record, journal, essay, biography, narrative, monograph

memoirs = **autobiography**, diary, life story, experiences, memories, journals, recollections, reminiscences

memorable = **noteworthy**, celebrated, historic, striking, famous, significant, remarkable, notable OPPOSITE: forgettable

m

memorandum = note, minute, message, communication, reminder, memo, jotting

memorial NOUN
1 = monument, shrine, plaque, cenotaph
▷ ADJECTIVE
2 = commemorative, remembrance, monumental

memory 1 = recall, mind, retention, ability to remember, powers of recall, powers of retention 2 = recollection, reminder, reminiscence, impression, echo, remembrance 3 = commemoration, respect, honour, recognition, tribute, remembrance, observance

menace NOUN 1 (Informal) = nuisance, plague, pest, annoyance, troublemaker
2 = threat, warning, intimidation, ill-omen, ominousness
▷ VERB 3 = bully, threaten, intimidate, terrorize, frighten, scare

menacing = threatening, frightening, forbidding, looming, intimidating, ominous, louring or lowering
OPPOSITE: encouraging

mend 1 = repair, fix, restore, renew, patch up, renovate, refit, retouch 2 = darn, repair, patch, stitch, sew 3 = heal, improve, recover, get better, be all right, be cured, recuperate, pull through 4 = improve, reform, correct, revise, amend, rectify, ameliorate, emend
▷ PHRASES: on the mend
= convalescent, improving, recovering, getting better, recuperating

mental 1 = intellectual, rational, theoretical, cognitive, brain, conceptual, cerebral
2 (Informal) = insane, mad, disturbed, unstable, mentally ill, psychotic, unbalanced, deranged

mentality = attitude, character, personality, psychology, make-up, outlook, disposition, cast of mind

mentally = psychologically, intellectually, inwardly

mention VERB 1 = refer to, point out, bring up, state, reveal, declare, disclose, intimate
▷ NOUN 2 often with of
= reference to, observation, indication, remark on, allusion to 3 = acknowledgment, recognition, tribute, citation, honourable mention

mentor = guide, teacher, coach, adviser, tutor, instructor, counsellor, guru

menu = bill of fare, tariff (chiefly Brit.), set menu, table d'hôte (French), carte du jour (French)

merchandise = goods, produce, stock, products, commodities, wares

merchant = tradesman, dealer, trader, broker, retailer, supplier, seller, salesman

mercy 1 = compassion, pity, forgiveness, grace, kindness, clemency, leniency, forbearance **OPPOSITE:** cruelty 2 = **blessing**, boon, godsend

mere 1 = simple, nothing more than, common, plain, pure 2 = bare, slender, trifling, meagre, just, only, basic, no more than

merge 1 = combine, blend, fuse, amalgamate, unite, join, mix, mingle **OPPOSITE:** separate 2 = **join**, unite, combine, fuse **OPPOSITE:** separate 3 = **melt**, blend, mingle

merger = union, fusion, consolidation, amalgamation, combination, coalition, incorporation

merit NOUN 1 = advantage, value, quality, worth, strength, asset, virtue, strong point ▷ VERB 2 = **deserve**, warrant, be entitled to, earn, have a right to, be worthy of

merry 1 = cheerful, happy, carefree, jolly, festive, joyous, convivial, blithe **OPPOSITE:** gloomy 2 (*Brit. informal*) = tipsy, happy, mellow, tiddly (*slang, chiefly Brit.*), squiffy (*Brit. informal*)

mesh NOUN 1 = net, netting, network, web, tracery ▷ VERB 2 = **engage**, combine, connect, knit, coordinate, interlock, dovetail, harmonize

mess NOUN 1 = untidiness, disorder, confusion, chaos, litter, clutter, disarray, jumble 2 = **shambles** 3 = **difficulty**, dilemma, plight, hole (*informal*), fix (*informal*), jam (*informal*), muddle, pickle (*informal*), uphill (*S. African*)

▷ PHRASES: **mess about** or **around** = potter about, dabble, amuse yourself, fool about or around, muck about or around (*informal*), play about or around, trifle ▶ **mess something up** 1 = botch, muck something up (*Brit. slang*), muddle something up 2 = **dirty**, pollute, clutter, disarrange, dishevel ▶ **mess with something** or **someone** = interfere, play, fiddle (*informal*), tamper, tinker, meddle

message 1 = communication, note, bulletin, word, letter, dispatch, memorandum, communiqué 2 = **point**, meaning, idea, moral, theme, import, purport

messenger = courier, runner, carrier, herald, envoy, go-between, emissary, delivery boy

messy 1 = disorganized, sloppy (*informal*), untidy 2 = **dirty** 3 = **untidy**, disordered, chaotic, muddled, cluttered, shambolic, disorganized **OPPOSITE:** tidy 4 = **dishevelled**, ruffled, untidy, rumpled, bedraggled, tousled, uncombed 5 = **confusing**, difficult, complex, confused, tangled, chaotic, tortuous

m

metaphor = figure of speech, image, symbol, analogy, conceit (*literary*), allegory, trope, figurative expression

method 1 = manner, process, approach, technique, way, system, style, procedure 2 = orderliness, planning, order, system, purpose, pattern, organization, regularity

midday = noon, twelve o'clock, noonday

middle NOUN 1 = centre, heart, midst, halfway point, midpoint, midsection
▷ ADJECTIVE 2 = central, medium, mid, intervening, halfway, intermediate, median 3 = intermediate, intervening

middle-class = bourgeois, traditional, conventional

middling 1 = mediocre, all right, indifferent, so-so (*informal*), unremarkable, tolerable, run-of-the-mill, passable, half-pie (*N.Z. informal*) 2 = moderate, medium, average, fair, ordinary, modest, adequate

midnight = twelve o'clock, middle of the night, dead of night, the witching hour

midst PHRASES: in the midst of = among, during, in the middle of, surrounded by, amidst, in the thick of

midway ADJECTIVE, ADVERB = halfway, in the middle of, part-way, equidistant, at the midpoint, betwixt and between

might = power, force, energy, strength, vigour
▷ PHRASES: with all your might = forcefully, vigorously, mightily, manfully, lustily

mighty = powerful, strong, strapping, robust, vigorous, sturdy, forceful, lusty OPPOSITE: weak

migrant NOUN 1 = wanderer, immigrant, traveller, rover, nomad, emigrant, itinerant, drifter
▷ ADJECTIVE 2 = itinerant, wandering, drifting, roving, travelling, shifting, immigrant, transient

migrate = move, travel, journey, wander, trek, voyage, roam, emigrate

migration = wandering, journey, voyage, travel, movement, trek, emigration, roving

mild 1 = gentle, calm, easy-going, meek, placid, docile, peaceable, equable OPPOSITE: harsh 2 = temperate, warm, calm, moderate, tranquil, balmy OPPOSITE: cold 3 = bland, thin, smooth, tasteless, insipid, flavourless

militant = aggressive, active, vigorous, assertive, combative OPPOSITE: peaceful

military ADJECTIVE 1 = warlike, armed, soldierly, martial
▷ NOUN 2 = armed forces, forces, services, army

milk = **exploit**, pump, take advantage of

mill NOUN 1 = **grinder**, crusher, quern 2 = **factory**, works, plant, workshop, foundry
▷ VERB 3 = **grind**, pound, crush, powder, grate
▷ PHRASES: **mill about** or **around** = **swarm**, crowd, stream, surge, throng

mimic VERB 1 = **imitate**, do (*informal*), take off (*informal*), ape, parody, caricature, impersonate
▷ NOUN 2 = **imitator**, impressionist, copycat (*informal*), impersonator, caricaturist

mince 1 = **cut**, grind, crumble, dice, hash, chop up 2 = **tone down**, spare, moderate, weaken, soften

mincing = **affected**, camp (*informal*), precious, pretentious, dainty, sissy, effeminate, foppish

mind NOUN 1 = **memory**, recollection, remembrance, powers of recollection 2 = **intelligence**, reason, reasoning, understanding, sense, brain(s) (*informal*), wits, intellect 3 = **intention**, wish, desire, urge, fancy, leaning, notion, inclination 4 = **sanity**, reason, senses, judgment, wits, marbles (*informal*), rationality, mental balance
▷ VERB 5 = **take offence at**, dislike, care about, object to, resent, disapprove of, be bothered by, be affronted by 6 = **be careful**, watch, take care, be wary, be cautious, be on your guard 7 = **look after**, watch, protect, tend, guard, take care of, attend to, keep an eye on 8 = **pay attention to**, mark, note, listen to, observe, obey, heed, take heed of

mine NOUN 1 = **pit**, deposit, shaft, colliery, excavation 2 = **source**, store, fund, stock, supply, reserve, treasury, wealth
▷ VERB 3 = **dig up**, extract, quarry, unearth, excavate, hew, dig for

miner = **coalminer**, pitman (*Brit.*), collier (*Brit.*)

mingle 1 = **mix**, combine, blend, merge, unite, join, interweave, intermingle OPPOSITE: separate 2 = **associate**, consort, socialize, rub shoulders (*informal*), hobnob, fraternize, hang about or around OPPOSITE: dissociate

miniature = **small**, little, minute, tiny, toy, scaled-down, diminutive, minuscule OPPOSITE: giant

minimal = **minimum**, smallest, least, slightest, token, nominal, negligible, least possible

minimize 1 = **reduce**, decrease, shrink, diminish, prune, curtail, miniaturize OPPOSITE: increase 2 = **play down**, discount,

m

belittle, disparage, decry, underrate, deprecate, make light *or* little of **OPPOSITE:** praise

minimum ADJECTIVE

1 = **lowest**, smallest, least, slightest, minimal, least possible **OPPOSITE:** maximum

▷ NOUN 2 = **lowest**, least, lowest level, nadir

minister NOUN

1 = **clergyman**, priest, vicar, parson, preacher, pastor, cleric, rector

▷ VERB 2 *often with* **to** = **attend**, serve, tend, take care of, cater to, pander to, administer to

ministry 1 = **department**, office, bureau, government department

2 = **administration**, council

3 = **the priesthood**, the church, the cloth, holy orders

minor = **small**, lesser, slight, petty, trivial, insignificant, unimportant, inconsequential **OPPOSITE:** major

mint = **make**, produce, strike, cast, stamp, punch, coin

minute¹ NOUN 1 = **moment**, second, bit, flash, instant, tick (*Brit. informal*), sec (*informal*), short time

▷ PLURAL NOUN 2 = **record**, notes, proceedings, transactions, transcript, memorandum

minute² 1 = **small**, little, tiny, miniature, microscopic,

diminutive, minuscule, infinitesimal **OPPOSITE:** huge

2 = **precise**, close, detailed, critical, exact, meticulous, exhaustive, painstaking **OPPOSITE:** imprecise

miracle = **wonder**, phenomenon, sensation, marvel, amazing achievement, astonishing feat

miraculous = **wonderful**, amazing, extraordinary, incredible, astonishing, unbelievable, phenomenal, astounding **OPPOSITE:** ordinary

mirror NOUN 1 = **looking-glass**, glass (*Brit.*), reflector

▷ VERB 2 = **reflect**, follow, copy, echo, emulate

miscarriage = **failure**, error, breakdown, mishap, perversion

misconduct = **immorality**, wrongdoing, mismanagement, malpractice, impropriety

miserable 1 = **sad**, depressed, gloomy, forlorn, dejected, despondent, sorrowful, wretched **OPPOSITE:** happy

2 = **pathetic**, sorry, shameful, despicable, deplorable, lamentable **OPPOSITE:** respectable

misery 1 = **unhappiness**, distress, despair, grief, suffering, depression, gloom, torment **OPPOSITE:** happiness 2 (*Brit. informal*) = **moaner**, pessimist, killjoy, spoilsport, prophet of doom, wet blanket (*informal*), sourpuss (*informal*)

misfortune 1 *often plural* = **bad luck**, adversity, hard luck, ill luck, infelicity 2 = **mishap**, trouble, disaster, reverse, tragedy, setback, calamity, affliction, tribulation **OPPOSITE:** good luck

misguided = **unwise**, mistaken, misplaced, deluded, ill-advised, imprudent, injudicious

mislead = **deceive**, fool, delude, take someone in (*informal*), misdirect, misinform, hoodwink, misguide

misleading = **confusing**, false, ambiguous, deceptive, evasive, disingenuous **OPPOSITE:** straightforward

miss VERB 1 = **fail to notice**, overlook, pass over 2 = **long for**, yearn for, pine for, long to see, ache for, feel the loss of, regret the absence of 3 = **not go to**, skip, cut, omit, be absent from, fail to attend, skive off (*informal*), play truant from, bludge (*Austral. & N.Z. informal*) 4 = **avoid**, beat, escape, skirt, duck, cheat, bypass, dodge ▷ NOUN 5 = **mistake**, failure, error, blunder, omission, oversight

missile = **projectile**, weapon, shell, rocket

missing = **lost**, misplaced, not present, astray, unaccounted for, mislaid

mission = **task**, job, commission, duty, undertaking, quest, assignment, vocation

missionary = **evangelist**, preacher, apostle

mist = **fog**, cloud, steam, spray, film, haze, vapour, smog

mistake NOUN 1 = **error**, blunder, oversight, slip, gaffe (*informal*), miscalculation, faux pas 2 = **oversight**, error, slip, fault, howler (*informal*), erratum ▷ VERB 3 = **confuse with**, take for, mix up with 4 = **misunderstand**, misinterpret, misjudge, misread, misconstrue, misapprehend

mistaken 1 = **wrong**, incorrect, misguided, wide of the mark **OPPOSITE:** correct 2 = **inaccurate**, false, faulty, erroneous, unsound **OPPOSITE:** accurate

mistress = **lover**, girlfriend, concubine, kept woman, paramour

misunderstand
1 = **misinterpret**, misread, mistake, misjudge, misconstrue, misapprehend, be at cross-purposes with 2 = **miss the point**, get the wrong end of the stick

misunderstanding
= **mistake**, error, mix-up, misconception, misinterpretation, misjudgment

misuse NOUN 1 = **waste**, squandering 2 = **abuse** 3 = **misapplication**, abuse,

illegal use, wrong use
4 = **perversion**, desecration
5 = **misapplication**
▷ VERB **6** = **abuse**, misapply, prostitute **7** = **waste**, squander, embezzle, misappropriate

mix VERB **1** = **combine**, blend, merge, join, cross, fuse, mingle, jumble **2** = **socialize**, associate, hang out (*informal*), mingle, circulate, consort, hobnob, fraternize **3** *often with* **up** = **combine**, marry, blend, integrate, amalgamate, coalesce, meld
▷ NOUN **4** = **mixture**, combination, blend, fusion, compound, assortment, alloy, medley
▷ PHRASES: **mix something up 1** = **confuse**, scramble, muddle, confound **2** = **blend**, beat, mix, stir, fold

mixed 1 = **varied**, diverse, different, differing, cosmopolitan, assorted, jumbled, disparate **OPPOSITE:** homogeneous **2** = **combined**, blended, united, compound, composite, mingled, amalgamated **OPPOSITE:** pure

mixed-up = **confused**, disturbed, puzzled, bewildered, at sea, upset, distraught, muddled

mixture 1 = **blend**, mix, variety, fusion, assortment, brew, jumble, medley **2** = **composite**, compound, combination, blend **3** = **cross**, combination, blend

4 = **concoction**, compound, blend, brew, amalgam

mix-up = **confusion**, mistake, misunderstanding, mess, tangle, muddle

moan VERB **1** = **groan**, sigh, sob, whine, lament **2** (*Informal*) = **grumble**, complain, groan, whine, carp, grouse, whinge (*informal*), bleat
▷ NOUN **3** = **groan**, sigh, sob, lament, wail, grunt, whine
4 (*Informal*) = **complaint**, protest, grumble, whine, grouse, gripe (*informal*), grouch (*informal*)

mob NOUN **1** = **crowd**, pack, mass, host, drove, flock, swarm, horde **2** (*Slang*) = **gang**, group, set, lot, crew (*informal*)
▷ VERB **3** = **surround**, besiege, jostle, fall on, set upon, crowd around, swarm around

mobile = **movable**, moving, travelling, wandering, portable, itinerant, peripatetic

mobilize 1 = **rally**, organize, stimulate, excite, prompt, marshal, activate, awaken
2 = **deploy**, prepare, ready, rally, assemble, call up, marshal, muster

mock VERB **1** = **laugh at**, tease, ridicule, taunt, scorn, sneer, scoff, deride **OPPOSITE:** respect
▷ ADJECTIVE **2** = **imitation**, pretended, artificial, fake, false, dummy, sham, feigned
OPPOSITE: genuine

mocking = **scornful**, scoffing,

satirical, contemptuous, sarcastic, sardonic, disrespectful, disdainful

mode 1 = **method**, way, system, form, process, style, technique, manner
2 = **fashion**, style, trend, rage, vogue, look, craze

model NOUN
1 = **representation**, image, copy, miniature, dummy, replica, imitation, duplicate
2 = **pattern**, example, standard, original, ideal, prototype, paradigm, archetype 3 = **sitter**, subject, poser
▷ VERB 4 = **show off** (*informal*), wear, display, sport 5 = **shape**, form, design, fashion, carve, mould, sculpt

moderate ADJECTIVE 1 = **mild**, reasonable, controlled, limited, steady, modest, restrained, middle-of-the-road OPPOSITE: extreme 2 = **average**, middling, fair, ordinary, indifferent, mediocre, so-so (*informal*), passable, half-pie (*N.Z. informal*)
▷ VERB 3 = **soften**, control, temper, regulate, curb, restrain, subdue, lessen 4 = **lessen**, ease OPPOSITE: intensify

modern 1 = **current**, contemporary, recent, present-day, latter-day 2 = **up-to-date**, fresh, new, novel, newfangled OPPOSITE: old-fashioned

modest 1 = **moderate**, small, limited, fair, ordinary, middling, meagre, frugal

2 = **unpretentious**, reserved, retiring, shy, coy, reticent, self-effacing, demure

modesty = **reserve**, humility, shyness, reticence, timidity, diffidence, coyness, bashfulness OPPOSITE: conceit

modification = **change**, variation, qualification, adjustment, revision, alteration, refinement

modify 1 = **change**, reform, convert, alter, adjust, adapt, revise, remodel 2 = **tone down**, lower, qualify, ease, moderate, temper, soften, restrain

mogul = **tycoon**, baron, magnate, big shot (*informal*), big noise (*informal*), big hitter (*informal*), heavy hitter (*informal*), V.I.P.

moist = **damp**, wet, soggy, humid, clammy, dewy

moisture = **damp**, water, liquid, dew, wetness

molecule = **particle**, jot, speck

moment 1 = **instant**, second, flash, twinkling, split second, jiffy (*informal*), trice 2 = **time**, point, stage, juncture

momentous = **significant**, important, vital, critical, crucial, historic, pivotal, fateful OPPOSITE: unimportant

momentum = **impetus**, force, power, drive, push, energy, strength, thrust

monarch = **ruler**, king or queen, sovereign, tsar or tsarina, potentate, emperor or empress,

m

prince *or* princess

monarchy 1 = **sovereignty**, autocracy, kingship, royalism, monocracy 2 = **kingdom**, empire, realm, principality

monastery = **abbey**, convent, priory, cloister, nunnery, friary

monetary = **financial**, money, economic, capital, cash, fiscal, budgetary, pecuniary

money = **cash**, capital, currency, hard cash, readies (*informal*), riches, silver, coin

monitor VERB 1 = **check**, follow, watch, survey, observe, keep an eye on, keep track of, keep tabs on
▷ NOUN 2 = **guide**, observer, supervisor, invigilator
3 = **prefect** (*Brit.*), head girl, head boy, senior boy, senior girl

monk (*Loosely*) = **friar**, brother
● RELATED WORD
● *adjective:* monastic

monkey 1 = **simian**, ape, primate 2 = **rascal**, horror, devil, rogue, imp, tyke, scallywag, scamp, nointer (*Austral. slang*)
▷ See panel MONKEYS, APES AND OTHER PRIMATES

monster NOUN 1 = **giant**, mammoth, titan, colossus, monstrosity 2 = **brute**, devil, beast, demon, villain, fiend
▷ ADJECTIVE 3 = **huge**, massive, enormous, tremendous, immense, gigantic, mammoth, colossal

monstrous 1 = **outrageous**,

shocking, foul, intolerable, disgraceful, scandalous, inhuman, diabolical OPPOSITE: decent 2 = **huge**, massive, enormous, tremendous, immense, mammoth, colossal, prodigious OPPOSITE: tiny 3 = **unnatural**, horrible, hideous, grotesque, gruesome, frightful, freakish, fiendish OPPOSITE: normal

monument = **memorial**, cairn, marker, shrine, tombstone, mausoleum, commemoration, headstone

monumental 1 = **important**, significant, enormous, historic, memorable, awesome, majestic, unforgettable OPPOSITE: unimportant 2 (*Informal*) = **immense**, great, massive, staggering, colossal OPPOSITE: tiny

mood = **state of mind**, spirit, humour, temper, disposition, frame of mind

moody 1 = **changeable**, volatile, unpredictable, erratic, fickle, temperamental, impulsive, mercurial OPPOSITE: stable 2 = **sulky**, irritable, temperamental, touchy, ill-tempered, tooshie (*Austral. slang*) OPPOSITE: cheerful 3 = **gloomy**, sad, sullen, glum, morose OPPOSITE: cheerful 4 = **sad**, gloomy, melancholy, sombre

moon NOUN 1 = **satellite**
▷ VERB 2 = **idle**, drift, loaf,

MONKEYS, APES AND OTHER PRIMATES

baboon	loris
Barbary ape	macaque
bushbaby or galago	mandrill
capuchin	mangabey
chacma	marmoset
chimpanzee or chimp	mona
colobus	monkey or (archaic)
douroucouli	jackanapes
flying lemur or colugo	orang-outang, orang-utan, or
gelada	orang
gibbon	proboscis monkey
gorilla	rhesus monkey
green monkey	saki
grivet	siamang
guenon	sifaka
guereza	spider monkey
howler monkey	squirrel monkey
indris or indri	tamarin
langur	tarsier
lemur	vervet

languish, waste time, daydream, mope

moor¹ = moorland, fell (*Brit.*), heath

moor² = **tie up**, secure, anchor, dock, lash, berth, make fast

mop NOUN 1 = **squeegee**, sponge, swab 2 = **mane**, shock, mass, tangle, mat, thatch
▷ VERB 3 = **clean**, wash, wipe, sponge, swab

moral ADJECTIVE 1 = **good**, just, right, principled, decent, noble, ethical, honourable
OPPOSITE: immoral
▷ NOUN 2 = **lesson**, meaning, point, message, teaching,

import, significance, precept
▷ PLURAL NOUN 3 = **morality**, standards, conduct, principles, behaviour, manners, habits, ethics

morale = **confidence**, heart, spirit, self-esteem, team spirit, esprit de corps

morality 1 = **virtue**, justice, morals, honour, integrity, goodness, honesty, decency
2 = **ethics**, conduct, principles, morals, manners, philosophy, mores 3 = **rights and wrongs**, ethics

moratorium = **postponement**, freeze, halt, suspension, standstill

m

more ADJECTIVE 1 = **extra**, additional, new, other, added, further, new-found, supplementary

▷ ADVERB 2 = **to a greater extent**, longer, better, further, some more 3 = **moreover**, also, in addition, besides, furthermore, what's more, on top of that, to boot

moreover = **furthermore**, also, further, in addition, too, as well, besides, additionally

morning 1 = **before noon**, forenoon, morn (*poetic*), a.m. 2 = **dawn**, sunrise, first light, daybreak, break of day

mortal ADJECTIVE 1 = **human**, worldly, passing, fleshly, temporal, transient, ephemeral, perishable 2 = **fatal**, killing, terminal, deadly, destructive, lethal, murderous, death-dealing

▷ NOUN 3 = **human being**, being, man, woman, person, human, individual, earthling

mortality 1 = **humanity**, transience, impermanence, corporeality, impermanency 2 = **death**, dying, fatality

mostly 1 = **mainly**, largely, chiefly, principally, primarily, on the whole, predominantly 2 = **generally**, usually, on the whole, as a rule

moth
● RELATED WORDS
● *young:* caterpillar
● *enthusiast:* lepidopterist

▷ *See panel* BUTTERFLIES AND MOTHS

mother NOUN 1 = **female parent**, mum (*Brit. informal*), ma (*informal*), mater, dam, mummy (*Brit. informal*), foster mother, biological mother

▷ VERB 2 = **nurture**, raise, protect, tend, nurse, rear, care for, cherish

▷ ADJECTIVE 3 = **native**, natural, innate, inborn
● RELATED WORD
● *adjective:* maternal

motherly = **maternal**, loving, caring, comforting, sheltering, protective, affectionate

motif 1 = **design**, shape, decoration, ornament 2 = **theme**, idea, subject, concept, leitmotif

motion NOUN 1 = **movement**, mobility, travel, progress, flow, locomotion 2 = **proposal**, suggestion, recommendation, proposition, submission

▷ VERB 3 = **gesture**, direct, wave, signal, nod, beckon, gesticulate

motivate 1 = **inspire**, drive, stimulate, move, cause, prompt, stir, induce 2 = **stimulate**, drive, inspire, stir, arouse, galvanize, incentivize

motivation = **incentive**, inspiration, motive, stimulus, reason, spur, inducement, incitement

motive = **reason**, ground(s),

purpose, object, incentive, inspiration, stimulus, rationale

motto = **saying**, slogan, maxim, rule, adage, proverb, dictum, precept

mould¹ NOUN 1 = **cast**, shape, pattern 2 = **design**, style, fashion, build, form, kind, shape, pattern 3 = **nature**, character, sort, kind, quality, type, stamp, calibre ▷ VERB 4 = **shape**, make, work, form, create, model, fashion, construct 5 = **influence**, make, form, control, direct, affect, shape

mould² = **fungus**, blight, mildew

mound 1 = **heap**, pile, drift, stack, rick 2 = **hill**, bank, rise, dune, embankment, knoll, hillock, kopje or koppie (S. African)

mount VERB 1 = **increase**, build, grow, swell, intensify, escalate, multiply **OPPOSITE:** decrease 2 = **accumulate**, increase, collect, gather, build up, pile up, amass 3 = **ascend**, scale, climb (up), go up, clamber up **OPPOSITE:** descend 4 = **get (up) on**, jump on, straddle, climb onto, hop on to, bestride, get on the back of **OPPOSITE:** get off 5 = **display**, present, prepare, put on, organize, put on display ▷ NOUN 6 = **horse**, steed (literary) 7 = **backing**, setting, support, stand, base, frame

mountain 1 = **peak**, mount, horn, ridge, fell (Brit.), berg (S. African), alp, pinnacle 2 = **heap**, mass, masses, pile, a great deal, ton, stack, abundance

mourn 1 often with **for** = **grieve for**, lament, weep for, wail for 2 = **bemoan**, rue, deplore, bewail

mourning 1 = **grieving**, grief, bereavement, weeping, woe, lamentation 2 = **black**, sackcloth and ashes, widow's weeds

mouth 1 = **lips**, jaws, gob (slang, esp. Brit.), maw, cakehole (Brit. slang) 2 = **entrance**, opening, gateway, door, aperture, orifice 3 = **opening** 4 = **inlet**, outlet, estuary, firth, outfall, debouchment

move VERB 1 = **transfer**, change, switch, shift, transpose 2 = **go**, advance, progress, shift, proceed, stir, budge, make a move 3 = **relocate**, leave, remove, quit, migrate, emigrate, decamp, up sticks (Brit. informal) 4 = **drive**, cause, influence, persuade, shift, inspire, prompt, induce **OPPOSITE:** discourage 5 = **touch**, affect, excite, impress, stir, disquiet 6 = **propose**, suggest, urge, recommend, request, advocate, submit, put forward ▷ NOUN 7 = **action**, step, manoeuvre 8 = **ploy**, action, measure, step, initiative, stroke,

m

tactic, manoeuvre **9** = **transfer**, posting, shift, removal, relocation **10** = **turn**, go, play, chance, shot (*informal*), opportunity

movement 1 = **group**, party, organization, grouping, front, faction **2** = **campaign**, drive, push, crusade **3** = **move**, action, motion, manoeuvre **4** = **activity**, moving, stirring, bustle **5** = **advance**, progress, flow **6** = **transfer**, transportation, displacement **7** = **development**, change, variation, fluctuation **8** = **progression**, progress **9** (*Music*) = **section**, part, division, passage

movie = **film**, picture, feature, flick (*slang*)

moving 1 = **emotional**, touching, affecting, inspiring, stirring, poignant **OPPOSITE:** unemotional **2** = **mobile**, running, active, going, operational, in motion, driving, kinetic **OPPOSITE:** stationary

mow = **cut**, crop, trim, shear, scythe
▷ **PHRASES: mow something or someone down** = **massacre**, butcher, slaughter, cut down, shoot down, cut to pieces

much ADVERB 1 = **greatly**, a lot, considerably, decidedly, exceedingly, appreciably **OPPOSITE:** hardly **2** = **often**, a lot, routinely, a great deal, many times, habitually, on many occasions, customarily
▷ **DETERMINER 3** = **great**, a lot of, plenty of, considerable, substantial, piles of (*informal*), ample, abundant **OPPOSITE:** little
▷ **PRONOUN 4** = **a lot**, plenty, a great deal, lots (*informal*), masses (*informal*), loads (*informal*), tons (*informal*), heaps (*informal*) **OPPOSITE:** little

muck 1 = **dirt**, mud, filth, ooze, sludge, mire, slime, gunge (*informal*), kak (*S. African informal*) **2** = **manure**, dung, ordure

mud = **dirt**, clay, ooze, silt, sludge, mire, slime

muddle NOUN 1 = **confusion**, mess, disorder, chaos, tangle, mix-up, disarray, predicament
▷ **VERB 2** = **jumble**, disorder, scramble, tangle, mix up **3** = **confuse**, bewilder, daze, confound, perplex, disorient, stupefy, befuddle

muddy 1 = **boggy**, swampy, marshy, quaggy **2** = **dirty**, soiled, grimy, mucky, mud-caked, bespattered

mug¹ = **cup**, pot, beaker, tankard

mug² NOUN (*Informal*) **1** = **face**, features, countenance, visage
▷ **NOUN 2** = **fool**, sucker (*slang*), chump (*informal*), simpleton, easy or soft touch (*slang*), dorba or dorb (*Austral. slang*), bogan (*Austral. slang*)

mug³ = **attack**, assault, beat up, rob, set about or upon

▷ **PHRASES: mug up (on)**
something = study, cram
(*informal*), bone up on (*informal*),
swot up on (*Brit. informal*)
multiple = many, several,
various, numerous, sundry,
manifold, multitudinous
multiply 1 = increase, extend,
expand, spread, build up,
proliferate **OPPOSITE:** decrease
2 = reproduce, breed,
propagate
multitude 1 = great number,
host, army, mass, horde, myriad
2 = crowd, host, mass, mob,
swarm, horde, throng
mundane 1 = ordinary,
routine, commonplace, banal,
everyday, day-to-day, prosaic,
humdrum **OPPOSITE:**
extraordinary 2 = earthly,
worldly, secular, mortal,
terrestrial, temporal **OPPOSITE:**
spiritual
municipal = civic, public, local,
council, district, urban,
metropolitan
murder NOUN 1 = killing,
homicide, massacre,
assassination, slaying,
bloodshed, carnage, butchery
▷ **VERB** 2 = kill, massacre,
slaughter, assassinate,
eliminate (*slang*), butcher, slay,
bump off (*slang*)
murderer = killer, assassin,
slayer, butcher, slaughterer, cut-
throat, hit man (*slang*)
murderous = deadly, savage,
brutal, cruel, lethal, ferocious,

cut-throat, bloodthirsty
murky 1 = dark, gloomy, grey,
dull, dim, cloudy, misty,
overcast **OPPOSITE:** bright
2 = dark, cloudy
murmur VERB 1 = mumble,
whisper, mutter
▷ **NOUN** 2 = whisper, drone,
purr
muscle 1 = tendon, sinew
2 = strength, might, power,
weight, stamina, brawn
▷ **PHRASES: muscle in** (*Informal*)
= impose yourself, encroach,
butt in, force your way in
muscular = strong, powerful,
athletic, strapping, robust,
vigorous, sturdy, sinewy
muse = ponder, consider,
reflect, contemplate, deliberate,
brood, meditate, mull over
music NOUN ▷ *See panel*
MUSICAL EXPRESSIONS AND
TEMPO INSTRUCTIONS
musical = melodious, lyrical,
harmonious, melodic, tuneful,
dulcet, sweet-sounding,
euphonious **OPPOSITE:**
discordant
must = necessity, essential,
requirement, fundamental,
imperative, requisite,
prerequisite, sine qua non
(*Latin*)
muster VERB 1 = summon up,
marshal 2 = rally, gather,
assemble, marshal, mobilize,
call together 3 = assemble,
convene
▷ **NOUN** 4 = assembly,

m

MUSICAL EXPRESSIONS AND TEMPO INSTRUCTIONS

Instruction	Meaning
accelerando	with increasing speed
adagio	slowly
agitato	in an agitated manner
allegretto	fairly quickly or briskly
allegro	quickly, in a brisk, lively manner
amoroso	lovingly
andante	at a moderately slow tempo
andantino	slightly faster than andante
assai	(in combination) very
cantabile	in a singing style
con	(in combination) with
con amore	lovingly
con brio	vigorously
con moto	quickly
crescendo	gradual increase in loudness
diminuendo	gradual decrease in loudness
dolce	gently and sweetly
doloroso	in a sorrowful manner
espressivo	expressively
forte	loud or loudly
fortissimo	very loud
furioso	in a frantically rushing manner
giocoso	merry
grave	solemn and slow
grazioso	graceful
largo	slowly and broadly
larghetto	slowly and broadly, but less so than largo
legato	smoothly and connectedly
leggiero	light
lento	slowly
maestoso	majestically
mezzo	(in combination) moderately
moderato	at a moderate tempo
molto	(in combination) very
non troppo or non tanto	(in combination) not too much
pianissimo	very quietly

MUSICAL EXPRESSIONS AND TEMPO INSTRUCTIONS *continued*

Instruction	Meaning
piano	softly
più	(in combination) more
pizzicato	(in music for stringed instruments) to be plucked with the finger
poco *or* un poco	(in combination) a little
pomposo	in a pompous manner
presto	very fast
prestissimo	faster than presto
quasi	(in combination) almost, as if
rallentando	becoming slower
rubato	with a flexible tempo
scherzando	in jocular style
semplice	simple and unforced
sforzando	with strong initial attack
sostenuto	in a smooth and sustained manner
sotto voce	extremely quiet
staccato	(of notes) short, clipped, and separate
strepitoso	noisy
stringendo	with increasing speed
tanto	(in combination) too much
troppo	(in combination) too much
vivace	in a brisk lively manner

meeting, collection, gathering, rally, convention, congregation, roundup, hui (N.Z.), runanga (N.Z.)

mutation 1 = **anomaly**, variation, deviant, freak of nature 2 = **change**, variation, evolution, transformation, modification, alteration, metamorphosis, transfiguration

mute 1 = **close-mouthed**, silent 2 = **silent**, dumb, unspoken, tacit, wordless, voiceless, unvoiced 3 = **dumb**, speechless, voiceless

mutter = **grumble**, complain, murmur, rumble, whine, mumble, grouse, bleat

mutual = **shared**, common, joint, returned, reciprocal, interchangeable, requited

● **USAGE NOTE**
● *Mutual* is sometimes used, as
● in *a mutual friend*, to mean

- 'common to or shared by two
- or more people'. This use has
- sometimes been frowned on
- in the past because it does
- not reflect the two-way
- relationship contained in the
- origins of the word, which
- comes from Latin *mutuus*
- meaning 'reciprocal'.
- However, this usage is very
- common and is now
- generally regarded as
- acceptable.

myriad NOUN 1 = **multitude**, host, army, swarm, horde
▷ ADJECTIVE 2 = **innumerable**, countless, untold, incalculable, immeasurable, multitudinous

mysterious 1 = **strange**, puzzling, secret, weird, perplexing, uncanny, mystifying, arcane OPPOSITE: clear 2 = **secretive**, enigmatic, evasive, discreet, covert, reticent, furtive, inscrutable

mystery = **puzzle**, problem, question, secret, riddle, enigma, conundrum, teaser

mystic *or* **mystical** = **supernatural**, mysterious, transcendental, occult, metaphysical, paranormal, inscrutable, otherworldly

myth 1 = **legend**, story, fiction, saga, fable, allegory, fairy story, folk tale 2 = **illusion**, story, fancy, fantasy, imagination, invention, delusion, superstition

mythology = **legend**, folklore, tradition, lore

Nn

nab = **catch**, arrest, apprehend, seize, grab, capture, collar (*informal*), snatch

nag[1] VERB 1 = **scold**, harass, badger, pester, worry, plague, hassle (*informal*), upbraid
▷ NOUN 2 = **scold**, complainer, grumbler, virago, shrew, tartar, moaner, harpy

nag[2] = **horse** (*U.S.*), hack

nagging 1 = **continuous**, persistent, continual, niggling, repeated, constant, endless, perpetual 2 = **scolding**, shrewish

nail NOUN 1 = **tack**, spike, rivet, hobnail, brad (*technical*)
2 = **fingernail**, toenail, talon, thumbnail, claw
▷ VERB 3 = **fasten**, fix, secure, attach, pin, hammer, tack
4 (*informal*) = **catch**, arrest, capture, apprehend, trap, snare, ensnare, entrap

naive *or* **naïve** = **gullible**, trusting, credulous, unsuspicious, green, simple, innocent, callow OPPOSITE: worldly

naked = **nude**, stripped, exposed, bare, undressed,

starkers (*informal*), stark-naked, unclothed **OPPOSITE:** dressed

name NOUN 1 = **title**, nickname, designation, term, handle (*slang*), epithet, sobriquet, moniker *or* monicker (*slang*)
▷ VERB 2 = **call**, christen, baptize, dub, term, style, label, entitle 3 = **nominate**, choose, select, appoint, specify, designate

namely = **specifically**, to wit, viz.

nap¹ NOUN 1 = **sleep**, rest, kip (*Brit. slang*), siesta, catnap, forty winks (*informal*)
▷ VERB 2 = **sleep**, rest, drop off (*informal*), doze, kip (*Brit. slang*), snooze (*informal*), nod off (*informal*), catnap

nap² = **pile**, down, fibre, weave, grain

napkin = **serviette**, cloth

narcotic NOUN 1 = **drug**, anaesthetic, painkiller, sedative, opiate, tranquillizer, anodyne, analgesic
▷ ADJECTIVE 2 = **sedative**, calming, hypnotic, analgesic, soporific, painkilling

narrative = **story**, report, history, account, statement, tale, chronicle

narrator = **storyteller**, writer, author, reporter, commentator, chronicler

narrow ADJECTIVE 1 = **thin**, fine, slim, slender, tapering, attenuated **OPPOSITE:** broad

2 = **limited**, restricted, confined, tight, close, meagre, constricted **OPPOSITE:** wide
3 = **insular**, prejudiced, partial, dogmatic, intolerant, narrow-minded, small-minded, illiberal **OPPOSITE:** broad-minded
▷ VERB 4 = **restrict**, limit, reduce, constrict 5 = **get narrower**, taper, shrink, tighten, constrict

narrowly = **just**, barely, only just, scarcely, by the skin of your teeth

nasty 1 = **unpleasant**, ugly, disagreeable **OPPOSITE:** pleasant 2 = **spiteful**, mean, offensive, vicious, unpleasant, vile, malicious, despicable **OPPOSITE:** pleasant
3 = **disgusting**, unpleasant, offensive, vile, distasteful, obnoxious, objectionable, disagreeable, festy (*Austral. slang*), yucko (*Austral. slang*)
4 = **serious**, bad, dangerous, critical, severe, painful

nation 1 = **country**, state, realm 2 = **public**, people, society

national ADJECTIVE
1 = **nationwide**, public, widespread, countrywide
▷ NOUN 2 = **citizen**, subject, resident, native, inhabitant

nationalism = **patriotism**, loyalty to your country, chauvinism, jingoism, allegiance

nationality 1 = **citizenship**,

n

birth 2 = **race**, nation
nationwide = **national**,
general, widespread,
countrywide
native ADJECTIVE 1 = **mother**,
indigenous, vernacular
▷ NOUN 2 = **inhabitant**,
national, resident, citizen,
countryman, aborigine (*often
offensive*), dweller
natural 1 = **logical**, valid,
legitimate 2 = **normal**,
common, regular, usual,
ordinary, typical, everyday
OPPOSITE: abnormal
3 = **innate**, native,
characteristic, inherent,
instinctive, intuitive, inborn,
essential 4 = **unaffected**, open,
genuine, spontaneous,
unpretentious, unsophisticated,
dinkum (*Austral. & N.Z. informal*),
ingenuous, real **OPPOSITE:**
affected 5 = **pure**, plain,
organic, whole, unrefined
OPPOSITE: processed
naturally 1 = **of course**,
certainly 2 = **typically**, simply,
normally, spontaneously
nature 1 = **creation**, world,
earth, environment, universe,
cosmos, natural world
2 = **quality**, character, make-
up, constitution, essence,
complexion 3 = **temperament**,
character, personality,
disposition, outlook, mood,
humour, temper 4 = **kind**, sort,
style, type, variety, species,
category, description

naughty 1 = **disobedient**, bad,
mischievous, badly behaved,
wayward, wicked, impish,
refractory **OPPOSITE:** good
2 = **obscene**, vulgar, improper,
lewd, risqué, smutty, ribald
OPPOSITE: clean
nausea = **sickness**, vomiting,
retching, squeamishness,
queasiness, biliousness
naval = **nautical**, marine,
maritime
navigation = **sailing**, voyaging,
seamanship, helmsmanship
navy = **fleet**, flotilla, armada
near 1 = **close**, neighbouring,
nearby, adjacent, adjoining
OPPOSITE: far 2 = **imminent**,
forthcoming, approaching,
looming, impending, upcoming,
nigh, in the offing **OPPOSITE:**
far-off
nearby = **neighbouring**,
adjacent, adjoining
nearly 1 = **practically**, almost,
virtually, just about, as good as,
well-nigh 2 = **almost**,
approaching, roughly, just
about, approximately
neat ADJECTIVE 1 = **tidy**, trim,
orderly, spruce, shipshape,
spick-and-span **OPPOSITE:**
untidy 2 = **methodical**, tidy,
systematic, fastidious
OPPOSITE: disorganized
3 = **smart**, trim, tidy, spruce,
dapper, natty (*informal*), well-
groomed, well-turned out
4 = **graceful**, elegant, adept,
nimble, adroit, efficient

OPPOSITE: clumsy 5 = **clever**, efficient, handy, apt, well-judged **OPPOSITE:** inefficient 6 = **cool**, great (*informal*), excellent, brilliant, superb, fantastic (*informal*), tremendous, fabulous (*informal*), booshit (*Austral. slang*), exo (*Austral. slang*), sik (*Austral. slang*) **OPPOSITE:** terrible 7 (*of alcoholic drinks*) = **undiluted**, straight, pure, unmixed

neatly 1 = **tidily**, smartly, systematically, methodically, fastidiously 2 = **smartly**, elegantly, tidily, nattily 3 = **gracefully**, expertly, efficiently, adeptly, skilfully, nimbly, adroitly, dexterously 4 = **cleverly**, efficiently

necessarily 1 = **automatically**, naturally, definitely, undoubtedly, certainly 2 = **inevitably**, of necessity, unavoidably, incontrovertibly, nolens volens (*Latin*)

necessary 1 = **needed**, required, essential, vital, compulsory, mandatory, imperative, indispensable **OPPOSITE:** unnecessary 2 = **inevitable**, certain, unavoidable, inescapable **OPPOSITE:** avoidable

necessity NOUN 1 = **essential**, need, requirement, fundamental, requisite, prerequisite, sine qua non (*Latin*), desideratum

2 = **inevitability**, certainty ▷ PLURAL NOUN 3 = **essentials**, needs, requirements, fundamentals

need VERB 1 = **want**, miss, require, lack, have to have, demand 2 = **require**, want, demand, call for, entail, necessitate 3 = **have to**, be obliged to ▷ NOUN 4 = **requirement**, demand, essential, necessity, requisite, desideratum 5 = **necessity**, call, demand, obligation 6 = **emergency**, want, urgency, exigency 7 = **poverty**, deprivation, destitution, penury

needed = **necessary**, wanted, required, lacked, called for, desired

needle = **irritate**, provoke, annoy, harass, taunt, nag, goad, rile

needless = **unnecessary**, pointless, gratuitous, useless, unwanted, redundant, superfluous, groundless **OPPOSITE:** essential

needy = **poor**, deprived, disadvantaged, impoverished, penniless, destitute, poverty-stricken, underprivileged **OPPOSITE:** wealthy

negative ADJECTIVE 1 = **pessimistic**, cynical, unwilling, gloomy, jaundiced, uncooperative **OPPOSITE:** optimistic 2 = **dissenting**, contradictory, refusing,

n

denying, rejecting, opposing, resisting, contrary **OPPOSITE:** assenting
▷ **NOUN 3** = **denial**, no, refusal, rejection, contradiction
neglect VERB **1** = **disregard**, ignore, fail to look after **OPPOSITE:** look after **2** = **shirk**, forget, overlook, omit, evade, pass over, skimp, be remiss in or about **3** = **fail**, forget, omit
▷ **NOUN 4** = **negligence**, inattention **OPPOSITE:** care **5** = **shirking**, failure, oversight, carelessness, dereliction, slackness, laxity
neglected 1 = **uncared-for**, abandoned, underestimated, disregarded, undervalued, unappreciated **2** = **run down**, derelict, overgrown, uncared-for
negligence = **carelessness**, neglect, disregard, dereliction, slackness, inattention, laxity, thoughtlessness
negotiate 1 = **bargain**, deal, discuss, debate, mediate, hold talks, cut a deal, conciliate **2** = **arrange**, work out, bring about, transact **3** = **get round**, clear, pass, cross, get over, get past, surmount
negotiation 1 = **bargaining**, debate, discussion, transaction, dialogue, mediation, arbitration, wheeling and dealing (informal) **2** = **arrangement**, working out, transaction, bringing about
negotiator = **mediator**,

ambassador, diplomat, delegate, intermediary, moderator, honest broker
neighbourhood 1 = **district**, community, quarter, region, locality, locale **2** = **vicinity**, environs
neighbouring = **nearby**, next, near, bordering, surrounding, connecting, adjacent, adjoining **OPPOSITE:** remote
neighbourly = **helpful**, kind, friendly, obliging, harmonious, considerate, sociable, hospitable
nerve NOUN **1** = **bravery**, courage, bottle (Brit. slang), resolution, daring, guts (informal), pluck, grit **2** (Informal) = **impudence**, cheek (informal), audacity, boldness, temerity, insolence, impertinence, brazenness
▷ **PLURAL NOUN 3** = **tension**, stress, strain, anxiety, butterflies (in your stomach) (informal), nervousness, cold feet (informal), worry
▷ **PHRASES: nerve yourself** = **brace yourself**, prepare yourself, steel yourself, fortify yourself, gear yourself up, gee yourself up
nervous = **apprehensive**, anxious, uneasy, edgy, worried, tense, fearful, uptight (informal), toey (Austral. slang) **OPPOSITE:** calm
nest = **refuge**, retreat, haunt, den, hideaway

nestle = snuggle, cuddle, huddle, curl up, nuzzle

nestling = chick, fledgling, baby bird

net¹ NOUN 1 = mesh, netting, network, web, lattice, openwork
▷ VERB 2 = catch, bag, capture, trap, entangle, ensnare, enmesh

net² or **nett** ADJECTIVE
1 = after taxes, final, clear, take-home
▷ VERB 2 = earn, make, clear, gain, realize, bring in, accumulate, reap

network 1 = web, system, arrangement, grid, lattice
2 = maze, warren, labyrinth

neurotic = unstable, nervous, disturbed, abnormal, obsessive, compulsive, manic, unhealthy
OPPOSITE: rational

neutral 1 = unbiased, impartial, disinterested, even-handed, uninvolved, nonpartisan, unprejudiced, nonaligned OPPOSITE: biased
2 = expressionless, dull
3 = uncontroversial or noncontroversial, inoffensive
4 = colourless

never 1 = at no time, not once, not ever OPPOSITE: always
2 = under no circumstances, not at all, on no account, not ever

● USAGE NOTE
● Never is sometimes used in
● informal speech and writing

● as an emphatic form of not,
● with simple past tenses of
● certain verbs: I never said that
● - and in very informal speech
● as a denial in place of did not:
● he says I hit him, but I never.
● These uses of never should be
● avoided in careful writing.

nevertheless = even so, still, however, yet, regardless, nonetheless, notwithstanding, in spite of that

new 1 = modern, recent, contemporary, up-to-date, latest, current, original, fresh
OPPOSITE: old-fashioned
2 = brand new 3 = extra, more, added, new-found, supplementary 4 = unfamiliar, strange 5 = renewed, changed, improved, restored, altered, revitalized

newcomer 1 = new arrival, stranger 2 = beginner, novice, new arrival, parvenu, Johnny-come-lately (informal)

news = information, latest (informal), report, story, exposé, intelligence, rumour, revelation

next ADJECTIVE 1 = following, later, succeeding, subsequent
2 = adjacent, closest, nearest, neighbouring, adjoining
▷ ADVERB 3 = afterwards, then, later, following, subsequently, thereafter

nice 1 = pleasant, delightful, agreeable, good, attractive, charming, pleasurable, enjoyable OPPOSITE:

n

unpleasant **2** = **kind**, helpful, obliging, considerate **OPPOSITE:** unkind **3** = **likable** *or* **likeable**, friendly, engaging, charming, pleasant, agreeable **4** = **polite**, courteous, well-mannered **OPPOSITE:** vulgar **5** = **precise**, fine, careful, strict, subtle, delicate, meticulous, fastidious **OPPOSITE:** vague

nicely **1** = **pleasantly**, well, delightfully, attractively, charmingly, agreeably, acceptably, pleasurably **OPPOSITE:** unpleasantly **2** = **kindly**, politely, thoughtfully, amiably, courteously

niche **1** = **recess**, opening, corner, hollow, nook, alcove **2** = **position**, calling, place, slot (*informal*), vocation, pigeonhole (*informal*)

nick **VERB** **1** = (*Slang*) = **steal**, pinch (*informal*), swipe (*slang*), pilfer **2** = **cut**, mark, score, chip, scratch, scar, notch, dent ▷ **NOUN** **3** = **cut**, mark, scratch, chip, scar, notch, dent

nickname = **pet name**, label, diminutive, epithet, sobriquet, moniker *or* monicker (*slang*)

night = **darkness**, dark, night-time
  ● **RELATED WORD**
  ● *adjective:* nocturnal

nightly **ADJECTIVE** **1** = **nocturnal**, night-time ▷ **ADVERB** **2** = **every night**, nights (*informal*), each night, night after night

nightmare **1** = **bad dream**, hallucination **2** = **ordeal**, trial, hell, horror, torture, torment, tribulation, purgatory

nil **1** = **nothing**, love, zero **2** = **zero**, nothing, none, naught

nip[1] **1** = **pop**, go, run, rush, dash **2** = **bite** **3** = **pinch**, squeeze, tweak
▷ **PHRASES: nip something in the bud** = **thwart**, check, frustrate

nip[2] = **dram**, shot (*informal*), drop, sip, draught, mouthful, snifter (*informal*)

nirvana = **paradise**, peace, joy, bliss, serenity, tranquillity

no **INTERJECTION** **1** = **not at all**, certainly not, of course not, absolutely not, never, no way, nay **OPPOSITE:** yes
▷ **NOUN** **2** = **refusal**, rejection, denial, negation **OPPOSITE:** consent

noble **ADJECTIVE** **1** = **worthy**, generous, upright, honourable, virtuous, magnanimous **OPPOSITE:** despicable **2** = **dignified**, great, imposing, impressive, distinguished, splendid, stately **OPPOSITE:** lowly **3** = **aristocratic**, lordly, titled, patrician, blue-blooded, highborn **OPPOSITE:** humble
▷ **NOUN** **4** = **lord**, peer, aristocrat, nobleman **OPPOSITE:** commoner

nobody **PRONOUN** **1** = **no-one**
▷ **NOUN** **2** = **nonentity**,

lightweight (*informal*), zero, cipher **OPPOSITE:** celebrity

nod VERB 1 = **incline**, bow 2 = **signal**, indicate, motion, gesture 3 = **salute**, acknowledge
▷ NOUN 4 = **signal**, sign, motion, gesture, indication 5 = **salute**, greeting, acknowledgment

noise = **sound**, row, racket, clamour, din, uproar, commotion, hubbub **OPPOSITE:** silence

noisy 1 = **rowdy**, strident, boisterous, vociferous, uproarious, clamorous **OPPOSITE:** quiet 2 = **loud**, piercing, deafening, tumultuous, ear-splitting, cacophonous, clamorous **OPPOSITE:** quiet

nominal 1 = **titular**, formal, purported, in name only, supposed, so-called, theoretical, professed 2 = **token**, small, symbolic, minimal, trivial, trifling, insignificant, inconsiderable

nominate 1 = **propose**, suggest, recommend, put forward 2 = **appoint**, name, choose, select, elect, assign, designate

nomination 1 = **proposal**, suggestion, recommendation 2 = **appointment**, election, selection, designation, choice

nominee = **candidate**, applicant, entrant, contestant, aspirant, runner

none 1 = **not any**, nothing, zero, not one, nil 2 = **no-one**, nobody, not one

nonetheless = **nevertheless**, however, yet, even so, despite that, in spite of that

non-existent or **nonexistent** = **imaginary**, fictional, mythical, unreal, hypothetical, illusory **OPPOSITE:** real

nonsense 1 = **rubbish**, hot air (*informal*), twaddle, drivel, tripe (*informal*), gibberish, claptrap (*informal*), double Dutch (*Brit. informal*), bizzo (*Austral. slang*), bull's wool (*Austral. & N.Z. slang*) **OPPOSITE:** sense 2 = **idiocy**, stupidity

non-stop or **nonstop**
ADJECTIVE 1 = **continuous**, constant, relentless, uninterrupted, endless, unbroken, interminable, incessant **OPPOSITE:** occasional
▷ ADVERB 2 = **continuously**, constantly, endlessly, relentlessly, perpetually, incessantly, ceaselessly, interminably

noon NOUN 1 = **midday**, high noon, noonday, twelve noon, noontide
▷ ADJECTIVE 2 = **midday**, noonday, noontide

norm = **standard**, rule, pattern, average, par, criterion, benchmark, yardstick

normal 1 = **usual**, common,

n

standard, average, natural, regular, ordinary, typical **OPPOSITE:** unusual **2 = sane**, reasonable, rational, well-adjusted, compos mentis (*Latin*), in your right mind, mentally sound

normally 1 = usually, generally, commonly, regularly, typically, ordinarily, as a rule, habitually **2 = as usual**, naturally, properly, conventionally, in the usual way

north ADJECTIVE 1 = northern, polar, arctic, boreal, northerly ▷ ADVERB 2 = northward(s), in a northerly direction

nose NOUN 1 = snout, bill, beak, hooter (*slang*), proboscis ▷ VERB 2 = ease forward, push, edge, shove, nudge
● RELATED WORD
● *adjective*: nasal

nostalgia = reminiscence, longing, pining, yearning, remembrance, homesickness, wistfulness

nostalgic = sentimental, longing, emotional, homesick, wistful, maudlin, regretful

notable ADJECTIVE 1 = remarkable, striking, unusual, extraordinary, outstanding, memorable, uncommon, conspicuous **OPPOSITE:** imperceptible **2 = prominent**, famous **OPPOSITE:** unknown ▷ NOUN **3 = celebrity**, big name, dignitary, luminary,

personage, V.I.P., star

notably = remarkably, unusually, extraordinarily, noticeably, strikingly, singularly, outstandingly, uncommonly

notch NOUN 1 = level (*Informal*), step, degree, grade **2 = cut**, nick, incision, indentation, mark, score, cleft ▷ VERB **3 = cut**, mark, score, nick, scratch, indent

note NOUN 1 = message, letter, communication, memo, memorandum, epistle **2 = record**, reminder, memo, memorandum, jotting, minute **3 = annotation**, comment, remark **4 = document**, form, record, certificate **5 = symbol**, mark, sign, indication, token **6 = tone**, touch, trace, hint, sound ▷ VERB **7 = notice**, see, observe, perceive **8 = bear in mind**, be aware, take into account **9 = mention**, record, mark, indicate, register, remark **10 = write down**, record, scribble, set down, jot down

notebook = notepad, exercise book, journal, diary

noted = famous, celebrated, distinguished, well-known, prominent, acclaimed, notable, renowned **OPPOSITE:** unknown

nothing 1 = nought, zero, nil, not a thing, zilch (*slang*) **2 = a trifle 3 = nobody**, cipher, nonentity **4 = void**, emptiness, nothingness, nullity

notice VERB 1 = observe, see, note, spot, distinguish, perceive, detect, discern OPPOSITE: overlook
▷ NOUN 2 = notification, warning, advice, intimation, news, communication, announcement, instruction 3 = attention, interest, note, regard, consideration, observation, scrutiny, heed OPPOSITE: oversight 4 = the sack (*informal*), dismissal, the boot (*slang*), the push (*slang*), marching orders (*informal*)

noticeable = obvious, clear, striking, plain, evident, manifest, conspicuous, perceptible

notify = inform, tell, advise, alert to, announce, warn

notion 1 = idea, view, opinion, belief, concept, impression, sentiment, inkling 2 = whim, wish, desire, fancy, impulse, inclination, caprice

notorious = infamous, disreputable, opprobrious

notoriously = infamously, disreputably

notwithstanding = despite, in spite of, regardless of

nought (*Archaic or literary*) or **naught** = zero, nothing, nil

nourish 1 = feed, supply, sustain, nurture 2 = encourage, support, maintain, promote, sustain, foster

nourishing = nutritious,

beneficial, wholesome, nutritive

novel[1] = story, tale, fiction, romance, narrative

novel[2] = new, different, original, fresh, unusual, innovative, uncommon OPPOSITE: ordinary

novelty 1 = newness, originality, freshness, innovation, surprise, uniqueness, strangeness, unfamiliarity 2 = curiosity, rarity, oddity, wonder 3 = trinket, souvenir, memento, bauble, trifle, knick-knack

novice = beginner, pupil, amateur, newcomer, trainee, apprentice, learner, probationer OPPOSITE: expert

now 1 = nowadays, at the moment 2 = immediately, promptly, instantly, at once, straightaway
▷ PHRASES: now and then or again = occasionally, sometimes, from time to time, on and off, intermittently, infrequently, sporadically

nowadays = now, today, at the moment, in this day and age

nucleus = centre, heart, focus, basis, core, pivot, kernel, nub

nude = naked, stripped, bare, undressed, stark-naked, disrobed, unclothed, unclad OPPOSITE: dressed

nudge VERB 1 = push, touch, dig, jog, prod, elbow, shove, poke 2 = prompt, influence, persuade, spur, prod, coax
▷ NOUN 3 = push, touch, dig,

elbow, bump, shove, poke, jog
4 = **prompting**, push,
encouragement, prod

nuisance = **trouble**, problem,
trial, drag (*informal*), bother,
pest, irritation, hassle (*informal*)
OPPOSITE: benefit

numb ADJECTIVE **1** = **unfeeling**,
dead, frozen, paralysed,
insensitive, deadened,
immobilized, torpid **OPPOSITE:**
sensitive **2** = **stupefied**,
deadened, unfeeling
▷ VERB **3** = **stun**, knock out,
paralyse, daze **4** = **deaden**,
freeze, dull, paralyse,
immobilize, benumb

number NOUN **1** = **numeral**,
figure, character, digit, integer
2 = **amount**, quantity,
collection, aggregate **OPPOSITE:**
shortage **3** = **crowd**, horde,
multitude, throng **4** = **group**,
set, band, crowd, gang
5 = **issue**, copy, edition,
imprint, printing
▷ VERB **6** = **amount to**, come
to, total, add up to
7 = **calculate**, account, reckon,
compute, enumerate
OPPOSITE: guess **8** = **include**,
count

numerous = **many**, several,
countless, lots, abundant,
plentiful, innumerable, copious
OPPOSITE: few

nurse 1 = **look after**, treat,
tend, care for, take care of,
minister to **2** = **harbour**, have,
maintain, preserve, entertain,

cherish **3** = **breast-feed**, feed,
nurture, nourish, suckle, wet-
nurse

nursery = **crèche**, kindergarten,
playgroup

nurture VERB **1** = **bring up**,
raise, look after, rear, care for,
develop **OPPOSITE:** neglect
▷ NOUN **2** = **upbringing**,
training, education, instruction,
rearing, development

nut 1 (*Slang*) = **madman**, psycho
(*slang*), crank (*informal*), lunatic,
maniac, nutcase (*slang*)
2 (*Slang*) = **head**, skull

nutrition = **food**, nourishment,
sustenance, nutriment

Oo

oath 1 = **promise**, bond, pledge, vow, word, affirmation, avowal 2 = **swear word**, curse, obscenity, blasphemy, expletive, four-letter word, profanity

obedience = **compliance**, respect, reverence, observance, subservience, submissiveness, docility **OPPOSITE:** disobedience

obey 1 = **submit to**, surrender (to), give way to, bow to, give in to, yield to, do what you are told by **OPPOSITE:** disobey 2 = **carry out**, follow, implement, act upon, carry through **OPPOSITE:** disregard 3 = **abide by**, keep, follow, comply with, observe, heed, conform to, keep to

object¹ 1 = **thing**, article, body, item, entity 2 = **purpose**, aim, end, point, plan, idea, goal, design 3 = **target**, victim, focus, recipient

object² with to = **protest against**, oppose, argue against, draw the line at, take exception to, cry out against, complain against, expostulate against **OPPOSITE:** accept 2 = **disagree**, demur, remonstrate, express

disapproval **OPPOSITE:** agree

objection = **protest**, opposition, complaint, doubt, dissent, outcry, protestation, scruple **OPPOSITE:** agreement

objective NOUN 1 = **purpose**, aim, goal, end, plan, hope, idea, target
▷ ADJECTIVE 2 = **factual**, real 3 = **unbiased**, detached, fair, open-minded, impartial, impersonal, disinterested, even-handed **OPPOSITE:** subjective

objectively = **impartially**, neutrally, fairly, justly, without prejudice, dispassionately, with an open mind, equitably

obligation 1 = **duty**, compulsion 2 = **task**, job, duty, work, charge, role, function, mission 3 = **responsibility**, duty, liability, accountability, answerability

oblige 1 = **compel**, make, force, require, bind, constrain, necessitate, impel 2 = **help**, assist, benefit, please, humour, accommodate, indulge, gratify **OPPOSITE:** bother

obliged 1 = **forced**, required, bound, compelled, duty-bound 2 = **grateful**, in (someone's) debt, thankful, indebted, appreciative, beholden

obliging = **accommodating**, kind, helpful, willing, polite, cooperative, agreeable, considerate **OPPOSITE:** unhelpful

obscene 1 = **indecent**, dirty,

offensive, filthy, improper, immoral, pornographic, lewd **OPPOSITE:** decent **2** = **offensive**, shocking, evil, disgusting, outrageous, revolting, sickening, vile

obscure ADJECTIVE
1 = **unknown**, little-known, humble, unfamiliar, out-of-the-way, lowly, unheard-of, undistinguished **OPPOSITE:** famous **2** = **abstruse**, complex, confusing, mysterious, vague, unclear, ambiguous, enigmatic **OPPOSITE:** straightforward **3** = **unclear**, uncertain, confused, mysterious, doubtful, indeterminate **OPPOSITE:** well-known **4** = **indistinct**, vague, blurred, dark, faint, dim, gloomy, murky **OPPOSITE:** clear ▷ VERB **5** = **obstruct**, hinder **6** = **hide**, screen, mask, disguise, conceal, veil, cloak, camouflage **OPPOSITE:** expose

observation 1 = **watching**, study, survey, review, investigation, monitoring, examination, inspection **2** = **comment**, thought, note, statement, opinion, remark, explanation, reflection, utterance **3** = **observance of**, compliance with, honouring of, fulfilment of, carrying out of

observe 1 = **watch**, study, view, look at, check, survey, monitor, keep an eye on (*informal*) **2** = **notice**, see, note, discover, spot, regard, witness,

distinguish **3** = **remark**, say, comment, state, note, reflect, mention, opine **4** = **comply with**, keep, follow, respect, carry out, honour, discharge, obey **OPPOSITE:** disregard

observer 1 = **witness**, viewer, spectator, looker-on, watcher, onlooker, eyewitness, bystander **2** = **commentator**, reporter, special correspondent **3** = **monitor**, watchdog, supervisor, scrutineer

obsessed = **absorbed**, dominated, gripped, haunted, distracted, hung up (*slang*), preoccupied **OPPOSITE:** indifferent

obsession = **preoccupation**, thing (*informal*), complex, hang-up (*informal*), mania, phobia, fetish, fixation

obsessive = **compulsive**, gripping, consuming, haunting, irresistible, neurotic, besetting, uncontrollable

obsolete = **outdated**, old, passé, old-fashioned, discarded, extinct, out-of-date, archaic **OPPOSITE:** up-to-date

obstacle 1 = **obstruction**, block, barrier, hurdle, snag, impediment, blockage, hindrance **2** = **hindrance**, bar, difficulty, barrier, handicap, hurdle, hitch, drawback, uphill (S. *African*) **OPPOSITE:** help

obstruct 1 = **block**, close, bar, plug, barricade, stop up, bung up (*informal*) **2** = **hold up**, stop,

check, block, restrict, slow
down, hamper, hinder
3 = impede, hamper, hold back,
thwart, hinder **OPPOSITE:** help
4 = obscure, screen, cover
obtain 1 = get, gain, acquire,
land, net, pick up, secure,
procure **OPPOSITE:** lose
2 = achieve, get, gain,
accomplish, attain **3** (*Formal*)
= prevail, hold, exist, be the
case, abound, predominate, be
in force, be current
obvious = clear, plain,
apparent, evident, distinct,
manifest, noticeable,
conspicuous **OPPOSITE:** unclear
obviously 1 = clearly, of
course, without doubt,
assuredly **2 = plainly**, patently,
undoubtedly, evidently,
manifestly, markedly, without
doubt, unquestionably
occasion NOUN 1 = time,
moment, point, stage, instance,
juncture **2 = function**, event,
affair, do (*informal*), happening,
experience, gathering,
celebration **3 = opportunity**,
chance, time, opening, window
4 = reason, cause, call,
ground(s), excuse, incentive,
motive, justification
▷ **VERB 5** (*Formal*) **= cause**,
produce, lead to, inspire, result
in, generate, prompt, provoke
occasional = infrequent, odd,
rare, irregular, sporadic,
intermittent, few and far
between, periodic

occasionally = sometimes, at
times, from time to time, now
and then, irregularly, now and
again, periodically, once in a
while, every so often **OPPOSITE:**
constantly
occult NOUN 1 = magic,
witchcraft, sorcery, wizardry,
enchantment, black art,
necromancy
▷ **ADJECTIVE 2 = supernatural**,
magical, mysterious, psychic,
mystical, unearthly, esoteric,
uncanny
occupant = occupier, resident,
tenant, inmate, inhabitant,
incumbent, dweller, lessee
occupation 1 = job, calling,
business, line (of work), trade,
career, employment, profession
2 = hobby, pastime, diversion,
relaxation, leisure pursuit,
(leisure) activity **3 = invasion**,
seizure, conquest, incursion,
subjugation **4 = occupancy**,
residence, holding, control,
possession, tenure, tenancy
occupied 1 = in use, taken,
full, engaged, unavailable
2 = inhabited, peopled, lived-
in, settled, tenanted **OPPOSITE:**
uninhabited **3 = busy**, engaged,
employed, working, active, hard
at work, rushed off your feet
occupy 1 = inhabit, own, live
in, dwell in, reside in, abide in
OPPOSITE: vacate **2 = invade**,
take over, capture, seize,
conquer, overrun, annex,
colonize **OPPOSITE:** withdraw

3 = **hold**, control, dominate, possess 4 = **take up**, consume, tie up, use up, monopolize 5 *often passive* = **engage**, involve, employ, divert, preoccupy, engross 6 = **fill**, take up, cover, fill up, pervade, permeate, extend over

occur 1 = **happen**, take place, come about, turn up (*informal*), crop up (*informal*), transpire (*informal*), befall 2 = **exist**, appear, be found, develop, turn up, be present, manifest itself, present itself

▷ **PHRASES: occur to someone** = **come to mind**, strike someone, dawn on someone, spring to mind, cross someone's mind, enter someone's head, suggest itself to someone

● **USAGE NOTE**
● It is usually regarded as
● incorrect to talk of pre-
● arranged events *occurring* or
● *happening*. For this meaning a
● synonym such as *take place*
● would be more appropriate:
● *the wedding took place* (not
● *occurred* or *happened*) *in the*
● *afternoon*.

occurrence 1 = **incident**, happening, event, fact, matter, affair, circumstance, episode 2 = **existence**, instance, appearance, manifestation, materialization

odd 1 = **peculiar**, strange, unusual, extraordinary, bizarre, offbeat, freakish 2 = **unusual**,

strange, rare, extraordinary, remarkable, bizarre, peculiar, irregular **OPPOSITE:** normal 3 = **occasional**, various, random, casual, irregular, periodic, sundry, incidental **OPPOSITE:** regular 4 = **spare**, remaining, extra, surplus, solitary, leftover, unmatched, unpaired **OPPOSITE:** matched

odds 1 = **probability**, chances, likelihood

▷ **PHRASES: at odds** 1 = **in conflict**, arguing, quarrelling, at loggerheads, at daggers drawn 2 = **at variance**, conflicting, contrary to, at odds, out of line, out of step, at sixes and sevens (*informal*) ▶ **odds and ends** = **scraps**, bits, remains, fragments, debris, remnants, bits and pieces, bric-a-brac

odour = **smell**, scent, perfume, fragrance, stink, bouquet, aroma, stench

odyssey = **journey**, tour, trip, quest, trek, expedition, voyage, crusade

off ADVERB 1 = **away**, out, apart, elsewhere, aside, hence, from here

▷ ADJECTIVE 2 = **absent**, gone, unavailable 3 = **cancelled**, abandoned, postponed, shelved 4 = **bad**, rotten, rancid, mouldy, turned, spoiled, sour, decayed

offence 1 = **crime**, sin, fault, violation, wrongdoing, trespass (*formal*), felony, misdemeanour 2 = **outrage**, shock, anger,

trouble, bother, resentment, irritation, hassle (*informal*)
3 = insult, slight, hurt, outrage, injustice, snub, affront, indignity

offend 1 = distress, upset, outrage, wound, slight, insult, annoy, snub **OPPOSITE:** please
2 = break the law, sin, err, do wrong, fall, go astray

offended = upset, hurt, bothered, disturbed, distressed, outraged, stung, put out (*informal*), tooshie (*Austral. slang*)

offender = criminal, convict, crook, villain, culprit, sinner, delinquent, felon

offensive ADJECTIVE
1 = insulting, rude, abusive, degrading, contemptuous, disparaging, objectionable, disrespectful **OPPOSITE:** respectful **2 = disgusting**, gross, foul, unpleasant, revolting, vile, repellent, obnoxious, festy (*Austral. slang*), yucko (*Austral. slang*) **OPPOSITE:** pleasant **3 = attacking**, threatening, aggressive, striking, hostile, invading, combative **OPPOSITE:** defensive ▷ NOUN **4 = attack**, charge, campaign, strike, push (*informal*), assault, raid, drive

offer VERB **1 = provide**, present, furnish, afford **OPPOSITE:** withhold
2 = volunteer, come forward, offer your services **3 = propose**, suggest, advance, submit
4 = give, show, bring, provide, render, impart **5 = put up for sale**, sell **6 = bid**, submit, propose, tender, proffer (*formal*), ▷ NOUN **7 = proposal**, suggestion, proposition, submission **8 = bid**, tender, bidding price

offering 1 = contribution, gift, donation, present, subscription, hand-out **2 = sacrifice**, tribute, libation, burnt offering

office 1 = place of work, workplace, base, workroom, place of business **2 = branch**, department, division, section, wing, subdivision, subsection **3 = post**, place, role, situation, responsibility, function, occupation

officer 1 = official, executive, agent, representative, appointee, functionary, office-holder, office-bearer **2 = police officer**, detective, PC, police constable, policeman, policewoman

official ADJECTIVE
1 = authorized, formal, sanctioned, licensed, proper, legitimate, authentic, certified **OPPOSITE:** unofficial
2 = formal, bureaucratic, ceremonial, solemn, ritualistic ▷ NOUN **3 = officer**, executive, agent, representative, bureaucrat, appointee, functionary, office-holder

offset = cancel out, balance, set

off, make up for, compensate for, counteract, neutralize, counterbalance

offspring 1 = **child**, baby, kid (*informal*), youngster, infant, successor, babe, toddler, littlie (*Austral. informal*), ankle-biter (*Austral. slang*), tacker (*Austral. slang*) **OPPOSITE:** parent 2 = **children**, young, family, issue, stock, heirs, descendants, brood

often = **frequently**, generally, commonly, repeatedly, time and again, habitually, not infrequently **OPPOSITE:** never

oil VERB 1 = **lubricate**, grease ▷ NOUN 2 = **lubricant**, grease, lubrication, fuel oil 3 = **lotion**, cream, balm, salve, liniment, embrocation

oily = **greasy**, slimy, fatty, slippery, oleaginous

OK or **okay** ADJECTIVE (*Informal*) 1 = **all right**, fine, fitting, in order, permitted, suitable, acceptable, allowable **OPPOSITE:** unacceptable 2 = **fine**, good, average, fair, all right, acceptable, adequate, satisfactory **OPPOSITE:** unsatisfactory 3 = **well**, all right, safe, sound, healthy, unharmed, uninjured ▷ INTERJECTION 4 = **all right**, right, yes, agreed, very good, roger, very well, ya (*S. African*), righto (*Brit. informal*), yebo (*S. African informal*) ▷ VERB 5 = **approve**, allow,

agree to, permit, sanction, endorse, authorize, rubber-stamp (*informal*) ▷ NOUN 6 = **authorization**, agreement, sanction, approval, go-ahead (*informal*), blessing, permission, consent

old 1 = **aged**, elderly, ancient, mature, venerable, antiquated, senile, decrepit **OPPOSITE:** young 2 = **former**, earlier, past, previous, prior, one-time, erstwhile (*formal*), 3 = **long-standing**, established, fixed, enduring, abiding, long-lasting, long-established, time-honoured 4 = **stale**, worn-out, banal, threadbare, trite, overused, timeworn

old-fashioned 1 = **out-of-date**, dated, outdated, unfashionable, outmoded, passé, old hat, behind the times **OPPOSITE:** up-to-date 2 = **oldfangled**, square (*informal*), outdated, unfashionable, obsolescent

ominous = **threatening**, sinister, grim, fateful, foreboding, unpromising, portentous, inauspicious **OPPOSITE:** promising

omission 1 = **exclusion**, removal, elimination, deletion, excision **OPPOSITE:** inclusion 2 = **gap**, space, exclusion, lacuna 3 = **failure**, neglect, negligence, oversight, carelessness, dereliction, slackness, laxity

omit 1 = **leave out**, drop, exclude, eliminate, skip **OPPOSITE:** include 2 = **forget**, overlook, neglect, pass over, lose sight of

once ADVERB 1 = **on one occasion**, one time, one single time 2 = **at one time**, previously, formerly, long ago, once upon a time
▷ CONJUNCTION 3 = **as soon as**, when, after, the moment, immediately, the instant
▷ PHRASES: **at once** 1 = **immediately**, now, straight away, directly, promptly, instantly, right away, forthwith 2 = **simultaneously**, together, at the same time, concurrently

one-sided 1 = **unequal**, unfair, uneven, unjust, unbalanced, lopsided, ill-matched **OPPOSITE:** equal 2 = **biased**, prejudiced, weighted, unfair, partial, distorted, partisan, slanted **OPPOSITE:** unbiased

ongoing = **in progress**, developing, progressing, evolving, unfolding, unfinished

onlooker = **spectator**, witness, observer, viewer, looker-on, watcher, eyewitness, bystander

only ADJECTIVE 1 = **sole**, one, single, individual, exclusive, unique, lone, solitary
▷ ADVERB 2 = **just**, simply, purely, merely 3 = **hardly**, just, barely, only just, scarcely, at a push

onset = **beginning**, start, birth, outbreak, inception, commencement **OPPOSITE:** end

onslaught = **attack**, charge, campaign, strike, assault, raid, invasion, offensive **OPPOSITE:** retreat

onward *or* **onwards** = **forward**, on, forwards, ahead, beyond, in front, forth

ooze¹ 1 = **seep**, well, escape, leak, drain, filter, drip, trickle 2 = **emit**, release, leak, drip, dribble, give off, pour forth 3 = **exude**, emit

ooze² = **mud**, clay, dirt, silt, sludge, mire, slime, alluvium

open VERB 1 = **unfasten**, unlock **OPPOSITE:** close 2 = **unwrap**, uncover, undo, unravel, untie **OPPOSITE:** wrap 3 = **uncork** 4 = **unfold**, spread (out), expand, unfurl, unroll **OPPOSITE:** fold 5 = **clear**, unblock **OPPOSITE:** block 6 = **undo**, unbutton, unfasten **OPPOSITE:** fasten 7 = **begin business**, start trading 8 = **start**, begin, launch, trigger, kick off (*informal*), initiate, commence, get going **OPPOSITE:** end 9 = **begin**, start, commence **OPPOSITE:** end
▷ ADJECTIVE 10 = **unclosed**, unlocked, ajar, unfastened, yawning **OPPOSITE:** closed 11 = **unsealed**, unstoppered **OPPOSITE:** unopened 12 = **extended**, unfolded, stretched out, unfurled, straightened out, unrolled

OPPOSITE: shut **13** = **frank**, direct, straightforward, sincere, transparent, honest, candid, truthful **OPPOSITE:** sly **14** = **receptive**, sympathetic, responsive, amenable **15** = **unresolved**, unsettled, undecided, debatable, moot, arguable **16** = **clear**, passable, unhindered, unimpeded, navigable, unobstructed **OPPOSITE:** obstructed **17** = **available**, to hand, accessible, handy, at your disposal **18** = **general**, public, free, universal, blanket, across-the-board, unrestricted, overarching **OPPOSITE:** restricted **19** = **vacant**, free, available, empty, unoccupied, unfilled

open-air = **outdoor**, outside, out-of-door(s), alfresco

opening ADJECTIVE **1** = **first**, earliest, beginning, premier, primary, initial, maiden, inaugural

▷ NOUN **2** = **beginning**, start, launch, dawn, outset, initiation, inception, commencement **OPPOSITE:** ending **3** = **hole**, space, tear, crack, gap, slot, puncture, aperture **OPPOSITE:** blockage **4** = **opportunity**, chance, time, moment, occasion, look-in (*informal*) **5** = **job**, position, post, situation, opportunity, vacancy

openly = **frankly**, plainly, honestly, overtly, candidly,

unreservedly, unhesitatingly, forthrightly **OPPOSITE:** privately

open-minded = **unprejudiced**, liberal, balanced, objective, reasonable, tolerant, impartial, receptive **OPPOSITE:** narrow-minded

operate 1 = **manage**, run, direct, handle, supervise, be in charge of **2** = **function**, work, act **3** = **run**, work, use, control, manoeuvre **4** = **work**, go, run, perform, function **OPPOSITE:** break down

operation = **performance**, action, movement, motion

operational = **working**, going, running, ready, functioning, operative, viable, functional **OPPOSITE:** inoperative

operative ADJECTIVE **1** = **in force**, effective, functioning, active, in effect, operational, in operation **OPPOSITE:** inoperative

▷ NOUN **2** = **worker**, employee, labourer, workman, artisan **3** (*U.S. & Canad.*) = **spy**, undercover agent, mole, nark (*Brit., Austral. & N.Z. slang*)

operator = **worker**, driver, mechanic, operative, conductor, technician, handler

opinion 1 = **belief**, feeling, view, idea, theory, conviction, point of view, sentiment **2** = **estimation**, view, impression, assessment, judgment, appraisal, considered opinion

opponent 1 = **adversary**, rival, enemy, competitor, challenger, foe, contestant, antagonist **OPPOSITE:** ally 2 = **opposer**, dissident, objector **OPPOSITE:** supporter

opportunity = **chance**, opening, time, turn, moment, possibility, occasion, slot

oppose = **be against**, fight (against), block, take on, counter, contest, resist, combat **OPPOSITE:** support

opposed 1 *with* to = **against**, hostile, adverse, in opposition, averse, antagonistic, (dead) set against 2 = **contrary**, conflicting, clashing, counter, adverse, contradictory, dissentient

opposing 1 = **conflicting**, different, contrasting, opposite, differing, contrary, contradictory, incompatible 2 = **rival**, conflicting, competing, enemy, opposite, hostile

opposite PREPOSITION 1 = **facing**, face to face with, across from, eyeball to eyeball (*informal*) ▷ ADJECTIVE 2 = **facing**, other, opposing 3 = **different**, conflicting, contrasted, contrasting, unlike, contrary, dissimilar, divergent **OPPOSITE:** alike 4 = **rival**, conflicting, opposing, competing ▷ NOUN 5 = **reverse**, contrary, converse, antithesis,

contradiction, inverse, obverse

opposition 1 = **hostility**, resistance, resentment, disapproval, obstruction, animosity, antagonism, antipathy **OPPOSITE:** support 2 = **opponent(s)**, competition, rival(s), enemy, competitor(s), other side, challenger(s), foe

oppress 1 = **subjugate**, abuse, suppress, wrong, master, overcome, subdue, persecute **OPPOSITE:** liberate 2 = **depress**, burden, discourage, torment, harass, afflict, sadden, vex

oppression = **persecution**, control, abuse, injury, injustice, cruelty, domination, repression **OPPOSITE:** justice

oppressive 1 = **tyrannical**, severe, harsh, cruel, brutal, authoritarian, unjust, repressive **OPPOSITE:** merciful 2 = **stifling**, close, sticky, stuffy, humid, sultry, airless, muggy

opt = **choose**, decide, prefer, select, elect **OPPOSITE:** reject ▷ PHRASES: opt for something or someone = **choose**, pick, select, adopt, go for, designate, decide on, plump for

optimistic 1 = **hopeful**, positive, confident, encouraged, cheerful, rosy, buoyant, sanguine **OPPOSITE:** pessimistic 2 = **encouraging**, promising, bright, good, reassuring, rosy, heartening, auspicious **OPPOSITE:** discouraging

optimum *or* **optimal** = **ideal**,

SHADES OF ORANGE		
amber	ochre	tangerine
burnt sienna	peach	terracotta

best, highest, finest, perfect, supreme, peak, outstanding **OPPOSITE:** worst

option = choice, alternative, selection, preference, freedom of choice, power to choose

optional = voluntary, open, discretionary, possible, extra, elective **OPPOSITE:** compulsory

opus = work, piece, production, creation, composition, work of art, brainchild, oeuvre (*French*)

oral = spoken, vocal, verbal, unwritten

orange ▷ See panel SHADES OF ORANGE

orbit NOUN 1 = path, course, cycle, circle, revolution, rotation, trajectory, sweep 2 = sphere of influence, reach, range, influence, province, scope, domain, compass ▷ VERB 3 = circle, ring, go round, revolve around, encircle, circumscribe, circumnavigate

orchestrate 1 = organize, plan, run, set up, arrange, put together, marshal, coordinate 2 = score, set, arrange, adapt

ordain 1 = appoint, name, commission, select, invest, nominate, anoint, consecrate 2 (*Formal*) = order, will, rule, demand, require, direct, command, dictate

ordeal = hardship, trial,

difficulty, test, suffering, nightmare, torture, agony **OPPOSITE:** pleasure

order VERB 1 = command, instruct, direct, charge, demand, require, bid, compel **OPPOSITE:** forbid 2 = decree, rule, demand, prescribe, pronounce, ordain **OPPOSITE:** ban 3 = request, ask (for), book, seek, reserve, apply for, solicit, send away for 4 = arrange, group, sort, position, line up, organize, catalogue, sort out **OPPOSITE:** disarrange ▷ NOUN 5 = instruction, ruling, demand, direction, command, dictate, decree, mandate 6 = request, booking, demand, commission, application, reservation, requisition 7 = sequence, grouping, series, structure, chain, arrangement, line-up, array 8 = organization, system, method, pattern, symmetry, regularity, neatness, tidiness **OPPOSITE:** chaos 9 = peace, control, law, quiet, calm, discipline, law and order, tranquillity 10 = society, company, group, club, community, association, institute, organization 11 = class, set, rank, grade, caste **12** = **kind**, group, class, family, sort, type, variety, category

orderly 1 = **well-behaved**, controlled, disciplined, quiet, restrained, law-abiding, peaceable **OPPOSITE:** disorderly **2** = **well-organized**, regular, in order, organized, precise, neat, tidy, systematic **OPPOSITE:** disorganized

ordinary 1 = **usual**, standard, normal, common, regular, typical, conventional, routine **2** = **commonplace**, plain, modest, humble, mundane, banal, unremarkable, run-of-the-mill **OPPOSITE:** extraordinary

organ 1 = **body part**, part of the body, element, biological structure **2** = **newspaper**, medium, voice, vehicle, gazette, mouthpiece

organic 1 = **natural**, biological, living, live, animate **2** = **systematic**, ordered, structured, organized, integrated, orderly, methodical

organism = **creature**, being, thing, body, animal, structure, beast, entity

organization 1 = **group**, company, party, body, association, band, institution, corporation **2** = **management**, running, planning, control, operation, handling, structuring, administration **3** = **structure**, form, pattern,

make-up, arrangement, construction, format, formation

organize 1 = **arrange**, run, plan, prepare, set up, devise, put together, take care of, jack up (*N.Z. informal*) **OPPOSITE:** disrupt **2** = **put in order**, arrange, group, list, file, index, classify, inventory **OPPOSITE:** muddle

orient or **orientate 1** = **adjust**, adapt, alter, accustom, align, familiarize, acclimatize **2** = **get your bearings**, establish your location

orientation 1 = **inclination**, tendency, disposition, predisposition, predilection, proclivity, partiality **2** = **induction**, introduction, adjustment, settling in, adaptation, assimilation, familiarization, acclimatization **3** = **position**, situation, location, bearings, direction, arrangement, whereabouts

origin 1 = **beginning**, start, birth, launch, foundation, creation, emergence, onset **OPPOSITE:** end **2** = **root**, source, basis, base, seed, foundation, nucleus, derivation

original ADJECTIVE **1** = **first**, earliest, initial **2** = **initial**, first, starting, opening, primary, introductory **OPPOSITE:** final **3** = **new**, fresh, novel, unusual, unprecedented, innovative, unfamiliar, seminal **OPPOSITE:**

unoriginal 4 = **creative**, inspired, imaginative, artistic, fertile, ingenious, visionary, inventive
▷ NOUN 5 = **prototype**, master, pattern **OPPOSITE:** copy

originally 1 = **initially**, first, firstly, at first, primarily, to begin with, in the beginning

originate 1 = **begin**, start, emerge, come, happen, rise, appear, spring **OPPOSITE:** end 2 = **invent**, create, design, launch, introduce, institute, generate, pioneer

ornament NOUN
1 = **decoration**, trimming, accessory, festoon, trinket, bauble, knick-knack
2 = **embellishment**, decoration, embroidery, elaboration, adornment, ornamentation
▷ VERB 3 = **decorate**, adorn, array, do up (*informal*), embellish, festoon, beautify, prettify

orthodox 1 = **established**, official, accepted, received, common, traditional, normal, usual **OPPOSITE:** unorthodox 2 = **conformist**, conservative, traditional, strict, devout, observant **OPPOSITE:** nonconformist

orthodoxy 1 = **doctrine**, teaching, opinion, principle, belief, convention, creed, dogma 2 = **conformity**, received wisdom,

traditionalism, conventionality **OPPOSITE:** nonconformity

other 1 = **additional**, more, further, new, added, extra, fresh, spare 2 = **different**, alternative, contrasting, distinct, diverse, dissimilar, separate, alternative

otherwise 1 = **or else**, or, if not, or then 2 = **apart from that**, in other ways, in (all) other respects 3 = **differently**, any other way, contrarily

ounce = **shred**, bit, drop, trace, scrap, grain, fragment, atom

oust = **expel**, turn out, dismiss, exclude, exile, throw out, displace, topple

out ADJECTIVE 1 = **not in**, away, elsewhere, outside, gone, abroad, from home, absent 2 = **extinguished**, ended, finished, dead, exhausted, expired, used up, at an end **OPPOSITE:** alight 3 = **in bloom**, opening, open, flowering, blooming, in flower, in full bloom 4 = **available**, on sale, in the shops, to be had, purchasable 5 = **revealed**, exposed, common knowledge, public knowledge, (out) in the open **OPPOSITE:** kept secret
▷ VERB 6 = **expose**

outbreak 1 = **eruption**, burst, explosion, epidemic, rash, outburst, flare-up, upsurge 2 = **onset**, beginning, outset, opening, dawn, commencement

outburst = explosion, fit, surge, outbreak, flare-up, eruption, spasm, outpouring

outcome = result, end, consequence, conclusion, payoff (*informal*), upshot

outcry = protest, complaint, objection, dissent, outburst, clamour, uproar, commotion

outdated = old-fashioned, dated, obsolete, out-of-date, passé, archaic, unfashionable, antiquated **OPPOSITE:** modern

outdoor = open-air, outside, out-of-door(s), alfresco **OPPOSITE:** indoor

outer 1 = external, outside, outward, exterior, exposed, outermost **OPPOSITE:** inner 2 = surface 3 = outlying, distant, provincial, out-of-the-way, peripheral, far-flung **OPPOSITE:** central

outfit 1 = costume, dress, clothes, clothing, suit, get-up (*informal*), kit, ensemble 2 (*Informal*) = group, company, team, party, unit, crowd, squad, organization

outgoing 1 = leaving, former, previous, retiring, withdrawing, prior, departing, erstwhile **OPPOSITE:** incoming 2 = sociable, open, social, warm, friendly, expansive, affable, extrovert **OPPOSITE:** reserved

outgoings = expenses, costs, payments, expenditure, overheads, outlay

outing = journey, run, trip, tour, expedition, excursion, spin (*informal*), jaunt

outlaw VERB 1 = ban, bar, veto, forbid, exclude, prohibit, disallow, proscribe **OPPOSITE:** legalise 2 = banish, put a price on (someone's) head ▷ NOUN 3 (*History*) = bandit, criminal, thief, robber, fugitive, outcast, felon, highwayman

outlet 1 = shop, store, supermarket, market, boutique, emporium, hypermarket 2 = channel, release, medium, avenue, vent, conduit 3 = pipe, opening, channel, exit, duct

outline VERB 1 = summarize, draft, plan, trace, sketch (in), sum up, encapsulate, delineate 2 = silhouette, sketch ▷ NOUN 3 = summary, review, résumé, rundown, synopsis, précis, thumbnail sketch, recapitulation 4 = shape, lines, form, figure, profile, silhouette, configuration, contour(s)

outlook 1 = attitude, opinion, position, approach, mood, perspective, point of view, stance 2 = prospect(s), future, expectations, forecast, prediction, probability, prognosis

out of date 1 = old-fashioned, dated, outdated, obsolete, démodé (*French*), antiquated, outmoded, passé **OPPOSITE:** modern 2 = invalid, expired, lapsed, void, null and void

output = production, manufacture, manufacturing, yield, productivity

outrage VERB 1 = offend, shock, upset, wound, insult, infuriate, incense, madden
▷ NOUN 2 = indignation, shock, anger, rage, fury, hurt, resentment, scorn

outrageous 1 = atrocious, shocking, terrible, offensive, appalling, cruel, savage, horrifying OPPOSITE: mild
2 = unreasonable, unfair, steep (informal), shocking, extravagant, scandalous, preposterous, unwarranted OPPOSITE: reasonable

outright ADJECTIVE
1 = absolute, complete, total, perfect, sheer, thorough, unconditional, unqualified
2 = definite, clear, certain, flat, absolute, black-and-white, straightforward, unequivocal
▷ ADVERB 3 = openly, frankly, plainly, overtly, candidly, unreservedly, unhesitatingly, forthrightly 4 = absolutely, completely, totally, fully, entirely, thoroughly, wholly, utterly

outset = beginning, start, opening, onset, inauguration, inception, commencement, kickoff (informal) OPPOSITE: finish

outside NOUN 1 = exterior, face, front, covering, skin, surface, shell, coating

▷ ADJECTIVE 2 = external, outer, exterior, outward, extraneous OPPOSITE: inner
3 = remote, small, unlikely, slight, slim, distant, faint, marginal
▷ ADVERB 4 = outdoors, out of the house, out-of-doors OPPOSITE: inside
● USAGE NOTE
● The use of outside of and inside
● of, although fairly common, is
● generally thought to be
● incorrect or nonstandard: She
● waits outside (not outside of)
● the school.

outsider = stranger, incomer, visitor, newcomer, intruder, interloper, odd one out

outskirts = edge, boundary, suburbs, fringe, perimeter, periphery, suburbia, environs

outspan (S. African) = relax, chill out (slang, chiefly U.S.), take it easy, loosen up, put your feet up

outspoken = forthright, open, frank, straightforward, blunt, explicit, upfront (informal), unequivocal OPPOSITE: reserved

outstanding 1 = excellent, good, great, important, special, fine, brilliant, impressive, booshit (Austral. slang), exo (Austral. slang), sik (Austral. slang) OPPOSITE: mediocre
2 = unpaid, remaining, due, pending, payable, unsettled, uncollected 3 = undone, left, omitted, unfinished, unfulfilled,

unperformed, not done

outward = **apparent**, seeming, surface, ostensible **OPPOSITE:** inward

outwardly = **apparently**, externally, seemingly, it seems that, on the surface, it appears that, ostensibly, on the face of it

outweigh = **override**, cancel (out), eclipse, offset, compensate for, supersede, neutralize, counterbalance

oval = **elliptical**, egg-shaped, ovoid

ovation = **applause**, hand, cheers, praise, tribute, acclaim, clapping, accolade **OPPOSITE:** derision

over PREPOSITION 1 = **above**, on top of 2 = **on top of**, on, across, upon 3 = **across**, (looking) onto 4 = **more than**, above, exceeding, in excess of, upwards of 5 = **about**, regarding, relating to, concerning, apropos of
▷ ADVERB 6 = **above**, overhead, in the sky, on high, aloft, up above 7 = **extra**, more, further, beyond, additional, in addition, surplus, in excess
▷ ADJECTIVE 8 = **finished**, done (with), through, ended, closed, past, completed, complete
● RELATED WORDS
● *prefixes:* hyper-, super-

overall ADJECTIVE 1 = **total**, full, whole, general, complete, entire, global, comprehensive
▷ ADVERB 2 = **in general**, generally, mostly, all things considered, on average, on the whole, predominantly, in the main

overcome VERB 1 = **defeat**, beat, conquer, master, overwhelm, subdue, rout, overpower 2 = **conquer**, beat, master, subdue, triumph over, vanquish
▷ ADJECTIVE 3 = **overwhelmed**, moved, affected, emotional, choked, speechless, bowled over (*informal*), at a loss for words

overdue 1 = **delayed**, belated, late, behind schedule, tardy, unpunctual, behindhand **OPPOSITE:** early 2 = **unpaid**, owing

overflow VERB 1 = **spill over**, well over, run over, pour over, bubble over, brim over
▷ NOUN 2 = **flood**, spilling over 3 = **surplus**, extra, excess, overspill, overabundance, additional people *or* things

overhaul VERB 1 = **check**, service, maintain, examine, restore, tune (up), repair, go over 2 = **overtake**, pass, leave behind, catch up with, get past, outstrip, get ahead of, outdistance
▷ NOUN 3 = **check**, service, examination, going-over (*informal*), inspection, once-over (*informal*), checkup, reconditioning

overhead ADJECTIVE

1 = **raised**, suspended, elevated, aerial, overhanging
▷ ADVERB 2 = **above**, in the sky, on high, aloft, up above
OPPOSITE: underneath

overheads = **running costs**, expenses, outgoings, operating costs

overlook 1 = **look over or out on**, have a view of 2 = **miss**, forget, neglect, omit, disregard, pass over OPPOSITE: notice 3 = **ignore**, excuse, forgive, pardon, disregard, condone, turn a blind eye to, wink at

overpower 1 = **overcome**, master, overwhelm, overthrow, subdue, quell, subjugate, prevail over 2 = **beat**, defeat, crush, triumph over, vanquish 3 = **overwhelm**, overcome, bowl over (informal), stagger

override 1 = **outweigh**, eclipse, supersede, take precedence over, prevail over 2 = **overrule**, cancel, overturn, repeal, rescind, annul, nullify, countermand 3 = **ignore**, reject, discount, overlook, disregard, pass over, take no notice of

overrun 1 = **overwhelm**, attack, assault, occupy, raid, invade, penetrate, rout 2 = **spread over**, overwhelm, choke, swamp, infest, inundate, permeate, swarm over 3 = **exceed**, go beyond, surpass, overshoot, run over or on

overshadow 1 = **spoil**, ruin,

mar, wreck, blight, crool or cruel (Austral. slang), mess up, put a damper on 2 = **outshine**, eclipse, surpass, dwarf, tower above, leave or put in the shade

overt = **open**, obvious, plain, public, manifest, blatant, observable, undisguised
OPPOSITE: hidden

overtake 1 = **pass**, leave behind, overhaul, catch up with, get past, outdistance, go by or past 2 = **outdo**, top, exceed, eclipse, surpass, outstrip, get the better of, outclass 3 = **befall**, hit, happen to, catch off guard, catch unawares 4 = **engulf**, overwhelm, hit, strike, swamp, envelop, swallow up

overthrow VERB 1 = **defeat**, overcome, conquer, bring down, oust, topple, rout, overpower OPPOSITE: uphold
▷ NOUN 2 = **downfall**, fall, defeat, collapse, destruction, ousting, undoing, unseating
OPPOSITE: preservation

overturn 1 = **tip over**, topple, upturn, capsize, upend, keel over, overbalance 2 = **knock over or down**, upturn, tip over, upend 3 = **reverse**, change, cancel, abolish, overthrow, set aside, repeal, quash 4 = **overthrow**, defeat, destroy, overcome, bring down, oust, topple, depose

overweight = **fat**, heavy, stout, hefty, plump, bulky, chunky, chubby **OPPOSITE:** underweight

overwhelm 1 = **overcome**, devastate, stagger, bowl over (informal), knock (someone) for six (informal), sweep (someone) off his or her feet, take (someone's) breath away 2 = **destroy**, defeat, overcome, crush, massacre, conquer, wipe out, overthrow

overwhelming 1 = **overpowering**, strong, powerful, towering, stunning, crushing, devastating, shattering **OPPOSITE:** negligible 2 = **vast**, huge, massive, enormous, tremendous, immense, very large **OPPOSITE:** insignificant

owe = **be in debt (to)**, be in arrears (to), be overdrawn (by), be obligated or indebted (to)

owing to = **because of**, thanks to, as a result of, on account of, by reason of

own ADJECTIVE 1 = **personal**, special, private, individual, particular, exclusive ▷ VERB 2 = **possess**, have, keep, hold, enjoy, retain, be in possession of, have to your name

owner = **possessor**, holder, proprietor, titleholder, landlord or landlady

ownership = **possession**, occupation, tenure, dominion

Pp

pace NOUN 1 = **speed**, rate, tempo, velocity 2 = **step**, walk, stride, tread, gait 3 = **footstep**, step, stride ▷ VERB 4 = **stride**, walk, pound, patrol, march up and down

pack VERB 1 = **package**, load, store, bundle, stow 2 = **cram**, crowd, press, fill, stuff, jam, ram, compress ▷ NOUN 3 = **packet**, box, package, carton 4 = **bundle**, parcel, load, burden, rucksack, knapsack, backpack, kitbag 5 = **group**, crowd, company, band, troop, gang, bunch, mob ▷ PHRASES: **pack someone off** = **send away**, dismiss, send packing (informal) ▶ **pack something in** 1 (Brit. informal) = **resign from**, leave, give up, quit (informal), chuck (informal), jack in (informal) 2 = **stop**, give up, kick (informal), cease, chuck (informal)

package NOUN 1 = **parcel**, box, container, packet, carton 2 = **collection**, lot, unit, combination, compilation ▷ VERB 3 = **pack**, box, parcel

P

(up), batch

packet 1 = **container**, box, package, carton 2 = **package**, parcel 3 (*Slang*) = **a fortune**, a bomb (*Brit. slang*), a pile (*informal*), a small fortune, a tidy sum (*informal*), a king's ransom (*informal*)

pact = **agreement**, alliance, treaty, deal, understanding, bargain, covenant

pad¹ NOUN 1 = **wad**, dressing, pack, padding, compress, wadding 2 = **cushion**, filling, stuffing, pillow, bolster, upholstery 3 = **notepad**, block, notebook, jotter, writing pad 4 (*Slang*) = **home**, flat, apartment, place 5 = **paw**, foot, sole
▷ VERB 6 = **pack**, fill, protect, stuff, cushion

pad² = **sneak**, creep, steal, go barefoot

padding 1 = **filling**, stuffing, packing, wadding 2 = **waffle** (*informal, chiefly Brit.*), hot air (*informal*), verbiage, wordiness, verbosity

paddle¹ NOUN 1 = **oar**, scull
▷ VERB 2 = **row**, pull, scull

paddle² = **wade**, splash (about), slop

pagan ADJECTIVE 1 = **heathen**, infidel, polytheistic, idolatrous
▷ NOUN 2 = **heathen**, infidel, polytheist, idolater

page¹ = **folio**, side, leaf, sheet

page² VERB 1 = **call**, summon, send for
▷ NOUN 2 = **attendant**, pageboy 3 = **servant**, attendant, squire, pageboy

pain NOUN 1 = **suffering**, discomfort, hurt, irritation, tenderness, soreness 2 = **ache**, stinging, aching, cramp, throb, throbbing, pang, twinge 3 = **sorrow**, suffering, torture, distress, despair, misery, agony, sadness
▷ PLURAL NOUN 4 = **trouble**, effort, care, bother, diligence
▷ VERB 5 = **distress**, hurt, torture, grieve, torment, sadden, agonize, cut to the quick 6 = **hurt**, be sore

painful 1 = **sore**, smarting, aching, tender OPPOSITE: painless 2 = **distressing**, unpleasant, grievous, distasteful, agonizing OPPOSITE: pleasant 3 = **difficult**, arduous, trying, hard, troublesome, laborious OPPOSITE: easy

painfully = **distressingly**, clearly, sadly, unfortunately, dreadfully

paint NOUN 1 = **colouring**, colour, stain, dye, tint, pigment, emulsion
▷ VERB 2 = **colour**, cover, coat, stain, whitewash, daub, distemper, apply paint to 3 = **depict**, draw, portray, picture, represent, sketch

pair NOUN 1 = **set** 2 = **couple**, brace, duo
▷ VERB 3 = **team**, match (up),

join, couple, twin, bracket

● USAGE NOTE
● Like other collective nouns,
● *pair* takes a singular or a
● plural verb according to
● whether it is seen as a unit or
● as a collection of two things:
● *the pair are said to dislike each*
● *other; a pair of good shoes is*
● *essential.*

pal (*Informal*) = friend,
companion, mate (*informal*),
buddy (*informal*), comrade,
chum (*informal*), crony, cobber
(*Austral. & N.Z. old-fashioned
informal*), E hoa (*N.Z.*)

pale ADJECTIVE 1 = light, soft,
faded, subtle, muted, bleached,
pastel, light-coloured 2 = dim,
weak, faint, feeble, thin, wan,
watery 3 = white, pasty,
bleached, wan, colourless,
pallid, ashen OPPOSITE: rosy-
cheeked
▷ VERB 4 = become pale,
blanch, whiten, go white, lose
colour

pamper = spoil, indulge, pet,
cosset, coddle, mollycoddle

pamphlet = booklet, leaflet,
brochure, circular, tract

pan¹ NOUN 1 = pot, container,
saucepan
▷ VERB 2 (*Informal*) = criticize,
knock, slam (*slang*), censure,
tear into (*informal*) 3 = sift out,
look for, search for

pan² = move along or across,
follow, track, sweep

panic NOUN 1 = fear, alarm,
terror, anxiety, hysteria, fright,
trepidation, a flap (*informal*)
▷ VERB 2 = go to pieces,
become hysterical, lose your
nerve 3 = alarm, scare,
unnerve

panorama 1 = view, prospect,
vista 2 = survey, perspective,
overview, overall picture

pant = puff, blow, breathe, gasp,
wheeze, heave

pants 1 (*Brit.*) = underpants,
briefs, drawers, knickers,
panties, boxer shorts, broekies
(*S. African*), underdaks (*Austral.
slang*) 2 (*U.S.*) = trousers, slacks

paper NOUN 1 = newspaper,
daily, journal, gazette
2 = essay, article, treatise,
dissertation 3 = examination,
test, exam 4 = report
▷ PLURAL NOUN 5 = letters,
records, documents, file,
diaries, archive, paperwork,
dossier 6 = documents,
records, certificates,
identification, deeds, identity
papers, I.D. (*informal*)
▷ VERB 7 = wallpaper, hang

parade NOUN 1 = procession,
march, pageant, cavalcade
2 = show, display, spectacle
▷ VERB 3 = march, process,
promenade 4 = flaunt, display,
exhibit, show off (*informal*)
5 = strut, show off (*informal*),
swagger, swank

paradigm = model, example,
pattern, ideal

paradise 1 = heaven, Promised

p

Land, Happy Valley (*Islam*), Elysian fields **2** = **bliss**, delight, heaven, felicity, utopia

paradox = **contradiction**, puzzle, anomaly, enigma, oddity

paragraph = **section**, part, item, passage, clause, subdivision

parallel NOUN **1** = **equivalent**, counterpart, match, equal, twin, analogue **OPPOSITE:** opposite **2** = **similarity**, comparison, analogy, resemblance, likeness **OPPOSITE:** difference ▷ ADJECTIVE **3** = **matching**, corresponding, like, similar, resembling, analogous **OPPOSITE:** different **4** = **equidistant**, alongside, side by side **OPPOSITE:** divergent

paralyse **1** = **disable**, cripple, lame, incapacitate **2** = **freeze**, stun, numb, petrify, halt, immobilize **3** = **immobilize**, freeze, halt, disable, cripple, incapacitate, bring to a standstill

paralysis **1** = **immobility**, palsy **2** = **standstill**, breakdown, stoppage, halt

parameter (*Formal*) *usually plural* = **limit**, restriction, framework, limitation, specification

paramount = **principal**, prime, first, chief, main, primary, supreme, cardinal **OPPOSITE:** secondary

paranoid **1** (*Informal*) = **suspicious**, worried, nervous, fearful, antsy (*informal*) **2** (*Technical*) = **obsessive**, disturbed, manic, neurotic, mentally ill, psychotic, deluded, paranoiac

parasite = **sponger** (*informal*), leech, hanger-on, scrounger (*informal*), bloodsucker (*informal*), quandong (*Austral. slang*)

parcel NOUN **1** = **package**, case, box, pack, bundle ▷ VERB **2** *often with* **up** = **wrap**, pack, package, tie up, do up, gift-wrap, box up, fasten together

pardon VERB **1** = **forgive**, excuse **OPPOSITE:** condemn **2** = **acquit**, let off (*informal*), exonerate, absolve **OPPOSITE:** punish ▷ NOUN **3** = **forgiveness**, absolution **OPPOSITE:** condemnation **4** = **acquittal**, amnesty, exoneration **OPPOSITE:** punishment

parent = **father** or **mother**, sire, progenitor, procreator, old (*Austral. & N.Z. informal*), patriarch

parish **1** = **district**, community **2** = **community**, flock, church, congregation

park **1** = **recreation ground**, garden, playground, pleasure garden, playpark, domain (*N.Z.*), forest park (*N.Z.*) **2** = **parkland**, grounds, estate, lawns,

woodland, grassland 3 = **field**,
pitch, playing field
parliament 1 = **assembly**,
council, congress, senate,
convention, legislature
2 = **sitting**
parliamentary
= **governmental**, legislative,
law-making
parlour or (U.S.) **parlor** 1 (Old-
fashioned) = **sitting room**,
lounge, living room, drawing
room, front room
2 = **establishment**, shop, store,
salon
parody NOUN 1 = **takeoff**
(informal), satire, caricature,
send-up (Brit. informal), spoof
(informal), skit, burlesque
▷ VERB 2 = **take off** (informal),
caricature, send up (Brit.
informal), burlesque, satirize, do
a takeoff of (informal)
parrot = **repeat**, echo, imitate,
copy, mimic
parry 1 = **evade**, avoid, dodge,
sidestep 2 = **ward off**, block,
deflect, repel, rebuff, repulse
parson = **clergyman**, minister,
priest, vicar, preacher, pastor,
cleric, churchman
part NOUN 1 = **piece**, share,
proportion, percentage, bit,
section, scrap, portion
OPPOSITE: entirety 2 often plural
= **region**, area, district,
neighbourhood, quarter,
vicinity 3 = **component**, bit,
unit, constituent 4 = **branch**,
division, office, section, wing,

subdivision, subsection
5 = **organ**, member, limb
6 (Theatre) = **role**,
representation, persona,
portrayal, depiction, character
part 7 (Theatre) = **lines**, words,
script, dialogue 8 = **side**,
behalf
▷ VERB 9 = **divide**, separate,
break, tear, split, rend, detach,
sever **OPPOSITE:** join 10 = **part
company**, separate, split up
OPPOSITE: meet
▷ PHRASES: in good part
= **good-naturedly**, well,
cheerfully, without offence
partial 1 = **incomplete**,
unfinished, imperfect,
uncompleted **OPPOSITE:**
complete 2 = **biased**,
prejudiced, discriminatory,
partisan, unfair, one-sided,
unjust **OPPOSITE:** unbiased
partially = **partly**, somewhat,
in part, not wholly, fractionally,
incompletely
participant = **participator**,
member, player, contributor,
stakeholder
participate = **take part**, be
involved, perform, join, partake
OPPOSITE: refrain from
participation = **taking part**,
contribution, involvement,
sharing in, joining in, partaking
particle = **bit**, piece, scrap,
grain, shred, mite, jot, speck
particular ADJECTIVE
1 = **specific**, special, exact,
precise, distinct, peculiar

P

OPPOSITE: general **2** = special, exceptional, notable, uncommon, marked, unusual, remarkable, singular **3** = fussy, demanding, fastidious, choosy (*informal*), picky (*informal*), finicky (*informal*), pernickety (*informal*)
OPPOSITE: indiscriminate
▷ NOUN **4** *usually plural* = detail, fact, feature, item, circumstance, specification

particularly 1 = specifically, expressly, explicitly, especially, in particular, distinctly **2** = especially, notably, unusually, exceptionally, singularly, uncommonly

parting 1 = farewell, goodbye **2** = division, breaking, split, separation, rift, rupture

partisan ADJECTIVE
1 = prejudiced, one-sided, biased, partial, sectarian
OPPOSITE: unbiased
▷ NOUN **2** = supporter, devotee, adherent, upholder
OPPOSITE: opponent
3 = underground fighter, guerrilla, freedom fighter, resistance fighter

partition NOUN **1** = screen, wall, barrier **2** = division, separation, segregation
▷ VERB **3** = separate, screen, divide

partly 1 = partially, somewhat, slightly **OPPOSITE:** completely

● USAGE NOTE
● *Partly* and *partially* are to
● some extent interchangeable,
● but *partly* should be used
● when referring to a part or
● parts of something: *the*
● *building is partly* (not *partially*)
● *made of stone*, while *partially* is
● preferred for the meaning *to*
● *some extent*: *his mother is*
● *partially* (not *partly*) *sighted*.

partner 1 = spouse, consort, significant other (*U.S. informal*), mate, husband or wife **2** = companion, ally, colleague, associate, mate, comrade **3** = associate, colleague, collaborator

partnership 1 = cooperation, alliance, sharing, union, connection, participation, copartnership **2** = company, firm, house, interest, society, cooperative

party 1 = faction, set, side, league, camp, clique, coterie **2** = get-together (*informal*), celebration, do (*informal*), gathering, function, reception, festivity, social gathering **3** = group, team, band, company, unit, squad, crew, gang

pass VERB **1** = go by *or* past, overtake, drive past, lap, leave behind, pull ahead of **OPPOSITE:** stop **2** = go, move, travel, progress, flow, proceed **3** = run, move, stroke **4** = give, hand, send, transfer, deliver, convey **5** = be left, come, be bequeathed, be inherited by **6** = kick, hit, loft, head, lob

7 = **elapse**, progress, go by, lapse, wear on, go past, tick by 8 = **end**, go, cease, blow over 9 = **spend**, fill, occupy, while away 10 = **exceed**, beat, overtake, go beyond, surpass, outstrip, outdo 11 = **be successful in**, qualify (in), succeed (in), graduate (in), get through, do, gain a pass (in) OPPOSITE: fail 12 = **approve**, accept, decree, enact, ratify, ordain, legislate (for) OPPOSITE: ban ▷ NOUN 13 = **licence**, ticket, permit, passport, warrant, authorization 14 = **gap**, route, canyon, gorge, ravine ▷ PHRASES: **pass away** or **on** (Euphemistic) = **die**, pass on, expire, pass over, snuff it (informal), kick the bucket (slang), shuffle off this mortal coil, cark it (Austral. & N.Z. informal) ▶ **pass out** (Informal) = **faint**, black out (informal), lose consciousness, become unconscious ▶ **pass something over** = **disregard**, ignore, not dwell on ▶ **pass something up** (Informal) = **miss**, let slip, decline, neglect, forgo (formal), abstain from, give (something) a miss (informal)

● USAGE NOTE
● The past participle of pass is
● sometimes wrongly spelt
● past: the time for recriminations
● has passed (not past).

passage 1 = **corridor**, hall, lobby, vestibule 2 = **alley**, way, close (Brit.), course, road, channel, route, path 3 = **extract**, reading, piece, section, text, excerpt, quotation 4 = **journey**, crossing, trip, trek, voyage 5 = **safe-conduct**, right to travel, freedom to travel, permission to travel

passenger = **traveller**, rider, fare, commuter, fare payer

passer-by = **bystander**, witness, observer, viewer, spectator, looker-on, watcher, onlooker

passing 1 = **momentary**, fleeting, short-lived, transient, ephemeral, brief, temporary, transitory 2 = **superficial**, short, quick, glancing, casual, summary, cursory, perfunctory

passion 1 = **love**, desire, lust, infatuation, ardour 2 = **emotion**, feeling, fire, heat, excitement, intensity, warmth, zeal OPPOSITE: indifference 3 = **mania**, enthusiasm, obsession, bug (informal), craving, fascination, craze 4 = **rage**, fit, storm, anger, fury, outburst, frenzy, paroxysm

passionate 1 = **emotional**, eager, strong, intense, fierce, ardent, fervent, heartfelt OPPOSITE: unemotional 2 = **loving**, erotic, hot, ardent, amorous, lustful OPPOSITE: cold

passive 1 = **submissive**, compliant, receptive, docile, quiescent OPPOSITE: spirited

2 = **inactive**, uninvolved
OPPOSITE: active

past NOUN 1 = **former times**, long ago, days gone by, the olden days **OPPOSITE:** future
2 = **background**, life, history, past life, life story, career to date
▷ ADJECTIVE 3 = **former**, early, previous, ancient, bygone, olden **OPPOSITE:** future
4 = **previous**, former, one-time, ex- 5 = **last**, previous 6 = **over**, done, ended, finished, gone
▷ PREPOSITION 7 = **after**, beyond, later than 8 = **by**, across, in front of
▷ ADVERB 9 = **on**, by, along
● USAGE NOTE
● The past participle of *pass* is
● sometimes wrongly spelt
● *past: the time for recrimination*
● *has passed* (not *past*).

paste NOUN 1 = **adhesive**, glue, cement, gum 2 = **purée**, pâté, spread
▷ VERB 3 = **stick**, glue, cement, gum

pastel = **pale**, light, soft, delicate, muted **OPPOSITE:** bright

pastime = **activity**, game, entertainment, hobby, recreation, amusement, diversion

pastor = **clergyman**, minister, priest, vicar, parson, rector, curate, churchman

pastoral 1 = **ecclesiastical**, priestly, ministerial, clerical

2 = **rustic**, country, rural, bucolic

pasture = **grassland**, grass, meadow, grazing

pat VERB 1 = **stroke**, touch, tap, pet, caress, fondle
▷ NOUN 2 = **tap**, stroke, clap

patch NOUN 1 = **spot**, bit, scrap, shred, small piece
2 = **plot**, area, ground, land, tract 3 = **reinforcement**, piece of fabric, piece of cloth, piece of material, piece sewn on
▷ VERB 4 *often with* up = **mend**, cover, repair, reinforce, stitch (up), sew (up)

patent NOUN 1 = **copyright**, licence, franchise, registered trademark
▷ ADJECTIVE 2 = **obvious**, apparent, evident, clear, glaring, manifest

path 1 = **way**, road, walk, track, trail, avenue, footpath, berm (N.Z.) 2 = **route**, way, course, direction 3 = **course**, way, road, route

pathetic = **sad**, moving, touching, affecting, distressing, tender, poignant, plaintive **OPPOSITE:** funny

patience 1 = **forbearance**, tolerance, serenity, restraint, calmness, sufferance **OPPOSITE:** impatience 2 = **endurance**, resignation, submission, fortitude, long-suffering, perseverance, stoicism, constancy

patient NOUN 1 = **sick person**,

case, sufferer, invalid
▷ ADJECTIVE 2 = **forbearing**, understanding, forgiving, mild, tolerant, indulgent, lenient, even-tempered OPPOSITE: impatient 3 = **long-suffering**, resigned, calm, enduring, philosophical, persevering, stoical, submissive

patriot = **nationalist**, loyalist, chauvinist

patriotic = **nationalistic**, loyal, chauvinistic, jingoistic

patriotism = **nationalism**, jingoism

patrol VERB 1 = **police**, guard, keep watch (on), inspect, safeguard, keep guard (on)
▷ NOUN 2 = **guard**, watch, watchman, sentinel, patrolman

patron 1 = **supporter**, friend, champion, sponsor, backer, helper, benefactor, philanthropist 2 = **customer**, client, buyer, frequenter, shopper, habitué

patronage = **support**, promotion, sponsorship, backing, help, aid, assistance

pattern 1 = **order**, plan, system, method, sequence 2 = **design**, arrangement, motif, figure, device, decoration 3 = **plan**, design, original, guide, diagram, stencil, template

pause VERB 1 = **stop briefly**, delay, break, wait, rest, halt, cease, interrupt OPPOSITE: continue

▷ NOUN 2 = **stop**, break, interval, rest, gap, halt, respite, lull OPPOSITE: continuance

pave = **cover**, floor, surface, concrete, tile

paw (*Informal*) = **manhandle**, grab, maul, molest, handle roughly

pay VERB 1 = **reward**, compensate, reimburse, recompense, requite, remunerate 2 = **spend**, give, fork out (*informal*), remit, shell out (*informal*) 3 = **settle** 4 = **bring in**, earn, return, net, yield 5 = **be profitable**, make money, make a return 6 = **benefit**, repay, be worthwhile 7 = **give**, extend, present with, grant, hand out, bestow
▷ NOUN 8 = **wages**, income, payment, earnings, fee, reward, salary, allowance
▷ PHRASES: **pay off** = **succeed**, work, be effective ▶ **pay something off** = **settle**, clear, square, discharge, pay in full

payable = **due**, outstanding, owed, owing

payment 1 = **remittance**, advance, deposit, premium, instalment 2 = **settlement**, paying, discharge, remittance 3 = **wages**, fee, reward, hire, remuneration

peace 1 = **truce**, ceasefire, treaty, armistice OPPOSITE: war 2 = **stillness**, rest, quiet, silence, calm, hush, tranquillity, seclusion 3 = **serenity**, calm, composure, contentment, repose, equanimity, peacefulness, harmoniousness 4 = **harmony**, accord, agreement, concord

peaceful 1 = **at peace**, friendly, harmonious, amicable, nonviolent **OPPOSITE:** hostile 2 = **peace-loving**, conciliatory, peaceable, unwarlike **OPPOSITE:** belligerent 3 = **calm**, still, quiet, tranquil, restful **OPPOSITE:** agitated 4 = **serene**, placid, undisturbed

peak NOUN 1 = **high point**, crown, climax, culmination, zenith, acme 2 = **point**, top, tip, summit, brow, crest, pinnacle, apex ▷ VERB 3 = **culminate**, climax, come to a head

peasant = **rustic**, countryman

peck VERB 1 = **pick**, hit, strike, tap, poke, jab, prick 2 = **kiss**, plant a kiss, give someone a smacker, give someone a peck *or* kiss ▷ NOUN 3 = **kiss**, smacker, osculation (*rare*)

peculiar 1 = **odd**, strange, unusual, bizarre, funny, extraordinary, curious, weird **OPPOSITE:** ordinary 2 = **special**, particular, unique, characteristic **OPPOSITE:** common

peddle = **sell**, trade, push (*informal*), market, hawk, flog (*slang*)

pedestrian NOUN 1 = **walker**, foot-traveller **OPPOSITE:** driver ▷ ADJECTIVE 2 = **dull**, ordinary, boring, commonplace, mundane, mediocre, banal, prosaic, half-pie (*N.Z. informal*) **OPPOSITE:** exciting

pedigree ADJECTIVE 1 = **purebred**, thoroughbred, full-blooded ▷ NOUN 2 = **lineage**, family, line, race, stock, blood, breed, descent

peel NOUN 1 = **rind**, skin, peeling ▷ VERB 2 = **skin**, scale, strip, pare, shuck, flake off, take the skin or rind off

peep VERB 1 = **peek**, look, eyeball (*slang*), sneak a look, steal a look ▷ NOUN 2 = **look**, glimpse, peek, look-see (*slang*)

peer¹ = **squint**, look, spy, gaze, scan, inspect, peep, peek

peer² 1 = **noble**, lord, aristocrat, nobleman 2 = **equal**, like, fellow, contemporary, compeer

peg NOUN 1 = **pin**, spike, rivet, skewer, dowel, spigot ▷ VERB 2 = **fasten**, join, fix, secure, attach

pen¹ = **write (down)**, draft, compose, pencil, draw up, scribble, take down, inscribe

pen² NOUN 1 = **enclosure**, pound, fold, cage, coop, hutch, sty ▷ VERB 2 = **enclose**, confine, cage, fence in, coop up, hedge in, shut up *or* in, impound

penalty = punishment, price, fine, handicap, forfeit

pending ADJECTIVE

1 = **undecided**, unsettled, in the balance, undetermined

2 = **forthcoming**, imminent, prospective, impending, in the wind

▷ PREPOSITION 3 = **awaiting**, until, waiting for, till

penetrate 1 = **pierce**, enter, go through, bore, stab, prick

2 = **grasp**, work out, figure out (*informal*), comprehend, fathom, decipher, suss (out) (*slang*), get to the bottom of

penetrating 1 = **sharp**, harsh, piercing, carrying, piping, loud, strident, shrill **OPPOSITE:** sweet

2 = **pungent**, piercing

4 = **intelligent**, quick, sharp, keen, acute, shrewd, astute, perceptive **OPPOSITE:** dull

5 = **perceptive**, sharp, keen **OPPOSITE:** unperceptive

penetration 1 = **piercing**, entry, entrance, puncturing, incision 2 = **entry**, entrance

pension = **allowance**, benefit, welfare, annuity, superannuation

pensioner = **senior citizen**, retired person, retiree (*U.S.*), old-age pensioner, O.A.P.

people PLURAL NOUN

1 = **persons**, individuals, folk (*informal*), men and women, humanity, mankind, mortals, the human race 2 = **nation**,

public, community, subjects, population, residents, citizens, folk 3 = **race**, tribe 4 = **family**, parents, relations, relatives, folk, folks (*informal*), clan, kin

▷ VERB 5 = **inhabit**, occupy, settle, populate, colonize

pepper NOUN 1 = **seasoning**, flavour, spice

▷ VERB 2 = **pelt**, hit, shower, blitz, rake, bombard, assail, strafe 3 = **sprinkle**, spot, scatter, dot, fleck, intersperse, speck, spatter

perceive 1 = **see**, notice, note, identify, discover, spot, observe, recognize 2 = **understand**, gather, see, learn, realize, grasp, comprehend, suss (out) (*slang*)

3 = **consider**, believe, judge, suppose, rate, deem, adjudge (*formal*)

perception 1 = **awareness**, understanding, sense, impression, feeling, idea, notion, consciousness

2 = **understanding**, intelligence, observation, discrimination, insight, sharpness, cleverness, keenness

perch VERB 1 = **sit**, rest, balance, settle 2 = **place**, put, rest, balance 3 = **land**, alight, roost

▷ NOUN 4 = **resting place**, post, branch, pole

perennial = **continual**, lasting, constant, enduring, persistent, abiding, recurrent, incessant

perfect ADJECTIVE

1 = **faultless**, correct, pure, impeccable, exemplary, flawless, foolproof **OPPOSITE:** deficient **2** = **excellent**, ideal, supreme, superb, splendid, sublime, superlative
3 = **immaculate**, impeccable, flawless, spotless, unblemished **OPPOSITE:** flawed
4 = **complete**, absolute, sheer, utter, consummate, unmitigated **OPPOSITE:** partial
5 = **exact**, true, accurate, precise, correct, faithful, unerring
▷ VERB **6** = **improve**, develop, polish, refine **OPPOSITE:** mar

● USAGE NOTE
● For most of its meanings, the
● adjective *perfect* describes an
● absolute state, so that
● something either is or is not
● *perfect*, and cannot be
● referred to in terms of degree
● – thus, one thing should not
● be described as *more perfect* or
● *less perfect* than another
● thing. However, when *perfect*
● is used in the sense of
● 'excellent in all respects', *more*
● and *most* are acceptable, for
● example *the next day the*
● *weather was even more perfect*.

perfection = **excellence**, integrity, superiority, purity, wholeness, sublimity, exquisiteness, faultlessness

perfectly 1 = **completely**, totally, absolutely, quite, fully, altogether, thoroughly, wholly **OPPOSITE:** partially
2 = **flawlessly**, ideally, wonderfully, superbly, supremely, impeccably, faultlessly **OPPOSITE:** badly

perform 1 = **do**, achieve, carry out, complete, fulfil, accomplish, execute, pull off
2 = **fulfil**, carry out, execute, discharge **3** = **present**, act (out), stage, play, produce, represent, put on, enact
4 = **appear on stage**, act
5 = **function**, go, work, run, operate, handle, respond, behave

performance
1 = **presentation**, playing, acting (out), staging, production, exhibition, rendering, portrayal **2** = **show**, appearance, concert, gig (*informal*), recital **3** = **work**, acts, conduct, exploits, feats
4 = **carrying out**, practice, achievement, execution, completion, accomplishment, fulfilment

performer = **artiste**, player, Thespian, trouper, actor or actress

perfume 1 = **fragrance**, scent
2 = **scent**, smell, fragrance, bouquet, aroma, odour

perhaps = **maybe**, possibly, it may be, it is possible (that), conceivably, perchance (*archaic*), feasibly, happen (*Northern English dialect*)

peril 1 = **danger**, risk, threat,

hazard, menace, jeopardy, perilousness **2** *often plural* = **pitfall**, problem, risk, hazard **OPPOSITE:** safety

perimeter = **boundary**, edge, border, bounds, limit, margin, confines, periphery **OPPOSITE:** centre

period = **time**, term, season, space, run, stretch, spell, phase

periodic = **recurrent**, regular, repeated, occasional, cyclical, sporadic, intermittent

peripheral 1 = **secondary**, minor, marginal, irrelevant, unimportant, incidental, inessential **2** = **outermost**, outside, external, outer, exterior

perish 1 = **die**, be killed, expire, pass away, lose your life, cark it (*Austral. & N.Z. slang*) **2** = **be destroyed**, fall, decline, collapse, disappear, vanish **3** = **rot**, waste away, decay, disintegrate, decompose, moulder

perk (*Brit. informal*) = **bonus**, benefit, extra, plus, fringe benefit, perquisite

permanent 1 = **lasting**, constant, enduring, persistent, eternal, abiding, perpetual, everlasting **OPPOSITE:** temporary **2** = **long-term**, established, secure, stable, steady **OPPOSITE:** temporary

permission = **authorization**, sanction, licence, approval, leave, go-ahead (*informal*), liberty, consent **OPPOSITE:** prohibition

permit VERB **1** = **allow**, grant, sanction, let, entitle, license, authorize, consent to **OPPOSITE:** forbid **2** = **enable**, let, allow, cause ▷ NOUN **3** = **licence**, pass, document, certificate, passport, visa, warrant, authorization **OPPOSITE:** prohibition

perpetual 1 = **everlasting**, permanent, endless, eternal, lasting, perennial, infinite, never-ending **OPPOSITE:** temporary **2** = **continual**, repeated, constant, endless, continuous, persistent, recurrent, never-ending **OPPOSITE:** brief

perpetuate = **maintain**, preserve, keep going, immortalize **OPPOSITE:** end

persecute 1 = **victimize**, torture, torment, oppress, pick on, ill-treat, maltreat **OPPOSITE:** mollycoddle **2** = **harass**, bother, annoy, tease, hassle (*informal*), badger, pester **OPPOSITE:** leave alone

persist 1 = **continue**, last, remain, carry on, keep up, linger **2** = **persevere**, continue, go on, carry on, keep on, keep going, press on, not give up

persistence = **determination**, resolution, grit, endurance, tenacity, perseverance, doggedness, pertinacity

persistent 1 = **continuous**, constant, repeated, endless, perpetual, continual, never-ending, incessant **OPPOSITE:** occasional 2 = **determined**, dogged, steady, stubborn, persevering, tireless, tenacious, steadfast **OPPOSITE:** irresolute

person 1 = **individual**, being, body, human, soul, creature, mortal, man or woman
▷ **PHRASES: in person**
1 = **personally**, yourself 2 = **in the flesh**, actually, physically, bodily

personal 1 = **own**, special, private, individual, particular, peculiar 2 = **individual**, special, particular, exclusive 3 = **private** 4 = **offensive**, nasty, insulting, disparaging, derogatory

personality 1 = **nature**, character, make-up, identity, temperament, disposition, individuality 2 = **character**, charm, attraction, charisma, magnetism 3 = **celebrity**, star, notable, household name, famous name, personage, megastar (informal)

personally 1 = **in your opinion**, in your book, for your part, from your own viewpoint, in your own view 2 = **by yourself**, alone, independently, solely, on your own 3 = **individually**, specially, subjectively, individualistically 4 = **privately**, in private, off the record

personnel = **employees**, people, staff, workers, workforce, human resources, helpers

perspective 1 = **outlook**, attitude, context, angle, frame of reference 2 = **objectivity**, proportion, relation, relativity, relative importance

persuade 1 = **talk (someone) into**, urge, influence, win (someone) over, induce, sway, entice, coax **OPPOSITE:** dissuade 2 = **cause**, lead, move, influence, motivate, induce, incline, dispose 3 = **convince**, satisfy, assure, cause to believe

persuasion 1 = **urging**, inducement, wheedling, enticement, cajolery 2 = **belief**, views, opinion, party, school, side, camp, faith

persuasive = **convincing**, telling, effective, sound, compelling, influential, valid, credible **OPPOSITE:** unconvincing

pervasive = **widespread**, general, common, extensive, universal, prevalent, ubiquitous, rife

perverse 1 = **stubborn**, contrary, dogged, troublesome, rebellious, wayward, intractable, wilful **OPPOSITE:** cooperative 2 = **ill-natured**, cross, surly, fractious, churlish, ill-tempered, stroppy (Brit. slang), peevish **OPPOSITE:** good-natured 3 = **abnormal**, unhealthy, improper, deviant

pervert VERB 1 = **distort**, abuse, twist, misuse, warp, misrepresent, falsify 2 = **corrupt**, degrade, deprave, debase, debauch, lead astray ▷ NOUN 3 = **deviant**, degenerate, sicko (*informal*), weirdo *or* weirdie (*informal*)

pessimistic = **gloomy**, dark, despairing, bleak, depressed, cynical, hopeless, glum **OPPOSITE:** optimistic

pest 1 = **infection**, bug, insect, plague, epidemic, blight, scourge, pestilence, gogga (*S. African informal*) 2 = **nuisance**, trial, pain (*informal*), drag (*informal*), bother, irritation, annoyance, bane

pet ADJECTIVE 1 = **favourite**, favoured, dearest, cherished, fave (*informal*), dear to your heart ▷ NOUN 2 = **favourite**, treasure, darling, jewel, idol ▷ VERB 3 = **fondle**, pat, stroke, caress 4 = **pamper**, spoil, indulge, cosset, baby, dote on, coddle, mollycoddle 5 (*Informal*) = **cuddle**, kiss, snog (*Brit. slang*), smooch (*informal*), neck (*informal*), canoodle (*old-fashioned*)

petition NOUN 1 = **appeal**, round robin, list of signatures 2 = **entreaty**, appeal, suit, application, request, prayer, plea, solicitation ▷ VERB 3 = **appeal**, plead, ask, pray, beg, solicit, beseech, entreat, supplicate

petty 1 = **trivial**, insignificant, little, small, slight, trifling, negligible, unimportant **OPPOSITE:** important 2 = **small-minded**, mean, shabby, spiteful, ungenerous, mean-minded **OPPOSITE:** broad-minded

phantom = **spectre**, ghost, spirit, shade (*literary*), spook (*informal*), apparition, wraith (*literary*), phantasm

phase = **stage**, time, point, position, step, development, period, chapter ▷ PHRASES: **phase something in** = **introduce**, incorporate, ease in, start ▶ **phase something out** = **eliminate**, close, remove, withdraw, pull out, wind up, run down, terminate

phenomenal = **extraordinary**, outstanding, remarkable, fantastic, unusual, marvellous, exceptional, miraculous **OPPOSITE:** unremarkable

phenomenon 1 = **occurrence**, happening, fact, event, incident, circumstance, episode 2 = **wonder**, sensation, exception, miracle, marvel, prodigy, rarity

● USAGE NOTE
● Although *phenomena* is often
● treated as a singular, this is
● not grammatically correct.
● *Phenomenon* is the singular
● form of this word, and

- *phenomena* the plural; so
- *several new phenomena were*
- *recorded in his notes* is correct,
- but *that is an interesting*
- *phenomena* is not.

philosopher = thinker, theorist, sage, wise man, logician, metaphysician

philosophical *or* **philosophic** 1 = **theoretical**, abstract, wise, rational, logical, thoughtful, sagacious **OPPOSITE:** practical 2 = **stoical**, calm, composed, cool, collected, serene, tranquil, unruffled **OPPOSITE:** emotional

philosophy 1 = **thought**, knowledge, thinking, reasoning, wisdom, logic, metaphysics 2 = **outlook**, values, principles, convictions, thinking, beliefs, doctrine, ideology

phone NOUN 1 = **telephone**, blower (*informal*) 2 = **call**, ring (*informal, chiefly Brit.*), tinkle (*Brit. informal*)
▷ VERB 3 = **call**, telephone, ring (up) (*informal, chiefly Brit.*), give someone a call, give someone a ring (*informal, chiefly Brit.*), make a call, give someone a tinkle (*Brit. informal*), get on the blower (*informal*)

photograph NOUN 1 = **picture**, photo (*informal*), shot, print, snap (*informal*), snapshot, transparency
▷ VERB = **take a picture of**, record, film, shoot, snap (*informal*), take (someone's) picture

photographic 1 = **pictorial**, visual, graphic, cinematic, filmic 2 = **accurate**, exact, precise, faithful, retentive

phrase NOUN 1 = **expression**, saying, remark, construction, quotation, maxim, idiom, adage
▷ VERB 2 = **express**, say, word, put, voice, communicate, convey, put into words

physical 1 = **corporal**, fleshly, bodily, corporeal 2 = **earthly**, fleshly, mortal, incarnate 3 = **material**, real, substantial, natural, solid, tangible, palpable

physician = **doctor**, doc (*informal*), medic (*informal*), general practitioner, medical practitioner, doctor of medicine, G.P., M.D.

pick VERB 1 = **select**, choose, identify, elect, nominate, specify, opt for, single out **OPPOSITE:** reject 2 = **gather**, pull, collect, take in, harvest, pluck, garner 3 = **provoke**, start, cause, stir up, incite, instigate 4 = **open**, force, crack (*informal*), break into, break open
▷ NOUN 5 = **choice**, decision, option, selection, preference 6 = **best**, prime, finest, elect, elite, cream, jewel in the crown, crème de la crème (*French*)
▷ PHRASES: **pick on someone** 1 = **torment**, bully, bait, tease, get at (*informal*), badger, persecute, hector 2 = **choose**,

select, prefer, elect, single out, fix on, settle upon ▶ **pick something** or **someone out** = **identify**, recognize, distinguish, perceive, discriminate, make someone or something out, tell someone or something apart ▶ **pick something** or **someone up** 1 = **lift**, raise, gather, take up, grasp, uplift 2 = **collect**, get, call for ▶ **pick something up** 1 = **learn**, master, acquire, get the hang of (*informal*), become proficient in 2 = **obtain**, get, find, buy, discover, purchase, acquire, locate ▶ **pick up** 1 = **improve**, recover, rally, get better, bounce back, make progress, perk up, turn the corner 2 = **recover**, improve, rally, get better, mend, turn the corner, be on the mend, take a turn for the better

picket VERB 1 = **blockade**, boycott, demonstrate outside ▷ NOUN 2 = **demonstration**, strike, blockade 3 = **protester**, demonstrator, picketer 4 = **lookout**, watch, guard, patrol, sentry, sentinel 5 = **stake**, post, pale, paling, upright, stanchion

pickle VERB 1 = **preserve**, marinade, steep ▷ NOUN 2 = **chutney**, relish, piccalilli 3 (*Informal*) = **predicament**, fix (*informal*), difficulty, bind (*informal*), jam (*informal*), dilemma, scrape

(*informal*), hot water (*informal*), uphill (*S. African*)

pick-up = **improvement**, recovery, rise, rally, strengthening, revival, upturn, change for the better

picnic = **excursion**, barbecue, barbie (*informal*), cookout (*U.S. & Canad.*), alfresco meal, clambake (*U.S. & Canad.*), outdoor meal, outing

picture NOUN 1 = **representation**, drawing, painting, portrait, image, print, illustration, sketch 2 = **photograph**, photo, still, shot, image, print, frame, slide 3 = **film**, movie (*U.S. informal*), flick (*slang*), feature film, motion picture 4 = **idea**, vision, concept, impression, notion, visualization, mental picture, mental image 5 = **description**, impression, explanation, report, account, image, sketch, depiction 6 = **personification**, embodiment, essence, epitome ▷ VERB 7 = **imagine**, see, envision, visualize, conceive of, fantasize about, conjure up an image of 8 = **represent**, show, draw, paint, illustrate, sketch, depict 9 = **show**, photograph, capture on film

picturesque 1 = **interesting**, pretty, beautiful, attractive, charming, scenic, quaint OPPOSITE: unattractive 2 = **vivid**, striking, graphic, colourful, memorable

piece 1 = **bit**, slice, part, block, quantity, segment, portion, fragment 2 = **component**, part, section, bit, unit, segment, constituent, module 3 = **item**, report, story, study, review, article 4 = **composition**, work, production, opus 5 = **work of art**, work, creation 6 = **share**, cut (*informal*), slice, percentage, quantity, portion, quota, fraction

pier 1 = **jetty**, wharf, quay, promenade, landing place 2 = **pillar**, support, post, column, pile, upright, buttress

pierce = **penetrate**, stab, spike, enter, bore, drill, puncture, prick

piercing 1 = **penetrating**, sharp, loud, shrill, high-pitched, ear-splitting **OPPOSITE:** low 2 = **perceptive**, sharp, keen, alert, penetrating, shrewd, perspicacious, quick-witted **OPPOSITE:** unperceptive 3 = **sharp**, acute, severe, intense, painful, stabbing, excruciating, agonizing 4 = **cold**, biting, freezing, bitter, arctic, wintry, nippy

pig 1 = **hog**, sow, boar, swine, porker 2 (*Informal*) = **slob**, glutton 3 (*Informal*) = **brute**, monster, scoundrel, rogue, swine, rotter, boor

pigment = **colour**, colouring, paint, stain, dye, tint, tincture

pile¹ NOUN 1 = **heap**, collection, mountain, mass, stack, mound, accumulation, hoard 2 (*Informal*) often plural = **lot(s)**, mountain(s), load(s) (*informal*), oceans, wealth, great deal, stack(s), abundance 3 = **mansion**, building, residence, manor, country house, seat, big house, stately home ▷ VERB 4 = **load**, stuff, pack, stack, charge, heap, cram, lade 5 = **crowd**, pack, rush, climb, flood, stream, crush, squeeze ▷ PHRASES: pile up = **accumulate**, collect, gather (up), build up, amass

pile² = **foundation**, support, post, column, beam, upright, pillar

pile³ = **nap**, fibre, down, hair, fur, plush

pile-up (*Informal*) = **collision**, crash, accident, smash, smash-up (*informal*), multiple collision

pilgrim = **traveller**, wanderer, devotee, wayfarer

pilgrimage = **journey**, tour, trip, mission, expedition, excursion

pill = **tablet**, capsule, pellet

pillar 1 = **support**, post, column, prop, shaft, upright, pier, stanchion 2 = **supporter**, leader, mainstay, leading light (*informal*), upholder

pilot NOUN 1 = **airman**, flyer, aviator, aeronaut 2 = **helmsman**, navigator, steersman

▷ VERB **3** = **fly**, operate, be at the controls of **4** = **navigate**, drive, direct, guide, handle, conduct, steer **5** = **direct**, conduct, steer

▷ ADJECTIVE **6** = **trial**, test, model, sample, experimental

pin NOUN **1** = **tack**, nail, needle, safety pin **2** = **peg**, rod, brace, bolt

▷ VERB **3** = **fasten**, stick, attach, join, fix, secure, nail, clip **4** = **hold fast**, hold down, constrain, immobilize, pinion

▷ PHRASES: **pin someone down** = **force**, pressure, compel, put pressure on, pressurize, nail someone down, make someone commit themselves ▶ **pin something down** = **determine**, identify, locate, name, specify, establish, pinpoint

pinch VERB **1** = **nip**, press, squeeze, grasp, compress **2** = **hurt**, crush, squeeze, pain, cramp **3** (*Brit. informal*) = **steal**, lift (*informal*), nick (*slang, chiefly Brit.*), swipe (*slang*), knock off (*slang*), pilfer, purloin (*formal*), filch

▷ NOUN **4** = **nip**, squeeze **5** = **dash**, bit, mite, jot, speck, soupçon (*French*) **6** = **emergency**, crisis, difficulty, plight, scrape (*informal*), strait, uphill (*S. African*), predicament

pine = **waste**, decline, sicken, fade, languish

▷ PHRASES: **pine for something or someone 1** = **long**, ache,

crave, yearn, eat your heart out over **2** = **hanker after**, crave, wish for, yearn for, thirst for, hunger for

pink ADJECTIVE = **rosy**, rose, salmon, flushed, reddish, roseate

▷ *See panel* SHADES OF RED

pinnacle 1 = **summit**, top, height, peak **2** = **height**, top, crown, crest, zenith, apex, vertex

pinpoint 1 = **identify**, discover, define, distinguish, put your finger on **2** = **locate**, find, identify, zero in on

pioneer NOUN **1** = **founder**, leader, developer, innovator, trailblazer **2** = **settler**, explorer, colonist

▷ VERB **3** = **develop**, create, establish, start, discover, institute, invent, initiate

pipe NOUN **1** = **tube**, drain, canal, pipeline, line, main, passage, cylinder

▷ VERB **2** = **convey**, channel, conduct

▷ PHRASES: **pipe down** (*Informal*) = **be quiet**, shut up (*informal*), hush, stop talking, quieten down, shush, shut your mouth, hold your tongue

pipeline = **tube**, passage, pipe, conduit, duct

pirate NOUN **1** = **buccaneer**, raider, marauder, corsair, freebooter

▷ VERB **2** = **copy**, steal, reproduce, bootleg,

P

appropriate, poach, crib (*informal*), plagiarize

pit NOUN **1** = **coal mine**, mine, shaft, colliery, mine shaft **2** = **hole**, depression, hollow, crater, trough, cavity, abyss, chasm ▷ VERB **3** = **scar**, mark, dent, indent, pockmark

pitch NOUN **1** = **sports field**, ground, stadium, arena, park, field of play **2** = **tone**, sound, key, frequency, timbre, modulation **3** = **level**, point, degree, summit, extent, height, intensity, high point **4** = **talk**, patter, spiel (*informal*) ▷ VERB **5** = **throw**, cast, toss, hurl, fling, chuck (*informal*), sling, lob (*informal*) **6** = **fall**, drop, plunge, dive, tumble, topple, plummet, fall headlong **7** = **set up**, raise, settle, put up, erect **8** = **toss (about)**, roll, plunge, lurch ▷ PHRASES: **pitch in** (*Informal*) = **help**, contribute, participate, join in, cooperate, chip in (*informal*), get stuck in (*Brit. informal*), lend a hand

pitfall usually plural = **danger**, difficulty, peril, catch, trap, hazard, drawback, snag, uphill (*S. African*)

pity NOUN **1** = **compassion**, charity, sympathy, kindness, fellow feeling **OPPOSITE:** mercilessness **2** = **shame**, sin (*informal*), misfortune, bummer (*slang*), crying shame

3 = **mercy**, kindness, clemency, forbearance ▷ VERB **4** = **feel sorry for**, feel for, sympathize with, grieve for, weep for, bleed for, have compassion for

pivotal = **crucial**, central, vital, critical, decisive

place NOUN **1** = **spot**, point, position, site, area, location, venue, whereabouts **2** = **region**, quarter, district, neighbourhood, vicinity, locality, locale, dorp (*S. African*) **3** = **position**, point, spot, location **4** = **space**, position, seat, chair **5** = **rank**, standing, position, footing, station, status, grade, niche **6** = **situation**, position, circumstances, shoes (*informal*) **7** = **job**, position, post, situation, office, employment, appointment **8** = **home**, house, room, property, accommodation, pad (*slang*), residence, dwelling **9** (In this context, the construction is always negative) = **duty**, right, job, charge, concern, role, affair, responsibility ▷ VERB **10** = **lay (down)**, put (down), set (down), stand, position, rest, station, stick (*informal*) **11** = **put**, lay, set, invest, pin **12** = **classify**, class, group, put, order, sort, rank, arrange **13** = **entrust to**, give to, assign to, appoint to, allocate to, find a home for

14 = **identify**, remember, recognize, pin someone down, put your finger on, put a name to

▷ PHRASES: **take place** = **happen**, occur, go on, go down, arise, come about, crop up, transpire (*informal*)

plague NOUN **1** = **disease**, infection, epidemic, pestilence **2** = **infestation**, invasion, epidemic, influx, host, swarm, multitude

▷ VERB **3** = **torment**, trouble, torture **4** = **pester**, trouble, bother, annoy, tease, harry, harass, hassle (*informal*)

plain ADJECTIVE

1 = **unadorned**, simple, basic, severe, bare, stark, austere, spartan **OPPOSITE:** ornate **2** = **clear**, obvious, patent, evident, visible, distinct, understandable, manifest **OPPOSITE:** hidden **3** = **straightforward**, open, direct, frank, blunt, outspoken, honest, downright **OPPOSITE:** roundabout **4** = **ugly**, unattractive, homely (*U.S. & Canad.*), unlovely, unprepossessing, not beautiful, no oil painting (*informal*), ill-favoured **OPPOSITE:** attractive **5** = **ordinary**, common, simple, everyday, commonplace, unaffected, unpretentious **OPPOSITE:** sophisticated

▷ NOUN **6** = **flatland**, plateau, prairie, grassland, steppe, veld

plan NOUN **1** = **scheme**, system, design, programme, proposal, strategy, method, suggestion **2** = **diagram**, map, drawing, chart, representation, sketch, blueprint, layout

▷ VERB **3** = **devise**, arrange, scheme, plot, draft, organize, outline, formulate **4** = **intend**, aim, mean, propose, purpose **5** = **design**, outline, draw up a plan of

plane NOUN **1** = **aeroplane**, aircraft, jet, airliner, jumbo jet **2** = **flat surface**, the flat, horizontal, level surface **3** = **level**, position, stage, condition, standard, degree, rung, echelon

▷ ADJECTIVE **4** = **level**, even, flat, regular, smooth, horizontal

▷ VERB **5** = **skim**, sail, skate, glide

plant¹ NOUN **1** = **flower**, bush, vegetable, herb, weed, shrub

▷ VERB **2** = **sow**, scatter, transplant, implant, put in the ground **3** = **seed**, sow, implant **4** = **place**, put, set, fix **5** = **hide**, put, place, conceal **6** = **place**, put, establish, found, fix, insert

plant² **1** = **factory**, works, shop, yard, mill, foundry **2** = **machinery**, equipment, gear, apparatus

plaster NOUN **1** = **mortar**, stucco, gypsum, plaster of Paris **2** = **bandage**, dressing, sticking plaster, Elastoplast ®, adhesive plaster

▷ VERB **3** = **cover**, spread, coat, smear, overlay, daub

plastic = **pliant**, soft, flexible, supple, pliable, ductile, mouldable **OPPOSITE:** rigid

plate NOUN **1** = **platter**, dish, dinner plate, salver, trencher (*archaic*) **2** = **helping**, course, serving, dish, portion, platter, plateful **3** = **layer**, panel, sheet, slab **4** = **illustration**, picture, photograph, print, engraving, lithograph

▷ VERB **5** = **coat**, gild, laminate, cover, overlay

plateau 1 = **upland**, table, highland, tableland **2** = **levelling off**, level, stage, stability

platform 1 = **stage**, stand, podium, rostrum, dais, soapbox **2** = **policy**, programme, principle, objective(s), manifesto, party line

plausible 1 = **believable**, possible, likely, reasonable, credible, probable, persuasive, conceivable **OPPOSITE:** unbelievable **2** = **glib**, smooth, specious, smooth-talking, smooth-tongued

play VERB **1** = **amuse yourself**, have fun, sport, fool, romp, revel, trifle, entertain yourself **2** = **take part in**, be involved in, engage in, participate in, compete in **3** = **compete against**, challenge, take on,

oppose, contend against **4** = **perform**, carry out **5** = **act**, portray, represent, perform, act the part of **6** = **perform on**, strum, make music on

▷ NOUN **7** = **amusement**, pleasure, leisure, games, sport, fun, entertainment, relaxation **8** = **drama**, show, piece, comedy, tragedy, farce, soapie or soapie (*Austral. slang*), pantomime

▷ PHRASES: **play on** or **upon something** = **take advantage of**, abuse, exploit, impose on, trade on, capitalize on ▶ **play something down** = **minimize**, make light of, gloss over, talk down, underrate, underplay, pooh-pooh (*informal*), soft-pedal (*informal*) ▶ **play something up** = **emphasize**, highlight, underline, stress, accentuate ▶ **play up 1** (*Brit. informal*) = **hurt**, be painful, bother you, trouble you, be sore, pain you **2** (*Brit. informal*) = **malfunction**, not work properly, be on the blink (*slang*) **3** (*Brit. informal*) = **be awkward**, misbehave, give trouble, be disobedient, be stroppy (*Brit. slang*)

playboy = **womanizer**, philanderer, rake, lady-killer (*informal*), roué, ladies' man

player 1 = **sportsman** or **sportswoman**, competitor, participant, contestant **2** = **musician**, artist, performer, virtuoso, instrumentalist

3 = **performer**, entertainer, Thespian, trouper, actor *or* actress

plea 1 = **appeal**, request, suit, prayer, petition, entreaty, intercession, supplication 2 = **excuse**, defence, explanation, justification

plead = **appeal**, ask, request, beg, petition, implore, beseech, entreat

pleasant 1 = **pleasing**, nice, fine, lovely, amusing, delightful, enjoyable, agreeable, lekker (*S. African slang*) **OPPOSITE:** horrible 2 = **friendly**, nice, agreeable, likable *or* likeable, engaging, charming, amiable, genial **OPPOSITE:** disagreeable

please = **delight**, entertain, humour, amuse, suit, satisfy, indulge, gratify **OPPOSITE:** annoy

pleased = **happy**, delighted, contented, satisfied, thrilled, glad, gratified, over the moon (*informal*)

pleasing 1 = **enjoyable**, satisfying, charming, delightful, gratifying, agreeable, pleasurable **OPPOSITE:** unpleasant 2 = **likable** *or* **likeable**, engaging, charming, delightful, agreeable **OPPOSITE:** disagreeable

pleasure 1 = **happiness**, delight, satisfaction, enjoyment, bliss, gratification, gladness, delectation **OPPOSITE:** displeasure

2 = **amusement**, joy **OPPOSITE:** duty

pledge NOUN 1 = **promise**, vow, assurance, word, undertaking, warrant, oath, covenant 2 = **guarantee**, security, deposit, bail, collateral, pawn, surety ▷ VERB 3 = **promise**, vow, swear, contract, engage, give your word, give your oath

plentiful = **abundant**, liberal, generous, lavish, ample, overflowing, copious, bountiful **OPPOSITE:** scarce

plenty 1 = **abundance**, wealth, prosperity, fertility, profusion, affluence, plenitude, fruitfulness 2 *usually with* **of** = **lots of** (*informal*), enough, a great deal of, masses of, piles of (*informal*), stacks of, heaps of (*informal*), an abundance of

plight = **difficulty**, condition, state, situation, trouble, predicament

plot[1] NOUN 1 = **plan**, scheme, intrigue, conspiracy, cabal, stratagem, machination 2 = **story**, action, subject, theme, outline, scenario, narrative, story line ▷ VERB 3 = **plan**, scheme, conspire, intrigue, manoeuvre, contrive, collude, machinate 4 = **devise**, design, lay, conceive, hatch, contrive, concoct, cook up (*informal*) 5 = **chart**, mark, map, locate, calculate, outline

P

plot² = **patch**, lot, area, ground, parcel, tract, allotment

plough = **turn over**, dig, till, cultivate
▷ PHRASES: **plough through something** = **forge**, cut, drive, press, push, plunge, wade

ploy = **tactic**, move, trick, device, scheme, manoeuvre, dodge, ruse

pluck VERB 1 = **pull out** or **off**, pick, draw, collect, gather, harvest 2 = **tug**, catch, snatch, clutch, jerk, yank, tweak, pull at 3 = **strum**, pick, finger, twang
▷ NOUN 4 = **courage**, nerve, bottle (*Brit. slang*), guts (*informal*), grit, bravery, backbone, boldness

plug NOUN 1 = **stopper**, cork, bung, spigot 2 (*Informal*) = **mention**, advertisement, advert (*Brit. informal*), push, publicity, hype
▷ VERB 3 = **seal**, close, stop, fill, block, stuff, pack, cork 4 (*Informal*) = **mention**, push, promote, publicize, advertise, build up, hype
▷ PHRASES: **plug away** (*Informal*) = **slog away** (*informal*), labour, toil away, grind away (*informal*), peg away, plod away

plum = **choice**, prize, first-class

plumb VERB 1 = **delve into**, explore, probe, go into, penetrate, gauge, unravel, fathom
▷ ADVERB 2 = **exactly**, precisely, bang, slap, spot-on

(*Brit. informal*), slap-bang

plummet 1 = **drop**, fall, crash, nose-dive, descend rapidly 2 = **plunge**, fall, drop, crash, tumble, nosedive, descend rapidly

plump = **chubby**, fat, stout, round, tubby, dumpy, roly-poly, rotund OPPOSITE: scrawny

plunder = **loot**, strip, sack, rob, raid, rifle, ransack, pillage 2 = **steal**, rob, take, nick (*informal*), pinch (*informal*), embezzle, pilfer, thieve
▷ NOUN 3 = **pillage** 4 = **loot**, spoils, booty, swag (*slang*), ill-gotten gains

plunge VERB 1 = **descend**, fall, drop, crash, pitch, sink, dive, tumble 2 = **hurtle**, charge, career, jump, tear, rush, dive, dash 3 = **submerge**, dip 4 = **throw**, cast, pitch, propel 5 = **fall steeply**, drop, crash (*informal*), slump, plummet, take a nosedive (*informal*)
▷ NOUN 6 = **dive**, jump, duck, descent 7 = **fall**, crash (*informal*), slump, drop, tumble

plus PREPOSITION 1 = **and**, with, added to, coupled with
▷ NOUN 2 (*Informal*) = **advantage**, benefit, asset, gain, extra, bonus, good point
▷ ADJECTIVE 3 = **additional**, added, extra, supplementary, add-on

● USAGE NOTE
● When you have a sentence
● with more than one subject

- linked by *and*, this makes the
- subject plural and means it
- should take a plural verb: *the*
- *doctor and all the nurses were*
- (not *was*) *waiting for the*
- *patient*. However, where the
- subjects are linked by *plus*,
- *together with*, or *along with*,
- the number of the verb
- remains just as it would have
- been if the extra subjects had
- not been mentioned.
- Therefore you would say *the*
- *doctor, together with all the*
- *nurses, was* (not *were*) *waiting*
- *for the patient*.

plush = luxurious, luxury, lavish, rich, sumptuous, opulent, de luxe

ply = work at, follow, exercise, pursue, carry on, practise

pocket NOUN 1 = pouch, bag, sack, compartment, receptacle
▷ ADJECTIVE 2 = small, compact, miniature, portable, little
▷ VERB 3 = steal, take, lift (*informal*), appropriate, pilfer, purloin, filch (*informal*)

pod = shell, case, hull, husk, shuck

podium = platform, stand, stage, rostrum, dais

poem = verse, song, lyric, rhyme, sonnet, ode, verse composition

poet = bard, rhymer, lyricist, lyric poet, versifier, elegist

poetic 1 = figurative, creative, lyric, symbolic, lyrical

2 = lyrical, lyric, elegiac, metrical

poetry = verse, poems, rhyme, rhyming, verse composition

poignant = moving, touching, sad, bitter, intense, painful, distressing, pathetic

point NOUN 1 = essence, meaning, subject, question, heart, import, drift, thrust 2 = purpose, aim, object, end, reason, goal, intention, objective 3 = aspect, detail, feature, quality, particular, respect, item, characteristic 4 = place, area, position, site, spot, location, locality, locale 5 = moment, time, stage, period, phase, instant, juncture, moment in time 6 = stage, level, position, condition, degree, pitch, circumstance, extent 7 = end, tip, sharp end, top, spur, spike, apex, prong 8 = score, tally, mark 9 = pinpoint, mark, spot, dot, fleck
▷ VERB 10 = aim, level, train, direct 11 = indicate, show, signal, point to, gesture towards 12 = face, look, direct
▷ PHRASES: point at *or* to something *or* someone = indicate, point out, specify, designate, gesture towards

pointed 1 = sharp, edged, acute, barbed 2 = cutting, telling, biting, sharp, keen, acute, penetrating, pertinent

pointer 1 = hint, tip,

p

suggestion, recommendation, caution, piece of information, piece of advice **2** = **indicator**, hand, guide, needle, arrow

pointless = **senseless**, meaningless, futile, fruitless, stupid, silly, useless, absurd **OPPOSITE:** worthwhile

poised 1 = **ready**, waiting, prepared, standing by, all set **2** = **composed**, calm, together (*informal*), collected, dignified, self-confident, self-possessed **OPPOSITE:** agitated

poison NOUN 1 = **toxin**, venom, bane (*archaic*) ▷ **VERB 2** = **murder**, kill, give someone poison, administer poison to **3** = **contaminate**, foul, infect, spoil, pollute, blight, taint, befoul **4** = **corrupt**, colour, undermine, bias, sour, pervert, warp, taint

poisonous 1 = **toxic**, fatal, deadly, lethal, mortal, virulent, noxious, venomous **2** = **evil**, malicious, corrupting, pernicious, baleful

poke VERB 1 = **jab**, push, stick, dig, stab, thrust, shove, nudge **2** = **protrude**, stick, thrust, jut ▷ **NOUN 3** = **jab**, dig, thrust, nudge, prod

pole = **rod**, post, support, staff, bar, stick, stake, paling

police NOUN 1 = **the law** (*informal*), police force, constabulary, fuzz (*slang*), boys in blue (*informal*), the Old Bill (*slang*), rozzers (*slang*)

▷ **VERB 2** = **control**, patrol, guard, watch, protect, regulate

policy 1 = **procedure**, plan, action, practice, scheme, code, custom **2** = **line**, rules, approach

polish NOUN 1 = **varnish**, wax, glaze, lacquer, japan **2** = **sheen**, finish, glaze, gloss, brightness, lustre **3** = **style**, class (*informal*), finish, breeding, grace, elegance, refinement, finesse ▷ **VERB 4** = **shine**, wax, smooth, rub, buff, brighten, burnish **5** *often with* **up** = **perfect**, improve, enhance, refine, finish, brush up, touch up

polished 1 = **elegant**, sophisticated, refined, polite, cultivated, suave, well-bred **OPPOSITE:** unsophisticated **2** = **accomplished**, professional, masterly, fine, expert, skilful, adept, superlative **OPPOSITE:** amateurish **3** = **shining**, bright, smooth, gleaming, glossy, burnished **OPPOSITE:** dull

polite 1 = **mannerly**, civil, courteous, gracious, respectful, well-behaved, complaisant, well-mannered **OPPOSITE:** rude **2** = **refined**, cultured, civilized, polished, sophisticated, elegant, genteel, well-bred **OPPOSITE:** uncultured

politic = **wise**, diplomatic, sensible, prudent, advisable, expedient, judicious

political = governmental, government, state, parliamentary, constitutional, administrative, legislative, ministerial

politician = statesman or stateswoman, representative, senator (U.S.), congressman (U.S.), Member of Parliament, legislator, public servant, congresswoman (U.S.)

politics 1 = affairs of state, government, public affairs, civics 2 = political beliefs, party politics, political allegiances, political leanings, political sympathies 3 = political science, statesmanship, civics, statecraft

poll NOUN 1 = survey, figures, count, sampling, returns, ballot, tally, census 2 = election, vote, voting, referendum, ballot, plebiscite ▷ VERB 3 = question, interview, survey, sample, ballot, canvass 4 = gain, return, record, register, tally

pollute 1 = contaminate, dirty, poison, soil, foul, infect, spoil, stain OPPOSITE: decontaminate 2 = defile, corrupt, sully, deprave, debase, profane, desecrate, dishonour OPPOSITE: honour

pollution 1 = contamination, dirtying, corruption, taint, foulness, defilement, uncleanness 2 = waste, poisons, dirt, impurities

pond = pool, tarn, small lake, fish pond, duck pond, millpond

ponder = think about, consider, reflect on, contemplate, deliberate about, muse on, brood on, meditate on

pool[1] 1 = swimming pool, lido, swimming bath(s) (Brit.), bathing pool (archaic) 2 = pond, lake, mere, tarn 3 = puddle, drop, patch

pool[2] NOUN 1 = supply, reserve, fall-back 2 = kitty, bank, fund, stock, store, pot, jackpot, stockpile ▷ VERB 3 = combine, share, merge, put together, amalgamate, lump together, join forces on

poor ADJECTIVE 1 = impoverished, broke (informal), hard up (informal), short, needy, penniless, destitute, poverty-stricken OPPOSITE: rich 2 = unfortunate, unlucky, hapless, pitiful, luckless, wretched, ill-starred, pitiable OPPOSITE: fortunate 3 = inferior, unsatisfactory, mediocre, second-rate, rotten (informal), low-grade, below par, substandard, half-pie (N.Z. informal), bodger or bodgie (Austral. slang) OPPOSITE: excellent 4 = meagre, inadequate, insufficient, lacking, incomplete, scant, deficient, skimpy OPPOSITE: ample

P

poorly ADVERB 1 = **badly**, incompetently, inadequately, unsuccessfully, insufficiently, unsatisfactorily, inexpertly **OPPOSITE:** well
▷ ADJECTIVE 2 (*Informal*) = **ill**, sick, unwell, crook (*Austral. & N.Z. informal*), seedy (*informal*), below par, off colour, under the weather (*informal*), feeling rotten (*informal*) **OPPOSITE:** healthy

pop NOUN 1 = **bang**, report, crack, noise, burst, explosion
▷ VERB 2 = **burst**, crack, snap, bang, explode, go off (with a bang) 3 = **put**, insert, push, stick, slip, thrust, tuck, shove

pope = **Holy Father**, pontiff, His Holiness, Bishop of Rome, Vicar of Christ

popular 1 = **well-liked**, liked, in, accepted, favourite, approved, in favour, fashionable **OPPOSITE:** unpopular
2 = **common**, general, prevailing, current, conventional, universal, prevalent **OPPOSITE:** rare

popularity 1 = **favour**, esteem, acclaim, regard, approval, vogue 2 = **currency**, acceptance, circulation, vogue, prevalence

populate 1 = **inhabit**, people, live in, occupy, reside in, dwell in (*formal*) 2 = **settle**, occupy, pioneer, colonize

population = **inhabitants**, people, community, society, residents, natives, folk, occupants

pore = **opening**, hole, outlet, orifice

pornography = **obscenity**, porn (*informal*), dirt, filth, indecency, smut

port = **harbour**, haven, anchorage, seaport

portable = **light**, compact, convenient, handy, manageable, movable, easily carried

porter[1] (*Chiefly Brit.*) = **doorman**, caretaker, janitor, concierge, gatekeeper

porter[2] = **baggage attendant**, carrier, bearer, baggage-carrier

portion 1 = **part**, bit, piece, section, scrap, segment, fragment, chunk 2 = **helping**, serving, piece, plateful 3 = **share**, allowance, lot, measure, quantity, quota, ration, allocation

portrait 1 = **picture**, painting, image, photograph, representation, likeness 2 = **description**, profile, portrayal, depiction, characterization, thumbnail sketch

portray 1 = **play**, take the role of, act the part of, represent, personate (*rare*) 2 = **describe**, present, depict, evoke, delineate, put in words 3 = **represent**, draw, paint, illustrate, sketch, figure, picture, depict

p

4 = **characterize**, represent, depict

portrayal 1 = **performance**, interpretation, characterization 2 = **depiction**, picture, representation, sketch, rendering 3 = **description**, account, representation 4 = **characterization**, representation, depiction

pose VERB 1 = **position yourself**, sit, model, arrange yourself 2 = **put on airs**, posture, show off (*informal*) ▷ NOUN 3 = **posture**, position, bearing, attitude, stance 4 = **act**, façade, air, front, posturing, pretence, mannerism, affectation ▷ PHRASES: **pose as something or someone** = **impersonate**, pretend to be, profess to be, masquerade as, pass yourself off as

posh ADJECTIVE (*Informal, chiefly Brit.*) 1 = **smart**, grand, stylish, luxurious, classy (*informal*), swish (*informal, chiefly Brit.*), up-market, swanky (*informal*) ▷ ADJECTIVE 2 = **upper-class**, high-class

position NOUN 1 = **location**, place, point, area, post, situation, station, spot 2 = **posture**, attitude, arrangement, pose, stance 3 = **status**, place, standing, footing, station, rank, reputation, importance 4 = **job**, place, post, opening,

office, role, situation, duty 5 = **place**, standing, rank, status 6 = **attitude**, view, perspective, point of view, opinion, belief, stance, outlook ▷ VERB 7 = **place**, put, set, stand, arrange, locate, lay out

positive 1 = **beneficial**, useful, practical, helpful, progressive, productive, worthwhile, constructive **OPPOSITE:** harmful 2 = **certain**, sure, convinced, confident, satisfied, assured, free from doubt **OPPOSITE:** uncertain 3 = **definite**, real, clear, firm, certain, express, absolute, decisive **OPPOSITE:** inconclusive 4 (*Informal*) = **absolute**, complete, perfect, right (*Brit. informal*), real, total, sheer, utter

positively 1 = **definitely**, surely, firmly, certainly, absolutely, emphatically, unquestionably, categorically 2 = **really**, completely, simply, plain (*informal*), absolutely, thoroughly, utterly, downright

possess 1 = **own**, have, hold, be in possession of, be the owner of, have in your possession 2 = **be endowed with**, have, enjoy, benefit from, be possessed of, be gifted with 3 = **seize**, hold, control, dominate, occupy, take someone over, have power over, have mastery over

possession NOUN 1 = **ownership**, control,

P

custody, hold, hands, tenure
▷ **PLURAL NOUN** 2 = **property**, things, effects, estate, assets, belongings, chattels

possibility 1 = **feasibility**, likelihood, potentiality, practicability, workableness 2 = **likelihood**, chance, risk, odds, prospect, liability, probability 3 *often plural* = **potential**, promise, prospects, talent, capabilities, potentiality

possible 1 = **feasible**, viable, workable, achievable, practicable, attainable, doable, realizable **OPPOSITE:** unfeasible 2 = **likely**, potential, anticipated, probable, odds-on, on the cards **OPPOSITE:** improbable 3 = **conceivable**, likely, credible, plausible, hypothetical, imaginable, believable, thinkable **OPPOSITE:** inconceivable 4 = **aspiring**, would-be, promising, hopeful, prospective, wannabe (*informal*)

● **USAGE NOTE**
● Although it is very common
● to talk about something
● being *very possible* or *more*
● *possible*, many people object
● to such uses, claiming that
● *possible* describes an absolute
● state, and therefore
● something can only be either
● *possible* or *not possible*. If you
● want to refer to different
● degrees of probability, a word
● such as *likely* or *easy* may be
● more appropriate than

● *possible*, for example *it is very*
● *likely that he will resign* (not
● *very possible*).

possibly = perhaps, maybe, perchance (*archaic*)

post¹ NOUN 1 = **mail**, collection, delivery, postal service, snail mail (*informal*) 2 = **correspondence**, letters, cards, mail
▷ **VERB** 3 = **send (off)**, forward, mail, get off, transmit, dispatch, consign
▷ **PHRASES: keep someone posted** = **notify**, brief, advise, inform, report to, keep someone informed, keep someone up to date, apprise

post² NOUN 1 = **job**, place, office, position, situation, employment, appointment, assignment 2 = **position**, place, base, beat, station
▷ **VERB** 3 = **station**, assign, put, place, position, situate, put on duty

post³ NOUN 1 = **support**, stake, pole, column, shaft, upright, pillar, picket
▷ **VERB** 2 = **put something up**, display, affix, pin something up

poster = **notice**, bill, announcement, advertisement, sticker, placard, public notice

postpone = put off, delay, suspend, adjourn, shelve, defer, put back, put on the back burner (*informal*) **OPPOSITE:** go ahead with

posture NOUN 1 = **bearing**,

set, attitude, stance, carriage, disposition

▷ VERB 2 = **show off** (*informal*), pose, affect, put on airs

pot = **container**, bowl, pan, vessel, basin, cauldron, skillet

potent 1 = **powerful**, commanding, dynamic, dominant, influential, authoritative 2 = **strong**, powerful, mighty, vigorous, forceful **OPPOSITE:** weak

potential ADJECTIVE
1 = **possible**, future, likely, promising, probable
2 = **hidden**, possible, inherent, dormant, latent

▷ NOUN 3 = **ability**, possibilities, capacity, capability, aptitude, wherewithal, potentiality

potter *usually with* **around** *or* **about** = **mess about**, tinker, dabble, footle (*informal*)

pottery = **ceramics**, terracotta, crockery, earthenware, stoneware

pounce = **attack**, strike, jump, leap, swoop

pound[1] = **enclosure**, yard, pen, compound, kennels

pound[2] 1 *sometimes with on* = **beat**, strike, hammer, batter, thrash, thump, clobber (*slang*), pummel 2 = **crush**, powder, pulverize 3 = **pulsate**, beat, pulse, throb, palpitate
4 = **stomp**, tramp, march, thunder (*informal*)

pour 1 = **let flow**, spill, splash, dribble, drizzle, slop (*informal*), slosh (*informal*), decant 2 = **flow**, stream, run, course, rush, emit, cascade, gush
3 = **rain**, pelt (down), teem, bucket down (*informal*)
4 = **stream**, crowd, flood, swarm, gush, throng, teem

⬤ **USAGE NOTE**
● The spelling of pour (as in she
● poured cream on her strudel)
● should be carefully
● distinguished from that of
● pore or through (as in she
● pored over the manuscript).

pout VERB 1 = **sulk**, glower, look petulant, pull a long face

▷ NOUN 2 = **sullen look**, glower, long face

poverty 1 = **pennilessness**, want, need, hardship, insolvency, privation, penury, destitution **OPPOSITE:** wealth
2 = **scarcity**, lack, absence, want, deficit, shortage, deficiency, inadequacy
OPPOSITE: abundance

powder NOUN 1 = **dust**, talc, fine grains, loose particles

▷ VERB 2 = **dust**, cover, scatter, sprinkle, strew, dredge

power NOUN 1 = **control**, authority, influence, command, dominance, domination, mastery, dominion, mana (*N.Z.*)
2 = **ability**, capacity, faculty, property, potential, capability, competence, competency
OPPOSITE: inability
3 = **authority**, right, licence,

P

privilege, warrant, prerogative, authorization **4** = **strength**, might, energy, muscle, vigour, potency, brawn **OPPOSITE:** weakness **5** = **forcefulness**, force, strength, punch (*informal*), intensity, potency, eloquence, persuasiveness

powerful 1 = **influential**, dominant, controlling, commanding, prevailing, authoritative **OPPOSITE:** powerless **2** = **strong**, strapping, mighty, vigorous, potent, energetic, sturdy **OPPOSITE:** weak **3** = **persuasive**, convincing, telling, moving, striking, storming, dramatic, impressive

powerless 1 = **defenceless**, vulnerable, dependent, subject, tied, ineffective, unarmed **2** = **weak**, disabled, helpless, incapable, frail, feeble, debilitated, impotent **OPPOSITE:** strong

practical ADJECTIVE **1** = **functional**, realistic, pragmatic **OPPOSITE:** impractical **2** = **empirical**, real, applied, actual, hands-on, in the field, experimental, factual **OPPOSITE:** theoretical **3** = **sensible**, ordinary, realistic, down-to-earth, matter-of-fact, businesslike, hard-headed **OPPOSITE:** impractical **4** = **feasible**, possible, viable, workable, practicable, doable **OPPOSITE:** impractical

5 = **useful**, ordinary, appropriate, sensible, everyday, functional, utilitarian, serviceable **6** = **skilled**, experienced, efficient, accomplished, proficient **OPPOSITE:** inexperienced

- USAGE NOTE
- A distinction is usually made
- between *practical* and
- *practicable*. Practical refers to a
- person, idea, project, etc., as
- being more concerned with
- or relevant to practice than
- theory: *he is a very practical*
- *person; the idea had no practical*
- *application. Practicable* refers
- to a project or idea as being
- capable of being done or put
- into effect: *the plan was*
- *expensive, yet practicable.*

practically 1 = **almost**, nearly, essentially, virtually, basically, fundamentally, all but, just about **2** = **sensibly**, reasonably, matter-of-factly, realistically, rationally, pragmatically

practice 1 = **custom**, way, system, rule, method, tradition, habit, routine, tikanga (N.Z.) **2** = **training**, study, exercise, preparation, drill, rehearsal, repetition **3** = **profession**, work, business, career, occupation, pursuit, vocation **4** = **business**, company, office, firm, practice, partnership, outfit (*informal*) **5** = **use**, experience, action, operation, application, enactment

practise 1 = rehearse, study, prepare, perfect, repeat, go through, go over, refine 2 = do, train, exercise, drill 3 = carry out, follow, apply, perform, observe, engage in 4 = work at, pursue, carry on

practised = skilled, trained, experienced, seasoned, able, expert, accomplished, proficient OPPOSITE: inexperienced

pragmatic = practical, sensible, realistic, down-to-earth, utilitarian, businesslike, hard-headed OPPOSITE: idealistic

praise VERB 1 = acclaim, approve of, honour, cheer, admire, applaud, compliment, congratulate OPPOSITE: criticize 2 = give thanks to, bless, worship, adore, glorify, exalt ▷ NOUN 3 = approval, acclaim, tribute, compliment, congratulations, eulogy, commendation OPPOSITE: criticism 4 = thanks, glory, worship, homage, adoration

pray 1 = say your prayers, offer a prayer, recite the rosary 2 = beg, ask, plead, petition, request, solicit, implore, beseech

prayer 1 = supplication, devotion 2 = orison, litany, invocation, intercession 3 = plea, appeal, request, petition, entreaty, supplication

preach 1 often with **to** = deliver a sermon, address, evangelize, preach a sermon 2 = urge, teach, champion, recommend, advise, counsel, advocate, exhort

preacher = clergyman, minister, parson, missionary, evangelist

precarious 1 = insecure, dangerous, tricky, risky, dodgy (Brit., Austral. & N.Z. informal), unsure, hazardous, shaky OPPOSITE: secure 2 = dangerous, shaky, insecure, unsafe, unreliable OPPOSITE: stable

precaution 1 = safeguard, insurance, protection, provision, safety measure 2 = forethought, care, caution, prudence, providence, wariness

precede 1 = go before, antedate 2 = go ahead of, lead, head, go before 3 = preface, introduce, go before

precedent = instance, example, standard, model, pattern, prototype, paradigm, antecedent

precinct = area, quarter, section, sector, district, zone

precious 1 = valuable, expensive, fine, prized, dear, costly, invaluable, priceless OPPOSITE: worthless 2 = loved, prized, dear, treasured, darling, beloved, adored, cherished 3 = affected, artificial, twee (Brit. informal), over-refined, overnice, chichi

precipitate VERB 1 = **quicken**, trigger, accelerate, advance, hurry, speed up, bring on, hasten 2 = **throw**, launch, cast, hurl, fling, let fly
▷ ADJECTIVE 3 = **hasty**, rash, reckless, impulsive, precipitous, impetuous, heedless
4 = **sudden**, quick, brief, rushing, rapid, unexpected, swift, abrupt

precise 1 = **exact**, specific, particular, express, correct, absolute, accurate, explicit OPPOSITE: vague 2 = **strict**, particular, exact, formal, careful, stiff, rigid, meticulous OPPOSITE: inexact

precisely 1 = **exactly**, squarely, correctly, absolutely, strictly, accurately, plumb (*informal*), square on 2 = **just so**, yes, absolutely, exactly, quite so, you bet (*informal*), without a doubt, indubitably 3 = **just**, entirely, absolutely, altogether, exactly, in all respects 4 = **word for word**, literally, exactly, to the letter

precision = **exactness**, care, accuracy, particularity, meticulousness, preciseness

predecessor 1 = **previous job holder**, precursor, forerunner, antecedent 2 = **ancestor**, forebear, antecedent, forefather, tupuna or tipuna (*N.Z.*)

predicament = **fix** (*informal*),

situation, spot (*informal*), hole (*slang*), mess, jam (*informal*), dilemma, pinch

predict = **foretell**, forecast, divine, prophesy, augur, portend

predictable = **likely**, expected, sure, certain, anticipated, reliable, foreseeable OPPOSITE: unpredictable

prediction = **prophecy**, forecast, prognosis, divination, prognostication, augury

predominantly = **mainly**, largely, chiefly, mostly, generally, principally, primarily, for the most part

prefer 1 = **like better**, favour, go for, pick, fancy, opt for, incline towards, be partial to 2 = **choose**, opt for, pick, desire, would rather, would sooner, incline towards

● USAGE NOTE
● Normally, *to* (not *than*) is used
● after *prefer* and *preferable*.
● Therefore, you would say *I*
● *prefer skating to skiing*, and *a*
● *small income is preferable to no*
● *income at all*. However, when
● expressing a preference
● between two activities stated
● as infinitive verbs, for
● example *to skate* and *to ski*,
● use *than*, as in *I prefer to skate*
● *than to ski*.

preferable = **better**, best, chosen, preferred, recommended, favoured, superior, more suitable

opposite: undesirable

preferably = **ideally**, if possible, rather, sooner, by choice, in or for preference

preference 1 = **liking**, wish, taste, desire, leaning, bent, bias, inclination 2 = **first choice**, choice, favourite, pick, option, selection 3 = **priority**, first place, precedence, favouritism, favoured treatment

pregnant 1 = **expectant**, expecting (*informal*), with child, in the club (*Brit. slang*), big or heavy with child
2 = **meaningful**, pointed, charged, significant, telling, loaded, expressive, eloquent

prejudice NOUN
1 = **discrimination**, injustice, intolerance, bigotry, unfairness, chauvinism, narrow-mindedness 2 = **bias**, preconception, partiality, preconceived notion, prejudgment
▷ VERB 3 = **bias**, influence, colour, poison, distort, slant, predispose 4 = **harm**, damage, hurt, injure, mar, undermine, spoil, impair, crool or cruel (*Austral. slang*)

prejudiced = **biased**, influenced, unfair, one-sided, bigoted, intolerant, opinionated, narrow-minded
opposite: unbiased

preliminary ADJECTIVE
1 = **first**, opening, trial, initial, test, pilot, prior, introductory

2 = **qualifying**, eliminating
▷ NOUN 3 = **introduction**, opening, beginning, start, prelude, preface, overture, preamble

prelude 1 = **introduction**, beginning, start 2 = **overture**, opening, introduction, introductory movement

premature 1 = **early**, untimely, before time, unseasonable
2 = **hasty**, rash, too soon, untimely, ill-timed, overhasty

premier NOUN 1 = **head of government**, prime minister, chancellor, chief minister, P.M.
▷ ADJECTIVE 2 = **chief**, leading, first, highest, head, main, prime, primary

premiere = **first night**, opening, debut

premise = **assumption**, proposition, argument, hypothesis, assertion, supposition, presupposition, postulation

premises = **building(s)**, place, office, property, site, establishment

premium 1 = **fee**, charge, payment, instalment
2 = **surcharge**, extra charge, additional fee or charge
3 = **bonus**, reward, prize, perk (*Brit. informal*), bounty, perquisite
▷ PHRASES: **at a premium** = **in great demand**, rare, scarce, in short supply, hard to come by

preoccupation 1 = **obsession**,

P

fixation, bee in your bonnet (*informal*) **2 = absorption**, abstraction, daydreaming, immersion, reverie, absent-mindedness, engrossment, woolgathering

preoccupied 1 = absorbed, lost, wrapped up, immersed, engrossed, rapt **2 = lost in thought**, distracted, oblivious, absent-minded

preparation 1 = groundwork, preparing, getting ready **2** *usually plural* **= arrangement**, plan, measure, provision **3 = mixture**, medicine, compound, concoction

prepare 1 = make *or* get ready, arrange, jack up (*N.Z. informal*) **2 = train**, guide, prime, direct, brief, discipline, put someone in the picture **3 = make**, cook, put together, get, produce, assemble, muster, concoct **4 = get ready 5 = practise**, get ready, train, exercise, warm up, get into shape

prepared 1 = willing, inclined, disposed **2 = ready**, set **3 = fit**, primed, in order, arranged, in readiness

prescribe 1 = specify, order, direct, stipulate, write a prescription for **2 = ordain**, set, order, rule, recommend, dictate, lay down, decree

prescription 1 = instruction, direction, formula, script (*informal*), recipe **2 = medicine**, drug, treatment, preparation,

cure, mixture, dose, remedy

presence 1 = being, existence, residence, attendance, showing up, occupancy, inhabitance **2 = personality**, bearing, appearance, aspect, air, carriage, aura, poise ▷ **PHRASES: presence of mind = level-headedness**, assurance, composure, poise, cool (*slang*), wits, countenance, coolness

present¹ 1 = current, existing, immediate, contemporary, present-day, existent **2 = here**, there, near, ready, nearby, at hand **OPPOSITE:** absent **3 = in existence**, existing, existent, extant ▷ **PHRASES: the present = now**, today, the time being, here and now, the present moment

present² NOUN 1 = gift, offering, grant, donation, hand-out, endowment, boon, gratuity, bonsela (*S. African*), koha (*N.Z.*) ▷ **VERB 2 = give**, award, hand over, grant, hand out, confer, bestow **3 = put on**, stage, perform, give, show, render **4 = launch**, display, parade, exhibit, unveil **5 = introduce**, make known, acquaint someone with

presentation 1 = giving, award, offering, donation, bestowal, conferral **2 = appearance**, look, display, packaging, arrangement, layout **3 = performance**, production

presently 1 = **at present**, currently, now, today, these days, nowadays, at the present time, in this day and age
2 = **soon**, shortly, directly, before long, momentarily (*U.S. & Canad.*), by and by, in a jiffy (*informal*), erelong (*archaic poetic*)

preservation 1 = **upholding**, support, maintenance
2 = **protection**, safety, maintenance, conservation, salvation, safeguarding, safekeeping

preserve VERB 1 = **maintain**, keep, continue, sustain, keep up, prolong, uphold, conserve **OPPOSITE:** end 2 = **protect**, keep, save, maintain, defend, shelter, shield, care for **OPPOSITE:** attack
▷ NOUN 3 = **area**, department, field, territory, province, arena, sphere

preside = **officiate**, chair, moderate, be chairperson

press VERB 1 = **push (down)**, depress, lean on, press down, force down 2 = **push**, squeeze, jam, thrust, ram, wedge, shove
3 = **hug**, squeeze, embrace, clasp, crush, hold close, fold in your arms 4 = **urge**, beg, petition, exhort, implore, pressurize, entreat 5 = **plead**, present, lodge, submit, tender, advance insistently 6 = **steam**, iron, smooth, flatten
7 = **compress**, grind, reduce,

mill, crush, pound, squeeze, tread 8 = **crowd**, push, gather, surge, flock, herd, swarm, seethe

pressing = **urgent**, serious, vital, crucial, imperative, important, high-priority, importunate **OPPOSITE:** unimportant

pressure 1 = **force**, crushing, squeezing, compressing, weight, compression
2 = **power**, influence, force, constraint, sway, compulsion, coercion 3 = **stress**, demands, strain, heat, load, burden, urgency, hassle (*informal*), uphill (*S. African*)

prestige = **status**, standing, credit, reputation, honour, importance, fame, distinction, mana (*N.Z.*)

prestigious = **celebrated**, respected, prominent, great, important, esteemed, notable, renowned, illustrious **OPPOSITE:** unknown

presumably = **it would seem**, probably, apparently, seemingly, on the face of it, in all probability, in all likelihood

presume 1 = **believe**, think, suppose, assume, guess (*informal, chiefly U.S. & Canad.*), take for granted, infer, conjecture 2 = **dare**, venture, go so far as, take the liberty, make so bold as

pretend 1 = **feign**, affect, assume, allege, fake, simulate, profess, sham 2 = **make believe**, suppose, imagine, act, make up

pretty ADJECTIVE
1 = **attractive**, beautiful, lovely, charming, fair, good-looking, bonny, comely **OPPOSITE:** plain
▷ ADVERB 2 (*Informal*) = **fairly**, rather, quite, kind of (*informal*), somewhat, moderately, reasonably

prevail 1 = **win**, succeed, triumph, overcome, overrule, be victorious 2 = **be widespread**, abound, predominate, be current, be prevalent, exist generally

prevailing 1 = **widespread**, general, established, popular, common, current, usual, ordinary 2 = **predominating**, ruling, main, existing, principal

prevalent = **common**, established, popular, general, current, usual, widespread, universal **OPPOSITE:** rare

prevent = **stop**, avoid, frustrate, hamper, foil, inhibit, avert, thwart **OPPOSITE:** help

prevention = **elimination**, safeguard, precaution, thwarting, avoidance, deterrence

preview = **sample**, sneak preview, trailer, taster, foretaste, advance showing

previous 1 = **earlier**, former, past, prior, preceding, erstwhile (*formal*) **OPPOSITE:** later
2 = **preceding**, past, prior

previously = **before**, earlier, once, in the past, formerly, hitherto, beforehand, heretofore

prey 1 = **quarry**, game, kill 2 = **victim**, target, mug (*Brit. slang*), dupe, fall guy (*informal*)
▷ *See panel* BIRDS OF PREY

price NOUN 1 = **cost**, value, rate, charge, figure, worth, damage (*informal*), amount
2 = **consequences**, penalty, cost, result, toll, forfeit
▷ VERB 3 = **evaluate**, value, estimate, rate, cost, assess

priceless = **valuable**, expensive, precious, invaluable, dear, costly **OPPOSITE:** worthless

prick VERB 1 = **pierce**, stab, puncture, punch, lance, jab, perforate
▷ NOUN 2 = **puncture**, hole, wound, perforation, pinhole

prickly 1 = **spiny**, barbed, thorny, bristly 2 = **itchy**, sharp, smarting, stinging, crawling, tingling, scratchy

pride 1 = **satisfaction**, achievement, fulfilment, delight, content, pleasure, joy, gratification 2 = **self-respect**, honour, ego, dignity, self-esteem, self-image, self-worth
3 = **conceit**, vanity, arrogance, pretension, hubris, self-importance, egotism, self-love **OPPOSITE:** humility

priest = **clergyman**, minister, father, divine, vicar, pastor, cleric, curate

BIRDS OF PREY

accipiter	kestrel
Australian goshawk or chicken hawk	kite
	lammergeier, lammergeyer,
bald eagle	bearded vulture, or (archaic)
barn owl	ossifrage
buzzard	lanner
caracara	merlin
condor	mopoke or (N.Z.) ruru
duck hawk	osprey, fish eagle, or (archaic)
eagle	ossifrage
eagle-hawk or wedge-tailed eagle	owl
	peregrine falcon
falcon or (N.Z.) bush-hawk or karearea	saker
	screech owl
falconet	sea eagle, erne, or ern
golden eagle	secretary bird
goshawk	snowy owl
gyrfalcon or gerfalcon	sparrowhawk
harrier	tawny owl
hawk	turkey buzzard or vulture
hobby	vulture
honey buzzard	

primarily 1 = **chiefly**, largely, generally, mainly, essentially, mostly, principally, fundamentally **2** = **at first**, originally, initially, in the first place, in the beginning, first and foremost, at or from the start

primary = **chief**, main, first, highest, greatest, prime, principal, cardinal **OPPOSITE:** subordinate

prime ADJECTIVE **1** = **main**, leading, chief, central, major, key, primary, supreme **2** = **best**, top, select, highest, quality, choice, excellent, first-class

▷ NOUN **3** = **peak**, flower, bloom, height, heyday, zenith
▷ VERB **4** = **inform**, tell, train, coach, brief, fill in (informal), notify, clue in (informal) **5** = **prepare**, set up, load, equip, get ready, make ready

primitive 1 = **early**, first, earliest, original, primary, elementary, primordial, primeval **OPPOSITE:** modern **2** = **crude**, simple, rough, rudimentary, unrefined

prince = **ruler**, lord, monarch, sovereign, crown prince, liege, prince regent, crowned head

p

princely 1 = **substantial**, considerable, large, huge, massive, enormous, sizable or sizeable 2 = **regal**, royal, imperial, noble, sovereign, majestic

princess = **ruler**, lady, monarch, sovereign, liege, crowned head, crowned princess, dynast

principal ADJECTIVE 1 = **main**, leading, chief, prime, first, key, essential, primary **OPPOSITE:** minor
▷ NOUN 2 = **headmaster** or **headmistress**, head (informal), dean, head teacher, rector, master or mistress 3 = **star**, lead, leader, prima ballerina, leading man or lady, coryphée 4 = **capital**, money, assets, working capital

principally 1 = **mainly**, largely, chiefly, especially, mostly, primarily, predominantly

principle 1 = **morals**, standards, ideals, honour, virtue, ethics, integrity, conscience, kaupapa (N.Z.) 2 = **rule**, law, truth, precept
▷ PHRASES: **in principle** 1 = **in general** 2 = **in theory**, ideally, on paper, theoretically, in an ideal world, en principe (French)
● USAGE NOTE
● Principle and principal are
● often confused: the principal
● (not principle) reason for his
● departure; the plan was
● approved in principle (not
● principal).

print VERB 1 = **run off**, publish, copy, reproduce, issue, engrave 2 = **publish**, release, circulate, issue, disseminate 3 = **mark**, impress, stamp, imprint
▷ NOUN 4 = **photograph**, photo, snap 5 = **picture**, plate, etching, engraving, lithograph, woodcut, linocut 6 = **copy**, photo (informal), picture, reproduction, replica

prior = **earlier**, previous, former, preceding, foregoing, pre-existing, pre-existent
▷ PHRASES: **prior to** = **before**, preceding, earlier than, in advance of, previous to

priority 1 = **prime concern** 2 = **precedence**, preference, primacy, predominance 3 = **supremacy**, rank, precedence, seniority, right of way, pre-eminence

prison = **jail**, confinement, nick (Brit. slang), cooler (slang), jug (slang), dungeon, clink (slang), gaol, boob (Austral. slang)

prisoner 1 = **convict**, con (slang), lag (slang), jailbird (informal) 2 = **captive**, hostage, detainee, internee

privacy = **seclusion**, isolation, solitude, retirement, retreat

private ADJECTIVE 1 = **exclusive**, individual, privately owned, own, special, reserved **OPPOSITE:** public 2 = **secret**, confidential, covert, unofficial, clandestine, off the record, hush-hush (informal)

p

OPPOSITE: public 3 = **personal**, individual, secret, intimate, undisclosed, unspoken, innermost, unvoiced
4 = **secluded**, secret, separate, isolated, sequestered
OPPOSITE: busy 5 = **solitary**, reserved, retiring, withdrawn, discreet, secretive, self-contained, reclusive **OPPOSITE:** sociable

privilege = **right**, due, advantage, claim, freedom, liberty, concession, entitlement

privileged = **special**, advantaged, favoured, honoured, entitled, elite

prize¹ NOUN 1 = **reward**, cup, award, honour, medal, trophy, accolade 2 = **winnings**, haul, jackpot, stakes, purse
▷ ADJECTIVE 3 = **champion**, best, winning, top, outstanding, award-winning, first-rate

prize² = **value**, treasure, esteem, cherish, hold dear

prize³ *or* **prise** 1 = **force**, pull, lever 2 = **drag**, force, draw, wring, extort

probability 1 = **likelihood**, prospect, chance, odds, expectation, liability, likeliness 2 = **chance**, odds, possibility, likelihood

probable = **likely**, possible, apparent, reasonable to think, credible, plausible, feasible, presumable **OPPOSITE:** unlikely

probably = **likely**, perhaps, maybe, possibly, presumably, most likely, doubtless, perchance (*archaic*)

probation = **trial period**, trial, apprenticeship

probe VERB 1 *often with* **into** = **examine**, go into, investigate, explore, search, look into, analyze, dissect 2 = **explore**, examine, poke, prod, feel around
▷ NOUN 3 = **investigation**, study, inquiry, analysis, examination, exploration, scrutiny, scrutinization

problem 1 = **difficulty**, trouble, dispute, plight, obstacle, dilemma, headache (*informal*), complication 2 = **puzzle**, question, riddle, enigma, conundrum, poser

problematic = **tricky**, puzzling, doubtful, dubious, debatable, problematical **OPPOSITE:** clear

procedure = **method**, policy, process, course, system, action, practice, strategy

proceed 1 = **begin**, go ahead 2 = **continue**, go on, progress, carry on, go ahead, press on **OPPOSITE:** discontinue 3 = **go on**, continue, progress, carry on, go ahead, move on, move forward, press on **OPPOSITE:** stop 4 = **arise**, come, issue, result, spring, flow, stem, derive

proceeding = **action**, process, procedure, move, act, step, measure, deed

proceeds = **income**, profit,

p

revenue, returns, products, gain, earnings, yield

process NOUN 1 = **procedure**, means, course, system, action, performance, operation, measure 2 = **development**, growth, progress, movement, advance, evolution, progression 3 = **method**, system, practice, technique, procedure
▷ VERB 4 = **handle**, manage, action, deal with, fulfil

procession = **parade**, train, march, file, cavalcade, cortege

proclaim 1 = **announce**, declare, advertise, publish, indicate, herald, circulate, profess OPPOSITE: keep secret 2 = **pronounce**, announce, declare

prod VERB 1 = **poke**, push, dig, shove, nudge, jab 2 = **prompt**, move, urge, motivate, spur, stimulate, rouse, incite
▷ NOUN 3 = **poke**, push, dig, shove, nudge, jab 4 = **prompt**, signal, cue, reminder, stimulus

prodigy = **genius**, talent, wizard, mastermind, whizz (*informal*)

produce VERB 1 = **cause**, effect, generate, bring about, give rise to 2 = **make**, create, develop, manufacture, construct, invent, fabricate 3 = **create**, develop, write, turn out, compose, originate, churn out (*informal*) 4 = **yield**, provide, grow, bear, give, supply, afford, render 5 = **bring**

forth, bear, deliver, breed, give birth to, beget (*old-fashioned*), bring into the world 6 = **show**, provide, present, advance, demonstrate, offer, come up with, exhibit 7 = **display**, show, present, proffer 8 = **present**, stage, direct, put on, do, show, mount, exhibit
▷ NOUN 9 = **fruit and vegetables**, goods, food, products, crops, yield, harvest, greengrocery (*Brit.*)

producer 1 = **director**, promoter, impresario 2 = **maker**, manufacturer, builder, creator, fabricator 3 = **grower**, farmer

product 1 = **goods**, produce, creation, commodity, invention, merchandise, artefact 2 = **result**, consequence, effect, outcome, upshot

production 1 = **producing**, making, manufacture, manufacturing, construction, formation, fabrication 2 = **creation**, development, fashioning, composition, origination 3 = **management**, administration, direction 4 = **presentation**, staging, mounting

productive 1 = **fertile**, rich, prolific, plentiful, fruitful, fecund OPPOSITE: barren 2 = **creative**, inventive 3 = **useful**, rewarding, valuable, profitable, effective, worthwhile, beneficial, constructive **OPPOSITE:** useless

productivity = output, production, capacity, yield, efficiency, work rate

profess 1 = claim, allege, pretend, fake, make out, purport, feign 2 = state, admit, announce, declare, confess, assert, proclaim, affirm

professed 1 = supposed, would-be, alleged, so-called, pretended, purported, self-styled, ostensible 2 = declared, confirmed, confessed, proclaimed, self-confessed, avowed, self-acknowledged

profession = occupation, calling, business, career, employment, office, position, sphere

professional ADJECTIVE 1 = qualified, trained, skilled, white-collar 2 = expert, experienced, skilled, masterly, efficient, competent, adept, proficient **OPPOSITE:** amateurish

▷ NOUN 3 = expert, master, pro (informal), specialist, guru, adept, maestro, virtuoso, fundi (S. African)

professor = don (Brit.), fellow (Brit.), prof (informal)

profile 1 = outline, lines, form, figure, silhouette, contour, side view 2 = biography, sketch, vignette, characterization, thumbnail sketch

profit NOUN 1 often plural = earnings, return, revenue, gain, yield, proceeds, receipts, takings **OPPOSITE:** loss
2 = benefit, good, use, value, gain, advantage, advancement **OPPOSITE:** disadvantage

▷ VERB 3 = make money, gain, earn 4 = benefit, help, serve, gain, promote, be of advantage to

profitable 1 = money-making, lucrative, paying, commercial, worthwhile, cost-effective, fruitful, remunerative
2 = beneficial, useful, rewarding, valuable, productive, worthwhile, fruitful, advantageous **OPPOSITE:** useless

profound 1 = sincere, acute, intense, great, keen, extreme, heartfelt, deeply felt **OPPOSITE:** insincere 2 = wise, learned, deep, penetrating, philosophical, sage, abstruse, sagacious **OPPOSITE:** uninformed

programme 1 = schedule, plan, agenda, timetable, listing, list, line-up, calendar
2 = course, curriculum, syllabus
3 = show, performance, production, broadcast, episode, presentation, transmission, telecast

progress NOUN
1 = development, growth, advance, gain, improvement, breakthrough, headway **OPPOSITE:** regression
2 = movement forward,

passage, advancement, course, advance, headway **OPPOSITE:** movement backward
▷ **VERB 3** = **move on**, continue, travel, advance, proceed, go forward, make headway **OPPOSITE:** move back
4 = **develop**, improve, advance, grow, gain **OPPOSITE:** get behind
▷ **PHRASES: in progress** = going on, happening, continuing, being done, occurring, taking place, proceeding, under way

progression 1 = **progress**, advance, advancement, gain, headway, furtherance, movement forward
2 = **sequence**, course, series, chain, cycle, string, succession

progressive 1 = **enlightened**, liberal, modern, advanced, radical, revolutionary, avant-garde, reformist **2** = **growing**, continuing, increasing, developing, advancing, ongoing

prohibit 1 = **forbid**, ban, veto, outlaw, disallow, proscribe, debar **OPPOSITE:** permit
2 = **prevent**, restrict, stop, hamper, hinder, impede **OPPOSITE:** allow

prohibition = **ban**, boycott, embargo, bar, veto, prevention, exclusion, injunction

project NOUN **1** = **scheme**, plan, job, idea, campaign, operation, activity, venture
2 = **assignment**, task, homework, piece of research

▷ **VERB 3** = **forecast**, expect, estimate, predict, reckon, calculate, gauge, extrapolate
4 = **stick out**, extend, stand out, bulge, protrude, overhang, jut (out)

projection = **forecast**, estimate, reckoning, calculation, estimation, computation, extrapolation

proliferation = **multiplication**, increase, spread, expansion

prolific 1 = **productive**, creative, fertile, inventive, copious **2** = **fruitful**, fertile, abundant, luxuriant, profuse, fecund **OPPOSITE:** unproductive

prolong = **lengthen**, continue, perpetuate, draw out, extend, delay, stretch out, spin out **OPPOSITE:** shorten

prominence 1 = **fame**, name, reputation, importance, celebrity, distinction, prestige, eminence
2 = **conspicuousness**, markedness

prominent 1 = **famous**, leading, top, important, main, distinguished, well-known, notable **OPPOSITE:** unknown
2 = **noticeable**, obvious, outstanding, pronounced, conspicuous, eye-catching, obtrusive **OPPOSITE:** inconspicuous

promise VERB **1** = **guarantee**, pledge, vow, swear, contract, assure, undertake, warrant
2 = **seem likely**, look like, show

signs of, augur (*formal*), betoken (*formal*)
▷ NOUN 3 = **guarantee**, word, bond, vow, commitment, pledge, undertaking, assurance 4 = **potential**, ability, talent, capacity, capability, aptitude

promising 1 = **encouraging**, likely, bright, reassuring, hopeful, favourable, rosy, auspicious OPPOSITE: unpromising 2 = **talented**, able, gifted, rising

promote 1 = **help**, back, support, aid, forward, encourage, advance, boost OPPOSITE: impede 2 = **advertise**, sell, hype, publicize, push, plug (*informal*) 3 = **raise**, upgrade, elevate, exalt OPPOSITE: demote

promotion 1 = **rise**, upgrading, move up, advancement, elevation, exaltation, preferment 2 = **publicity**, advertising, plugging (*informal*) 3 = **encouragement**, support, boosting, advancement, furtherance

prompt VERB 1 = **cause**, occasion, provoke, give rise to, elicit 2 = **remind**, assist, cue, help out
▷ ADJECTIVE 3 = **immediate**, quick, rapid, instant, timely, early, swift, speedy OPPOSITE: slow
▷ ADVERB 4 (*Informal*) = **exactly**, sharp, promptly, on the dot, punctually

promptly 1 = **immediately**, swiftly, directly, quickly, at once, speedily 2 = **punctually**, on time, spot on (*informal*), bang on (*informal*), on the dot, on the button (U.S.), on the nail

prone 1 = **liable**, given, subject, inclined, tending, bent, disposed, susceptible OPPOSITE: disinclined 2 = **face down**, flat, horizontal, prostrate, recumbent OPPOSITE: face up

pronounce 1 = **say**, speak, sound, articulate, enunciate 2 = **declare**, announce, deliver, proclaim, decree, affirm

pronounced = **noticeable**, decided, marked, striking, obvious, evident, distinct, definite OPPOSITE: imperceptible

proof NOUN 1 = **evidence**, demonstration, testimony, confirmation, verification, corroboration, authentication, substantiation
▷ ADJECTIVE 2 = **impervious**, strong, resistant, impenetrable, repellent

prop VERB 1 = **lean**, place, set, stand, position, rest, lay, balance 2 *often with* **up** = **support**, sustain, hold up, brace, uphold, bolster, buttress
▷ NOUN 3 = **support**, stay, brace, mainstay, buttress, stanchion 4 = **mainstay**, support, sustainer, anchor, backbone, cornerstone

p

propaganda = information, advertising, promotion, publicity, hype, disinformation, newspeak

propel 1 = **drive**, launch, force, send, shoot, push, thrust, shove **OPPOSITE:** stop 2 = **impel**, drive, push, prompt, spur, motivate **OPPOSITE:** hold back

proper 1 = **real**, actual, genuine, true, bona fide, dinkum (Austral. & N.Z. informal) 2 = **correct**, accepted, established, appropriate, right, formal, conventional, precise **OPPOSITE:** improper 3 = **polite**, right, becoming, seemly, fitting, fit, mannerly, suitable **OPPOSITE:** unseemly

properly 1 = **correctly**, rightly, fittingly, appropriately, accurately, suitably, aptly **OPPOSITE:** incorrectly 2 = **politely**, decently, respectably **OPPOSITE:** badly

property 1 = **possessions**, goods, effects, holdings, capital, riches, estate, assets 2 = **land**, holding, estate, real estate, freehold 3 = **quality**, feature, characteristic, attribute, trait, hallmark

prophecy 1 = **prediction**, forecast, prognostication, augury 2 = **second sight**, divination, augury, telling the future, soothsaying

prophet or **prophetess** = soothsayer, forecaster, diviner, oracle, seer, sibyl

proportion NOUN 1 = **part**, share, amount, division, percentage, segment, quota, fraction 2 = **relative amount**, relationship, ratio 3 = **balance**, harmony, correspondence, symmetry, concord, congruity

▷ PLURAL NOUN

4 = **dimensions**, size, volume, capacity, extent, expanse, amplitude

proportional or **proportionate** = **correspondent**, corresponding, even, balanced, consistent, compatible, equitable, in proportion **OPPOSITE:** disproportionate

proposal = **suggestion**, plan, programme, scheme, offer, project, bid, recommendation

propose 1 = **put forward**, present, suggest, advance, submit 2 = **intend**, mean, plan, aim, design, scheme, have in mind 3 = **nominate**, name, present, recommend 4 = **offer marriage**, pop the question (informal), ask for someone's hand (in marriage)

proposition NOUN 1 = **task**, problem, activity, job, affair, venture, undertaking 2 = **theory**, idea, argument, concept, thesis, hypothesis, theorem, premise 3 = **proposal**, plan, suggestion, scheme, bid, recommendation 4 = **advance**, pass (informal), proposal, overture, improper

suggestion, come-on (*informal*)
▷ VERB 5 = **make a pass at**, solicit, accost, make an improper suggestion to

proprietor *or* **proprietress** = **owner**, titleholder, landlord or landlady

prosecute (*Law*) = **take someone to court**, try, sue, indict, arraign, put someone on trial, litigate, bring someone to trial

prospect NOUN 1 = **likelihood**, chance, possibility, hope, promise, odds, expectation, probability 2 = **idea**, outlook 3 = **view**, landscape, scene, sight, outlook, spectacle, vista
▷ PLURAL NOUN
4 = **possibilities**, chances, future, potential, expectations, outlook, scope
▷ VERB 5 = **look**, search, seek, dowse

prospective 1 = **potential**, possible 2 = **expected**, coming, future, likely, intended, anticipated, forthcoming, imminent

prospectus = **catalogue**, list, programme, outline, syllabus, synopsis

prosper = **succeed**, advance, progress, thrive, get on, do well, flourish

prosperity = **success**, riches, plenty, fortune, wealth, luxury, good fortune, affluence
OPPOSITE: poverty

prosperous 1 = **wealthy**, rich, affluent, well-off, well-heeled (*informal*), well-to-do, moneyed OPPOSITE: poor 2 = **successful**, booming, thriving, flourishing, doing well OPPOSITE: unsuccessful

prostitute NOUN 1 = **whore**, hooker (*chiefly U.S. slang*), pro (*slang*), tart (*informal*), call girl, harlot, streetwalker, loose woman
▷ VERB 2 = **cheapen**, sell out, pervert, degrade, devalue, squander, demean, debase

protagonist 1 = **supporter**, champion, advocate, exponent 2 = **leading character**, principal, central character, hero or heroine

protect = **keep someone safe**, defend, support, save, guard, preserve, look after, shelter OPPOSITE: endanger

protection 1 = **safety**, care, defence, protecting, security, custody, safeguard, aegis (*formal*) 2 = **safeguard**, cover, guard, shelter, screen, barrier, shield, buffer 3 = **armour**, cover, screen, barrier, shelter, shield

protective 1 = **protecting** 2 = **caring**, defensive, motherly, fatherly, maternal, vigilant, watchful, paternal

protector 1 = **defender**, champion, guard, guardian, patron, bodyguard 2 = **guard**, screen, protection, shield, pad, cushion, buffer

p

protest VERB 1 = **object**, demonstrate, oppose, complain, disagree, cry out, disapprove, demur 2 = **assert**, insist, maintain, declare, affirm, profess, attest, avow
▷ NOUN 3 = **demonstration**, march, rally, sit-in, demo (*informal*), hikoi (*N.Z.*)
4 = **objection**, complaint, dissent, outcry, protestation, remonstrance

protocol = **code of behaviour**, manners, conventions, customs, etiquette, propriety, decorum

prototype = **original**, model, first, example, standard

protracted = **extended**, prolonged, drawnout, spun out, dragged out, long-drawn-out

proud 1 = **satisfied**, pleased, content, thrilled, glad, gratified, joyful, well-pleased **OPPOSITE:** dissatisfied 2 = **conceited**, arrogant, lordly, imperious, overbearing, haughty, snobbish, self-satisfied **OPPOSITE:** humble

prove 1 = **turn out**, come out, end up 2 = **verify**, establish, determine, show, confirm, demonstrate, justify, substantiate **OPPOSITE:** disprove

proven = **established**, proved, confirmed, tested, reliable, definite, verified, attested

provide 1 = **supply**, give, distribute, fit out, outfit (*chiefly U.S.*), equip, donate, furnish, dispense **OPPOSITE:** withhold
2 = **give**, bring, add, produce, present, serve, afford, yield
▷ PHRASES: **provide for someone** = **support**, care for, keep, maintain, sustain, take care of, fend for ▶ **provide for something** = **take precautions against**, plan for, prepare for, anticipate, plan ahead for, forearm for

provided *often with* **that** = **if**, given that, on condition that, as long as

provider 1 = **supplier**, giver, source, donor
2 = **breadwinner**, supporter, earner, wage earner

providing *often with* **that** = **on condition that**, given that, as long as

province = **region**, section, district, zone, patch, colony, domain

provincial 1 = **regional**, state, local, county, district, territorial, parochial 2 = **rural**, country, local, rustic, homespun, hick (*informal, chiefly U.S. & Canad.*), backwoods **OPPOSITE:** urban
3 = **parochial**, insular, narrow-minded, unsophisticated, limited, narrow, small-town (*chiefly U.S.*), inward-looking **OPPOSITE:** cosmopolitan

provision NOUN
1 = **supplying**, giving, providing, supply, delivery, distribution, catering, presentation 2 = **condition**,

term, requirement, demand, rider, restriction, qualification, clause
▷ PLURAL NOUN 3 = **food**, supplies, stores, fare, rations, foodstuff, kai (*N.Z. informal*), victuals, edibles

provisional 1 = **temporary**, interim **OPPOSITE:** permanent 2 = **conditional**, limited, qualified, contingent, tentative **OPPOSITE:** definite

provocation 1 = **cause**, reason, grounds, motivation, stimulus, incitement 2 = **offence**, challenge, insult, taunt, injury, dare, grievance, annoyance

provocative = **offensive**, provoking, insulting, stimulating, annoying, galling, goading

provoke 1 = **anger**, annoy, irritate, infuriate, hassle (*informal*), aggravate (*informal*), incense, enrage **OPPOSITE:** pacify 2 = **rouse**, cause, produce, promote, occasion, prompt, stir, induce **OPPOSITE:** curb

prowess 1 = **skill**, ability, talent, expertise, genius, excellence, accomplishment, mastery **OPPOSITE:** inability 2 = **bravery**, daring, courage, heroism, mettle, valour, fearlessness, valiance **OPPOSITE:** cowardice

proximity = **nearness**, closeness

proxy = **representative**, agent, deputy, substitute, factor, delegate

prudent 1 = **cautious**, careful, wary, discreet, vigilant **OPPOSITE:** careless 2 = **wise**, politic, sensible, shrewd, discerning, judicious **OPPOSITE:** unwise 3 = **thrifty**, economical, sparing, careful, canny, provident, frugal, far-sighted **OPPOSITE:** extravagant

prune 1 = **cut**, trim, clip, dock, shape, shorten, snip 2 = **reduce**, cut, cut back, trim, cut down, pare down, make reductions in

psyche = **soul**, mind, self, spirit, personality, individuality, anima, wairua (*N.Z.*)

psychiatrist = **psychotherapist**, analyst, therapist, psychologist, shrink (*slang*), psychoanalyst, headshrinker (*slang*)

psychic ADJECTIVE 1 = **supernatural**, mystic, occult 2 = **mystical**, spiritual, magical, other-worldly, paranormal, preternatural 3 = **psychological**, emotional, mental, spiritual, inner, psychiatric, cognitive
▷ NOUN = **clairvoyant**, fortune teller

psychological 1 = **mental**, emotional, intellectual, inner, cognitive, cerebral 2 = **imaginary**, psychosomatic, irrational, unreal, all in the mind

P

psychology
1 = **behaviourism**, study of personality, science of mind
2 (*Informal*) = **way of thinking**, attitude, behaviour, temperament, mentality, thought processes, mental processes, what makes you tick

pub *or* **public house** = **tavern**, bar, inn, saloon

public NOUN 1 = **people**, society, community, nation, everyone, citizens, electorate, populace
▷ ADJECTIVE 2 = **civic**, government, state, national, local, official, community, social
3 = **general**, popular, national, shared, common, widespread, universal, collective 4 = **open**, accessible, communal, unrestricted OPPOSITE: private
5 = **well-known**, leading, important, respected, famous, celebrated, recognized, distinguished 6 = **known**, open, obvious, acknowledged, plain, patent, overt OPPOSITE: secret

publication 1 = **pamphlet**, newspaper, magazine, issue, title, leaflet, brochure, periodical 2 = **announcement**, publishing, broadcasting, reporting, declaration, disclosure, proclamation, notification

publicity 1 = **advertising**, press, promotion, hype, boost, plug (*informal*) 2 = **attention**, exposure, fame, celebrity, fuss, public interest, limelight, notoriety

publish 1 = **put out**, issue, produce, print 2 = **announce**, reveal, spread, advertise, broadcast, disclose, proclaim, circulate

pudding = **dessert**, afters (*Brit. informal*), sweet, pud (*informal*)

puff VERB 1 = **smoke**, draw, drag (*slang*), suck, inhale, pull at or on 2 = **breathe heavily**, pant, exhale, blow, gasp, gulp, wheeze, fight for breath
▷ NOUN 3 = **drag**, pull (*slang*), smoke 4 = **blast**, breath, whiff, draught, gust

pull VERB 1 = **draw**, haul, drag, trail, tow, tug, jerk, yank OPPOSITE: push 2 = **extract**, pick, remove, gather, take out, pluck, uproot, draw out OPPOSITE: insert 3 (*Informal*) = **attract**, draw, bring in, tempt, lure, interest, entice, pull in OPPOSITE: repel 4 = **strain**, tear, stretch, rip, wrench, dislocate, sprain
▷ NOUN 5 = **tug**, jerk, yank, twitch, heave OPPOSITE: shove
6 = **puff**, drag (*slang*), inhalation 7 (*Informal*) = **influence**, power, weight, muscle, clout (*informal*), kai (*N.Z. informal*)
▷ PHRASES: **pull out (of)** 1 = **withdraw**, quit 2 = **leave**, abandon, get out, quit, retreat from, depart, evacuate ▶ **pull someone up** = **reprimand**,

rebuke, admonish, read the riot act to (*informal*), tell someone off (*informal*), reprove, bawl someone out (*informal*), tear someone off a strip (*Brit. informal*) ▸ **pull something off** (*Informal*) = **succeed in**, manage, carry out, accomplish ▸ **pull something out** = **produce**, draw, bring out, draw out ▸ **pull up** = **stop**, halt, brake

pulp NOUN 1 = **paste**, mash, mush 2 = **flesh**, meat, soft part
▷ ADJECTIVE 3 = **cheap**, lurid, trashy, rubbishy
▷ VERB 4 = **crush**, squash, mash, pulverize

pulse NOUN 1 = **beat**, rhythm, vibration, beating, throb, throbbing, pulsation
▷ VERB 2 = **beat**, throb, vibrate, pulsate

pump 1 = **supply**, send, pour, inject 2 = **interrogate**, probe, quiz, cross-examine

punch¹ VERB 1 = **hit**, strike, box, smash, belt (*informal*), sock (*slang*), swipe (*informal*), bop (*informal*)
▷ NOUN 2 = **blow**, hit, sock (*slang*), jab, swipe (*informal*), bop (*informal*), wallop (*informal*) 3 (*Informal*) = **effectiveness**, bite, impact, drive, vigour, verve, forcefulness

punch² = **pierce**, cut, bore, drill, stamp, puncture, prick, perforate

punctuate = **interrupt**, break, pepper, sprinkle, intersperse

puncture NOUN 1 = **flat tyre**, flat, flattie (*N.Z.*) 2 = **hole**, opening, break, cut, nick, leak, slit
▷ VERB 3 = **pierce**, cut, nick, penetrate, prick, rupture, perforate, bore a hole (in)

punish = **discipline**, correct, castigate, chastise, sentence, chasten, penalize

punishing = **hard**, taxing, wearing, tiring, exhausting, gruelling, strenuous, arduous
OPPOSITE: easy

punishment 1 = **penalizing**, discipline, correction, retribution, chastening, chastisement 2 = **penalty**, penance

punitive = **retaliatory**, in reprisal, retaliative

punt VERB 1 = **bet**, back, stake, gamble, lay, wager
▷ NOUN 2 = **bet**, stake, gamble, wager

punter 1 = **gambler**, better, backer 2 (*Informal*) = **person**, man in the street

pupil 1 = **student**, schoolboy or schoolgirl, schoolchild
OPPOSITE: teacher 2 = **learner**, novice, beginner, disciple
OPPOSITE: instructor

puppet 1 = **marionette**, doll, glove puppet, finger puppet 2 = **pawn**, tool, instrument, mouthpiece, stooge, cat's-paw

purchase VERB 1 = **buy**, pay

SHADES OF PURPLE

amethyst	lavender	plum
aubergine	lilac	puce
burgundy	magenta	Tyrian purple
claret	mauve	violet
heather	mulberry	wine
indigo		

for, obtain, get, score (*slang*), gain, pick up, acquire **OPPOSITE:** sell
▷ NOUN 2 = **acquisition**, buy, investment, property, gain, asset, possession 3 = **grip**, hold, support, leverage, foothold

pure 1 = **unmixed**, real, simple, natural, straight, genuine, neat, authentic **OPPOSITE:** adulterated 2 = **clean**, wholesome, sanitary, spotless, sterilized, squeaky-clean, untainted, uncontaminated **OPPOSITE:** contaminated 3 = **complete**, total, perfect, absolute, sheer, patent, utter, outright **OPPOSITE:** qualified 4 = **innocent**, modest, good, moral, impeccable, righteous, virtuous, squeaky-clean **OPPOSITE:** corrupt

purely = **absolutely**, just, only, completely, simply, entirely, exclusively, merely

purge VERB 1 = **rid**, clear, cleanse, strip, empty, void 2 = **get rid of**, remove, expel, wipe out, eradicate, do away with, exterminate
▷ NOUN 3 = **removal**,

elimination, expulsion, eradication, ejection

purity 1 = **cleanness**, cleanliness, wholesomeness, pureness, faultlessness, immaculateness **OPPOSITE:** impurity 2 = **innocence**, virtue, integrity, honesty, decency, virginity, chastity, chasteness **OPPOSITE:** immorality

purple ▷ See panel SHADES OF PURPLE

purport = **claim**, allege, assert, profess

purpose 1 = **reason**, point, idea, aim, object, intention 2 = **aim**, end, plan, hope, goal, wish, desire, object 3 = **determination**, resolve, will, resolution, ambition, persistence, tenacity, firmness
▷ PHRASES: **on purpose** = **deliberately**, purposely, intentionally, knowingly, designedly

● **USAGE NOTE**
● The two concepts *purposeful*
● and *on purpose* should be
● carefully distinguished. *On*
● *purpose* and *purposely* have
● roughly the same meaning,
● and imply that a person's

- action is deliberate, rather
- than accidental. However,
- *purposeful* and its related
- adverb *purposefully* refer to
- the way that someone acts as
- being full of purpose or
- determination.

purposely = deliberately, expressly, consciously, intentionally, knowingly, with intent, on purpose **OPPOSITE:** accidentally

purse NOUN 1 = pouch, wallet, money-bag 2 (*U.S.*) = handbag, bag, shoulder bag, pocket book (*U.S. & Canad.*), clutch bag 3 = funds, means, money, resources, treasury, wealth, exchequer

▷ VERB 4 = pucker, contract, tighten, pout, press together

pursue 1 = engage in, perform, conduct, carry on, practise 2 = try for, seek, desire, search for, aim for, work towards, strive for 3 = continue, maintain, carry on, keep on, persist in, proceed in, persevere in 4 = follow, track, hunt, chase, dog, shadow, tail (*informal*), hound **OPPOSITE:** flee

pursuit 1 = quest, seeking, search, aim of, aspiration, striving towards 2 = pursuing, seeking, search, hunt, chase, trailing 3 = occupation, activity, interest, line, pleasure, hobby, pastime

push VERB 1 = shove, force, press, thrust, drive, knock,

sweep, plunge **OPPOSITE:** pull 2 = press, operate, depress, squeeze, activate, hold down 3 = make or force your way, move, shoulder, inch, squeeze, thrust, elbow, shove 4 = urge, encourage, persuade, spur, press, incite, impel **OPPOSITE:** discourage

▷ NOUN 5 = shove, thrust, butt, elbow, nudge **OPPOSITE:** pull 6 (*Informal*) = drive, go (*informal*), energy, initiative, enterprise, ambition, vitality, vigour

▷ PHRASES: the push (*Informal, chiefly Brit.*) = dismissal, the sack (*informal*), discharge, the boot (*slang*), your cards (*informal*)

put VERB 1 = place, leave, set, position, rest, park (*informal*), plant, lay 2 = express, state, word, phrase, utter

▷ PHRASES: put someone off 1 = discourage, intimidate, deter, daunt, dissuade, demoralize, scare off, dishearten 2 = disconcert, confuse, unsettle, throw (*informal*), dismay, perturb, faze (*informal*), discomfit (*literary*)

▶ put someone up 1 = accommodate, house, board, lodge, quarter, take someone in, billet 2 = nominate, put forward, offer, present, propose, recommend, submit ▶ put something across or over

= **communicate**, explain, convey, make clear, get across, make yourself understood ▶ **put something off** = **postpone**, delay, defer, adjourn, hold over, put on the back burner (*informal*), take a rain check on (*U.S. & Canad. informal*) ▶ **put something up 1** = **build**, raise, set up, construct, erect, fabricate **2** = **offer**, present, mount, put forward

puzzle VERB **1** = **perplex**, confuse, baffle, stump, bewilder, confound, mystify, faze (*informal*)
▷ NOUN **2** = **problem**, riddle, question, conundrum, poser **3** = **mystery**, problem, paradox, enigma, conundrum

puzzling = **perplexing**, baffling, bewildering, involved, enigmatic, incomprehensible, mystifying, abstruse **OPPOSITE:** simple

Qq

quake = **shake**, tremble, quiver, move, rock, shiver, shudder, vibrate

qualification 1 = **eligibility**, quality, ability, skill, fitness, attribute, capability, aptitude **2** = **condition**, proviso, requirement, rider, reservation, limitation, modification, caveat

qualified 1 = **capable**, trained, experienced, seasoned, able, fit, expert, chartered **OPPOSITE:** untrained **2** = **restricted**, limited, provisional, conditional, reserved, bounded, adjusted, moderated **OPPOSITE:** unconditional

qualify 1 = **certify**, equip, empower, train, prepare, fit, ready, permit **OPPOSITE:** disqualify **2** = **restrict**, limit, reduce, ease, moderate, regulate, diminish, temper

quality 1 = **standard**, standing, class, condition, rank, grade, merit, classification **2** = **excellence**, status, merit, position, value, worth, distinction, virtue **3** = **characteristic**, feature, attribute, point, side, mark,

q

property, aspect **4 = nature**, character, make, sort, kind

quantity 1 = amount, lot, total, sum, part, number **2 = size**, measure, mass, volume, length, capacity, extent, bulk

● **USAGE NOTE**
● The use of a plural noun after
● *quantity of*, as in a large
● *quantity of bananas*, used to be
● considered incorrect, the
● objection being that the word
● *quantity* should only be used
● to refer to an uncountable
● amount, which was
● grammatically regarded as a
● singular concept. Nowadays,
● however, most people
● consider the use of *quantity*
● with a plural noun to be
● acceptable.

quarrel NOUN
1 = disagreement, fight, row, argument, dispute, controversy, breach, contention, biffo (*Austral. slang*) **OPPOSITE:** accord

▷ **VERB 2 = disagree**, fight, argue, row, clash, dispute, differ, fall out (*informal*) **OPPOSITE:** get on *or* along (with)

quarry = prey, victim, game, goal, aim, prize, objective

quarter NOUN 1 = district, region, neighbourhood, place, part, side, area, zone **2 = mercy**, pity, compassion, charity, sympathy, tolerance, kindness, forgiveness

▷ **PLURAL NOUN 3 = lodgings**, rooms, chambers, residence, dwelling, barracks, abode, habitation

▷ **VERB 4 = accommodate**, house, lodge, place, board, post, station, billet

quash 1 = annul, overturn, reverse, cancel, overthrow, revoke, overrule, rescind **2 = suppress**, crush, put down, beat, overthrow, squash, subdue, repress

queen 1 = sovereign, ruler, monarch, leader, Crown, princess, majesty, head of state **2 = leading light**, star, favourite, celebrity, darling, mistress, big name

queer 1 = strange, odd, funny, unusual, extraordinary, curious, weird, peculiar **OPPOSITE:** normal **2 = faint**, dizzy, giddy, queasy, light-headed

● **USAGE NOTE**
● Although the term *queer*
● meaning 'homosexual' is still
● considered derogatory when
● used by non-gays, it is now
● being used by gay people
● themselves as a positive term
● in certain contexts, such as
● *queer politics, queer cinema*.
● Nevertheless, many gay
● people would not wish to
● have the term applied to
● them, nor would they use it
● of themselves.

query NOUN 1 = question, inquiry, problem **2 = doubt**,

q

suspicion, objection

▷ VERB 3 = **question**, challenge, doubt, suspect, dispute, object to, distrust, mistrust 4 = **ask**, inquire or enquire, question

quest 1 = **search**, hunt, mission, enterprise, crusade 2 = **expedition**, journey, adventure

question NOUN 1 = **inquiry**, enquiry, query, investigation, examination, interrogation **OPPOSITE:** answer 2 = **difficulty**, problem, doubt, argument, dispute, controversy, query, contention 3 = **issue**, point, matter, subject, problem, debate, proposal, theme

▷ VERB 4 = **interrogate**, cross-examine, interview, examine, probe, quiz, ask questions 5 = **dispute**, challenge, doubt, suspect, oppose, query, mistrust, disbelieve **OPPOSITE:** accept

▷ PHRASES: out of the question = **impossible**, unthinkable, inconceivable, not on (informal), hopeless, unimaginable, unworkable, unattainable

questionable = **dubious**, suspect, doubtful, controversial, suspicious, dodgy (Brit., Austral. & N.Z. informal), debatable, moot **OPPOSITE:** indisputable

queue = **line**, row, file, train, series, chain, string, column

quick ADJECTIVE 1 = **fast**, swift, speedy, express, cracking (Brit.

informal), smart, rapid, fleet **OPPOSITE:** slow 2 = **brief**, passing, hurried, flying, fleeting, summary, lightning, short-lived **OPPOSITE:** long 3 = **immediate**, instant, prompt, sudden, abrupt, instantaneous 4 = **excitable**, passionate, irritable, touchy, irascible, testy **OPPOSITE:** calm 5 = **intelligent**, bright (informal), alert, sharp, acute, smart, clever, shrewd **OPPOSITE:** stupid

quicken 1 = **speed up**, hurry, accelerate, hasten, gee up (informal) 2 = **stimulate**, inspire, arouse, excite, revive, incite, energize, invigorate

quickly 1 = **swiftly**, rapidly, hurriedly, fast, hastily, briskly, apace **OPPOSITE:** slowly 2 = **soon**, speedily, as soon as possible, momentarily (U.S.), instantaneously, pronto (informal), a.s.a.p. (informal) 3 = **immediately**, at once, directly, promptly, abruptly, without delay

quiet ADJECTIVE 1 = **soft**, low, muted, lowered, whispered, faint, suppressed, stifled **OPPOSITE:** loud 2 = **peaceful**, silent, hushed, soundless, noiseless **OPPOSITE:** noisy 3 = **calm**, peaceful, tranquil, mild, serene, placid, restful **OPPOSITE:** exciting 4 = **still**, calm, peaceful, tranquil **OPPOSITE:** troubled 5 = **undisturbed**, isolated,

secluded, private, sequestered, unfrequented **OPPOSITE:** crowded **6** = **silent**, dumb **7** = **reserved**, retiring, shy, gentle, mild, sedate, meek **OPPOSITE:** excitable
▷ NOUN **8** = **peace**, rest, tranquillity, ease, silence, solitude, serenity, stillness **OPPOSITE:** noise

quietly 1 = **noiselessly**, silently **2** = **softly**, inaudibly, in an undertone, under your breath **3** = **calmly**, serenely, placidly, patiently, mildly **4** = **silently**, mutely

quilt = **bedspread**, duvet, coverlet, eiderdown, counterpane, doona (*Austral.*), continental quilt

quip = **joke**, sally, jest, riposte, wisecrack (*informal*), retort, pleasantry, gibe

quirky = **odd**, unusual, eccentric, idiosyncratic, peculiar, offbeat

quit 1 = **resign (from)**, leave, retire (from), pull out (of), step down (from) (*informal*), abdicate **2** = **stop**, give up, cease, end, drop, abandon, halt, discontinue **OPPOSITE:** continue **3** = **leave**, depart from, go out of, go away from, pull out from

quite 1 = **somewhat**, rather, fairly, reasonably, relatively, moderately **2** = **absolutely**, perfectly, completely, totally, fully, entirely, wholly

quiz NOUN **1** = **examination**,

questioning, interrogation, interview, investigation, grilling (*informal*), cross-examination, cross-questioning
▷ VERB **2** = **question**, ask, interrogate, examine, investigate

quota = **share**, allowance, ration, part, limit, slice, quantity, portion

quotation 1 = **passage**, quote (*informal*), excerpt, reference, extract, citation **2** (*Commerce*) = **estimate**, price, tender, rate, cost, charge, figure, quote (*informal*)

quote 1 = **repeat**, recite, recall **2** = **refer to**, cite, give, name, detail, relate, mention, instance

q

Rr

race¹ NOUN 1 = **competition**, contest, chase, dash, pursuit 2 = **contest**, competition, rivalry ▷ VERB 3 = **compete against**, run against 4 = **compete**, run, contend, take part in a race 5 = **run**, fly, career, speed, tear, dash, hurry, dart

race² = **people**, nation, blood, stock, type, folk, tribe

racial = **ethnic**, ethnological, national, folk, genetic, tribal, genealogical

rack NOUN 1 = **frame**, stand, structure, framework ▷ VERB 2 = **torture**, torment, afflict, oppress, harrow, crucify, agonize, pain

● USAGE NOTE
● The use of the spelling *wrack*
● rather than *rack* in sentences
● such as *she was wracked by*
● *grief* or *the country was wracked*
● *by civil war* is very common,
● but is thought by many
● people to be incorrect.

racket 1 = **noise**, row, fuss, disturbance, outcry, clamour, din, pandemonium 2 = **fraud**, scheme

radiate 1 = **emit**, spread, send out, pour, shed, scatter 2 = **shine**, be diffused 3 = **show**, display, demonstrate, exhibit, emanate, give off or out 4 = **spread out**, diverge, branch out

radical ADJECTIVE 1 = **extreme**, complete, entire, sweeping, severe, thorough, drastic 2 = **revolutionary**, extremist, fanatical 3 = **fundamental**, natural, basic, profound, innate, deep-seated OPPOSITE: superficial ▷ NOUN 4 = **extremist**, revolutionary, militant, fanatic OPPOSITE: conservative

rage NOUN 1 = **fury**, temper, frenzy, rampage, tantrum, foulie (*Austral. slang*) OPPOSITE: calmness 2 = **anger**, passion, madness, wrath, ire 3 = **craze**, fashion, enthusiasm, vogue, fad (*informal*), latest thing ▷ VERB 4 = **be furious**, blow up (*informal*), fume, lose it (*informal*), seethe, lose the plot (*informal*), go ballistic (*slang, chiefly U.S.*), lose your temper OPPOSITE: stay calm

ragged 1 = **tatty**, worn, torn, run-down, shabby, seedy, scruffy, in tatters OPPOSITE: smart 2 = **rough**, rugged, unfinished, uneven, jagged, serrated

raid VERB 1 = **steal from**, plunder, pillage, sack 2 = **attack**, invade, assault

3 = **make a search of**, search, bust (*informal*), make a raid on, make a swoop on

▷ NOUN **4** = **attack**, invasion, foray, sortie, incursion, sally, inroad **5** = **bust** (*informal*), swoop **6** = **robbery**, sacking

raider = **attacker**, thief, robber, plunderer, invader, marauder

railing = **fence**, rails, barrier, paling, balustrade

rain NOUN **1** = **rainfall**, fall, showers, deluge, drizzle, downpour, raindrops, cloudburst

▷ VERB **2** = **pour**, pelt (down), teem, bucket down (*informal*), drizzle, come down in buckets (*informal*) **3** = **fall**, shower, be dropped, sprinkle, be deposited

rainy = **wet**, damp, drizzly, showery **OPPOSITE:** dry

raise VERB **1** = **lift**, elevate, uplift, heave **2** = **set upright**, lift, elevate **3** = **increase**, intensify, heighten, advance, boost, strengthen, enhance, enlarge **OPPOSITE:** reduce **4** = **make louder**, heighten, amplify, louden **5** = **collect**, gather, obtain **6** = **cause**, start, produce, create, occasion, provoke, originate, engender **7** = **put forward**, suggest, introduce, advance, broach, moot **8** = **bring up**, develop, rear, nurture **9** = **build**, construct, put up, erect **OPPOSITE:** demolish

rake¹ 1 = **gather**, collect, remove **2** = **search**, comb, scour, scrutinize, fossick (*Austral. & N.Z.*)

rake² = libertine, playboy, swinger (*slang*), lecher, roué, debauchee **OPPOSITE:** puritan

rally NOUN **1** = **gathering**, convention, meeting, congress, assembly, hui (*N.Z.*) **2** = **recovery**, improvement, revival, recuperation **OPPOSITE:** relapse

▷ VERB **3** = **gather together**, unite, regroup, reorganize, reassemble **4** = **recover**, improve, revive, get better, recuperate **OPPOSITE:** get worse

ram 1 = **hit**, force, drive into, crash, impact, smash, dash, butt **2** = **cram**, force, stuff, jam, thrust

ramble NOUN **1** = **walk**, tour, stroll, hike, roaming, roving, saunter

▷ VERB **2** = **walk**, range, wander, stroll, stray, roam, rove, saunter, go walkabout (*Austral.*) **3** *often with* **on** = **babble**, rabbit (on) (*Brit. informal*), waffle (*informal, chiefly Brit.*), witter on (*informal*)

ramp = **slope**, incline, gradient, rise

rampage = **go berserk**, storm, rage, run riot, run amok

▷ PHRASES: **on the rampage** = **berserk**, wild, violent, raging, out of control, amok, riotous, berko (*Austral. slang*)

r

rampant 1 = **widespread**, prevalent, rife, uncontrolled, unchecked, unrestrained, profuse, spreading like wildfire 2 (*Heraldry*) = **upright**, standing, rearing, erect

random 1 = **chance**, casual, accidental, incidental, haphazard, fortuitous, hit or miss, adventitious **OPPOSITE:** planned 2 = **casual**, arbitrary ▷ **PHRASES: at random** = **haphazardly**, randomly, arbitrarily, by chance, willy-nilly, unsystematically

randy (*Informal*) = **lustful**, hot, turned-on (*slang*), aroused, horny (*slang*), amorous, lascivious

range NOUN 1 = **series**, variety, selection, assortment, lot, collection, gamut 2 = **limits**, reach 3 = **scope**, area, bounds, province, orbit, radius ▷ VERB 4 = **vary**, run, reach, extend, stretch 5 = **roam**, wander, rove, ramble, traverse

rank¹ NOUN 1 = **status**, level, position, grade, order, sort, type, division 2 = **class**, caste 3 = **row**, line, file, column, group, range, series, tier ▷ VERB 4 = **order**, dispose 5 = **arrange**, sort, line up, array, align

rank² 1 = **absolute**, complete, total, gross, sheer, utter, thorough, blatant 2 = **foul**, bad, offensive, disgusting, revolting, stinking, noxious,

rancid, festy (*Austral. slang*) 3 = **abundant**, lush, luxuriant, dense, profuse

ransom = **payment**, money, price, payoff

rant = **shout**, roar, yell, rave, cry, declaim

rap VERB 1 = **hit**, strike, knock, crack, tap ▷ NOUN 2 = **blow**, knock, crack, tap, clout (*informal*) 3 (*Slang*) = **rebuke**, blame, responsibility, punishment

rape VERB 1 = **sexually assault**, violate, abuse, ravish, force, outrage ▷ NOUN 2 = **sexual assault**, violation, ravishment, outrage

rapid 1 = **sudden**, prompt, speedy, express, swift **OPPOSITE:** gradual 2 = **quick**, fast, hurried, swift, brisk, hasty **OPPOSITE:** slow

rapidly = **quickly**, fast, swiftly, briskly, promptly, hastily, hurriedly, speedily

rare 1 = **uncommon**, unusual, few, strange, scarce, singular, sparse, infrequent **OPPOSITE:** common 2 = **superb**, great, fine, excellent, superlative, choice, peerless

rarely = **seldom**, hardly, hardly ever, infrequently **OPPOSITE:** often

● USAGE NOTE
● Since the meaning of *rarely* is
● 'hardly ever', the combination
● *rarely ever* is repetitive and
● should be avoided in careful

- writing, even though you
- may sometimes hear this
- phrase used in informal
- speech.

raring (in construction *raring to do something*) = **eager**, impatient, longing, ready, keen, desperate, enthusiastic

rarity 1 = **curio**, find, treasure, gem, collector's item **2** = **uncommonness**, scarcity, infrequency, unusualness, shortage, strangeness, sparseness

rash¹ = **reckless**, hasty, impulsive, imprudent, careless, ill-advised, foolhardy, impetuous **OPPOSITE:** cautious

rash² **1** = **outbreak of spots**, (skin) eruption **2** = **spate**, series, wave, flood, plague, outbreak

rate NOUN **1** = **speed**, pace, tempo, velocity, frequency **2** = **degree**, standard, scale, proportion, ratio **3** = **charge**, price, cost, fee, figure ▷ VERB **4** = **evaluate**, consider, rank, reckon, value, measure, estimate, count **5** = **deserve**, merit, be entitled to, be worthy of ▷ PHRASES: **at any rate** = **in any case**, anyway, anyhow, at all events

rather 1 = **preferably**, sooner, more readily, more willingly **2** = **to some extent**, quite, a little, fairly, relatively,

somewhat, moderately, to some degree

- USAGE NOTE
- It is acceptable to use either
- *would rather* or *had rather* in
- sentences such as *I would*
- *rather* (or *had rather*) *see a film*
- *than a play. Had rather*,
- however, is less common
- than *would rather*, and sounds
- a little old-fashioned
- nowadays.

ratify = **approve**, establish, confirm, sanction, endorse, uphold, authorize, affirm **OPPOSITE:** annul

rating = **position**, placing, rate, order, class, degree, rank, status

ratio = **proportion**, rate, relation, percentage, fraction

ration NOUN **1** = **allowance**, quota, allotment, helping, part, share, measure, portion ▷ VERB **2** = **limit**, control, restrict, budget

rational = **sensible**, sound, wise, reasonable, intelligent, realistic, logical, sane **OPPOSITE:** insane

rationale = **reason**, grounds, theory, principle, philosophy, logic, motivation, raison d'être (French)

rattle 1 = **clatter**, bang, jangle **2** = **shake**, jolt, vibrate, bounce, jar **3** (*Informal*) = **fluster**, shake, upset, disturb, disconcert, perturb, faze (*informal*)

ravage VERB **1** = **destroy**, ruin, devastate, spoil, demolish,

ransack, lay waste, despoil
▷ **PLURAL NOUN** 2 = **damage**, destruction, devastation, ruin, havoc, ruination, spoliation

rave 1 = **rant**, rage, roar, go mad (*informal*), babble, be delirious 2 (*Informal*) = **enthuse**, praise, gush, be mad about (*informal*), be wild about (*informal*)

raving = **mad**, wild, crazy, hysterical, insane, irrational, crazed, delirious, berko (*Austral. slang*), off the air (*Austral. slang*)

raw 1 = **unrefined**, natural, crude, unprocessed, basic, rough, coarse, unfinished **OPPOSITE:** refined
2 = **uncooked**, natural, fresh **OPPOSITE:** cooked
3 = **inexperienced**, new, green, immature, callow **OPPOSITE:** experienced 4 = **chilly**, biting, cold, freezing, bitter, piercing, parky (*Brit. informal*)

ray = **beam**, bar, flash, shaft, gleam

re = **concerning**, about, regarding, with regard to, with reference to, apropos
● USAGE NOTE
● In contexts such as *re your*
● *letter*, your remarks have been
● *noted* or he spoke to me *re your*
● *complaint*, *re* is common in
● business or official
● correspondence. In spoken
● and in general written
● English *with reference to* is
● preferable in the former case

● and *about* or *concerning* in the
● latter. Even in business
● correspondence, the use of *re*
● is often restricted to the
● letter heading.

reach **VERB** 1 = **arrive at**, get to, make, attain 2 = **attain**, get to 3 = **touch**, grasp, extend to, stretch to, contact
4 = **contact**, get in touch with, get through to, communicate with, get hold of
▷ **NOUN** 5 = **grasp**, range, distance, stretch, capacity, extent, extension, scope
6 = **jurisdiction**, power, influence

react = **respond**, act, proceed, behave

reaction 1 = **response**, answer, reply 2 = **counteraction**, backlash, recoil
3 = **conservatism**, the right
● USAGE NOTE
● Some people say that *reaction*
● should always refer to an
● instant response to
● something (as in *his reaction*
● *was one of amazement*), and
● that this word should not be
● used to refer to a considered
● response given in the form of
● a statement (as in *the Minister*
● *gave his reaction to the court's*
● *decision*). Use *response*
● instead.

reactionary **ADJECTIVE**
1 = **conservative**, right-wing
▷ **NOUN** 2 = **conservative**, die-hard, right-winger **OPPOSITE:**

radical

read 1 = **scan**, study, look at, pore over, peruse
2 = **understand**, interpret, comprehend, construe, decipher, see, discover
3 = **register**, show, record, display, indicate

readily 1 = **willingly**, freely, quickly, gladly, eagerly **OPPOSITE:** reluctantly
2 = **promptly**, quickly, easily, smoothly, effortlessly, speedily, unhesitatingly **OPPOSITE:** with difficulty

readiness 1 = **willingness**, eagerness, keenness
2 = **promptness**, facility, ease, dexterity, adroitness

reading 1 = **perusal**, study, examination, inspection, scrutiny 2 = **learning**, education, knowledge, scholarship, erudition
3 = **recital**, performance, lesson, sermon
4 = **interpretation**, version, impression, grasp

ready 1 = **prepared**, set, primed, organized **OPPOSITE:** unprepared 2 = **completed**, arranged 3 = **mature**, ripe, mellow, ripened, seasoned
4 = **willing**, happy, glad, disposed, keen, eager, inclined, prone **OPPOSITE:** reluctant
5 = **prompt**, smart, quick, bright, sharp, keen, alert, clever **OPPOSITE:** slow 6 = **available**, handy, present, near, accessible,

convenient **OPPOSITE:** unavailable

real 1 = **true**, genuine, sincere, factual, dinkum (*Austral. & N.Z. informal*), unfeigned
2 = **genuine**, authentic, dinkum (*Austral. & N.Z. informal*) **OPPOSITE:** fake 3 = **proper**, true, valid 4 = **true**, actual
5 = **typical**, true, genuine, sincere, dinkum (*Austral. & N.Z. informal*), unfeigned
6 = **complete**, total, perfect, utter, thorough

realistic 1 = **practical**, real, sensible, common-sense, down-to-earth, matter-of-fact, level-headed **OPPOSITE:** impractical
2 = **attainable**, sensible
3 = **lifelike**, true to life, authentic, true, natural, genuine, faithful

reality 1 = **fact**, truth, realism, validity, verity, actuality
2 = **truth**, fact, actuality

realization 1 = **awareness**, understanding, recognition, perception, grasp, conception, comprehension, cognizance
2 = **achievement**, accomplishment, fulfilment

realize 1 = **become aware of**, understand, take in, grasp, comprehend, get the message
2 = **fulfil**, achieve, accomplish, make real 3 = **achieve**, do, effect, complete, perform, fulfil, accomplish, carry out *or* through

really 1 = **certainly**, genuinely,

positively, surely **2** = **truly**, actually, in fact, indeed, in actuality

realm 1 = **field**, world, area, province, sphere, department, branch, territory **2** = **kingdom**, country, empire, land, domain, dominion

reap 1 = **get**, gain, obtain, acquire, derive **2** = **collect**, gather, train, bring in, harvest, garner, cut

rear¹ NOUN **1** = **back part**, back **OPPOSITE:** front **2** = **back**, end, tail, rearguard, tail end
▷ ADJECTIVE **3** = **back**, hind, last, following **OPPOSITE:** front

rear² 1 = **bring up**, raise, educate, train, foster, nurture **2** = **breed**, keep **3** = **rise**, tower, soar, loom

reason NOUN **1** = **cause**, grounds, purpose, motive, goal, aim, object, intention **2** = **sense**, mind, understanding, judgment, logic, intellect, sanity, rationality **OPPOSITE:** emotion
▷ VERB **3** = **deduce**, conclude, work out, train, infer, think
▷ PHRASES: **reason with someone** = **persuade**, bring round, urge, win over, prevail upon (*formal*), talk into or out of

● USAGE NOTE
● Many people object to the
● expression *the reason is*
● *because*, on the grounds that
● it is repetitive. It is therefore
● advisable to use either *this is*

● *because* or *the reason is that*.

reasonable 1 = **sensible**, sound, practical, wise, logical, sober, plausible, sane **OPPOSITE:** irrational **2** = **fair**, just, right, moderate, equitable, tenable **OPPOSITE:** unfair **3** = **within reason**, fit, proper **OPPOSITE:** impossible **4** = **low**, cheap, competitive, moderate, modest, inexpensive **5** = **average**, fair, moderate, modest, O.K. or okay (*informal*)

reassure = **encourage**, comfort, hearten, gee up (*informal*), restore confidence to, put or set your mind at rest

rebate = **refund**, discount, reduction, bonus, allowance, deduction

rebel NOUN **1** = **revolutionary**, insurgent, secessionist, revolutionist **2** = **nonconformist**, dissenter, heretic, apostate, schismatic
▷ VERB **3** = **revolt**, resist, rise up, mutiny **4** = **defy**, dissent, disobey
▷ ADJECTIVE **5** = **rebellious**, revolutionary, insurgent, insurrectionary

rebellion 1 = **resistance**, rising, revolution, revolt, uprising, mutiny **2** = **nonconformity**, defiance, heresy, schism

rebellious 1 = **defiant**, difficult, resistant, unmanageable, refractory **OPPOSITE:** obedient **2** = **revolutionary**, rebel, disorderly, unruly, insurgent, disloyal, seditious, mutinous **OPPOSITE:** obedient

rebound 1 = **bounce**, ricochet, recoil 2 = **misfire**, backfire, recoil, boomerang

rebuff VERB 1 = **reject**, refuse, turn down, cut, slight, snub, spurn, knock back (*informal*) **OPPOSITE:** encourage
▷ NOUN 2 = **rejection**, snub, knock-back (*informal*), slight, refusal, repulse, cold shoulder, slap in the face (*informal*) **OPPOSITE:** encouragement

rebuke VERB 1 = **scold**, censure, reprimand, castigate, chide, dress down (*informal*), admonish, tell off (*informal*) **OPPOSITE:** praise
▷ NOUN 2 = **scolding**, censure, reprimand, row, dressing-down (*informal*), telling-off (*informal*), admonition **OPPOSITE:** praise

recall VERB 1 = **recollect**, remember, evoke, call to mind 2 = **call back** 3 = **annul**, withdraw, cancel, repeal, revoke, retract, countermand
▷ NOUN 4 = **recollection**, memory, remembrance 5 = **annulment**, withdrawal, repeal, cancellation, retraction, rescindment

recede = **fall back**, withdraw, retreat, return, retire, regress

receipt 1 = **sales slip**, proof of purchase, counterfoil 2 = **receiving**, delivery, reception, acceptance

receive 1 = **get**, accept, be given, pick up, collect, obtain, acquire, take 2 = **experience**, suffer, bear, encounter, sustain, undergo 3 = **greet**, meet, admit, welcome, entertain, accommodate

recent = **new**, modern, up-to-date, late, current, fresh, novel, present-day **OPPOSITE:** old

recently = **not long ago**, newly, lately, currently, freshly, of late, latterly

reception 1 = **party**, gathering, get-together, social gathering, function, celebration, festivity, soirée 2 = **response**, reaction, acknowledgment, treatment, welcome, greeting

recess 1 = **break**, rest, holiday, interval, vacation, respite, intermission 2 = **alcove**, corner, bay, hollow, niche, nook

recession = **depression**, drop, decline, slump **OPPOSITE:** boom

recipe = **directions**, instructions, ingredients

recital 1 = **performance**, rendering, rehearsal, reading 2 = **account**, telling, statement, relation, narrative 3 = **recitation**

recite = **perform**, deliver, repeat, declaim

reckless = **careless**, wild, rash, precipitate, hasty, mindless, headlong, thoughtless **OPPOSITE:** cautious

reckon 1 (*Informal*) = **think**, believe, suppose, imagine, assume, guess (*informal, chiefly U.S. & Canad.*) **2** = **consider**, rate, account, judge, regard, count, esteem, deem **3** = **count**, figure, total, calculate, compute, add up, tally, number

reckoning = count, estimate, calculation, addition

reclaim **1** = **retrieve**, regain **2** = **regain**, salvage, recapture

recognition **1** = **identification**, recollection, discovery, remembrance **2** = **acceptance**, admission, allowance, confession

recognize **1** = **identify**, know, place, remember, spot, notice, recall, recollect **2** = **acknowledge**, allow, accept, admit, grant, concede **OPPOSITE:** ignore **3** = **appreciate**, respect, notice

recollection = memory, recall, impression, remembrance, reminiscence

recommend **1** = **advocate**, suggest, propose, approve, endorse, commend **OPPOSITE:** disapprove of **2** = **put forward**, approve, endorse, commend, praise **3** = **advise**, suggest, advance, propose, counsel, advocate, prescribe, put forward

recommendation **1** = **advice**, proposal, suggestion, counsel **2** = **commendation**, reference, praise, sanction, approval, endorsement, advocacy,

testimonial, approbation

reconcile **1** = **resolve**, settle, square, adjust, compose, rectify, put to rights **2** = **reunite**, bring back together, conciliate **3** = **make peace between**, reunite, propitiate

reconciliation = reunion, conciliation, pacification, reconcilement **OPPOSITE:** separation

reconsider = rethink, review, revise, think again, reassess

reconstruct **1** = **rebuild**, restore, recreate, remake, renovate, remodel, regenerate **2** = **build up a picture of**, build up, piece together, deduce

record NOUN **1** = **document**, file, register, log, report, account, entry, journal **2** = **evidence**, trace, documentation, testimony, witness **3** = **disc**, single, album, LP, vinyl **4** = **background**, history, performance, career ▷ VERB **5** = **set down**, minute, note, enter, document, register, log, chronicle **6** = **make a recording of**, video, tape, video-tape, tape-record **7** = **register**, show, indicate, give evidence of

recorder = chronicler, archivist, historian, clerk, scribe, diarist

recording = record, video, tape, disc

recount = tell, report, describe, relate, repeat, depict, recite, narrate

recover 1 = **get better**, improve, get well, recuperate, heal, revive, mend, convalesce **OPPOSITE:** relapse 2 = **rally** 3 = **save**, rescue, retrieve, salvage, reclaim **OPPOSITE:** abandon 4 = **recoup**, restore, get back, regain, retrieve, reclaim, redeem, recapture **OPPOSITE:** lose

recovery 1 = **improvement**, healing, revival, mending, recuperation, convalescence 2 = **retrieval**, repossession, reclamation, restoration

recreation = **leisure**, play, sport, fun, entertainment, relaxation, enjoyment, amusement

recruit VERB 1 = **gather**, obtain, engage, procure 2 = **assemble**, raise, levy, muster, mobilize 3 = **enlist**, draft, enrol **OPPOSITE:** dismiss ▷ NOUN 4 = **beginner**, trainee, apprentice, novice, convert, initiate, helper, learner

recur = **happen again**, return, repeat, persist, revert, reappear, come again

recycle = **reprocess**, reuse, salvage, reclaim, save

red NOUN ▷ ADJECTIVE 1 = **crimson**, scarlet, ruby, vermilion, cherry, coral, carmine 2 = **flushed**, embarrassed, blushing, florid, shamefaced 3 = (of hair) = **chestnut**, reddish, flame-coloured, sandy, Titian, carroty

▷ PHRASES: **in the red** (Informal) = **in debt**, insolvent, in arrears, overdrawn ▶ **see red** (Informal) = **lose your temper**, lose it (informal), go mad (informal), crack up (informal), lose the plot (informal), go ballistic (slang, chiefly U.S.), fly off the handle (informal), blow your top (informal)

▷ See panel SHADES OF RED

redeem 1 = **reinstate**, absolve, restore to favour 2 = **make up for**, compensate for, atone for, make amends for 3 = **buy back**, recover, regain, retrieve, reclaim, repurchase 4 = **save**, free, deliver, liberate, ransom, emancipate

redemption 1 = **compensation**, amends, reparation, atonement 2 = **salvation**, release, rescue, liberation, emancipation, deliverance

redress VERB 1 = **make amends for**, make up for, compensate for 2 = **put right**, balance, correct, adjust, regulate, rectify, even up ▷ NOUN 3 = **amends**, payment, compensation, reparation, atonement, recompense

reduce 1 = **lessen**, cut, lower, moderate, weaken, diminish, decrease, cut down **OPPOSITE:** increase 2 = **degrade**, downgrade, break, humble, bring low **OPPOSITE:** promote

redundancy 1 = **layoff**,

r

SHADES OF RED

auburn	coral	mulberry	rosy
baby pink	crimson	old rose	ruby
burgundy	damask	oxblood	russet
burnt sienna	flame	oyster pink	rust
cardinal red	flesh	peach	sandy
carmine	foxy	pink	scarlet
carnation	fuchsia	plum	strawberry
carroty	ginger	poppy	tea rose
cerise	henna	puce	terracotta
cherry	liver	raspberry	Titian
chestnut	magenta	rose	vermilion
cinnabar	maroon	roseate	wine
copper or coppery			

sacking, dismissal
2 = **unemployment**, the sack
(*informal*), the axe (*informal*),
joblessness

redundant = **superfluous**,
extra, surplus, unnecessary,
unwanted, inessential,
supernumerary **OPPOSITE:**
essential

reel 1 = **stagger**, rock, roll,
pitch, sway, lurch 2 = **whirl**,
spin, revolve, swirl

refer 1 = **direct**, point, send,
guide
▷ **PHRASES: refer to something
or someone** 1 = **allude to**,
mention, cite, speak of, bring
up 2 = **relate to**, concern, apply
to, pertain to, be relevant to
3 = **consult**, go, apply, turn to,
look up

* **USAGE NOTE**
* It is usually unnecessary to
* add *back* to the verb *refer*,
* since the sense of *back* is

* already contained in the *re-*
* part of this word. For
* example, you might say *This
* refers to* (not *refers back to*)
* *what has already been said*.
* *Refer back* is only considered
* acceptable when used to
* mean 'return a document or
* question to the person it
* came from for further
* consideration', as in *he referred
* the matter back to me*.

referee NOUN 1 = **umpire**,
judge, ref (*informal*), arbiter,
arbitrator, adjudicator
▷ **VERB** 2 = **umpire**, judge,
mediate, adjudicate, arbitrate

reference 1 = **allusion**, note,
mention, quotation
2 = **citation** 3 = **testimonial**,
recommendation, credentials,
endorsement, character
reference

referendum = **public vote**,
popular vote, plebiscite

refine 1 = **purify**, process, filter, cleanse, clarify, distil
2 = **improve**, perfect, polish, hone

refined 1 = **purified**, processed, pure, filtered, clean, clarified, distilled **OPPOSITE:** unrefined
2 = **cultured**, polished, elegant, polite, cultivated, civilized, well-bred **OPPOSITE:** coarse
3 = **discerning**, fine, sensitive, delicate, precise, discriminating, fastidious

reflect 1 = **show**, reveal, display, indicate, demonstrate, manifest 2 = **throw back**, return, mirror, echo, reproduce
3 = **consider**, think, muse, ponder, meditate, ruminate, cogitate, wonder

reflection 1 = **image**, echo, mirror image
2 = **consideration**, thinking, thought, idea, opinion, observation, musing, meditation

reflective = **thoughtful**, contemplative, meditative, pensive

reform NOUN
1 = **improvement**, amendment, rehabilitation, betterment
▷ VERB 2 = **improve**, correct, restore, amend, mend, rectify
3 = **mend your ways**, go straight (*informal*), shape up (*informal*), turn over a new leaf, clean up your act (*informal*), pull your socks up (*Brit. informal*)

refrain¹ = **stop**, avoid, cease, renounce, abstain, leave off, desist, forbear (*formal*)

refrain² = **chorus**, tune, melody

refresh 1 = **revive**, freshen, revitalize, stimulate, brace, enliven, invigorate
2 = **stimulate**, prompt, renew, jog

refreshing 1 = **new**, original, novel 2 = **stimulating**, fresh, bracing, invigorating **OPPOSITE:** tiring

refreshment = **food and drink**, drinks, snacks, titbits, kai (*N.Z. informal*)

refuge 1 = **protection**, shelter, asylum 2 = **haven**, retreat, sanctuary, hide-out

refugee = **exile**, émigré, displaced person, escapee

refund NOUN 1 = **repayment**, reimbursement, return
▷ VERB 2 = **repay**, return, restore, pay back, reimburse

refurbish = **renovate**, restore, repair, clean up, overhaul, revamp, mend, do up (*informal*)

refusal = **rejection**, denial, rebuff, knock-back (*slang*)

refuse¹ 1 = **decline**, reject, turn down, say no to 2 = **deny**, decline, withhold **OPPOSITE:** allow

refuse² = **rubbish**, waste, junk (*informal*), litter, garbage (*chiefly U.S.*), trash

regain 1 = **recover**, get back, retrieve, recapture, win back, take back, recoup 2 = **get back to**, return to, reach again

r

regal = royal, majestic, kingly or queenly, noble, princely, magnificent

regard VERB 1 = consider, see, rate, view, judge, think of, esteem, deem 2 = look at, view, eye, watch, observe, clock (*Brit. slang*), check out (*informal*), gaze at
▷ NOUN 3 = respect, esteem, thought, concern, care, consideration 4 = look, gaze, scrutiny, stare, glance
▷ PLURAL NOUN 5 = good wishes, respects, greetings, compliments, best wishes
▷ PHRASES: as regards = concerning, regarding, relating to, pertaining to

● USAGE NOTE
● The word *regard* in the
● expression *with regard to* is
● singular, and has no *s* at the
● end. People often make the
● mistake of saying *with regards*
● *to*, perhaps being influenced
● by the phrase *as regards*.

regarding = concerning, about, on the subject of, re, respecting, as regards, with reference to, in or with regard to

regardless 1 = in spite of everything, anyway, nevertheless, in any case 2 with of = irrespective of, heedless of, unmindful of

regime 1 = government, rule, management, leadership, reign 2 = plan, course, system, policy, programme, scheme, regimen

region = area, place, part, quarter, section, sector, district, territory

regional = local, district, provincial, parochial, zonal

register NOUN 1 = list, record, roll, file, diary, catalogue, log, archives
▷ VERB 2 = enrol, enlist, list, note, enter 3 = record, catalogue, chronicle
4 = indicate, show 5 = show, mark, indicate, manifest
6 = express, show, reveal, display, exhibit

regret VERB 1 = be or feel sorry about, rue, deplore, bemoan, repent (of), bewail OPPOSITE: be satisfied with 2 = mourn, miss, grieve for or over
▷ NOUN 3 = remorse, compunction, bitterness, repentance, contrition, penitence 4 = sorrow, disappointment OPPOSITE: satisfaction

regular 1 = frequent, daily OPPOSITE: infrequent
2 = normal, common, usual, ordinary, typical, routine, customary, habitual
3 = steady, consistent
4 = even, level, balanced, straight, flat, fixed, smooth, uniform OPPOSITE: uneven

regulate 1 = control, run, rule, manage, direct, guide, handle, govern 2 = moderate, control, modulate, fit, tune, adjust

regulation 1 = rule, order, law,

dictate, decree, statute, edict, precept **2 = control**, government, management, direction, supervision

rehearsal = practice, rehearsing, run-through, preparation, drill

rehearse = practise, prepare, run through, go over, train, repeat, drill, recite

reign VERB **1 = be supreme**, prevail, predominate, hold sway **2 = rule**, govern, be in power, influence, command
▷ NOUN **3 = rule**, power, control, command, monarchy, dominion

● USAGE NOTE
● The words *rein* and *reign*
● should not be confused. Note
● the correct spellings in *he gave*
● *full rein to his feelings* (not
● *reign*), and it *will be necessary*
● *to rein in public spending* (not
● *reign in*).

rein = control, harness, bridle, hold, check, brake, curb, restraint

reincarnation = rebirth

reinforce 1 = support, strengthen, fortify, toughen, stress, prop, supplement, emphasize **2 = increase**, extend, add to, strengthen, supplement

reinforcement NOUN **1 = strengthening**, increase, fortification, augmentation **2 = support**, stay, prop, brace, buttress
▷ PLURAL NOUN **3 = reserves**, support, auxiliaries, additional or fresh troops

reinstate = restore, recall, re-establish, return

reiterate (*Formal*) **= repeat**, restate, say again, do again

reject VERB **1 = rebuff**, jilt, turn down, spurn, refuse, say no to, repulse OPPOSITE: accept **2 = deny**, exclude, veto, relinquish, renounce, disallow, forsake, disown OPPOSITE: approve **3 = discard**, decline, eliminate, scrap, jettison, throw away or out OPPOSITE: accept
▷ NOUN **4 = castoff**, second, discard OPPOSITE: treasure **5 = failure**, loser, flop

rejection 1 = denial, veto, dismissal, exclusion, disowning, thumbs down, renunciation, repudiation OPPOSITE: approval **2 = rebuff**, refusal, knock-back (*slang*), kick in the teeth (*slang*), brushoff (*slang*) OPPOSITE: acceptance

rejoice = be glad, celebrate, be happy, glory, be overjoyed, exult OPPOSITE: lament

rejoin = reply, answer, respond, retort, riposte

relate 1 = tell, recount, report, detail, describe, recite, narrate
▷ PHRASES: **relate to something** *or* **someone 1 = concern**, refer to, apply to, have to do with, pertain to, be relevant to **2 = connect with**, associate with, link with, couple

with, join with, correlate to

related 1 = **associated**, linked, joint, connected, affiliated, akin, interconnected **OPPOSITE:** unconnected **2** = **akin**, kindred **OPPOSITE:** unrelated

relation NOUN **1** = **similarity**, link, bearing, bond, comparison, correlation, connection **2** = **relative**, kin, kinsman or kinswoman
▷ **PLURAL NOUN 3** = **dealings**, relationship, affairs, contact, connections, interaction, intercourse **4** = **family**, relatives, tribe, clan, kin, kindred, kinsmen, kinsfolk, ainga (N.Z.)

relationship 1 = **association**, bond, connection, affinity, rapport, kinship **2** = **affair**, romance, liaison, amour, intrigue **3** = **connection**, link, parallel, similarity, tie-up, correlation

relative NOUN **1** = **relation**, kinsman or kinswoman, member of your or the family
▷ **ADJECTIVE 2** = **comparative**, reasonable **3** = **corresponding**, respective **4** = **in proportion to**, with **to** = **in proportion to**, proportionate to

relatively = **comparatively**, rather, somewhat

relax 1 = **be** or **feel at ease**, chill out (slang, chiefly U.S.), take it easy, lighten up (slang), outspan (S. African) **OPPOSITE:** be alarmed **2** = **calm down**, calm,

unwind **3** = **make less tense**, rest **4** = **lessen**, reduce, ease, relieve, weaken, loosen, let up, slacken **OPPOSITE:** tighten **5** = **moderate**, ease, relieve, weaken, slacken **OPPOSITE:** tighten up

relaxation = **leisure**, rest, fun, pleasure, recreation, enjoyment

relay = **broadcast**, carry, spread, communicate, transmit, send out

release VERB **1** = **set free**, free, discharge, liberate, drop, loose, undo, extricate **OPPOSITE:** imprison **2** = **acquit**, let go, let off, exonerate, absolve **3** = **issue**, publish, make public, make known, launch, distribute, put out, circulate **OPPOSITE:** withhold
▷ **NOUN 4** = **liberation**, freedom, liberty, discharge, emancipation, deliverance **OPPOSITE:** imprisonment **5** = **acquittal**, exemption, absolution, exoneration **6** = **issue**, publication, proclamation

relegate = **demote**, degrade, downgrade

relentless 1 = **merciless**, fierce, cruel, ruthless, unrelenting, implacable, remorseless, pitiless **OPPOSITE:** merciful **2** = **unremitting**, persistent, unrelenting, incessant, nonstop, unrelieved

relevant = **significant**, appropriate, related, fitting, to the point, apt, pertinent, apposite **OPPOSITE:** irrelevant

reliable 1 = **dependable**, trustworthy, sure, sound, true, faithful, staunch **OPPOSITE:** unreliable 2 = **safe**, dependable 3 = **definitive**, sound, dependable, trustworthy

reliance 1 = **dependency**, dependence 2 = **trust**, confidence, belief, faith

relic = **remnant**, vestige, memento, trace, fragment, souvenir, keepsake

relief 1 = **ease**, release, comfort, cure, remedy, solace, deliverance, mitigation 2 = **rest**, respite, relaxation, break, breather (*informal*) 3 = **aid**, help, support, assistance, succour

relieve 1 = **ease**, soothe, alleviate, relax, comfort, calm, cure, soften **OPPOSITE:** intensify 2 = **help**, support, aid, sustain, assist, succour (*formal*)

religion = **belief**, faith, theology, creed
▷ *See panel* RELIGION

religious 1 = **spiritual**, holy, sacred, devotional 2 = **conscientious**, faithful, rigid, meticulous, scrupulous, punctilious

relinquish (*Formal*) = **give up**, leave, drop, abandon, surrender, let go, renounce, forsake (*formal*)

relish VERB 1 = **enjoy**, like, savour, revel in **OPPOSITE:**
dislike 2 = **look forward to**, fancy, delight in
▷ NOUN 3 = **enjoyment**, liking, love, taste, fancy, penchant, fondness, gusto **OPPOSITE:** distaste 4 = **condiment**, seasoning, sauce

reluctance = **unwillingness**, dislike, loathing, distaste, aversion, disinclination, repugnance

reluctant = **unwilling**, hesitant, loath, disinclined, unenthusiastic **OPPOSITE:** willing

● **USAGE NOTE**
● *Reticent* is quite commonly
● used nowadays as a synonym
● of *reluctant* and followed by to
● and a verb. In careful writing
● it is advisable to avoid this
● use, since many people would
● regard it as mistaken.

rely on 1 = **depend on**, lean on 2 = **be confident of**, bank on, trust, count on, bet on

remain 1 = **stay**, continue, go on, stand, dwell 2 = **stay behind**, wait, delay **OPPOSITE:** go 3 = **continue**, be left, linger

remainder = **rest**, remains, balance, excess, surplus, remnant, residue, leavings

remains 1 = **remnants**, leftovers, rest, debris, residue, dregs, leavings 2 = **corpse**, body, carcass, cadaver 3 = **relics**

remark VERB 1 = **comment**, say, state, reflect, mention,

RELIGION
Religions

animism
Babi or Babism
Baha'ism
Buddhism
Christianity
Confucianism
druidism
heliolatry
Hinduism or Hindooism
Islam
Jainism

Judaism
Macumba
Manichaeism or Manicheism
Mithraism or Mithraicism
Orphism
paganism
Rastafarianism
Ryobu Shinto
Santeria
Satanism

Scientology ®
shamanism
Shango
Shembe
Shinto
Sikhism
Taoism
voodoo or voodooism
Yezidis
Zoroastrianism or Zoroastrism

Religious festivals

Advent
Al Hijrah
Ascension Day
Ash Wednesday
Baisakhi
Bodhi Day
Candlemas
Chanukah or Hanukkah
Ching Ming
Christmas
Corpus Christi
Day of Atonement
Dhammacakka
Diwali
Dragon Boat Festival
Dussehra
Easter
Eid ul-Adha or Id-ul-Adha
Eid ul-Fitr or Id-ul-Fitr

Epiphany
Feast of Tabernacles
Good Friday
Guru Nanak's Birthday
Hirja
Hola Mohalla
Holi
Janamashtami
Lailat ul-Barah
Lailat ul-Isra Wal Mi'raj
Lailat ul-Qadr
Lent
Mahashivaratri
Maundy Thursday
Michaelmas
Moon Festival
Palm Sunday
Passion Sunday
Passover

Pentecost
Pesach
Purim
Quadragesima
Quinquagesima
Raksha Bandhan
Ramadan
Rama Naumi
Rogation
Rosh Hashanah
Septuagesima
Sexagesima
Shavuot
Shrove Tuesday
Sukkoth or Succoth
Trinity
Wesak
Whitsuntide
Winter Festival
Yom Kippur
Yuan Tan

r

declare, observe, pass comment
2 = notice, note, observe, perceive, see, mark, make out, espy
▷ NOUN **3 = comment**, observation, reflection, statement, utterance
remarkable = extraordinary, striking, outstanding, wonderful, rare, unusual, surprising, notable OPPOSITE: ordinary
remedy NOUN **1 = cure**, treatment, medicine, nostrum
▷ VERB **2 = put right**, rectify, fix, correct, set to rights
remember 1 = recall, think back to, recollect, reminisce about, call to mind OPPOSITE: forget **2 = bear in mind**, keep in mind **3 = look back (on)**, commemorate
remembrance
1 = commemoration, memorial
2 = souvenir, token, reminder, monument, memento, keepsake **3 = memory**, recollection, thought, recall, reminiscence
remind = jog your memory, prompt, make you remember
reminiscent = suggestive, evocative, similar
remnant = remainder, remains, trace, fragment, end, rest, residue, leftovers
remorse = regret, shame, guilt, grief, sorrow, anguish, repentance, contrition
remote 1 = distant, far,

isolated, out-of-the-way, secluded, inaccessible, in the middle of nowhere OPPOSITE: nearby **2 = far**, distant **3 = slight**, small, outside, unlikely, slim, faint, doubtful, dubious OPPOSITE: strong **4 = aloof**, cold, reserved, withdrawn, distant, abstracted, detached, uncommunicative OPPOSITE: outgoing
removal 1 = extraction, withdrawal, uprooting, eradication, dislodgment, taking away or off or out **2 = dismissal**, expulsion, elimination, ejection **3 = move**, transfer, departure, relocation, flitting (Scot. & Northern English dialect)
remove 1 = take out, withdraw, extract OPPOSITE: insert **2 = take off**, doff OPPOSITE: put on **3 = erase**, eliminate, take out **4 = dismiss**, eliminate, get rid of, discharge, abolish, expel, throw out, oust OPPOSITE: appoint **5 = get rid of**, erase, eradicate, expunge (formal) **6 = take away**, detach, displace OPPOSITE: put back **7 = delete**, get rid of, erase, excise **8 = move**, depart, relocate, flit (Scot. & Northern English dialect)
renaissance or **renascence = rebirth**, revival, restoration, renewal, resurgence, reappearance, reawakening
rend (Literary) **= tear**, rip,

separate, wrench, rupture
render 1 = **make**, cause to
become, leave 2 = **provide**,
give, pay, present, supply,
submit, tender, hand out
3 = **represent**, portray, depict,
do, give, play, act, perform
renew 1 = **recommence**,
continue, extend, repeat,
resume, reopen, recreate,
reaffirm 2 = **reaffirm**, resume,
recommence 3 = **replace**,
refresh, replenish, restock
4 = **restore**, repair, overhaul,
mend, refurbish, renovate, refit,
modernize
renounce 1 = **disown**, quit,
forsake (*literary*), recant (*formal*),
forswear (*formal*), abjure (*formal*)
2 = **disclaim**, deny, give up,
relinquish, waive, abjure (*formal*)
OPPOSITE: assert
renovate = **restore**, repair,
refurbish, do up (*informal*),
renew, overhaul, refit,
modernize
renowned = **famous**, noted,
celebrated, well-known,
distinguished, esteemed,
notable, eminent **OPPOSITE:**
unknown
rent¹ VERB 1 = **hire**, lease
2 = **let**, lease
▷ NOUN 3 = **hire**, rental, lease,
fee, payment
rent² 1 = **tear**, split, rip, slash,
slit, gash, hole 2 = **opening**,
hole
repair VERB 1 = **mend**, fix,
restore, heal, patch, renovate,

patch up **OPPOSITE:** damage
2 = **put right**, make up for,
compensate for, rectify, redress
▷ NOUN 3 = **mend**, restoration,
overhaul 4 = **darn**, mend,
patch 5 = **condition**, state,
form, shape (*informal*)
repay = **pay back**, refund, settle
up, return, square, compensate,
reimburse, recompense
repeal VERB 1 = **abolish**,
reverse, revoke, annul, recall,
cancel, invalidate, nullify
OPPOSITE: pass
▷ NOUN 2 = **abolition**,
cancellation, annulment,
invalidation, rescindment
OPPOSITE: passing
repeat VERB 1 = **reiterate**,
restate 2 = **retell**, echo, replay,
reproduce, rerun, reshow
▷ NOUN 3 = **repetition**, echo,
reiteration 4 = **rerun**, replay,
reshowing
● **USAGE NOTE**
● Since the sense of *again* is
● already contained within the
● *re-* part of the word *repeat*, it
● is unnecessary to say that
● something is *repeated again*.
repeatedly = **over and over**,
often, frequently, many times
repel 1 = **drive off**, fight, resist,
parry, hold off, rebuff, ward off,
repulse **OPPOSITE:** submit to
2 = **disgust**, offend, revolt,
sicken, nauseate, gross out (*U.S.
slang*) **OPPOSITE:** delight
repertoire = **range**, list, stock,
supply, store, collection,

repertory, repository

repetition 1 = **recurrence**, repeating, echo 2 = **repeating**, replication, restatement, reiteration, tautology

replace 1 = **take the place of**, follow, succeed, oust, take over from, supersede, supplant 2 = **substitute**, change, exchange, switch, swap 3 = **put back**, restore

replacement 1 = **replacing** 2 = **successor**, double, substitute, stand-in, proxy, surrogate, understudy

replica 1 = **reproduction**, model, copy, imitation, facsimile, carbon copy **OPPOSITE:** original 2 = **duplicate**, copy, carbon copy

replicate = **copy**, reproduce, recreate, mimic, duplicate, reduplicate

reply VERB 1 = **answer**, respond, retort, counter, rejoin, retaliate, reciprocate ▷ NOUN 2 = **answer**, response, reaction, counter, retort, retaliation, counterattack, rejoinder

report VERB 1 = **inform of**, communicate, recount 2 *often with* on = **communicate**, tell, state, detail, describe, relate, broadcast, pass on 3 = **present yourself**, come, appear, arrive, turn up ▷ NOUN 4 = **article**, story, piece, write-up 5 = **account**, record, statement, communication, description, narrative 6 *often plural* = **news**, word 7 = **bang**, sound, crack, noise, blast, boom, explosion, discharge 8 = **rumour**, talk, buzz, gossip, hearsay

reporter = **journalist**, writer, correspondent, hack (*derogatory*), pressman, journo (*slang*)

represent 1 = **act for**, speak for 2 = **stand for**, serve as 3 = **express**, correspond to, symbolize, mean 4 = **exemplify**, embody, symbolize, typify, personify, epitomize 5 = **depict**, show, describe, picture, illustrate, outline, portray, denote

representation 1 = **picture**, model, image, portrait, illustration, likeness 2 = **portrayal**, depiction, account, description

representative NOUN 1 = **delegate**, member, agent, deputy, proxy, spokesman *or* spokeswoman 2 = **agent**, salesman, rep, commercial traveller ▷ ADJECTIVE 3 = **typical**, characteristic, archetypal, exemplary **OPPOSITE:** uncharacteristic 4 = **symbolic**

repress 1 = **control**, suppress, hold back, bottle up, check, curb, restrain, inhibit **OPPOSITE:** release 2 = **hold back**, suppress, stifle 3 = **subdue**, abuse, wrong, persecute, quell, subjugate, maltreat **OPPOSITE:** liberate

repression 1 = subjugation, control, constraint, domination, tyranny, despotism
2 = suppression, crushing, quashing 3 = inhibition, control, restraint, bottling up

reprieve VERB 1 = grant a stay of execution to, pardon, let off the hook (*slang*)
▷ NOUN 2 = stay of execution, amnesty, pardon, remission, deferment, postponement of punishment

reproduce 1 = copy, recreate, replicate, duplicate, match, mirror, echo, imitate 2 = print, copy 3 (*Biology*) = breed, procreate, multiply, spawn, propagate

reproduction 1 = copy, picture, print, replica, imitation, duplicate, facsimile **OPPOSITE:** original 2 (*Biology*) = breeding, increase, generation, multiplication

reptile ▷ *See panel* REPTILES

Republican ADJECTIVE
1 = right-wing, Conservative
▷ NOUN 2 = right-winger, Conservative

reputation = name, standing, character, esteem, stature, renown, repute

request VERB 1 = ask for, appeal for, put in for, demand, desire 2 = invite, entreat
3 = seek, ask (for), solicit

▷ NOUN 4 = appeal, call, demand, plea, desire, entreaty, suit 5 = asking, plea

require 1 = need, crave, want, miss, lack, wish, desire
2 = order, demand, command, compel, exact, oblige, call upon, insist upon 3 = ask

● USAGE NOTE
● The use of *require to* as in *I*
● *require to see the manager* or
● *you require to complete a special*
● *form* is thought by many
● people to be incorrect. Useful
● alternatives are: *I need to see*
● *the manager* and *you are*
● *required to complete a special*
● *form*.

requirement = necessity, demand, stipulation, want, need, must, essential, prerequisite

rescue VERB 1 = save, get out, release, deliver, recover, liberate **OPPOSITE:** desert 2 = salvage, deliver, redeem
▷ NOUN 3 = saving, salvage, deliverance, release, recovery, liberation, salvation, redemption

research NOUN
1 = investigation, study, analysis, examination, probe, exploration
▷ VERB 2 = investigate, study, examine, explore, probe, analyse

resemblance = similarity, correspondence, parallel, likeness, kinship, sameness,

REPTILES

adder
agama
agamid
alligator
amphisbaena
anaconda or (Caribbean) camoodi
asp
bandy-bandy
black snake or red-bellied black snake
blind snake
blue tongue
boa
boa constrictor
box turtle
brown snake or (Austral.) mallee snake
bull snake or gopher snake
bushmaster
carpet snake or python
cayman or caiman
chameleon
chuckwalla
cobra
constrictor
copperhead
coral snake
crocodile
death adder or deaf adder
diamondback, diamondback terrapin, or diamondback turtle
diamond snake or diamond python
elapid
fer-de-lance
frill-necked lizard, frilled lizard, bicycle lizard, cycling lizard, or (Austral. informal) frillie
gaboon viper
garter snake
gecko
giant tortoise
Gila monster
glass snake
goanna, bungarra (Austral.), or go (Austral. informal)
grass snake
green turtle
harlequin snake
hawksbill or hawksbill turtle
hognose snake or puff adder
horned toad or lizard
horned viper
iguana
jew lizard, bearded lizard, or bearded dragon
king cobra or hamadryad
king snake
Komodo dragon or Komodo lizard
krait
leatherback or (Brit.) leathery turtle
lizard
loggerhead or loggerhead turtle
mamba
massasauga
milk snake
monitor
mud turtle
ngarara (N.Z.)

r

REPTILES *continued*	
perentie *or* perenty	smooth snake
pit viper	snake
puff adder	snapping turtle
python	soft-shelled turtle
rat snake	taipan
rattlesnake *or (U.S. & Canad.*	terrapin
informal) rattler	tiger snake
rock snake, rock python,	tokay
amethystine python, *or*	tortoise
Schneider python	tree snake
saltwater crocodile *or*	tuatara *or (technical)*
(Austral. informal) saltie	sphenodon *(N.Z.)*
sand lizard	turtle
sand viper	viper
sea snake	wall lizard
sidewinder	water moccasin, moccasin,
skink	*or* cottonmouth
slowworm *or*	water snake
blindworm	whip snake

similitude **OPPOSITE:**
dissimilarity

resemble = be like, look like,
mirror, parallel, be similar to,
bear a resemblance to

resent = be bitter about, object
to, grudge, begrudge, take
exception to, take offence at
OPPOSITE: be content with

resentment = bitterness,
indignation, ill feeling, ill will,
grudge, animosity, pique,
rancour

reservation 1 *often plural*
= doubt, scruples, hesitancy
2 = reserve, territory, preserve,
sanctuary

reserve VERB 1 = book,
prearrange, engage 2 = put by,

secure 3 = keep, hold, save,
store, retain, set aside,
stockpile, hoard
▷ NOUN 4 = store, fund,
savings, stock, supply, reservoir,
hoard, cache 5 = park,
reservation, preserve,
sanctuary, tract, forest park
(N.Z.) 6 = shyness, silence,
restraint, constraint, reticence,
secretiveness, taciturnity
7 = reservation, doubt, delay,
uncertainty, indecision,
hesitancy, vacillation,
irresolution
▷ ADJECTIVE 8 = substitute,
extra, spare, secondary, fall-
back, auxiliary

reserved

1 = **uncommunicative**, retiring, silent, shy, restrained, secretive, reticent, taciturn **OPPOSITE:** uninhibited 2 = **set aside**, taken, kept, held, booked, retained, engaged, restricted

reservoir 1 = **lake**, pond, basin 2 = **store**, stock, source, supply, reserves, pool

reside (*Formal*) = **live**, lodge, dwell, stay, abide **OPPOSITE:** visit

residence = **home**, house, dwelling, place, flat, lodging, abode, habitation

resident 1 = **inhabitant**, citizen, local **OPPOSITE:** nonresident 2 = **tenant**, occupant, lodger 3 = **guest**, lodger

residue = **remainder**, remains, remnant, leftovers, rest, extra, excess, surplus

resign 1 = **quit**, leave, step down (*informal*), vacate, abdicate, give or hand in your notice 2 = **give up**, abandon, yield, surrender, relinquish, renounce, forsake, forgo ▷ **PHRASES: resign yourself to something** = **accept**, succumb to, submit to, give in to, yield to, acquiesce to

resignation 1 = **leaving**, departure, abandonment, abdication 2 = **acceptance**, patience, submission, compliance, endurance, passivity, acquiescence, sufferance **OPPOSITE:** resistance

resigned = **stoical**, patient, subdued, long-suffering, compliant, unresisting

resist 1 = **oppose**, battle against, combat, defy, stand up to, hinder **OPPOSITE:** accept 2 = **refrain from**, avoid, keep from, forgo, abstain from, forbear **OPPOSITE:** indulge in 3 = **withstand**, be proof against

resistance 1 = **opposition**, hostility, aversion 2 = **fighting**, fight, battle, struggle, defiance, obstruction, impediment, hindrance

resistant 1 = **opposed**, hostile, unwilling, intractable, antagonistic, intransigent 2 = **impervious**, hard, strong, tough, unaffected

resolution 1 = **declaration** 2 = **decision**, resolve, intention, aim, purpose, determination, intent 3 = **determination**, purpose, resolve, tenacity, perseverance, willpower, firmness, steadfastness

resolve VERB 1 = **work out**, answer, clear up, crack, fathom 2 = **decide**, determine, agree, purpose, intend, fix, conclude ▷ NOUN 3 = **determination**, resolution, willpower, firmness, steadfastness, resoluteness **OPPOSITE:** indecision 4 = **decision**, resolution, objective, purpose, intention

resort 1 = **holiday centre**, spot, retreat, haunt, tourist centre 2 = **recourse to**, reference to

r

resound 1 = echo, resonate, reverberate, re-echo **2** = ring

resounding = echoing, full, ringing, powerful, booming, reverberating, resonant, sonorous

resource NOUN **1** = facility **2** = means, course, resort, device, expedient
▷ PLURAL NOUN **3** = funds, holdings, money, capital, riches, assets, wealth **4** = reserves, supplies, stocks

respect VERB **1** = think highly of, value, honour, admire, esteem, look up to, defer to, have a good or high opinion of **2** = show consideration for, honour, observe, heed **3** = abide by, follow, observe, comply with, obey, heed, keep to, adhere to **OPPOSITE:** disregard
▷ NOUN **4** = regard, honour, recognition, esteem, admiration, estimation **OPPOSITE:** contempt **5** = consideration, kindness, deference, tact, thoughtfulness, considerateness **6** = particular, way, point, matter, sense, detail, feature, aspect

respectable 1 = honourable, good, decent, worthy, upright, honest, reputable, estimable **OPPOSITE:** disreputable **2** = decent, neat, spruce **3** = reasonable, considerable, substantial, fair, ample, appreciable, sizable or sizeable **OPPOSITE:** paltry

respective = specific, own, individual, particular, relevant

respite = pause, break, rest, relief, halt, interval, recess, lull

respond 1 = answer, return, reply, counter, retort, rejoin **OPPOSITE:** remain silent **2** often with to = reply to, answer **3** = react, retaliate, reciprocate

response 1 = answer, return, reply, reaction, feedback, retort, counterattack, rejoinder

responsibility 1 = duty, business, job, role, task, accountability, answerability **2** = fault, blame, liability, guilt, culpability **3** = obligation, duty, liability, charge, care **4** = authority, power, importance, mana (N.Z.) **5** = job, task, function, role **6** = level-headedness, rationality, dependability, trustworthiness, conscientiousness, sensibleness

responsible 1 = to blame, guilty, at fault, culpable **2** = in charge, in control, in authority **3** = accountable, liable, answerable **OPPOSITE:** unaccountable **4** = sensible, reliable, rational, dependable, trustworthy, level-headed **OPPOSITE:** unreliable

responsive = sensitive, open, alive, susceptible, receptive, reactive, impressionable **OPPOSITE:** unresponsive

rest¹ VERB **1** = relax, take it

easy, sit down, be at ease, put your feet up, outspan (*S. African*) **OPPOSITE:** work 2 = **stop**, have a break, break off, take a breather (*informal*), halt, cease **OPPOSITE:** keep going
3 = **place**, repose, sit, lean, prop
4 = **be placed**, sit, lie, be supported, recline
▷ NOUN 5 = **relaxation**, repose, leisure **OPPOSITE:** work
6 = **pause**, break, stop, halt, interval, respite, lull, interlude
7 = **refreshment**, release, relief, ease, comfort, cure, remedy, solace 8 = **inactivity**
9 = **support**, stand, base, holder, prop 10 = **calm**, tranquillity, stillness

rest² = **remainder**, remains, excess, remnants, others, balance, surplus, residue

restaurant = **café**, diner (*chiefly U.S. & Canad.*), bistro, cafeteria, tearoom, eatery *or* eaterie

restless 1 = **unsettled**, nervous, edgy, fidgeting, on edge, restive (*formal*), jumpy, fidgety **OPPOSITE:** relaxed
2 = **moving**, wandering, unsettled, unstable, roving, transient, nomadic **OPPOSITE:** settled

restoration
1 = **reinstatement**, return, revival, restitution, re-establishment, replacement **OPPOSITE:** abolition 2 = **repair**, reconstruction, renewal, renovation, revitalization

OPPOSITE: demolition

restore 1 = **reinstate**, re-establish, reintroduce **OPPOSITE:** abolish 2 = **revive**, build up, strengthen, refresh, revitalize **OPPOSITE:** make worse 3 = **re-establish**, replace, reinstate, give back
4 = **repair**, refurbish, renovate, reconstruct, fix (up), renew, rebuild, mend **OPPOSITE:** demolish 5 = **return**, replace, recover, bring back, send back, hand back

restrain 1 = **hold back**, control, check, contain, restrict, curb, hamper, hinder **OPPOSITE:** encourage 2 = **control**, inhibit

restrained 1 = **controlled**, moderate, self-controlled, calm, mild, undemonstrative **OPPOSITE:** hot-headed
2 = **unobtrusive**, discreet, subdued, tasteful, quiet **OPPOSITE:** garish

restraint 1 = **limitation**, limit, check, ban, embargo, curb, rein, interdict **OPPOSITE:** freedom
2 = **self-control**, self-discipline, self-restraint, self-possession **OPPOSITE:** self-indulgence
3 = **constraint**, limitation, inhibition, control, restriction

restrict 1 = **limit**, regulate, curb, ration **OPPOSITE:** widen
2 = **hamper**, handicap, restrain, inhibit

restriction 1 = **control**, rule, regulation, curb, restraint, confinement 2 = **limitation**,

r

handicap, inhibition, limit

result NOUN 1 = **consequence**, effect, outcome, end result, product, sequel, upshot **OPPOSITE:** cause 2 = **outcome**, end

▷ VERB 3 = **arise**, follow, issue, happen, appear, develop, spring, derive

resume = **begin again**, continue, go on with, proceed with, carry on, reopen, restart **OPPOSITE:** discontinue

résumé = **summary**, synopsis, précis, rundown, recapitulation

resumption = **continuation**, carrying on, reopening, renewal, restart, resurgence, re-establishment

resurgence = **revival**, return, renaissance, resurrection, resumption, rebirth, re-emergence

resurrect 1 = **revive**, renew, bring back, reintroduce 2 = **restore to life**, raise from the dead

resurrection 1 = **revival**, restoration, renewal, resurgence, return, renaissance, rebirth, reappearance **OPPOSITE:** killing off 2 usually caps = **raising** or **rising from the dead**, return from the dead **OPPOSITE:** demise

retain 1 = **maintain**, reserve, preserve, keep up, continue to have 2 = **keep**, save **OPPOSITE:** let go

retaliate = **pay someone back**, hit back, strike back, reciprocate, take revenge, get even with (informal), get your own back (informal) **OPPOSITE:** turn the other cheek

retaliation = **revenge**, repayment, vengeance, reprisal, an eye for an eye, reciprocation, requital, counterblow

retard = **slow down**, check, arrest, delay, handicap, hinder, impede, set back **OPPOSITE:** speed up

retire 1 = **stop working**, give up work 2 = **withdraw**, leave, exit, go away, depart 3 = **go to bed**, turn in (informal), hit the sack (slang), hit the hay (slang)

retirement = **withdrawal**, retreat, privacy, solitude, seclusion

retiring = **shy**, reserved, quiet, timid, unassuming, self-effacing, bashful, unassertive **OPPOSITE:** outgoing

retort VERB 1 = **reply**, return, answer, respond, counter, come back with, riposte

▷ NOUN 2 = **reply**, answer, response, comeback, riposte, rejoinder

retreat VERB 1 = **withdraw**, back off, draw back, leave, go back, depart, fall back, pull back **OPPOSITE:** advance

▷ NOUN 2 = **flight**, retirement, departure, withdrawal, evacuation **OPPOSITE:** advance 3 = **refuge**, haven, shelter, sanctuary, hideaway, seclusion

retrieve 1 = get back, regain, recover, restore, recapture **2** = redeem, save, win back, recoup

retrospect = hindsight, review, re-examination **OPPOSITE:** foresight

return VERB **1** = come back, go back, retreat, turn back, revert, reappear **OPPOSITE:** depart **2** = put back, replace, restore, reinstate **OPPOSITE:** keep **3** = give back, repay, refund, pay back, reimburse, recompense **OPPOSITE:** keep **4** = recur, repeat, persist, revert, happen again, reappear, come again **5** = elect, choose, vote in ▷ NOUN **6** = reappearance, homecoming **OPPOSITE:** departure **7** = restoration, reinstatement, re-establishment **OPPOSITE:** removal **8** = recurrence, repetition, reappearance, reversion, persistence **9** = profit, interest, gain, income, revenue, yield, proceeds, takings **10** = statement, report, form, list, account, summary

revamp = renovate, restore, overhaul, refurbish, do up (informal), recondition

reveal 1 = make known, disclose, give away, make public, tell, announce, proclaim, let out (informal) **OPPOSITE:** keep secret **2** = show, display, exhibit, unveil, uncover, manifest, unearth, unmask **OPPOSITE:** hide

revel VERB **1** = celebrate, carouse, live it up (informal), make merry ▷ NOUN **2** often plural = merrymaking, party, celebration, spree, festivity, carousal

revelation 1 = disclosure, news, announcement, publication, leak, confession, divulgence **2** = exhibition, publication, exposure, unveiling, uncovering, unearthing, proclamation

revenge NOUN **1** = retaliation, vengeance, reprisal, retribution, an eye for an eye ▷ VERB **2** = avenge, repay, take revenge for, get your own back for (informal)

revenue = income, returns, profits, gain, yield, proceeds, receipts, takings **OPPOSITE:** expenditure

revere = be in awe of, respect, honour, worship, reverence, exalt, look up to, venerate **OPPOSITE:** despise

reverse VERB **1** (Law) = change, cancel, overturn, overthrow, undo, repeal, quash, revoke **OPPOSITE:** implement **2** = turn round, turn over, turn upside down, upend **3** = transpose, change, move, exchange, transfer, switch, shift, alter **4** = go backwards,

retreat, back up, turn back, move backwards, back **OPPOSITE:** go forward
▷ NOUN 5 = **opposite**, contrary, converse, inverse
6 = **misfortune**, blow, failure, disappointment, setback, hardship, reversal, adversity
7 = **back**, rear, other side, wrong side, underside **OPPOSITE:** front
▷ ADJECTIVE 8 = **opposite**, contrary, converse

revert 1 = **go back**, return, come back, resume 2 = **return**
● USAGE NOTE
● Since the concept *back* is
● already contained in the *re-*
● part of the word *revert*, it is
● unnecessary to say that
● someone *reverts back* to a
● particular type of behaviour.

review NOUN 1 = **survey**, study, analysis, examination, scrutiny 2 = **critique**, commentary, evaluation, notice, criticism, judgment 3 = **inspection**, parade, march past 4 = **magazine**, journal, periodical, zine (*informal*)
▷ VERB 5 = **reconsider**, revise, rethink, reassess, re-examine, re-evaluate, think over
6 = **assess**, study, judge, evaluate, criticize 7 = **inspect**, check, survey, examine, vet
8 = **look back on**, remember, recall, reflect on, recollect

reviewer = **critic**, judge, commentator

revise 1 = **change**, review
2 = **edit**, correct, alter, update, amend, rework, redo, emend
3 = **study**, go over, run through, cram (*informal*), swot up on (*Brit. informal*)

revision 1 = **emendation**, updating, correction
2 = **change**, amendment
3 = **studying**, cramming (*informal*), swotting (*Brit. informal*), homework

revival 1 = **resurgence**, improvement **OPPOSITE:** decline
2 = **reawakening**, renaissance, renewal, resurrection, rebirth, revitalization

revive 1 = **revitalize**, restore, renew, rekindle, invigorate, reanimate 2 = **bring round**, awaken 3 = **come round**, recover 4 = **refresh**, reinvigorate **OPPOSITE:** exhaust

revolt NOUN 1 = **uprising**, rising, revolution, rebellion, mutiny, insurrection, insurgency
▷ VERB 2 = **rebel**, rise up, resist, mutiny 3 = **disgust**, sicken, repel, repulse, nauseate, gross out (*U.S. slang*), turn your stomach (*informal*), make your flesh creep (*informal*)

revolting = **disgusting**, foul, horrible, sickening, horrid, repellent, repulsive, nauseating, yucko (*Austral. slang*) **OPPOSITE:** delightful

revolution 1 = **revolt**, rising, coup, rebellion, uprising,

mutiny, insurgency
2 = **transformation**, shift, innovation, upheaval, reformation, sea change
3 = **rotation**, turn, cycle, circle, spin, lap, circuit, orbit

revolutionary ADJECTIVE

1 = **rebel**, radical, extremist, subversive, insurgent OPPOSITE: reactionary

2 = **innovative**, new, different, novel, radical, progressive, drastic, ground-breaking OPPOSITE: conventional
▷ NOUN **3** = **rebel**, insurgent, revolutionist OPPOSITE: reactionary

revolve 1 = **go round**, circle, orbit **2** = **rotate**, turn, wheel, spin, twist, whirl

reward NOUN

1 = **punishment**, retribution, comeuppance (slang), just deserts **2** = **payment**, return, prize, wages, compensation, bonus, premium, repayment OPPOSITE: penalty
▷ VERB **3** = **compensate**, pay, repay, recompense, remunerate OPPOSITE: penalize

rewarding = **satisfying**, fulfilling, valuable, profitable, productive, worthwhile, beneficial, enriching OPPOSITE: unrewarding

rhetoric 1 = **hyperbole**, bombast, wordiness, verbosity, grandiloquence, magniloquence **2** = **oratory**, eloquence, public speaking, speech-making,

elocution, declamation, grandiloquence, whaikorero (N.Z.)

rhetorical = **high-flown**, bombastic, verbose, oratorical, grandiloquent, declamatory, arty-farty (informal), magniloquent

rhyme = **poem**, song, verse, ode

rhythm 1 = **beat**, swing, accent, pulse, tempo, cadence, lilt **2** = **metre**, time

rich 1 = **wealthy**, affluent, well-off, loaded (slang), prosperous, well-heeled (informal), well-to-do, moneyed OPPOSITE: poor **2** = **well-stocked**, full, productive, ample, abundant, plentiful, copious, well-supplied OPPOSITE: scarce **3** = **full-bodied**, sweet, fatty, tasty, creamy, luscious, succulent OPPOSITE: bland **4** = **fruitful**, productive, fertile, prolific OPPOSITE: barren **5** = **abounding**, luxurious, lush, abundant

riches 1 = **wealth**, assets, plenty, fortune, substance, treasure, affluence OPPOSITE: poverty **2** = **resources**, treasures

richly 1 = **elaborately**, lavishly, elegantly, splendidly, exquisitely, expensively, luxuriously, gorgeously **2** = **fully**, well, thoroughly, amply, appropriately, properly, suitably

rid = **free**, clear, deliver, relieve,

purge, unburden, make free, disencumber
▷ **PHRASES: get rid of something** or **someone** = **dispose of**, throw away or out, dump (*informal*), remove, eliminate, expel, eject

riddle¹ 1 = **puzzle**, problem, conundrum, poser **2** = **enigma**, question, secret, mystery, puzzle, conundrum, teaser, problem

riddle² 1 = **pierce**, pepper, puncture, perforate, honeycomb **2** = **pervade**, fill, spread through

riddled = **filled**, spoilt, pervaded, infested, permeated

ride VERB **1** = **control**, handle, manage **2** = **travel**, be carried, go, move
▷ NOUN **3** = **journey**, drive, trip, lift, outing, jaunt

ridicule VERB **1** = **laugh at**, mock, make fun of, sneer at, jeer at, deride, poke fun at, chaff
▷ NOUN **2** = **mockery**, scorn, derision, laughter, jeer, chaff, gibe, raillery

ridiculous = **laughable**, stupid, silly, absurd, ludicrous, farcical, comical, risible **OPPOSITE:** sensible

rife = **widespread**, rampant, general, common, universal, frequent, prevalent, ubiquitous

rifle = **ransack**, rob, burgle, loot, strip, sack, plunder, pillage

rift 1 = **breach**, division, split, separation, falling out (*informal*), disagreement, quarrel **2** = **split**, opening, crack, gap, break, fault, flaw, cleft

rig 1 = **fix**, engineer (*informal*), arrange, manipulate, tamper with, gerrymander **2** (*Nautical*) = **equip**, fit out, kit out, outfit, supply, furnish
▷ **PHRASES: rig something up** = **set up**, build, construct, put up, arrange, assemble, put together, erect

right ADJECTIVE **1** = **correct**, true, genuine, accurate, exact, precise, valid, factual, dinkum (*Austral. & N.Z. informal*) **OPPOSITE:** wrong **2** = **proper**, done, becoming, seemly, fitting, fit, appropriate, suitable **OPPOSITE:** inappropriate **3** = **just**, good, fair, moral, proper, ethical, honest, equitable **OPPOSITE:** unfair
▷ ADVERB **4** = **correctly**, truly, precisely, exactly, genuinely, accurately **OPPOSITE:** wrongly **5** = **suitably**, fittingly, appropriately, properly, aptly **OPPOSITE:** improperly **6** = **exactly**, squarely, precisely **7** = **directly**, straight, precisely, exactly, unswervingly, without deviation, by the shortest route, in a beeline **8** = **straight**, directly, quickly, promptly, straightaway **OPPOSITE:** indirectly
▷ NOUN **9** = **prerogative**,

business, power, claim, authority, due, freedom, licence **10** = **justice**, truth, fairness, legality, righteousness, lawfulness **OPPOSITE:** injustice
▷ VERB **11** = **rectify**, settle, fix, correct, sort out, straighten, redress, put right

right away = **immediately**, now, directly, instantly, at once, straightaway, forthwith, pronto (*informal*)

righteous = **virtuous**, good, just, fair, moral, pure, ethical, upright **OPPOSITE:** wicked

rigid 1 = **strict**, set, fixed, exact, rigorous, stringent **OPPOSITE:** flexible **2** = **inflexible**, uncompromising, unbending **3** = **stiff**, inflexible, inelastic **OPPOSITE:** pliable

rigorous = **strict**, hard, demanding, tough, severe, exacting, harsh, stern **OPPOSITE:** soft

rim 1 = **edge**, lip, brim **2** = **border**, edge, trim **3** = **margin**, border, verge, brink

ring¹ VERB **1** = **phone**, call, telephone, buzz (*informal, chiefly Brit.*) **2** = **chime**, sound, toll, reverberate, clang, peal **3** = **reverberate**, echo
▷ NOUN **4** = **call**, phone call, buzz (*informal, chiefly Brit.*) **5** = **chime**, knell, peal
● USAGE NOTE
● *Rang* is the past tense of the verb *ring*, as in *he rang the bell*.
● *Rung* is the past participle, as

● in *he has already rung the bell*,
● and care should be taken not
● to use it as if it were a variant
● form of the past tense.

ring² NOUN **1** = **circle**, round, band, circuit, loop, hoop, halo **2** = **arena**, enclosure, circus, rink **3** = **gang**, group, association, band, circle, mob, syndicate, cartel
▷ VERB **4** = **encircle**, surround, enclose, girdle, gird

rinse VERB **1** = **wash**, clean, dip, splash, cleanse, bathe
▷ NOUN **2** = **wash**, dip, splash, bath

riot NOUN **1** = **disturbance**, disorder, confusion, turmoil, upheaval, strife, turbulence, lawlessness **2** = **display**, show, splash, extravaganza, profusion **3** = **laugh**, joke, scream (*informal*), hoot (*informal*), lark (*informal*)
▷ VERB **4** = **rampage**, run riot, go on the rampage
▷ PHRASES: **run riot**
1 = **rampage**, go wild, be out of control **2** = **grow profusely**, spread like wildfire

rip VERB **1** = **tear**, cut, split, burst, rend, slash, claw, slit **2** = **be torn**, tear, split, burst
▷ NOUN **3** = **tear**, cut, hole, split, rent, slash, slit, gash
▷ PHRASES: **rip someone off**
(*Slang*) = **cheat**, rob, con (*informal*), skin (*slang*), fleece (*informal*), defraud, swindle

ripe 1 = **ripened**, seasoned,

ready, mature, mellow
OPPOSITE: unripe 2 = **right**,
suitable 3 = **mature**, old
4 = **suitable**, timely, ideal,
favourable, auspicious,
opportune **OPPOSITE:**
unsuitable

rip-off or **ripoff** (Slang) = **cheat**,
con (informal), scam (slang), con
trick (informal), fraud, theft,
swindle

rise VERB 1 = **get up**, stand up,
get to your feet 2 = **arise**
3 = **go up**, climb, ascend
OPPOSITE: descend 4 = **loom**,
tower 5 = **get steeper**, ascend,
go uphill, slope upwards
OPPOSITE: drop 6 = **increase**,
mount **OPPOSITE:** decrease
7 = **grow**, go up, intensify
8 = **rebel**, revolt, mutiny
9 = **advance**, progress, get on,
prosper
▷ NOUN 10 = **upward slope**,
incline, elevation, ascent, kopje
or koppie (S. African)
11 = **increase**, upturn, upswing,
upsurge **OPPOSITE:** decrease
12 = **pay increase**, raise (chiefly
U.S.), increment
13 = **advancement**, progress,
climb, promotion
▷ PHRASES: **give rise to
something** = **cause**, produce,
effect, result in, bring about

risk NOUN 1 = **danger**, chance,
possibility, hazard 2 = **gamble**,
chance, speculation, leap in the
dark 3 = **peril**, jeopardy
▷ VERB 4 = **stand a chance of**,

venture 5 = **dare**, endanger,
jeopardize, imperil, venture,
gamble, hazard

risky = **dangerous**, hazardous,
unsafe, perilous, uncertain,
dodgy (Brit., Austral. & N.Z.
informal), dicey (informal, chiefly
Brit.), chancy (informal)
OPPOSITE: safe

rite = **ceremony**, custom, ritual,
practice, procedure, observance

ritual NOUN 1 = **ceremony**,
rite, observance 2 = **custom**,
tradition, routine, convention,
practice, procedure, habit,
protocol, tikanga (N.Z.)
▷ ADJECTIVE 3 = **ceremonial**,
conventional, routine,
customary, habitual

rival NOUN 1 = **opponent**,
competitor, contender,
contestant, adversary
OPPOSITE: supporter
▷ VERB 2 = **compete with**,
match, equal, compare with,
come up to, be a match for
▷ ADJECTIVE 3 = **competing**,
conflicting, opposing

rivalry = **competition**,
opposition, conflict, contest,
contention

river 1 = **stream**, brook, creek,
waterway, tributary, burn (Scot.)
2 = **flow**, rush, flood, spate,
torrent

riveting = **enthralling**,
gripping, fascinating,
absorbing, captivating,
hypnotic, engrossing,
spellbinding

r

road 1 = **roadway**, highway, motorway, track, route, path, lane, pathway 2 = **way**, path

roam = **wander**, walk, range, travel, stray, ramble, prowl, rove

roar VERB 1 = **thunder** 2 = **guffaw**, laugh heartily, hoot, split your sides (*informal*) 3 = **cry**, shout, yell, howl, bellow, bawl, bay
▷ NOUN 4 = **guffaw**, hoot 5 = **cry**, shout, yell, howl, outcry, bellow

rob 1 = **steal from**, hold up, mug (*informal*) 2 = **raid**, hold up, loot, plunder, burgle, pillage 3 = **dispossess**, con (*informal*), cheat, defraud 4 = **deprive**, do out of (*informal*)

robber = **thief**, raider, burglar, looter, fraud, cheat, bandit, plunderer

robbery 1 = **burglary**, raid, hold-up, rip-off (*slang*), stick-up (*slang, chiefly U.S.*) 2 = **theft**, stealing, mugging (*informal*), plunder, swindle, pillage, larceny

robe = **gown**, costume, habit

robot = **machine**, automaton, android, mechanical man

robust = **strong**, tough, powerful, fit, healthy, strapping, hardy, vigorous OPPOSITE: weak

rock[1] = **stone**, boulder

rock[2] 1 = **sway**, pitch, swing, reel, toss, lurch, roll 2 = **shock**, surprise, shake, stun, astonish, stagger, astound

rocky[1] = **rough**, rugged, stony, craggy, boulder-strewn

rocky[2] = **unstable**, shaky, wobbly, rickety, unsteady

rod 1 = **stick**, bar, pole, shaft, cane 2 = **staff**, baton, wand

rodent ▷ See panel RODENTS

rogue 1 = **scoundrel**, crook (*informal*), villain, fraud, blackguard, skelm (*S. African*), rorter (*Austral. slang*) 2 = **scamp**, rascal, scally (*Northwest English dialect*), nointer (*Austral. slang*)

role 1 = **job**, part, position, post, task, duty, function, capacity 2 = **part**, character, representation, portrayal

roll VERB 1 = **turn**, wheel, spin, go round, revolve, rotate, whirl, swivel 2 = **trundle**, go, move 3 = **flow**, run, course 4 *often with* up = **wind**, bind, wrap, swathe, envelop, furl, enfold 5 = **level**, even, press, smooth, flatten 6 = **toss**, rock, lurch, reel, tumble, sway
▷ NOUN 7 = **rumble**, boom, roar, thunder, reverberation 8 = **register**, record, list, index, census 9 = **turn**, spin, rotation, cycle, wheel, revolution, reel, whirl

romance 1 = **love affair**, relationship, affair, attachment, liaison, amour 2 = **excitement**, colour, charm, mystery, glamour, fascination 3 = **story**, tale, fantasy, legend, fairy tale, love story, melodrama

romantic ADJECTIVE

RODENTS

agouti	jerboa
beaver	kangaroo rat
capybara	kiore (N.Z.)
cavy	lemming
chinchilla	Māori rat or (N.Z.) kiore
chipmunk	marmot
coypu or nutria	mouse
desert rat	muskrat or musquash
dormouse	paca
fieldmouse	pack rat
flying squirrel	porcupine
gerbil, gerbille, or jerbil	rat
gopher or pocket gopher	red squirrel or chickaree
gopher or ground squirrel	spinifex hopping mouse or
grey squirrel	(Austral.) dargawarra
groundhog or woodchuck	springhaas
guinea pig or cavy	squirrel
hamster	suslik or souslik
harvest mouse	viscacha or vizcacha
hedgehog	vole
house mouse	water rat or water vole

1 = **loving**, tender, passionate, fond, sentimental, amorous, icky (*informal*) **OPPOSITE:** unromantic 2 = **idealistic**, unrealistic, impractical, dreamy, starry-eyed **OPPOSITE:** realistic 3 = **exciting**, fascinating, mysterious, colourful, glamorous **OPPOSITE:** unexciting
▷ NOUN 4 = **idealist**, dreamer, sentimentalist
romp VERB 1 = **frolic**, sport, have fun, caper, cavort, frisk, gambol
▷ NOUN 2 = **frolic**, lark (*informal*), caper

room 1 = **chamber**, office, apartment 2 = **space**, area, capacity, extent, expanse 3 = **opportunity**, scope, leeway, chance, range, occasion, margin
root[1] NOUN 1 = **stem**, tuber, rhizome 2 = **source**, cause, heart, bottom, base, seat, seed, foundation
▷ PLURAL NOUN 3 = **sense of belonging**, origins, heritage, birthplace, home, family, cradle
▷ PHRASES: **root something or someone out** = **get rid of**, remove, eliminate, abolish, eradicate, do away with, weed out, exterminate

r

root² = dig, burrow, ferret
rope = cord, line, cable, strand, hawser
▷ **PHRASES: know the ropes** = be experienced, be knowledgeable, be an old hand
▶ **rope someone in** or **into something** (Brit.) = persuade, involve, engage, enlist, talk into, inveigle (formal)
rosy ADJECTIVE 1 = glowing, blooming, radiant, ruddy, healthy-looking **OPPOSITE:** pale
2 = promising, encouraging, bright, optimistic, hopeful, cheerful, favourable, auspicious **OPPOSITE:** gloomy
▷ NOUN 3 = pink, red
▷ See panel SHADES OF RED
rot VERB 1 = decay, spoil, deteriorate, perish, decompose, moulder, go bad, putrefy
2 = crumble 3 = deteriorate, decline, waste away
▷ NOUN 4 = decay, decomposition, corruption, mould, blight, canker, putrefaction 5 (Informal) = nonsense, rubbish, drivel, twaddle, garbage (chiefly U.S.), trash, tripe (informal), claptrap (informal), bizzo (Austral. slang), bull's wool (Austral. & N.Z. slang)
● **RELATED WORD**
● adjective: putrid
rotate 1 = revolve, turn, wheel, spin, reel, go round, swivel, pivot 2 = follow in sequence, switch, alternate, take turns
rotation 1 = revolution,

turning, turn, wheel, spin, spinning, reel, orbit
2 = sequence, switching, cycle, succession, alternation
rotten ADJECTIVE 1 = decaying, bad, rank, corrupt, sour, stinking, perished, festering, festy (Austral. slang) **OPPOSITE:** fresh 2 = crumbling, perished
3 (Informal) = despicable, mean, base, dirty, nasty, contemptible
4 (Informal) = inferior, poor, inadequate, duff (Brit. informal), unsatisfactory, lousy (slang), substandard, crummy (slang), bodger or bodgie (Austral. slang)
5 = corrupt, immoral, crooked (informal), dishonest, dishonourable, perfidious **OPPOSITE:** honourable
rough ADJECTIVE 1 = uneven, broken, rocky, irregular, jagged, bumpy, stony, craggy **OPPOSITE:** even 2 = boisterous, hard, tough, arduous
3 = ungracious, blunt, rude, coarse, brusque, uncouth, impolite, uncivil **OPPOSITE:** refined 4 = unpleasant, hard, difficult, tough, uncomfortable **OPPOSITE:** easy
5 = approximate, estimated **OPPOSITE:** exact 6 = vague, general, sketchy, imprecise, inexact 7 = basic, crude, unfinished, incomplete, imperfect, rudimentary, sketchy, unrefined **OPPOSITE:** complete 8 = stormy, wild, turbulent, choppy, squally

r

OPPOSITE: calm 9 = **harsh**, tough, nasty, cruel, unfeeling **OPPOSITE:** gentle
▷ NOUN = **outline**, draft, mock-up, preliminary sketch
▷ PHRASES: **rough and ready** 1 = **makeshift**, crude, provisional, improvised, sketchy, stopgap
2 = **unrefined**, shabby, untidy, unkempt, unpolished, ill-groomed ▶ **rough something out** = **outline**, plan, draft, sketch

round NOUN 1 = **series**, session, cycle, sequence, succession 2 = **stage**, turn, level, period, division, session, lap 3 = **sphere**, ball, band, ring, circle, disc, globe, orb
4 = **course**, tour, circuit, beat, series, schedule, routine
▷ ADJECTIVE 5 = **spherical**, rounded, curved, circular, cylindrical, rotund, globular
6 = **plump**, full, ample, fleshy, rotund, full-fleshed
▷ VERB 7 = **go round**, circle, skirt, flank, bypass, encircle, turn
▷ PHRASES: **round something or someone up** = **gather**, muster, group, drive, collect, rally, herd, marshal

roundabout 1 = **indirect**, devious, tortuous, circuitous, evasive, discursive **OPPOSITE:** direct 2 = **oblique**, implied, indirect, circuitous

roundup = **muster**, collection,

rally, assembly, herding
rouse 1 = **wake up**, call, wake, awaken 2 = **excite**, move, stir, provoke, anger, animate, agitate, inflame 3 = **stimulate**, provoke, incite
rousing = **lively**, moving, spirited, exciting, inspiring, stirring, stimulating **OPPOSITE:** dull
rout VERB 1 = **defeat**, beat, overthrow, thrash (*informal*), destroy, crush, conquer, wipe the floor with (*informal*)
▷ NOUN 2 = **defeat**, beating, overthrow, thrashing (*informal*), pasting (*slang*), debacle, drubbing
route 1 = **way**, course, road, direction, path, journey, itinerary 2 = **beat**, circuit

● USAGE NOTE
● When adding -*ing* to the verb
● *route* to form the present
● participle, it is more
● conventional, and clearer, to
● keep the final *e* from the end
● of the verb stem: *routeing*. The
● spelling *routing* in this sense is
● also possible, but keeping the
● *e* distinguishes it from *routing*,
● which is the participle formed
● from the verb *rout* meaning
● 'to defeat'.

routine NOUN 1 = **procedure**, programme, order, practice, method, pattern, custom
▷ ADJECTIVE 2 = **usual**, standard, normal, customary, ordinary, typical, everyday,

habitual **OPPOSITE:** unusual
3 = boring, dull, predictable,
tedious, tiresome, humdrum
row¹ = line, bank, range, series,
file, string, column
▷ **PHRASES: in a row**
= **consecutively**, running, in
turn, one after the other,
successively, in sequence
row² NOUN (*Informal*)
1 = quarrel, dispute, argument,
squabble, tiff, trouble, brawl
▷ **NOUN 2 = disturbance**,
noise, racket, uproar,
commotion, rumpus, tumult
▷ **VERB 3 = quarrel**, fight,
argue, dispute, squabble,
wrangle
royal 1 = regal, kingly, queenly,
princely, imperial, sovereign
2 = splendid, grand, impressive,
magnificent, majestic, stately
rub VERB 1 = stroke, massage,
caress **2 = polish**, clean, shine,
wipe, scour **3 = chafe**, scrape,
grate, abrade (*formal*)
▷ **NOUN 4 = massage**, caress,
kneading **5 = polish**, stroke,
shine, wipe
▷ **PHRASES: rub something out**
= **erase**, remove, cancel, wipe
out, delete, obliterate, efface
rubbish 1 = waste, refuse,
scrap, junk (*informal*), litter,
garbage (*chiefly U.S.*), trash,
lumber **2 = nonsense**, garbage
(*chiefly U.S.*), twaddle (*informal*),
rot, trash, hot air (*informal*),
tripe (*informal*), claptrap
(*informal*), bizzo (*Austral. slang*),

bull's wool (*Austral. & N.Z. slang*)
rude 1 = impolite, insulting,
cheeky, abusive, disrespectful,
impertinent, insolent, impudent
OPPOSITE: polite
2 = uncivilized, rough, coarse,
brutish, boorish, uncouth,
loutish, graceless **3 = vulgar**,
crude **OPPOSITE:** refined
4 = unpleasant, sharp, sudden,
harsh, startling, abrupt
5 = roughly-made, simple,
rough, raw, crude, primitive,
makeshift, artless **OPPOSITE:**
well-made
rue (*Literary*) **= regret**, mourn,
lament, repent, be sorry for,
kick yourself for (*informal*)
ruffle 1 = disarrange, disorder,
mess up, rumple, tousle,
dishevel **2 = annoy**, upset,
irritate, agitate, nettle, fluster,
peeve (*informal*) **OPPOSITE:** calm
rugged 1 = rocky, broken,
rough, craggy, difficult, ragged,
irregular, uneven **OPPOSITE:**
even **2 = strong-featured**,
rough-hewn, weather-beaten
OPPOSITE: delicate **3 = well-
built**, strong, tough, robust,
sturdy **4 = tough**, strong,
robust, muscular, sturdy, burly,
husky (*informal*), brawny
OPPOSITE: delicate
ruin VERB 1 = destroy,
devastate, wreck, defeat,
smash, crush, demolish, lay
waste **OPPOSITE:** create
2 = bankrupt, break,
impoverish, beggar, pauperize

r

3 = **spoil**, damage, mess up, blow (*slang*), screw up (*informal*), botch (*informal*), make a mess of, crool or cruel (*Austral. slang*) **OPPOSITE:** improve
▷ NOUN 4 = **bankruptcy**, insolvency, destitution
5 = **disrepair**, decay, disintegration, ruination, wreckage 6 = **destruction**, fall, breakdown, defeat, collapse, wreck, undoing, downfall **OPPOSITE:** preservation

rule NOUN 1 = **regulation**, law, direction, guideline, decree
2 = **precept**, principle, canon, maxim, tenet, axiom
3 = **custom**, procedure, practice, routine, tradition, habit, convention
4 = **government**, power, control, authority, command, regime, reign, jurisdiction, mana (*N.Z.*)
▷ VERB 5 = **govern**, control, direct, have power over, command over, have charge of
6 = **reign**, govern, be in power, be in authority 7 = **decree**, decide, judge, settle, pronounce
8 = **be prevalent**, prevail, predominate, be customary, preponderate
▷ PHRASES: **as a rule** = usually, generally, mainly, normally, on the whole, ordinarily ▶ **rule someone out** = exclude, eliminate, disqualify, ban, reject, dismiss, prohibit, leave out ▶ **rule something out**

= reject, exclude, eliminate
ruler 1 = **governor**, leader, lord, commander, controller, monarch, sovereign, head of state 2 = **measure**, rule, yardstick

ruling ADJECTIVE
1 = **governing**, reigning, controlling, commanding
2 = **predominant**, dominant, prevailing, preponderant, chief, main, principal, pre-eminent **OPPOSITE:** minor
▷ NOUN 3 = **decision**, verdict, judgment, decree, adjudication, pronouncement

rumour = **story**, news, report, talk, word, whisper, buzz, gossip

run VERB 1 = **race**, rush, dash, hurry, sprint, bolt, gallop, hare (*Brit. informal*) **OPPOSITE:** dawdle 2 = **flee**, escape, take off (*informal*), bolt, beat it (*slang*), leg it (*informal*), take flight, do a runner (*slang*) **OPPOSITE:** stay 3 = **take part**, compete 4 = **continue**, go, stretch, reach, extend, proceed **OPPOSITE:** stop 5 (*Chiefly U.S. & Canad.*) = **compete**, stand, contend, be a candidate, put yourself up for, take part
6 = **manage**, lead, direct, be in charge of, head, control, operate, handle 7 = **go**, work, operate, perform, function
8 = **perform**, carry out
9 = **work**, go, operate, function
10 = **pass**, go, move, roll, glide,

skim 11 = **flow**, pour, stream, go, leak, spill, discharge, gush 12 = **publish**, feature, display, print 13 = **melt**, dissolve, liquefy, go soft 14 = **smuggle**, traffic in, bootleg

▷ NOUN 15 = **race**, rush, dash, sprint, gallop, jog, spurt 16 = **ride**, drive, trip, spin (*informal*), outing, excursion, jaunt 17 = **sequence**, period, stretch, spell, course, season, series, string 18 = **enclosure**, pen, coop

▷ PHRASES: run away = **flee**, escape, bolt, abscond (*formal*), do a runner (*slang*), make a run for it, scram (*informal*), fly the coop (*U.S. & Canad. informal*)

▶ run into someone = **meet**, encounter, bump into, run across, come across *or* upon

▶ run into something 1 = **be beset by** (*formal*), encounter, come across *or* upon, face, experience 2 = **collide with**, hit, strike ▶ run out 1 = **be used up**, dry up, give out, fail, finish, be exhausted 2 = **expire**, end, terminate ▶ run over something 1 = **exceed**, overstep, go over the top of, go over the limit of 2 = **review**, check, go through, go over, run through, rehearse ▶ run over something *or* someone = **knock down**, hit, run down, knock over ▶ run something *or* someone down 1 = **criticize**, denigrate, belittle, knock

(*informal*), rubbish (*informal*), slag (off) (*slang*), disparage, decry 2 = **downsize**, cut, reduce, trim, decrease, cut back, curtail 3 = **knock down**, hit, run into, run over, knock over

run-down *or* **rundown**
1 = **exhausted**, weak, drained, weary, unhealthy, worn-out, debilitated, below par
OPPOSITE: fit 2 = **dilapidated**, broken-down, shabby, worn-out, seedy, ramshackle, decrepit

runner 1 = **athlete**, sprinter, jogger 2 = **messenger**, courier, errand boy, dispatch bearer

running NOUN
1 = **management**, control, administration, direction, leadership, organization, supervision 2 = **working**, performance, operation, functioning, maintenance
▷ ADJECTIVE 3 = **continuous**, constant, perpetual, uninterrupted, incessant 4 = **in succession**, unbroken 5 = **flowing**, moving, streaming, coursing

rupture NOUN 1 = **break**, tear, split, crack, rent, burst, breach, fissure
▷ VERB 2 = **break**, separate, tear, split, crack, burst, sever

rural 1 = **agricultural**, country 2 = **rustic**, country, pastoral, sylvan OPPOSITE: urban

rush VERB 1 = **hurry**, run, race, shoot, fly, career, speed, tear

r

OPPOSITE: dawdle 2 = push,
hurry, press, hustle 3 = **attack**,
storm, charge at
▷ NOUN 4 = **dash**, charge, race,
scramble, stampede 5 = **hurry**,
haste, hustle 6 = **surge**, flow,
gush 7 = **attack**, charge,
assault, onslaught
▷ ADJECTIVE 8 = **hasty**, fast,
quick, hurried, rapid, urgent,
swift **OPPOSITE:** leisurely

rust NOUN 1 = **corrosion**,
oxidation 2 = **mildew**, must,
mould, rot, blight
▷ VERB 3 = **corrode**, oxidize

rusty 1 = **corroded**, rusted,
oxidized, rust-covered 2 = **out
of practice**, weak, stale,
unpractised 3 = **reddish-
brown**, chestnut, reddish,
russet, coppery, rust-coloured
▷ See panel SHADES OF RED

ruthless = **merciless**, harsh,
cruel, brutal, relentless, callous,
heartless, remorseless
OPPOSITE: merciful

Ss

sabotage VERB 1 = **damage**,
destroy, wreck, disable, disrupt,
subvert, incapacitate, vandalize
▷ NOUN 2 = **damage**,
destruction, wrecking

sack¹ NOUN 1 = **bag**, pocket,
sac, pouch, receptacle
2 = **dismissal**, discharge, the
boot (slang), the axe (informal),
the push (slang)
▷ VERB 3 (Informal) = **dismiss**,
fire (informal), axe (informal),
discharge, kiss off (slang, chiefly
U.S. & Canad.), give (someone)
the push (informal)

sack² VERB 1 = **plunder**, loot,
pillage, strip, rob, raid, ruin
▷ NOUN 2 = **plundering**,
looting, pillage

sacred 1 = **holy**, hallowed,
blessed, divine, revered,
sanctified **OPPOSITE:** secular
2 = **religious**, holy,
ecclesiastical, hallowed
OPPOSITE: unconsecrated
3 = **inviolable**, protected,
sacrosanct, hallowed,
inalienable, unalterable

sacrifice VERB 1 = **offer**, offer
up, immolate 2 = **give up**,
abandon, relinquish, lose,

surrender, let go, do without, renounce

▷ NOUN 3 = **offering**, oblation 4 = **surrender**, loss, giving up, rejection, abdication, renunciation, repudiation, forswearing

sad 1 = **unhappy**, down, low, blue, depressed, melancholy, mournful, dejected OPPOSITE: happy 2 = **tragic**, moving, upsetting, depressing, dismal, pathetic, poignant, harrowing 3 = **deplorable**, bad, sorry, terrible, unfortunate, regrettable, lamentable, wretched OPPOSITE: good

sadden = **upset**, depress, distress, grieve, make sad, deject

saddle = **burden**, load, lumber (Brit. informal), encumber

sadness = **unhappiness**, sorrow, grief, depression, the blues, misery, melancholy, poignancy OPPOSITE: happiness

safe ADJECTIVE 1 = **protected**, secure, impregnable, out of danger, safe and sound, in safe hands, out of harm's way OPPOSITE: endangered 2 = **all right**, intact, unscathed, unhurt, unharmed, undamaged, O.K. or okay (informal) 3 = **risk-free**, sound, secure, certain, impregnable

▷ NOUN 4 = **strongbox**, vault, coffer, repository, deposit box, safe-deposit box

safeguard VERB 1 = **protect**,

guard, defend, save, preserve, look after, keep safe

▷ NOUN 2 = **protection**, security, defence, guard

safely = **in safety**, with impunity, without risk, safe and sound

safety 1 = **security**, protection, safeguards, precautions, safety measures, impregnability OPPOSITE: risk 2 = **shelter**, haven, protection, cover, retreat, asylum, refuge, sanctuary

sag 1 = **sink**, bag, droop, fall, slump, dip, give way, hang loosely 2 = **drop**, sink, slump, flop, droop, loll 3 = **decline**, tire, flag, weaken, wilt, wane, droop

saga 1 = **carry-on** (informal, chiefly Brit.), performance (informal), pantomime (informal) 2 = **epic**, story, tale, narrative, yarn

sage NOUN 1 = **wise man**, philosopher, guru, master, elder, tohunga (N.Z.)

▷ ADJECTIVE 2 = **wise**, sensible, judicious, sagacious, sapient

sail NOUN 1 = **sheet**, canvas

▷ VERB 2 = **go by water**, cruise, voyage, ride the waves, go by sea 3 = **set sail**, embark, get under way, put to sea, put off, leave port, hoist sail, cast or weigh anchor 4 = **pilot**, steer 5 = **glide**, sweep, float, fly, wing, soar, drift, skim

sailor = **mariner**, marine,

seaman, sea dog, seafarer

sake = **purpose**, interest, reason, end, aim, objective, motive

▷ PHRASES: **for someone's sake** = **in someone's interests**, to someone's advantage, on someone's account, for the benefit of, for the good of, for the welfare of, out of respect for, out of consideration for

salary = **pay**, income, wage, fee, payment, wages, earnings, allowance

sale 1 = **selling**, marketing, dealing, transaction, disposal 2 = **auction**, fair, mart, bazaar

salt NOUN 1 = **seasoning** ▷ ADJECTIVE 2 = **salty**, saline, brackish, briny

salute VERB 1 = **greet**, welcome, acknowledge, address, hail, mihi (N.Z.) 2 = **honour**, acknowledge, recognize, pay tribute or homage to ▷ NOUN 3 = **greeting**, recognition, salutation, address

salvage = **save**, recover, rescue, get back, retrieve, redeem

salvation = **saving**, rescue, recovery, salvage, redemption, deliverance **OPPOSITE:** ruin

same 1 = **identical**, similar, alike, equal, twin, corresponding, duplicate **OPPOSITE:** different 2 = **the very same**, one and the same, selfsame 3 = **aforementioned**, aforesaid 4 = **unchanged**, consistent, constant, unaltered, invariable, unvarying, changeless **OPPOSITE:** altered

● USAGE NOTE
● The use of *same* as in *if you*
● *send us your order for the*
● *materials, we will deliver same*
● *tomorrow* is common in
● business and official English.
● In general English, however,
● this use of the word is best
● avoided, as it may sound
● rather stilted: *may I borrow*
● *your book? I will return it* (not
● *same*) *tomorrow*.

sample NOUN 1 = **specimen**, example, model, pattern, instance 2 = **cross section** ▷ VERB 3 = **test**, try, experience, taste, inspect ▷ ADJECTIVE 4 = **test**, trial, specimen, representative

sanction VERB 1 = **permit**, allow, approve, endorse, authorize **OPPOSITE:** forbid ▷ NOUN 2 *often plural* = **ban**, boycott, embargo, exclusion, penalty, coercive measures **OPPOSITE:** permission 3 = **permission**, backing, authority, approval, authorization, O.K. or okay (*informal*), stamp or seal of approval **OPPOSITE:** ban

sanctuary 1 = **protection**, shelter, refuge, haven, retreat, asylum 2 = **reserve**, park, preserve, reservation, national park, tract, nature reserve, conservation area

sane 1 = rational, all there (*informal*), of sound mind, compos mentis (*Latin*), in your right mind, mentally sound **OPPOSITE:** insane 2 = sensible, sound, reasonable, balanced, judicious, level-headed **OPPOSITE:** foolish

sap¹ 1 = juice, essence, vital fluid, lifeblood 2 (*Slang*) = fool, jerk (*slang, chiefly U.S. & Canad.*), idiot, wally (*slang*), twit (*informal*), simpleton, ninny, dorba *or* dorb (*Austral. slang*), bogan (*Austral. slang*)

sap² = weaken, drain, undermine, exhaust, deplete

satanic = evil, demonic, hellish, black, wicked, devilish, infernal, fiendish **OPPOSITE:** godly

satire 1 = mockery, irony, ridicule 2 = parody, mockery, caricature, lampoon, burlesque

satisfaction 1 = fulfilment, pleasure, achievement, relish, gratification, pride **OPPOSITE:** dissatisfaction

2 = contentment, content, comfort, pleasure, happiness, enjoyment, satiety, repletion **OPPOSITE:** discontent

satisfactory = adequate, acceptable, good enough, average, fair, all right, sufficient, passable **OPPOSITE:** unsatisfactory

satisfy 1 = content, please, indulge, gratify, pander to, assuage, pacify, quench **OPPOSITE:** dissatisfy

2 = convince, persuade, assure, reassure **OPPOSITE:** dissuade
3 = comply with, meet, fulfil, answer, serve, fill, observe, obey **OPPOSITE:** fail to meet

saturate 1 = flood, overwhelm, swamp, overrun 2 = soak, steep, drench, imbue, suffuse, wet through, waterlog, souse

saturated = soaked, soaking (wet), drenched, sodden, dripping, waterlogged, sopping (wet), wet through

sauce = dressing, dip, relish, condiment

savage ADJECTIVE 1 = cruel, brutal, vicious, fierce, harsh, ruthless, ferocious, sadistic **OPPOSITE:** gentle 2 = wild, fierce, ferocious, unbroken, feral, untamed, undomesticated **OPPOSITE:** tame 3 = primitive, undeveloped, uncultivated, uncivilized 4 = uncultivated, rugged, unspoilt, uninhabited, rough, uncivilized **OPPOSITE:** cultivated

▷ NOUN 5 = lout, yob (*Brit. slang*), barbarian, yahoo, hoon (*Austral. & N.Z.*), boor, cougan (*Austral. slang*), scozza (*Austral. slang*), bogan (*Austral. slang*)

▷ VERB 6 = maul, tear, claw, attack, mangle, lacerate, mangulate (*Austral. slang*)

save 1 = rescue, free, release, deliver, recover, get out, liberate, salvage **OPPOSITE:** endanger 2 = keep, reserve, set

s

aside, store, collect, gather, hold, hoard **OPPOSITE:** spend **3 = protect**, keep, guard, preserve, look after, safeguard, salvage, conserve **4 = put aside**, keep, reserve, collect, retain, set aside, put by

saving NOUN **1 = economy**, discount, reduction, bargain ▷ PLURAL NOUN **2 = nest egg**, fund, store, reserves, resources

saviour = rescuer, deliverer, defender, protector, liberator, redeemer, preserver

Saviour = Christ, Jesus, the Messiah, the Redeemer

savour VERB **1 = relish**, delight in, revel in, luxuriate in **2 = enjoy**, appreciate, relish, delight in, revel in, luxuriate in ▷ NOUN **3 = flavour**, taste, smell, relish, smack, tang, piquancy

say VERB **1 = state**, declare, remark, announce, maintain, mention, assert, affirm **2 = speak**, utter, voice, express, pronounce **3 = suggest**, express, imply, communicate, disclose, give away, convey, divulge **4 = suppose**, supposing, imagine, assume, presume **5 = estimate**, suppose, guess, conjecture, surmise ▷ NOUN **6 = influence**, power, control, authority, weight, clout (*informal*), mana (N.Z.) **7 = chance to speak**, vote, voice

saying = proverb, maxim, adage, dictum, axiom, aphorism

scale[1] **= flake**, plate, layer, lamina

scale[2] NOUN **1 = degree**, size, range, extent, dimensions, scope, magnitude, breadth **2 = system of measurement**, measuring system **3 = ranking**, ladder, hierarchy, series, sequence, progression **4 = ratio**, proportion ▷ VERB **5 = climb up**, mount, ascend, surmount, clamber up, escalade

scan 1 = glance over, skim, look over, eye, check, examine, check out (*informal*), run over **2 = survey**, search, investigate, sweep, scour, scrutinize

scandal 1 = disgrace, crime, offence, sin, embarrassment, wrongdoing, dishonourable behaviour, discreditable behaviour **2 = gossip**, talk, rumours, dirt, slander, tattle, aspersion **3 = shame**, disgrace, stigma, infamy, opprobrium **4 = outrage**, shame, insult, disgrace, injustice, crying shame

scant = inadequate, meagre, sparse, little, minimal, barely sufficient **OPPOSITE:** adequate

scapegoat = fall guy, whipping boy

scar NOUN **1 = mark**, injury, wound, blemish **2 = trauma**, suffering, pain, torture

▷ VERB 3 = **mark**, disfigure, damage, mar, mutilate, blemish, deface

scarce 1 = **in short supply**, insufficient **OPPOSITE:** plentiful 2 = **rare**, few, uncommon, few and far between, infrequent **OPPOSITE:** common

scarcely 1 = **hardly**, barely 2 (*Often used ironically*) = **by no means**, hardly, definitely not, under no circumstances

● **USAGE NOTE**
● Since *scarcely*, *hardly*, and
● *barely* already have negative
● force, it is unnecessary to use
● another negative word with
● them. Therefore, say *he had*
● *hardly had time to think* (not *he*
● *hadn't hardly had time to think*);
● and *there was scarcely any*
● *bread left* (not *there was*
● *scarcely no bread left*). When
● *scarcely*, *hardly*, and *barely* are
● used at the beginning of a
● sentence, the following clause
● should start with *when*:
● *scarcely had I arrived when I was*
● *asked to chair a meeting*. The
● word *before* can be used in
● place of *when* in this context,
● but the word *than* used in the
● same way is considered
● incorrect by many people,
● though this use is becoming
● increasingly common.

scare VERB 1 = **frighten**, alarm, terrify, panic, shock, startle, intimidate, dismay

▷ NOUN 2 = **fright**, shock, start 3 = **panic**, hysteria 4 = **alert**, warning, alarm

scared = **afraid**, alarmed, frightened, terrified, shaken, startled, fearful, petrified

scary (*Informal*) = **frightening**, alarming, terrifying, chilling, horrifying, spooky (*informal*), creepy (*informal*), spine-chilling

scatter 1 = **throw about**, spread, sprinkle, strew, shower, fling, diffuse, disseminate **OPPOSITE:** gather 2 = **disperse**, dispel, disband, dissipate **OPPOSITE:** assemble

scenario 1 = **situation** 2 = **story line**, résumé, outline, summary, synopsis

scene 1 = **act**, part, division, episode 2 = **setting**, set, background, location, backdrop 3 = **site**, place, setting, area, position, spot, locality 4 (*Informal*) = **world**, business, environment, arena 5 = **view**, prospect, panorama, vista, landscape, outlook 6 = **fuss**, to-do, row, performance, exhibition, carry-on (*informal*, *chiefly Brit.*), tantrum, commotion

scenery 1 = **landscape**, view, surroundings, terrain, vista 2 (*Theatre*) = **set**, setting, backdrop, flats, stage set

scenic = **picturesque**, beautiful, spectacular, striking, panoramic

scent NOUN 1 = **fragrance**, smell, perfume, bouquet,

S

aroma, odour **2** = **trail**, track, spoor

▷ VERB **3** = **smell**, sense, detect, sniff, discern, nose out

scented = **fragrant**, perfumed, aromatic, sweet-smelling, odoriferous

sceptic **1** = **doubter**, cynic, disbeliever **2** = **agnostic**, doubter, unbeliever, doubting Thomas

sceptical = **doubtful**, cynical, dubious, unconvinced, disbelieving, incredulous, mistrustful **OPPOSITE:** convinced

scepticism = **doubt**, suspicion, disbelief, cynicism, incredulity

schedule NOUN **1** = **plan**, programme, agenda, calendar, timetable

▷ VERB **2** = **plan**, set up, book, programme, arrange, organize

scheme NOUN **1** = **plan**, programme, strategy, system, project, proposal, tactics **2** = **plot**, ploy, ruse, intrigue, conspiracy, manoeuvre, subterfuge, stratagem

▷ VERB **3** = **plot**, plan, intrigue, manoeuvre, conspire, contrive, collude, machinate

scheming = **calculating**, cunning, sly, tricky, wily, artful, conniving, underhand **OPPOSITE:** straightforward

scholar **1** = **intellectual**, academic, savant, acca (Austral. slang) **2** = **student**, pupil, learner, schoolboy or schoolgirl

scholarly = **learned**, academic, intellectual, lettered, erudite, scholastic, bookish **OPPOSITE:** uneducated

scholarship **1** = **grant**, award, payment, endowment, fellowship, bursary **2** = **learning**, education, knowledge, erudition, book-learning

school NOUN **1** = **academy**, college, institution, institute, seminary **2** = **group**, set, circle, faction, followers, disciples, devotees, denomination

▷ VERB **3** = **train**, coach, discipline, educate, drill, tutor, instruct

science = **discipline**, body of knowledge, branch of knowledge

scientific = **systematic**, accurate, exact, precise, controlled, mathematical

scientist = **researcher**, inventor, boffin (informal), technophile

scoff[1] = **scorn**, mock, laugh at, ridicule, knock (informal), despise, sneer, jeer

scoff[2] = **gobble (up)**, wolf, devour, bolt, guzzle, gulp down, gorge yourself on

scoop VERB **1** = **win**, get, land, gain, achieve, earn, secure, obtain

▷ NOUN **2** = **ladle**, spoon, dipper **3** = **exclusive**, exposé, revelation, sensation

▷ PHRASES: **scoop something**

or **someone up** = gather up, lift, pick up, take up, sweep up *or* away ▶ **scoop something out** **1** = take out, empty, spoon out, bail *or* bale out **2** = dig, shovel, excavate, gouge, hollow out

scope 1 = opportunity, room, freedom, space, liberty, latitude **2** = range, capacity, reach, area, outlook, orbit, span, sphere

scorch = burn, sear, roast, wither, shrivel, parch, singe

scorching = burning, boiling, baking, flaming, roasting, searing, fiery, red-hot

score VERB **1** = gain, win, achieve, make, get, attain, notch up (*informal*), chalk up (*informal*) **2** (*Music*) = arrange, set, orchestrate, adapt **3** = cut, scratch, mark, slash, scrape, graze, gouge, deface ▷ NOUN **4** = rating, mark, grade, percentage **5** = points, result, total, outcome **6** = composition, soundtrack, arrangement, orchestration **7** = grievance, wrong, injury, injustice, grudge ▷ PLURAL NOUN **8** = lots, loads, many, millions, hundreds, masses, swarms, multitudes ▷ PHRASES: **score something out** *or* **through** = cross out, delete, strike out, cancel, obliterate

scorn NOUN **1** = contempt, disdain, mockery, derision, sarcasm, disparagement **OPPOSITE:** respect

▷ VERB **2** = despise, reject, disdain, slight, be above, spurn, deride, flout **OPPOSITE:** respect

scour¹ = scrub, clean, polish, rub, buff, abrade

scour² = search, hunt, comb, ransack

scout NOUN **1** = vanguard, lookout, precursor, outrider, reconnoitrer, advance guard ▷ VERB **2** = reconnoitre, investigate, watch, survey, observe, spy, probe, recce (*slang*)

scramble VERB **1** = struggle, climb, crawl, swarm, scrabble **2** = strive, rush, contend, vie, run, push, jostle **3** = jumble, mix up, muddle, shuffle ▷ NOUN **4** = clamber, ascent **5** = race, competition, struggle, rush, confusion, commotion, melee *or* mêlée

scrap¹ NOUN **1** = piece, fragment, bit, grain, particle, portion, part, crumb **2** = waste, junk, off cuts ▷ PLURAL NOUN **3** = leftovers, remains, bits, leavings ▷ VERB **4** = get rid of, drop, abandon, ditch (*slang*), discard, write off, jettison, throw away *or* out **OPPOSITE:** bring back

scrap² (*Informal*) NOUN **1** = fight, battle, row, argument, dispute, disagreement, quarrel, squabble, biffo (*Austral. slang*) ▷ VERB **2** = fight, argue, row, squabble, wrangle

S

scrape VERB 1 = **rake**, sweep, drag, brush 2 = **grate**, grind, scratch, squeak, rasp 3 = **graze**, skin, scratch, bark, scuff, rub 4 = **clean**, remove, scour
▷ NOUN 5 (*Informal*) = **predicament**, difficulty, fix (*informal*), mess, dilemma, plight, tight spot, awkward situation

scratch VERB 1 = **rub**, scrape, claw at 2 = **mark**, cut, score, damage, grate, graze, etch, lacerate
▷ NOUN 3 = **mark**, scrape, graze, blemish, gash, laceration, claw mark
▷ PHRASES: up to scratch (*Informal*) = **adequate**, acceptable, satisfactory, sufficient, up to standard

scream VERB 1 = **cry**, yell, shriek, screech, bawl, howl
▷ NOUN 2 = **cry**, yell, howl, shriek, screech, yelp

screen NOUN 1 = **cover**, guard, shade, shelter, shield, partition, cloak, canopy
▷ VERB 2 = **broadcast**, show, put on, present, air, cable, beam, transmit 3 = **cover**, hide, conceal, shade, mask, veil, cloak 4 = **investigate**, test, check, examine, scan 5 = **process**, sort, examine, filter, scan, evaluate, gauge, sift 6 = **protect**, guard, shield, defend, shelter

screw NOUN 1 = **nail**, pin, tack, rivet, fastener, spike
▷ VERB 2 = **fasten**, fix, attach, bolt, clamp, rivet 3 = **turn**, twist, tighten 4 (*Informal*) = **cheat**, do (*slang*), rip (someone) off (*slang*), skin (*slang*), trick, con, sting (*informal*), fleece 5 (*Informal*) *often with* out of = **squeeze**, wring, extract, wrest
▷ PHRASES: screw something up 1 = **contort**, wrinkle, distort, pucker 2 (*Informal*) = **bungle**, botch, mess up, spoil, mishandle, make a mess of (*slang*), make a hash of (*informal*), crool or cruel (*Austral. slang*)

scribble = **scrawl**, write, jot, dash off

script NOUN 1 = **text**, lines, words, book, copy, dialogue, libretto 2 = **handwriting**, writing, calligraphy, penmanship
▷ VERB 3 = **write**, draft

scripture = **The Bible**, The Gospels, The Scriptures, The Good Book, Holy Scripture, Holy Writ, Holy Bible

scrub 1 = **scour**, clean, polish, rub, wash, cleanse, buff 2 (*Informal*) = **cancel**, drop, give up, abolish, forget about, call off, delete

scrutiny = **examination**, study, investigation, search, analysis, inspection, exploration, perusal

sculpture NOUN 1 = **statue**, figure, model, bust, effigy,

figurine, statuette
▷ VERB 2 = **carve**, form, model, fashion, shape, mould, sculpt, chisel

sea 1 = **ocean**, the deep, the waves, main 2 = **mass**, army, host, crowd, mob, abundance, swarm, horde
▷ PHRASES: at sea
= **bewildered**, lost, confused, puzzled, baffled, perplexed, mystified, flummoxed
● RELATED WORDS
● *adjectives:* marine, maritime

sea bird ▷ *See panel* SEA BIRDS

seal VERB 1 = **settle**, clinch, conclude, consummate, finalize
▷ NOUN 2 = **sealant**, sealer, adhesive 3 = **authentication**, stamp, confirmation, ratification, insignia, imprimatur

seam 1 = **joint**, closure 2 = **layer**, vein, stratum, lode

sea mammal ▷ *See panel* SEA MAMMALS

sear = **wither**, burn, scorch, sizzle

search VERB 1 = **examine**, investigate, explore, inspect, comb, scour, ransack, scrutinize, fossick (*Austral. & N.Z.*)
▷ NOUN 2 = **hunt**, look, investigation, examination, pursuit, quest, inspection, exploration
▷ PHRASES: **search for something** *or* **someone** = **look for**, hunt for, pursue

searching = **keen**, sharp, probing, close, intent, piercing, penetrating, quizzical
OPPOSITE: superficial

searing 1 = **acute**, intense, shooting, severe, painful, stabbing, piercing, gut-wrenching 2 = **cutting**, biting, bitter, harsh, barbed, hurtful, caustic

season NOUN 1 = **period**, time, term, spell
▷ VERB 2 = **flavour**, salt, spice, enliven, pep up

seasoned = **experienced**, veteran, practised, hardened, time-served OPPOSITE: inexperienced

seasoning = **flavouring**, spice, salt and pepper, condiment

seat NOUN 1 = **chair**, bench, stall, stool, pew, settle 2 = **membership**, place, constituency, chair, incumbency 3 = **centre**, place, site, heart, capital, situation, source, hub 4 = **mansion**, house, residence, abode, ancestral hall
▷ VERB 5 = **sit**, place, settle, set, fix, locate, install 6 = **hold**, take, accommodate, sit, contain, cater for

second¹ ADJECTIVE 1 = **next**, following, succeeding, subsequent 2 = **additional**, other, further, extra, alternative 3 = **inferior**, secondary, subordinate, lower, lesser
▷ NOUN 4 = **supporter**, assistant, aide, colleague,

S

SEA BIRDS

albatross or (*informal*) gooney bird
auk
black-backed gull
black shag or kawau (*N.Z.*)
blue penguin, korora or little blue penguin (*N.Z.*)
blue shag (*N.Z.*)
caspian tern or taranui (*N.Z.*)
coot
cormorant
fairy penguin, little penguin, or (*N.Z.*) korora
fish hawk
fulmar
gannet
guillemot
gull or (*archaic or dialect*) cob(b)
herring gull

kittiwake
man-of-war bird or frigate bird
oystercatcher
petrel
razorbill or razor-billed auk
scoter
sea eagle, erne, or ern
seagull
shearwater
short-tailed shearwater, (Tasmanian) mutton bird, or (*N.Z.*) titi
skua
storm petrel, stormy petrel, or Mother Carey's chicken
wandering albatross
white-fronted tern, black cap, kahawai bird, sea swallow or tara (*N.Z.*)

SEA MAMMALS

dugong
elephant seal
harp seal
manatee

sea cow
seal
sea lion
walrus or (*archaic*) sea horse

s

backer, helper, right-hand man
▷ **VERB** 5 = **support**, back, endorse, approve, go along with
second² = **moment**, minute, instant, flash, sec (*informal*), jiffy (*informal*), trice
secondary 1 = **subordinate**, minor, lesser, lower, inferior, unimportant **OPPOSITE:** main
2 = **resultant**, contingent, derived, indirect **OPPOSITE:** original

second-hand = **used**, old, hand-me-down (*informal*), nearly new
secondly = **next**, second, moreover, furthermore, also, in the second place
secrecy 1 = **mystery**, stealth, concealment, furtiveness, secretiveness, clandestineness, covertness 2 = **confidentiality**, privacy 3 = **privacy**, silence, seclusion

secret ADJECTIVE
1 = **undisclosed**, unknown, confidential, underground, undercover, unrevealed
2 = **concealed**, hidden, disguised OPPOSITE: unconcealed 3 = **undercover**, furtive OPPOSITE: open
4 = **secretive**, reserved, close OPPOSITE: frank
5 = **mysterious**, cryptic, abstruse, occult, clandestine, arcane OPPOSITE: straightforward
▷ NOUN 6 = **private affair**
▷ PHRASES: in secret = **secretly**, surreptitiously, slyly

secretive = **reticent**, reserved, close, deep, uncommunicative, tight-lipped OPPOSITE: open

secretly = **in secret**, privately, surreptitiously, quietly, covertly, furtively, stealthily, clandestinely

sect = **group**, division, faction, party, camp, denomination, schism

section 1 = **part**, piece, portion, division, slice, passage, segment, fraction 2 = **district**, area, region, sector, zone

sector 1 = **part**, division
2 = **area**, part, region, district, zone, quarter

secular = **worldly**, lay, earthly, civil, temporal, nonspiritual OPPOSITE: religious

secure VERB 1 = **obtain**, get, acquire, score (*slang*), gain, procure OPPOSITE: lose

2 = **attach**, stick, fix, bind, fasten OPPOSITE: detach
▷ ADJECTIVE 3 = **safe**, protected, immune, unassailable OPPOSITE: unprotected 4 = **fast**, firm, fixed, stable, steady, fastened, immovable OPPOSITE: insecure
5 = **confident**, sure, easy, certain, assured, reassured OPPOSITE: uneasy

security 1 = **precautions**, defence, safeguards, protection, safety measures
2 = **assurance**, confidence, conviction, certainty, reliance, sureness, positiveness OPPOSITE: insecurity
3 = **pledge**, insurance, guarantee, hostage, collateral, pawn, gage, surety
4 = **protection**, safety, custody, refuge, sanctuary, safekeeping OPPOSITE: vulnerability

sediment = **dregs**, grounds, residue, lees, deposit

seduce 1 = **tempt**, lure, entice, mislead, deceive, beguile, lead astray, inveigle 2 = **corrupt**, deprave, dishonour, debauch, deflower

seductive = **tempting**, inviting, attractive, enticing, provocative, alluring, bewitching

see VERB 1 = **perceive**, spot, notice, sight, witness, observe, distinguish, glimpse
2 = **understand**, get, follow, realize, appreciate, grasp,

S

comprehend, fathom **3 = find out**, learn, discover, determine, verify, ascertain **4 = consider**, decide, reflect, deliberate, think over **5 = make sure**, ensure, guarantee, make certain, see to it **6 = accompany**, show, escort, lead, walk, usher **7 = speak to**, receive, interview, consult, confer with **8 = meet**, come across, happen on, bump into, run across, chance on **9 = go out with**, court, date (*informal, chiefly U.S.*), go steady with (*informal*)

▷ **PHRASES: seeing as = since**, as, in view of the fact that, inasmuch as

● **USAGE NOTE**
● It is common to hear *seeing as*
● *how*, as in *seeing as how the bus*
● *is always late, I don't need to*
● *hurry.* However, the use of
● *how* here is considered
● incorrect or nonstandard, and
● should be avoided.

seed 1 = grain, pip, germ, kernel, egg, embryo, spore, ovum **2 = beginning**, start, germ **3 = origin**, source, nucleus **4** (*Chiefly Bible*) **= offspring**, children, descendants, issue, progeny

▷ **PHRASES: go** *or* **run to seed = decline**, deteriorate, degenerate, decay, go downhill (*informal*), let yourself go, go to pot

seek 1 = look for, pursue, search for, be after, hunt

2 = try, attempt, aim, strive, endeavour, essay, aspire to

seem = appear, give the impression of being, look

seep = ooze, well, leak, soak, trickle, exude, permeate

seethe 1 = be furious, rage, fume, simmer, see red (*informal*), be livid, go ballistic (*slang, chiefly U.S.*) **2 = boil**, bubble, foam, fizz, froth

segment = section, part, piece, division, slice, portion, wedge

segregate = set apart, divide, separate, isolate, discriminate against, dissociate **OPPOSITE:** unite

segregation = separation, discrimination, apartheid, isolation

seize 1 = grab, grip, grasp, take, snatch, clutch, snap up, pluck **OPPOSITE: let go 2 = take by storm**, take over, acquire, occupy, conquer **3 = capture**, catch, arrest, apprehend, take captive **OPPOSITE:** release

seizure 1 = attack, fit, spasm, convulsion, paroxysm **2 = taking**, grabbing, annexation, confiscation, commandeering **3 = capture**, arrest, apprehension

seldom = rarely, not often, infrequently, hardly ever **OPPOSITE:** often

select VERB **1 = choose**, take, pick, opt for, decide on, single out, adopt, settle upon **OPPOSITE:** reject

s

▷ **ADJECTIVE 2** = **choice**, special, excellent, superior, first-class, hand-picked, top-notch (informal) **OPPOSITE:** ordinary
3 = **exclusive**, elite, privileged, cliquish **OPPOSITE:** indiscriminate

selection 1 = **choice**, choosing, pick, option, preference
2 = **anthology**, collection, medley, choice

selective = **particular**, discriminating, careful, discerning, tasteful, fastidious **OPPOSITE:** indiscriminate

selfish = **self-centred**, self-interested, greedy, ungenerous, egoistic or egoistical, egotistic or egoistical **OPPOSITE:** unselfish

sell 1 = **trade**, exchange, barter **OPPOSITE:** buy **2** = **deal in**, market, trade in, stock, handle, retail, peddle, traffic in **OPPOSITE:** buy
▷ **PHRASES: sell out of something** = **run out of**, be out of stock of

seller = **dealer**, merchant, vendor, agent, retailer, supplier, purveyor, salesman or saleswoman

send 1 = **dispatch**, forward, direct, convey, remit
2 = **propel**, hurl, fling, shoot, fire, cast, let fly
▷ **PHRASES: send something or someone up** (Brit. informal) = **mock**, mimic, parody, spoof (informal), imitate, take off

(informal), make fun of, lampoon

send-off = **farewell**, departure, leave-taking, valediction

senior 1 = **higher ranking**, superior **OPPOSITE:** subordinate
2 = **the elder**, major (Brit.) **OPPOSITE:** junior

sensation 1 = **feeling**, sense, impression, perception, awareness, consciousness
2 = **excitement**, thrill, stir, furore, commotion

sensational 1 = **amazing**, dramatic, thrilling, astounding **OPPOSITE:** dull **2** = **shocking**, exciting, melodramatic, shock-horror (facetious) **OPPOSITE:** unexciting **3** (Informal) = **excellent**, superb, mean (slang), impressive, smashing (informal), fabulous (informal), marvellous, out of this world (informal), booshit (Austral. slang), exo (Austral. slang), sik (Austral. slang) **OPPOSITE:** ordinary

sense NOUN 1 = **faculty**
2 = **feeling**, impression, perception, awareness, consciousness, atmosphere, aura **3** = **understanding**, awareness **4** sometimes plural = **intelligence**, reason, understanding, brains (informal), judgment, wisdom, wit(s), common sense **OPPOSITE:** foolishness **5** = **meaning**, significance, import, implication, drift, gist
▷ **VERB 6** = **perceive**, feel,

S

understand, pick up, realize, be aware of, discern, get the impression **OPPOSITE:** be unaware of

sensibility *often plural* = **feelings**, emotions, sentiments, susceptibilities, moral sense

sensible 1 = **wise**, practical, prudent, shrewd, judicious **OPPOSITE:** foolish
2 = **intelligent**, practical, rational, sound, realistic, sage, shrewd, down-to-earth **OPPOSITE:** senseless

sensitive 1 = **thoughtful**, kindly, concerned, patient, attentive, tactful, unselfish
2 = **delicate**, tender
3 = **susceptible to**, responsive to, easily affected by
4 = **touchy**, oversensitive, easily upset, easily offended, easily hurt **OPPOSITE:** insensitive
5 = **precise**, fine, acute, keen, responsive **OPPOSITE:** imprecise

sensitivity 1 = **susceptibility**, responsiveness, receptiveness, sensitiveness
2 = **consideration**, patience, thoughtfulness
3 = **touchiness**, oversensitivity
4 = **responsiveness**, precision, keenness, acuteness

sensual 1 = **sexual**, erotic, raunchy (*slang*), lewd, lascivious, lustful, lecherous
2 = **physical**, bodily, voluptuous, animal, luxurious, fleshly, carnal

sentence NOUN
1 = **punishment**, condemnation
2 = **verdict**, order, ruling, decision, judgment, decree
▷ **VERB 3** = **condemn**, doom
4 = **convict**, condemn, penalize

sentiment 1 = **feeling**, idea, view, opinion, attitude, belief, judgment **2** = **sentimentality**, emotion, tenderness, romanticism, sensibility, emotionalism, mawkishness

sentimental = **romantic**, touching, emotional, nostalgic, maudlin, weepy (*informal*), slushy (*informal*), schmaltzy (*slang*) **OPPOSITE:** unsentimental

separate ADJECTIVE
1 = **unconnected**, individual, particular, divided, divorced, isolated, detached, disconnected **OPPOSITE:** connected **2** = **individual**, independent, apart, distinct **OPPOSITE:** joined
▷ **VERB 3** = **divide**, detach, disconnect, disjoin **OPPOSITE:** combine **4** = **come apart**, split, come away **OPPOSITE:** connect
5 = **sever**, break apart, split in two, divide in two **OPPOSITE:** join **6** = **split up**, part, divorce, break up, part company, get divorced, be estranged
7 = **distinguish**, mark, single out, set apart **OPPOSITE:** link

separated 1 = **estranged**, parted, separate, apart, disunited **2** = **disconnected**, parted, divided, separate, disassociated, disunited, sundered

separately 1 = **alone**, apart, not together, severally **OPPOSITE:** together 2 = **individually**, singly

separation 1 = **division**, break, dissociation, disconnection, disunion 2 = **split-up**, parting, split, divorce, break-up, rift

sequel 1 = **follow-up**, continuation, development 2 = **consequence**, result, outcome, conclusion, end, upshot

sequence = **succession**, course, series, order, chain, cycle, arrangement, progression

series 1 = **sequence**, course, chain, succession, run, set, order, train 2 = **drama**, serial, soap (*informal*), sitcom (*informal*), soap opera, soapie or soapie (*Austral. slang*), situation comedy

serious 1 = **grave**, bad, critical, dangerous, acute, severe 2 = **important**, crucial, urgent, pressing, worrying, significant, grim, momentous **OPPOSITE:** unimportant 3 = **thoughtful**, detailed, careful, deep, profound, in-depth 4 = **deep**, sophisticated 5 = **solemn**, earnest, grave, sober, staid, humourless, unsmiling **OPPOSITE:** light-hearted 6 = **sincere**, earnest, genuine,

honest, in earnest **OPPOSITE:** insincere

seriously 1 = **truly**, in earnest, all joking aside 2 = **badly**, severely, gravely, critically, acutely, dangerously

seriousness 1 = **importance**, gravity, urgency, significance 2 = **solemnity**, gravity, earnestness, gravitas

sermon = **homily**, address

servant = **attendant**, domestic, slave, maid, help, retainer, skivvy (*chiefly Brit.*)

serve 1 = **work for**, help, aid, assist, be in the service of 2 = **perform**, do, complete, fulfil, discharge 3 = **be adequate**, do, suffice, suit, satisfy, be acceptable, answer the purpose 4 = **present**, provide, supply, deliver, set out, dish up

service NOUN 1 = **facility**, system, resource, utility, amenity 2 = **ceremony**, worship, rite, observance 3 = **work**, labour, employment, business, office, duty 4 = **check**, maintenance check ▷ VERB 5 = **overhaul**, check, maintain, tune (up), go over, fine tune

session = **meeting**, hearing, sitting, period, conference, congress, discussion, assembly

set[1] VERB 1 = **put**, place, lay, position, rest, plant, station, stick 2 = **arrange**, decide (upon), settle, establish, determine, fix, schedule, appoint **3 = assign**, give, allot, prescribe **4 = harden**, stiffen, solidify, cake, thicken, crystallize, congeal **5 = go down**, sink, dip, decline, disappear, vanish, subside **6 = prepare**, lay, spread, arrange, make ready

▷ **ADJECTIVE 7 = established**, planned, decided, agreed, arranged, rigid, definite, inflexible **8 = strict**, rigid, stubborn, inflexible **OPPOSITE:** flexible **9 = conventional**, traditional, stereotyped, unspontaneous

▷ **NOUN 10 = scenery**, setting, scene, stage set **11 = position**, bearing, attitude, carriage, posture

▷ **PHRASES: be set on** or **upon something = be determined to**, be intent on, be bent on, be resolute about ▶ **set something up 1 = arrange**, organize, prepare, prearrange **2 = establish**, begin, found, institute, initiate **3 = build**, raise, construct, put up, assemble, put together, erect **4 = assemble**, put up

set² 1 = series, collection, assortment, batch, compendium, ensemble **2 = group**, company, crowd, circle, band, gang, faction, clique

setback = hold-up, check, defeat, blow, reverse, disappointment, hitch, misfortune

setting = surroundings, site, location, set, scene, background, context, backdrop

settle 1 = resolve, work out, put an end to, straighten out **2 = pay**, clear, square (up), discharge **3 = move to**, take up residence in, live in, dwell in, inhabit, reside in, set up home in, put down roots in **4 = colonize**, populate, people, pioneer **5 = land**, alight, descend, light, come to rest **6 = calm**, quiet, relax, relieve, reassure, soothe, lull, quell **OPPOSITE:** disturb

settlement 1 = agreement, arrangement, working out, conclusion, establishment, confirmation **2 = payment**, clearing, discharge **3 = colony**, community, outpost, encampment, kainga or kaika (N.Z.)

settler = colonist, immigrant, pioneer, frontiersman

set-up (Informal) **= arrangement**, system, structure, organization, conditions, regime

sever 1 = cut, separate, split, part, divide, detach, disconnect, cut in two **OPPOSITE:** join **2 = discontinue**, terminate, break off, put an end to, dissociate **OPPOSITE:** continue

several ADJECTIVE 1 = some, a

few, a number of, a handful of
▷ PRONOUN 2 = **various**,
different, diverse, sundry
severe ADJECTIVE 1 = **serious**,
critical, terrible, desperate,
extreme, awful, drastic,
catastrophic 2 = **acute**,
intense, violent, piercing,
harrowing, unbearable,
agonizing, insufferable
3 = **strict**, hard, harsh, cruel,
rigid, drastic, oppressive,
austere **OPPOSITE:** lenient
4 = **grim**, serious, grave,
forbidding, stern, unsmiling,
tight-lipped **OPPOSITE:** genial
5 = **plain**, simple, austere,
classic, restrained, Spartan,
unadorned, unfussy **OPPOSITE:**
fancy
severely 1 = **seriously**, badly,
extremely, gravely, acutely
2 = **strictly**, harshly, sternly,
sharply
severity = **strictness**,
harshness, toughness,
hardness, sternness, severeness
sew = **stitch**, tack, seam, hem
sex 1 = **gender** 2 (*Informal*)
= **lovemaking**, sexual relations,
copulation, fornication, coitus,
coition
sexual 1 = **carnal**, erotic,
intimate 2 = **sexy**, erotic,
sensual, arousing, naughty,
provocative, seductive,
sensuous
sexuality = **desire**, lust,
eroticism, sensuality, sexiness
(*informal*), carnality

sexy = **erotic**, sensual,
seductive, arousing, naughty,
provocative, sensuous,
suggestive
shabby 1 = **tatty**, worn,
ragged, scruffy, tattered,
threadbare **OPPOSITE:** smart
2 = **run-down**, seedy, mean,
dilapidated 3 = **mean**, low,
rotten (*informal*), cheap, dirty,
despicable, contemptible,
scurvy **OPPOSITE:** fair
shack = **hut**, cabin, shanty,
whare (*N.Z.*)
shade NOUN 1 = **hue**, tone,
colour, tint 2 = **shadow**
3 = **dash**, trace, hint,
suggestion 4 = **nuance**,
difference, degree 5 = **screen**,
covering, cover, blind, curtain,
shield, veil, canopy 6 (*Literary*)
= **ghost**, spirit, phantom,
spectre, apparition, kehua
(*N.Z.*)
▷ VERB 7 = **darken**, shadow,
cloud, dim 8 = **cover**, protect,
screen, hide, shield, conceal,
obscure, veil
shadow NOUN 1 = **silhouette**,
shape, outline, profile
2 = **shade**, dimness, darkness,
gloom, cover, dusk
▷ VERB 3 = **shade**, screen,
shield, darken, overhang
4 = **follow**, tail (*informal*), trail,
stalk
shady 1 = **shaded**, cool, dim
OPPOSITE: sunny 2 (*Informal*)
= **crooked**, dodgy (*Brit., Austral.
& N.Z. informal*), unethical,

S

suspect, suspicious, dubious, questionable, shifty **OPPOSITE:** honest

shaft 1 = **tunnel**, hole, passage, burrow, passageway, channel 2 = **handle**, staff, pole, rod, stem, baton, shank 3 = **ray**, beam, gleam

shake VERB 1 = **jiggle**, agitate 2 = **tremble**, shiver, quake, quiver 3 = **rock**, totter 4 = **wave**, wield, flourish, brandish 5 = **upset**, shock, frighten, disturb, distress, rattle (informal), unnerve, traumatize ▷ NOUN 6 = **vibration**, trembling, quaking, jerk, shiver, shudder, jolt, tremor

Shakespeare ▷ See panel SHAKESPEARE

shaky 1 = **unstable**, weak, precarious, rickety **OPPOSITE:** stable 2 = **unsteady**, faint, trembling, faltering, quivery 3 = **uncertain**, suspect, dubious, questionable, iffy (informal) **OPPOSITE:** reliable

shallow = **superficial**, surface, empty, slight, foolish, trivial, meaningless, frivolous **OPPOSITE:** deep

sham NOUN 1 = **fraud**, imitation, hoax, pretence, forgery, counterfeit, humbug, impostor **OPPOSITE:** the real thing ▷ ADJECTIVE 2 = **false**, artificial, bogus, pretended, mock, imitation, simulated, counterfeit **OPPOSITE:** real

shambles 1 = **chaos**, mess, disorder, confusion, muddle, havoc, disarray, madhouse 2 = **mess**, jumble, untidiness

shame NOUN 1 = **embarrassment**, humiliation, ignominy, mortification, abashment **OPPOSITE:** shamelessness 2 = **disgrace**, scandal, discredit, smear, disrepute, reproach, dishonour, infamy **OPPOSITE:** honour ▷ VERB 3 = **embarrass**, disgrace, humiliate, humble, mortify, abash **OPPOSITE:** make proud 4 = **dishonour**, degrade, stain, smear, blot, debase, defile **OPPOSITE:** honour

shameful = **disgraceful**, outrageous, scandalous, mean, low, base, wicked, dishonourable **OPPOSITE:** admirable

shape NOUN 1 = **appearance**, form, aspect, guise, likeness, semblance 2 = **form**, profile, outline, lines, build, figure, silhouette, configuration 3 = **pattern**, model, frame, mould 4 = **condition**, state, health, trim, fettle ▷ VERB 5 = **form**, make, produce, create, model, fashion, mould 6 = **mould**, form, make, fashion, model, frame

share NOUN 1 = **part**, portion, quota, ration, lot, due, contribution, allowance ▷ VERB 2 = **divide**, split,

SHAKESPEARE

Characters in Shakespeare	Play
Sir Andrew Aguecheek	Twelfth Night
Antonio	The Merchant of Venice
Antony	Antony and Cleopatra, Julius Caesar
Ariel	The Tempest
Aufidius	Coriolanus
Autolycus	The Winter's Tale
Banquo	Macbeth
Bassanio	The Merchant of Venice
Beatrice	Much Ado About Nothing
Sir Toby Belch	Twelfth Night
Benedick	Much Ado About Nothing
Bolingbroke	Richard II
Bottom	A Midsummer Night's Dream
Brutus	Julius Caesar
Caliban	The Tempest
Casca	Julius Caesar
Cassio	Othello
Cassius	Julius Caesar
Claudio	Much Ado About Nothing, Measure for Measure
Claudius	Hamlet
Cleopatra	Antony and Cleopatra
Cordelia	King Lear
Coriolanus	Coriolanus
Cressida	Troilus and Cressida
Demetrius	A Midsummer Night's Dream
Desdemona	Othello
Dogberry	Much Ado About Nothing
Edmund	King Lear
Enobarbus	Antony and Cleopatra
Falstaff	Henry IV Parts I and II, The Merry Wives of Windsor
Ferdinand	The Tempest
Feste	Twelfth Night
Fluellen	Henry V
Fool	King Lear

S

SHAKESPEARE *continued*

Characters in Shakespeare	Play
Gertrude	Hamlet
Gloucester	King Lear
Goneril	King Lear
Guildenstern	Hamlet
Hamlet	Hamlet
Helena	All's Well that Ends Well, A Midsummer Night's Dream
Hermia	A Midsummer Night's Dream
Hero	Much Ado About Nothing
Hotspur	Henry IV Part I
Iago	Othello
Jaques	As You Like It
John of Gaunt	Richard II
Juliet	Romeo and Juliet
Julius Caesar	Julius Caesar
Katharina or Kate	The Taming of the Shrew
Kent	King Lear
Laertes	Hamlet
Lear	King Lear
Lysander	A Midsummer Night's Dream
Macbeth	Macbeth
Lady Macbeth	Macbeth
Macduff	Macbeth
Malcolm	Macbeth
Malvolio	Twelfth Night
Mercutio	Romeo and Juliet
Miranda	The Tempest
Oberon	A Midsummer Night's Dream
Octavius	Antony and Cleopatra
Olivia	Twelfth Night
Ophelia	Hamlet
Orlando	As You Like It
Orsino	Twelfth Night
Othello	Othello
Pandarus	Troilus and Cressida
Perdita	The Winter's Tale

SHAKESPEARE continued

Characters in Shakespeare	Play
Petruchio	The Taming of the Shrew
Pistol	Henry IV Part II, Henry V, The Merry Wives of Windsor
Polonius	Hamlet
Portia	The Merchant of Venice
Prospero	The Tempest
Puck	A Midsummer Night's Dream
Mistress Quickly	The Merry Wives of Windsor
Regan	King Lear
Romeo	Romeo and Juliet
Rosalind	As You Like It
Rosencrantz	Hamlet
Sebastian	The Tempest, Twelfth Night
Shylock	The Merchant of Venice
Thersites	Troilus and Cressida
Timon	Timon of Athens
Titania	A Midsummer Night's Dream
Touchstone	As You Like It
Troilus	Troilus and Cressida
Tybalt	Romeo and Juliet
Viola	Twelfth Night

Plays of Shakespeare

All's Well that Ends Well	Julius Caesar
Antony and Cleopatra	King John
As You Like It	King Lear
The Comedy of Errors	Love's Labour's Lost
Coriolanus	Macbeth
Cymbeline	Measure for Measure
Hamlet	The Merchant of Venice
Henry IV Part I	The Merry Wives of Windsor
Henry IV Part II	A Midsummer Night's Dream
Henry V	Much Ado About Nothing
Henry VI Part I	Othello
Henry VI Part II	Pericles, Prince of Tyre
Henry VI Part III	Richard II
Henry VIII	Richard III

SHAKESPEARE *continued*

Romeo and Juliet
The Taming of the Shrew
The Tempest
Timon of Athens
Titus Andronicus

Troilus and Cressida
Twelfth Night
The Two Gentlemen of Verona
The Winter's Tale

SHARKS

angel shark, angelfish, or
  monkfish
basking shark, sailfish or (N.Z.)
  reremai
blue pointer or (N.Z.) blue shark
  or blue whaler
bronze whaler (Austral.)
carpet shark or (Austral.)
  wobbegong
dogfish or (Austral.) dog
  shark
gummy (shark)

hammerhead
mako
nurse shark
porbeagle or mackerel shark
requiem shark
school shark (Austral.)
seven-gill shark (Austral.)
shovelhead
thresher or thresher shark
tiger shark
tope
whale shark

---

distribute, assign **3** = **go halves
on**, go fifty-fifty on (*informal*)
shark ▷ *See panel* SHARKS
sharp ADJECTIVE **1** = **keen**,
jagged, serrated OPPOSITE:
blunt **2** = **quick-witted**, clever,
astute, knowing, quick, bright,
alert, penetrating OPPOSITE:
dim **3** = **cutting**, biting, bitter,
harsh, barbed, hurtful, caustic
OPPOSITE: gentle **4** = **sudden**,
marked, abrupt, extreme,
distinct OPPOSITE: gradual
5 = **clear**, distinct, well-defined,
crisp OPPOSITE: indistinct
6 = **sour**, tart, pungent, hot,
acid, acrid, piquant OPPOSITE:
bland **7** = **acute**, severe,

intense, painful, shooting,
stabbing, piercing, gut-
wrenching
▷ ADVERB **8** = **promptly**,
precisely, exactly, on time, on
the dot, punctually OPPOSITE:
approximately
sharpen = **make sharp**, hone,
whet, grind, edge
shatter 1 = **smash**, break,
burst, crack, crush, pulverize
2 = **destroy**, ruin, wreck,
demolish, torpedo
shattered 1 = **devastated**,
crushed, gutted (*slang*)
2 (*Informal*) = **exhausted**,
drained, worn out, done in
(*informal*), all in (*slang*),

knackered (*slang*), tired out, ready to drop

shave 1 = **trim**, crop
2 = **scrape**, trim, shear, pare

shed¹ = **hut**, shack, outhouse, whare (*N.Z.*)

shed² 1 = **drop**, spill, scatter
2 = **cast off**, discard, moult, slough off 3 = **give out**, cast, emit, give, radiate

sheen = **shine**, gleam, gloss, polish, brightness, lustre

sheer 1 = **total**, complete, absolute, utter, pure, downright, out-and-out, unmitigated **OPPOSITE:** moderate 2 = **steep**, abrupt, precipitous **OPPOSITE:** gradual 3 = **fine**, thin, transparent, see-through, gossamer, diaphanous, gauzy **OPPOSITE:** thick

sheet 1 = **page**, leaf, folio, piece of paper 2 = **plate**, piece, panel, slab 3 = **coat**, film, layer, surface, stratum, veneer, overlay, lamina 4 = **expanse**, area, stretch, sweep, covering, blanket

shell NOUN 1 = **husk**, case, pod
2 = **carapace** 3 = **frame**, structure, hull, framework, chassis
▷ VERB 4 = **bomb**, bombard, attack, blitz, strafe
▷ PHRASES: **shell something out** (with money or a specified sum of money as object) = **pay out**, fork out (*slang*), give, hand over

shelter NOUN 1 = **cover**, screen
2 = **protection**, safety, refuge, cover 3 = **refuge**, haven, sanctuary, retreat, asylum
▷ VERB 4 = **take shelter**, hide, seek refuge, take cover
5 = **protect**, shield, harbour, safeguard, cover, hide, guard, defend **OPPOSITE:** endanger

sheltered 1 = **screened**, covered, protected, shielded, secluded **OPPOSITE:** exposed
2 = **protected**, screened, shielded, quiet, isolated, secluded, cloistered

shelve = **postpone**, defer, freeze, suspend, put aside, put on ice, put on the back burner (*informal*), take a rain check on (*U.S. & Canad. informal*)

shepherd NOUN 1 = **drover**, stockman, herdsman, grazier
▷ VERB 2 = **guide**, conduct, steer, herd, usher
● RELATED WORD
● *adjective:* pastoral

shield NOUN 1 = **protection**, cover, defence, screen, guard, shelter, safeguard
▷ VERB 2 = **protect**, cover, screen, guard, defend, shelter, safeguard

shift VERB 1 = **move**, move around, budge 2 = **remove**, move, displace, relocate, rearrange, reposition
▷ NOUN 3 = **change**, shifting, displacement 4 = **move**, rearrangement

shimmer VERB 1 = **gleam**,

twinkle, glisten, scintillate
▷ NOUN 2 = **gleam**, iridescence

shine VERB 1 = **gleam**, flash,
beam, glow, sparkle, glitter,
glare, radiate 2 = **polish**, buff,
burnish, brush 3 = **be
outstanding**, stand out, excel,
be conspicuous
▷ NOUN 4 = **polish**, gloss,
sheen, lustre 5 = **brightness**,
light, sparkle, radiance

shining = **bright**, brilliant,
gleaming, beaming, sparkling,
shimmering, radiant, luminous

shiny = **bright**, gleaming,
glossy, glistening, polished,
lustrous

ship = **vessel**, boat, craft

shiver VERB 1 = **shudder**,
shake, tremble, quake, quiver
▷ NOUN 2 = **tremble**, shudder,
quiver, trembling, flutter,
tremor

shock NOUN 1 = **upset**, blow,
trauma, bombshell, turn
(_informal_), distress, disturbance
2 = **impact**, blow, clash,
collision 3 = **start**, scare, fright,
turn, jolt
▷ VERB 4 = **shake**, stun,
stagger, jolt, stupefy
5 = **horrify**, appal, disgust,
revolt, sicken, nauseate,
scandalize

shocking 1 (_Informal_)
= **terrible**, appalling, dreadful,
bad, horrendous, ghastly,
deplorable, abysmal
2 = **appalling**, outrageous,
disgraceful, disgusting,

dreadful, horrifying, revolting,
sickening OPPOSITE: wonderful

shoot VERB 1 = **open fire on**,
blast (_slang_), hit, kill, plug
(_slang_), bring down 2 = **fire**,
launch, discharge, project, hurl,
fling, propel, emit 3 = **speed**,
race, rush, charge, fly, tear,
dash, barrel (along) (_informal,
chiefly U.S. & Canad._)
▷ NOUN 4 = **sprout**, branch,
bud, sprig, offshoot

shop = **store**, supermarket,
boutique, emporium,
hypermarket, dairy (_N.Z._)

shore = **beach**, coast, sands,
strand (_poetic_), seashore

short ADJECTIVE 1 = **brief**,
fleeting, momentary OPPOSITE:
long 2 = **concise**, brief,
succinct, summary,
compressed, terse, laconic,
pithy OPPOSITE: lengthy
3 = **small**, little, squat,
diminutive, petite, dumpy
OPPOSITE: tall 4 = **abrupt**,
sharp, terse, curt, brusque,
impolite, discourteous, uncivil
OPPOSITE: polite 5 = **scarce**,
wanting, low, limited, lacking,
scant, deficient OPPOSITE:
plentiful
▷ ADVERB 6 = **abruptly**,
suddenly, without warning
OPPOSITE: gradually

shortage = **deficiency**, want,
lack, scarcity, dearth, paucity,
insufficiency OPPOSITE:
abundance

shortcoming = **failing**, fault,

weakness, defect, flaw, imperfection

shorten 1 = **cut**, reduce, decrease, diminish, lessen, curtail, abbreviate, abridge **OPPOSITE:** increase 2 = **turn up**

shortly = **soon**, presently, before long, in a little while

shot 1 = **discharge**, gunfire, crack, blast, explosion, bang 2 = **ammunition**, bullet, slug, pellet, projectile, lead, ball 3 = **marksman**, shooter, markswoman 4 (Informal) = **strike**, throw, lob 5 = **attempt**, go (informal), try, turn, effort, stab (informal), endeavour

shoulder 1 = **bear**, carry, take on, accept, assume, be responsible for 2 = **push**, elbow, shove, jostle, press

shout VERB 1 = **cry (out)**, call (out), yell, scream, roar, bellow, bawl, holler (informal)
▷ NOUN 2 = **cry**, call, yell, scream, roar, bellow
▷ PHRASES: **shout someone down** = **drown out**, overwhelm, drown, silence

shove VERB 1 = **push**, thrust, elbow, drive, press, propel, jostle, impel
▷ NOUN 2 = **push**, knock, thrust, elbow, bump, nudge, jostle
▷ PHRASES: **shove off** (Informal) = **go away**, leave, clear off (informal), depart, push off (informal), scram (informal)

shovel 1 = **move**, scoop, dredge, load, heap 2 = **stuff**, ladle

show VERB 1 = **indicate**, demonstrate, prove, reveal, display, point out, manifest, testify to **OPPOSITE:** disprove 2 = **display**, exhibit 3 = **guide**, lead, conduct, accompany, direct, escort 4 = **demonstrate**, describe, explain, teach, illustrate, instruct 5 = **be visible**, be seen **OPPOSITE:** be invisible 6 = **express**, display, reveal, indicate, register, demonstrate, manifest **OPPOSITE:** hide 7 = **turn up**, appear, attend 8 = **broadcast**, transmit, air, beam, relay, televise, put on the air
▷ NOUN 9 = **display**, sight, spectacle, array 10 = **exhibition**, fair, display, parade, pageant 11 = **appearance**, display, pose, parade 12 = **pretence**, appearance, illusion, affectation 13 = **programme**, broadcast, presentation, production 14 = **entertainment**, production, presentation
▷ PHRASES: **show off** (Informal) = **boast**, brag, blow your own trumpet, swagger ▶ **show someone up** (Informal) = **embarrass**, let down, mortify, put to shame ▶ **show something off** = **exhibit**, display, parade, demonstrate,

S

flaunt ▶ **show something up** = **reveal**, expose, highlight, lay bare

showdown (*Informal*) = **confrontation**, clash, face-off (*slang*)

shower NOUN 1 = **deluge** ▷ VERB 2 = **cover**, dust, spray, sprinkle 3 = **inundate**, heap, lavish, pour, deluge

show-off (*Informal*) = **exhibitionist**, boaster, poseur, braggart

shred 1 = **strip**, bit, piece, scrap, fragment, sliver, tatter 2 = **particle**, trace, scrap, grain, atom, jot, iota

shrewd = **astute**, clever, sharp, keen, smart, calculating, intelligent, cunning **OPPOSITE:** naive

shriek VERB 1 = **scream**, cry, yell, screech, squeal ▷ NOUN 2 = **scream**, cry, yell, screech, squeal

shrink = **decrease**, dwindle, lessen, grow *or* get smaller, contract, narrow, diminish, shorten **OPPOSITE:** grow

shroud NOUN 1 = **winding sheet**, grave clothes 2 = **covering**, veil, mantle, screen, pall ▷ VERB 3 = **conceal**, cover, screen, hide, blanket, veil, cloak, envelop

shudder VERB 1 = **shiver**, shake, tremble, quake, quiver, convulse ▷ NOUN 2 = **shiver**, tremor,

quiver, spasm, convulsion

shuffle 1 = **shamble**, stagger, stumble, dodder 2 = **scuffle**, drag, scrape 3 = **rearrange**, jumble, mix, disorder, disarrange

shun = **avoid**, steer clear of, keep away from

shut VERB 1 = **close**, secure, fasten, seal, slam **OPPOSITE:** open ▷ ADJECTIVE 2 = **closed**, fastened, sealed, locked **OPPOSITE:** open ▷ PHRASES: shut down = **stop work**, halt work, close down

shuttle = **go back and forth**, commute, go to and fro, alternate

shy ADJECTIVE 1 = **timid**, self-conscious, bashful, retiring, shrinking, coy, self-effacing, diffident **OPPOSITE:** confident 2 = **cautious**, wary, hesitant, suspicious, distrustful, chary **OPPOSITE:** reckless ▷ VERB 3 *sometimes with* **off** *or* **away** = **recoil**, flinch, draw back, start, balk

sick 1 = **unwell**, ill, poorly (*informal*), diseased, crook (*Austral. & N.Z. informal*), ailing, under the weather, indisposed **OPPOSITE:** well 2 = **nauseous**, ill, queasy, nauseated 3 = **tired**, bored, fed up, weary, jaded 4 (*Informal*) = **morbid**, sadistic, black, macabre, ghoulish

sicken 1 = **disgust**, revolt, nauseate, repel, gross out (*U.S.*

slang), turn your stomach
2 = **fall ill**, take sick, ail

sickening = **disgusting**,
revolting, offensive, foul,
distasteful, repulsive,
nauseating, loathsome, yucko
(*Austral. slang*) **OPPOSITE:**
delightful

sickness 1 = **illness**, disorder,
ailment, disease, complaint,
bug (*informal*), affliction, malady
2 = **nausea**, queasiness
3 = **vomiting**

side NOUN **1** = **border**, margin,
boundary, verge, flank, rim,
perimeter, edge **OPPOSITE:**
middle **2** = **face**, surface, facet
3 = **party**, camp, faction, cause
4 = **point of view**, viewpoint,
position, opinion, angle, slant,
standpoint **5** = **team**, squad,
line-up **6** = **aspect**, feature,
angle, facet
▷ ADJECTIVE **7** = **subordinate**,
minor, secondary, subsidiary,
lesser, marginal, incidental,
ancillary **OPPOSITE:** main
▷ PHRASES: **side with someone**
= **support**, agree with, stand up
for, favour, go along with, take
the part of, ally yourself with

sidewalk (*U.S. & Canad.*)
= **pavement**, footpath (*Austral.
& N.Z.*)

sideways ADVERB
1 = **indirectly**, obliquely **2** = **to
the side**, laterally
▷ ADJECTIVE **3** = **sidelong**,
oblique

sift 1 = **part**, filter, strain,

separate, sieve **2** = **examine**,
investigate, go through,
research, analyse, work over,
scrutinize

sight NOUN **1** = **vision**, eyes,
eyesight, seeing, eye
2 = **spectacle**, show, scene,
display, exhibition, vista,
pageant **3** = **view**, range of
vision, visibility **4** (*Informal*)
= **eyesore**, mess, monstrosity
▷ VERB **5** = **spot**, see, observe,
distinguish, perceive, make out,
discern, behold
● RELATED WORDS
● *adjectives*: optical, visual

sign NOUN **1** = **symbol**, mark,
device, logo, badge, emblem
2 = **figure 3** = **notice**, board,
warning, placard
4 = **indication**, evidence, mark,
signal, symptom, hint, proof,
gesture **5** = **omen**, warning,
portent, foreboding, augury,
auspice
▷ VERB **6** = **gesture**, indicate,
signal, beckon, gesticulate
7 = **autograph**, initial, inscribe

signal NOUN **1** = **flare**, beam,
beacon **2** = **cue**, sign,
prompting, reminder **3** = **sign**,
gesture, indication, mark, note,
expression, token
▷ VERB **4** = **gesture**, sign,
wave, indicate, motion, beckon,
gesticulate

significance = **importance**,
consequence, moment, weight

significant 1 = **important**,
serious, material, vital, critical,

S

momentous, weighty, noteworthy **OPPOSITE:** insignificant **2 = meaningful**, expressive, eloquent, indicative, suggestive **OPPOSITE:** meaningless

signify = indicate, mean, suggest, imply, intimate, be a sign of, denote, connote

silence NOUN 1 = quiet, peace, calm, hush, lull, stillness **OPPOSITE:** noise **2 = reticence**, dumbness, taciturnity, muteness **OPPOSITE:** speech ▷ **VERB 3 = quieten**, still, quiet, cut off, stifle, cut short, muffle, deaden **OPPOSITE:** make louder

silent 1 = mute, dumb, speechless, wordless, voiceless **OPPOSITE:** noisy
2 = uncommunicative, quiet, taciturn **3 = quiet**, still, hushed, soundless, noiseless, muted **OPPOSITE:** loud

silently 1 = quietly, in silence, soundlessly, noiselessly, inaudibly, without a sound
2 = mutely, in silence, wordlessly

silhouette NOUN 1 = outline, form, shape, profile ▷ **VERB 2 = outline**, etch

silly 1 = stupid, ridiculous, absurd, daft, inane, senseless, idiotic, fatuous **OPPOSITE:** clever **2 = foolish**, stupid, unwise, rash, irresponsible, thoughtless, imprudent **OPPOSITE:** sensible

similar 1 = alike, resembling, comparable **OPPOSITE:** different
2 with **to = like**, comparable to, analogous to, close to
● **USAGE NOTE**
● As should not be used after
● similar - so Wilson held a similar
● position to Jones is correct, but
● not Wilson held a similar
● position as Jones; and the
● system is similar to the one in
● France is correct, but not the
● system is similar as in France.

similarity = resemblance, likeness, sameness, agreement, correspondence, analogy, affinity, closeness **OPPOSITE:** difference

simmer 1 = bubble, boil gently, seethe **2 = fume**, seethe, smoulder, rage, be angry ▷ **PHRASES:** simmer down (Informal) **= calm down**, control yourself, cool off or down

simple ADJECTIVE
1 = uncomplicated, clear, plain, understandable, lucid, recognizable, comprehensible, intelligible **OPPOSITE:** complicated **2 = easy**, straightforward, not difficult, effortless, painless, uncomplicated, undemanding **3 = plain**, natural, classic, unfussy, unembellished **OPPOSITE:** elaborate **4 = pure**, mere, sheer, unalloyed **5 = artless**, innocent, naive, natural, sincere, unaffected, childlike, unsophisticated **OPPOSITE:** sophisticated

6 = **unpretentious**, modest, humble, homely, unfussy, unembellished **OPPOSITE:** fancy

simplicity
1 = **straightforwardness**, ease, clarity, clearness **OPPOSITE:** complexity 2 = **plainness**, restraint, purity, lack of adornment **OPPOSITE:** elaborateness

simplify = **make simpler**, streamline, disentangle, dumb down, reduce to essentials

simply 1 = **just**, only, merely, purely, solely 2 = **totally**, completely, absolutely, wholly, utterly 3 = **clearly**, straightforwardly, directly, plainly, intelligibly 4 = **plainly**, naturally, modestly, unpretentiously 5 = **without doubt**, surely, certainly, definitely, beyond question

simulate = **pretend**, act, feign, affect, put on, sham

simultaneous = **coinciding**, concurrent, contemporaneous, coincident, synchronous, happening at the same time

simultaneously = **at the same time**, together, concurrently

sin NOUN 1 = **wickedness**, evil, crime, error, transgression, iniquity 2 = **crime**, offence, error, wrongdoing, misdeed, transgression, act of evil, guilt ▷ VERB 3 = **transgress**, offend, lapse, err, go astray, do wrong

sincere = **honest**, genuine, real, true, serious, earnest, frank, candid, dinkum (*Austral. & N.Z. informal*) **OPPOSITE:** false

sincerely = **honestly**, truly, genuinely, seriously, earnestly, wholeheartedly, in earnest

sincerity = **honesty**, truth, candour, frankness, seriousness, genuineness

sing 1 = **croon**, carol, chant, warble, yodel, pipe 2 = **trill**, chirp, warble

● USAGE NOTE
● *Sang* is the past tense of the
● verb *sing*, as in *she sang*
● *sweetly*. *Sung* is the past
● participle, as in *we have sung*
● *our song*, and care should be
● taken not to use it as if it
● were a variant form of the
● past tense.

singer = **vocalist**, crooner, minstrel, soloist, chorister, balladeer

single 1 = **one**, sole, lone, solitary, only, only one 2 = **individual**, separate, distinct 3 = **unmarried**, free, unattached, unwed 4 = **separate**, individual, exclusive, undivided, unshared 5 = **simple**, unmixed, unblended
▷ PHRASES: **single something or someone out** = **pick**, choose, select, separate, distinguish, fix on, set apart, pick on or out

singly = **one by one**, individually, one at a time, separately

singular 1 = **single**, individual

S

2 = **remarkable**, outstanding, exceptional, notable, eminent, noteworthy **OPPOSITE:** ordinary
3 = **unusual**, odd, strange, extraordinary, curious, peculiar, eccentric, queer **OPPOSITE:** conventional

sinister = **threatening**, evil, menacing, dire, ominous, malign, disquieting **OPPOSITE:** reassuring

sink 1 = **go down**, founder, go under, submerge, capsize
2 = **slump**, drop **3** = **fall**, drop, slip, plunge, subside, abate
4 = **drop**, fall **5** = **stoop**, be reduced to, lower yourself
6 = **decline**, fade, fail, flag, weaken, diminish, decrease, deteriorate **OPPOSITE:** improve
7 = **dig**, bore, drill, drive, excavate

sip VERB **1** = **drink**, taste, sample, sup
▷ NOUN **2** = **swallow**, drop, taste, thimbleful

sit 1 = **take a seat**, perch, settle down **2** = **place**, set, put, position, rest, lay, settle, deposit **3** = **be a member of**, serve on, have a seat on, preside on **4** = **convene**, meet, assemble, officiate

site NOUN **1** = **area**, plot
2 = **location**, place, setting, point, position, situation, spot
▷ VERB **3** = **locate**, put, place, set, position, establish, install, situate

situation 1 = **position**, state,

case, condition, circumstances, equation, plight, state of affairs
2 = **scenario**, state of affairs
3 = **location**, place, setting, position, site, spot

● USAGE NOTE
● It is common to hear the
● word situation used in
● sentences such as the
● company is in a crisis situation.
● This use of situation is
● considered bad style and the
● word should be left out, since
● it adds nothing to the
● sentence's meaning.

size = **dimensions**, extent, range, amount, mass, volume, proportions, bulk
▷ PHRASES: size something or someone up (Informal) = **assess**, evaluate, appraise, take stock of

sizeable or **sizable** = **large**, considerable, substantial, goodly, decent, respectable, largish

sizzle = **hiss**, spit, crackle, fry, frizzle

skeleton = **bones**, bare bones

sketch NOUN **1** = **drawing**, design, draft, delineation
▷ VERB **2** = **draw**, outline, represent, draft, depict, delineate, rough out

skilful = **expert**, skilled, masterly, able, professional, clever, practised, competent **OPPOSITE:** clumsy

skill = **expertise**, ability, proficiency, art, technique, facility, talent, craft, finesse

OPPOSITE: clumsiness

skilled = expert, professional, able, masterly, skilful, proficient **OPPOSITE:** unskilled

skim 1 = **remove**, separate, cream 2 = **glide**, fly, coast, sail, float 3 *usually with* **over** *or* **through** = **scan**, glance, run your eye over

skin NOUN 1 = **hide**, pelt, fell 2 = **peel**, rind, husk, casing, outside, crust 3 = **film**, coating ▷ VERB 4 = **peel** 5 = **scrape**, flay

skinny = **thin**, lean, scrawny, emaciated, undernourished **OPPOSITE:** fat

skip 1 = **hop**, dance, bob, trip, bounce, caper, prance, frisk 2 = **miss out**, omit, leave out, overlook, pass over, eschew, give (something) a miss

skirt 1 = **border**, edge, flank 2 *often with* **around** *or* **round** = **go round**, circumvent 3 *often with* **around** *or* **round** = **avoid**, evade, steer clear of, circumvent

sky = **heavens**, firmament, rangi (N.Z.)

● **RELATED WORD**
● *adjective:* celestial

slab = **piece**, slice, lump, chunk, wedge, portion

slack ADJECTIVE 1 = **limp**, relaxed, loose, lax 2 = **loose**, baggy **OPPOSITE:** taut 3 = **slow**, quiet, inactive, dull, sluggish, slow-moving **OPPOSITE:** busy 4 = **negligent**, lazy, lax, idle, inactive, slapdash,

neglectful, slipshod **OPPOSITE:** strict

▷ VERB 5 = **shirk**, idle, dodge, skive (*Brit. slang*), bludge (*Austral. & N.Z. informal*)

▷ NOUN 6 = **surplus**, excess, glut, surfeit, superabundance, superfluity 7 = **room**, excess, leeway, give (*informal*)

slam 1 = **bang**, crash, smash 2 = **throw**, dash, hurl, fling

slant VERB 1 = **slope**, incline, tilt, list, bend, lean, heel, cant 2 = **bias**, colour, twist, angle, distort

▷ NOUN 3 = **slope**, incline, tilt, gradient, camber 4 = **bias**, emphasis, prejudice, angle, point of view, one-sidedness

slanting = **sloping**, angled, inclined, tilted, tilting, bent, diagonal, oblique

slap VERB 1 = **smack**, beat, clap, cuff, swipe, spank, clobber (*slang*), wallop (*informal*)

▷ NOUN 2 = **smack**, blow, cuff, swipe, spank

slash VERB 1 = **cut**, slit, gash, lacerate, score, rend, rip, hack 2 = **reduce**, cut, decrease, drop, lower, moderate, diminish, cut down

▷ NOUN 3 = **cut**, slit, gash, rent, rip, incision, laceration

slate (*Informal, chiefly Brit.*) = **criticize**, censure, rebuke, scold, tear into (*informal*)

slaughter VERB 1 = **kill**, murder, massacre, destroy, execute, assassinate

s

2 = **butcher**, kill, slay, massacre
▷ NOUN 3 = **slaying**, killing, murder, massacre, bloodshed, carnage, butchery

slave NOUN 1 = **servant**, serf, vassal 2 = **drudge**, skivvy (*chiefly Brit.*)
▷ VERB 3 = **toil**, drudge, slog

slavery = **enslavement**, servitude, subjugation, captivity, bondage **OPPOSITE:** freedom

slay 1 (*Archaic or literary*) = **kill**, slaughter, massacre, butcher 2 = **murder**, kill, massacre, slaughter, mow down

sleaze (*Informal*) = **corruption**, fraud, dishonesty, bribery, extortion, venality, unscrupulousness

sleek = **glossy**, shiny, lustrous, smooth **OPPOSITE:** shaggy

sleep NOUN 1 = **slumber(s)**, nap, doze, snooze (*informal*), hibernation, siesta, forty winks (*informal*), zizz (*Brit. informal*)
▷ VERB 2 = **slumber**, doze, snooze (*informal*), hibernate, take a nap, catnap, drowse

sleepy = **drowsy**, sluggish, lethargic, heavy, dull, inactive **OPPOSITE:** wide-awake

slender 1 = **slim**, narrow, slight, lean, willowy **OPPOSITE:** chubby 2 = **faint**, slight, remote, slim, thin, tenuous **OPPOSITE:** strong 3 = **meagre**, little, small, scant, scanty **OPPOSITE:** large

slice NOUN 1 = **piece**, segment, portion, wedge, sliver, helping, share, cut
▷ VERB 2 = **cut**, divide, carve, sever, dissect, bisect

slick ADJECTIVE 1 = **skilful**, deft, adroit, dexterous, professional, polished **OPPOSITE:** clumsy 2 = **glib**, smooth, plausible, polished, specious
▷ VERB 3 = **smooth**, sleek, plaster down

slide = **slip**, slither, glide, skim, coast

slight ADJECTIVE 1 = **small**, minor, insignificant, trivial, feeble, trifling, meagre, unimportant **OPPOSITE:** large 2 = **slim**, small, delicate, spare, fragile, lightly-built **OPPOSITE:** sturdy
▷ VERB 3 = **snub**, insult, ignore, affront, scorn, disdain **OPPOSITE:** compliment
▷ NOUN 4 = **insult**, snub, affront, rebuff, slap in the face (*informal*), (the) cold shoulder **OPPOSITE:** compliment

slightly = **a little**, a bit, somewhat

slim ADJECTIVE 1 = **slender**, slight, trim, thin, narrow, lean, svelte, willowy **OPPOSITE:** chubby 2 = **slight**, remote, faint, slender **OPPOSITE:** strong
▷ VERB 3 = **lose weight**, diet **OPPOSITE:** put on weight

sling 1 (*Informal*) = **throw**, cast, toss, hurl, fling, chuck (*informal*), lob (*informal*), heave 2 = **hang**, suspend

slip VERB 1 = **fall**, skid
2 = **slide**, slither 3 = **sneak**,
creep, steal
▷ NOUN 4 = **mistake**, failure,
error, blunder, lapse, omission,
oversight
▷ PHRASES: **give someone the
slip** = **escape from**, get away
from, evade, elude, lose
(someone), flee, dodge ▶ **slip up**
= **make a mistake**, blunder, err,
miscalculate

slippery 1 = **smooth**, icy,
greasy, glassy, slippy (informal,
dialect), unsafe
2 = **untrustworthy**, tricky,
cunning, dishonest, devious,
crafty, evasive, shifty

slit VERB 1 = **cut (open)**, rip,
slash, knife, pierce, lance, gash
▷ NOUN 2 = **cut**, gash, incision,
tear, rent 3 = **opening**, split

slogan = **catch phrase**, motto,
tag-line, catchword

slope NOUN 1 = **inclination**,
rise, incline, tilt, slant, ramp,
gradient
▷ VERB 2 = **slant**, incline, drop
away, fall, rise, lean, tilt
▷ PHRASES: **slope off** (Informal)
= **slink away**, slip away, creep
away

sloping = **slanting**, leaning,
inclined, oblique

sloppy 1 (Informal) = **careless**,
slovenly, slipshod, messy, untidy
2 (Informal) = **sentimental**,
soppy (Brit. informal), slushy
(informal), gushing, mawkish,
icky (informal)

slot NOUN 1 = **opening**, hole,
groove, vent, slit, aperture
2 (Informal) = **place**, time,
space, opening, position,
vacancy
▷ VERB 3 = **fit**, insert

slow ADJECTIVE 1 = **unhurried**,
sluggish, leisurely, lazy,
ponderous, dawdling, laggard,
lackadaisical OPPOSITE: quick
2 = **prolonged**, protracted,
long-drawn-out, lingering,
gradual 3 = **late**, behind, tardy
4 = **stupid**, dim, dense, thick,
retarded, dozy (Brit. informal),
obtuse, braindead (informal)
OPPOSITE: bright
▷ VERB 5 often with **down**
= **decelerate**, brake 6 often
with **down** = **delay**, hold up,
handicap, retard OPPOSITE:
speed up
● USAGE NOTE
● While not as unkind as thick
● and stupid, words like slow
● and backward, when used to
● talk about a person's mental
● abilities, are both unhelpful
● and likely to cause offence. It
● is preferable to say that a
● person has special educational
● needs or learning difficulties.

slowly = **gradually**, unhurriedly
OPPOSITE: quickly

slug ▷ See panel SNAILS, SLUGS
AND OTHER GASTROPODS

sluggish = **inactive**, slow,
lethargic, heavy, dull, inert,
indolent, torpid OPPOSITE:
energetic

S

slum = hovel, ghetto, shanty
slump VERB 1 = fall, sink, plunge, crash, collapse, slip **OPPOSITE:** increase 2 = sag, hunch, droop, slouch, loll
▷ NOUN 3 = fall, drop, decline, crash, collapse, reverse, downturn, trough **OPPOSITE:** increase 4 = recession, depression, stagnation, inactivity, hard or bad times
slur = insult, stain, smear, affront, innuendo, calumny, insinuation, aspersion
sly 1 = roguish, knowing, arch, mischievous, impish
2 = cunning, scheming, devious, secret, clever, subtle, wily, crafty **OPPOSITE:** open
▷ PHRASES: on the sly
= secretly, privately, covertly, surreptitiously, on the quiet
smack VERB 1 = slap, hit, strike, clap, cuff, swipe, spank
2 = drive, hit, strike
▷ NOUN 3 = slap, blow, cuff, swipe, spank
▷ ADVERB 4 (Informal)
= directly, right, straight, squarely, precisely, exactly, slap (informal)
small 1 = little, minute, tiny, mini, miniature, minuscule, diminutive, petite **OPPOSITE:** big 2 = young, little, junior, wee, juvenile, youthful, immature 3 = unimportant, minor, trivial, insignificant, little, petty, trifling, negligible **OPPOSITE:** important

4 = modest, humble, unpretentious **OPPOSITE:** grand
smart ADJECTIVE 1 = chic, trim, neat, stylish, elegant, spruce, snappy, natty (informal) **OPPOSITE:** scruffy 2 = clever, bright, intelligent, quick, sharp, keen, acute, shrewd **OPPOSITE:** stupid 3 = brisk, quick, lively, vigorous
▷ VERB 4 = sting, burn, hurt
smash VERB 1 = break, crush, shatter, crack, demolish, pulverize 2 = shatter, break, disintegrate, crack, splinter 3 = collide, crash, meet head-on, clash, come into collision 4 = destroy, ruin, wreck, trash (slang), lay waste
▷ NOUN 5 = collision, crash, accident
smashing (Informal, chiefly Brit.)
= excellent, mean (slang), great (informal), wonderful, brilliant (informal), cracking (Brit. informal), superb, fantastic (informal), boshit (Austral. slang), exo (Austral. slang), sik (Austral. slang) **OPPOSITE:** awful
smear VERB 1 = spread over, daub, rub on, cover, coat, bedaub 2 = slander, malign, blacken, besmirch 3 = smudge, soil, dirty, stain, sully
▷ NOUN 4 = smudge, daub, streak, blot, blotch, splotch
5 = slander, libel, defamation, calumny
smell NOUN 1 = odour, scent, fragrance, perfume, bouquet,

aroma 2 = **stink**, stench, pong (*Brit. informal*), fetor

▷ VERB 3 = **stink**, reek, pong (*Brit. informal*) 4 = **sniff**, scent

smile VERB 1 = **grin**, beam, smirk, twinkle, grin from ear to ear

▷ NOUN 2 = **grin**, beam, smirk

smooth ADJECTIVE 1 = **even**, level, flat, plane, flush, horizontal OPPOSITE: uneven 2 = **sleek**, polished, shiny, glossy, silky, velvety OPPOSITE: rough 3 = **mellow**, pleasant, mild, agreeable 4 = **flowing**, steady, regular, uniform, rhythmic 5 = **easy**, effortless, well-ordered 6 = **suave**, slick, persuasive, urbane, glib, facile, unctuous, smarmy (*Brit. informal*)

▷ VERB 7 = **flatten**, level, press, plane, iron 8 = **ease**, facilitate OPPOSITE: hinder

smother 1 = **extinguish**, put out, stifle, snuff 2 = **suffocate**, choke, strangle, stifle 3 = **suppress**, stifle, repress, hide, conceal, muffle

smug = **self-satisfied**, superior, complacent, conceited

snack = **light meal**, bite, refreshment(s)

snag NOUN 1 = **difficulty**, hitch, problem, obstacle, catch, disadvantage, complication, drawback

▷ VERB 2 = **catch**, tear, rip

snail ▷ *See panel* SNAILS, SLUGS AND OTHER GASTROPODS

snake = **serpent**

● RELATED WORD

● *adjective:* serpentine

▷ *See panel* REPTILES

snap VERB 1 = **break**, crack, separate 2 = **pop**, click, crackle 3 = **speak sharply**, bark, lash out at, jump down (someone's) throat (*informal*) 4 = **bite at**, bite, nip

▷ ADJECTIVE 5 = **instant**, immediate, sudden, spur-of-the-moment

▷ PHRASES: snap something up = **grab**, seize, take advantage of, pounce upon

snare NOUN 1 = **trap**, net, wire, gin, noose

▷ VERB 2 = **trap**, catch, net, wire, seize, entrap

snatch VERB 1 = **grab**, grip, grasp, clutch 2 = **steal**, take, nick (*slang, chiefly Brit.*), pinch (*informal*), lift (*informal*), pilfer, filch, thieve 3 = **win** 4 = **save**, recover, get out, salvage

▷ NOUN 5 = **bit**, part, fragment, piece, snippet

sneak VERB 1 = **slink**, slip, steal, pad, skulk 2 = **slip**, smuggle, spirit

▷ NOUN 3 = **informer**, betrayer, telltale, Judas, accuser, stool pigeon, nark (*Brit., Austral. & N.Z. slang*), fizgig (*Austral. slang*)

sneaking 1 = **nagging**, worrying, persistent, uncomfortable 2 = **secret**, private, hidden, unexpressed, unvoiced, undivulged

S

SNAILS, SLUGS AND OTHER GASTROPODS

abalone or ear shell
conch
cowrie or cowry
limpet
murex

nudibranch or sea slug
ormer or sea-ear
periwinkle or winkle
slug
snail

triton
wentletrap
whelk

---

sneer VERB 1 = **scorn**, mock, ridicule, laugh, jeer, disdain, deride 2 = **say contemptuously**, snigger
▷ NOUN 3 = **scorn**, ridicule, mockery, derision, jeer, gibe

sniff 1 = **breathe in**, inhale 2 = **smell**, scent 3 = **inhale**, breathe in, suck in, draw in

snub VERB 1 = **insult**, slight, put down, humiliate, cut (informal), rebuff, cold-shoulder
▷ NOUN 2 = **insult**, put-down, affront, slap in the face (informal)

so = **therefore**, thus, hence, consequently, then, as a result, accordingly, thence

soak 1 = **steep** 2 = **wet**, damp, saturate, drench, moisten, suffuse, wet through, waterlog 3 = **penetrate**, permeate, seep
▷ PHRASES: **soak something up** = **absorb**, suck up, assimilate

soaking = **soaked**, dripping, saturated, drenched, sodden, streaming, sopping, wet through

soar 1 = **rise**, increase, grow, mount, climb, go up, rocket, escalate 2 = **fly**, wing, climb, ascend OPPOSITE: plunge 3 = **tower**, climb, go up

sob VERB 1 = **cry**, weep, howl, shed tears
▷ NOUN 2 = **cry**, whimper, howl

sober 1 = **abstinent**, temperate, abstemious, moderate OPPOSITE: drunk 2 = **serious**, cool, grave, reasonable, steady, composed, rational, solemn OPPOSITE: frivolous 3 = **plain**, dark, sombre, quiet, subdued, drab OPPOSITE: bright

so-called = **alleged**, supposed, professed, pretended, self-styled

social ADJECTIVE 1 = **communal**, community, collective, group, public, general, common 2 = **organized**, gregarious
▷ NOUN 3 = **get-together** (informal), party, gathering, function, reception, social gathering

society 1 = **the community**, people, the public, humanity, civilization, mankind 2 = **culture**, community, population 3 = **organization**, group, club, union, league, association, institute, circle 4 = **upper classes**, gentry, elite, high society, beau monde 5 (Old-fashioned)

= **companionship**, company, fellowship, friendship

sofa = **couch**, settee, divan, chaise longue

soft ADJECTIVE 1 = **velvety**, smooth, silky, feathery, downy, fleecy OPPOSITE: rough 2 = **yielding**, elastic OPPOSITE: hard 3 = **soggy**, swampy, marshy, boggy 4 = **squashy**, sloppy, mushy, spongy, gelatinous, pulpy 5 = **pliable**, flexible, supple, malleable, plastic, elastic, bendable, mouldable 6 = **quiet**, gentle, murmured, muted, dulcet, soft-toned OPPOSITE: loud 7 = **lenient**, easy-going, lax, indulgent, permissive, spineless, overindulgent OPPOSITE: harsh 8 = **kind**, tender, sentimental, compassionate, sensitive, gentle, tenderhearted, touchy-feely (informal) 9 (Informal) = **easy**, comfortable, undemanding, cushy (informal) 10 = **pale**, light, subdued, pastel, bland, mellow OPPOSITE: bright 11 = **dim**, faint, dimmed OPPOSITE: bright 12 = **mild**, temperate, balmy

soften 1 = **melt**, tenderize 2 = **lessen**, moderate, temper, ease, cushion, subdue, allay, mitigate

soil[1] 1 = **earth**, ground, clay, dust, dirt 2 = **territory**, country, land

soil[2] = **dirty**, foul, stain, pollute, tarnish, sully, defile, besmirch

OPPOSITE: sanitize

soldier = **fighter**, serviceman, trooper, warrior, man-at-arms, squaddie or squaddy (Brit. slang)

sole = **only**, one, single, individual, alone, exclusive, solitary

solely = **only**, completely, entirely, exclusively, alone, merely

solemn 1 = **serious**, earnest, grave, sober, sedate, staid OPPOSITE: cheerful 2 = **formal**, grand, grave, dignified, ceremonial, stately, momentous OPPOSITE: informal

solid 1 = **firm**, hard, compact, dense, concrete OPPOSITE: unsubstantial 2 = **strong**, stable, sturdy, substantial, unshakable OPPOSITE: unstable 3 = **reliable**, dependable, upstanding, worthy, upright, trusty OPPOSITE: unreliable 4 = **sound**, real, reliable, good, genuine, dinkum (Austral. & N.Z. informal) OPPOSITE: unsound

solidarity = **unity**, unification, accord, cohesion, team spirit, unanimity, concordance, like-mindedness, kotahitanga (N.Z.)

solitary 1 = **unsociable**, reclusive, unsocial, isolated, lonely, cloistered, lonesome, friendless OPPOSITE: sociable 2 = **lone**, alone 3 = **isolated**, remote, out-of-the-way, hidden, unfrequented OPPOSITE: busy

solution 1 = **answer**, key, result, explanation

S

2 (*Chemistry*) = **mixture**, mix, compound, blend, solvent

solve = **answer**, work out, resolve, crack, clear up, unravel, decipher, suss (out) (*slang*)

sombre 1 = **gloomy**, sad, sober, grave, dismal, mournful, lugubrious, joyless **OPPOSITE:** cheerful **2** = **dark**, dull, gloomy, sober, drab **OPPOSITE:** bright

somebody = **celebrity**, name, star, notable, household name, dignitary, luminary, personage **OPPOSITE:** nobody

somehow = **one way or another**, come what may, come hell or high water (*informal*), by fair means or foul, by hook or (by) crook, by some means or other

sometimes = **occasionally**, at times, now and then **OPPOSITE:** always

song = **ballad**, air, tune, carol, chant, chorus, anthem, number, waiata (*N.Z.*)

soon = **before long**, shortly, in the near future

soothe 1 = **calm**, still, quiet, hush, appease, lull, pacify, mollify **OPPOSITE:** upset **2** = **relieve**, ease, alleviate, assuage **OPPOSITE:** irritate

soothing 1 = **calming**, relaxing, peaceful, quiet, calm, restful **2** = **emollient**, palliative

sophisticated 1 = **complex**, advanced, complicated, subtle, delicate, elaborate, refined, intricate **OPPOSITE:** simple

2 = **cultured**, refined, cultivated, worldly, cosmopolitan, urbane **OPPOSITE:** unsophisticated

sophistication = **poise**, worldliness, savoir-faire, urbanity, finesse, worldly wisdom

sore 1 = **painful**, smarting, raw, tender, burning, angry, sensitive, irritated **2** = **annoyed**, cross, angry, pained, hurt, upset, stung, irritated, tooshie (*Austral. slang*), hoha (*N.Z.*) **3** = **annoying**, troublesome **4** (*Literary*) = **urgent**, desperate, extreme, dire, pressing, critical, acute

sorrow NOUN 1 = **grief**, sadness, woe, regret, distress, misery, mourning, anguish **OPPOSITE:** joy **2** = **hardship**, trial, tribulation, affliction, trouble, woe, misfortune **OPPOSITE:** good fortune ▷ **VERB 3** = **grieve**, mourn, lament, be sad, bemoan, agonize, bewail **OPPOSITE:** rejoice

sorry 1 = **regretful**, apologetic, contrite, repentant, remorseful, penitent, shamefaced, conscience-stricken **OPPOSITE:** unapologetic **2** = **sympathetic**, moved, full of pity, compassionate, commiserative **OPPOSITE:** unsympathetic **3** = **wretched**, miserable, pathetic, mean, poor, sad, pitiful, deplorable

sort NOUN 1 = **kind**, type, class, make, order, style, quality, nature
▷ VERB 2 = **arrange**, group, order, rank, divide, grade, classify, categorize

- USAGE NOTE
- It is common in informal
- speech to combine singular
- and plural in sentences like
- *these sort of distinctions are*
- *becoming blurred*. This is not
- acceptable in careful writing,
- where the plural must be
- used consistently: *these sorts*
- *of distinctions are becoming*
- *blurred.*

soul 1 = **spirit**, essence, life, vital force, wairua (N.Z.)
2 = **embodiment**, essence, epitome, personification, quintessence, type 3 = **person**, being, individual, body, creature, man *or* woman

sound¹ NOUN 1 = **noise**, din, report, tone, reverberation
2 = **idea**, impression, drift
3 = **cry**, noise, peep, squeak
4 = **tone**, music, note
▷ VERB 5 = **toll**, set off
6 = **resound**, echo, go off, toll, set off, chime, reverberate, clang 7 = **seem**, seem to be, appear to be

- RELATED WORDS
- *adjectives*: sonic, acoustic

sound² 1 = **fit**, healthy, perfect, intact, unhurt, uninjured, unimpaired OPPOSITE: frail
2 = **sturdy**, strong, solid, stable

3 = **sensible**, wise, reasonable, right, correct, proper, valid, rational OPPOSITE: irresponsible
4 = **deep**, unbroken, undisturbed, untroubled OPPOSITE: troubled

sour 1 = **sharp**, acid, tart, bitter, pungent, acetic OPPOSITE: sweet 2 = **rancid**, turned, gone off, curdled, gone bad, off OPPOSITE: fresh 3 = **bitter**, tart, acrimonious, embittered, disagreeable, ill-tempered, waspish, ungenerous OPPOSITE: good-natured

source 1 = **cause**, origin, derivation, beginning, author
2 = **informant**, authority
3 = **origin**, fount

souvenir = **keepsake**, reminder, memento

sovereign ADJECTIVE
1 = **supreme**, ruling, absolute, royal, principal, imperial, kingly *or* queenly 2 = **excellent**, efficient, effectual
▷ NOUN 3 = **monarch**, ruler, king *or* queen, chief, potentate, emperor *or* empress, prince *or* princess

sovereignty = **supreme power**, domination, supremacy, primacy, kingship, rangatiratanga (N.Z.)

sow = **scatter**, plant, seed, implant

space 1 = **room**, capacity, extent, margin, scope, play, expanse, leeway 2 = **period**, interval, time, while, span, duration 3 = **outer space**, the universe, the galaxy, the solar system, the cosmos 4 = **blank**, gap, interval

spacious = **roomy**, large, huge, broad, extensive, ample, expansive, capacious **OPPOSITE:** limited

span NOUN 1 = **period**, term, duration, spell 2 = **extent**, reach, spread, length, distance, stretch
▷ VERB 3 = **extend across**, cross, bridge, cover, link, traverse

spar = **argue**, row, squabble, scrap (*informal*), wrangle, bicker

spare ADJECTIVE 1 = **back-up**, reserve, second, extra, additional, auxiliary 2 = **extra**, surplus, leftover, over, free, odd, unwanted, unused **OPPOSITE:** necessary 3 = **free**, leisure, unoccupied 4 = **thin**, lean, meagre, gaunt, wiry **OPPOSITE:** plump
▷ VERB 5 = **afford**, give, grant, do without, part with, manage without, let someone have 6 = **have mercy on**, pardon, leave, let off (*informal*), go easy on (*informal*), save (from harm) **OPPOSITE:** show no mercy to

sparing = **economical**, frugal, thrifty, saving, careful, prudent **OPPOSITE:** lavish

spark NOUN 1 = **flicker**, flash, gleam, glint, flare 2 = **trace**, hint, scrap, atom, jot, vestige
▷ VERB 3 *often with* **off** = **start**, stimulate, provoke, inspire, trigger (off), set off, precipitate

sparkle VERB 1 = **glitter**, flash, shine, gleam, shimmer, twinkle, dance, glint
▷ NOUN 2 = **glitter**, flash, gleam, flicker, brilliance, twinkle, glint 3 = **vivacity**, life, spirit, dash, vitality, élan, liveliness

spate = **flood**, flow, torrent, rush, deluge, outpouring

speak 1 = **talk**, say something 2 = **articulate**, say, pronounce, utter, tell, state, talk, express 3 = **converse**, talk, chat, discourse, confer, commune, exchange views, korero (*N.Z.*) 4 = **lecture**, address an audience

speaker = **orator**, public speaker, lecturer, spokesperson, spokesman or spokeswoman

spearhead = **lead**, head, pioneer, launch, set off, initiate, set in motion

special 1 = **exceptional**, important, significant, particular, unique, unusual, extraordinary, memorable **OPPOSITE:** ordinary 2 = **specific**, particular, distinctive, individual, appropriate, precise **OPPOSITE:** general

specialist = **expert**, authority, professional, master, consultant, guru, buff (*informal*), connoisseur, fundi (*S. African*)

speciality = **forte**, métier,

specialty, bag (*slang*), pièce de résistance (*French*)

species = kind, sort, type, group, class, variety, breed, category

specific 1 = particular, special, characteristic, distinguishing **OPPOSITE:** general 2 = precise, exact, explicit, definite, express, clear-cut, unequivocal **OPPOSITE:** vague 3 = peculiar, appropriate, individual, particular, unique

specification = requirement, detail, particular, stipulation, condition, qualification

specify = state, designate, stipulate, name, detail, mention, indicate, define

specimen 1 = sample, example, model, type, pattern, instance, representative, exemplification 2 = example, model, type

spectacle 1 = show, display, exhibition, event, performance, extravaganza, pageant 2 = sight, wonder, scene, phenomenon, curiosity, marvel

spectacular ADJECTIVE 1 = impressive, striking, dramatic, stunning (*informal*), grand, magnificent, splendid, dazzling **OPPOSITE:** unimpressive ▷ NOUN 2 = show, display, spectacle

spectator = onlooker, observer, viewer, looker-on, watcher, bystander

spectre = ghost, spirit, phantom, vision, apparition, wraith, kehua (*N.Z.*)

speculate 1 = conjecture, consider, wonder, guess, surmise, theorize, hypothesize 2 = gamble, risk, venture, hazard

speculation 1 = theory, opinion, hypothesis, conjecture, guess, surmise, guesswork, supposition 2 = gamble, risk, hazard

speculative = hypothetical, academic, theoretical, notional, conjectural, suppositional, abstract

speech 1 = communication, talk, conversation, discussion, dialogue 2 = diction, pronunciation, articulation, delivery, fluency, inflection, intonation, elocution 3 = language, tongue, jargon, dialect, idiom, parlance, articulation, diction 4 = talk, address, lecture, discourse, homily, oration, spiel (*informal*), whaikorero (*N.Z.*)

speed NOUN 1 = rate, pace 2 = swiftness, rush, hurry, haste, rapidity, quickness **OPPOSITE:** slowness ▷ VERB 3 = race, rush, hurry, zoom, career, tear, barrel (along) (*informal, chiefly U.S. & Canad.*), gallop **OPPOSITE:** crawl 4 = help, advance, aid, boost, assist, facilitate, expedite **OPPOSITE:** hinder

S

● USAGE NOTE
● The past tense of *speed up* is
● *speeded up* (not *sped up*), for
● example *I speeded up to*
● *overtake the lorry.* The past
● participle is also *speeded up*,
● for example *I had already*
● *speeded up when I spotted the*
● *police car.*

speedy = **quick**, fast, rapid,
swift, express, immediate,
prompt, hurried **OPPOSITE:**
slow

spell¹ = **indicate**, mean, signify,
point to, imply, augur, portend

spell² 1 = **incantation**, charm,
makutu (N.Z.)

2 = **enchantment**, magic,
fascination, glamour, allure,
bewitchment

spell³ = **period**, time, term,
stretch, course, season,
interval, bout

spend 1 = **pay out**, fork out
(slang), expend, disburse
OPPOSITE: save 2 = **pass**, fill,
occupy, while away 3 = **use up**,
waste, squander, empty, drain,
exhaust, consume, run through
OPPOSITE: save

sphere 1 = **ball**, globe, orb,
globule, circle 2 = **field**,
department, function, territory,
capacity, province, patch, scope

spice 1 = **seasoning**
2 = **excitement**, zest, colour,
pep, zing (informal), piquancy

spicy 1 = **hot**, seasoned,
aromatic, savoury, piquant
2 (Informal) = **risqué**, racy,
ribald, hot (informal),
suggestive, titillating, indelicate

spider
● RELATED WORD
● *fear:* arachnophobia
▷ *See panel* SPIDERS AND OTHER
ARACHNIDS

spike NOUN 1 = **point**, stake,
spine, barb, prong
▷ VERB 2 = **impale**, spit, spear,
stick

spill 1 = **tip over**, overturn,
capsize, knock over 2 = **shed**,
discharge, disgorge 3 = **slop**,
flow, pour, run, overflow

spin VERB 1 = **revolve**, turn,
rotate, reel, whirl, twirl, gyrate,
pirouette 2 = **reel**, swim, whirl
▷ NOUN 3 (Informal) = **drive**,
ride, joy ride (informal)
4 = **revolution**, roll, whirl,
gyration
▷ PHRASES: **spin something**
out = **prolong**, extend,
lengthen, draw out, drag out,
delay, amplify

spine 1 = **backbone**, vertebrae,
spinal column, vertebral column
2 = **barb**, spur, needle, spike,
ray, quill

spiral ADJECTIVE 1 = **coiled**,
winding, whorled, helical
▷ NOUN 2 = **coil**, helix,
corkscrew, whorl

spirit NOUN 1 = **soul**, life
2 = **life force**, vital spark, mauri
(N.Z.) 3 = **ghost**, phantom,
spectre, apparition, atua (N.Z.),
kehua (N.Z.) 4 = **courage**, guts
(informal), grit, backbone, spunk

SPIDERS AND OTHER ARACHNIDS

black widow
chigger, chigoe, or (U.S. &
 Canad.) redbug
chigoe, chigger, jigger, or sand
 flea
harvestman or (U.S. & Canad.)
 daddy-longlegs
katipo (N.Z.)
mite

red-back (spider) (Austral.)
spider
spider mite
tarantula
tick
trap-door spider
whip scorpion
wolf spider or hunting
 spider

(informal), gameness
5 = **liveliness**, energy, vigour,
life, force, fire, enthusiasm,
animation **6** = **attitude**,
character, temper, outlook,
temperament, disposition
7 = **heart**, sense, nature, soul,
core, substance, essence,
quintessence **8** = **intention**,
meaning, purpose, purport, gist
9 = **feeling**, atmosphere,
character, tone, mood, tenor,
ambience
▷ **PLURAL NOUN 10** = **mood**,
feelings, morale, temper,
disposition, state of mind,
frame of mind
spirited = **lively**, energetic,
animated, active, feisty
(informal, chiefly U.S. & Canad.),
vivacious, mettlesome
OPPOSITE: lifeless
spiritual 1 = **nonmaterial**,
immaterial, incorporeal
OPPOSITE: material **2** = **sacred**,
religious, holy, divine,
devotional
spit VERB **1** = **expectorate**
2 = **eject**, throw out

▷ NOUN **3** = **saliva**, dribble,
spittle, drool, slaver
spite NOUN **1** = **malice**,
malevolence, ill will, hatred,
animosity, venom, spleen,
spitefulness **OPPOSITE:**
kindness
▷ VERB **2** = **annoy**, hurt, injure,
harm, vex **OPPOSITE:** benefit
▷ PHRASES: in spite of
= **despite**, regardless of,
notwithstanding, (even) though
splash VERB **1** = **paddle**,
plunge, bathe, dabble, wade,
wallow **2** = **scatter**, shower,
spray, sprinkle, wet, spatter,
slop **3** = **spatter**, mark, stain,
speck, speckle
▷ NOUN **4** = **dash**, touch,
spattering **5** = **spot**, burst,
patch, spurt **6** = **blob**, spot,
smudge, stain, smear, fleck,
speck
splendid 1 = **excellent**,
wonderful, marvellous, great
(informal), cracking (Brit.
informal), fantastic (informal),
first-class, glorious, booshit
(Austral. slang), exo (Austral.

S

slang), sik (*Austral. slang*)
OPPOSITE: poor
2 = **magnificent**, grand,
impressive, rich, superb, costly,
gorgeous, lavish **OPPOSITE:**
squalid

splendour = **magnificence**,
grandeur, show, display,
spectacle, richness, nobility,
pomp **OPPOSITE:** squalor

splinter NOUN 1 = **sliver**,
fragment, chip, flake
▷ VERB 2 = **shatter**, split,
fracture, disintegrate

split VERB 1 = **break**, crack,
burst, open, give way, come
apart, come undone 2 = **cut**,
break, crack, snap, chop
3 = **divide**, separate, disunite,
disband, cleave 4 = **diverge**,
separate, branch, fork, part
5 = **tear**, rend, rip 6 = **share
out**, divide, distribute, halve,
allocate, partition, allot,
apportion
▷ NOUN 7 = **division**, breach,
rift, rupture, discord, schism,
estrangement, dissension
8 = **separation**, break-up, split-
up 9 = **crack**, tear, rip, gap,
rent, breach, slit, fissure
▷ ADJECTIVE 10 = **divided**
11 = **broken**, cracked, fractured,
ruptured, cleft

spoil VERB 1 = **ruin**, destroy,
wreck, damage, injure, harm,
mar, trash (*slang*), crool or cruel
(*Austral. slang*) **OPPOSITE:**
improve 2 = **overindulge**,
indulge, pamper, cosset, coddle,

mollycoddle **OPPOSITE:** deprive
3 = **indulge**, pamper, satisfy,
gratify, pander to 4 = **go bad**,
turn, go off (*Brit. informal*), rot,
decay, decompose, curdle,
addle
▷ PLURAL NOUN 5 = **booty**,
loot, plunder, prey, swag (*slang*)

spoken = **verbal**, voiced,
expressed, uttered, oral, said,
told, unwritten

spokesperson = **speaker**,
official, spokesman *or*
spokeswoman, voice, spin
doctor (*informal*), mouthpiece

sponsor VERB 1 = **back**, fund,
finance, promote, subsidize,
patronize
▷ NOUN 2 = **backer**, patron,
promoter

spontaneous = **unplanned**,
impromptu, unprompted,
willing, natural, voluntary,
instinctive, impulsive **OPPOSITE:**
planned

sport NOUN 1 = **game**,
exercise, recreation, play,
amusement, diversion, pastime
2 = **fun**, joking, teasing, banter,
jest, badinage
▷ VERB 3 (*Informal*) = **wear**,
display, flaunt, exhibit, flourish,
show off, vaunt

sporting = **fair**, sportsmanlike,
game (*informal*) **OPPOSITE:**
unfair

sporty = **athletic**, outdoor,
energetic

spot NOUN 1 = **mark**, stain,
speck, scar, blot, smudge,

blemish, speckle **2 = pimple**, pustule, zit (*slang*) **3 = place**, site, point, position, scene, location **4** (*Informal*) **= predicament**, trouble, difficulty, mess, plight, hot water (*informal*), quandary, tight spot

▷ VERB **5 = see**, observe, catch sight of, sight, recognize, detect, make out, discern **6 = mark**, stain, soil, dirty, fleck, spatter, speckle, splodge

spotlight NOUN **1 = attention**, limelight, public eye, fame

▷ VERB **2 = highlight**, draw attention to, accentuate

spotted = speckled, dotted, flecked, mottled, dappled

spouse = partner, mate, husband *or* wife, consort, significant other (*U.S. informal*)

sprawl = loll, slump, lounge, flop, slouch

spray¹ NOUN **1 = droplets**, fine mist, drizzle **2 = aerosol**, sprinkler, atomizer

▷ VERB **3 = scatter**, shower, sprinkle, diffuse

spray² = sprig, floral arrangement, branch, corsage

spread VERB **1 = open (out)**, extend, stretch, unfold, sprawl, unroll **2 = extend**, open, stretch **3 = grow**, increase, expand, widen, escalate, proliferate, multiply, broaden **4 = circulate**, broadcast, propagate, disseminate, make known **OPPOSITE:** suppress

5 = diffuse, cast, shed, radiate

▷ NOUN **6 = increase**, development, advance, expansion, proliferation, dissemination, dispersal **7 = extent**, span, stretch, sweep

spree = fling, binge (*informal*), orgy

spring NOUN **1 = flexibility**, bounce, resilience, elasticity, buoyancy

▷ VERB **2 = jump**, bound, leap, bounce, vault **3** *often with* **from = originate**, come, derive, start, issue, proceed, arise, stem

● **RELATED WORD**

● *adjective*: vernal

sprinkle = scatter, dust, strew, pepper, shower, spray, powder, dredge

sprinkling = scattering, dusting, few, dash, handful, sprinkle

sprint = run, race, shoot, tear, dash, dart, hare (*Brit. informal*)

sprout 1 = germinate, bud, shoot, spring **2 = grow**, develop, ripen

spur VERB **1 = incite**, drive, prompt, urge, stimulate, animate, prod, prick

▷ NOUN **2 = stimulus**, incentive, impetus, motive, impulse, inducement, incitement

▷ PHRASES: **on the spur of the moment = on impulse**, impulsively, on the spot, impromptu, without planning

spurn = reject, slight, scorn, rebuff, snub, despise, disdain, repulse **OPPOSITE:** accept

spy NOUN 1 = undercover agent, mole, nark (Brit., Austral. & N.Z. slang)
▷ VERB 2 = catch sight of, spot, notice, observe, glimpse, espy

squabble VERB 1 = quarrel, fight, argue, row, dispute, wrangle, bicker
▷ NOUN 2 = quarrel, fight, row, argument, dispute, disagreement, tiff

squad = team, group, band, company, force, troop, crew, gang

squander = waste, spend, fritter away, blow (slang), misuse, expend, misspend **OPPOSITE:** save

square ADJECTIVE 1 = fair, straight, genuine, ethical, honest, on the level (informal), kosher (informal), dinkum (Austral. & N.Z. informal), above board
▷ VERB 2 often with **with** = agree, match, fit, correspond, tally, reconcile

squash 1 = crush, press, flatten, mash, smash, distort, pulp, compress 2 = suppress, quell, silence, crush, annihilate 3 = embarrass, put down, shame, degrade, mortify

squeeze VERB 1 = press, crush, squash, pinch 2 = clutch, press, grip, crush, pinch,

squash, compress, wring 3 = cram, press, crowd, force, stuff, pack, jam, ram 4 = hug, embrace, cuddle, clasp, enfold
▷ NOUN 5 = press, grip, clasp, crush, pinch, squash, wring 6 = crush, jam, squash, press, crowd, congestion 7 = hug, embrace, clasp

stab VERB 1 = pierce, stick, wound, knife, thrust, spear, jab, transfix
▷ NOUN 2 (Informal) = attempt, go, try, endeavour 3 = twinge, prick, pang, ache

stability = firmness, strength, soundness, solidity, steadiness **OPPOSITE:** instability

stable 1 = secure, lasting, strong, sound, fast, sure, established, permanent **OPPOSITE:** insecure 2 = well-balanced, balanced, sensible, reasonable, rational 3 = solid, firm, fixed, substantial, durable, well-made, well-built, immovable **OPPOSITE:** unstable

stack NOUN 1 = pile, heap, mountain, mass, load, mound 2 = lot, mass, load (informal), ton (informal), heap (informal), great amount
▷ VERB 3 = pile, heap up, load, assemble, accumulate, amass

staff 1 = workers, employees, personnel, workforce, team 2 = stick, pole, rod, crook, cane, stave, wand, sceptre

stage = step, leg, phase, point, level, period, division, lap

stagger 1 = totter, reel, sway, lurch, wobble 2 = **astound**, amaze, stun, shock, shake, overwhelm, astonish, confound

stain NOUN 1 = mark, spot, blot, blemish, discoloration, smirch 2 = **stigma**, shame, disgrace, slur, dishonour 3 = dye, colour, tint
▷ VERB 4 = mark, soil, discolour, dirty, tinge, spot, blot, blemish 5 = dye, colour, tint

stake¹ = pole, post, stick, pale, paling, picket, palisade

stake² NOUN 1 = bet, ante, wager
▷ VERB 2 = bet, gamble, wager, chance, risk, venture, hazard
▷ NOUN 3 = interest, share, involvement, concern, investment

stale 1 = old, hard, dry, decayed **OPPOSITE:** fresh 2 = musty, fusty 3 = tasteless, flat, sour 4 = **unoriginal**, banal, trite, stereotyped, worn-out, threadbare, hackneyed, overused **OPPOSITE:** original

stalk = pursue, follow, track, hunt, shadow, haunt

stall VERB 1 = play for time, delay, hedge, temporize 2 = stop dead, jam, seize up, catch, stick, stop short
▷ NOUN 3 = stand, table, counter, booth, kiosk

stalwart 1 = loyal, faithful, firm, true, dependable, steadfast 2 = **strong**,

strapping, sturdy, stout **OPPOSITE:** puny

stamina = staying power, endurance, resilience, force, power, energy, strength

stammer = stutter, falter, pause, hesitate, stumble over your words

stamp NOUN 1 = imprint, mark, brand, signature, earmark, hallmark
▷ VERB 2 = print, mark, impress 3 = trample, step, tread, crush 4 = **identify**, mark, brand, label, reveal, show to be, categorize
▷ PHRASES: stamp something out = eliminate, destroy, eradicate, crush, suppress, put down, scotch, quell

stance 1 = attitude, stand, position, viewpoint, standpoint 2 = **posture**, carriage, bearing, deportment

stand VERB 1 = be upright, be erect, be vertical 2 = get to your feet, rise, stand up, straighten up 3 = be located, be, sit, be positioned, be situated or located 4 = be valid, continue, exist, prevail, remain valid 5 = put, place, position, set, mount 6 = sit, mellow 7 = resist, endure, tolerate, stand up to 8 = tolerate, bear, abide, stomach, endure, brook 9 = take, bear, handle, endure, put up with (*informal*), countenance

▷ NOUN 10 = **position**, attitude, stance, opinion, determination 11 = **stall**, booth, kiosk, table

▷ PHRASES: stand by = **be prepared**, wait ▸ stand for something 1 = **represent**, mean, signify, denote, indicate, symbolize, betoken

▷ VERB 2 (*Informal*) = **tolerate**, bear, endure, put up with, brook ▸ stand in for someone = **be a substitute for**, represent, cover for, take the place of, deputize for ▸ stand up for something *or* someone = **support**, champion, defend, uphold, stick up for (*informal*)

standard NOUN 1 = **level**, grade 2 = **criterion**, measure, guideline, example, model, average, norm, gauge 3 *often plural* = **principles**, ideals, morals, ethics 4 = **flag**, banner, ensign

▷ ADJECTIVE 5 = **usual**, normal, customary, average, basic, regular, typical, orthodox **OPPOSITE:** unusual 6 = **accepted**, official, established, approved, recognized, definitive, authoritative **OPPOSITE:** unofficial

stand-in = **substitute**, deputy, replacement, reserve, surrogate, understudy, locum, stopgap

standing NOUN 1 = **status**, position, footing, rank, reputation, eminence, repute 2 = **duration**, existence, continuance

▷ ADJECTIVE 3 = **permanent**, lasting, fixed, regular 4 = **upright**, erect, vertical

staple = **principal**, chief, main, key, basic, fundamental, predominant

star NOUN 1 = **heavenly body**, celestial body 2 = **celebrity**, big name, megastar (*informal*), name, luminary 3 = **leading man** *or* **lady**, hero or heroine, principal, main attraction

▷ VERB 4 = **play the lead**, appear, feature, perform

▷ ADJECTIVE 5 = **leading**, major, celebrated, brilliant, well-known, prominent

● RELATED WORDS
● *adjectives:* astral, stellar

stare = **gaze**, look, goggle, watch, gape, eyeball (*slang*), gawp (*Brit. slang*), gawk

stark ADJECTIVE 1 = **plain**, harsh, basic, grim, straightforward, blunt 2 = **sharp**, clear, striking, distinct, clear-cut 3 = **austere**, severe, plain, bare, harsh 4 = **bleak**, grim, barren, hard 5 = **absolute**, pure, sheer, utter, downright, out-and-out, unmitigated

▷ ADVERB 6 = **absolutely**, quite, completely, entirely, altogether, wholly, utterly

start VERB 1 = **set about**, begin, proceed, embark upon, take the first step, make a beginning **OPPOSITE:** stop **2** = **begin**, arise, originate, issue, appear, commence **OPPOSITE:** end **3** = **set in motion**, initiate, instigate, open, trigger, originate, get going, kick-start **OPPOSITE:** stop **4** = **establish**, begin, found, create, launch, set up, institute, pioneer **OPPOSITE:** terminate **5** = **start up**, activate, get something going **OPPOSITE:** turn off **6** = **jump**, shy, jerk, flinch, recoil ▷ **NOUN 7** = **beginning**, outset, opening, birth, foundation, dawn, onset, initiation **OPPOSITE:** end **8** = **jump**, spasm, convulsion

startle = **surprise**, shock, frighten, scare, make (someone) jump

starving = **hungry**, starved, ravenous, famished

state NOUN 1 = **country**, nation, land, republic, territory, federation, commonwealth, kingdom **2** = **government**, ministry, administration, executive, regime, powers-that-be **3** = **condition**, shape **4** = **frame of mind**, condition, spirits, attitude, mood, humour **5** = **ceremony**, glory, grandeur, splendour, majesty, pomp **6** = **circumstances**, situation, position, predicament ▷ **VERB 7** = **say**, declare, present, voice, express, assert,

utter, articulate

stately = **grand**, majestic, dignified, royal, august, noble, regal, lofty **OPPOSITE:** lowly

statement
1 = **announcement**, declaration, communication, communiqué, proclamation **2** = **account**, report

station NOUN 1 = **railway station**, stop, stage, halt, terminal, train station, terminus **2** = **headquarters**, base, depot **3** = **position**, rank, status, standing, post, situation **4** = **post**, place, location, position, situation ▷ **VERB 5** = **assign**, post, locate, set, establish, install

stature 1 = **height**, build, size **2** = **importance**, standing, prestige, rank, prominence, eminence

status 1 = **position**, rank, grade **2** = **prestige**, standing, authority, influence, weight, honour, importance, fame, mana (N.Z.) **3** = **state of play**, development, progress, condition, evolution

staunch = **loyal**, faithful, stalwart, firm, sound, true, trusty, steadfast

stay VERB 1 = **remain**, continue to be, linger, stop, wait, halt, pause, abide **OPPOSITE:** go **2** *often with* **at** = **lodge**, visit, sojourn, put up at, be accommodated at **3** = **continue**, remain, go on,

S

survive, endure

▷ NOUN 4 = **visit**, stop, holiday, stopover, sojourn

5 = **postponement**, delay, suspension, stopping, halt, deferment

steady 1 = **continuous**, regular, constant, consistent, persistent, unbroken, uninterrupted, incessant **OPPOSITE:** irregular 2 = **stable**, fixed, secure, firm, safe **OPPOSITE:** unstable

3 = **regular**, established

4 = **dependable**, sensible, reliable, secure, calm, supportive, sober, level-headed **OPPOSITE:** undependable

steal 1 = **take**, nick (*slang, chiefly Brit.*), pinch (*informal*), lift (*informal*), embezzle, pilfer, misappropriate, purloin

2 = **copy**, take, appropriate, pinch (*informal*) 3 = **sneak**, slip, creep, tiptoe, slink

stealth = **secrecy**, furtiveness, slyness, sneakiness, unobtrusiveness, stealthiness, surreptitiousness

steep¹ 1 = **sheer**, precipitous, abrupt, vertical **OPPOSITE:** gradual 2 = **sharp**, sudden, abrupt, marked, extreme, distinct 3 (*Informal*) = **high**, exorbitant, extreme, unreasonable, overpriced, extortionate **OPPOSITE:** reasonable

steep² = **soak**, immerse, marinate (*Cookery*), submerge,

drench, moisten, souse

steeped = **saturated**, pervaded, permeated, filled, infused, imbued, suffused

steer 1 = **drive**, control, direct, handle, pilot 2 = **direct**, lead, guide, conduct, escort

stem¹ = **stalk**, branch, trunk, shoot, axis

▷ PHRASES: stem from something = **originate from**, be caused by, derive from, arise from

stem² = **stop**, hold back, staunch, check, dam, curb

step NOUN 1 = **pace**, stride, footstep 2 = **footfall**

3 = **move**, measure, action, means, act, deed, expedient

4 = **stage**, point, phase

5 = **level**, rank, degree

▷ VERB 6 = **walk**, pace, tread, move

▷ PHRASES: step in (*Informal*) = **intervene**, take action, become involved ▶ step something up = **increase**, intensify, raise

stereotype NOUN

1 = **formula**, pattern

▷ VERB 2 = **categorize**, typecast, pigeonhole, standardize

sterile 1 = **germ-free**, sterilized, disinfected, aseptic **OPPOSITE:** unhygienic 2 = **barren**, infertile, unproductive, childless **OPPOSITE:** fertile

sterling = **excellent**, sound, fine, superlative

stern 1 = **strict**, harsh, hard, grim, rigid, austere, inflexible **OPPOSITE:** lenient 2 = **severe**, serious, forbidding **OPPOSITE:** friendly

stick¹ 1 = **twig**, branch 2 = **cane**, staff, pole, rod, crook, baton 3 (*Slang*) = **abuse**, criticism, flak (*informal*), fault-finding

stick² VERB 1 (*Informal*) = **put**, place, set, lay, deposit 2 = **poke**, dig, stab, thrust, pierce, penetrate, spear, prod 3 = **fasten**, fix, bind, hold, bond, attach, glue, paste 4 = **adhere**, cling, become joined, become welded 5 = **stay**, remain, linger, persist 6 (*Slang*) = **tolerate**, take, stand, stomach, abide ▷ PHRASES: **stick out** = **protrude**, stand out, jut out, show, project, bulge, obtrude ▶ **stick up for someone** (*Informal*) = **defend**, support, champion, stand up for

sticky 1 = **adhesive**, gummed, adherent 2 = **gooey**, tacky (*informal*), viscous, glutinous, gummy, icky (*informal*), gluey, clinging 3 (*Informal*) = **difficult**, awkward, tricky, embarrassing, nasty, delicate, unpleasant, barro (*Austral. slang*) 4 = **humid**, close, sultry, oppressive, sweltering, clammy, muggy

stiff 1 = **inflexible**, rigid, unyielding, hard, firm, tight, solid, tense **OPPOSITE:** flexible

2 = **formal**, constrained, forced, unnatural, stilted, unrelaxed **OPPOSITE:** informal 3 = **vigorous**, great, strong 4 = **severe**, strict, harsh, hard, heavy, extreme, drastic 5 = **difficult**, hard, tough, exacting, arduous

stifle 1 = **suppress**, repress, stop, check, silence, restrain, hush, smother 2 = **restrain**, suppress, repress, smother

stigma = **disgrace**, shame, dishonour, stain, slur, smirch

still ADJECTIVE 1 = **motionless**, stationary, calm, peaceful, serene, tranquil, undisturbed, restful **OPPOSITE:** moving 2 = **silent**, quiet, hushed **OPPOSITE:** noisy ▷ VERB 3 = **quieten**, calm, settle, quiet, silence, soothe, hush, lull **OPPOSITE:** get louder ▷ ADVERB 4 = **however**, but, yet, nevertheless, notwithstanding

stimulate = **encourage**, inspire, prompt, fire, spur, provoke, arouse, rouse

stimulating = **exciting**, inspiring, stirring, rousing, provocative, exhilarating **OPPOSITE:** boring

stimulus = **incentive**, spur, encouragement, impetus, inducement, goad, incitement, fillip

sting 1 = **hurt**, burn, wound 2 = **smart**, burn, pain, hurt, tingle

S

stink VERB 1 = **reek**, pong (*Brit. informal*)
▷ NOUN 2 = **stench**, pong (*Brit. informal*), foul smell, fetor

stint NOUN 1 = **term**, time, turn, period, share, shift, stretch, spell
▷ VERB 2 = **be mean**, hold back, be sparing, skimp on, be frugal

stipulate = **specify**, agree, require, contract, settle, covenant, insist upon

stir VERB 1 = **mix**, beat, agitate 2 = **stimulate**, move, excite, spur, provoke, arouse, awaken, rouse OPPOSITE: inhibit 3 = **spur**, drive, prompt, stimulate, prod, urge, animate, prick
▷ NOUN 4 = **commotion**, excitement, activity, disorder, fuss, disturbance, bustle, flurry

stock NOUN 1 = **shares**, holdings, securities, investments, bonds, equities 2 = **property**, capital, assets, funds 3 = **goods**, merchandise, wares, range, choice, variety, selection, commodities 4 = **supply**, store, reserve, fund, stockpile, hoard 5 = **livestock**, cattle, beasts, domestic animals
▷ VERB 6 = **sell**, supply, handle, keep, trade in, deal in 7 = **fill**, supply, provide with, equip, furnish, fit out
▷ ADJECTIVE 8 = **hackneyed**,

routine, banal, trite, overused 9 = **regular**, usual, ordinary, conventional, customary

stomach NOUN 1 = **belly**, gut (*informal*), abdomen, tummy (*informal*), puku (*N.Z.*) 2 = **tummy**, pot, spare tyre 3 = **inclination**, taste, desire, appetite, relish
▷ VERB 4 = **bear**, take, tolerate, endure, swallow, abide
● RELATED WORD
● *adjective*: gastric

stone NOUN 1 = **masonry**, rock 2 = **rock**, pebble 3 = **pip**, seed, pit, kernel

stoop VERB 1 = **hunch** 2 = **bend**, lean, bow, duck, crouch
▷ NOUN 3 = **slouch**, bad posture, round-shoulderedness

stop VERB 1 = **quit**, cease, refrain, put an end to, discontinue, desist OPPOSITE: start 2 = **prevent**, cut short, arrest, restrain, hold back, hinder, repress, impede OPPOSITE: facilitate 3 = **end**, conclude, finish, terminate OPPOSITE: continue 4 = **cease**, shut down, discontinue, desist OPPOSITE: continue 5 = **halt**, pause OPPOSITE: keep going 6 = **pause**, wait, rest, take a break, have a breather (*informal*), stop briefly 7 = **stay**, rest, lodge
▷ NOUN 8 = **halt**, standstill 9 = **station**, stage, depot, terminus 10 = **stay**, break, rest

store NOUN 1 = **shop**, outlet, market, mart 2 = **supply**, stock, reserve, fund, quantity, accumulation, stockpile, hoard 3 = **repository**, warehouse, depository, storeroom
▷ VERB 4 *often with* **away** *or* **up** = **put by**, save, hoard, keep, reserve, deposit, garner, stockpile 5 = **put away**, put in storage, put in store 6 = **keep**, hold, preserve, maintain, retain, conserve

storm NOUN 1 = **tempest**, hurricane, gale, blizzard, squall 2 = **outburst**, row, outcry, furore, outbreak, turmoil, disturbance, strife
▷ VERB 3 = **rush**, stamp, flounce, fly 4 = **rage**, rant, thunder, rave, bluster 5 = **attack**, charge, rush, assault, assail

stormy 1 = **wild**, rough, raging, turbulent, windy, blustery, inclement, squally 2 = **rough**, wild, turbulent, raging 3 = **angry**, heated, fierce, passionate, fiery, impassioned

story 1 = **tale**, romance, narrative, history, legend, yarn 2 = **anecdote**, account, tale, report 3 = **report**, news, article, feature, scoop, news item

stout 1 = **fat**, big, heavy, overweight, plump, bulky, burly, fleshy OPPOSITE: slim 2 = **strong**, strapping, muscular, robust, sturdy, stalwart, brawny, able-bodied OPPOSITE: puny 3 = **brave**, bold, courageous, fearless, resolute, gallant, intrepid, valiant OPPOSITE: timid

straight ADJECTIVE 1 = **direct**, undeviating OPPOSITE: indirect 2 = **level**, even, right, square, true, smooth, aligned, horizontal OPPOSITE: crooked 3 = **frank**, plain, straightforward, blunt, outright, honest, candid, forthright OPPOSITE: evasive 4 = **successive**, consecutive, continuous, running, solid, nonstop OPPOSITE: discontinuous 5 (*Slang*) = **conventional**, conservative, bourgeois OPPOSITE: fashionable 6 = **honest**, just, fair, reliable, respectable, upright, honourable, law-abiding OPPOSITE: dishonest 7 = **undiluted**, pure, neat, unadulterated, unmixed 8 = **in order**, organized, arranged, neat, tidy, orderly, shipshape OPPOSITE: untidy
▷ ADVERB 9 = **directly**, precisely, exactly, unswervingly, by the shortest route, in a beeline 10 = **immediately**, directly, promptly, instantly, at once, straight away, without delay, forthwith

straight away = **immediately**, now, at once, directly, instantly, right away

straighten = **neaten**, arrange,

tidy (up), order, put in order

straightforward 1 (*Chiefly Brit.*) = **simple**, easy, uncomplicated, routine, elementary, easy-peasy (*slang*) **OPPOSITE:** complicated
2 = **honest**, open, direct, genuine, sincere, candid, truthful, forthright, dinkum (*Austral. & N.Z. informal*) **OPPOSITE:** devious

strain[1] NOUN 1 = **pressure**, stress, demands, burden
2 = **stress**, anxiety 3 = **worry**, effort, struggle **OPPOSITE:** ease
4 = **burden**, tension 5 = **injury**, wrench, sprain, pull
▷ VERB 6 = **stretch**, tax, overtax 7 = **strive**, struggle, endeavour, labour, go for it (*informal*), bend over backwards (*informal*), give it your best shot (*informal*), knock yourself out (*informal*) **OPPOSITE:** relax
8 = **sieve**, filter, sift, purify

strain[2] 1 = **trace**, suggestion, tendency, streak 2 = **breed**, family, race, blood, descent, extraction, ancestry, lineage

strained 1 = **tense**, difficult, awkward, embarrassed, stiff, uneasy **OPPOSITE:** relaxed
2 = **forced**, put on, false, artificial, unnatural **OPPOSITE:** natural

strait NOUN 1 *often plural*
= **channel**, sound, narrows
▷ PLURAL NOUN 2 = **difficulty**, dilemma, plight, hardship, uphill (*S. African*), predicament, extremity, perplexity

strand = **filament**, fibre, thread, string

stranded 1 = **beached**, grounded, marooned, ashore, shipwrecked, aground
2 = **helpless**, abandoned, high and dry

strange 1 = **odd**, curious, weird, wonderful, extraordinary, bizarre, peculiar, abnormal **OPPOSITE:** ordinary
2 = **unfamiliar**, new, unknown, foreign, novel, alien, exotic, untried **OPPOSITE:** familiar

stranger 1 = **unknown person**
2 = **newcomer**, incomer, foreigner, guest, visitor, alien, outlander

strangle 1 = **throttle**, choke, asphyxiate, strangulate
2 = **suppress**, inhibit, subdue, stifle, repress, overpower, quash, quell

strap NOUN 1 = **tie**, thong, belt
▷ VERB 2 = **fasten**, tie, secure, bind, lash, buckle

strapping = **well-built**, big, powerful, robust, sturdy, husky (*informal*), brawny

strategic 1 = **tactical**, calculated, deliberate, planned, politic, diplomatic 2 = **crucial**, important, key, vital, critical, decisive, cardinal

strategy 1 = **policy**, procedure, approach, scheme 2 = **plan**, approach, scheme

stray VERB 1 = **wander**, go

astray, drift 2 = **drift**, wander, roam, meander, rove 3 = **digress**, diverge, deviate, get off the point
▷ ADJECTIVE 4 = **lost**, abandoned, homeless, roaming, vagrant 5 = **random**, chance, accidental

streak NOUN 1 = **band**, line, strip, stroke, layer, slash, vein, stripe 2 = **trace**, touch, element, strain, dash, vein
▷ VERB 3 = **speed**, fly, tear, flash, sprint, dart, zoom, whizz (*informal*)

stream NOUN 1 = **river**, brook, burn (*Scot.*), beck, tributary, bayou, rivulet 2 = **flow**, current, rush, run, course, drift, surge, tide
▷ VERB 3 = **flow**, run, pour, issue, flood, spill, cascade, gush 4 = **rush**, fly, speed, tear, flood, pour

streamlined = **efficient**, organized, rationalized, slick, smooth-running

street = **road**, lane, avenue, terrace, row, roadway

strength 1 = **might**, muscle, brawn OPPOSITE: weakness 2 = **will**, resolution, courage, character, nerve, determination, pluck, stamina 3 = **health**, fitness, vigour 4 = **mainstay** 5 = **toughness**, soundness, robustness, sturdiness 6 = **force**, power, intensity OPPOSITE: weakness 7 = **potency**, effectiveness,

efficacy 8 = **strong point**, skill, asset, advantage, talent, forte, speciality OPPOSITE: failing

strengthen 1 = **fortify**, harden, toughen, consolidate, stiffen, gee up, brace up OPPOSITE: weaken 2 = **reinforce**, support, intensify, bolster, buttress 3 = **bolster**, harden, reinforce 4 = **heighten**, intensify 5 = **make stronger**, build up, invigorate, restore, give strength to 6 = **support**, brace, reinforce, consolidate, harden, bolster, augment, buttress 7 = **become stronger**, intensify, gain strength

stress VERB 1 = **emphasize**, underline, dwell on 2 = **place the emphasis on**, emphasize, give emphasis to, lay emphasis upon
▷ NOUN 3 = **emphasis**, significance, force, weight 4 = **strain**, pressure, worry, tension, burden, anxiety, trauma 5 = **accent**, beat, emphasis, accentuation

stretch VERB 1 = **extend**, cover, spread, reach, put forth, unroll 2 = **last**, continue, go on, carry on, reach 3 = **expand** 4 = **pull**, distend, strain, tighten, draw out, elongate
▷ NOUN 5 = **expanse**, area, tract, spread, distance, extent 6 = **period**, time, spell, stint, term, space

strict 1 = **severe**, harsh, stern,

S

firm, stringent **OPPOSITE:** easygoing 2 = **stern**, firm, severe, harsh, authoritarian 3 = **exact**, accurate, precise, close, true, faithful, meticulous, scrupulous 4 = **absolute**, total, utter

strife = **conflict**, battle, clash, quarrel, friction, discord, dissension

strike NOUN 1 = **walkout**, industrial action, mutiny, revolt ▷ VERB 2 = **walk out**, down tools, revolt, mutiny 3 = **hit**, smack, thump, beat, knock, punch, hammer, slap 4 = **drive**, hit, smack, wallop (*informal*) 5 = **collide with**, hit, run into, bump into 6 = **knock**, smack, thump, beat 7 = **affect**, touch, devastate, overwhelm, leave a mark on 8 = **attack**, assault someone, set upon someone, lay into someone (*informal*) 9 = **occur to**, hit, come to, register (*informal*), dawn on or upon 10 = **seem to**, appear to, look to, give the impression to 11 = **move**, touch, hit, affect, overcome, stir, disturb, perturb

striking = **impressive**, dramatic, outstanding, noticeable, conspicuous, jaw-dropping **OPPOSITE:** unimpressive

string 1 = **cord**, twine, fibre 2 = **series**, line, row, file, sequence, succession, procession 3 = **sequence**, run, series, chain, succession

stringent = **strict**, tough, rigorous, tight, severe, rigid, inflexible **OPPOSITE:** lax

strip^1 1 = **undress**, disrobe, unclothe 2 = **plunder**, rob, loot, empty, sack, ransack, pillage, divest

strip^2 1 = **piece**, shred, band, belt 2 = **stretch**, area, tract, expanse, extent

strive = **try**, labour, struggle, attempt, toil, go all out (*informal*), bend over backwards (*informal*), do your best

stroke VERB 1 = **caress**, rub, fondle, pet ▷ NOUN 2 = **apoplexy**, fit, seizure, attack, collapse 3 = **blow**, hit, knock, pat, rap, thump, swipe

stroll VERB 1 = **walk**, ramble, amble, promenade, saunter ▷ NOUN 2 = **walk**, promenade, constitutional, ramble, breath of air

strong ADJECTIVE 1 = **powerful**, muscular, tough, athletic, strapping, hardy, sturdy, burly **OPPOSITE:** weak 2 = **fit**, robust, lusty 3 = **durable**, substantial, sturdy, heavy-duty, well-built, hard-wearing **OPPOSITE:** flimsy 4 = **extreme**, radical, drastic, strict, harsh, rigid, forceful, uncompromising 5 = **decisive**, firm, forceful, decided, determined, resolute, incisive 6 = **persuasive**, convincing, compelling, telling, sound, effective, potent, weighty

7 = **keen**, deep, acute, fervent, zealous, vehement **8** = **intense**, deep, passionate, ardent, fierce, fervent, vehement, fervid **9** = **staunch**, firm, fierce, ardent, enthusiastic, passionate, fervent **10** = **distinct**, marked, clear, unmistakable **OPPOSITE:** slight **11** = **bright**, brilliant, dazzling, bold **OPPOSITE:** dull

stronghold 1 = **bastion**, fortress, bulwark **2** = **refuge**, haven, retreat, sanctuary, hide-out

structure NOUN
  1 = **arrangement**, form, make-up, design, organization, construction, formation, configuration **2** = **building**, construction, erection, edifice ▷ VERB **3** = **arrange**, organize, design, shape, build up, assemble

struggle VERB **1** = **strive**, labour, toil, work, strain, go all out (*informal*), give it your best shot (*informal*), exert yourself **2** = **fight**, battle, wrestle, grapple, compete, contend ▷ NOUN **3** = **effort**, labour, toil, work, pains, scramble, exertion **4** = **fight**, battle, conflict, clash, contest, brush, combat, tussle, biffo (*Austral. slang*)

strut = **swagger**, parade, peacock, prance

stubborn = **obstinate**, dogged, inflexible, persistent, intractable, tenacious, recalcitrant, unyielding **OPPOSITE:** compliant

stuck 1 = **fastened**, fast, fixed, joined, glued, cemented **2** (*Informal*) = **baffled**, stumped, beaten

student 1 = **undergraduate**, scholar **2** = **pupil**, scholar, schoolchild, schoolboy or schoolgirl **3** = **learner**, trainee, apprentice, disciple

studied = **planned**, deliberate, conscious, intentional, premeditated **OPPOSITE:** unplanned

studio = **workshop**, workroom, atelier

study VERB **1** = **learn**, cram (*informal*), swot (up) (*Brit. informal*), read up, mug up (*Brit. slang*) **2** = **examine**, survey, look at, scrutinize **3** = **contemplate**, read, examine, consider, go into, pore over ▷ NOUN **4** = **examination**, investigation, analysis, consideration, inspection, scrutiny, contemplation **5** = **piece of research**, survey, report, review, inquiry, investigation **6** = **learning**, lessons, school work, reading, research, swotting (*Brit. informal*)

stuff NOUN **1** = **things**, gear, possessions, effects, equipment, objects, tackle, kit **2** = **substance**, material, essence, matter

▷ VERB 3 = **shove**, force, push, squeeze, jam, ram 4 = **cram**, fill, pack, crowd

stuffing = **wadding**, filling, packing

stumble 1 = **trip**, fall, slip, reel, stagger, falter, lurch 2 = **totter**, reel, lurch, wobble
▷ PHRASES: **stumble across** or **on** or **upon something** or **someone** = **discover**, find, come across, chance upon

stump NOUN 1 = **tail end**, end, remnant, remainder
▷ VERB 2 = **baffle**, confuse, puzzle, bewilder, perplex, mystify, flummox, nonplus

stun 1 = **overcome**, shock, confuse, astonish, stagger, bewilder, astound, overpower 2 = **daze**, knock out, stupefy, numb, benumb

stunning (*Informal*) = **wonderful**, beautiful, impressive, striking, lovely, spectacular, marvellous, splendid OPPOSITE: unimpressive

stunt = **feat**, act, trick, exploit, deed

stunted = **undersized**, little, small, tiny, diminutive

stupid 1 = **unintelligent**, thick, simple, slow, dim, dense, simple-minded, moronic OPPOSITE: intelligent 2 = **silly**, foolish, daft (*informal*), rash, pointless, senseless, idiotic, fatuous OPPOSITE: sensible 3 = **senseless**, dazed, groggy, insensate, semiconscious

sturdy 1 = **robust**, hardy, powerful, athletic, muscular, lusty, brawny OPPOSITE: puny 2 = **substantial**, solid, durable, well-made, well-built OPPOSITE: flimsy

style NOUN 1 = **manner**, way, method, approach, technique, mode 2 = **elegance**, taste, chic, flair, polish, sophistication, panache, élan 3 = **design**, form, cut 4 = **type**, sort, kind, variety, category, genre 5 = **fashion**, trend, mode, vogue, rage 6 = **luxury**, ease, comfort, elegance, grandeur, affluence
▷ VERB 7 = **design**, cut, tailor, fashion, shape, arrange, adapt 8 = **call**, name, term, label, entitle, dub, designate

stylish = **smart**, chic, fashionable, trendy (*Brit. informal*), modish, dressy (*informal*), voguish OPPOSITE: scruffy

subdue 1 = **overcome**, defeat, master, break, control, crush, conquer, tame 2 = **moderate**, suppress, soften, mellow, tone down, quieten down OPPOSITE: arouse

subdued 1 = **quiet**, serious, sad, chastened, dejected, downcast, crestfallen, down in the mouth OPPOSITE: lively 2 = **hushed**, soft, quiet, muted OPPOSITE: loud

subject NOUN 1 = **topic**,

S

question, issue, matter, point, business, affair, object

2 = **citizen**, resident, native, inhabitant, national

3 = **dependant**, subordinate

▷ ADJECTIVE **4** = **subordinate**, dependent, satellite, inferior, obedient

▷ VERB **5** = **put through**, expose, submit, lay open

▷ PHRASES: **subject to**

1 = **liable to**, open to, exposed to, vulnerable to, prone to, susceptible to **2** = **bound by**

3 = **dependent on**, contingent on, controlled by, conditional on

subjective = **personal**, prejudiced, biased, nonobjective **OPPOSITE:** objective

sublime = **noble**, glorious, high, great, grand, elevated, lofty, exalted **OPPOSITE:** lowly

submerge 1 = **flood**, swamp, engulf, overflow, inundate, deluge **2** = **immerse**, plunge, duck **3** = **sink**, plunge, go under water **4** = **overwhelm**, swamp, engulf, deluge

submission 1 = **surrender**, yielding, giving in, cave-in (*informal*), capitulation

2 = **presentation**, handing in, entry, tendering

3 = **compliance**, obedience, meekness, resignation, deference, passivity, docility

submit 1 = **surrender**, yield, give in, agree, endure, tolerate, comply, succumb **2** = **present**, hand in, tender, put forward,

table, proffer, commit

subordinate NOUN

1 = **inferior**, junior, assistant, aide, second, attendant **OPPOSITE:** superior

▷ ADJECTIVE **2** = **inferior**, lesser, lower, junior, subject, minor, secondary, dependent **OPPOSITE:** superior

subscribe 1 = **support**, advocate, endorse

2 = **contribute**, give, donate

subscription (*Chiefly Brit.*)
= **membership fee**, dues, annual payment

subsequent = **following**, later, succeeding, after, successive, ensuing **OPPOSITE:** previous

subsequently = **later**, afterwards

subside 1 = **decrease**, diminish, lessen, ease, wane, ebb, abate, slacken **OPPOSITE:** increase

2 = **collapse**, sink, cave in, drop, lower, settle

subsidiary NOUN **1** = **branch**, division, section, office, department, wing, subdivision, subsection

▷ ADJECTIVE **2** = **secondary**, lesser, subordinate, minor, supplementary, auxiliary, ancillary **OPPOSITE:** main

subsidy = **aid**, help, support, grant, assistance, allowance

substance 1 = **material**, body, stuff, fabric **2** = **importance**, significance, concreteness

3 = **meaning**, main point, gist, import, significance, essence

S

4 = **wealth**, means, property, assets, resources, estate

substantial = **big**, significant, considerable, large, important, ample, sizable or sizeable **OPPOSITE:** small

substitute VERB 1 = **replace**, exchange, swap, change, switch, interchange

▷ NOUN 2 = **replacement**, reserve, surrogate, deputy, sub, proxy, locum

▷ ADJECTIVE 3 = **replacement**, reserve, surrogate, second, alternative, fall-back, proxy

● USAGE NOTE
● Although *substitute* and
● *replace* have the same
● meaning, the structures they
● are used in are different. You
● replace A with B, while you
● substitute B for A.
● Accordingly, *he replaced the*
● *worn tyre with a new one*, and
● *he substituted a new tyre for the*
● *worn one* are both correct
● ways of saying the same
● thing.

subtle 1 = **faint**, slight, implied, delicate, understated **OPPOSITE:** obvious 2 = **crafty**, cunning, sly, shrewd, ingenious, devious, wily, artful **OPPOSITE:** straightforward 3 = **muted**, soft, subdued, low-key, toned down 4 = **fine**, minute, narrow, tenuous, hair-splitting

subtlety 1 = **fine point**, refinement, sophistication, delicacy 2 = **skill**, ingenuity,

cleverness, deviousness, craftiness, artfulness, slyness, wiliness

subversive ADJECTIVE 1 = **seditious**, riotous, treasonous

▷ NOUN 2 = **dissident**, terrorist, saboteur, fifth columnist

succeed 1 = **triumph**, win, prevail 2 = **work out**, work, be successful 3 = **make it** (*informal*), do well, be successful, triumph, thrive, flourish, make good, prosper **OPPOSITE:** fail 4 = **take over from**, assume the office of 5 *with* **to** = **take over**, assume, attain, come into, inherit, accede to, come into possession of 6 = **follow**, come after, follow after **OPPOSITE:** precede

success 1 = **victory**, triumph **OPPOSITE:** failure 2 = **prosperity**, fortune, luck, fame 3 = **hit** (*informal*), winner, smash (*informal*), triumph, sensation **OPPOSITE:** flop (*informal*) 4 = **big name**, star, hit (*informal*), celebrity, sensation, megastar (*informal*) **OPPOSITE:** nobody

successful 1 = **triumphant**, victorious, lucky, fortunate 2 = **thriving**, profitable, rewarding, booming, flourishing, fruitful **OPPOSITE:** unprofitable 3 = **top**, prosperous, wealthy

successfully = **well**, favourably,

with flying colours, victoriously

succession 1 = **series**, run, sequence, course, order, train, chain, cycle 2 = **taking over**, assumption, inheritance, accession

successive = **consecutive**, following, in succession

succumb 1 *often with* **to** = **surrender**, yield, submit, give in, cave in (*informal*), capitulate **OPPOSITE:** beat 2 *with* **to** (with an illness as object) = **catch**, fall ill with

suck 1 = **drink**, sip, draw 2 = **take**, draw, pull, extract

sudden = **quick**, rapid, unexpected, swift, hurried, abrupt, hasty **OPPOSITE:** gradual

suddenly = **abruptly**, all of a sudden, unexpectedly

sue (*Law*) = **take (someone) to court**, prosecute, charge, summon, indict

suffer 1 = **be in pain**, hurt, ache 2 = **be affected**, have trouble with, be afflicted, be troubled with 3 = **undergo**, experience, sustain, bear, go through, endure 4 = **tolerate**, stand, put up with (*informal*), bear, endure

suffering = **pain**, distress, agony, misery, ordeal, discomfort, torment, hardship

suffice = **be enough**, do, be sufficient, be adequate, serve, meet requirements

sufficient = **adequate**, enough, ample, satisfactory **OPPOSITE:** insufficient

suggest 1 = **recommend**, propose, advise, advocate, prescribe 2 = **indicate** 3 = **hint at**, imply, intimate 4 = **bring to mind**, evoke

suggestion 1 = **recommendation**, proposal, proposition, plan, motion 2 = **hint**, insinuation, intimation 3 = **trace**, touch, hint, breath, indication, whisper, intimation

suit NOUN 1 = **outfit**, costume, ensemble, dress, clothing, habit 2 = **lawsuit**, case, trial, proceeding, cause, action, prosecution ▷ VERB 3 = **be acceptable to**, please, satisfy, do, gratify 4 = **agree with**, become, match, go with, harmonize with

suitable 1 = **appropriate**, right, fitting, fit, becoming, satisfactory, apt, befitting **OPPOSITE:** inappropriate 2 = **seemly**, fitting, becoming, proper, correct **OPPOSITE:** unseemly 3 = **suited**, appropriate, in keeping with **OPPOSITE:** out of keeping 4 = **pertinent**, relevant, applicable, fitting, appropriate, to the point, apt **OPPOSITE:** irrelevant 5 = **convenient**, timely, appropriate, well-timed, opportune **OPPOSITE:** inopportune

suite = **rooms**, apartment

S

sum 1 = **amount**, quantity, volume 2 = **calculation**, figures, arithmetic, mathematics, maths (*Brit. informal*), tally, math (*U.S. informal*), arithmetical problem 3 = **total**, aggregate 4 = **totality**, whole

summarize = **sum up**, condense, encapsulate, epitomize, abridge, précis

summary = **synopsis**, résumé, précis, review, outline, rundown, abridgment

summit 1 = **peak**, top, tip, pinnacle, apex, head **OPPOSITE:** base 2 = **height**, pinnacle, peak, zenith, acme **OPPOSITE:** depths

summon 1 = **send for**, call, bid, invite 2 *often with* **up** = **gather**, muster, draw on

sumptuous = **luxurious**, grand, superb, splendid, gorgeous, lavish, opulent **OPPOSITE:** plain

sunny 1 = **bright**, clear, fine, radiant, sunlit, summery, unclouded **OPPOSITE:** dull 2 = **cheerful**, happy, cheery, buoyant, joyful, light-hearted **OPPOSITE:** gloomy

sunset = **nightfall**, dusk, eventide, close of (the) day

superb 1 = **splendid**, excellent, magnificent, fine, grand, superior, marvellous, world-class, booshit (*Austral. slang*), exo (*Austral. slang*), sik (*Austral. slang*) **OPPOSITE:** inferior

2 = **magnificent**, superior, marvellous, exquisite, superlative **OPPOSITE:** terrible

superficial 1 = **shallow**, frivolous, empty-headed, silly, trivial **OPPOSITE:** serious 2 = **hasty**, cursory, perfunctory, hurried, casual, sketchy, desultory, slapdash **OPPOSITE:** thorough 3 = **slight**, surface, external, on the surface, exterior **OPPOSITE:** profound

superintendent = **supervisor**, director, manager, chief, governor, inspector, controller, overseer

superior ADJECTIVE 1 = **better**, higher, greater, grander, surpassing, unrivalled **OPPOSITE:** inferior 2 = **first-class**, excellent, first-rate, choice, exclusive, exceptional, de luxe, booshit (*Austral. slang*), exo (*Austral. slang*), sik (*Austral. slang*) **OPPOSITE:** average 3 = **supercilious**, patronizing, condescending, haughty, disdainful, lordly, lofty, pretentious

▷ NOUN 4 = **boss**, senior, director, manager, chief (*informal*), principal, supervisor, baas (*S. African*) **OPPOSITE:** subordinate

- USAGE NOTE
- *Superior* should not be used
- with *than*: *he is a better* (not *a*
- *superior*) *poet than his brother*;
- *his poetry is superior to* (not
- *than*) *his brother's*.

superiority = supremacy, lead, advantage, excellence, ascendancy, predominance

supernatural = paranormal, unearthly, uncanny, ghostly, psychic, mystic, miraculous, occult

supervise 1 = **observe**, guide, monitor, oversee, keep an eye on 2 = **oversee**, run, manage, control, direct, handle, look after, superintend

supervision = superintendence, direction, control, charge, care, management, guidance

supervisor = boss (*informal*), manager, chief, inspector, administrator, foreman, overseer, baas (*S. African*)

supplement VERB 1 = **add to**, reinforce, augment, extend ▷ NOUN 2 = **pull-out**, insert 3 = **appendix**, add-on, postscript 4 = **addition**, extra

supply VERB 1 = **provide**, give, furnish, produce, stock, grant, contribute, yield 2 = **furnish**, provide, equip, endow ▷ NOUN 3 = **store**, fund, stock, source, reserve, quantity, hoard, cache ▷ PLURAL NOUN 4 = **provisions**, necessities, stores, food, materials, equipment, rations

support VERB 1 = **help**, back, champion, second, aid, defend, assist, side with **OPPOSITE:** oppose 2 = **provide for**, maintain, look after, keep, fund,

finance, sustain **OPPOSITE:** live off 3 = **bear out**, confirm, verify, substantiate, corroborate **OPPOSITE:** refute 4 = **bear**, carry, sustain, prop (up), reinforce, hold, brace, buttress ▷ NOUN 5 = **furtherance**, backing, promotion, assistance, encouragement 6 = **help**, loyalty **OPPOSITE:** opposition 7 = **aid**, help, benefits, relief, assistance 8 = **prop**, post, foundation, brace, pillar 9 = **supporter**, prop, mainstay, tower of strength, second, backer **OPPOSITE:** antagonist 10 = **upkeep**, maintenance, keep, subsistence, sustenance

supporter = follower, fan, advocate, friend, champion, sponsor, patron, helper **OPPOSITE:** opponent

supportive = helpful, encouraging, understanding, sympathetic

suppose 1 = **imagine**, consider, conjecture, postulate, hypothesize 2 = **think**, imagine, expect, assume, guess (*informal, chiefly U.S. & Canad.*), presume, conjecture

supposed 1 *usually with* to = **meant**, expected, required, obliged 2 = **presumed**, alleged, professed, accepted, assumed

supposedly = presumably, allegedly, ostensibly, theoretically, hypothetically **OPPOSITE:** actually

suppress 1 = **stamp out**, stop,

check, crush, conquer, subdue,
put an end to, overpower
OPPOSITE: encourage
2 = **check**, inhibit, subdue,
stop, quell 3 = **restrain**, stifle,
contain, silence, conceal, curb,
repress, smother
suppression 1 = **elimination**,
crushing, check, quashing
2 = **inhibition**, blocking,
restraint, smothering
supremacy = **domination**,
sovereignty, sway, mastery,
primacy, predominance,
supreme power
supreme 1 = **paramount**,
sovereign **OPPOSITE:** least
2 = **chief**, leading, principal,
highest, head, top, prime,
foremost **OPPOSITE:** lowest
3 = **ultimate**, highest, greatest
supremo (*Brit. informal*) = **head**,
leader, boss (*informal*), director,
master, governor, commander,
principal, baas (*S. African*)
sure 1 = **certain**, positive,
decided, convinced, confident,
assured, definite **OPPOSITE:**
uncertain 2 = **inevitable**,
guaranteed, bound, assured,
inescapable **OPPOSITE:** unsure
3 = **reliable**, accurate,
dependable, undoubted,
undeniable, foolproof, infallible,
unerring **OPPOSITE:** unreliable
surely 1 = **it must be the case
that** 2 = **undoubtedly**,
certainly, definitely, without
doubt, unquestionably,
indubitably, doubtlessly

surface NOUN 1 = **covering**,
face, exterior, side, top, veneer
2 = **façade**
▷ VERB 3 = **emerge**, come up,
come to the surface
4 = **appear**, emerge, arise,
come to light, crop up (*informal*),
transpire, materialize
surge NOUN 1 = **rush**, flood
2 = **flow**, wave, rush, roller,
gush, outpouring 3 = **tide**,
swell, billowing 4 = **rush**,
wave, storm, torrent, eruption
▷ VERB 5 = **rush**, pour, rise,
gush 6 = **roll**, rush, heave
7 = **sweep**, rush, storm
surpass = **outdo**, beat, exceed,
eclipse, excel, transcend,
outstrip, outshine
surpassing = **supreme**,
extraordinary, outstanding,
exceptional, unrivalled,
incomparable, matchless
surplus NOUN 1 = **excess**,
surfeit **OPPOSITE:** shortage
▷ ADJECTIVE 2 = **extra**, spare,
excess, remaining, odd,
superfluous **OPPOSITE:**
insufficient
surprise NOUN 1 = **shock**,
revelation, jolt, bombshell, eye-
opener (*informal*)
2 = **amazement**, astonishment,
wonder, incredulity
▷ VERB 3 = **amaze**, astonish,
stun, startle, stagger, take
aback 4 = **catch unawares** or
off-guard, spring upon
surprised = **amazed**,
astonished, speechless,

S

thunderstruck

surprising = amazing, remarkable, incredible, astonishing, unusual, extraordinary, unexpected, staggering

surrender VERB 1 = give in, yield, submit, give way, succumb, cave in (*informal*), capitulate OPPOSITE: resist 2 = give up, abandon, relinquish, yield, concede, part with, renounce, waive
▷ NOUN 3 = submission, cave-in (*informal*), capitulation, resignation, renunciation, relinquishment

surround = enclose, ring, encircle, encompass, envelop, hem in

surrounding ADJECTIVE
1 = nearby, neighbouring
▷ PLURAL NOUN
2 = environment, setting, background, location, milieu

surveillance = observation, watch, scrutiny, supervision, inspection

survey NOUN 1 = poll, study, research, review, inquiry, investigation 2 = examination, inspection, scrutiny
3 = valuation, estimate, assessment, appraisal
▷ VERB 4 = interview, question, poll, research, investigate 5 = look over, view, examine, observe, contemplate, inspect, eyeball (*slang*), scrutinize 6 = measure, estimate, assess, appraise

survive 1 = remain alive, last, live on, endure 2 = continue, last, live on 3 = live longer than, outlive, outlast

susceptible 1 = responsive, sensitive, receptive, impressionable, suggestible OPPOSITE: unresponsive
2 *usually with* to = liable, inclined, prone, given, subject, vulnerable, disposed OPPOSITE: resistant

suspect VERB 1 = believe, feel, guess, consider, suppose, speculate OPPOSITE: know
2 = distrust, doubt, mistrust OPPOSITE: trust
▷ ADJECTIVE 3 = dubious, doubtful, questionable, iffy (*informal*) OPPOSITE: innocent

suspend 1 = postpone, put off, cease, interrupt, shelve, defer, cut short, discontinue OPPOSITE: continue 2 = hang, attach, dangle

suspension = postponement, break, breaking off, interruption, abeyance, deferment, discontinuation

suspicion 1 = distrust, scepticism, mistrust, doubt, misgiving, qualm, wariness, dubiety 2 = idea, notion, hunch, guess, impression
3 = trace, touch, hint, suggestion, shade, streak, tinge, soupçon (*French*)

suspicious 1 = distrustful, sceptical, doubtful, unbelieving,

S

wary **OPPOSITE:** trusting
2 = **suspect**, dubious, questionable, doubtful, dodgy (Brit., Austral. & N.Z. informal), fishy (informal) **OPPOSITE:** beyond suspicion

sustain 1 = **maintain**, continue, keep up, prolong, protract 2 = **suffer**, experience, undergo, feel, bear, endure, withstand 3 = **help**, aid, assist 4 = **keep alive**, nourish, provide for 5 = **support**, bear, uphold

sustained = **continuous**, constant, steady, prolonged, perpetual, unremitting, nonstop **OPPOSITE:** periodic

swallow 1 = **eat**, consume, devour, swig (informal) 2 = **gulp**, drink

swamp NOUN 1 = **bog**, marsh, quagmire, slough, fen, mire, morass, pakihi (N.Z.)
▷ VERB 2 = **flood**, engulf, submerge, inundate
3 = **overload**, overwhelm, inundate

swap or **swop** = **exchange**, trade, switch, interchange, barter

swarm NOUN 1 = **multitude**, crowd, mass, army, host, flock, herd, horde
▷ VERB 2 = **crowd**, flock, throng, mass, stream
3 = **teem**, crawl, abound, bristle

swathe NOUN 1 = **area**, section, tract
▷ VERB 2 = **wrap**, drape, envelop, cloak, shroud,

bundle up, muffle up,

sway VERB 1 = **move from side to side**, rock, roll, swing, bend, lean 2 = **influence**, affect, guide, persuade, induce
▷ NOUN 3 = **power**, control, influence, authority, clout (informal)

swear 1 = **curse**, blaspheme, be foul-mouthed 2 = **vow**, promise, testify, attest
3 = **declare**, assert, affirm

swearing = **bad language**, cursing, profanity, blasphemy, foul language

sweat NOUN 1 = **perspiration** 2 (Informal) = **panic**, anxiety, worry, distress, agitation
▷ VERB 3 = **perspire**, glow
4 (Informal) = **worry**, fret, agonize, torture yourself

sweep VERB 1 = **brush**, clean 2 = **clear**, remove, brush, clean 3 = **sail**, pass, fly, tear, zoom, glide, skim
▷ NOUN 4 = **movement**, move, swing, stroke 5 = **extent**, range, stretch, scope

sweeping 1 = **indiscriminate**, blanket, wholesale, exaggerated, overstated, unqualified 2 = **wide-ranging**, global, comprehensive, wide, broad, extensive, all-inclusive, all-embracing **OPPOSITE:** limited

sweet ADJECTIVE 1 = **sugary**, cloying, saccharine, icky (informal) **OPPOSITE:** sour
2 = **fragrant**, aromatic

s

OPPOSITE: stinking 3 = **fresh**, clean, pure 4 = **melodious**, musical, harmonious, mellow, dulcet **OPPOSITE:** harsh 5 = **charming**, kind, agreeable **OPPOSITE:** nasty 6 = **delightful**, appealing, cute, winning, engaging, lovable, likable *or* likeable **OPPOSITE:** unpleasant ▷ **NOUN** 7 *usually plural* = **confectionery**, candy (*U.S.*), lolly (*Austral. & N.Z.*), bonbon 8 (*Brit.*) = **dessert**, pudding

sweetheart 1 = **dearest**, beloved, sweet, angel, treasure, honey, dear, sweetie (*informal*) 2 = **love**, boyfriend *or* girlfriend, beloved, lover, darling

swell **VERB** 1 = **increase**, rise, grow, mount, expand, accelerate, escalate, multiply **OPPOSITE:** decrease 2 = **expand**, increase, grow, rise, balloon, enlarge, bulge, dilate **OPPOSITE:** shrink ▷ **NOUN** 3 = **wave**, surge, billow

swelling = **enlargement**, lump, bump, bulge, inflammation, protuberance, distension

swift 1 = **quick**, prompt, rapid 2 = **fast**, quick, rapid, hurried, speedy **OPPOSITE:** slow

swiftly 1 = **quickly**, rapidly, speedily 2 = **fast**, promptly, hurriedly

swing **VERB** 1 = **brandish**, wave, shake, flourish, wield, dangle 2 = **sway**, rock, wave, veer, oscillate 3 *usually with* **round** = **turn**, swivel, curve,

rotate, pivot 4 = **hit out**, strike, swipe, lash out at, slap 5 = **hang**, dangle, suspend ▷ **NOUN** 6 = **swaying**, sway 7 = **fluctuation**, change, shift, switch, variation

swirl = **whirl**, churn, spin, twist, eddy

switch **NOUN** 1 = **control**, button, lever, on/off device 2 = **change**, shift, reversal ▷ **VERB** 3 = **change**, shift, divert, deviate 4 = **exchange**, swap, substitute

swollen = **enlarged**, bloated, inflamed, puffed up, distended

swoop 1 = **pounce**, attack, charge, rush, descend 2 = **drop**, plunge, dive, sweep, descend, pounce, stoop

symbol 1 = **metaphor**, image, sign, representation, token 2 = **representation**, sign, figure, mark, image, token, logo, badge

symbolic 1 = **representative**, emblematic, allegorical 2 = **representative**, figurative

sympathetic 1 = **caring**, kind, understanding, concerned, interested, warm, pitying, supportive **OPPOSITE:** uncaring 2 = **like-minded**, compatible, agreeable, friendly, congenial, companionable **OPPOSITE:** uncongenial

sympathy 1 = **compassion**, understanding, pity, commiseration, aroha (*N.Z.*) **OPPOSITE:** indifference

S

2 = **affinity**, agreement,
rapport, fellow feeling
OPPOSITE: opposition
symptom 1 = **sign**, mark,
indication, warning
2 = **manifestation**, sign,
indication, mark, evidence,
expression, proof, token
synthetic = **artificial**, fake,
man-made **OPPOSITE:** real
system 1 = **arrangement**,
structure, organization,
scheme, classification
2 = **method**, practice,
technique, procedure, routine
systematic = **methodical**,
organized, efficient, orderly
OPPOSITE: unmethodical

Tt

table NOUN 1 = **counter**,
bench, stand, board, surface,
work surface 2 = **list**, chart,
tabulation, record, roll, register,
diagram, itemization
▷ VERB 3 (*Brit.*) = **submit**,
propose, put forward, move,
suggest, enter, file, lodge
taboo NOUN 1 = **prohibition**,
ban, restriction, anathema,
interdict, proscription, tapu
(*N.Z.*)
▷ ADJECTIVE 2 = **forbidden**,
banned, prohibited,
unacceptable, outlawed,
anathema, proscribed,
unmentionable **OPPOSITE:**
permitted
tack NOUN 1 = **nail**, pin,
drawing pin
▷ VERB 2 = **fasten**, fix, attach,
pin, nail, affix 3 (*Brit.*) = **stitch**,
sew, hem, bind, baste
▷ PHRASES: tack something on
to something = **append**, add,
attach, tag
tackle VERB 1 = **deal with**, set
about, get stuck into (*informal*),
come *or* get to grips with
2 = **undertake**, attempt,
embark upon, get stuck into

t

(*informal*), have a go *or* stab at (*informal*) 3 = **intercept**, stop, challenge

▷ NOUN 4 = **block**, challenge 5 = **rig**, apparatus

tactic NOUN 1 = **policy**, approach, move, scheme, plans, method, manoeuvre, ploy

▷ PLURAL NOUN 2 = **strategy**, campaigning, manoeuvres, generalship

tactical = **strategic**, shrewd, smart, diplomatic, cunning OPPOSITE: impolitic

tag NOUN 1 = **label**, tab, note, ticket, slip, identification, marker, flap

▷ VERB 2 = **label**, mark

tail NOUN 1 = **extremity**, appendage, brush, rear end, hindquarters, hind part 2 = **train**, end, trail, tailpiece

▷ VERB 3 (*Informal*) = **follow**, track, shadow, trail, stalk

▷ PHRASES: turn tail = **run away**, flee, run off, retreat, cut and run, take to your heels

tailor NOUN 1 = **outfitter**, couturier, dressmaker, seamstress, clothier, costumier

▷ VERB 2 = **adapt**, adjust, modify, style, fashion, shape, alter, mould

taint = **spoil**, ruin, contaminate, damage, stain, corrupt, pollute, tarnish OPPOSITE: purify

take VERB 1 = **grip**, grab, seize, catch, grasp, clasp, take hold of 2 = **carry**, bring, bear, transport, ferry, haul, convey,

fetch OPPOSITE: send 3 = **accompany**, lead, bring, guide, conduct, escort, convoy, usher 4 = **remove**, draw, pull, fish, withdraw, extract 5 = **steal**, appropriate, pocket, pinch (*informal*), misappropriate, purloin OPPOSITE: return 6 = **capture**, seize, take into custody, lay hold of OPPOSITE: release 7 = **tolerate**, stand, bear, stomach, endure, abide, put up with (*informal*), withstand OPPOSITE: avoid 8 = **require**, need, involve, demand, call for, entail, necessitate 9 = **understand**, follow, comprehend, get, see, grasp, apprehend 10 = **regard as**, believe to be, consider to be, perceive to be, presume to be 11 = **have room for**, hold, contain, accommodate, accept

▷ PHRASES: take off 1 = **lift off**, take to the air 2 (*Informal*) = **depart**, go, leave, disappear, abscond, decamp, slope off ▶ take someone in = **deceive**, fool, con (*informal*), trick, cheat, mislead, dupe, swindle ▶ take someone off (*Informal*) = **parody**, imitate, mimic, mock, caricature, send up (*Brit. informal*), lampoon, satirize ▶ take something in = **understand**, absorb, grasp, digest, comprehend, assimilate, get the hang of (*informal*) ▶ take something up 1 = **start**, begin, engage in, adopt, become

t

involved in 2 = **occupy**, absorb, consume, use up, cover, fill, waste, squander

takeover = **merger**, coup, incorporation

tale = **story**, narrative, anecdote, account, legend, saga, yarn (*informal*) fable

talent = **ability**, gift, aptitude, capacity, genius, flair, knack

talented = **gifted**, able, expert, master, masterly, brilliant, ace (*informal*) consummate

talk VERB 1 = **speak**, chat, chatter, converse, communicate, natter 2 = **discuss**, confer, negotiate, parley, confabulate, korero (*N.Z.*) 3 = **inform**, grass (*Brit. slang*), tell all, give the game away, blab, let the cat out of the bag ▷ NOUN 4 = **speech**, lecture, presentation, report, address, discourse, sermon, symposium, whaikorero (*N.Z.*)

talking-to (*Informal*) = **reprimand**, lecture, rebuke, scolding, criticism, reproach, ticking-off (*informal*), dressing-down (*informal*) **OPPOSITE:** praise

tall 1 = **lofty**, big, giant, long-legged, lanky, leggy 2 = **high**, towering, soaring, steep, elevated, lofty **OPPOSITE:** short 3 (*Informal*) = **implausible**, incredible, far-fetched, exaggerated, absurd, unbelievable, preposterous, cock-and-bull (*informal*) **OPPOSITE:** plausible 4 = **difficult**, hard, demanding, unreasonable, well-nigh impossible

tally NOUN 1 = **record**, score, total, count, reckoning, running total ▷ VERB 2 = **agree**, match, accord, fit, square, coincide, correspond, conform **OPPOSITE:** disagree

tame ADJECTIVE 1 = **domesticated**, docile, broken, gentle, obedient, amenable, tractable **OPPOSITE:** wild 2 = **submissive**, meek, compliant, subdued, manageable, obedient, docile, unresisting **OPPOSITE:** stubborn 3 = **unexciting**, boring, dull, bland, uninspiring, humdrum, uninteresting, insipid **OPPOSITE:** exciting ▷ VERB 4 = **domesticate**, train, break in, house-train **OPPOSITE:** make fiercer 5 = **subdue**, suppress, master, discipline, humble, conquer, subjugate **OPPOSITE:** arouse

tangible = **definite**, real, positive, material, actual, concrete, palpable, perceptible **OPPOSITE:** intangible

tangle NOUN 1 = **knot**, twist, web, jungle, coil, entanglement 2 = **mess**, jam, fix (*informal*), confusion, complication, mix-up, shambles, entanglement ▷ VERB 3 = **twist**, knot, mat,

t

coil, mesh, entangle, interweave, ravel **OPPOSITE:** disentangle

▷ **PHRASES: tangle with someone = come into conflict with**, come up against, cross swords with, dispute with, contend with, contest with, lock horns with

tantrum = outburst, temper, hysterics, fit, flare-up, foulie (*Austral. slang*)

tap¹ VERB 1 = **knock**, strike, pat, rap, beat, touch, drum
▷ NOUN 2 = **knock**, pat, rap, touch, drumming

tap² NOUN 1 = **valve**, stopcock
▷ VERB 2 = **listen in on**, monitor, bug (*informal*), spy on, eavesdrop on, wiretap
▷ **PHRASES: on tap** 1 (*Informal*) = **available**, ready, standing by, to hand, on hand, at hand, in reserve 2 = **on draught**, cask-conditioned, from barrels, not bottled *or* canned

tape NOUN 1 = **binding**, strip, band, string, ribbon
▷ VERB 2 = **record**, video, tape-record, make a recording of 3 *sometimes with* **up** = **bind**, secure, stick, seal, wrap

target 1 = **mark**, goal 2 = **goal**, aim, objective, end, mark, object, intention, ambition 3 = **victim**, butt, prey, scapegoat

tariff 1 = **tax**, duty, toll, levy, excise 2 = **price list**, schedule

tarnish VERB 1 = **damage**, taint, blacken, sully, smirch **OPPOSITE:** enhance 2 = **stain**, discolour, darken, blot, blemish **OPPOSITE:** brighten
▷ NOUN 3 = **stain**, taint, discoloration, spot, blot, blemish

tart¹ = pie, pastry, pasty, tartlet, patty

tart² = **sharp**, acid, sour, bitter, pungent, tangy, piquant, vinegary **OPPOSITE:** sweet

tart³ (*Informal*) = **slut**, prostitute, whore, call girl, trollop, floozy (*slang*)

task = job, duty, assignment, exercise, mission, enterprise, undertaking, chore
▷ **PHRASES: take someone to task** = **criticize**, blame, censure, rebuke, reprimand, reproach, scold, tell off (*informal*)

taste NOUN 1 = **flavour**, savour, relish, smack, tang **OPPOSITE:** blandness 2 = **bit**, bite, mouthful, sample, dash, spoonful, morsel, titbit 3 = **liking**, preference, penchant, fondness, partiality, fancy, appetite, inclination **OPPOSITE:** dislike 4 = **refinement**, style, judgment, discrimination, appreciation, elegance, sophistication, discernment **OPPOSITE:** lack of judgment
▷ VERB 5 = **have a flavour of**, smack of, savour of 6 = **sample**, try, test, sip, savour 7 = **distinguish**,

perceive, discern, differentiate
8 = **experience**, know, undergo, partake of, encounter, meet with **OPPOSITE:** miss

tasty = **delicious**, luscious, palatable, delectable, savoury, full-flavoured, scrumptious (*informal*), appetizing, lekker (*S. African slang*), yummo (*Austral. slang*) **OPPOSITE:** bland

taunt VERB **1** = **jeer**, mock, tease, ridicule, provoke, insult, torment, deride
▷ NOUN **2** = **jeer**, dig, insult, ridicule, teasing, provocation, derision, sarcasm

tavern = **inn**, bar, pub (*informal, chiefly Brit.*), public house, hostelry, alehouse (*archaic*)

tax NOUN **1** = **charge**, duty, toll, levy, tariff, excise, tithe
▷ VERB **2** = **charge**, rate, assess **3** = **strain**, stretch, try, test, load, burden, exhaust, weaken

teach VERB = **instruct**, train, coach, inform, educate, drill, tutor, enlighten
▷ VERB = **show**, train

teacher = **instructor**, coach, tutor, guide, trainer, lecturer, mentor, educator

team 1 = **side**, squad **2** = **group**, company, set, body, band, gang, line-up, bunch
▷ PHRASES: **team up** = **join**, unite, work together, cooperate, couple, link up, get together, band together

tear VERB **1** = **rip**, split, rend, shred, rupture **2** = **run**

3 = **scratch**, cut (open), gash, lacerate, injure, mangle, cut to pieces, cut to ribbons, mangulate (*Austral. slang*)
4 = **pull apart**, claw, lacerate, mutilate, mangle, mangulate (*Austral. slang*) **5** = **rush**, run, charge, race, fly, speed, dash, hurry
▷ NOUN **6** = **hole**, split, rip, rent, snag, rupture

tears = **crying**, weeping, sobbing, wailing, blubbering
▷ PHRASES: **in tears** = **weeping**, crying, sobbing, blubbering

tease 1 = **mock**, provoke, torment, taunt, goad, pull someone's leg (*informal*), make fun of **2** = **tantalize**, lead on, flirt with, titillate

technical = **scientific**, technological, skilled, specialist, specialized, hi-tech or high-tech

technique 1 = **method**, way, system, approach, means, style, manner, procedure **2** = **skill**, performance, craft, touch, execution, artistry, craftsmanship, proficiency

tedious = **boring**, dull, dreary, monotonous, drab, tiresome, laborious, humdrum **OPPOSITE:** exciting

teenager = **youth**, minor, adolescent, juvenile, girl, boy

telephone NOUN **1** = **phone**, mobile (phone), handset, dog and bone (*slang*)
▷ VERB **2** = **call**, phone, ring (*chiefly Brit.*), dial

telescope NOUN 1 = glass, scope (*informal*), spyglass ▷ VERB 2 = **shorten**, contract, compress, shrink, condense, abbreviate, abridge **OPPOSITE:** lengthen

television = TV, telly (*Brit. informal*), small screen (*informal*), the box (*Brit. informal*), the tube (*slang*)

tell VERB 1 = **inform**, notify, state to, reveal to, express to, disclose to, proclaim to, divulge 2 = **describe**, relate, recount, report, portray, depict, chronicle, narrate 3 = **instruct**, order, command, direct, bid 4 = **distinguish**, discriminate, discern, differentiate, identify 5 = **have** *or* **take effect**, register, weigh, count, take its toll, carry weight, make its presence felt ▷ PHRASES: **tell someone off** = **reprimand**, rebuke, scold, lecture, censure, reproach, berate, chide

telling = **effective**, significant, considerable, marked, striking, powerful, impressive, influential **OPPOSITE:** unimportant

temper NOUN 1 = **irritability**, irascibility, passion, resentment, petulance, surliness, hot-headedness **OPPOSITE:** good humour 2 = **frame of mind**, nature, mind, mood, constitution, humour, temperament, disposition 3 = **rage**, fury, bad mood, passion, tantrum, foulie (*Austral. slang*) 4 = **self-control**, composure, cool (*slang*), calmness, equanimity **OPPOSITE:** anger ▷ VERB 5 = **moderate**, restrain, tone down, soften, soothe, lessen, mitigate, assuage **OPPOSITE:** intensify 6 = **strengthen**, harden, toughen, anneal **OPPOSITE:** soften

temperament 1 = **nature**, character, personality, make-up, constitution, bent, humour, temper 2 = **moods**, anger, volatility, petulance, excitability, moodiness, hot-headedness

temple = **shrine**, church, sanctuary, house of God

temporarily = **briefly**, for the time being, momentarily, fleetingly, pro tem

temporary 1 = **impermanent**, transitory, brief, fleeting, interim, short-lived, momentary, ephemeral **OPPOSITE:** permanent 2 = **short-term**, acting, interim, supply, stand-in, fill-in, caretaker, provisional

tempt 1 = **attract**, allure 2 = **entice**, lure, lead on, invite, seduce, coax **OPPOSITE:** discourage

temptation 1 = **enticement**, lure, inducement, pull, seduction, allurement, tantalization 2 = **appeal**, attraction

t

tempting = inviting, enticing, seductive, alluring, attractive, mouthwatering, appetizing **OPPOSITE:** uninviting

tenant = leaseholder, resident, renter, occupant, inhabitant, occupier, lodger, boarder

tend¹ = be inclined, be liable, have a tendency, be apt, be prone, lean, incline, gravitate

tend² 1 = take care of, look after, keep, attend, nurture, watch over **OPPOSITE:** neglect 2 = maintain, take care of, nurture, cultivate, manage **OPPOSITE:** neglect

tendency = inclination, leaning, liability, disposition, propensity, susceptibility, proclivity, proneness

tender¹ 1 = gentle, loving, kind, caring, sympathetic, affectionate, compassionate, considerate **OPPOSITE:** harsh 2 = vulnerable, young, sensitive, raw, youthful, inexperienced, immature, impressionable **OPPOSITE:** experienced 3 = sensitive, painful, sore, raw, bruised, inflamed

tender² NOUN 1 = offer, bid, estimate, proposal, submission ▷ VERB 2 = offer, present, submit, give, propose, volunteer, hand in, put forward

tense ADJECTIVE 1 = strained, uneasy, stressful, fraught, charged, difficult, worrying, exciting 2 = nervous, edgy, strained, anxious, apprehensive, uptight (*informal*), on edge, jumpy **OPPOSITE:** calm 3 = rigid, strained, taut, stretched, tight **OPPOSITE:** relaxed ▷ VERB 4 = tighten, strain, brace, stretch, flex, stiffen **OPPOSITE:** relax

tension 1 = strain, stress, nervousness, pressure, anxiety, unease, apprehension, suspense **OPPOSITE:** calmness 2 = friction, hostility, unease, antagonism, antipathy, enmity 3 = rigidity, tightness, stiffness, pressure, stress, stretching, tautness

tentative 1 = unconfirmed, provisional, indefinite, test, trial, pilot, preliminary, experimental **OPPOSITE:** confirmed 2 = hesitant, cautious, uncertain, doubtful, faltering, unsure, timid, undecided **OPPOSITE:** confident

term NOUN 1 = word, name, expression, title, label, phrase 2 = period, time, spell, while, season, interval, span, duration ▷ PLURAL NOUN 3 = conditions, particulars, provisions, provisos, stipulations, qualifications, specifications 4 = relationship, standing, footing, relations, status ▷ VERB 5 = call, name, label, style, entitle, tag, dub, designate

terminal ADJECTIVE 1 = **fatal**, deadly, lethal, killing, mortal, incurable, inoperable, untreatable 2 = **final**, last, closing, finishing, concluding, ultimate, terminating **OPPOSITE:** initial
▷ NOUN 3 = **terminus**, station, depot, end of the line

terminate 1 = **end**, stop, conclude, finish, complete, discontinue **OPPOSITE:** begin 2 = **cease**, end, close, finish 3 = **abort**, end

terrain = **ground**, country, land, landscape, topography, going

terrestrial = **earthly**, worldly, global

terrible 1 = **awful**, shocking, terrifying, horrible, dreadful, horrifying, fearful, horrendous 2 (Informal) = **bad**, awful, dreadful, dire, abysmal, poor, rotten (informal) **OPPOSITE:** wonderful 3 = **serious**, desperate, severe, extreme, dangerous, insufferable **OPPOSITE:** mild

terribly 1 = **very much**, very, dreadfully, seriously, extremely, desperately, thoroughly, decidedly 2 = **extremely**, very, dreadfully, seriously, desperately, thoroughly, decidedly, awfully (informal)

terrific 1 (Informal) = **excellent**, wonderful, brilliant, amazing, outstanding, superb, fantastic (informal), magnificent, booshit (Austral. slang), exo (Austral.

slang), sik (Austral. slang), ka pai (N.Z.) **OPPOSITE:** awful 2 = **intense**, great, huge, enormous, tremendous, fearful, gigantic

terrified = **frightened**, scared, petrified, alarmed, panic-stricken, horror-struck

terrify = **frighten**, scare, alarm, terrorize

territory = **district**, area, land, region, country, zone, province, patch

terror 1 = **fear**, alarm, dread, fright, panic, anxiety 2 = **nightmare**, monster, bogeyman, devil, fiend, bugbear

test VERB 1 = **check**, investigate, assess, research, analyse, experiment with, try out, put something to the test 2 = **examine**, put someone to the test
▷ NOUN 3 = **trial**, research, check, investigation, analysis, assessment, examination, evaluation 4 = **examination**, paper, assessment, evaluation

testament 1 = **proof**, evidence, testimony, witness, demonstration, tribute 2 = **will**, last wishes

testify = **bear witness**, state, swear, certify, assert, affirm, attest, corroborate **OPPOSITE:** disprove

testimony 1 = **evidence**, statement, submission, affidavit, deposition 2 = **proof**, evidence, demonstration, indication, support, manifestation, verification, corroboration

testing = **difficult**, demanding, taxing, challenging, searching, tough, exacting, rigorous **OPPOSITE:** undemanding

text 1 = **contents**, words, content, wording, body, subject matter 2 = **words**, wording 3 = **transcript**, script

texture = **feel**, consistency, structure, surface, tissue, grain

thank = **say thank you to**, show your appreciation to

thanks = **gratitude**, appreciation, credit, recognition, acknowledgment, gratefulness
▷ **PHRASES: thanks to**
= **because of**, through, due to, as a result of, owing to

thaw = **melt**, dissolve, soften, defrost, warm, liquefy, unfreeze **OPPOSITE:** freeze

theatrical 1 = **dramatic**, stage, Thespian 2 = **exaggerated**, dramatic, melodramatic, histrionic, affected, mannered, showy, ostentatious **OPPOSITE:** natural

theft = **stealing**, robbery, thieving, fraud, embezzlement, pilfering, larceny, purloining

theme 1 = **motif**, leitmotif 2 = **subject**, idea, topic, essence, subject matter, keynote, gist

theological = **religious**, ecclesiastical, doctrinal

theoretical 1 = **abstract**, speculative **OPPOSITE:** practical 2 = **hypothetical**, academic, notional, unproven, conjectural, postulatory

theory = **belief**, feeling, speculation, assumption, hunch, presumption, conjecture, surmise

therapeutic = **beneficial**, healing, restorative, good, corrective, remedial, salutary, curative **OPPOSITE:** harmful

therapist = **psychologist**, analyst, psychiatrist, shrink (*informal*), counsellor, healer, psychotherapist, psychoanalyst

therapy = **remedy**, treatment, cure, healing, method of healing

therefore = **consequently**, so, thus, as a result, hence, accordingly, thence, ergo

thesis 1 = **proposition**, theory, hypothesis, idea, view, opinion, proposal, contention 2 = **dissertation**, paper, treatise, essay, monograph

thick **ADJECTIVE** 1 = **bulky**, broad, big, large, fat, solid, substantial, hefty **OPPOSITE:** thin 2 = **wide**, across, deep, broad, in extent *or* diameter 3 = **dense**, close, heavy, compact, impenetrable, lush 4 = **heavy**, heavyweight, dense, chunky, bulky, woolly 5 = **opaque**, heavy, dense, impenetrable 6 = **viscous**, concentrated, stiff, condensed, gelatinous, semi-solid, viscid **OPPOSITE:** runny **7** = **crowded**, full, covered, bursting, bristling, brimming **OPPOSITE:** empty **8** (*Informal*) = **stupid**, slow, dense, dopey (*informal*), moronic, obtuse, brainless, dumb-ass (*informal*) **OPPOSITE:** clever **9** (*Informal*) = **friendly**, close, intimate, familiar, pally (*informal*), devoted, inseparable **OPPOSITE:** unfriendly

thicken = **set**, condense, congeal, clot, jell, coagulate **OPPOSITE:** thin

thief = **robber**, burglar, stealer, plunderer, shoplifter, embezzler, pickpocket, pilferer

thin ADJECTIVE **1** = **narrow**, fine, attenuated **OPPOSITE:** thick **2** = **slim**, spare, lean, slight, slender, skinny, skeletal, bony **OPPOSITE:** fat **3** = **meagre**, sparse, scanty, poor, scattered, inadequate, insufficient, deficient **OPPOSITE:** plentiful **4** = **fine**, delicate, flimsy, sheer, skimpy, gossamer, diaphanous, filmy **OPPOSITE:** thick **5** = **unconvincing**, inadequate, feeble, poor, weak, superficial, lame, flimsy **OPPOSITE:** convincing **6** = **wispy**, thinning, sparse, scarce, scanty

thing NOUN **1** = **substance**, stuff, being, body, material, fabric, entity **2** (*Informal*) = **phobia**, fear, complex, horror, terror, hang-up (*informal*),

aversion, neurosis **3** (*Informal*) = **obsession**, liking, preoccupation, mania, fetish, fixation, soft spot, predilection

▷ PLURAL NOUN

4 = **possessions**, stuff, gear, belongings, effects, luggage, clobber (*Brit. slang*), chattels **5** = **equipment**, gear, tools, stuff, tackle, implements, kit, apparatus **6** = **circumstances**, the situation, the state of affairs, matters, life, affairs

think 1 = **believe**, be of the opinion, be of the view **2** = **judge**, consider, estimate, reckon, deem, regard as **3** = **ponder**, reflect, contemplate, deliberate, meditate, ruminate, cogitate, be lost in thought

▷ PHRASES: **think something up** = **devise**, create, come up with, invent, contrive, visualize, concoct, dream something up

thinker = **philosopher**, intellect (*informal*), wise man, sage, brain (*informal*), theorist, mastermind

thinking NOUN **1** = **reasoning**, idea, view, position, theory, opinion, judgment, conjecture

▷ ADJECTIVE **2** = **thoughtful**, intelligent, reasoning, rational, philosophical, reflective, contemplative, meditative

thirst NOUN **1** = **dryness**, thirstiness, drought **2** = **craving**, appetite, longing, desire, passion, yearning, hankering, keenness **OPPOSITE:** aversion

thorn = prickle, spike, spine, barb

thorough 1 = comprehensive, full, complete, sweeping, intensive, in-depth, exhaustive **OPPOSITE:** cursory 2 = careful, conscientious, painstaking, efficient, meticulous, exhaustive, assiduous **OPPOSITE:** careless 3 = complete, total, absolute, utter, perfect, outright, unqualified, out-and-out **OPPOSITE:** partial

thoroughly 1 = carefully, fully, efficiently, meticulously, painstakingly, scrupulously, assiduously, intensively **OPPOSITE:** carelessly 2 = fully 3 = completely, quite, totally, perfectly, absolutely, utterly, downright, to the hilt **OPPOSITE:** partly

though CONJUNCTION 1 = although, while, even if, even though, notwithstanding ▷ ADVERB 2 = nevertheless, still, however, yet, nonetheless, for all that, notwithstanding

thought 1 = thinking, consideration, reflection, deliberation, musing, meditation, rumination, cogitation 2 = opinion, view, idea, concept, notion, judgment 3 = consideration, study, attention, care, regard, scrutiny, heed 4 = intention, plan, idea, design, aim, purpose, object, notion 5 = hope, expectation, prospect, aspiration, anticipation

thoughtful 1 = reflective, pensive, contemplative, meditative, serious, studious, deliberative, ruminative **OPPOSITE:** shallow 2 = considerate, kind, caring, kindly, helpful, attentive, unselfish, solicitous **OPPOSITE:** inconsiderate

thrash 1 = defeat, beat, crush, slaughter (informal), rout, trounce, run rings around (informal), wipe the floor with (informal) 2 = beat, wallop, whip, belt (informal), cane, flog, scourge, spank 3 = thresh, flail, jerk, writhe, toss and turn ▷ PHRASES: thrash something out = settle, resolve, discuss, debate, solve, argue out, have something out, talk something over

thrashing 1 = defeat, beating, hammering (informal), hiding (informal), rout, trouncing, drubbing 2 = beating, hiding (informal), belting (informal), whipping, flogging

thread NOUN 1 = strand, fibre, yarn, filament, line, string, twine 2 = theme, train of thought, direction, plot, drift, story line ▷ VERB 3 = move, pass, ease, thrust, squeeze through, pick your way

threat 1 = danger, risk, hazard, menace, peril 2 = threatening

remark, menace 3 = **warning**, foreshadowing, foreboding

threaten 1 = **intimidate**, bully, menace, terrorize, lean on (*slang*), pressurize, browbeat **OPPOSITE:** defend 2 = **endanger**, jeopardize, put at risk, imperil, put in jeopardy, put on the line **OPPOSITE:** protect 3 = **be imminent**, impend

threshold 1 = **entrance**, doorway, door, doorstep 2 = **start**, beginning, opening, dawn, verge, brink, inception **OPPOSITE:** end 3 = **limit**, margin, starting point, minimum

thrift = **economy**, prudence, frugality, saving, parsimony, carefulness, thriftiness **OPPOSITE:** extravagance

thrill NOUN 1 = **pleasure**, kick (*informal*), buzz (*slang*), high, stimulation, tingle, titillation **OPPOSITE:** tedium ▷ VERB 2 = **excite**, stimulate, arouse, move, stir, electrify, titillate, give someone a kick

thrilling = **exciting**, gripping, stimulating, stirring, sensational, rousing, riveting, electrifying **OPPOSITE:** boring

thrive = **prosper**, do well, flourish, increase, grow, develop, succeed, get on **OPPOSITE:** decline

thriving = **successful**, flourishing, healthy, booming, blooming, prosperous,

burgeoning **OPPOSITE:** unsuccessful

throb VERB 1 = **pulsate**, pound, beat, pulse, thump, palpitate 2 = **vibrate**, pulsate, reverberate, shake, judder (*informal*) ▷ NOUN 3 = **pulse**, pounding, beat, thump, thumping, pulsating, palpitation 4 = **vibration**, throbbing, reverberation, judder (*informal*), pulsation

throng NOUN 1 = **crowd**, mob, horde, host, pack, mass, crush, swarm ▷ VERB 2 = **crowd**, flock, congregate, converge, mill around, swarm around **OPPOSITE:** disperse 3 = **pack**, crowd

throttle = **strangle**, choke, garrotte, strangulate

through PREPOSITION 1 = **via**, by way of, by, between, past, from one side to the other of 2 = **because of**, by way of, by means of 3 = **using**, via, by way of, by means of, by virtue of, with the assistance of 4 = **during**, throughout, for the duration of, in ▷ ADJECTIVE 5 = **completed**, done, finished, ended ▷ PHRASES: through and through = **completely**, totally, fully, thoroughly, entirely, altogether, wholly, utterly

throughout PREPOSITION 1 = **right through**, everywhere

in, during the whole of, through the whole of **2** = **all over**, everywhere in, through the whole of
▷ ADVERB **3** = **from start to finish**, right through **4** = **all through**, right through

throw VERB **1** = **hurl**, toss, fling, send, launch, cast, pitch, chuck (*informal*) **2** = **toss**, fling, chuck (*informal*), cast, hurl, sling **3** (*Informal*) = **confuse**, baffle, faze, astonish, confound, disconcert, dumbfound
▷ NOUN **4** = **toss**, pitch, fling, sling, lob (*informal*), heave

thrust VERB **1** = **push**, force, shove, drive, plunge, jam, ram, propel
▷ NOUN **2** = **stab**, pierce, lunge **3** = **push**, shove, poke, prod **4** = **momentum**, impetus, drive

thug = **ruffian**, hooligan, tough, heavy (*slang*), gangster, bully boy, bruiser (*informal*), tsotsi (*S. African*)

thump VERB **1** = **strike**, hit, punch, pound, beat, knock, smack, clout (*informal*)
▷ NOUN **2** = **blow**, knock, punch, rap, smack, clout (*informal*), whack, swipe **3** = **thud**, crash, bang, clunk, thwack

thunder NOUN **1** = **rumble**, crash, boom, explosion
▷ VERB **2** = **rumble**, crash, boom, roar, resound, reverberate, peal **3** = **shout**, roar, yell, bark, bellow

thus 1 = **therefore**, so, hence, consequently, accordingly, for this reason, ergo, on that account **2** = **in this way**, so, like this, as follows

thwart = **frustrate**, foil, prevent, snooker, hinder, obstruct, outwit, stymie
OPPOSITE: assist

tick NOUN **1** = **check mark**, mark, line, stroke, dash **2** = **click**, tapping, clicking, ticktock **3** (*Brit. informal*) = **moment**, second, minute, flash, instant, twinkling, split second, trice
▷ VERB **4** = **mark**, indicate, check off **5** = **click**, tap, ticktock

ticket 1 = **voucher**, pass, coupon, card, slip, certificate, token, chit **2** = **label**, tag, marker, sticker, card, slip, tab, docket

tide 1 = **current**, flow, stream, ebb, undertow, tideway **2** = **course**, direction, trend, movement, tendency, drift

tidy ADJECTIVE **1** = **neat**, orderly, clean, spruce, well-kept, well-ordered, shipshape
OPPOSITE: untidy
2 = **organized**, neat, methodical **3** (*Informal*) = **considerable**, large, substantial, goodly, healthy, generous, handsome, ample
OPPOSITE: small
▷ VERB **4** = **neaten**, straighten, order, clean, groom, spruce up

OPPOSITE: disorder

tie VERB 1 = **fasten**, bind, join, link, connect, attach, knot **OPPOSITE:** unfasten 2 = **tether**, secure 3 = **restrict**, limit, confine, bind, restrain, hamper, hinder **OPPOSITE:** free 4 = **draw**, be level, match, equal
▷ NOUN 5 = **fastening**, binding, link, bond, knot, cord, fetter, ligature 6 = **bond**, relationship, connection, commitment, liaison, allegiance, affiliation 7 = **draw**, dead heat, deadlock, stalemate

tier = **row**, bank, layer, line, level, rank, storey, stratum

tight ADJECTIVE 1 = **close-fitting**, narrow, cramped, snug, constricted, close **OPPOSITE:** loose 2 = **secure**, firm, fast, fixed 3 = **taut**, stretched, rigid **OPPOSITE:** slack 4 = **close**, even, well-matched, hard-fought, evenly-balanced **OPPOSITE:** uneven 5 (Informal) = **miserly**, mean, stingy, grasping, parsimonious, niggardly, tightfisted **OPPOSITE:** generous 6 (Informal) = **drunk**, intoxicated, plastered (slang), under the influence (informal), tipsy, paralytic (informal), inebriated, out to it (Austral. & N.Z. slang) **OPPOSITE:** sober

tighten = **close**, narrow, strengthen, squeeze, harden, constrict **OPPOSITE:** slacken

till¹ = **cultivate**, dig, plough, work, turnover

till² = **cash register**, cash box

tilt VERB 1 = **slant**, tip, slope, list, lean, heel, incline
▷ NOUN 2 = **slope**, angle, inclination, list, pitch, incline, slant, camber 3 (Medieval history) = **joust**, fight, tournament, lists, combat, duel

timber 1 = **beams**, boards, planks 2 = **wood**, logs

time NOUN 1 = **period**, term, space, stretch, spell, span 2 = **occasion**, point, moment, stage, instance, point in time, juncture 3 = **age**, duration 4 = **tempo**, beat, rhythm, measure
▷ VERB 5 = **schedule**, set, plan, book, programme, set up, fix, arrange

timeless = **eternal**, lasting, permanent, enduring, immortal, everlasting, ageless, changeless **OPPOSITE:** temporary

timely = **opportune**, appropriate, well-timed, suitable, convenient, judicious, propitious, seasonable **OPPOSITE:** untimely

timetable 1 = **schedule**, programme, agenda, list, diary, calendar 2 = **syllabus**, course, curriculum, programme, teaching programme

tinge NOUN 1 = **tint**, colour, shade 2 = **trace**, bit, drop, touch, suggestion, dash, sprinkling, smattering

t

▷ VERB **3** = **tint**, colour

tinker = **meddle**, play, potter, fiddle (*informal*), dabble, mess about

tint NOUN **1** = **shade**, colour, tone, hue **2** = **dye**, wash, rinse, tinge, tincture
▷ VERB **3** = **dye**, colour

tiny = **small**, little, minute, slight, miniature, negligible, microscopic, diminutive
OPPOSITE: huge

tip¹ NOUN **1** = **end**, point, head, extremity, sharp end, nib, prong **2** = **peak**, top, summit, pinnacle, zenith, spire, acme, vertex
▷ VERB **3** = **cap**, top, crown, surmount, finish

tip² VERB **1** = **reward**, remunerate, give a tip to, sweeten (*informal*) **2** = **predict**, back, recommend, think of
▷ NOUN **3** = **gratuity**, gift, reward, present, sweetener (*informal*) **4** = **hint**, suggestion, piece of advice, pointer

tip³ VERB **1** = **pour**, drop, empty, dump, drain, discharge, unload, jettison **2** (*Brit.*) = **dump**, empty, unload, pour out
▷ NOUN **3** (*Brit.*) = **dump**, midden, rubbish heap, refuse heap

tire 1 = **exhaust**, drain, fatigue, weary, wear out OPPOSITE: refresh **2** = **flag**, become tired, fail **3** = **bore**, weary, exasperate, irritate, irk

tired 1 = **exhausted**, fatigued, weary, flagging, drained, sleepy, worn out, drowsy, tuckered out (*Austral. & N.Z. informal*)
OPPOSITE: energetic **2** = **bored**, fed up, weary, sick, hoha (*N.Z.*)
OPPOSITE: enthusiastic about **3** = **hackneyed**, stale, well-worn, old, corny (*slang*), threadbare, trite, clichéd
OPPOSITE: original

tiring = **exhausting**, demanding, wearing, tough, exacting, strenuous, arduous, laborious

title 1 = **name**, designation, term, handle (*slang*), moniker or monicker (*slang*) **2** (*Sport*) = **championship**, trophy, bays, crown, honour **3** (*Law*) = **ownership**, right, claim, privilege, entitlement, tenure, prerogative, freehold

toast¹ 1 = **brown**, grill, crisp, roast **2** = **warm (up)**, heat (up), thaw, bring back to life

toast² NOUN **1** = **tribute**, compliment, salute, health, pledge, salutation **2** = **favourite**, celebrity, darling, talk, pet, focus of attention, hero or heroine, blue-eyed boy or girl (*Brit. informal*)
▷ VERB **3** = **drink to**, honour, salute, drink (to) the health of

together ADVERB **1** = **collectively**, jointly, as one, with each other, in conjunction, side by side, mutually, in partnership OPPOSITE: separately **2** = **at the same**

time, simultaneously, concurrently, contemporaneously, at one fell swoop
▷ ADJECTIVE **3** (*Informal*) = **self-possessed**, composed, well-balanced, well-adjusted

toil VERB **1** = **labour**, work, struggle, strive, sweat (*informal*), slave, graft (*informal*), slog **2** = **struggle**, trek, slog, trudge, fight your way, footslog
▷ NOUN **3** = **hard work**, effort, application, sweat, graft (*informal*), slog, exertion, drudgery OPPOSITE: idleness

toilet **1** = **lavatory**, bathroom, loo (*Brit. informal*), privy, cloakroom (*Brit.*), urinal, latrine, washroom, dunny (*Austral. & N.Z. old-fashioned informal*), bogger (*Austral. slang*), brasco (*Austral. slang*) **2** = **bathroom**, gents or ladies (*Brit. informal*), privy, latrine, water closet, ladies' room, W.C.

token NOUN **1** = **symbol**, mark, sign, note, expression, indication, representation, badge
▷ ADJECTIVE **2** = **nominal**, symbolic, minimal, hollow, superficial, perfunctory

tolerance 1 = **broad-mindedness**, indulgence, forbearance, permissiveness, open-mindedness OPPOSITE: intolerance **2** = **endurance**, resistance, stamina, fortitude, resilience, toughness, staying

power, hardiness **3** = **resistance**, immunity, resilience, non-susceptibility

tolerant = **broad-minded**, understanding, open-minded, catholic, long-suffering, permissive, forbearing, unprejudiced OPPOSITE: intolerant

tolerate 1 = **endure**, stand, take, stomach, put up with (*informal*) **2** = **allow**, accept, permit, take, brook, put up with (*informal*), condone OPPOSITE: forbid

toll¹ VERB **1** = **ring**, sound, strike, chime, knell, clang, peal
▷ NOUN **2** = **ringing**, chime, knell, clang, peal

toll² **1** = **charge**, tax, fee, duty, payment, levy, tariff **2** = **damage**, cost, loss, roll, penalty, sum, number, roster **3** = **adverse effects**, price, cost, suffering, damage, penalty, harm

tomb = **grave**, vault, crypt, mausoleum, sarcophagus, catacomb, sepulchre

tone NOUN **1** = **pitch**, inflection, intonation, timbre, modulation **2** = **volume**, timbre **3** = **character**, style, feel, air, spirit, attitude, manner, mood **4** = **colour**, shade, tint, tinge, hue
▷ VERB **5** = **harmonize**, match, blend, suit, go well with
▷ PHRASES: **tone something down** = **moderate**, temper,

soften, restrain, subdue, play down = **reduce**, moderate

tongue = **language**, speech, dialect, parlance

tonic = **stimulant**, boost, pick-me-up (*informal*), fillip, shot in the arm (*informal*), restorative

too 1 = **also**, as well, further, in addition, moreover, besides, likewise, to boot
2 = **excessively**, very, extremely, overly, unduly, unreasonably, inordinately, immoderately

tool 1 = **implement**, device, appliance, machine, instrument, gadget, utensil, contraption 2 = **puppet**, creature, pawn, stooge (*slang*), minion, lackey, flunkey, hireling

top NOUN 1 = **peak**, summit, head, crown, height, ridge, brow, crest **OPPOSITE:** bottom
2 = **lid**, cover, cap, plug, stopper, bung 3 = **first place**, head, peak, lead, high point
▷ ADJECTIVE 4 = **highest**, loftiest, furthest up, uppermost
5 = **leading**, best, first, highest, head, finest, elite, foremost **OPPOSITE:** lowest 6 = **chief**, most important, principal, most powerful, highest, head, leading, main 7 = **prime**, best, select, first-class, quality, choice, excellent, premier
▷ VERB 8 = **lead**, head, be at the top of, be first in 9 = **cover**, garnish, finish, crown, cap
10 = **surpass**, better, beat, improve on, cap, exceed,

eclipse, excel **OPPOSITE:** not be as good as

topic = **subject**, point, question, issue, matter, theme, subject matter

topical = **current**, popular, contemporary, up-to-date, up-to-the-minute, newsworthy

topple 1 = **fall over**, fall, collapse, tumble, overturn, totter, keel over, overbalance
2 = **knock over** 3 = **overthrow**, overturn, bring down, oust, unseat, bring low

torment NOUN 1 = **suffering**, distress, misery, pain, hell, torture, agony, anguish **OPPOSITE:** bliss
▷ VERB 2 = **torture**, distress, rack, crucify **OPPOSITE:** comfort
3 = **tease**, annoy, bother, irritate, harass, hassle (*informal*), pester, vex

torn 1 = **cut**, split, rent, ripped, ragged, slit, lacerated
2 = **undecided**, uncertain, unsure, wavering, vacillating, in two minds (*informal*), irresolute

tornado = **whirlwind**, storm, hurricane, gale, cyclone, typhoon, tempest, squall

torture VERB 1 = **torment**, abuse, persecute, afflict, scourge, molest, crucify, mistreat **OPPOSITE:** comfort
2 = **distress**, torment, worry, trouble, rack, afflict, harrow, inflict anguish on
▷ NOUN 3 = **ill-treatment**, abuse, torment, persecution,

maltreatment, harsh treatment
4 = **agony**, suffering, anguish, distress, torment, heartbreak **OPPOSITE:** bliss

toss VERB **1** = **throw**, pitch, hurl, fling, launch, cast, flip, sling **2** = **shake 3** = **thrash (about)**, twitch, wriggle, squirm, writhe
▷ NOUN **4** = **throw**, pitch, lob (*informal*)

tot 1 = **infant**, child, baby, toddler, mite, littlie (*Austral. informal*), ankle-biter (*Austral. slang*), tacker (*Austral. slang*) **2** = **measure**, shot (*informal*), finger, nip, slug, dram, snifter (*informal*)
▷ PHRASES: **tot something up** = **add up**, calculate, total, reckon, compute, tally, enumerate, count up

total NOUN **1** = **sum**, entirety, grand total, whole, aggregate, totality, full amount, sum total **OPPOSITE:** part
▷ ADJECTIVE **2** = **complete**, absolute, utter, whole, entire, undivided, overarching, thoroughgoing **OPPOSITE:** partial
▷ VERB **3** = **amount to**, make, come to, reach, equal, run to, number, add up to **4** = **add up**, work out, compute, reckon, tot up **OPPOSITE:** subtract

totally = **completely**, entirely, absolutely, fully, comprehensively, thoroughly, wholly, utterly **OPPOSITE:** partly

touch VERB **1** = **feel**, handle, finger, stroke, brush, make contact with, caress, fondle **2** = **come into contact**, meet, contact, border, graze, adjoin, be in contact, abut **3** = **tap 4** = **affect**, influence, inspire, impress **5** = **consume**, take, drink, eat, partake of **6** = **move**, stir, disturb **7** = **match**, rival, equal, compare with, parallel, hold a candle to (*informal*)
▷ NOUN **8** = **contact**, push, stroke, brush, press, tap, poke, nudge **9** = **feeling**, handling, physical contact **10** = **bit**, spot, trace, drop, dash, small amount, jot, smattering **11** = **style**, method, technique, way, manner, trademark
▷ PHRASES: **touch and go** = **risky**, close, near, critical, precarious, nerve-racking
▶ **touch on** or **upon something** = **refer to**, cover, raise, deal with, mention, bring in, speak of, hint at

touching = **moving**, affecting, sad, stirring, pathetic, poignant, emotive, pitiable

tough ADJECTIVE **1** = **strong**, unyielding **OPPOSITE:** weak **2** = **hardy**, strong, seasoned, strapping, vigorous, sturdy, stout **3** = **violent**, rough, ruthless, pugnacious, hard-bitten **4** = **strict**, severe, stern, hard, firm, resolute, merciless, unbending **OPPOSITE:** lenient

t

5 = **hard**, difficult, troublesome, uphill, strenuous, arduous, laborious **6** = **resilient**, hard, resistant, durable, strong, solid, rugged, sturdy **OPPOSITE:** fragile

▷ **NOUN 7** = **ruffian**, bully, thug, hooligan, bruiser (*informal*), roughneck (*slang*), tsotsi (*S. African*)

tour NOUN **1** = **journey**, expedition, excursion, trip, outing, jaunt, junket
▷ **VERB 2** = **travel round**, travel through, journey round, trek round, go on a trip through **3** = **visit**, explore, go round, inspect, walk round, drive round, sightsee

tourist = **traveller**, voyager, tripper, globetrotter, holiday-maker, sightseer, excursionist

tournament = **competition**, meeting, event, series, contest

tow = **drag**, draw, pull, haul, tug, yank, lug

towards 1 = **in the direction of**, to, for, on the way to, en route for **2** = **regarding**, about, concerning, respecting, in relation to, with regard to, with respect to, apropos

tower = **column**, pillar, turret, belfry, steeple, obelisk

toxic = **poisonous**, deadly, lethal, harmful, pernicious, noxious, septic, pestilential **OPPOSITE:** harmless

toy = **plaything**, game, doll
▷ **PHRASES:** toy with

something = **play with**, consider, trifle with, dally with, entertain the possibility of, amuse yourself with, think idly of

trace VERB **1** = **search for**, track, unearth, hunt down **2** = **find**, track (down), discover, detect, unearth, hunt down, ferret out, locate **3** = **outline**, sketch, draw **4** = **copy**, map, draft, outline, sketch, reproduce, draw over
▷ **NOUN 5** = **bit**, drop, touch, shadow, suggestion, hint, suspicion, tinge **6** = **remnant**, sign, record, mark, evidence, indication, vestige **7** = **track**, trail, footstep, path, footprint, spoor, footmark

track NOUN **1** = **path**, way, road, route, trail, pathway, footpath **2** = **course**, line, path, orbit, trajectory **3** = **line**, tramline
▷ **VERB 4** = **follow**, pursue, chase, trace, tail (*informal*), shadow, trail, stalk
▷ **PHRASES:** track something or someone down = **find**, discover, trace, unearth, dig up, hunt down, sniff out, run to earth or ground

tract¹ = **area**, region, district, stretch, territory, extent, plot, expanse

tract² = **treatise**, essay, booklet, pamphlet, dissertation, monograph, homily

trade NOUN **1** = **commerce**,

business, transactions, dealing, exchange, traffic, truck, barter **2** = **job**, employment, business, craft, profession, occupation, line of work, métier
▷ VERB **3** = **deal**, do business, traffic, truck, bargain, peddle, transact, cut a deal
4 = **exchange**, switch, swap, barter **5** = **operate**, run, deal, do business

trader = **dealer**, supplier, merchant, seller, purveyor

tradition 1 = **customs**, institution, ritual, folklore, lore, tikanga (*N.Z.*) **2** = **established practice**, custom, convention, habit, ritual

traditional 1 = **old-fashioned**, old, established, conventional, usual, accustomed, customary, time-honoured **OPPOSITE:** revolutionary **2** = **folk**, old

traffic NOUN **1** = **transport**, vehicles, transportation, freight **2** = **trade**, commerce, business, exchange, truck, dealings, peddling
▷ VERB **3** = **trade**, deal, exchange, bargain, do business, peddle, cut a deal, have dealings

tragedy = **disaster**, catastrophe, misfortune, adversity, calamity **OPPOSITE:** fortune

tragic 1 = **distressing**, sad, appalling, deadly, unfortunate, disastrous, dreadful, dire **OPPOSITE:** fortunate **2** = **sad**, miserable, pathetic, mournful

OPPOSITE: happy

trail NOUN **1** = **path**, track, route, way, course, road, pathway, footpath **2** = **tracks**, path, marks, wake, trace, scent, footprints, spoor **3** = **wake**, stream, tail
▷ VERB **4** = **follow**, track, chase, pursue, dog, hunt, shadow, trace **5** = **drag**, draw, pull, sweep, haul, tow, dangle, droop **6** = **lag**, follow, drift, wander, linger, trudge, plod, meander

train VERB **1** = **instruct**, school, prepare, coach, teach, guide, educate, drill **2** = **exercise**, prepare, work out, practise, do exercise, get into shape **3** = **aim**, point, level, position, direct, focus, sight, zero in
▷ NOUN **4** = **sequence**, series, chain, string, set, cycle, trail, succession

trainer = **coach**, manager, guide, adviser, tutor, instructor, counsellor, guru

trait = **characteristic**, feature, quality, attribute, quirk, peculiarity, mannerism, idiosyncrasy

traitor = **betrayer**, deserter, turncoat, renegade, defector, Judas, quisling, apostate, fizgig (*Austral. slang*) **OPPOSITE:** loyalist

tramp VERB **1** = **trudge**, stump, toil, plod, traipse (*informal*) **2** = **hike**, walk, trek, roam, march, ramble, slog,

rove, footslog
▷ NOUN 3 = **vagrant**, derelict, drifter, down-and-out, derro (*Austral. slang*) 4 = **tread**, stamp, footstep, footfall 5 = **hike**, march, trek, ramble, slog

trample *often with* **on** = **stamp**, crush, squash, tread, flatten, run over, walk over

trance = **daze**, dream, abstraction, rapture, reverie, stupor, unconsciousness

transaction = **deal**, negotiation, business, enterprise, bargain, undertaking

transcend = **surpass**, exceed, go beyond, rise above, eclipse, excel, outstrip, outdo

transcript = **copy**, record, manuscript, reproduction, duplicate, transcription

transfer VERB 1 = **move**, transport, shift, relocate, transpose, change
▷ NOUN 2 = **transference**, move, handover, change, shift, transmission, translation, relocation

transform 1 = **change**, convert, alter, transmute 2 = **make over**, remodel, revolutionize

transformation 1 = **change**, conversion, alteration, metamorphosis, transmutation 2 = **revolution**, sea change

transit = **movement**, transfer, transport, passage, crossing,

transportation, carriage, conveyance

transition = **change**, passing, development, shift, conversion, alteration, progression, metamorphosis

transitional 1 = **changing**, passing, fluid, intermediate, unsettled, developmental 2 = **temporary**, working, acting, short-term, interim, fill-in, caretaker, provisional

translate = **render**, put, change, convert, interpret, decode, construe, paraphrase

translation = **interpretation**, version, rendering, rendition, decoding, paraphrase

transmission 1 = **transfer**, spread, spreading, passing on, circulation, dispatch, relaying, mediation 2 = **broadcasting**, showing, putting out, relaying, sending 3 = **programme**, broadcast, show, production, telecast

transmit 1 = **broadcast**, televise, relay, air, radio, send out, disseminate, beam out 2 = **pass on**, carry, spread, send, bear, transfer, hand on, convey

transparent 1 = **clear**, sheer, see-through, lucid, translucent, crystalline, limpid, diaphanous **OPPOSITE:** opaque 2 = **obvious**, plain, patent, evident, explicit, manifest, recognizable, unambiguous **OPPOSITE:** uncertain

transplant 1 = implant, transfer, graft 2 = transfer, take, bring, carry, remove, transport, shift, convey

transport NOUN 1 = vehicle, transportation, conveyance 2 = transference, carrying, delivery, distribution, transportation, shipment, freight, haulage 3 *often plural* = ecstasy, delight, heaven, bliss, euphoria, rapture, enchantment, ravishment **OPPOSITE:** despondency ▷ VERB 4 = convey, take, move, bring, send, carry, bear, transfer 5 = enrapture, move, delight, entrance, enchant, captivate, ravish 6 (*History*) = exile, banish, deport

trap NOUN 1 = snare, net, gin, pitfall, noose 2 = ambush, set-up (*informal*) 3 = trick, set-up (*informal*), deception, ploy, ruse, trickery, subterfuge, stratagem ▷ VERB 4 = catch, snare, ensnare, entrap, take, corner, bag, lay hold of 5 = trick, fool, cheat, lure, seduce, deceive, dupe, beguile 6 = capture, catch, arrest, seize, take, secure, collar (*informal*), apprehend

trash 1 = nonsense, rubbish, rot, drivel, twaddle, tripe (*informal*), moonshine, hogwash, kak (*S. African taboo slang*), bizzo (*Austral. slang*), bull's wool (*Austral. & N.Z. slang*) **OPPOSITE:** sense 2 (*Chiefly U.S.*

& *Canad.*) = litter, refuse, waste, rubbish, junk (*informal*), garbage, dross

trauma 1 = shock, suffering, pain, torture, ordeal, anguish 2 = injury, damage, hurt, wound, agony

traumatic = shocking, upsetting, alarming, awful, disturbing, devastating, painful, distressing **OPPOSITE:** calming

travel VERB 1 = go, journey, move, tour, progress, wander, trek, voyage ▷ NOUN 2 *usually plural* = journey, wandering, expedition, globetrotting, tour, trip, voyage, excursion

traveller *or* (*U.S.*) **traveler** = voyager, tourist, explorer, globetrotter, holiday-maker, wayfarer

tread VERB 1 = step, walk, march, pace, stamp, stride, hike ▷ NOUN 2 = step, walk, pace, stride, footstep, gait, footfall

treason = disloyalty, mutiny, treachery, duplicity, sedition, perfidy, lese-majesty, traitorousness **OPPOSITE:** loyalty

treasure NOUN 1 = riches, money, gold, fortune, wealth, valuables, jewels, cash 2 (*Informal*) = angel, darling, jewel, gem, paragon, nonpareil ▷ VERB 3 = prize, value, esteem, adore, cherish, revere, hold dear, love

t

treasury = **storehouse**, bank, store, vault, hoard, cache, repository

treat VERB 1 = **behave towards**, deal with, handle, act towards, use, consider, serve, manage 2 = **take care of**, minister to, attend to, give medical treatment to, doctor (*informal*), nurse, care for, prescribe medicine for 3 = **provide**, stand (*informal*), entertain, lay on, regale ▷ NOUN 4 = **entertainment**, party, surprise, gift, celebration, feast, outing, excursion 5 = **pleasure**, delight, joy, thrill, satisfaction, enjoyment, source of pleasure, fun

treatment 1 = **care**, medical care, nursing, medicine, surgery, therapy, healing, medication 2 = **cure**, remedy, medication, medicine 3 *often with of* = **handling**, dealings with, behaviour towards, conduct towards, management, manipulation, action towards

treaty = **agreement**, pact, contract, alliance, convention, compact, covenant, entente

trek VERB 1 = **journey**, march, hike, tramp, rove, go walkabout (*Austral.*) 2 = **trudge**, traipse (*informal*), footslog, slog ▷ NOUN 3 = **slog**, tramp 4 = **journey**, hike, expedition, safari, march, odyssey

tremble VERB 1 = **shake**, shiver, quake, shudder, quiver,

totter 2 = **vibrate**, shake, quake, wobble ▷ NOUN 3 = **shake**, shiver, quake, shudder, wobble, tremor, quiver, vibration

tremendous 1 = **huge**, great, enormous, terrific, formidable, immense, gigantic, colossal OPPOSITE: tiny 2 = **excellent**, great, wonderful, brilliant, amazing, extraordinary, fantastic (*informal*), marvellous, booshit (*Austral. slang*), exo (*Austral. slang*), sik (*Austral. slang*) OPPOSITE: terrible

trench = **ditch**, channel, drain, gutter, trough, furrow, excavation

trend 1 = **tendency**, swing, drift, inclination, current, direction, flow, leaning 2 = **fashion**, craze, fad (*informal*), mode, thing, style, rage, vogue

trendy (*Brit. informal*) = **fashionable**, with it (*informal*), stylish, in fashion, in vogue, modish, voguish

trial 1 (*Law*) = **hearing**, case, court case, inquiry, tribunal, lawsuit, appeal, litigation 2 = **test**, experiment, evaluation, audition, dry run (*informal*), assessment, probation, appraisal 3 = **hardship**, suffering, trouble, distress, ordeal, adversity, affliction, tribulation

tribe = **race**, people, family, clan, hapu (*N.Z.*), iwi (*N.Z.*)

tribunal = hearing, court, trial

tribute = accolade, testimonial, eulogy, recognition, compliment, commendation, panegyric **OPPOSITE:** criticism

trick NOUN 1 = joke, stunt, spoof (*informal*), prank, practical joke, antic, jape, leg-pull (*Brit. informal*) 2 = deception, trap, fraud, manoeuvre, ploy, hoax, swindle, ruse 3 = sleight of hand, stunt, legerdemain 4 = secret, skill, knack, hang (*informal*), technique, know-how (*informal*) 5 = mannerism, habit, characteristic, trait, quirk, peculiarity, foible, idiosyncrasy
▷ VERB 6 = deceive, trap, take someone in (*informal*), fool, cheat, con (*informal*), kid (*informal*), mislead

trickle VERB 1 = dribble, run, drop, stream, drip, ooze, seep, exude
▷ NOUN 2 = dribble, drip, seepage, thin stream

tricky 1 = difficult, sensitive, complicated, delicate, risky, hairy (*informal*), problematic, thorny **OPPOSITE:** simple 2 = crafty, scheming, cunning, slippery, sly, devious, wily, artful **OPPOSITE:** open

trifle = knick-knack, toy, plaything, bauble, bagatelle

trifling = insignificant, trivial, worthless, negligible, unimportant, paltry, measly **OPPOSITE:** significant

trigger = bring about, start, cause, produce, generate, prompt, provoke, set off **OPPOSITE:** prevent

trim ADJECTIVE 1 = neat, smart, tidy, spruce, dapper, natty (*informal*), well-groomed, shipshape **OPPOSITE:** untidy 2 = slender, fit, slim, sleek, streamlined, shapely, svelte, willowy
▷ VERB 3 = cut, crop, clip, shave, tidy, prune, pare, even up 4 = decorate, dress, array, adorn, ornament, embellish, deck out, beautify
▷ NOUN 5 = decoration, edging, border, piping, trimming, frill, embellishment, adornment 6 = condition, health, shape (*informal*), fitness, wellness, fettle 7 = cut, crop, clipping, shave, pruning, shearing, tidying up

trimming NOUN 1 = decoration, edging, border, piping, frill, embellishment, adornment, ornamentation
▷ PLURAL NOUN 2 = extras, accessories, ornaments, accompaniments, frills, trappings, paraphernalia

trinity = threesome, trio, triad, triumvirate

trio = threesome, trinity, trilogy, triad, triumvirate

trip NOUN 1 = journey, outing, excursion, day out, run, drive, tour, spin (*informal*) 2 = stumble, fall, slip, misstep

t

▷ VERB 3 = **stumble**, fall, fall over, slip, tumble, topple, stagger, misstep 4 = **skip**, dance, hop, gambol
▷ PHRASES: trip someone up = **catch out**, trap, wrongfoot

triple ADJECTIVE 1 = **treble**, three times 2 = **three-way**, threefold, tripartite
▷ VERB 3 = **treble**, increase threefold

triumph NOUN 1 = **success**, victory, accomplishment, achievement, coup, feat, conquest, attainment OPPOSITE: failure 2 = **joy**, pride, happiness, rejoicing, elation, jubilation, exultation
▷ VERB 3 often with over = **succeed**, win, overcome, prevail, prosper, vanquish OPPOSITE: fail 4 = **rejoice**, celebrate, glory, revel, gloat, exult, crow

triumphant 1 = **victorious**, winning, successful, conquering OPPOSITE: defeated 2 = **celebratory**, jubilant, proud, elated, exultant, cock-a-hoop

trivial = **unimportant**, small, minor, petty, meaningless, worthless, trifling, insignificant OPPOSITE: important

troop NOUN 1 = **group**, company, team, body, unit, band, crowd, squad
▷ PLURAL NOUN 2 = **soldiers**, men, armed forces, servicemen, army, soldiery

▷ VERB 3 = **flock**, march, stream, swarm, throng, traipse (informal)

trophy 1 = **prize**, cup, award, laurels 2 = **souvenir**, spoils, relic, memento, booty, keepsake

tropical = **hot**, stifling, steamy, torrid, sultry, sweltering OPPOSITE: cold

trot VERB 1 = **run**, jog, scamper, lope, canter
▷ NOUN 2 = **run**, jog, lope, canter

trouble NOUN 1 = **bother**, problems, concern, worry, stress, difficulty (informal), anxiety, distress 2 usually plural = **distress**, problem, worry, pain, anxiety, grief, torment, sorrow OPPOSITE: pleasure 3 = **ailment**, disease, failure, complaint, illness, disorder, defect, malfunction 4 = **disorder**, fighting, conflict, bother, unrest, disturbance, to-do (informal), furore, biffo (Austral. slang) OPPOSITE: peace 5 = **effort**, work, thought, care, labour, pains, hassle (informal), inconvenience OPPOSITE: convenience
▷ VERB 6 = **bother**, worry, upset, disturb, distress, plague, pain, sadden OPPOSITE: please 7 = **afflict**, hurt, bother, cause discomfort to, pain, grieve 8 = **inconvenience**, disturb, burden, put out, impose upon, incommode OPPOSITE: relieve

9 = **take pains**, take the time, make an effort, exert yourself **OPPOSITE:** avoid

troublesome
1 = **bothersome**, trying, taxing, demanding, difficult, worrying, annoying, tricky **OPPOSITE:** simple **2** = **disorderly**, violent, turbulent, rebellious, unruly, rowdy, undisciplined, uncooperative **OPPOSITE:** well-behaved

trough = **manger**, water trough

truce = **ceasefire**, peace, moratorium, respite, lull, cessation, let-up (*informal*), armistice

true 1 = **correct**, right, accurate, precise, factual, truthful, veracious **OPPOSITE:** false **2** = **actual**, real, genuine, proper, authentic, dinkum (*Austral. & N.Z. informal*) **3** = **faithful**, loyal, devoted, dedicated, steady, reliable, staunch, trustworthy **OPPOSITE:** unfaithful **4** = **exact**, perfect, accurate, precise, spot-on (*Brit. informal*), on target, unerring **OPPOSITE:** inaccurate

truly 1 = **genuinely**, correctly, truthfully, rightly, precisely, exactly, legitimately, authentically **OPPOSITE:** falsely **2** = **really**, very, greatly, indeed, extremely **3** = **faithfully**, steadily, sincerely, staunchly, dutifully, loyally, devotedly

trumpet NOUN **1** = **horn**, clarion, bugle

▷ VERB **2** = **proclaim**, advertise, tout (*informal*), announce, broadcast, shout from the rooftops **OPPOSITE:** keep secret

trunk 1 = **stem**, stalk, bole **2** = **chest**, case, box, crate, coffer, casket **3** = **body**, torso **4** = **snout**, nose, proboscis

trust VERB **1** = **believe in**, have faith in, depend on, count on, bank on, rely upon **OPPOSITE:** distrust **2** = **entrust**, commit, assign, confide, consign, put into the hands of, allow to look after, hand over **3** = **expect**, hope, suppose, assume, presume, surmise

▷ NOUN **4** = **confidence**, credit, belief, faith, expectation, conviction, assurance, certainty **OPPOSITE:** distrust

trusting *or* **trustful** = **unsuspecting**, naive, gullible, unwary, credulous, unsuspicious **OPPOSITE:** suspicious

truth 1 = **reality**, fact(s), real life **2** = **truthfulness**, fact, accuracy, precision, validity, legitimacy, veracity, genuineness **OPPOSITE:** inaccuracy

try VERB **1** = **attempt**, seek, aim, strive, struggle, endeavour, have a go, make an effort **2** = **experiment with**, try out, put to the test, test, taste, examine, investigate, sample

▷ NOUN **3** = **attempt**, go

(*informal*), shot (*informal*), effort, crack (*informal*), stab (*informal*), bash (*informal*), whack (*informal*)

trying = **annoying**, hard, taxing, difficult, tough, stressful, exasperating, tiresome
OPPOSITE: straightforward

tuck VERB 1 = **push**, stick, stuff, slip, ease, insert, pop (*informal*) ▷ NOUN 2 (*Brit. informal*) = **food**, grub (*slang*), kai (*N.Z. informal*), nosh (*slang*) 3 = **fold**, gather, pleat, pinch

tug VERB 1 = **pull**, pluck, jerk, yank, wrench 2 = **drag**, pull, haul, tow, lug, heave, draw ▷ NOUN 3 = **pull**, jerk, yank

tuition = **training**, schooling, education, teaching, lessons, instruction, tutoring, tutelage

tumble VERB 1 = **fall**, drop, topple, plummet, stumble, flop ▷ NOUN 2 = **fall**, drop, trip, plunge, spill, stumble

tumour = **growth**, cancer, swelling, lump, carcinoma (*Pathology*), sarcoma (*Medical*)

tune NOUN 1 = **melody**, air, song, theme, strain(s), jingle, ditty 2 = **harmony**, pitch, euphony ▷ VERB 3 = **tune up**, adjust 4 = **regulate**, adapt, modulate, harmonize, attune, pitch

tunnel NOUN 1 = **passage**, underpass, passageway, subway, channel, hole, shaft ▷ VERB 2 = **dig**, burrow, mine, bore, drill, excavate

turbulent = **stormy**, rough,

raging, tempestuous, furious, foaming, agitated, tumultuous
OPPOSITE: calm

turf 1 = **grass**, sward 2 = **sod** ▷ PHRASES: **the turf** = **horse-racing**, the flat, racing

turmoil = **confusion**, disorder, chaos, upheaval, disarray, uproar, agitation, commotion
OPPOSITE: peace

turn VERB 1 = **change course**, swing round, wheel round, veer, move, switch, shift, swerve 2 = **rotate**, spin, go round (and round), revolve, roll, circle, twist, spiral 3 = **change**, transform, shape, convert, alter, mould, remodel, mutate 4 = **shape**, form, fashion, cast, frame, mould, make 5 = **go bad**, go off (*Brit. informal*), curdle 6 = **make rancid**, spoil, sour, taint ▷ NOUN 7 = **rotation**, cycle, circle, revolution, spin, twist, whirl, swivel 8 = **change of direction**, shift, departure, deviation 9 = **direction**, course, tack, tendency, drift 10 = **opportunity**, go, time, try, chance, crack (*informal*) 11 = **deed**, service, act, action, favour, gesture ▷ PHRASES: **turn on someone** = **attack**, assault, fall on, round on, lash out at, assail, lay into (*informal*), let fly at ▷ **turn someone on** (*Informal*) = **arouse**, attract, excite, thrill, stimulate, please, titillate

▶ **turn something down**
1 = **refuse**, decline, reject, spurn, rebuff, repudiate
2 = **lower**, soften, mute, lessen, muffle, quieten ▶ **turn something in** = **hand in**, return, deliver, give up, hand over, submit, surrender, tender
▶ **turn something off** = **switch off**, turn out, put out, stop, cut out, shut down, unplug, flick off
▶ **turn something on** = **switch on**, activate, start, start up, ignite, kick-start ▶ **turn something up** 1 = **find**, reveal, discover, expose, disclose, unearth, dig up 2 = **increase**, raise, boost, enhance, intensify, amplify ▶ **turn up** 1 = **arrive**, come, appear, show up (*informal*), attend, put in an appearance, show your face
2 = **come to light**, show up, pop up, materialize
turning = **turn-off**, turn, bend, curve, junction, crossroads, side road, exit
turning point = **crossroads**, change, crisis, crux, moment of truth
turnout = **attendance**, crowd, audience, gate, assembly, congregation, number, throng
turnover 1 = **output**, business, productivity 2 = **movement**, coming and going, change
turtle ▷ *See panel* REPTILES
tutor NOUN 1 = **teacher**, coach, instructor, educator, guide, guardian, lecturer, guru

▷ VERB 2 = **teach**, educate, school, train, coach, guide, drill, instruct
twig = **branch**, stick, sprig, shoot, spray
twilight 1 = **dusk**, evening, sunset, early evening, nightfall, sundown, gloaming (*Scot. poetic*), close of day, evo (*Austral. slang*) OPPOSITE: dawn
2 = **half-light**, gloom, dimness, semi-darkness
twin NOUN 1 = **double**, counterpart, mate, match, fellow, clone, duplicate, lookalike
▷ VERB 2 = **pair**, match, join, couple, link, yoke
twinkle VERB 1 = **sparkle**, flash, shine, glitter, gleam, blink, flicker, shimmer
▷ NOUN 2 = **sparkle**, flash, spark, gleam, flicker, shimmer, glimmer
twist VERB 1 = **coil**, curl, wind, wrap, screw, twirl
2 = **intertwine** 3 = **distort**, screw up, contort, mangle, mangulate (*Austral. slang*)
OPPOSITE: straighten
▷ NOUN 4 = **surprise**, change, turn, development, revelation
5 = **development**, emphasis, variation, slant 6 = **wind**, turn, spin, swivel, twirl 7 = **curve**, turn, bend, loop, arc, kink, zigzag, dog-leg
twitch VERB 1 = **jerk**, flutter, jump, squirm 2 = **pull (at)**, tug (at), pluck (at), yank (at)

t

▷ NOUN 3 = **jerk**, tic, spasm, jump, flutter

tycoon = **magnate**, capitalist, baron, industrialist, financier, fat cat (*slang, chiefly U.S.*), mogul, plutocrat

type = **kind**, sort, class, variety, group, order, style, species

typical 1 = **archetypal**, standard, model, normal, stock, representative, usual, regular
OPPOSITE: unusual
2 = **characteristic**
3 = **average**, normal, usual, routine, regular, orthodox, predictable, run-of-the-mill

tyranny = **oppression**, cruelty, dictatorship, authoritarianism, despotism, autocracy, absolutism, high-handedness
OPPOSITE: liberality

Uu

ubiquitous = **ever-present**, pervasive, omnipresent, everywhere, universal

ugly 1 = **unattractive**, homely (*chiefly U.S.*), plain, unsightly, unlovely, unprepossessing, ill-favoured **OPPOSITE:** beautiful
2 = **unpleasant**, shocking, terrible, nasty, distasteful, horrid, objectionable, disagreeable **OPPOSITE:** pleasant 3 = **bad-tempered**, dangerous, menacing, sinister, baleful

ulcer = **sore**, abscess, peptic ulcer, gumboil

ultimate 1 = **final**, last, end
2 = **supreme**, highest, greatest, paramount, superlative
3 = **worst**, greatest, utmost, extreme 4 = **best**, greatest, supreme, optimum, quintessential

ultimately 1 = **finally**, eventually, in the end, after all, at last, sooner or later, in due time 2 = **fundamentally**, essentially, basically, primarily, at heart, deep down

umpire NOUN 1 = **referee**, judge, arbiter, arbitrator

u

▷ VERB 2 = **referee**, judge, adjudicate, arbitrate

unable = **incapable**, powerless, unfit, impotent, unqualified, ineffectual **OPPOSITE:** able

unanimous 1 = **agreed**, united, in agreement, harmonious, like-minded, of the same mind **OPPOSITE:** divided 2 = **united**, common, concerted, solid, consistent, harmonious, undivided, congruent **OPPOSITE:** split

unarmed = **defenceless**, helpless, unprotected **OPPOSITE:** armed

unaware = **ignorant**, unconscious, oblivious, uninformed, unknowing, not in the loop (*informal*) **OPPOSITE:** aware

unbearable = **intolerable**, insufferable, too much (*informal*), unacceptable **OPPOSITE:** tolerable

unborn = **expected**, awaited, embryonic

uncertain = **unsure**, undecided, vague, unclear, dubious, hazy, irresolute **OPPOSITE:** sure

uncertainty
1 = **unpredictability**, precariousness, ambiguity, unreliability, fickleness, chanciness, changeableness **OPPOSITE:** predictability
2 = **doubt**, confusion **OPPOSITE:** confidence
3 = **hesitancy**, indecision

uncomfortable 1 = **uneasy**, troubled, disturbed, embarrassed, awkward, discomfited **OPPOSITE:** comfortable 2 = **painful**, awkward, rough

uncommon 1 = **rare**, unusual, odd, novel, strange, peculiar, scarce, queer **OPPOSITE:** common 2 = **extraordinary**, remarkable, special, outstanding, distinctive, exceptional, notable **OPPOSITE:** ordinary

uncompromising = **inflexible**, strict, rigid, firm, tough, inexorable, intransigent, unbending

unconditional = **absolute**, full, complete, total, positive, entire, outright, unlimited **OPPOSITE:** qualified

unconscious 1 = **senseless**, knocked out, out cold (*informal*), out, stunned, dazed, in a coma, stupefied **OPPOSITE:** awake 2 = **unaware**, ignorant, oblivious, unknowing **OPPOSITE:** aware 3 = **unintentional**, unwitting, inadvertent, accidental **OPPOSITE:** intentional

uncover 1 = **reveal**, expose, disclose, divulge, make known **OPPOSITE:** conceal 2 = **open**, unveil, unwrap, show, strip, expose, bare, lay bare

under PREPOSITION 1 = **below**, beneath, underneath **OPPOSITE:** over

u

2 = **subordinate to**, subject to, governed by, secondary to
▷ ADVERB **3** = **below**, down, beneath **OPPOSITE:** up

undercover = **secret**, covert, private, hidden, concealed **OPPOSITE:** open

underdog = **weaker party**, little fellow (*informal*), outsider

underestimate
1 = **undervalue**, understate, diminish, play down, minimize, downgrade, miscalculate, trivialize **OPPOSITE:** overestimate **2** = **underrate**, undervalue, belittle **OPPOSITE:** overrate

● USAGE NOTE
● *Underestimate* is sometimes
● wrongly used where
● *overestimate* is meant: *the*
● *importance of his work cannot*
● *be overestimated* (not *cannot be*
● *underestimated*).

undergo = **experience**, go through, stand, suffer, bear, sustain, endure

underground
1 = **subterranean**, basement, lower-level, sunken, covered, buried, subterrestrial
2 = **secret**, covert, hidden, guerrilla, revolutionary, confidential, dissident, closet
▷ PHRASES: **the underground**
1 = **the tube** (*Brit.*), the subway, the metro **2** = **the Resistance**, partisans, freedom fighters

underline 1 = **emphasize**, stress, highlight, accentuate

OPPOSITE: minimize
2 = **underscore**, mark

underlying = **fundamental**, basic, prime, primary, elementary, intrinsic

undermine = **weaken**, sabotage, subvert, compromise, disable **OPPOSITE:** reinforce

understand 1 = **comprehend**, get, take in, perceive, grasp, see, follow, realize **2** = **believe**, gather, think, see, suppose, notice, assume, fancy

understandable
= **reasonable**, natural, justified, expected, inevitable, legitimate, predictable, accountable

understanding NOUN
1 = **perception**, knowledge, grasp, sense, know-how (*informal*), judgment, awareness, appreciation **OPPOSITE:** ignorance
2 = **agreement**, deal, promise, arrangement, accord, contract, bond, pledge **OPPOSITE:** disagreement **3** = **belief**, view, opinion, impression, interpretation, feeling, idea, notion
▷ ADJECTIVE **4** = **sympathetic**, kind, compassionate, considerate, patient, sensitive, tolerant **OPPOSITE:** unsympathetic

undertake = **agree**, promise, contract, guarantee, engage, pledge

undertaking 1 = **task**, business, operation, project,

attempt, effort, affair, venture
2 = **promise**, commitment,
pledge, word, vow, assurance
underwear = **underclothes**,
lingerie, undies (*informal*),
undergarments, underthings,
broekies (*S. African informal*),
underdaks (*Austral. slang*)
underworld 1 = **criminals**,
gangsters, organized crime,
gangland (*informal*) **2** = **nether
world**, Hades, nether regions
underwrite = **finance**, back,
fund, guarantee, sponsor,
insure, ratify, subsidize
undesirable = **unwanted**,
unwelcome, disagreeable,
objectionable, unacceptable,
unsuitable, unattractive,
distasteful **OPPOSITE:** desirable
undo 1 = **open**, unfasten, loose,
untie, unbutton, disentangle
2 = **reverse**, cancel, offset,
neutralize, invalidate, annul
3 = **ruin**, defeat, destroy, wreck,
shatter, upset, undermine,
overturn
undone = **unfinished**, left,
neglected, omitted, unfulfilled,
unperformed **OPPOSITE:**
finished
undoubtedly = **certainly**,
definitely, surely, doubtless,
without doubt, assuredly
unearth 1 = **discover**, find,
reveal, expose, uncover **2** = **dig
up**, excavate, exhume,
dredge up
unearthly = **eerie**, strange,
supernatural, ghostly, weird,

phantom, uncanny, spooky
(*informal*)
uneasy 1 = **anxious**, worried,
troubled, nervous, disturbed,
uncomfortable, edgy, perturbed
OPPOSITE: relaxed
2 = **precarious**, strained,
uncomfortable, tense,
awkward, shaky, insecure
unemployed = **out of work**,
redundant, laid off, jobless, idle
OPPOSITE: working
unfair 1 = **biased**, prejudiced,
unjust, one-sided, partial,
partisan, bigoted
2 = **unscrupulous**, dishonest,
unethical, wrongful, unsporting
OPPOSITE: ethical
unfit 1 = **out of shape**, feeble,
unhealthy, flabby, in poor
condition **OPPOSITE:** healthy
2 = **incapable**, inadequate,
incompetent, no good, useless,
unqualified **OPPOSITE:** capable
3 = **unsuitable**, inadequate,
useless, unsuited **OPPOSITE:**
suitable
unfold 1 = **reveal**, tell, present,
show, disclose, uncover,
divulge, make known **2** = **open**,
spread out, undo, expand,
unfurl, unwrap, unroll
unfortunate 1 = **disastrous**,
calamitous, adverse, ill-fated
OPPOSITE: opportune
2 = **regrettable**, deplorable,
lamentable, unsuitable,
unbecoming **OPPOSITE:**
becoming **3** = **unlucky**,
unhappy, doomed, cursed,

u

unsuccessful, hapless, wretched **OPPOSITE:** fortunate

unhappy 1 = **sad**, depressed, miserable, blue, melancholy, mournful, dejected, despondent **OPPOSITE:** happy 2 = **unlucky**, unfortunate, hapless, cursed, wretched, ill-fated **OPPOSITE:** fortunate

unhealthy 1 = **harmful**, detrimental, unwholesome, insanitary, insalubrious **OPPOSITE:** beneficial 2 = **sick**, sickly, unwell, delicate, crook (*Austral. & N.Z. informal*), ailing, frail, feeble, invalid **OPPOSITE:** well 3 = **weak**, ailing **OPPOSITE:** strong

unification = **union**, uniting, alliance, coalition, federation, confederation, amalgamation, coalescence

uniform NOUN 1 = **regalia**, suit, livery, colours, habit 2 = **outfit**, dress, costume, attire, gear (*informal*), get-up (*informal*), ensemble, garb ▷ ADJECTIVE 3 = **consistent**, unvarying, similar, even, same, matching, regular, constant **OPPOSITE:** varying 4 = **alike**, similar, like, same, equal

unify = **unite**, join, combine, merge, consolidate, confederate, amalgamate **OPPOSITE:** divide

union 1 = **joining**, uniting, unification, combination, coalition, merger, mixture, blend 2 = **alliance**, league,

association, coalition, federation, confederacy

unique 1 = **distinct**, special, exclusive, peculiar, only, single, lone, solitary 2 = **unparalleled**, unmatched, unequalled, matchless, without equal

- USAGE NOTE
- *Unique* with the meaning
- 'being the only one' or 'having
- no equal' describes an
- absolute state: *a case unique*
- *in British law*. In this use it
- cannot therefore be qualified;
- something is either *unique* or
- *not unique*. However, *unique* is
- also very commonly used in
- the sense of 'remarkable' or
- 'exceptional', particularly in
- the language of advertising,
- and in this meaning it can be
- used with qualifying words
- such as *rather*, *quite*, etc. Since
- many people object to this
- use, it is best avoided in
- formal and serious writing.

unit 1 = **entity**, whole, item, feature 2 = **section**, company, group, force, detail, division, cell, squad 3 = **measure**, quantity, measurement 4 = **part**, section, segment, class, element, component, constituent, tutorial

unite 1 = **join**, link, combine, couple, blend, merge, unify, fuse **OPPOSITE:** separate 2 = **cooperate**, ally, join forces, band, pool, collaborate **OPPOSITE:** split

u

unity 1 = union, unification, coalition, federation, integration, confederation, amalgamation 2 = wholeness, integrity, oneness, union, entity, singleness **OPPOSITE:** disunity 3 = agreement, accord, consensus, harmony, solidarity, unison, assent, concord **OPPOSITE:** disagreement

universal 1 = widespread, general, common, whole, total, unlimited, overarching 2 = global, worldwide, international, pandemic

universally = without exception, everywhere, always, invariably

universe = cosmos, space, creation, nature, heavens, macrocosm, all existence

unknown 1 = strange, new, undiscovered, uncharted, unexplored, virgin, remote, alien 2 = unidentified, mysterious, anonymous, unnamed, nameless, incognito 3 = obscure, humble, unfamiliar **OPPOSITE:** famous

unlike 1 = different from, dissimilar to, distinct from, unequal to **OPPOSITE:** similar to 2 = contrasted with, not like, in contradiction to, in contrast with or to, as opposed to, differently from, opposite to

unlikely 1 = improbable, doubtful, remote, slight, faint **OPPOSITE:** probable 2 = unbelievable, incredible,

implausible, questionable **OPPOSITE:** believable

unload 1 = empty, clear, unpack, dump, discharge 2 = unburden

unnatural 1 = abnormal, odd, strange, unusual, extraordinary, perverted, queer, irregular **OPPOSITE:** normal 2 = false, forced, artificial, affected, stiff, feigned, stilted, insincere **OPPOSITE:** genuine

unpleasant 1 = nasty, bad, horrid, distasteful, displeasing, objectionable, disagreeable **OPPOSITE:** nice 2 = obnoxious, rude **OPPOSITE:** likable or likeable

unravel 1 = solve, explain, work out, resolve, figure out (informal) 2 = undo, separate, disentangle, free, unwind, untangle

unrest = discontent, rebellion, protest, strife, agitation, discord, sedition, dissension **OPPOSITE:** peace

unsettled 1 = unstable, shaky, insecure, disorderly, unsteady 2 = restless, tense, shaken, confused, disturbed, anxious, agitated, flustered 3 = inconstant, changing, variable, uncertain

unstable 1 = changeable, volatile, unpredictable, variable, fluctuating, fitful, inconstant **OPPOSITE:** constant 2 = insecure, shaky, precarious, unsettled, wobbly, tottering,

u

unsteady 3 = **unpredictable**, irrational, erratic, inconsistent, temperamental, capricious, changeable **OPPOSITE:** level-headed

unthinkable 1 = **impossible**, out of the question, inconceivable, absurd, unreasonable **2** = **inconceivable**, incredible, unimaginable

untold 1 = **indescribable**, unthinkable, unimaginable, undreamed of, unutterable, inexpressible **2** = **countless**, incalculable, innumerable, myriad, numberless, uncountable

untrue 1 = **false**, lying, wrong, mistaken, incorrect, inaccurate, dishonest, deceptive **OPPOSITE:** true **2** = **unfaithful**, disloyal, deceitful, treacherous, faithless, false, untrustworthy, inconstant **OPPOSITE:** faithful

unusual 1 = **rare**, odd, strange, extraordinary, different, curious, queer, uncommon **OPPOSITE:** common **2** = **extraordinary**, unique, remarkable, exceptional, uncommon, singular, unconventional **OPPOSITE:** average

upbeat (*Informal*) = **cheerful**, positive, optimistic, encouraging, hopeful, cheery

upbringing = **education**, training, breeding, rearing, raising

update = **bring up to date**,

improve, correct, renew, revise, upgrade, amend, overhaul

upgrade 1 = **improve**, better, update, reform, add to, enhance, refurbish, renovate **2** = **promote**, raise, advance, boost, move up, elevate, kick upstairs (*informal*), give promotion to **OPPOSITE:** demote

upheaval = **disturbance**, revolution, disorder, turmoil, disruption

uphill 1 = **ascending**, rising, upward, mounting, climbing **OPPOSITE:** descending **2** = **arduous**, hard, taxing, difficult, tough, exhausting, gruelling, strenuous

uphold 1 = **support**, back, defend, aid, champion, maintain, promote, sustain **2** = **confirm**, endorse

uplift **VERB 1** = **improve**, better, raise, advance, inspire, refine, edify
▷ **NOUN 2** = **improvement**, enlightenment, advancement, refinement, enhancement, enrichment, edification

upper 1 = **topmost**, top **OPPOSITE:** bottom **2** = **higher**, high **OPPOSITE:** lower **3** = **superior**, senior, higher-level, greater, top, important, chief, most important **OPPOSITE:** inferior

upper class = **aristocratic**, upper-class, noble, high-class, patrician, blue-blooded

u

upright 1 = **vertical**, straight, standing up, erect, perpendicular, bolt upright **OPPOSITE:** horizontal
2 = **honest**, good, principled, just, ethical, honourable, righteous, conscientious, unimpeachable **OPPOSITE:** dishonourable

uprising = **rebellion**, rising, revolution, revolt, disturbance, mutiny, insurrection, insurgence

uproar 1 = **commotion**, noise, racket, riot, turmoil, mayhem, din, pandemonium 2 = **protest**, outrage, complaint, objection, fuss, stink (*informal*), outcry, furore

upset ADJECTIVE
1 = **distressed**, shaken, disturbed, worried, troubled, hurt, bothered, unhappy
2 = **sick**, queasy, bad, ill
3 = **overturned**, upside down, capsized, spilled
▷ VERB 4 = **distress**, trouble, disturb, worry, alarm, bother, grieve, agitate 5 = **tip over**, overturn, capsize, knock over, spill 6 = **mess up**, spoil, disturb, change, confuse, disorder, unsettle, disorganize
▷ NOUN 7 = **distress**, worry, trouble, shock, bother, disturbance, agitation
8 = **reversal**, shake-up (*informal*), defeat 9 = **illness**, complaint, disorder, bug (*informal*), sickness, malady

upside down *or* **upside-**

down ADVERB 1 = **wrong side up**
▷ ADJECTIVE 2 = **inverted**, overturned, upturned
3 (*Informal*) = **confused**, disordered, chaotic, muddled, topsy-turvy, higgledy-piggledy (*informal*)

up-to-date = **modern**, fashionable, trendy (*Brit. informal*), current, stylish, in vogue, up-to-the-minute **OPPOSITE:** out-of-date

urban = **civic**, city, town, metropolitan, municipal, dorp (*S. African*)

urge VERB 1 = **beg**, exhort, plead, implore, beseech, entreat
2 = **advocate**, recommend, advise, support, counsel **OPPOSITE:** discourage
▷ NOUN 3 = **impulse**, longing, wish, desire, drive, yearning, itch (*informal*), thirst **OPPOSITE:** reluctance

urgency = **importance**, need, necessity, gravity, pressure, hurry, seriousness, extremity

urgent = **crucial**, desperate, pressing, great, important, crying, critical, immediate **OPPOSITE:** unimportant

usage 1 = **use**, operation, employment, running, control, management, handling
2 = **practice**, method, procedure, habit, regime, custom, routine, convention

use VERB 1 = **employ**, utilize, work, apply, operate, exercise,

u

practise, resort to **2** *sometimes with up* = **consume**, exhaust, spend, run through, expend **3** = **take advantage of**, exploit, manipulate ▷ NOUN **4** = **usage**, employment, operation, application **5** = **purpose**, end, reason, object **6** = **good**, point, help, service, value, benefit, profit, advantage

used = **second-hand**, cast-off, nearly new, shopsoiled **OPPOSITE:** new

used to = **accustomed to**, familiar with

useful = **helpful**, effective, valuable, practical, profitable, worthwhile, beneficial, fruitful **OPPOSITE:** useless

useless 1 = **worthless**, valueless, impractical, fruitless, unproductive, ineffectual, unsuitable **OPPOSITE:** useful **2** = **pointless**, futile, vain **OPPOSITE:** worthwhile **3** (*Informal*) = **inept**, no good, hopeless, incompetent, ineffectual

usher VERB **1** = **escort**, lead, direct, guide, conduct ▷ NOUN **2** = **attendant**, guide, doorman, escort, doorkeeper

usual = **normal**, customary, regular, general, common, standard, ordinary, typical **OPPOSITE:** unusual

usually = **normally**, generally, mainly, commonly, mostly, on the whole, as a rule, habitually

utility = **usefulness**, benefit, convenience, practicality, efficacy, serviceableness

utilize = **use**, employ, deploy, take advantage of, make use of, put to use, bring into play, avail yourself of

utmost ADJECTIVE **1** = **greatest**, highest, maximum, supreme, paramount, pre-eminent **2** = **farthest**, extreme, last, final ▷ NOUN **3** = **best**, greatest, maximum, highest, hardest

utter[1] = **say**, state, speak, voice, express, deliver, declare, mouth

utter[2] = **absolute**, complete, total, sheer, outright, thorough, downright, unmitigated

utterly = **totally**, completely, absolutely, perfectly, fully, entirely, extremely, thoroughly

u

Vv

vacancy 1 = **opening**, job, post, place, position, role, situation, opportunity
2 = **room**, space, available accommodation, unoccupied room

vacant 1 = **empty**, free, available, abandoned, deserted, for sale, on the market, void **OPPOSITE:** occupied
2 = **unfilled**, unoccupied **OPPOSITE:** taken 3 = **blank**, vague, dreamy, empty, abstracted, idle, vacuous, inane **OPPOSITE:** thoughtful

vacuum 1 = **gap**, lack, absence, space, deficiency, void
2 = **emptiness**, space, void, gap, nothingness, vacuity

vague 1 = **unclear**, indefinite, hazy, confused, loose, uncertain, unsure, superficial **OPPOSITE:** clear 2 = **imprecise**, unspecified, generalized, rough, loose, ambiguous, hazy, equivocal 3 = **absent-minded**, distracted, vacant, preoccupied, oblivious, inattentive
4 = **indistinct**, unclear, faint, hazy, indeterminate, nebulous, ill-defined **OPPOSITE:** distinct

vain 1 = **futile**, useless, pointless, unsuccessful, idle, worthless, senseless, fruitless **OPPOSITE:** successful
2 = **conceited**, narcissistic, proud, arrogant, swaggering, egotistical, self-important **OPPOSITE:** modest
▷ **PHRASES: in vain** 1 = **useless**, to no avail, unsuccessful, fruitless, vain 2 = **uselessly**, to no avail, unsuccessfully, fruitlessly, vainly, ineffectually

valid 1 = **sound**, good, reasonable, telling, convincing, rational, logical, viable **OPPOSITE:** unfounded 2 = **legal**, official, legitimate, genuine, authentic, lawful, bona fide **OPPOSITE:** invalid

validity 1 = **soundness**, force, power, weight, strength, cogency 2 = **legality**, authority, legitimacy, right, lawfulness

valley = **hollow**, dale, glen, vale, depression, dell

valuable ADJECTIVE 1 = **useful**, important, profitable, worthwhile, beneficial, helpful **OPPOSITE:** useless
2 = **treasured**, prized, precious
3 = **precious**, expensive, costly, dear, high-priced, priceless, irreplaceable **OPPOSITE:** worthless
▷ **PLURAL NOUN** 4 = **treasures**, prized possessions, precious items, heirlooms, personal effects, costly article

value NOUN 1 = **importance**,

benefit, worth, merit, point, service, sense, profit **OPPOSITE:** worthlessness **2** = **cost**, price, worth, rate, market price, face value, asking price, selling price
▷ **PLURAL NOUN 3** = **principles**, morals, ethics, mores, standards of behaviour, (moral) standards
▷ **VERB 4** = **appreciate**, rate, prize, regard highly, respect, admire, treasure, esteem **OPPOSITE:** undervalue
5 = **evaluate**, price, estimate, rate, cost, assess, set at, appraise

vanish 1 = **disappear**, dissolve, evaporate, fade away, melt away, evanesce **OPPOSITE:** appear **2** = **die out**, disappear, pass away, end, fade, dwindle, cease to exist, become extinct

vanity = **pride**, arrogance, conceit, narcissism, egotism, conceitedness **OPPOSITE:** modesty

variable = **changeable**, unstable, fluctuating, shifting, flexible, uneven, temperamental, unsteady **OPPOSITE:** constant

variant NOUN 1 = **variation**, form, version, development, alternative, adaptation, revision, modification
▷ **ADJECTIVE 2** = **different**, alternative, modified, divergent

variation 1 = **alternative**, variety, modification, departure, innovation, variant **2** = **variety**, change, deviation, difference, diversity, diversion, novelty **OPPOSITE:** uniformity

varied = **different**, mixed, various, diverse, assorted, miscellaneous, sundry, motley **OPPOSITE:** unvarying

variety 1 = **diversity**, change, variation, difference, diversification, heterogeneity, multifariousness **OPPOSITE:** uniformity **2** = **range**, selection, assortment, mix, collection, line-up, mixture, array **3** = **type**, sort, kind, class, brand, species, breed, strain

various 1 = **different**, assorted, miscellaneous, varied, distinct, diverse, disparate, sundry **OPPOSITE:** similar **2** = **many**, numerous, countless, several, abundant, innumerable, sundry, profuse

● **USAGE NOTE**
● The use of *different* after
● *various*, which seems to be
● most common in speech, is
● unnecessary and should be
● avoided in serious writing: *the*
● *disease exists in various forms*
● (not *in various different forms*).

varnish NOUN 1 = **lacquer**, polish, glaze, gloss
▷ **VERB 2** = **lacquer**, polish, glaze, gloss

vary 1 = **differ**, be different, be dissimilar, disagree, diverge **2** = **change**, shift, swing, alter, fluctuate, oscillate, see-saw **3** = **alternate**

vast = **huge**, massive, enormous, great, wide, immense, gigantic, monumental **OPPOSITE:** tiny

vault¹ 1 = **strongroom**, repository, depository 2 = **crypt**, tomb, catacomb, cellar, mausoleum, charnel house, undercroft

vault² = **jump**, spring, leap, clear, bound, hurdle

veer = **change direction**, turn, swerve, shift, sheer, change course

vehicle 1 = **conveyance**, machine, motor vehicle 2 = **medium**, means, channel, mechanism, organ, apparatus

veil NOUN 1 = **mask**, cover, shroud, film, curtain, cloak 2 = **screen**, mask, disguise, blind 3 = **film**, cover, curtain, cloak, shroud ▷ VERB 4 = **cover**, screen, hide, mask, shield, disguise, conceal, obscure **OPPOSITE:** reveal

veiled = **disguised**, implied, hinted at, covert, masked, concealed, suppressed

vein 1 = **blood vessel** 2 = **mood**, style, note, tone, mode, temper, tenor 3 = **seam**, layer, stratum, course, current, bed, deposit, streak

velocity = **speed**, pace, rapidity, quickness, swiftness

vengeance = **revenge**, retaliation, reprisal, retribution, requital **OPPOSITE:** forgiveness

vent NOUN 1 = **outlet**, opening, aperture, duct, orifice ▷ VERB 2 = **express**, release, voice, air, discharge, utter, emit, pour out **OPPOSITE:** hold back

venture NOUN 1 = **undertaking**, project, enterprise, campaign, risk, operation, activity, scheme ▷ VERB 2 = **go**, travel, journey, set out, wander, stray, plunge into, rove 3 = **dare**, presume, have the courage to, be brave enough, hazard, go out on a limb (*informal*), take the liberty, go so far as 4 = **put forward**, volunteer

verbal = **spoken**, oral, word-of-mouth, unwritten

verdict = **decision**, finding, judgment, opinion, sentence, conclusion, conviction, adjudication

verge 1 = **brink**, point, edge, threshold 2 = **border**, edge, margin, limit, boundary, threshold, brim ▷ PHRASES: **verge on something** = **come near to**, approach, border on, resemble, incline to, be similar to, touch on, be more or less

verify 1 = **check**, make sure, examine, monitor, inspect 2 = **confirm**, prove, substantiate, support, validate, bear out, corroborate, authenticate **OPPOSITE:** disprove

versatile 1 = **adaptable**, flexible, all-round, resourceful, multifaceted **OPPOSITE:** unadaptable **2 = all-purpose**, variable, adjustable **OPPOSITE:** limited

versed = knowledgeable, experienced, seasoned, familiar, practised, well-informed, proficient **OPPOSITE:** ignorant

version 1 = form, variety, variant, sort, class, design, style, model **2 = adaptation**, edition, interpretation, form, copy, rendering, reproduction, portrayal **3 = account**, report, description, record, reading, story, view, understanding

vertical = upright sheer, perpendicular, straight (up and down), erect, plumb, on end, precipitous, vertiginous **OPPOSITE:** horizontal

very ADVERB **1 = extremely**, highly, greatly, really, deeply, unusually, profoundly, decidedly

▷ ADJECTIVE **2 = exact**, precise, selfsame **3 = ideal**

● USAGE NOTE
● In strict usage, adverbs of
● degree such as *very*, *too*, *quite*,
● *really*, and *extremely* are used
● only to qualify adjectives: *he*
● *is very happy; she is too sad*. By
● this rule, these words should
● not be used to qualify past
● participles that follow the
● verb *to be*, since they would
● then be technically qualifying
● verbs. With the exception of

● certain participles, such as
● *tired* or *disappointed*, that have
● come to be regarded as
● adjectives, all other past
● participles are qualified by
● adverbs such as *much*, *greatly*,
● *seriously*, or *excessively*: *he has*
● *been much* (not *very*)
● *inconvenienced; she has been*
● *excessively* (not *too*) *criticized*.

vessel 1 = ship, boat, craft **2 = container**, receptacle, can, bowl, tank, pot, drum, barrel

vest PHRASES: **vest in something** or **someone** *usually passive* **= place**, invest, entrust, settle, confer, endow, bestow, consign ▶ **vest with something** *usually passive* **= endow with**, entrust with

vet = check, examine, investigate, review, appraise, scrutinize

veteran NOUN **1 = old hand**, past master, warhorse (*informal*), old stager **OPPOSITE:** novice

▷ ADJECTIVE **2 = long-serving**, seasoned, experienced, old, established, qualified, mature, practised

veto VERB **1 = ban**, block, reject, rule out, turn down, forbid, boycott, prohibit **OPPOSITE:** pass

▷ NOUN **2 = ban**, dismissal, rejection, vetoing, boycott, embargo, prohibiting, prohibition **OPPOSITE:** ratification

v

viable = workable, practical, feasible, suitable, realistic, operational, applicable, usable **OPPOSITE:** unworkable

vibrant 1 = energetic, dynamic, sparkling, vivid, spirited, storming, alive, vigorous 2 = vivid, bright, brilliant, intense, clear, rich, glowing

vice 1 = fault, failing, weakness, limitation, defect, deficiency, flaw, shortcoming **OPPOSITE:** good point 2 = wickedness, evil, corruption, sin, depravity, immorality, iniquity, turpitude **OPPOSITE:** virtue

vice versa = the other way round, conversely, in reverse, contrariwise

vicious 1 = savage, brutal, violent, cruel, ferocious, barbarous **OPPOSITE:** gentle 2 = malicious, vindictive, spiteful, mean, cruel, venomous

victim 1 = casualty, sufferer, fatality **OPPOSITE:** survivor 2 = scapegoat, sacrifice, martyr

victor = winner, champion, conqueror, vanquisher, prizewinner **OPPOSITE:** loser

victorious = winning, successful, triumphant, first, champion, conquering, vanquishing, prizewinning **OPPOSITE:** losing

victory = win, success, triumph, conquest, walkover (informal) **OPPOSITE:** defeat

vie = compete, struggle,

contend, strive, be rivals

view NOUN 1 sometimes plural = opinion, belief, feeling, attitude, impression, conviction, point of view, sentiment 2 = scene, picture, sight, prospect, perspective, landscape, outlook, spectacle 3 = vision, sight, visibility, perspective, eyeshot ▷ VERB 4 = regard, see, consider, perceive, treat, estimate, reckon, deem

viewer = watcher, observer, spectator, onlooker

vigorous 1 = strenuous, energetic, arduous, hard, taxing, active, rigorous 2 = spirited, lively, energetic, active, dynamic, animated, forceful, feisty (informal) **OPPOSITE:** lethargic 3 = strong, powerful, lively, lusty **OPPOSITE:** weak

vigorously 1 = energetically, hard, forcefully, strongly, strenuously, lustily 2 = forcefully, strongly, vehemently, strenuously

vigour or (U.S.) **vigor** = energy, vitality, power, spirit, strength, animation, verve, gusto **OPPOSITE:** weakness

vile 1 = wicked, evil, corrupt, perverted, degenerate, depraved, nefarious **OPPOSITE:** honourable 2 = disgusting, foul, revolting, offensive, nasty, sickening, horrid, repulsive **OPPOSITE:** pleasant

v

villain 1 = **evildoer**, criminal, rogue, scoundrel, wretch, reprobate, miscreant, blackguard 2 = **baddy** (*informal*), antihero **OPPOSITE:** hero

vindicate 1 = **clear**, acquit, exonerate, absolve, let off the hook, exculpate **OPPOSITE:** condemn 2 = **support**, defend, excuse, justify

vintage NOUN (always used of wines) = **harvest**
▷ ADJECTIVE 1 (always used of wines) = **high-quality**, best, prime, quality, choice, select, superior 2 = **classic**, old, veteran, historic, heritage, enduring, antique, timeless, ageless

violate 1 = **break**, infringe, disobey, transgress, ignore, defy, disregard, flout **OPPOSITE:** obey 2 = **invade**, infringe on, disturb, upset, shatter, disrupt, impinge on, encroach on 3 = **desecrate**, profane, defile, abuse, pollute, deface, dishonour, vandalize **OPPOSITE:** honour 4 = **rape**, molest, sexually assault, ravish, abuse, assault, interfere with, sexually abuse

violation 1 = **breach**, abuse, infringement, contravention, abuse, trespass, transgression, infraction 2 = **invasion**, intrusion, trespass, breach, disturbance, disruption, interruption, encroachment

3 = **desecration**, sacrilege, defilement, profanation, spoliation 4 = **rape**, sexual assault, molesting, ravishing (*old-fashioned*), abuse, sexual abuse, indecent assault, molestation

violence 1 = **brutality**, bloodshed, savagery, fighting, terrorism 2 = **force**, power, strength, might, ferocity, forcefulness, powerfulness 3 = **intensity**, force, cruelty, severity, fervour, vehemence

violent 1 = **brutal**, aggressive, savage, wild, fierce, bullying, cruel, vicious **OPPOSITE:** gentle 2 = **passionate**, uncontrollable, unrestrained 4 = **fiery**, fierce, passionate

VIP = **celebrity**, big name, star, somebody, luminary, big hitter (*informal*), heavy hitter (*informal*)

virgin NOUN 1 = **maiden**, girl (*archaic*)
▷ ADJECTIVE 2 = **pure**, chaste, immaculate, virginal, vestal, uncorrupted, undefiled **OPPOSITE:** corrupted

virtual = **practical**, essential, in all but name

virtually = **practically**, almost, nearly, in effect, in essence, as good as, in all but name

virtue 1 = **goodness**, integrity, worth, morality, righteousness, probity, rectitude, incorruptibility **OPPOSITE:** vice 2 = **merit**, strength, asset, plus (*informal*), attribute, good point,

strong point **OPPOSITE:** failing
3 = **advantage**, benefit, merit,
credit, usefulness, efficacy
visible = **perceptible**,
observable, clear, apparent,
evident, manifest, in view,
discernible **OPPOSITE:** invisible
vision 1 = **image**, idea, dream,
plans, hopes, prospect, ideal,
concept 2 = **hallucination**,
illusion, apparition, revelation,
delusion, mirage, chimera
3 = **sight**, seeing, eyesight,
view, perception 4 = **foresight**,
imagination, perception,
insight, awareness, inspiration,
innovation, creativity
visionary NOUN 1 = **idealist**,
romantic, dreamer, daydreamer
OPPOSITE: realist 2 = **prophet**,
diviner, mystic, seer, soothsayer,
sibyl, scryer, spaewife (Scot.)
▷ ADJECTIVE 3 = **idealistic**,
romantic, unrealistic, utopian,
speculative, impractical,
unworkable, quixotic **OPPOSITE:**
realistic 4 = **prophetic**,
mystical, predictive, oracular,
sibylline
visit VERB 1 = **call on**, drop in
on (informal), stay at, stay with,
stop by, spend time with, look
someone up, go see (U.S.)
2 = **stay in**, stop by
▷ NOUN 3 = **call**, social call
4 = **trip**, stop, stay, break, tour,
holiday, vacation (informal),
stopover
visitor = **guest**, caller, company,
manu(w)hiri (N.Z.)

vista = **view**, scene, prospect,
landscape, panorama,
perspective
visual 1 = **optical**, optic, ocular
2 = **observable**, visible,
perceptible, discernible
OPPOSITE: imperceptible
vital 1 = **essential**, important,
necessary, key, basic,
significant, critical, crucial
OPPOSITE: unnecessary
2 = **lively**, vigorous, energetic,
spirited, dynamic, animated,
vibrant, vivacious **OPPOSITE:**
lethargic
vitality = **energy**, vivacity, life,
strength, animation, vigour,
exuberance, liveliness
OPPOSITE: lethargy
vivid 1 = **clear**, detailed,
realistic, telling, moving,
affecting, arresting, powerful
OPPOSITE: vague 2 = **bright**,
brilliant, intense, clear, rich,
glowing, colourful **OPPOSITE:**
dull
vocabulary 1 = **language**,
words, lexicon 2 = **wordbook**,
dictionary, glossary, lexicon
vocal 1 = **outspoken**, frank,
forthright, strident, vociferous,
articulate, expressive, eloquent
OPPOSITE: quiet 2 = **spoken**,
voiced, uttered, oral, said
vocation = **profession**, calling,
job, trade, career, mission,
pursuit
vogue = **fashion**, trend, craze,
style, mode, passing fancy,
dernier cri (French)

voice NOUN 1 = **tone**, sound, articulation 2 = **utterance** 3 = **opinion**, will, feeling, wish, desire 4 = **say**, view, vote, comment, input
▷ VERB 5 = **express**, declare, air, raise, reveal, mention, mouth, pronounce
● RELATED WORD
● *adjective:* vocal

void NOUN 1 = **gap**, space, lack, hole, emptiness
2 = **emptiness**, space, vacuum, oblivion, blankness, nullity, vacuity
▷ ADJECTIVE 3 = **invalid**, null and void, inoperative, useless, ineffective, worthless
▷ VERB 4 = **invalidate**, nullify, cancel, withdraw, reverse, undo, repeal, quash

volatile 1 = **changeable**, shifting, variable, unsettled, unstable, explosive, unreliable, unsteady OPPOSITE: stable
2 = **temperamental**, erratic, mercurial, up and down (*informal*), fickle, over-emotional OPPOSITE: calm

volley = **barrage**, blast, burst, shower, hail, bombardment, salvo, fusillade

volume 1 = **amount**, quantity, level, body, total, measure, degree, mass 2 = **capacity**, size, mass, extent, proportions, dimensions, bulk, measurements 3 = **book**, work, title, opus, publication, manual, tome, treatise 4 = **loudness**,

sound, amplification

voluntarily = **willingly**, freely, by choice, off your own bat, of your own accord, of your own volition

voluntary 1 = **intentional**, deliberate, planned, calculated, wilful OPPOSITE: unintentional
2 = **optional**, discretionary, up to the individual, open, unforced, at your discretion, open to choice OPPOSITE: obligatory 3 = **unpaid**, free, willing, pro bono (*Law*)

volunteer = **offer**, step forward OPPOSITE: refuse

vomit 1 = **be sick**, throw up (*informal*), spew, chuck (*Austral. & N.Z. informal*), heave (*slang*), retch 2 *often with* **up** = **bring up**, throw up, regurgitate, emit (*informal*), disgorge, spew out or up

vote NOUN 1 = **poll**, election, ballot, referendum, popular vote, plebiscite, straw poll, show of hands
▷ VERB 2 = **cast your vote**

voucher = **ticket**, token, coupon, pass, slip, chit, chitty (*Brit. informal*), docket

vow VERB 1 = **promise**, pledge, swear, commit, engage, affirm, avow, bind yourself
▷ NOUN 2 = **promise**, commitment, pledge, oath, profession, avowal

voyage NOUN 1 = **journey**, trip, passage, expedition, crossing, sail, cruise, excursion

▷ VERB 2 = **travel**, journey, tour, cruise, steam, take a trip, go on an expedition

vulgar 1 = **tasteless**, common **OPPOSITE:** tasteful 2 = **crude**, rude, coarse, indecent, tasteless, risqué, ribald 3 = **uncouth**, unrefined, impolite, ill-bred **OPPOSITE:** refined

vulnerable 1 = **susceptible**, helpless, unprotected, defenceless, exposed, weak, sensitive, tender **OPPOSITE:** immune 2 = **exposed**, open, unprotected, defenceless, accessible, wide open, assailable **OPPOSITE:** well-protected

Ww

waddle = **shuffle**, totter, toddle, sway, wobble

wade 1 = **paddle**, splash, splash about, slop 2 = **walk through**, cross, ford, travel across

wag VERB 1 = **wave**, shake, waggle, stir, quiver, vibrate, wiggle 2 = **waggle**, wave, shake, flourish, brandish, wobble, wiggle 3 = **shake**, bob, nod
▷ NOUN 4 = **wave**, shake, quiver, vibration, wiggle, waggle 5 = **nod**, bob, shake

wage NOUN 1 *often plural* = **payment**, pay, remuneration, fee, reward, income, allowance, recompense
▷ VERB 2 = **engage in**, conduct, pursue, carry on, undertake, practise, prosecute, proceed with

wail VERB 1 = **cry**, weep, grieve, lament, howl, bawl, yowl
▷ NOUN 2 = **cry**, moan, howl, lament, yowl

wait VERB 1 = **stay**, remain, stop, pause, rest, linger, loiter, tarry **OPPOSITE:** go 2 = **stand by**, hold back, hang fire 3 = **be postponed**, be suspended, be

delayed, be put off, be put back, be deferred, be put on hold (*informal*), be shelved
▷ NOUN 4 = **delay**, gap, pause, interval, stay, rest, halt, hold-up

waiter *or* **waitress** = **attendant**, server, flunkey, steward *or* stewardess, servant

waive 1 = **give up**, relinquish, renounce, forsake, drop, abandon, set aside, dispense with OPPOSITE: claim
2 = **disregard**, ignore, discount, overlook, set aside, pass over, dispense with, brush aside

wake¹ VERB 1 = **awake**, stir, awaken, come to, arise, get up, rouse, get out of bed OPPOSITE: fall asleep 2 = **awaken**, arouse, rouse, waken 3 = **evoke**, recall, renew, stimulate, revive, induce, arouse, call up
▷ NOUN 4 = **vigil**, watch, funeral, deathwatch, tangi (N.Z.)

● USAGE NOTE
● Both *wake* and its synonym
● *waken* can be used either with
● or without an object: I woke/
● wakened my sister, and also I
● woke/wakened (up) at noon.
● *Wake*, *wake up*, and
● occasionally *waken*, can also
● be used in a figurative sense,
● for example *seeing him again*
● *woke painful memories*; and *it's*
● *time he woke up to his*
● *responsibilities*. The verbs
● *awake* and *awaken* are more
● commonly used in the

● figurative than the literal
● sense, for example *he awoke*
● *to the danger he was in*.

wake² = **slipstream**, wash, trail, backwash, train, track, waves, path
▷ PHRASES: **in the wake of** = **in the aftermath of**, following, because of, as a result of, on account of, as a consequence of

walk VERB 1 = **stride**, stroll, go, move, step, march, pace, hike
2 = **travel on foot** 3 = **escort**, take, see, show, partner, guide, conduct, accompany
▷ NOUN 4 = **stroll**, hike, ramble, march, trek, trudge, promenade, saunter 5 = **gait**, step, bearing, carriage, tread
6 = **path**, footpath, track, way, road, lane, trail, avenue, berm (N.Z.)
▷ PHRASES: **walk of life** = **area**, calling, business, line, trade, class, field, career

walker = **hiker**, rambler, wayfarer, pedestrian

wall 1 = **partition**, screen, barrier, enclosure 2 = **barrier**, obstacle, barricade, obstruction, check, bar, fence, impediment

wallet = **purse**, pocketbook, pouch, case, holder, money-bag

wander VERB 1 = **roam**, walk, drift, stroll, range, stray, ramble, prowl
▷ NOUN 2 = **excursion**, walk, stroll, cruise, ramble, meander, promenade, mosey (*informal*)

wanderer = traveller, rover, nomad, drifter, gypsy, explorer, rambler, voyager

wane 1 = decline, weaken, diminish, fail, fade, decrease, dwindle, lessen **OPPOSITE:** grow 2 = diminish, decrease, dwindle **OPPOSITE:** wax

want VERB 1 = wish for, desire, long for, crave, covet, hope for, yearn for, thirst for **OPPOSITE:** have 2 = need, demand, require, call for 3 = should, need, must, ought 4 = desire, long for, crave, wish for, yearn for, thirst for, hanker after, burn for 5 = lack, need, require, miss ▷ NOUN 6 = lack, need, absence, shortage, deficiency, famine, scarcity, dearth **OPPOSITE:** abundance 7 = poverty, hardship, privation, penury, destitution, neediness, pennilessness **OPPOSITE:** wealth 8 = wish, will, need, desire, requirement, longing, appetite, craving

wanting 1 = deficient, poor, inadequate, insufficient, faulty, defective, imperfect, unsound, bodger or bodgie (*Austral. slang*) **OPPOSITE:** adequate 2 = lacking, missing, absent, incomplete, short, shy **OPPOSITE:** complete

war NOUN 1 = conflict, drive, attack, fighting, fight, operation, battle, movement **OPPOSITE:** peace

2 = campaign, drive, attack, operation, movement, push, mission, offensive ▷ VERB 3 = fight, battle, clash, wage war, campaign, combat, do battle, take up arms **OPPOSITE:** make peace

ward NOUN 1 = room, department, unit, quarter, division, section, apartment, cubicle 2 = district, constituency, area, division, zone, parish, precinct 3 = dependant, charge, pupil, minor, protégé ▷ PHRASES: ward someone off = drive off, resist, fight off, hold off, repel, fend off ▶ ward something off 1 = avert, fend off, stave off, avoid, frustrate, deflect, repel 2 = parry, avert, deflect, avoid, repel, turn aside

warden 1 = steward, guardian, administrator, superintendent, caretaker, curator, custodian 2 = jailer, prison officer, guard, screw (*slang*) 3 = governor, head, leader, director, manager, chief, executive, commander, baas (*S. African*) 4 = ranger, keeper, guardian, protector, custodian, official

wardrobe 1 = clothes cupboard, cupboard, closet (*U.S.*), cabinet 2 = clothes, apparel, attire

warehouse = store, depot, storehouse, repository, depository, stockroom

wares = goods, produce, stock,

products, stuff, commodities, merchandise

warfare = war, fighting, battle, conflict, combat, hostilities, enmity **OPPOSITE:** peace

warm ADJECTIVE 1 = balmy, mild, temperate, pleasant, fine, bright, sunny, agreeable **OPPOSITE:** cool 2 = cosy, snug, toasty (informal), comfortable, homely, comfy (informal) 3 = moderately hot, heated **OPPOSITE:** cool 4 = thermal, winter, thick, chunky, woolly **OPPOSITE:** cool 5 = mellow, relaxing, pleasant, agreeable, restful 6 = affable, kindly, friendly, affectionate, loving, tender, amicable, cordial **OPPOSITE:** unfriendly 7 = near, close, hot, near to the truth
▷ VERB 8 = warm up, heat, thaw (out), heat up **OPPOSITE:** cool down
▷ PHRASES: warm something or someone up = heat, thaw, heat up

warmth 1 = heat, snugness, warmness, comfort, homeliness, hotness **OPPOSITE:** coolness 2 = affection, feeling, love, goodwill, kindness, tenderness, cordiality, kindliness **OPPOSITE:** hostility

warn 1 = notify, tell, remind, inform, alert, tip off, give notice, make someone aware 2 = advise, urge, recommend, counsel, caution, commend, exhort, admonish

warning 1 = caution, information, advice, injunction, notification 2 = notice, notification, sign, alarm, announcement, alert, tip-off (informal) 3 = omen, sign, forecast, indication, prediction, prophecy, foreboding, portent, rahui (N.Z.) 4 = reprimand, admonition

warp VERB 1 = distort, bend, twist, buckle, deform, disfigure, contort, malform 2 = become distorted, bend, twist, contort, become deformed, become misshapen 3 = pervert, twist, corrupt, degrade, deprave, debase, debauch, lead astray
▷ NOUN 4 = twist, bend, defect, flaw, distortion, imperfection, kink, contortion

warrant VERB 1 = call for, demand, require, merit, rate, earn, deserve, permit 2 = guarantee, declare, pledge, promise, ensure, affirm, certify, attest
▷ NOUN 3 = authorization, permit, licence, permission, authority, sanction 4 = justification, reason, grounds, basis, licence, rationale, vindication, authority

warranty = guarantee, promise, contract, bond, pledge, certificate, assurance, covenant

warrior = soldier, combatant, fighter, gladiator, trooper, man-at-arms

wary 1 = suspicious, sceptical, guarded, distrustful, chary 2 = watchful, careful, alert, cautious, vigilant, circumspect, heedful OPPOSITE: careless

wash VERB 1 = clean, scrub, sponge, rinse, scour, cleanse 2 = launder, clean, rinse, dry-clean 3 = rinse, clean, scrub, lather 4 = bathe, bath, clean yourself, soak, douse, scrub yourself down 5 = move, overcome, touch, upset, stir, disturb, perturb, surge through 6 (*Informal*) (always used in negative constructions) = be plausible, stand up, hold up, pass muster, hold water, stick, carry weight, be convincing ▷ NOUN 7 = laundering, cleaning, clean, cleansing 8 = bathe, dip, soak, scrub, rinse 9 = backwash, slipstream, path, trail, train, track, waves, aftermath 10 = splash, surge, swell, rise and fall, undulation 11 = coat, film, covering, layer, coating, overlay ▷ PHRASES: wash something away = erode, wear something away ▸ wash something or someone away = sweep away, carry off, bear away

wasp ▷ See panel ANTS, BEES, AND WASPS

waste VERB 1 = squander, throw away, blow (*slang*), lavish, misuse, dissipate, fritter away OPPOSITE: save 2 = wear out, wither, corrode ▷ NOUN 3 = squandering, misuse, dissipation, frittering away, extravagance, wastefulness, prodigality OPPOSITE: saving 4 = rubbish, refuse, debris, scrap, litter, garbage, trash, leftovers ▷ PLURAL NOUN 5 = desert, wilderness, wasteland ▷ ADJECTIVE 6 = unwanted, useless, worthless, unused, leftover, superfluous, unusable, supernumerary OPPOSITE: necessary 6 = uncultivated, wild, bare, barren, empty, desolate, unproductive, uninhabited OPPOSITE: cultivated ▷ PHRASES: waste away = decline, dwindle, wither, fade, crumble, decay, wane, wear out

● USAGE NOTE
● *Waste* and *wastage* are to
● some extent interchangeable,
● but many people think that
● *wastage* should not be used to
● refer to loss resulting from
● human carelessness,
● inefficiency, etc.: *a waste* (not
● *a wastage*) *of time, money,*
● *effort*, etc.

watch VERB 1 = look at, observe, regard, eye, see, view, contemplate, eyeball (*slang*) 2 = spy on, follow, track, monitor, keep an eye on, stake out, keep tabs on (*informal*), keep watch on 3 = guard, keep, mind, protect, tend, look

W

after, shelter, take care of
▷ NOUN 4 = **wristwatch**, timepiece, chronometer
5 = **guard**, surveillance, observation, vigil, lookout
watchdog 1 = **guardian**, monitor, protector, custodian, scrutineer 2 = **guard dog**
water NOUN 1 = **liquid**, H_2O, wai (N.Z.)
▷ PLURAL NOUN 2 = **sea**, main, waves, ocean, depths, briny
▷ VERB 3 = **sprinkle**, spray, soak, irrigate, hose, dampen, drench, douse 4 = **get wet**, cry, weep, become wet, exude water
▷ PHRASES: water something down = **dilute**, weaken, water, doctor, thin
● RELATED WORD
● adjective: aquatic
waterfall = **cascade**, fall, cataract
wave VERB 1 = **signal**, sign, gesture, gesticulate 2 = **guide**, point, direct, indicate, signal, motion, gesture, nod
3 = **brandish**, swing, flourish, wag, shake 4 = **flutter**, flap, stir, shake, swing, wag, oscillate
▷ NOUN 5 = **gesture**, sign, signal, indication, gesticulation
6 = **ripple**, breaker, swell, ridge, roller, billow 7 = **outbreak**, rash, upsurge, flood, surge, ground swell 8 = **stream**, flood, surge, spate, current, flow, rush, tide

waver 1 = **hesitate**, dither (chiefly Brit.), vacillate, falter, fluctuate, seesaw, hum and haw OPPOSITE: be decisive
2 = **flicker**, shake, tremble, wobble, quiver, totter
wax 1 = **increase**, grow, develop, expand, swell, enlarge, magnify OPPOSITE: wane
2 = **become fuller**, enlarge
way NOUN 1 = **method**, means, system, process, technique, manner, procedure, mode
2 = **manner**, style, fashion, mode 3 often plural = **custom**, manner, habit, style, practice, nature, personality, wont, tikanga (N.Z.) 4 = **route**, direction, course, road, path
5 = **access**, road, track, channel, route, path, trail, pathway 6 = **journey**, approach, passage
7 = **distance**, length, stretch
wayward = **erratic**, unruly, unmanageable, unpredictable, capricious, ungovernable, inconstant OPPOSITE: obedient
weak ADJECTIVE 1 = **feeble**, frail, debilitated, fragile, sickly, puny, unsteady, infirm
OPPOSITE: strong 2 = **slight**, faint, feeble, pathetic, hollow
3 = **fragile**, brittle, flimsy, fine, delicate, frail, dainty, breakable
4 = **unsafe**, exposed, vulnerable, helpless, unprotected, defenceless, unguarded OPPOSITE: secure
5 = **unconvincing**,

unsatisfactory, lame, flimsy, pathetic **OPPOSITE:** convincing
6 = **tasteless**, thin, diluted, watery, runny, insipid **OPPOSITE:** strong

weaken 1 = **reduce**, undermine, moderate, diminish, lessen, sap **OPPOSITE:** boost
2 = **wane**, diminish, dwindle, lower, flag, fade, lessen **OPPOSITE:** grow 3 = **sap the strength of**, debilitate **OPPOSITE:** strengthen

weakness NOUN 1 = **frailty**, fatigue, exhaustion, fragility, infirmity, feebleness, decrepitude **OPPOSITE:** strength
2 = **liking**, appetite, penchant, soft spot, passion, inclination, fondness, partiality **OPPOSITE:** aversion 3 = **powerlessness**, vulnerability, meekness, spinelessness, timorousness, cravenness, cowardliness
4 = **inadequacy**, deficiency, transparency, lameness, hollowness, implausibility, flimsiness, unsoundness
5 = **failing**, fault, defect, deficiency, flaw, shortcoming, blemish, imperfection **OPPOSITE:** strong point

wealth 1 = **riches**, fortune, prosperity, affluence, money, opulence **OPPOSITE:** poverty
2 = **property**, capital, fortune
3 = **abundance**, plenty, richness, profusion, fullness, cornucopia, copiousness **OPPOSITE:** lack

wealthy = **rich**, prosperous, affluent, well-off, flush (informal), opulent, well-heeled (informal), well-to-do **OPPOSITE:** poor

wear VERB 1 = **be dressed in**, have on, sport (informal), put on
2 = **show**, present, bear, display, assume, put on, exhibit
3 = **deteriorate**, fray, wear thin
▷ NOUN 4 = **clothes**, things, dress, gear (informal), attire, costume, garments, apparel
5 = **damage**, wear and tear, erosion, deterioration, attrition, corrosion, abrasion **OPPOSITE:** repair
▷ PHRASES: **wear off** = **subside**, disappear, fade, diminish, decrease, dwindle, wane, peter out

wearing = **tiresome**, trying, fatiguing, oppressive, exasperating, irksome, wearisome **OPPOSITE:** refreshing

weary ADJECTIVE 1 = **tired**, exhausted, drained, worn out, done in (informal), flagging, fatigued, sleepy, clapped out (Austral. & N.Z. informal) **OPPOSITE:** energetic 2 = **tiring**, arduous, tiresome, laborious, wearisome **OPPOSITE:** refreshing
▷ VERB 3 = **grow tired**, tire, become bored **OPPOSITE:** invigorate

weather NOUN 1 = **climate**, conditions, temperature,

W

forecast, outlook, meteorological conditions, elements
▷ VERB 2 = **withstand**, stand, survive, overcome, resist, brave, endure, come through **OPPOSITE:** surrender to

weave 1 = **knit**, intertwine, plait, braid, entwine, interlace 2 = **zigzag**, wind, crisscross 3 = **create**, tell, recount, narrate, build, relate, make up, spin

web 1 = **cobweb**, spider's web 2 = **mesh**, lattice 3 = **tangle**, network

wed 1 = **get married to**, be united to **OPPOSITE:** divorce 2 = **get married**, marry, be united, tie the knot (*informal*), take the plunge (*informal*) **OPPOSITE:** divorce 3 = **unite**, combine, join, link, ally, blend, merge, interweave **OPPOSITE:** divide

wedding = **marriage**, nuptials, wedding ceremony, marriage service, wedding service

wedge VERB 1 = **squeeze**, force, lodge, jam, crowd, stuff, pack, thrust
▷ NOUN 2 = **block**, lump, chunk

weep = **cry**, shed tears, sob, whimper, mourn, lament, blubber, snivel **OPPOSITE:** rejoice

weigh 1 = **have a weight of**, tip the scales at (*informal*) 2 *often with* **up** = **consider**, examine, contemplate, evaluate, ponder,

think over, reflect upon, meditate upon 3 = **compare**, balance, contrast, juxtapose, place side by side 4 = **matter**, carry weight, count

weight NOUN 1 = **heaviness**, mass, poundage, load, tonnage 2 = **importance**, force, power, value, authority, influence, impact, import, mana (*N.Z.*)
▷ VERB 3 *often with* **down** = **load** 4 = **bias**, load, slant, unbalance

weird 1 = **strange**, odd, unusual, bizarre, mysterious, queer, eerie, unnatural **OPPOSITE:** normal 2 = **bizarre**, odd, strange, unusual, queer, unnatural, creepy (*informal*), freakish **OPPOSITE:** ordinary

welcome VERB 1 = **greet**, meet, receive, embrace, hail, karanga (*N.Z.*), mihi (*N.Z.*) **OPPOSITE:** reject 2 = **accept gladly**, appreciate, embrace, approve of, be pleased by, give the thumbs up to (*informal*), be glad about, express pleasure *or* satisfaction at
▷ NOUN 3 = **greeting**, welcoming, reception, acceptance, hail, hospitality, salutation **OPPOSITE:** rejection
▷ ADJECTIVE 4 = **pleasing**, appreciated, acceptable, pleasant, desirable, refreshing, delightful, gratifying **OPPOSITE:** unpleasant 5 = **wanted**, at home **OPPOSITE:** unwanted 6 = **free**

W

weld 1 = join, link, bond, bind, connect, fuse, solder 2 = **unite**, combine, blend, unify, fuse

welfare 1 = wellbeing, good, interest, health, security, benefit, safety, protection 2 = **state benefit**, support, benefits, pensions, dole (*slang*), social security, unemployment benefit, state benefits

well¹ ADVERB 1 = **skilfully**, expertly, adeptly, professionally, correctly, properly, efficiently, adequately **OPPOSITE:** badly 2 = **satisfactorily**, nicely, smoothly, successfully, pleasantly, splendidly, agreeably **OPPOSITE:** badly 3 = **thoroughly**, completely, fully, carefully, effectively, efficiently, rigorously 4 = **intimately**, deeply, fully, profoundly **OPPOSITE:** slightly 5 = **favourably**, highly, kindly, warmly, enthusiastically, approvingly, admiringly, with admiration **OPPOSITE:** unfavourably 6 = **considerably**, easily, very much, significantly, substantially, markedly 7 = **fully**, highly, greatly, amply, very much, thoroughly, considerably, substantially 8 = **possibly**, probably, certainly, reasonably, conceivably, justifiably 9 = **decently**, right, kindly, fittingly, fairly, properly, politely, suitably **OPPOSITE:** unfairly 10 = **prosperously**, comfortably, splendidly, in comfort, in (the lap of) luxury, without hardship ▷ ADJECTIVE 11 = **healthy**, sound, fit, blooming, in fine fettle, in good condition **OPPOSITE:** ill 12 = **satisfactory**, right, fine, pleasing, proper, thriving **OPPOSITE:** unsatisfactory 13 = **advisable**, proper, agreeable **OPPOSITE:** inadvisable

well² NOUN 1 = **hole**, bore, pit, shaft ▷ VERB 2 = **flow**, spring, pour, jet, surge, gush, spurt, spout 3 = **rise**, increase, grow, mount, surge, intensify

wet ADJECTIVE 1 = **damp**, soaking, saturated, moist, watery, soggy, sodden, waterlogged **OPPOSITE:** dry 2 = **rainy**, damp, drizzly, showery, raining, pouring, drizzling, teeming **OPPOSITE:** sunny 3 (*Informal*) = **feeble**, soft, weak, ineffectual, weedy (*informal*), spineless, effete, timorous ▷ VERB 4 = **moisten**, spray, dampen, water, soak, saturate, douse, irrigate **OPPOSITE:** dry ▷ NOUN 5 = **rain**, drizzle **OPPOSITE:** fine weather 6 = **moisture**, water, liquid, damp, humidity, condensation, dampness, wetness **OPPOSITE:** dryness

whack (*Informal*) VERB 1 = **strike**, hit, belt (*informal*),

WHALES AND DOLPHINS	
beluga	porpoise
baleen whale	right whale or (*Austral.*) bay whale
blue whale or sulphur-bottom	rorqual
bottlenose dolphin	sperm whale or cachalot
bowhead	toothed whale
humpback whale	whalebone whale
killer whale, grampus, or orca	white whale
narwhal	

bang, smack, thrash, thump, swipe
▷ **NOUN 2** = **blow**, hit, stroke, belt (*informal*), bang, smack, thump, swipe **3** (*Informal*) = **share**, part, cut (*informal*), bit, portion, quota **4** (*Informal*) = **attempt**, go (*informal*), try, turn, shot (*informal*), crack (*informal*), stab (*informal*), bash (*informal*)

whale ▷ *See panel* WHALES AND DOLPHINS

wharf = **dock**, pier, berth, quay, jetty, landing stage

wheel NOUN **1** = **disc**, ring, hoop
▷ **VERB 2** = **push**, trundle, roll **3** = **turn**, swing, spin, revolve, rotate, whirl, swivel **4** = **circle**, go round, twirl, gyrate

whereabouts = **position**, situation, site, location

whiff = **smell**, hint, scent, sniff, aroma, odour

whim = **impulse**, caprice, fancy, urge, notion

whine VERB **1** = **cry**, sob, wail, whimper, sniffle, snivel, moan **2** = **complain**, grumble, gripe

(*informal*), whinge (*informal*), moan, grouse, grizzle (*informal*, *chiefly Brit.*), grouch (*informal*)
▷ **NOUN 3** = **cry**, moan, sob, wail, whimper **4** = **drone**, note, hum **5** = **complaint**, moan, grumble, grouse, gripe (*informal*), whinge (*informal*), grouch (*informal*)

whip NOUN **1** = **lash**, cane, birch, crop, scourge, cat-o'-nine-tails
▷ **VERB 2** = **lash**, cane, flog, beat, strap, thrash, birch, scourge **3** (*Informal*) = **dash**, shoot, fly, tear, rush, dive, dart, whisk **4** = **whisk**, beat, mix vigorously, stir vigorously **5** = **incite**, drive, stir, spur, work up, get going, agitate, inflame

whirl VERB **1** = **spin**, turn, twist, rotate, twirl **2** = **rotate**, roll, twist, revolve, swirl, twirl, pirouette **3** = **feel dizzy**, swim, spin, reel, go round
▷ **NOUN 4** = **revolution**, turn, roll, spin, twist, swirl, rotation, twirl **5** = **bustle**, round, series, succession, flurry, merry-go-round **6** = **confusion**, daze,

dither (*chiefly Brit.*), giddiness
7 = **tumult**, spin

whisk VERB 1 = **flick**, whip,
sweep, brush 2 = **beat**, mix
vigorously, stir vigorously, whip,
fluff up
▷ NOUN 3 = **flick**, sweep, brush,
whip 4 = **beater**, mixer, blender

whisper VERB 1 = **murmur**,
breathe OPPOSITE: shout
2 = **rustle**, sigh, hiss, swish
▷ NOUN 3 = **murmur**, mutter,
mumble, undertone
4 (*Informal*) = **rumour**, report,
gossip, innuendo, insinuation
5 = **rustle**, sigh, hiss, swish

white = **pale**, wan, pasty, pallid,
ashen
▷ *See panel* SHADES FROM BLACK
TO WHITE

white-collar = **clerical**,
professional, salaried,
nonmanual

whittle = **carve**, cut, hew,
shape, trim, shave, pare
▷ PHRASES: whittle something
away = **undermine**, reduce,
consume, erode, eat away, wear
away ▶ whittle something or
someone down = **reduce**, cut
down, cut, decrease, prune,
scale down

whole NOUN 1 = **unit**,
ensemble, entirety, totality
OPPOSITE: part
▷ ADJECTIVE 2 = **complete**, full,
total, entire, uncut, undivided,
unabridged OPPOSITE: partial
3 = **undamaged**, intact,
unscathed, unbroken,

untouched, unharmed, in one
piece OPPOSITE: damaged
▷ PHRASES: on the whole
1 = **all in all**, altogether, all
things considered, by and large
2 = **generally**, in general, as a
rule, chiefly, mainly, mostly,
principally, on average

wholesale ADJECTIVE
1 = **extensive**, total, mass,
sweeping, broad,
comprehensive, wide-ranging,
blanket OPPOSITE: limited
▷ ADVERB 2 = **extensively**,
comprehensively, across the
board, indiscriminately

wholly = **completely**, totally,
perfectly, fully, entirely,
altogether, thoroughly, utterly
OPPOSITE: partly

whore = **prostitute**, tart
(*informal*), streetwalker, call girl

wide ADJECTIVE 1 = **spacious**,
broad, extensive, roomy,
commodious OPPOSITE:
confined 2 = **baggy**, full, loose,
ample, billowing, roomy,
voluminous, capacious
3 = **expanded**, dilated,
distended OPPOSITE: shut
4 = **broad**, extensive, wide-
ranging, large, sweeping, vast,
immense, expansive OPPOSITE:
restricted 5 = **extensive**,
general, far-reaching,
overarching 6 = **large**, broad,
vast, immense 7 = **distant**,
remote, off course, off target
▷ ADVERB 8 = **fully**, completely
OPPOSITE: partly 9 = **off target**,

W

astray, off course, off the mark

widen 1 = **broaden**, expand, enlarge, dilate, spread, extend, stretch **OPPOSITE:** narrow
2 = **get wider**, spread, extend, expand, broaden **OPPOSITE:** narrow

widespread = **common**, general, popular, broad, extensive, universal, far-reaching, pervasive **OPPOSITE:** limited

width = **breadth**, extent, span, scope, diameter, compass, thickness, girth

wield 1 = **brandish**, flourish, manipulate, swing, use, manage, handle, employ
2 = **exert**, maintain, exercise, have, possess

wife = **spouse**, partner, mate, bride, better half (*humorous*), vrou (*S. African*), wahine (*N.Z.*)

wild ADJECTIVE 1 = **untamed**, fierce, savage, ferocious, unbroken, feral, undomesticated, free, warrigal (*Austral. literary*) **OPPOSITE:** tame 2 = **uncultivated**, natural **OPPOSITE:** cultivated
3 = **stormy**, violent, rough, raging, choppy, tempestuous, blustery 4 = **excited**, crazy (*informal*), enthusiastic, raving, hysterical **OPPOSITE:** unenthusiastic
5 = **uncontrolled**, disorderly, turbulent, wayward, unruly, rowdy, unfettered, riotous **OPPOSITE:** calm 6 = **mad**

(*informal*), furious, fuming, infuriated, incensed, enraged, very angry, irate, tooshie (*Austral. slang*), off the air (*Austral. slang*) 7 = **uncivilized**, fierce, savage, primitive, ferocious, barbaric, brutish, barbarous **OPPOSITE:** civilized
▷ PLURAL NOUN
8 = **wilderness**, desert, wasteland, middle of nowhere (*informal*), backwoods, back of beyond (*informal*)

wilderness = **wilds**, desert, wasteland, uncultivated region

will NOUN 1 = **determination**, drive, purpose, commitment, resolution, resolve, spine, backbone 2 = **wish**, mind, desire, intention, fancy, preference, inclination
3 = **choice**, prerogative, volition
4 = **decree**, wish, desire, command, dictate, ordinance
5 = **testament**, bequest(s), last wishes, last will and testament
▷ VERB 6 = **wish**, want, prefer, desire, see fit 7 = **bequeath**, give, leave, transfer, gift, hand on, pass on, confer

willing 1 = **inclined**, prepared, consenting, agreeable, compliant, amenable **OPPOSITE:** unwilling 2 = **ready**, game (*informal*) **OPPOSITE:** reluctant

willingly = **readily**, freely, gladly, happily, eagerly, voluntarily, cheerfully, by choice **OPPOSITE:** unwillingly

willingness = **inclination**, will, agreement, wish, consent, volition **OPPOSITE:** reluctance

wilt 1 = **droop**, wither, sag, shrivel 2 = **weaken**, languish, droop 3 = **wane**, flag, fade

win VERB 1 = **be victorious in**, succeed in, prevail in, come first in, be the victor in **OPPOSITE:** lose 2 = **be victorious**, succeed, triumph, overcome, prevail, conquer, come first, sweep the board **OPPOSITE:** lose 3 = **gain**, get, land, achieve, earn, secure, obtain, acquire **OPPOSITE:** forfeit
▷ NOUN 4 = **victory**, success, triumph, conquest **OPPOSITE:** defeat
▷ PHRASES: win someone over or round = **convince**, influence, persuade, convert, sway, prevail upon, bring or talk round

wince VERB 1 = **flinch**, start, shrink, cringe, quail, recoil, cower, draw back
▷ NOUN 2 = **flinch**, start, cringe

wind¹ 1 = **air**, blast, hurricane, breeze, draught, gust, zephyr 2 = **breath**, puff, respiration 4 = **nonsense**, talk, boasting, hot air, babble, bluster, humbug, twaddle (*informal*), bizzo (*Austral. slang*), bull's wool (*Austral. & N.Z. slang*)
▷ PHRASES: get wind of something = **hear about**, learn of, find out about, become aware of, be told about, be informed of, be made aware of,

hear on the grape vine

wind² VERB 1 = **meander**, turn, bend, twist, curve, snake, ramble, twist and turn 2 = **wrap**, twist, reel, curl, loop, coil 3 = **coil**, curl, spiral, encircle
▷ PHRASES: wind someone up (*Informal*) 4 = **irritate**, excite, anger, annoy, exasperate, nettle, work someone up, pique 5 = **tease**, kid (*informal*), have someone on (*informal*), annoy, rag (*informal*), rib (*informal*), josh (*informal*), vex ▶ wind something up 1 = **end**, finish, settle, conclude, tie up, wrap up, finalize 2 = **close down**, close, dissolve, terminate, put something into liquidation
▶ wind up = **end up**, be left, finish up, fetch up (*informal*), land up

windfall = **godsend**, find, jackpot, bonanza, manna from heaven **OPPOSITE:** misfortune

windy = **breezy**, wild, stormy, windswept, blustery, gusty, squally, blowy **OPPOSITE:** calm

wing NOUN 1 = **faction**, group, arm, section, branch
▷ VERB 2 = **fly**, soar, glide, take wing 3 = **wound**, hit, clip

wink VERB 1 = **blink**, bat, flutter 2 = **twinkle**, flash, shine, sparkle, gleam, shimmer, glimmer
▷ NOUN 3 = **blink**, flutter

winner = **victor**, champion, master, champ (*informal*),

W

conqueror, prizewinner
OPPOSITE: loser
winning ADJECTIVE
1 = **victorious**, first, top, successful, unbeaten, conquering, triumphant, undefeated 2 = **charming**, pleasing, attractive, engaging, cute, disarming, enchanting, endearing **OPPOSITE:** unpleasant
▷ PLURAL NOUN 3 = **spoils**, profits, gains, prize, proceeds, takings
wipe VERB 1 = **clean**, polish, brush, rub, sponge, mop, swab 2 = **erase**, remove
▷ NOUN 3 = **rub**, brush
▷ PHRASES: wipe something or someone out = **destroy**, massacre, erase, eradicate, obliterate, annihilate, exterminate, expunge
wisdom = **understanding**, learning, knowledge, intelligence, judgment, insight, enlightenment, erudition
OPPOSITE: foolishness
wise 1 = **sage**, clever, intelligent, sensible, enlightened, discerning, perceptive, erudite **OPPOSITE:** foolish 2 = **sensible**, clever, intelligent, prudent, judicious
OPPOSITE: unwise
wish NOUN 1 = **desire**, want, hope, urge, intention, fancy (*informal*), ambition, fancy (*informal*) **OPPOSITE:** aversion
▷ VERB 2 = **want**, feel, choose,

please, desire, think fit
▷ PHRASES: wish for something = **desire**, want, hope for, long for, crave, aspire to, yearn for, hanker for
wit 1 = **humour**, quips, banter, puns, repartee, wordplay, witticisms, badinage **OPPOSITE:** seriousness 2 = **humorist**, card (*informal*), comedian, wag, joker, dag (*N.Z. informal*) 3 *often plural* = **cleverness**, sense, brains, wisdom, common sense, intellect, ingenuity, acumen
OPPOSITE: stupidity
witch = **enchantress**, magician, hag, crone, sorceress, Wiccan
witchcraft = **magic**, voodoo, wizardry, black magic, enchantment, occultism, sorcery, Wicca, makutu (*N.Z.*)
withdraw 1 = **remove**, take off, pull out, extract, take away, pull back, draw out, draw back 2 = **take out**, extract, draw out
withdrawal = **removal**, ending, stopping, taking away, abolition, elimination, cancellation, termination
withdrawn = **uncommunicative**, reserved, retiring, distant, shy, taciturn, introverted, unforthcoming
OPPOSITE: outgoing
wither 1 = **wilt**, decline, decay, disintegrate, perish, shrivel
OPPOSITE: flourish 2 = **waste**, decline, shrivel 3 = **fade**, decline, perish **OPPOSITE:** increase

w

withering = scornful, devastating, humiliating, snubbing, hurtful, mortifying

withhold 1 = keep secret, refuse, hide, reserve, retain, conceal, suppress, hold back **OPPOSITE:** reveal 2 = hold back, suppress, keep back **OPPOSITE:** release

withstand = resist, suffer, bear, oppose, cope with, endure, tolerate, stand up to **OPPOSITE:** give in to

witness NOUN 1 = observer, viewer, spectator, looker-on, watcher, onlooker, eyewitness, bystander 2 = testifier ▷ VERB 3 = see, view, watch, note, notice, observe, perceive 4 = countersign, sign, endorse, validate

witty = humorous, funny, clever, amusing, sparkling, whimsical, droll, piquant **OPPOSITE:** dull

wizard = magician, witch, shaman, sorcerer, occultist, magus, conjuror, warlock, tohunga (N.Z.)

wobble VERB 1 = shake, rock, sway, tremble, teeter, totter 2 = tremble, shake ▷ NOUN 3 = unsteadiness, shake, tremble 4 = unsteadiness, shake, tremor

woe 1 = misery, distress, grief, agony, gloom, sadness, sorrow, anguish **OPPOSITE:** happiness 2 = problem, grief, misery,

sorrow, tribulation

woman = lady, girl, female, sheila (Austral. & N.Z. informal), vrou (S. African), adult female, charlie (Austral. slang), chook (Austral. slang), wahine (N.Z.) **OPPOSITE:** man

womanly 1 = feminine, motherly, female, warm, tender, matronly, ladylike 2 = curvaceous, ample, voluptuous, shapely, curvy (informal), busty (informal), buxom, full-figured

wonder VERB 1 = think, question, puzzle, speculate, query, ponder, meditate, conjecture 2 = be amazed, stare, marvel, be astonished, gape ▷ NOUN 3 = amazement, surprise, admiration, awe, fascination, astonishment, bewilderment, wonderment 4 = phenomenon, sight, miracle, spectacle, curiosity, marvel, prodigy, rarity

wonderful 1 = excellent, great (informal), brilliant, outstanding, superb, fantastic (informal), tremendous, magnificent, booshit (Austral. slang), exo (Austral. slang), sik (Austral. slang) **OPPOSITE:** terrible 2 = remarkable, amazing, extraordinary, incredible, astonishing, staggering, startling, phenomenal **OPPOSITE:** ordinary

woo 1 = seek, cultivate

W

2 = **court**, pursue
wood 1 = **timber**, planks, planking, lumber (U.S.) 2 *Also* **woods** = **woodland**, forest, grove, thicket, copse, coppice 3 = **firewood**, fuel, logs, kindling
wooded = **tree-covered**, forested, timbered, sylvan (*poetic*), tree-clad
wooden 1 = **made of wood**, timber, woody, ligneous 2 = **expressionless**, lifeless, deadpan, unresponsive
wool 1 = **fleece**, hair, coat 2 = **yarn**
word NOUN 1 = **term**, name, expression 2 = **chat**, tête-à-tête, talk, discussion, consultation, confab (*informal*), heart-to-heart, powwow (*informal*) 3 = **comment**, remark, utterance 4 = **message**, news, report, information, notice, intelligence, dispatch, communiqué 5 = **promise**, guarantee, pledge, vow, assurance, oath 6 = **command**, order, decree, bidding, mandate ▷ VERB = **express**, say, state, put, phrase, utter, couch, formulate
● RELATED WORDS
● *adjectives:* lexical, verbal
wording = **phraseology**, words, language, phrasing, terminology
work VERB 1 = **be employed**, be in work 2 = **labour**, sweat,

slave, toil, slog (away), drudge, peg away, exert yourself OPPOSITE: relax 3 = **function**, go, run, operate, be in working order OPPOSITE: be out of order 4 = **succeed**, work out, pay off (*informal*), be successful, be effective, do the trick (*informal*), do the business (*informal*), get results 5 = **cultivate**, farm, dig, till, plough 6 = **operate**, use, move, control, drive, manage, handle, manipulate 7 = **manipulate**, form, fashion, shape, mould, knead ▷ NOUN 8 = **employment**, business, job, trade, duty, profession, occupation, livelihood OPPOSITE: play 9 = **effort**, industry, labour, sweat, toil, exertion, drudgery, elbow grease (*facetious*) OPPOSITE: leisure 10 = **task**, jobs, projects, commissions, duties, assignments, chores, yakka (*Austral. & N.Z. informal*) 11 = **handiwork**, doing, act, feat, deed 12 = **creation**, piece, production, opus, achievement, composition, handiwork ▷ PLURAL NOUN 13 = **factory**, plant, mill, workshop 14 = **writings**, output, canon, oeuvre (*French*) 15 = **mechanism**, workings, parts, action, movement, machinery ▷ PHRASES: work something out = **solve**, find out, calculate, figure out

worker = employee, hand, labourer, workman, craftsman, artisan, tradesman

workman = labourer, hand, worker, employee, mechanic, operative, craftsman, artisan

workshop 1 = factory, plant, mill 2 = workroom, studio

world 1 = earth, planet, globe 2 = mankind, man, everyone, the public, everybody, humanity, humankind 3 = sphere, area, field, environment, realm, domain 4 (usually used in phrase *a world of difference*) = huge amount, mountain, wealth, great deal, good deal, abundance, enormous amount, vast amount

worldly 1 = earthly, physical, secular, terrestrial, temporal, profane **OPPOSITE:** spiritual 2 = materialistic, grasping, selfish, greedy **OPPOSITE:** nonmaterialistic 3 = worldly-wise, knowing, experienced, sophisticated, cosmopolitan, urbane, blasé **OPPOSITE:** naive

worn 1 = ragged, frayed, shabby, tattered, tatty, threadbare, the worse for wear

worried = anxious, concerned, troubled, afraid, frightened, nervous, tense, uneasy **OPPOSITE:** unworried

worry VERB 1 = be anxious, be concerned, be worried, obsess, brood, fret, agonize, get in a lather (*informal*) **OPPOSITE:** be

unconcerned 2 = trouble, upset, bother, disturb, annoy, unsettle, pester, vex **OPPOSITE:** soothe

▷ NOUN 3 = anxiety, concern, fear, trouble, unease, apprehension, misgiving, trepidation **OPPOSITE:** peace of mind 4 = problem, care, trouble, bother, hassle (*informal*)

worsen 1 = deteriorate, decline, sink, decay, get worse, degenerate, go downhill (*informal*) **OPPOSITE:** improve 2 = aggravate, damage, exacerbate, make worse **OPPOSITE:** improve

worship VERB 1 = revere, praise, honour, adore, glorify, exalt, pray to, venerate **OPPOSITE:** dishonour 2 = love, adore, idolize, put on a pedestal **OPPOSITE:** despise

▷ NOUN 3 = reverence, praise, regard, respect, honour, glory, devotion, adulation

worth 1 = value, price, rate, cost, estimate, valuation **OPPOSITE:** worthlessness 2 = merit, value, quality, importance, excellence, goodness, worthiness **OPPOSITE:** unworthiness 3 = usefulness, value, quality, importance, excellence, goodness **OPPOSITE:** uselessness

worthless 1 = valueless, rubbishy, negligible **OPPOSITE:** valuable 2 = useless, unimportant, ineffectual, negligible **OPPOSITE:** useful **3** = **good-for-nothing**, vile, despicable, contemptible **OPPOSITE:** honourable

worthwhile = **useful**, valuable, helpful, profitable, productive, beneficial, meaningful, constructive **OPPOSITE:** useless

worthy = **praiseworthy**, deserving, valuable, worthwhile, admirable, virtuous, creditable, laudable **OPPOSITE:** disreputable

would-be = **budding**, self-styled, wannabe (*informal*), unfulfilled, self-appointed

wound NOUN **1** = **injury**, cut, hurt, trauma (*Pathology*), gash, lesion, laceration **2** *often plural* = **trauma**, offence, slight, insult ▷ VERB **3** = **injure**, cut, wing, hurt, pierce, gash, lacerate **4** = **offend**, hurt, annoy, sting, mortify, cut to the quick

wrangle VERB **1** = **argue**, fight, row, dispute, disagree, contend, quarrel, squabble ▷ NOUN **2** = **argument**, row, dispute, quarrel, squabble, bickering, tiff, altercation

wrap VERB **1** = **cover**, enclose, shroud, swathe, encase, enfold, bundle up **2** = **pack**, package, parcel (up), tie up, gift-wrap **OPPOSITE:** unpack **3** = **bind**, swathe **OPPOSITE:** unwind ▷ NOUN **4** = **cloak**, cape, stole, mantle, shawl ▷ PHRASES: wrap something

up 1 = **giftwrap**, pack, package, bundle up **2** (*Informal*) = **end**, conclude, wind up, terminate, finish off, round off, polish off

wrath = **anger**, rage, temper, fury, resentment, indignation, ire, displeasure **OPPOSITE:** satisfaction

wreck VERB **1** = **destroy**, break, smash, ruin, devastate, shatter, spoil, demolish **OPPOSITE:** build **2** = **spoil**, ruin, devastate, shatter, crool *or* cruel (*Austral. slang*) **OPPOSITE:** save ▷ NOUN **3** = **shipwreck**, hulk

wreckage = **remains**, pieces, ruin, fragments, debris, rubble

wrench VERB **1** = **twist**, force, pull, tear, rip, tug, jerk, yank **2** = **sprain**, strain, rick ▷ NOUN **3** = **twist**, pull, rip, tug, jerk, yank **4** = **sprain**, strain, twist **5** = **blow**, shock, upheaval, pang **6** = **spanner**, adjustable spanner

wrestle = **fight**, battle, struggle, combat, grapple, tussle, scuffle

wrinkle NOUN **1** = **line**, fold, crease, furrow, crow's-foot, corrugation **2** = **crease**, fold, crumple, furrow, crinkle, corrugation ▷ VERB **3** = **crease**, gather, fold, crumple, furrow, rumple, pucker, corrugate **OPPOSITE:** smooth

writ = **summons**, document, decree, indictment, court order, subpoena, arraignment

write 1 = **record**, scribble,

inscribe, set down, jot down
2 = **compose**, draft, pen, draw
up **3** = **correspond**, get in
touch, keep in touch, write a
letter, drop a line, drop a note
writer = **author**, novelist, hack,
scribbler, scribe, wordsmith,
penpusher
writing = **script**, hand, printing,
fist (*informal*), scribble,
handwriting, scrawl, calligraphy
wrong ADJECTIVE **1** = **amiss**,
faulty, unsatisfactory, not right,
defective, awry **2** = **incorrect**,
mistaken, false, inaccurate,
untrue, erroneous, wide of the
mark, fallacious **OPPOSITE:**
correct **3** = **inappropriate**,
incorrect, unsuitable,
unacceptable, undesirable,
incongruous, unseemly,
unbecoming **OPPOSITE:** correct
4 = **bad**, criminal, illegal, evil,
unlawful, immoral, unjust,
dishonest **OPPOSITE:** moral
5 = **defective**, faulty, awry,
askew
▷ ADVERB **6** = **incorrectly**,
badly, wrongly, mistakenly,
erroneously, inaccurately
OPPOSITE: correctly **7** = **amiss**,
astray, awry, askew
▷ NOUN **8** = **offence**, injury,
crime, error, sin, injustice,
misdeed, transgression
OPPOSITE: good deed
▷ VERB **9** = **mistreat**, abuse,
hurt, harm, cheat, take
advantage of, oppress, malign
OPPOSITE: treat well

Xx

xenophobia = **racism**,
nationalism, bigotry,
isolationism, racialism,
ethnocentrism, jingoism, racial
hatred
xenophobic = **racist**,
nationalist, bigoted, parochial
insular, isolationist,
ethnocentric
Xerox® = **photocopy**, copy,
reproduce, run off, print,
replicate, duplicate
Xmas = **Christmas**, Noel, festive
season, Yule (*archaic*), Yuletide,
(*archaic*), Christmastime,
Christmastide
X-ray® = **radiograph**, x-ray image

Yy

yank VERB 1 = **pull**, tug, jerk, seize, snatch, pluck, hitch, wrench
▷ NOUN 2 = **pull**, tug, jerk, snatch, hitch, wrench, tweak
yarn 1 = **thread**, fibre, cotton, wool 2 (*Informal*) = **story**, tale, anecdote, account, narrative, fable, reminiscence, urban myth
yawning = **gaping**, wide, huge, vast, cavernous
yearly ADJECTIVE 1 = **annual**, each year, every year, once a year
▷ ADVERB 2 = **annually**, every year, by the year, once a year, per annum
yearn *often with* **for** = **long**, desire, hunger, ache, crave, covet, itch, hanker after
yell VERB 1 = **scream**, shout,

cry out, howl, call out, wail, shriek, screech OPPOSITE: whisper
▷ NOUN 2 = **scream**, cry, shout, roar, howl, shriek, whoop, screech OPPOSITE: whisper
yellow ▷ *See panel* SHADES OF YELLOW
yen = **longing**, desire, craving, yearning, passion, hunger, ache, itch
yet ADVERB 1 = **so far**, until now, up to now, still, as yet, even now, thus far, up till now 2 = **now**, right now, just now, so soon 3 = **still**, in addition, besides, to boot, into the bargain
▷ CONJUNCTION
4 = **nevertheless**, still, however, for all that, notwithstanding, just the same, be that as it may
yield VERB 1 = **bow**, submit, give in, surrender, succumb, cave in (*informal*), capitulate OPPOSITE: resist 2 = **relinquish**, resign, hand over, surrender, turn over, make over, give over, bequeath OPPOSITE: retain

SHADES OF YELLOW

amber	lemon	saffron
buff	maize	straw
canary yellow	mustard	tea rose
champagne	oatmeal	topaz
cinnamon	ochre	tortoiseshell
daffodil	old gold	
gold or golden	primrose	

y

3 = **produce**, give, provide, return, supply, bear, net, earn **OPPOSITE:** use up
▷ NOUN **4** = **produce**, crop, harvest, output **5** = **profit**, return, income, revenue, earnings, takings **OPPOSITE:** loss

yielding 1 = **soft**, pliable, springy, elastic, supple, spongy, unresisting **2** = **submissive**, obedient, compliant, docile, flexible, accommodating, pliant, acquiescent **OPPOSITE:** obstinate

yob or **yobbo** = **thug**, hooligan, lout, hoon (Austral. & N.Z. slang), ruffian, roughneck (slang), tsotsi (S. African), cougan (Austral. slang), scozza (Austral. slang), bogan (Austral. slang)

young ADJECTIVE
1 = **immature**, juvenile, youthful, little, green, junior, infant, adolescent **OPPOSITE:** old **2** = **early**, new, undeveloped, fledgling **OPPOSITE:** advanced
▷ PLURAL NOUN **3** = **offspring**, babies, litter, family, issue, brood, progeny **OPPOSITE:** parents

youngster = **youth**, girl, boy, kid (informal), lad, teenager, juvenile, lass

youth 1 = **immaturity**, adolescence, boyhood or girlhood, salad days **OPPOSITE:** old age **2** = **boy**, lad, youngster, kid (informal), teenager, young

man, adolescent, teen (informal) **OPPOSITE:** adult

youthful = **young**, juvenile, childish, immature, boyish, girlish **OPPOSITE:** elderly

y

Zz

zeal = enthusiasm, passion, zest, spirit, verve, fervour, eagerness, gusto **OPPOSITE:** apathy

zero 1 = nought, nothing, nil 2 = rock bottom, the bottom, an all-time low, a nadir, as low as you can get

zip VERB 1 = speed, shoot, fly, flash, zoom, whizz (*informal*) ▷ NOUN 2 (*Informal*) = energy, drive, vigour, verve, zest, gusto, liveliness **OPPOSITE:** lethargy

zone = area, region, section, sector, district, territory, belt, sphere

zoom = speed, shoot, fly, rush, flash, dash, whizz (*informal*), hurtle